THE ANGLO-AMERICAN
LEGAL HERITAGE

THE ANGLO-AMERICAN LEGAL HERITAGE

INTRODUCTORY MATERIALS

Second Edition

Daniel R. Coquillette

J. Donald Monan, S.J. University Professor
Boston College Law School

Reporter, Committee on Rules of Practice and Procedure,
Judicial Conference of the United States

Carolina Academic Press
Durham, North Carolina

ISBN 1-59460-038-4
LCCN 2004102563

CAROLINA ACADEMIC PRESS
700 Kent St.
Durham, North Carolina 27701
Telephone (919) 489-7486
Fax (919) 493-5668
e-mail cap@cap-press.com

Printed in the United States of America

"No freeman shall be captured or imprisoned or disseised or outlawed or exiled or in any way destroyed, nor will we go against him or send against him, except by the lawful judgment of his peers or by the law of the land."

Magna Carta, Sec. 39
(1215)

"For a Common-wealth without lawes is like a ship without rigging and steerage."

The Book of the General
Lawes and Libertyes
Concerning the Inhabitants
of the Massachusets
(1648)

CONTENTS

TABLE OF STATUTES

TABLE OF CASES

ACKNOWLEDGMENTS

This revised edition was greatly advanced by the selfless generosity of two valued friends and colleagues, Christopher Mislow and William Wiecek, and by the extraordinary efforts of my excellent editorial assistant, Brendan M. Farmer. Their intelligence and judgment has improved nearly every page.

The Author gratefully acknowledges permission to reprint the following:

Pages 24–26 reprinted from Francis de Zulueta, *The Institutes of Gaius*, Part II. Copyright © 1953 by Oxford University Press. Reprinted by permission of Oxford University Press.

Pages 26–29 reprinted from *The Digest of Justinian* (A. Watson, ed.). Copyright © 1985 by University of Pennsylvania Press. Reprinted by permission of University of Pennsylvania Press.

Pages 33–35 reprinted by permission of the publisher from *The Diary and Autobiography of John Adams* by L.H. Butterfield, Leonard C. Faber, Wendell D. Gannett (eds.), Cambridge, Mass.: Harvard University Press, Copyright © 1961 by the Massachusetts Historical Society.

Pages 45–48, 64–65, 66–71, 80–88, 92–93, 117–118 reprinted from *Sources of English Constitutional History* (Stephenson and Marcham, eds.). Copyright © 1937 Harper & Brothers. Reprinted by permission of Addison Wesley Educational Publishers Inc.

Pages 48–50, approximately 1,224 words (pp. 112–113, 298–299) reprinted from *Njal's Saga*, translated by Magnus Magnusson and Hermann Palsson (Penguin Classics, 1960) copyright © Magnus Magnusson and Hermann Palsson, 1960. Reproduced by permission of Penguin Books Ltd.

Pages 51–52 reprinted from Robert Redfield, "Primitive Law," 33 *University of Cincinnati Law Review* 1. Copyright © 1964 by the University of Cincinnati Law Review. Reprinted by permission of University of Cincinnati Law Review.

Pages 52–53 reprinted from Margaret Hasluck, "The Albanian Blood Feud," *Law and Warfare* (Bohannan, ed.). Copyright © 1967 by Natural History Press. Reprinted by permission of Cambridge University Press.

Page 53 reprinted from *The Bramble Bush* by Karl Llewellyn. Copyright © 1960 by Oceana Publishing Inc. Reprinted by permission of Oceana Publishing Inc.

Pages 72–80 reprinted with permission from *Historical Foundations of the Common Law* (2d ed.) by S.F.C. Milsom. Copyright © 1981, Lexis Law Publishing, Charlottesville, VA (800) 446-3410. All rights reserved.

Pages 88–92 and 118–120 reprinted by permission of the publisher from *Bracton on the Laws and Customs of England* by Henry de Bracton, Cambridge, Mass.: Harvard University Press, Copyright © 1968 by the President and Fellows of Harvard College.

Pages 127–130 reprinted from *The Open Fields* by C.S. Orwin. Copyright © 1954 by Oxford University Press. Reprinted by permission of Oxford University Press.

Pages 133–135 reprinted from *The Law of Real Property* (fourth edition, 1975) by R. Megarry and H.W.R. Wade. Copyright © 1975 by Stevens & Sons Ltd. Reprinted by permission of Sweet & Maxwell.

Pages 145–146 reprinted from *A Concise History of the Common Law* (fifth edition) by T.F.T. Plucknett. Copyright © 1956 by Little, Brown and Company. Reprinted by permission of Aspen Publishers, Inc.

Pages 165–166 reprinted from *Royal Writs in England from the Conquest to Glanvill* (ed., R.C. Van Caenegem). Copyright © 1958 by Selden Society. Reprinted by permission of Selden Society.

Pages 176–179 reprinted by permission of the publisher from *A History of Lay Judges* by J.P. Dawson, Cambridge, Mass.: Harvard University Press, Copyright © 1960 by the President and Fellows of Harvard College.

Pages 191–195 reprinted from Daniel R. Coquillette, "Equity," *Dictionary of the Middle Ages*. Copyright © 1981 by American Council of Learned Societies. Reprinted by permission of American Council of Learned Societies.

Pages 196–202 reprinted from St. German's *Doctor and Student* (eds., T.F.T. Plucknett, J.L. Barton, 1974). Copyright © 1974 by Selden Society. Reprinted by permission of Selden Society.

Pages 238–241 reprinted from Daniel R. Coquillette, "Justinian in Braintree," from *Law in Colonial Massachusetts* (eds., Coquillette, Brink, and Menand). Copyright © 1984 by Colonial Society of Massachusetts. Reprinted by permission of Colonial Society of Massachusetts.

Pages 287–289 reprinted from *Glanvill* (trans. G.D.G. Hall). Copyright © 1965 by Selden Society, Oxford University Press and Thomas Nelson & Sons Ltd. Reprinted by permission of Selden Society and Oxford University Press.

Pages 289–291, 42 lines (pp. 29, 37) reprinted from *The Canterbury Tales* by Geoffrey Chaucer, translated by Nevill Coghill (Penguin Classics 1951, Fourth revised edition 1977) copyright © 1951 by Nevill Coghill, 1958, 1960, 1975, 1977. Reproduced by permission of Penguin Books Ltd.

Pages 291–295 reprinted from *De Laudibus Legum Anglie* by Sir John Fortescue (trans. S.B. Chrimes). Copyright © 1942 by Cambridge University Press. Reprinted by permission of Cambridge University Press.

Page 296 reprinted from *Year Books of Richard II, 2 Richard II 1378-1379* (ed., Morris S. Arnold) 69–70. Copyright © 1975 by Ames Foundation. Reprinted by permission of Ames Foundation.

Pages 301–303 reprinted from *An Introduction to the History of the Land Law* (1961) by A.W.B. Simpson. Copyright © 1961 A.W.B. Simpson. Reprinted by permission of Oxford University Press.

Pages 400–417 reprinted from Daniel R. Coquillette, "Radical Lawmakers in Colonial Massachusetts: The 'Countenance of Authoritie' and the *Lawes and Libertyes*," 67 *The New England Quarterly* 179. Copyright © 1994 by The New England Quarterly. Reprinted by permission of The New England Quarterly.

Pages 460–473 reprinted from *Albion's Fatal Tree* (eds., D. Hay, P. Linebaugh, John G. Rule, E.P. Thompson). Copyright © 1975 by Editors. Reprinted by permission of Douglas Hay.

Pages 577–583 reprinted by permission of the publisher from *Max Weber on Law in Economy and Society* by Max Rheinstein, (ed., tr.) and Edward Shils (tr.), Cambridge, Mass.: Harvard University Press, Copyright © 1954 by the President and Fellows of Harvard College.

Pages 583–585 reprinted from Duncan Kennedy, "The Structure of *Blackstone's Commentaries*," 28 *Buffalo Law Review* 209. Copyright © 1979 by Duncan Kennedy and the Buffalo Law Review. Reprinted by permission of Duncan Kennedy and Buffalo Law Review.

Pages 585–596 reprinted with the permission of The Free Press, a Division of Simon & Schuster from *Law in Modern Society: Toward a Criticism of Social Theory* by Roberto Mangabeira Unger. Copyright © 1976 by Roberto Mangabeira Unger.

Pages 616–623 reprinted by permission of the publisher from *Law and Revolution* by Harold J. Berman. Copyright © 1983 by Harvard University Press. Reprinted by permission of Harvard University Press.

Pages 623–627 reprinted from *The Strange Career of Legal Liberalism* by Laura Kalman. Copyright © 1996 by Yale University Press. Reprinted by permission of Yale University Press.

Pages 627–630 reprinted from Daniel R. Coquillette, "Introduction: The 'Countenance of Authoritie'," from *Law in Colonial Massachusetts* (eds., Coquillette, Brink, and Menand). Copyright © 1984 by The Colonial Society of Massachusetts. Reprinted by permission of The Colonial Society of Massachusetts.

For illustrations, see each individual illustration. Copyright permissions were obtained through the invaluable help of my research assistants, Kaitlin Carroll and Adam Kraus.

INTRODUCTION

Felix Frankfurter was once asked why he, a man whose parents originally could not speak English, devoted himself to the study of English legal history. It was not a friendly question. His reply was reported to be as follows: "American law is the beneficiary of a great heritage, and by my study, I make that heritage part of my own."[1] We are a nation strong in diversity, and we draw wealth from all our cultures. All of us, however, are touched directly by the great Anglo-American legal culture, for it permeates our courts, our legislatures, our Constitution, and even our daily language. It, in turn, is part of what Maitland termed the "seamless web" of all history.[2] As we shall see, in the Anglo-American "web" there are Roman, Talmudic, and Islamic strands. Early English and American lawyers built their rule of law from whatever materials were at hand. The English settlers of Massachusetts, clinging to a hostile shore in 1641, were often fluent in Latin, and the opening lines of their first legal treatises borrowed not only from the *Magna Carta* of 1215 A.D., but also from the Digest of the Emperor Justinian, completed in 533 A.D.

Today, we face unprecedented problems in our system of justice and in our legal profession. The experience of the centuries is available to us, as it was to the founders of our legal order in ages gone. It is, as Frankfurter said, only necessary to reach out to make it part of our own strength. Full of dark and stormy pages, as well as pages of courage and compassion, it is part of what it means to be an American lawyer today.

My fundamental purpose in preparing the materials that follow is to provide a "road map" into this vast resource. It is meant to be simple enough for any mo-

---

1. I am indebted to Paul Freund, a great teacher and scholar, for this story. It has been truly said that "More than any other contemporary did Felix Frankfurter bring to the judiciary an increased sense and perception of Anglo-American legal history." See *Essays in Legal History in Honor of Felix Frankfurter* (M. D. Forkosch, ed., New York, 1966), v.

2. "Such is the unity of all history that anyone who endeavours to tell a piece of it must feel that his first sentence tears a seamless web.... The web must be rent; but as we rend it, we may watch the whence and whither of a few of the severed and ravelling threads which have been making a pattern too large for any man's eye." Frederick Pollock, Frederic Williams Maitland, *The History of English Law Before the Time of Edward I* (1968 ed., S.F.C. Milsom ed.), vol. 1, 1.

tivated law student to follow, regardless of prior educational experience. Equally important, I have tried to include original material as much as possible. Too often, legal historians try to get between their students and the lawyers of the past. The actual documents are not obscure where properly translated and explained, and they scintillate with real life in a way no secondary source can. The historical record can be read directly by anyone, and that record is controversial, challenging, and, above all, directly relevant to ideological and moral struggles that threaten to divide us today.

There is one other purpose. As a law school dean, I have met with literally thousands of lawyers, at every stage of their careers. As diverse and multifaceted as these careers were, one simple distinction could usually be made. Some graduates were having fun being lawyers, and many were not. Those that genuinely enjoyed what they did usually had a perspective that gave their daily work meaning on a grander scale. These were the lawyers who implicitly understood their role in the vast, ever-shifting backdrop of the developing law; who could see and understand the connections that span the generations and the centuries. It is to these lawyers that I dedicate this book, for legal history should be fun.

Finally, it has been my great privilege to know and work with certain teachers and scholars who have changed my own life, and the lives of thousands of others. One of these teachers was certainly Samuel E. Thorne and another John P. Dawson. Jack Dawson took a special interest in helping me with the earliest stages of these materials, and generously gave me many of the excerpts to be used here. He and Sam were true friends to their students and colleagues. I am also most grateful to Charles Donahue Jr., for many kindnesses, small and large.

NOTE OF GRATITUDE

I have been assembling these materials for more than twenty years. They reflect the kind suggestions of hundreds of students and colleagues. I am particularly grateful to my devoted research assistants, particularly Kadesha Bagwell, Kaitlin Carroll, Susan Easton, Adam Krauss, Melinda McDermott, and Shelagh Newton, and to my editorial assistants, Brendan Farmer and Tasha Hansen, whose intelligence and hard work are apparent on every page. I received expert help from Boston College Law School's fine librarians and library staff. I am also most grateful to Tim Colton and the talented staff at Carolina Academic Press. Finally, there is my family; my wise parents, my beautiful and intelligent spouse and daughters, and my talented sons-in-law. To them I owe more than I could ever say.

THE ANGLO-AMERICAN
LEGAL HERITAGE

I

THE GLORY THAT WAS ROME

A. WHY ROMAN LAW?

It might seem somewhat curious to start a book on the Anglo-American legal heritage with a section about its great rival, the Roman Law. Almost all legal systems in the world today trace their ancestry to one or the other, and both the English and Americans have long defined the uniqueness of their "common law" systems by contrasting them with the "civil law" of Rome and its "continental" progeny.[1]

One could always justify this choice by pointing out that England was actually ruled by Roman law for more than three hundred years, from subjugation in about 45 A.D. to the famous letter of 410 A.D. from the Emperor Honorius to the

---

1. "Common law" is one of many inherently confusing terms in legal history with multiple meanings. Its first meaning was in reference to the law of the royal courts of England, a law that was "common" throughout the Kingdom. Now there are at least five different distinctions based on the term "common law": 1) English "common law" as a royal law opposed to merely local customs; 2) English "common law" as a secular national law opposed to religious "canon" law and "civilian" Roman law; 3) English "common law" as an English law opposed to all kinds of foreign legal procedures and doctrines; 4) English "common law" as case law as opposed to legislation; 5) English "common law" as fixed legal doctrine as opposed to "equity." Thus, the common law was seen as distinct from the "local" customary law of the feudal and shire courts. The royal "common" law was also seen as distinct from the religious "canon" law of the church courts and the Roman law curricular of the English universities. The third distinction was between the "common law" as the "national" law of England and all foreign legal systems, including the laws of the continent and the Church. A fourth distinction was the idea of "common" law as the judge made "law of the royal judges, as opposed to the written statutory laws. (As the statutes were largely Latin, and Roman law emphasized written texts, this distinction evolved from the earlier ones.) Finally, during the Renaissance, "common" law was contrasted to the "equity" of the Chancellor's court. (The former was a law of binding precedent applicable to all, and the latter an exercise of mercy in a particular case.) Needless to say, we will be discussing all of these important distinctions at length, particularly in Chapter V "Courts of Record," Chapter VI "Equity" and Chapter VII "Specialized Courts."

1

Illustration 1-1   Hadrian's Wall (*circa* 124 A.D.). This extended for 74 miles from the east to west coast of England to protect the Northern Border. See F. Haverfield, "The Roman Army in Britain," *Social England* (London, Cassell & Co.) (ed. H.D. Traill, J.S. Hann), vol 1., 76–106 (1894). The photograph is by Thomas Ashby. *Id.*, vol. 1, 85.

English *civitates*, or citizens, telling them to look "to their own defense."[2] But this would be a fraud. Not a trace of the Roman law in England survived the collapse of the Western Empire.[3] In fact, this catastrophic loss of a legal culture forms another, very different reason for beginning this course with Roman law. We like to think of history as a progression, an advance in civilization, technique, and knowledge. But the history of law in England begins with a great legal culture that was overrun and lost. Just compare the elegant sophistication of the excerpts from Gaius and Justinian included here, excerpts that anticipated the Uniform Commercial Code, with the brutal, laconic provisions of the *Dooms* of Alfred that follow in Chapter II. ("If an ear is cut off, 30 shillings shall be paid...."). But Alfred's laws (890 A.D.–901 A.D.) are more "modern" than those

---

2. See three fine paperback accounts: Peter H. Blair, *Roman Britain and Early England* (New York, 1963); J.A. Richmond, *Roman Britain* (London, 2d ed., 1963); Malcolm Todd, *Roman Britain* (London, 1981). The earliest attempts to conquer England were Caesar's famous expeditions in 55 B.C. Romanized Britons clung to their civilization many years after Honorius abandoned England in 410 A.D.

3. This loss occurred despite the fact that "Romanized" populations persisted in places like Verulamium (St. Albans) for many years. The absence of actual traces of Roman law in the later Anglo-Saxon *dooms* is in remarkable contrast to the massive Roman ruins, many of which still survive in England. Hadrian's Wall and the ruins at St. Albans and Bath are just examples. For an impressive photographic account, see T.W. Potter, *Roman Britain* (Cambridge, 1983).

of Gaius (*circa* 161 A.D.) by more than seven hundred years, the rough difference between today and the time of the *Magna Carta*. Thus, one reason for beginning with Roman law is to appreciate the fragility of legal culture, a fragility demonstrated by the shocking events of our own century.

There is, however, another reason. Roman law was never actually isolated from the development of the common law, at least not completely. Commencing with the discovery in medieval Italy of important Roman law manuscripts, documents that survived from the Byzantine period, educated English lawyers have been familiar with the *Institutes* and *Digest*. As early as 1149 A.D., Roman law teachers like Vacarius addressed audiences in England, and English students traveled to Bologna to learn civilian principles. At first the great texts were inadequately understood, although venerated. But time led to more understanding, and to a learning that influenced jurists throughout Europe. Certainly, the transnational law of the Catholic Church, which so influenced the English law of equity, had Roman roots. In every century, whether it be the age of *Bracton*, Bacon or of Bentham, Roman law influenced English law because it influenced educated English jurists and judges.

Illustration 1-2   This bronze head of the Emperor Hadrian (117–138 A.D.) was found in the Thames where the London Bridge is now. It is more than life sized. See T.W. Potter, *Roman Britain* (1983, British Museum), 41. Courtesy, British Museum. © The British Museum, British Museum Press.

America was influenced, too. Recent research has now begun to uncover the full extent of Roman law influence on the early development of American law. We have always known that Roman law texts were found in the best colonial libraries, such as at Harvard, but it now appears that early colonial attempts at treatise writing and codification were directly influenced by the *Institutes*. The seventeenth century settlers in colonies such as Massachusetts were fluent in Latin, and sought alternatives to royal English models for a number of reasons.[4] The founders of the American republic, most notably John Adams, were also students of Roman law, as the excerpts from Adams' *Diary* in this introductory section demonstrates. Adams used this knowledge, both in his law practice and in drafting the Constitution of Massachusetts.[5] As we shall see in Chapter XIII, *infra*, the nineteenth century codification movement, led by the likes of Livingstone and Field, is another example. The list goes on.

There is one final reason to get acquainted with the Roman texts. They were beautifully drafted and written. Indeed, in this book, I have left the Latin text with the translation in certain sections, so that those with an elementary familiarity with Latin can see for themselves the economy and precision of the language. Even the English translations show the clarity of the Roman style, the logical nature of their expositions, and their wonderful use of plain examples to demonstrate difficult points, a technique now used by the American Law Institute's *Restatements*. The excellent Roman numbering system has been borrowed by modern codification schemes, including the Uniform Commercial Code.

B. THE ROMAN TEXTS

The history of Roman jurisprudence is complex, and covers nearly a thousand years. This is far longer than the life, so far, of our American republic or its immediate civilization. Such an epic story cannot be summarized here, but, fortunately, there are a number of very readable introductions for the curious. These range from Edward Gibbon's classic *Decline and Fall of the Roman Empire* (1776) to Haus Julius Wolff's concise contemporary paperback, *Roman Law* (Norman, Okla., 1951, reprinted 1982).

In addition, Roman law comes down to us in the form of a highly organized set of texts, all dating from a massive project undertaken by the Emperor Justinian near the end of the Roman Empire in the period from 529 to 535 A.D. Justinian was proud of his military advances (temporary) in recapturing Roman glory from his base in Constantinople. He ordered his chief jurists, Tribonian, Theophilus, and Dorotheus, to perform an arduous task, to excerpt the best and most reliable sections from the earlier Roman texts, and to assemble these ex-

---

4. See Daniel R. Coquillette, "Introduction: The 'Countenance of Authoritie'" in *Law in Colonial Massachusetts* (ed. D.R. Coquillette, R. J. Brink, C.S. Menand, Boston, 1984) xxi–xlv.

5. See *id.*, Daniel R. Coquillette, "Justinian in Braintree: John Adams, Civilian Learning, and Legal Elitism, 1758–1775," 359–418.

cerpts under appropriate headings in a massive *Digest*. Justinian then ordered all the earlier texts destroyed throughout the Empire, ostensibly to eliminate repetition and error! In addition to the *Digest*, which was ready by 533 A.D., Justinian ordered his jurists to prepare an elementary text book for students, the *Institutes*, which drew on the *Digest*. The *Institutes* proved to be one of the most widely read law books of all time, and possibly the most influential. It had clear organization, conciseness, and simple illustrations. It reached audiences all over the known world, and far into the future. Even today, it is required reading for law students in many countries. The *Institutes* was also ready by 533 A.D. The next year Justinian's jurists completed their great task, which Justinian himself described as "a work that once seemed beyond hope," by issuing a final version of a collection of all Imperial statutes, the famous *Codex*. These three books, the *Digest*, the *Institutes*, and the *Codex* together became known as the *Corpus Juris*, the "Body of the Law."

We are, of course, familiar with the idea of legal texts, of which the *Institutes* was the founder, and the idea of codifications, or collections of statutes, of which the *Codex* remains the greatest example in history. These are actually good examples of Roman ideas that passed to us. The *Digest*, however, has a more unfamiliar basis, for it was largely composed of "opinions," not of "judges," but of "jurists." To fully understand those "opinions," we need to know a little more about Roman legal procedures, which are described in the next section.

Most of the "opinions," or excerpts, contained in the *Digest* were first written in the "golden age" of Roman Law, around the first two centuries A.D., the so-called "Classical" period. With only a few exceptions, these writings were all destroyed by Justinian following the completion of the *Digest* in 535 A.D., so all we know of those writings is what Justinian's jurists selected nearly two centuries later. The most important exception was the chance discovery, by B.G. Niebuhr in 1816, of a manuscript of the work of the "Classical" jurist, Gaius, now called the *Institutes of Gaius*. A thrifty librarian, rather than burn a valuable book at the Emperor's order, had painted over its pages and used it again, a so-called "palimpsest." Hidden underneath the paint, Gaius' text survived.

A great game for legal scholars has been to try to isolate the "pure" or "Classical" Roman law of the "golden age" from any changes, or "interpolations" introduced by Justinian's compilers.[6] With the exception of Gaius' text, however, no "pure" Classical law has survived in more than fragments. Indeed, Justinian's compilers often changed fragments included in the *Digest* to eliminate any conflicts or ambiguities, or to bring a particular doctrine "up to date" for conditions four centuries later. The Latin of Justinian's compilers, however, was not as concise and elegant as that of the Classical jurists, and experts usually can identify the later changes and additions. For fun, I have included a section from the "pure" Gaius, discovered in the palimpsest, so that you can directly compare it to the later sections from Justinian. Do you think the older text is better? Worse?

---

6. In particular, the work of Fritz Schulz has permitted us to understand the true state of the "Classical" Roman Law. His book, *Classical Roman Law* (Oxford, 1951) is a monument of scholarship.

C. HOW ROMAN "COURTS" WORKED

All of these Roman texts reflected the special nature of the Roman legal process during the "Classical" period. The texts were not court opinions or decisions, but were either statutes or the "opinions" of jurists. The former "codes" are familiar enough to us. Indeed, our word "codification" come directly from the Latin, and the idea comes largely from the *Codex*. The *Digest*, however, is an unfamiliar notion, being a collected series of opinions by experts, seemingly outside an actual case context. To understand this idea, we must know something of the "Classical" Roman way of resolving legal disputes.

When two Roman citizens had a legal dispute, they went to the representatives of the Praetor, the elected official responsible for enforcing the law of Rome. They would then be asked to choose the name of a "judge," or *judex*, from a list of qualified Roman citizens, called the *album*.[7] If they could not agree, the Praetor would choose a name for them.

The most interesting thing about the *album* is that none of the names would be trained professional lawyers or judges in the sense that we know today. They would be private citizens who served as "judges" as a public service, and would include lay persons of all kind. Indeed, parties might specially choose a *judex* who was a merchant or a trader or had other non-legal experience. The *judex* alone would hear the case, and make a decision as to the facts. The Praetor would then enforce the *judex's* decision. But what if there was a purely legal problem?

This is where the jurists came in. Jurists were private Roman citizens, who neither held an official government post nor actually heard cases. As a public service, they would answer questions put to them by any *judex* puzzled by the right legal standard or rule to apply to a particular set of facts. Those answers to *judex* inquiries, called *responsa*, were frequently written down and collected. They became the basis for the Republican treatises, such as Gaius' *Institutes*, and were the basic material for Justinian's *Digest*.

Here is an example that is actually addressed in Book iii, 23, 3 of *Justinian's Institutes*, which sets out the Roman law of sale ("*De Emptione et Venditione*"). Suppose a buyer and seller agree on the sale of a house, including the specific price. Before the buyer pays or takes possession, the house burns down. The buyer wants to rescind the sale, and refuses to pay. The *judex* is clear as to the facts, but doesn't know what to do. He asks the jurist Paul. Paul gives the correct rule of Roman law, i.e., once the price has been agreed, the risk in the transaction shifts to the buyer, even if the property has not been delivered or occupied. See *Justinian's Institutes* iii, 23, 3; *Digest* xviii 6, 8, pr. (Paul). The *judex* will enter a judgment requiring the buyer to pay the purchase price to the seller, and accept the burned house in return. If the buyer refuses, the Praetor will enforce the judg-

---

7. Of course, not all inhabitants of Rome were citizens, and not all Roman citizens were of "full legal personality." Only the senior male of a family, the *pater familias*, had a complete legal personality. At the other end of the scale were slaves. Even slaves, however, were protected in some ways, and many Roman slaves were in fact quite important managers and experts. Romans also did not practice the horror of race slavery, as we did in America. For a fascinating view of Roman social hierarchies, see Barry Nicholas, *An Introduction to Roman Law* (Oxford, 1962), 65–80. Of particular interest is the Roman treatment of women, including the law of marriage and divorce. See *id.*, 80–90. See also Aaron Kirschenbaum, *Sons, Slaves and Freedmen in Roman Commerce* (Jerusalem, 1987).

ment. Later, Paul's opinion will be saved, and included with the other opinions in a book. That "treatise" will then be used to guide future parties and judges.

What happened if there was disagreement among the jurists? Like legal experts of all ages, the jurists did disagree, and actually had "schools," or opposing camps, that squabbled regularly over even very small issues. The two best known "schools" were the followers of Proculus, or the Proculeans, and the followers of Sabinus, known as the Sabinians. For your amusement, I have included an example of one of their squabbles in the following materials. It was about whether the price in a sale can consist of something other than money. See the excerpts from *Gaius, Institutes*, iii, 139 and *Justinian's Institutes*, iii, 22, 2, set out below. A *judex* could consult with up to three jurists, and apparently could chose among conflicting opinions. If, however, all these agreed, the *judex* had to follow the *jurists*.

There was a great difference between the Roman "jurist" system and Anglo-American "judicial precedent." This persists as one of the major differences between the two systems to this day. (Although, ironically, the modern American tendency towards arbitration is very reminiscent of the Classical *judex*!) The decision of the *judex* did not establish a "precedent" that was binding on future jurists or a future *judex*, even in a very similar case. What was binding was the legislative code, or the persuasiveness of the opinion of the jurist. This stood on its own inherent authority, not because of any past decision. Roman influenced legal systems still rely primarily on expert treatises and codes for law, which are applied prospectively. In such a system, the case decision itself does not "make" any law. It is merely the result of the pre-existing rule. Roman jurists would ask why a badly decided case should have any authority, or why even a well decided case should make law *ex post facto*. Why is it fair to subject someone to a rule established *after* the acts involved? For a "civilian" the true source of law is never past practice, but present authority as incorporated in codes or expert treatises.

D. THE ROMAN VIEW OF LAW AND LEGAL AUTHORITY

Anglo-American lawyers have only one term for "law." "Law" is a Danish-Germanic term encompassing everything from sophisticated statutory schemes to primitive customs. The Romans, on the other hand, had no fewer than five different words for "law." To illustrate this, I have included in these materials the opening sections of both the *Institutes* and *Gaius*. Notice how the Romans logically set out the different definitions of law, and how sophisticated they were about difficult juristic distinctions. Just as the Inuit-Americans have many different words for "snow," because snow is so important to their lives, law was very important to Roman life, and one word was simply inadequate to accurately describe all of its functions.

Take, for example, the Latin word "*ius*." It refers to law in an abstract or "broad" sense. We get our term "jurisprudence" from this Latin word, and also "jurist" and "justice."

The Romans recognized three important different kinds of "*ius*." "*Ius naturale*" was the law of nature. It included everything that was beyond the power of human law making, and included "that law which nature teaches to all animals"—such as sex and procreation. It also included the laws of physics. One test of whether a rule was part of the "natural law" was this: Can human power change it? If not, it was *ius naturale*. (Later jurists would derive the idea of "natural law"—including the idea of human rights that can never be taken away by human law—from this Roman concept.) By definition, "*ius naturale*" applied to all human beings, and all animals.

"*Ius gentium*," or "law of all nations," referred to human made laws "common to all mankind." By this the Romans meant "common to all civilized peoples" and many examples of the *ius gentium* were quite advanced. For example, according to Justinian, "from this law of nations almost all contracts were at first introduced, as, for instance, buying and selling, letting and hiring, partnership, deposits, loans returnable in kind, and very many others." *Institutes*, i, 11, 2. The "*ius gentium*" was analogous to what today we would call "international law." It encompassed both rules of diplomacy and state relations, our "public international law," and also commercial practices and principles of fairness in trading, what we would call "private international law." Indeed, most of our ideas about international law have their origins in the Roman *ius gentium*.

The third kind of "*ius*" was the *ius civile*, the national law "of the particular state." It is from "*ius civile*" or the law of the Roman state that we get the term "civil law" as referring to Roman based legal doctrine. Jurists who study the Roman-based "civil law" are called "civilians." Thus, we will see sentences like this: "He was not a common lawyer (i.e., an expert in English national "common" law), but a civilian" (i.e., an expert in the Roman based "civil" law of the Continent or of the specialized English courts that looked to Roman and international law, such as the Admiralty.)

The "*ius civile*" was equivalent to what we would call "positive law," the statutes and judicially enforced rules of each state. But even here, the Romans drew more distinctions. Specific "laws," usually written laws enacted by legislative authorities, were referred to as *leges* or *lex*, from which root we get the word "legal." These were often concrete and technical. On the other extreme, there was the Roman idea of *equitas*, from which we get the term "equity." This referred to the idea of doing justice in a particular factual situation, even if it meant "bending" or ignoring a particular rule of law, or *lege*. In a sense, both the idea of *lex* and the idea of *equitas* are part of the operation of the *ius civile*, but represent opposite poles of legal specificity and judicial discretion.

To a Roman, our notion of "law" would include all of the above: the *ius naturale*, the *ius gentium*, the *ius civile*, the idea of *lex* and the idea of *equitas*, five different terms. The Romans were certainly advanced in theoretical legal analysis, and from their different juristic categories come many of our fundamental legal ideas today. Until very recently, all well-educated English and American students learned Latin. We often forget that it was a true second language to both medieval lawyers and American patriots. If you were fluent in Latin, it was natural to pick up Roman law books, particularly a book so clearly written as Justinian's *Institutes*. John Adams did, and so did Joseph Story and Roscoe Pound.

E. THE ROMAN INFLUENCE

In these materials, we will constantly come across the effect of Roman Law on English and American thought. For your amusement, I have included two particularly striking examples in the "Roman Law" Chapter itself, selections from the work of Francis Bacon and John Adams.

Francis Bacon (1561–1626) was one of the most brilliant stars of the English Renaissance. Not only was he a pioneer of modern scientific theory and a major philosopher, he also wrote beautifully. (He wrote so well, in fact, that he has been accused of writing Shakespeare's works.) He wrote as fluently in Latin as in English, and was a man of immense learning.

First and foremost, however, Bacon was a lawyer. He was the cruelly disinherited son of a Lord Keeper, and he vowed to rise to his father's place at the head of the English legal system. Against all odds, he succeeded, rising from Solicitor General, to Attorney General, and then to Lord Chancellor. But his political career was not free from controversy, and he was eventually impeached by Parliament, largely for political reasons. Nevertheless, he was a great voice for legal reform, practically inventing the modern system of official law reporters. He also suggested a radical "pruning" of all old and contradictory laws and law reports, leaving only those that were accurate and clear. This project, set out in 1616 in *A Proposition to His Majesty* (James I), was clearly inspired by that of Justinian, more than a thousand years before.[8] Today, we look to Francis Bacon as the founder of Anglo-American analytical jurisprudence, but his debts to Rome were large and obvious.[9]

John Adams would, at first glance, seem a far cry from a great Renaissance noble like Bacon. Bacon was an elegant man. He had several great houses, and hundreds of retainers. Adams was dumpy and homespun. He lived in a modest Boston home and a small farm house in Braintree, near Boston. Bacon was the right hand advisor to a King, but Adams was to become a courageous revolutionary, and eventually, one of the first elected presidents of a new and great republic, founded on a Constitution which he himself helped to write.

But there were also some remarkable similarities. Bacon and Adams were both fluent in Latin. They both valued Roman law, and studied Justinian's *Institutes* and *Digest* with great care. Both obtained major ideas from the Romans: Bacon focusing on internal law reform, and Adams focusing on constitutionalism and the "self-evident" rights of the *ius gentium* and the *ius naturale*. Indeed, Adams practiced in the British Vice-Admiralty court in colonial Boston, and used Roman law sources in that civil law jurisdiction with genuine expertise.[10] Much of Adams' legal thought shows traces of his Roman law studies, candidly described in the amusing pages of his youthful diary included in this chapter.

He was not alone. American jurists from the early Massachusetts drafters of the *Body of Laws and Liberties* in 1641, to the codifiers of the nineteenth century such as David Dudley Field and Edward Livingston, to the creative "realists" of the twentieth century, such as Karl Llewellyn and Roscoe Pound, all looked to Roman law for inspiration, as we shall see.[11]

---

8. See Daniel R. Coquillette, *Francis Bacon* (Stanford, 1992), 105–117; Daniel R. Coquillette, *The Civilian Writers of Doctors' Commons, London* (Berlin, 1988), 257–259.

9. *Id.* n. 16, 20–21, 257–259.

10. Coquillette, "Justinian in Braintree: John Adams, Civilian Learning, and Legal Elitism, 1758–1775," *supra* note 5, 359–418.

11. See Chapters XIII, XIV, *infra*, and Lawrence M. Friedman, *A History of American Law* (New York, 1973), 351–355.

F. THE "IDEOLOGY" OF ROMAN LAW

Roman law had many characteristics, and a history of over one thousand years. Even so, it is possible to emphasize five particularly important lessons it taught its students. First, the Emperor Justinian, building on the writing of the Classical jurists, achieved his dreams of a concise and highly structured *Corpus Juris*, an entire legal system in a *Digest*, a *Codex* and an *Institutes*. The Romans showed the world that a sophisticated legal system could be achieved based on written sources which were both intelligible and manageable in length. Second, the Roman *judex* system provided reliable and efficient justice without a large professional bar, under the supervision of the jurists and the Praetor. Third, the Romans conceived of elements of the legal order which extend beyond national borders, the *ius naturale* and *ius gentium,* which are today the conceptual cornerstone of international law and the international protection of human rights. Fourth, the Romans believed in a prospective legal system based on pre-established codes or treatises, rather than reliance as *ex post facto* judicial determinations. Fifth, and perhaps most important, the Romans believed in law as a perfectible science, capable of being tested by the results achieved in a rational manner.[12] These five elements, as we shall see, contrast sharply with many of the characteristics of the early English common law, to which we now will turn. Yet, as remote as medieval England may seem from the world of the Roman jurists, hidden away in the English universities, in the courts of the church, and in the personal libraries of the most learned were magnificent Roman law texts, always capable of teaching unexpected and important lessons.

FOR FURTHER READING

I.   THE ORIGINAL TEXTS

Nothing really duplicates reading the original Roman texts, particularly if you can read the Latin. Even if your Latin is very weak, there is a wonderful little book, *Latin for Lawyers* (Sweet & Maxwell, London, 1960) which is extraordinarily easy to follow and helpful. There are also excellent translations, such as J.B. Moyle's translation of *The Institutes of Justinian* (Oxford, 5th ed. 1913), Thomas Collett Sandars' translation of *The Institutes of Justinian* (parallel texts, London, 7th ed. 1883) and Francis de Zulueta's masterful translation of *The Institutes of Gaius* (Oxford, 1946). These have been reprinted many times and are in every law library. For a taste of the *Digest,* try Francis de Zulueta's selected translation in *The Roman Law of Sale* (Oxford, 1945). The great Latin text of the entire *Digest,* edited by Theodor Mommsen, has now been completely translated into English by a team of scholars under the supervision of Alan Watson. See *The Digest of Justinian* (Alan Watson, ed., Philadelphia, 1985).

---

12. See D. R. Coquillette, *The Civilian Writers of Doctors' Commons, London, supra* note 8, 32–41.

II. HELPFUL INTRODUCTIONS

The two great "students' friends" are Barry Nicholas' *Introduction to Roman Law* (Oxford, 1962) and Hans Julius Wolff's *Roman Law: An Historical Introduction* (Norman, Oklahoma, 1951). Also very helpful is J.M. Kelly's translation of Wolfgang Kunkel's classic, *An Introduction to Roman Legal and Constitutional History* (Oxford, 2d ed. 1973).

III. ROMAN BRITAIN

Please see the excellent collection of introductory books, all now in paperback, listed in notes 2 and 3, above.

IV. LATER INFLUENCE ON ANGLO-AMERICAN LAW

I will immodestly recommend my own books cited in notes 8, 9, and 10, above. There are also good summaries in Theodore F.T. Plucknett's *A Concise History of The Common Law* (5th ed. Boston, 1956), 294–300, Frederick Pollock, F.W. Maitland, *The History of English Law* (Cambridge, 3d ed., S.F.C. Milsom, 1968), vol. 1, 111–135 and John P. Dawson's *The Oracles of the Law* (Ann Arbor, 1968), 100–147. More complete scholarly treatments are in W.W. Buckland, Arnold D. McNair, *Roman Law and Common Law* (Cambridge, 2d ed. 1952), R.H. Helmholz's *Canon Law and the Law of England* (London, 1987), which focuses on Roman influence through the Church canon law, and Peter Stein's excellent series of essays, *The Character and Influence of the Roman Civil Law: Historical Essays* (London, 1988). Francis de Zulueta's great edition of *The Liber Pauperum of Vacarias* (Selden Society volume 44, London, 1927) sets out in full an original text, a "book for poor students" about Roman law, studied by English students as early as 1149 A.D. See also Francis de Zulueta, Peter Stein, *The Teaching of Roman Law in England Around 1200* (London, 1940).

For those interested in how Roman law became the foundation for the legal systems of most of Western Europe and Latin America, I would highly recommend John H. Merryman, *The Civil Law Tradition: An Introduction to the Legal Systems of Western Europe and Latin America* (Stanford, 1969). See also F.H. Lawson, *A Common Lawyer Looks at the Civil Law* (Ann Arbor, 1953).

Illustration 1-3   This is the frontispiece of a famous seventeenth century text on Roman law. The figure on the left represents the Emperor Justinian. The center figure is "Justice," from the latin *"ius."* The text in her hand is the *Corpus Iuris* of Justinian. On the right is a modern sovereign, possibly the Holy Roman Emperor. Below is a picture of the modern sovereign with his legal counselors, his judges or jurists. Note this Roman law treatise was published in Holland in 1664. The Dutch still have a civil law system. South Africa, a former Dutch colony, has been remarkably influenced by Roman law. [Author's Collection.]

MATERIALS

JUSTINIAN'S INSTITUTES (533 A.D.)

Note: This is the famous introduction to *Justinian's Institutes* (533 A.D.), prepared by the Emperor Justinian and his jurists as a text book for law students.
The translation was prepared by Thomas Collett Sandars and comes from T.C.
Sandars, *The Institutes of Justinian* (7th ed., 1883), Longman's. Note the text is
"in the mouth of the Emperor" himself, and is directly addressed to the Roman
law students. As the Emperor's words, the text book itself had the force of law.
Note what the Emperor says about legal education. Do you agree?

INSTITUTIONUM JUSTINIANI
PROŒMIUM.

IN NOMINE DOMINI NOSTRI
JESU CHRISTI.

IN THE NAME OF OUR LORD
JESUS CHRIST.

IMPERATOR CÆSAR FLAVIUS
JUSTINIANUS ALAMANNICUS
GOTHICUS FRANCICUS ANTICUS
ALANICUS VANDALICUS
AFRICANUS PIUS FELIX IN-
CLYTUS VICTOR AC TRIUMPHA-
TOR SEMPER AUGUSTUS CUPIDÆ
LEGUM JUVENTUTI.

THE EMPEROR CÆSAR FLAVIUS
JUSTINIANUS, VANQUISHER OF
THE ALAMANI, GOTHS, FRANCS,
GERMANS, ANTES, ALANI, VAN-
DALS, AFRICANS, PIOUS, HAPPY,
GLORIOUS, TRIUMPHANT CON-
QUEROR, EVER AUGUST, TO THE
YOUTH DESIROUS OF STUDYING
THE LAW, GREETING.

Imperatoriam majestatem non
solum armis decoratam, sed etiam
legibus oportet esse armatam, ut
utrumque tempus et bellorum et pacis
recte possit gubernari et princeps Romanus victor existat non solum in
hostilibus proeliis, sed etiam per legi-
timos tramites calumniatium iniqui-
tates expellens, et fiat tam juris reli-
giosissimus quam victis hostibus
triumphator.

The imperial majesty should be not
only made glorious by arms, but also
strengthened by laws, that, alike in
time of peace and in time of war, the
state may be well governed, and that
the emperor may not only be victorious
in the field of battle, but also may by
every legal means repel the iniquities of
men who abuse the laws, and may at
once religiously uphold justice and triumph over his conquered enemies.

1. Quorum utramque viam cum
summis vigiliis et summa providentia
adnuente Deo perfecimus. Et bellicos
quidem sudores nostros barbaricæ
gentes sub juga nostra deductæ cog-
noscunt et tiam Africa quam aliæ in-
numerosæ provinciæ post tanta tem-
porum spatia nostris victoriis a cælesti
numine præstitis iterum dicioni Romanæ nostroque additæ imperio
protestantur. Omnes vero populi leg-

1. By our incessant labours and
great care, with the blessing of God, we
have attained this double end. The barbarian nations reduced under our yoke
know our efforts in war; to which also
Africa and very many other provinces
bear witness, which, after so long an
interval, have been restored to the dominion of Rome and our empire, by
our victories gained through the favour
of heaven. All nations moreover are

ibus jam a nobis promulgatis vel compositis reguntur.

2. Et cum sacratissimas constitutiones antea confusas in luculentam oreximus consonantiam, tunc nostram extendimus curam et ad immensa prudentiæ veteris volumina et opus desperatum, quasi per medium profundum euntes, cælesti favore jam adimplevimus.

3. Cumque hoc Deo propitio peractum est, Triboniano, viro magnifico, magistro et ex quæstore sacri palatii nostri, nec non Theophilo et Dorotheo, viris illustribus, antecessoribus, quorum omnium sollertiam et legum scientiam

governed by laws which we have already either promulgated or compiled.

2. When we had arranged and brought into perfect harmony the hitherto confused mass of imperial constitutions, we then extended our care to the vast volumes of ancient law; and, sailing as it were across the mid-ocean, have now completed, through the favour of heaven, a work that once seemed beyond hope.

3. When by the blessing of God this task was accomplished, we summoned the most eminent Tribonian, master and ex-quæstor of our palace, together with the illustrious Theophilus and

Illustration 1-4   This is part of the first page of the Ravensberch edition of the *Institutes of Justinian* (1507). The text in the middle is the actual Roman law text, the same one reproduced in this book. (The medieval Latin uses abbreviations.) The small text in the margin is the "gloss," or scholarly commentary. Medieval scholars literally wrote in the margins of manuscripts, commenting on the "sacred" text in the middle. The Roman text of Justinian's *Institutes* was treated like such a sacred text, like the Bible or the Talmud. The scholars who wrote these glosses were called the "Glossators." [Author's Collection.]

et circa nostras jussiones fidem jam ex multis rerum argumentis accepimus, convocatis, specialiter mandavimus, ut nostra auctoritate nostrisque suasionibus componant institutiones: ut licent vobis prima legum cunabula non ab antiquis fabulis discere, sed ab imperiali splendore appetere, et tam aures quam animæ vestræ nihil inutile nilhilque perperam positum, sed quod in ipsis rerum optinet argumentis, accipiant et quod in priore tempore vix post triennium inferioribus contingebat, ut tunc constitutiones imperatorias legerent, hoc vos a primordio ingrediamini, digni tanto honore tantaque reperti felicitate, ut et initium vobis et finis legum eruditiones a voce principali procedat.

4. Igitur post libros quinquaginta digestorum seu pandectarum, in quos omne jus antiquum collatum est (quos per eundem virum excelsum Tribonianum nec non ceteros viros illustres et facundissimos confecimus), in hos quattuor libros easdem institutiones partiri jussimus, ut sint totius legitimæ scientiæ prima elementa.

5. Quibus breviter expositum est et quod antea optinebat, et quod postea desuetudine inumbratum ab imperiali remedio illuminatum est.

6. Quas ex omnibus antiquorum institutionibus et præcipue ex commentariis Gaii nostri tam institutionum quam rerum cottidianarum, aliisque multis commentariis compositas cum tres prædicti viri prudentes nobis optulerunt, et legimus et cognovimus et plenissimum nostrarum constitutionum robur eis accommodavimus.

Dorotheus, professors of law, all of whom have on many occasions proved to us their ability, legal knowledge, and obedience to our orders; and we have specially charged them to compose, under our authority and advice, Institutes, so that you may no more learn the first elements of law from old and erroneous sources, but apprehend them by the clear light of imperial wisdom; and that your minds and ears may receive nothing that is useless or misplaced, but only what obtains in actual practice. So that, whereas, formerly, the junior students could scarcely, after three years' study, read the imperial constitutions, you may now commence your studies by reading them, you who have been thought worthy of an honour and a happiness so great as that the first and last lessons in the knowledge of the law should issue for you from the mouth of the emperor.

4. When, therefore, by the assistance of the same eminent person Tribonian and that of other illustrious and learned men, we had compiled the fifty books, called Digests or Pandects, in which is collected the whole ancient law, we directed that these Institutes should be divided into four books, which might serve as the first elements of the whole science of law.

5. In these books a brief exposition is given of the ancient laws, and of those also which, overshadowed by disuse, have been again brought to light by our imperial authority.

6. These four books of Institutes thus complied, from all the Institutes left us by the ancients, and chiefly from the commentaries of our Gaius, both in his Institutes, and in his work on daily affairs, and also from many other commentaries, were presented to us by the three learned men we have above named. We have read and examined them and have accorded to them all the force of our constitutions.

7. Summa itaque ope et alacri studio has leges nostras accipite et vosmet ipsos sic eruditos ostendite, ut spes vos pulcherrima foveat, toto legitimo opere perfecto, posse etiam nostram rem publicam in partibus ejus vobis credendis gubernare.

Data undecimo kalendas Decembres Constantinopoli domino nostro Justiniano perpetuo Augusto tertium consula.

7. Receive, therefore, with eagerness, and study with cheerful diligence, these our laws, and show yourselves persons of such learning that you may conceive the flattering hope of yourselves being able, when your course of legal study is completed, to govern our empire in the different portions that may be entrusted to your care.

Given at Constantinople on the eleventh day of the calends of December, in the third consulate of the Emperor Justinian, ever August (533).

LIBER PRIMUS
TIT. I. DE JUSTITIA ET JURE.

JUSTITIA est constans et perpetua voluntas jus suum cuique tribuens.

1. Jurisprudentia est divinarum atque humanarum rerum notitis, justi atque injusti scientia.

2. His generaliter cognitis et incipientibus nobis exponere jura populi Romani ita maxime videntur posse tradi commodissime, si primo levi ac simplici, post deinde diligentissima atque exactissima interpretatione singula tradantur. Alioquin si statim ab initio rudem adhuc et infirmum animum studiosi multitudine ac varietate rerum oneraverimus, duorum alterum aut desertorem studiorum efficiemus aut cum magno labore ejus, sæpe etiam cum diffidentia, quæ plerumque juvenes avertit, serius ad id perducemus, ad quod leniore via ductus sine magno labore et sine ulla diffidentia maturius perduci potuisset.

Justice is the constant and perpetual wish to render every one his due.

1. Jurisprudence is the knowledge of things divine and human; the science of the just and the unjust.

2. Having explained these general terms, we think we shall commence our exposition of the law of the Roman people most advantageously, if our explanation is at first plain and easy, and is then carried on into details with the utmost care and exactness. For, if at the outset we overload the mind of the student, while yet new to the subject and unable to bear much, with a multitude and variety of topics, one of two things will happen—we shall either cause him wholly to abandon his studies, or, after great toil, and often after great distrust of himself (the most frequent stumbling-block in the way of youth), we shall at least conduct him to the point, to which, if he had been led by a smoother road, he might, without great labour, and without any distrust of his own powers, have been sooner conducted.

3. Juris præcepta sunt hæc: honeste vivere, alterum non lædere, suum cuique tribuere.

4. Hujus studii duæ sunt positiones, publicum et privatum. Publicum jus est quod ad statum rei Romanæ spec-

3. The maxims of the laws are these: to live honestly, to hurt no one, to give every one his due.

4. The study of law is divided into two branches; that of public and that of private law. Public law is that

tat, privatum, quod ad singulorum utilitatum pertinet. Dicendum est igitur de jure privato, quod tripertitum est; collectum est enim ex naturalibus præceptis aut gentium aut civilibus.

which regards the government of the Roman Empire; private law, that which concerns the interests of individuals. We are now to treat of the latter, which is composed of three elements, and consists of precepts belonging to natural law, to the law of nations and to the civil law.

LIB. I. TIT. II.
TIT. II. DE JURE NATURALI, GENTIUM ET CIVILI.

Jus naturale est, quod natura omnia animalia docuit. Nam jus istud non humani generis proprium est, sed omnium animalium, quæ in cælo, quæ in terra, quæ in mari nascuntur. Hinc descendit maris atque feminæ conjugatio, quam nos matrimonium appellamus, hinc liberorum procreatio et educatio: videmus etenim cetera quoque animalia istius juris peritia censeri.

The law of nature is that law which nature teaches to all animals. For this law does not belong exclusively to the human race, but belongs to all animals, whether of the air, the earth, or the sea. Hence comes that yoking together of male and female, which we term matrimony; hence the procreation and the bringing up of children. We see, indeed, that all the other animals besides man are considered as having knowledge of this law.

1. Jus autem civile vel gentium ita dividitur: omnes populi, qui legibus et moribus reguntur, partim suo proprio, partim communi omnium hominum jure utuntur: nam quod quisque populus ipse sibi jus constituit, id ipsius civitatis: quod vero naturalis ratio inter omnes homines constituit, id apud omnes populos peræque custoditur vocaturque jus gentium, quasi quo jure omnes gentes utuntur. Et populos itaque Romanus partim suo proprio, partim communi omnium hominum jure utitur. Quæ singula qualia sunt, suis locis proponemus.

1. Civil law is thus distinguished from the law of nations. Every community governed by laws and customs uses partly its own law, partly laws common to all mankind. The law which a people makes for its own government belongs exclusively to that state, and is called the civil law, as being the law of the particular state. But the law which natural reason appoints for all mankind obtains equally among all nations, and is called the law of nations, because all nations make use of it. The people of Rome, then, are governed partly by their own laws, and partly by the laws which are common to all mankind. What is the nature of these two component parts of our law we will set forth in the proper place.

2. Sed jus quidem civile ex unaquaque civitate appellatur, veluti Atheniensium: nam si quis velit Solonis vel Draconis leges appellare jus civile Atheniensium, non erraverit. Sic enim et jus, quo populus Romanus utitur, jus

2. Civil law takes its name from the state which it governs, as, for instance, from Athens; for it would be very proper to speak of the laws of Solon or Draco as the civil law of Athens. And thus the law which the Roman people

civile Romanorum appellamus vel jus Quiritium, quo Quirites utuntur; Romani enim a Quirino Quirites appellantur. Sed quotiens non addimus, cujus sit civitatis, nostrum jus significamus: sicuti cum poetam dicimus nec addimus nomen, subauditur apud Græcos egregius Homerus, apud nos Vergilius. Jus autem gentium omni humano generi commune est. Nam usu exigente et humanis necessitatibus gentes humanæ quædam sibi constituerunt: bella etenim orta sunt et captivitates secutæ et servitutes, quæ sunt juri naturali contrariæ (jure enim naturali ab initio omnes homines liberi nascebantur); ex hoc jure gentium et omnes pæne contractus introducti sunt, ut emptio venditio, locatio conductio, societas, depositum, mutuum et alii innumerabiles.

3. Constat autem jus nostrum aut ex scripto aut ex non scripto, ut apud Græcos: [Greek quotation.] Scriptum jus est lex, plebiscita, senatusconsulta, principum placita, magistratuum edicta, responsa prudentium.

4. Lex est, quod populus Romanus senatorio magistratu interrogante, veluti consule, constituebat. Plebiscitum est, quod plebs plebeio magistratu interrogante, veluti tribuno, constituebat. Plebs autem a populo eo differt, quo species a genere: nam appllatione populi universi cives significantur, connumeratis etiam patriciis et senatoribus: plebis autem appellatione sine patriciis et senatoribus ceteri cives significantur. Sed et plebiscita, lege Hortensia lata, non minus valere quam leges coeperunt.

5. Senatusconsultum est, quod senatus jubet atque constituit. Nam cum auctus est populus Romanus in eum

make use of is called the civil law of the Romans, or that of the Quirites, as being used by the Quirites; for the Romans are called Quirites from Quirinus. But whenever we speak of civil law, without adding of what state we are speaking, we mean our own law: just as when "the poet" is spoken of without any name being expressed, the Greeks mean the great Homer, and we Romans mean Virgil. The law of nations is common to all mankind, for nations have established certain laws, as occasion and the necessities of human life required. Wars arose, and in their train followed captivity and then slavery, which is contrary to the law of nature; for by that law all men are originally born free. Further, from this law of nations almost all contracts were at first introduced, as, for instance, buying and selling, letting and hiring, partnership, deposits, loans returnable in kind, and very many others.

3. Our law is written and unwritten, just as among the Greeks some of their laws were written and others not written. The written part consists of laws, *plebiscita*, *senatusconsulta*, enactments of emperors, edicts of magistrates, and answers of jurisprudents.

4. A law is that which was enacted by the Roman people on its being proposed by a senatorian magistrate, as a consul. A *plebiscitum* is that which was enacted by the plebs on its being proposed by a plebeian magistrate, as a tribune. The *plebs* differs from the people as a species from its genus; for all the citizens, including patricians and senators, are comprehended in the people; but the *plebs* only includes citizens, not being patricians or senators. But *plebiscita*, after the Hortensian law had been passed, began to have the same force as laws.

5. A *senatus-consultum* is that which the senate commands and appoints: for, when the Roman people

modum, ut difficile sit in unum eum convocari legis sanciendæ causa, æquum visum est senatum vice populi consuli.

6. Sed et quod principi placuit, legis habet vigorem, cum lege regia, quæ de imperio ejus lata est, populus ei et in eum omne suum imperium et potestatem concessit. Quodcumque igitur imperator per epistulam constituit vel cognoscens decrevit vel edicto præcepit, legem esse constat: hæ sunt, quæ constitutiones appellantur. Plane ex his quædam sunt personales, quæ nec ad exemplum trahuntur, quoniam non hoc princeps vult: nam quod alicui ob merita indulsit, vel si cui poenam irrogavit, vel si cui sine exemplo subvenit, personam non egreditur. Aliæ autem, cum generales sunt, omnes procul dubio tenent.

7. Prætorum quoque edicta non modicam juris optinent auctoritatem. Hæc etiam jus honorarium solemus appellare, quod qui honorem gerunt, id est magistratus, auctoritatem huic juri dederunt. Proponebant et ædiles curules edictum de quibusdam casibus, quod edictum juris honorarii portio est.

8. Responsa prudentium sunt sententiæ et opiniones eorum, quibus permissum erat jura condere. Nam antiquitus institutum erat, ut essent qui jura publice interpretarentur, quibus a Cæsare jus respondendi datum est, qui jurisconsulti appellabantur. Quorum omnium sententiæ et opiniones cam auctoritatem tenebant, ut judici recedere a responso eorum non liceret, ut est constitutum.

was so increased that it was difficult to assemble it together to pass laws, it seemed right that the senate should be consulted in the place of the people.

6. That which seems good to the emperor has also the force of law; for the people, by the *lex regia*, which is passed to confer on him his power, make over to him their whole power and authority. Therefore whatever the emperor ordains by rescript, or decides in adjudging a cause, or lays down by edict, is unquestionably law; and it is these enactments of the emperor that are called constitutions. Of these, some are personal, and are not to be drawn into precedent, such not being the intention of the emperor. Supposing the emperor has granted a favour to any man on account of his merits, or inflicted some punishment, or granted some extraordinary relief, the application of these acts does not extend beyond the particular individual. But the other constitutions, being general, are undoubtedly binding on all.

7. The edicts of the praetors are also of great authority. These edicts are called the *jus honorarium*, because those who bear honours in the state, that is, the magistrates, have given it their sanction. The curule aediles also used to publish an edict relative to certain subjects, which edict also became part of the *jus honorarium*.

8. The answers of the jurisprudents are the decisions and opinions of persons who were authorized to determine the law. For anciently it was provided that there should be persons to interpret publicly the law, who were permitted by the emperor to give answers on questions of law. They were called jurisconsults; and the authority of their decisions and opinions, when they were all unanimous, was such, that the judge could not according to the constitutions, refuse to be guided by their answers.

9. Ex non scripto jus venit, quod usus comprobavit. Nam diuturni mores consensu utentium comprobati legem imitantur.

10. Et non ineleganter in duas species jus civile distributum videtur. Nam origo ejus ab institutis duarum civitatium, Athenarum scilicet et Lacedæmonis, fluxisse videtur: in his enim civitatibus ita agi solitum erat, ut Lacedæmonii quidem magis ea, quæ pro legibus observarent, memoriæ mandarent, Athenienses vero ea, quæ in legibus scripta reprehendissent, custodirent.

11. Sed naturalia quidem jura, quæ apud omnes gentes peræque servantur, divina quadam providentia constituta, semper firma atque immutabilia permanent: ea vero, quæ ipsa sibi quæque civitas constituit, sæpe mutari solent vel tacito consensu populi vel alia postea lege lata.

12. Omne autem jus, quo utimur, vel ad personas pertinet vel ad res vel ad actiones. Ac prius de personis videamus. Nam parum est jus nosse, si personæ, quarum causa statutum est, ignorentur.

9. The unwritten law is that which usage has established; for ancient customs, being sanctioned by the consent of those who adopt them, are like laws.

10. The civil law is not improperly divided into two kinds, for the division seems to have had its origin in the customs of the two states Athens and Lacedaemon. For in these states it used to be the case, that the Lacedaemonians rather committed to memory what they were to observe as law, while the Athenians rather kept safely what they had found written in their laws.

11. The laws of nature, which all nations observe alike, being established by a divine providence, remain ever fixed and immutable. But the laws which every state has enacted, undergo frequent changes, either by the tacit consent of the people, or by a new law being subsequently passed.

12. All our law relates either to persons, or to things, or to actions. Let us first speak of persons; as it is of little purpose to know the law, if we do not know the persons for whom the law was made.

*   *   *   *

Note: The following excerpts come from another famous part of *Justinian's Institutes*, the section on Law of Sale, book III, titles 22–23. The Romans were great merchants and built a business empire throughout their military empire — not unlike, some would argue, the present economic power of the United States. Note how modern this law seems and how clearly it is written. This first section is cited "*Inst.* iii, 22," meaning book three, section 22. (Often there are subsections, say *Inst.* iii, 23, 3, below.) The Uniform Commercial Code adopted a similar system. It is only when we begin to see examples involving the sale of human beings that we realize we are in a different world, although this was done in America only a century ago. Note also the reference to the controversies between the rival groups of jurists, the Sabinians and the Proculians, discussed above in the chapter introduction. See *Inst.* iii, 23, 2.

TIT. XXII.
DE CONSENSU OBLIGATIONE.

Consensu fiunt obligationes in emptionibus venditionibus, locationibus conductionibus, societatibus, mandatis. Ideo autem istis modis consensu dicitur obligatio contrahi, quia neque scriptura neque præsentia omnimodo opus est, ac ne dari quidquam necesse est, ut substantiam capiat obligatio, sed sufficit eos, qui negotium gerunt, consentire. Unde inter absentes quoque talia negotia contrahuntur, veluti per epistulam aut per nuntium. Item in his contractibus alter alteri obligatur in id, quod alterum alteri ex bono et æquo præstare oportet, cum alioquin in verborum obligationibus alius stipuletur, alius promittat.

Obligations are formed by the mere consent of the parties in the contracts of sale, of letting to hire, of partnership, and of mandate. An obligation is, in these cases, said to be made by the mere consent of the parties, because there is no necessity for any writing, nor even for the presence of the parties; nor is it requisite that anything should be given to make the contract binding, but the mere consent of those between who the transaction is carried on suffices. Thus these contracts may be entered into by those who are at a distance from each other by means of letters, for instance, or of messengers. In these contracts each party is bound to the other to render him all that equity demands, while in verbal obligations one party stipulates and the other promises.

TIT. XXIII.
DE EMPTIONE ET VENDITIONE.

Emptio et venditio contrahitur, simulatque de pretio convenerit, quamvis nondum pretium numeratum sit ac ne arra quidem data fuerit. Nam quod arræ nomine datur, argumentum est emptionis et venditionis contractæ. Sed hæc quidem de emptionibus et venditionibus, quæ sine scriptura conficiuntur, non aliter perfectam esse emptionem et venditionem constituimus, nisi et instrumenta emptionis fuerint conscripta vel manu propria contrahentium, vel ab alio quidem scripta, a contrahente autem subscripta et, si per tabellionem fiunt, nisi et completiones acceperint et fuerint partibus absoluta. Donec enim aliquid ex his deest, et poenitentiæ locus est et potest emptor vel venditor sine poena recedere ab emptione. Ita tamen impune recedere eis concedimus, nisi jam arrarum nomine aliquid fuerit datum: hoc

The contract of sale is formed as soon as the price is agreed upon, although it has not yet been paid, nor even an earnest given; for what is given as an earnest only serves as proof that the contract has been made. This must be understood of sales made without writing; for with regard to these we have made no alteration in the law. But, where there is a written contract, we have enacted that a sale is not to be considered completed unless an instrument of sale has been drawn up, being either written by the contracting parties, or at least signed by them, if written by others; or if drawn up by a *tabellio* [a professional person who drew up written documents for clients], it must be formally complete and finished throughout; for as long as any of these requirements is wanting, there is room

etenim subsecuto, sive in scriptis sive sine scriptis venditio celebrata est, is, qui recusat adimplere contractum, si quidem emptor est, perdit, quod dedit, si vero venditor, duplum restituere compellitur, licet nihil super arris expressum est.

1. Pretium autem constitui oportet: nam nulla emptio sine pretio esse potest. Sed et certum pretium esse debet. Alioquin si ita inter aliquos convenerit, ut, quanti Titius rem æstimaverit, tanti sit empta: inter veteres satis abundeque hoc dubitabatur, sive constat venditio sive non. Sed nostra decisio ita hoc constituit, ut, quotiens sic composita sit venditio 'quanti ille æstimaverit,' sub hac condicione staret contractus, ut, si quidem ipse, qui nominatus est, pretium definierit, omnimodo secundum ejus æstimationem et pretium persolvatur et res tradatur, ut venditio ad effectum perducatur, emptore quidem ex empto actione, venditore autem ex venditio agente. Sin, autem ille, qui nominatus est, vel noluerit vel non potuerit pretium definire, tunc pro nihilo esse venditionem, quasi nullo pretio statuto. Quod jus cum in venditionibus nobis placuit, non est absurdum et in locationibus et conductionibus trahere.

2. Item pretium in numerata pecunia consistere debet. Nam in ceteris rebus an pretium esse possit, veluti homo aut fundus aut toga alterius rei pretium esse possit, valde quærebatur. Sabinus et Cassius etiam in alia re putant posse pretium consistere: unde illud est, quod vulgo dicebatur, per permutationem rerum emptionem et venditionem contrahi eamque speciem emptionis venditionisque vetustissimam esse: argumentoque utebantur Græco poeta Homero,

to retract, and either the buyer or seller may retract without suffering loss: that is, if no earnest has been given. If earnest has been given, then, whether the contract was written or unwritten, the purchaser, if he refuses to fulfill it, loses what he has given as earnest, and the seller, if he refuses, has to restore double; although no agreement on the subject of the earnest was expressly made.

1. It is necessary that a price should be agreed upon, for there can be no sale without a price. And the price must be fixed and certain. If the parties agree that the thing shall be sold at a sum at which Titius shall value it, it was a question much debated among the ancients, whether in such a case there is a sale or not. We have decided, that when a sale is made for a price to be fixed by a third person, the contract shall be binding under this condition—that if this third person does fix a price, the price to be paid shall be that which he fixes, and the thing shall be delivered, so that the sale becomes complete, the purchaser having the *actio ex empto*, and the seller having that *ex vendito*. But if he will not or cannot fix a price, the sale is then void, as being made without any price being fixed on. This decision, which we have adopted with respect to sales, may reasonably be made to apply to contracts of letting on hire.

2. The price should consist in a sum of money. It has been much doubted whether it can consist in anything else, as in a slave, a piece of land, or a toga. Sabinus and Cassius thought that it could. And it is thus that it is commonly said that exchange is a sale, and that this form of sale is the most ancient. The testimony of Homer was quoted, who in one place says that the army of the Greeks procured wine by an exchange

qui aliqua parte exercitum Achivorum vinum sibi comparasse sit permutatis quibusdam rebus, his verbis:—

[Greek quote.]

Diversæ scholæ auctores contra sentiebant aliudque esse existimabant permutationem rerum, aliud emptionem et venditionem. Alioquin non posse rem expediri, permutatis rebus, quæ videatur res venisse et quæ pretii nomine data esse: nam utramque videri et venisse et pretii nomine datam esse, rationem non pati. Sed Proculi sententia dicentis, permutationem propriam esse speciem contractus a venditione separatam, merito prævaluit, cum ipse aliis Homericis veraibus adjuvatur et validioribus rationibus argumentatur. Quod et anteriores divi principes admiserunt et in nostris digestis latius significatur.

3. Cum autem emptio et venditio contracta sit (quod effici diximus, simulatque de pretio convenerit, cum sine scriptura res agitur), periculum rei venditæ statim ad emptorem pertinet, tametsi adhuc ea res emptori tradita non sit. Itaque si homo mortuus sit vel aliqua parte corporis læsus fuerit, aut ædes totæ aut aliqua ex parte incedio consumptæ fuerint, aut fundus vi fluminis totus vel aliqua ex parte ablatus sit, sive etiam inundatione aquæ aut arboribus turbine dejectis longe minor aut deterior esse coeperit: emptoris damnum est, cui necesse est, licet rem non fuerit nactus, pertium solvere. Quidquid enim sine dolo et culpa venditoris accidit, in eo venditor securus est. Sed et si post emptionem fundo aliquid per alluvionem accessit, ad emptoris commodum pertinet: nam et commodum pertinet: nam et commodum ejus esse debet, cujus periculum est. Quodsi fugerit homo, qui veniit, aut subreptus fuerit, ita ut neque dolus

of certain things. The passage is this:—

'The long-haired Achæans procured wine, some by giving copper, others by giving shining steel, others by giving oxen, others by giving slaves'.

The authors of the opposite school were of a contrary opinion: they thought that exchange was one thing and sale another. Otherwise, in an exchange, it would be impossible to say which was the thing sold, and which the thing given as the price; for it was contrary to reason to consider each thing as at once sold, and given as the price. The opinion of Proculus, who maintained that exchange is a particular kind of contract distinct from sale, has deservedly prevailed, as it is supported by other lines from Homer, and still more weighty reasons. This view has been fully treated of in our Digest.

3. As soon as the sale is contracted, that is, in the case of a sale made without writing, when the parties have agreed upon the price, all risk attaching to the thing sold falls upon the purchaser, although the thing has not yet been delivered to him. Therefore, if the slave sold dies or receives an injury in any part of his body, or the whole or a portion of the house is burnt, or the whole or a portion of the land is carried away by the force of a flood, or is diminished or deteriorated by an inundation, or by a tempest making havoc with the trees, the loss falls on the purchaser, and although he does not receive the thing, he is obliged to pay the price, for the seller does not suffer for anything which happens without any fraud or fault of his. On the other hand, if after the sale the land is increased by alluvion, it is the purchaser who receives the advantage, for he who bears the risk of harm ought to receive the benefit of all that

neque culpa venditoris interveniat, animadvertendum erit, an custodiam ejus usque as traditionem venditor susceperit. Sane enim, si susceperit, ad ipsius periculum is casus pertinet: si non susceperit, securus erit. Idem et in ceteris animalibus ceterisque rebus intellegimus. Utique tamen vindicationem rei et condictionem exhibere debebit emptori, quia sane, qui rem nondum emptori tradidit, adhuc ipse dominus est. Idem est etiam de furti et de damni injuriæ actione.

is advantageous. But if a slave who has been sold runs away or is stolen, without any fraud or fault on the part of the seller, we must inquire whether the seller undertook to keep him safely until he was delivered over; if he undertook this what happens is at his risk; if he did not undertake it, he is not responsible. The same would hold in the case of any other animal or any other thing. But the seller is in any case bound to make over to the purchaser his right to a real or personal action, for the person who has not delivered the thing is still its owner; and it is the same with regard to the action of theft, and the action *damni injuriæ*.

INSTITUTES OF GAIUS (circa 161 A.D.)

Note: As discussed in the introduction to this chapter, all Roman texts predating Justinian's *Corpus Juris* were destroyed by order of the Emperor. This text, *Gaius' Institutes*, dates from about 161 A.D. It was preserved by accident, and discovered by B.G. Niebuhr in 1816 in the chapter library of Verona. Included are the sections comparable to those you just read from *Justinian's Institutes*, cited *Gai.* i, 1–9 and *Gai.* iii, 97, 139. The first section, from book i, deals with fundamental classifications of types of laws. The latter sections, from book iii, are Roman contract law, including doctrines of voidness for mistake and shifting of the risk by a contract of sale. Note, again, the reference to the disputes between the Sabinians and the Proculians. See *Gai.* iii, 139. Notice also how the Gaius uses simple examples to illustrate difficult ideas, something always popular with law students. Again, the examples relating to slavery are shocking, given the modern "feel" and elegance of this text. See *Gai.* iii, 97.

These passages were translated by the great Roman law scholar, Francis de Zulueta. See *The Institutes of Gaius, Part I* (trans. Francis de Zulueta, 1946), 3, 5, 183, 197, 199. [Reproduced courtesy Oxford University Press.]

THE INSTITUTES OF GAIUS

Part I

Text with Critical Notes and Translation by
Francis de Zulueta, D.C.L., F.B.A.

BOOK I

1. Every people that is governed by statutes and customs observes partly its own peculiar law and partly the common law of all mankind. That law which a

people establishes for itself is peculiar to it, and is called *ius ciuile* (civil law) as being the special law of that *ciuitas* (State), while the law that natural reason establishes among all mankind is followed by all peoples alike, and is called *ius gentium* (law of nations, or law of the world) as being the law observed by all mankind. Thus the Roman people observes partly its own peculiar law and partly the common law of mankind. This distinction we shall apply in detail at the proper places.

2. The laws of the Roman people consist of *leges* (comitial enactments), plebiscites, senatusconsults, imperial constitutions, edicts of those possessing the rights to issue them, and answers of the learned. 3. A *lex* is a command and ordinance of the *populus*. A plebiscite is a command or ordinance of the *plebs*. The *plebs* differs from the *populus* in that the term *populus* designates all citizens including patricians, while the term *plebs* designates all citizens excepting patricians. Hence in former times the patricians used to maintain that they were not bound by plebiscites, these having been made without their authorization. But later a *L. Hortensia* was passed, which provided that plebiscites should bind the entire *populus*. Thereby plebiscites were equated to *leges*. 4. A senatusconsult is a command and ordinance of the senate; it has the force of *lex*, though this has been questioned. 5. An imperial constitution is what the emperor by decree, edict, or letter ordains; it has never been doubted that this has the force of *lex*, seeing that the emperor himself receives his *imperium* (sovereign power) through a *lex*. 6. The right of issuing edicts is possessed by magistrates of the Roman people. Very extensive law is contained in the edicts of the two praetors, the urban and the peregrine, whose jurisdiction is possessed in the provinces by the provincial governors; also in the edicts of the curule aediles, whose jurisdiction is possessed in the provinces of the Roman people by quaestors; no quaestors are sent to the provinces of Caesar, and consequently the aedilician edict is not published there. 7. The answers of the learned are the decisions and opinions of those who are authorized to lay down the law. If the decisions of all of them agree, what they so hold has the force of *lex*, but if they disagree, the judge is at liberty to follow whichever decision he pleases. This is declared by a rescript of the late emperor Hadrian.

8. The whole of the law observed by us relates either to persons or to things or to actions. Let us first consider persons.

9. The primary distinction in the law of persons is this, that all men are either free or slaves. 10. Next, free men are either *ingenui* (freeborn) or *libertini* (freedmen). 11. *Ingenui* are those born free, *libertini* those manumitted from lawful slavery. 12. Next, of freedom there are three classes: they are either Roman citizens or Latins or in the category of *dediticii*. Let us consider each class separately, and first *dediticii*.

* * * *

BOOK III
VOID STIPULATIONS

97. If the thing for conveyance of which we stipulate is one that cannot be conveyed, our stipulation is void, for instance if one were to stipulate for conveyance of a free man whom one believed to be a slave, or of a dead slave whom one believed to be alive, or of sacred or religious land which one thought to be subject to human law. 97a. Again, if one stipulates for a thing which cannot exist

at all, such as a hippocentaur, the stipulation is likewise void. 98. Again, if one stipulates subject to a condition that one touches the sky with one's finger, the stipulation is void. Yet a legacy left subject to an impossible condition is held by our teachers to be due precisely as though it had been left unconditionally, whereas the authorities of the other school consider a legacy to be as void as a stipulation in such a case. One must admit that it is not easy to give a satisfactory ground for distinguishing. 99. Further, a stipulation is void in which a man, not knowing that a thing belongs to him, stipulates for its conveyance to himself, obviously because what belongs to a man cannot be conveyed to him. 100. Then again, a stipulation is void in which a man stipulates for conveyance thus: 'Do you solemnly promise conveyance after my death?' or 'after your death?'. Yet it is valid in the form 'when I am dying' or 'when you are dying', so that the obligation is made to begin at the last moment of the stipulator's or the promisor's life; for it was felt to be against principle that an obligation should start from the heir. But again, we cannot stipulate thus: 'Do you solemnly promise conveyance on the day before I die?' or 'on the day before you die?', because the day before a death cannot be known till the death has taken place, but when that has happened, the obligation is carried back into the past and is something like a stipulation: 'Do you solemnly promise conveyance to my heir?', which is of course void.

*   *   *   *

CONSENSUAL CONTRACTS: SALE

139. A contract of sale is concluded when the price has been agreed, although it have not yet been paid and even no earnest have been given. For what is given by way of earnest is evidence of a contract of sale having been concluded. 140. The price must be definite. Thus, if we agree that the thing be bought at the value to be put on it by Titius, Labeo said that this transaction was of no effect, and Cassius approves his view. But Ofilius thought it was a sale, and Proculus followed his view. 141. Also, the price must be in money. There is, however, much question whether the price can consist of other things, for example whether a slave or a robe or land can be the price of something else. Our teachers hold that the price can consist of another thing. Hence their opinion commonly is that by exchange of things a sale is contracted and that this is the most ancient form of sale. They argue from the Greek poet Homer, who somewhere says: 'Thence the long-haired Achaeans bought wine, some for copper, some for gleaming steel, some for hides, some for the cattle themselves, and some for slaves.' The other school dissent, holding that exchange or barter is one thing and sale another; for if not, so they argue, one cannot, when things are exchanged, determine which is the thing sold and which that given as price, while on the other hand it seems absurd that both things should be considered as both sold and given as price. Caelius Sabinus, however, says that if I give you a slave as the price of something, for instance land, which you are offering for sale, then the land is to be considered as having been sold and the slave as having been given as price for the land.

THE DIGEST OF JUSTINIAN (533 A.D.)

Note: The following short passages show how Justinian's jurists composed the great *Digest*. Note that the section again focuses on "mistake" doctrine in contract law. It actually consists of excerpts from a number of jurists, Paul, Ulpian, and Pomponius. They were carefully chosen by Justinian's compilers to "accurately" state the law, and then the underlying texts were destroyed. These translations, by Dr. Peter Garnesy, come from the new edition of the entire *Digest* edited by Alan Watson. See *The Digest of Justinian*, vol 2, 515, 517 (A. Watson, ed., 1985, University of Pennsylvania Press). [Reproduced courtesy University of Pennsylvania Press.] Again, the examples given shock us, although the legal principles are quite familiar to any first year contracts student. The classic account is F. de Zulueta, *The Roman Law of Sale* (1945).

Digest, Book 18, 1, 9–14

9. ULPIAN, *Sabinus, book 28*: It is obvious that agreement is of the essence in sale and purchase; the purchase is not valid if there be disagreement over the contract itself, the price, or any other element of the sale. Hence, if I thought that I was buying the Cornelian farm and you that you were selling the Sempronian, the sale is void because we were not agreed upon the thing sold. The same is true if I intended to sell Stichus and you thought I was selling you Pamphilus, the slave himself not being there: Because there is no agreement on the object of sale, there is manifestly no sale. 1. Of course, if we are merely in disagreement over the name but at one on the actual thing, there is no doubt that the sale is good; for if the thing be identified, a mistake over its name is irrelevant. 2. The next question is whether there is a good sale when there is no mistake over the identity of the thing but there is over its substance: Suppose that vinegar is sold as wine, copper as gold or lead, or something else similar to silver as silver. Marcellus, in the sixth book of his *Digest*, writes that there is a sale because there is agreement on the thing despite the mistake over its substance. I would agree in the case of the wine, because the essence is much the same, that is, if the wine has gone sour; if it be not sour wine, however, but was vinegar from the beginning such as brewed vinegar, then it emerges that one thing has been sold as another. But in the other cases, I think that there is no sale by reason of the error over the material.

10. PAUL, *Sabinus, book 5*: It would be different if the thing was gold, although of a quality inferior to that supposed by the purchaser. In such a case, the sale is good.

11. ULPIAN, *Sabinus, book 28*: Now what if the purchaser were blind or a mistake over the material were made by a purchaser unskilled in distinguishing materials? Do we say that the parties are agreed on the thing? How can a man agree who cannot see it? 1. If, however, I think that I am buying a virgin when she is, in fact, a woman, the sale is valid, there being no mistake over her sex. But if I sell you a woman and you think that you are buying a male slave, the error over sex makes the sale void.

12. POMPONIUS, *Quintus Mucius, book 31*: In questions of this kind, we must look to the persons of the actual contracting parties, not to those to whom an action will accrue from the contract; if, say, my slave or son-in-power buy something in my presence but in his own name, it is his intention not mine which must be investigated.

13. POMPONIUS, *Sabinus, book 9*: However, it is true that if you knowingly sell a fugitive to my slave or mandatory who is ignorant of the fact but I do know, you will not be liable to the action on purchase.

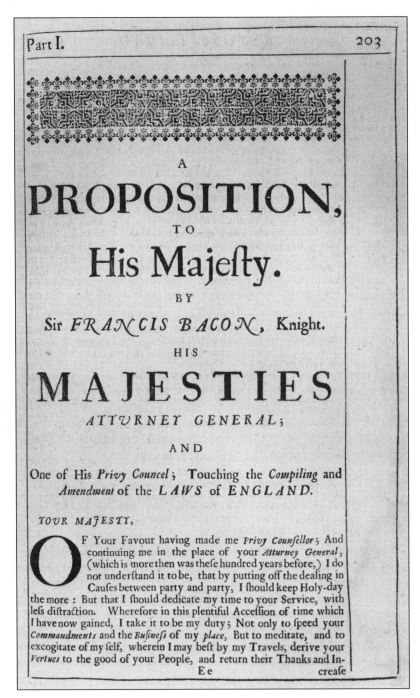

A

PROPOSITION,

T O

His Majesty.

B Y

Sir *FRANCIS BACON*, Knight.

H I S

MAJESTIES

ATTURNEY GENERAL;

A N D

One of His *Privy Councel*; Touching the *Compiling* and *Amendment* of the *LAWS* of *ENGLAND*.

YOUR MAJESTY,

OF Your Favour having made me *Privy Counsellor*; And continuing me in the place of your *Atturney General*, (which is more then was these hundred years before,) I do not understand it to be, that by putting off the dealing in Causes between party and party, I should keep Holy-day the more : But that I should dedicate my time to your Service, with less distraction. Wherefore in this plentiful Accession of time which I have now gained, I take it to be my duty; Not only to speed your *Commandments* and the *Business* of my *place*, But to meditate, and to excogitate of my self, wherein I may best by my Travels, derive your *Vertues* to the good of your People, and return their Thanks and In-
E e   crease

Illustration 1-5 This is the beginning of Francis Bacon's famous "Proposition" from the *Resuscitatio* of his works by his chaplain after Bacon's death, 1671 ed. [Author's Collection].

14. ULPIAN, *Sabinus, book 28*: Now what are we to say when both parties are in error over both the material and its quality? Suppose that I think that I am selling and you that you are buying gold, when it is, in fact, copper, or, again, that co-heirs sell to one of their number, for a substantial price, a bracelet said to be gold which proves to be largely copper? It is settled law that the sale holds good because there is some gold in it. Even if a thing be of gold alloy, though I think it solid gold, the sale is good. But if copper be sold as gold, there is no contract.

A PROPOSITION TO HIS MAJESTY BY SIR FRANCIS BACON, Knight, His Majesty's Attorney-General, and One of His Privy Council; Touching the Compiling and Amendment of the Laws of England.

Note: Francis Bacon (1561–1626) was a great legal theorist, as well as a brilliant writer and a scientific pioneer. Under the patronage of James I, he became Lord Chancellor of England in 1618. Nevertheless, his life was full of controversy and intrigue, as we shall see in Chapter X. The following are excerpts from his famous "A Proposition to His Majesty" for a complete reform of the English system of legal authority. It is taken from *The Works of Francis Bacon* (ed. Spedding, Ellis Heath, 1872), vol xiii, 61, 64–65, 68–73. [Notes omitted.] Note the strong influence of the Roman law. Do you think Bacon's colleagues at the bar liked this proposal? Why not? See D.R. Coquillette, *Francis Bacon* (1992), 105–117.

*   *   *   *

But certain it is, that our laws, as they now stand, are subject to great incertainties, and a variety of opinion, delays, and evasions: whereof ensueth,

1. That the multiplicity and length of suits is great.
2. That the contentious person is armed, and the honest subject wearied and oppressed.
3. That the judge is more absolute; who, in doubtful cases, hath a greater stroke and liberty.
4. That the chancery courts are more filled, the remedy of law being often obscure and doubtful.
5. That the ignorant lawyer shroudeth his ignorance of law in that doubts are so frequent and many.
6. That men's assurances of their lands and estates by patents, deeds, wills, are often subject to question, and hollow; and many the like inconveniences.

It is a good rule and direction (for that all laws, *secundum magis et minus*, do participate of incertainties,) that followeth: Mark, whether the doubts that arise are only in cases not of ordinary experience; or which happen every day. If in the first only, impute it to frailty of man's foresight, that cannot reach by law to all cases; but if in the latter, be assured there is a fault in the law. Of this I say no more, but that (to give every man his due) had it not been for Sir Edward Coke's *Reports* (which though they may have errors, and some peremptory and extrajudicial resolutions more than are warranted, yet they contain infinite good decisions and rulings over of cases), the law by this time had been almost like a ship without ballast; for that the cases of modern experience are fled from those that are adjudged and ruled in former time.

But the necessity of this work is yet greater in the statute law. For first, there are a number of ensnaring penal laws, which lie upon the subject; and if in bad times they should be awaked and put in execution, would grind them to powder.

There is a learned civilian that expoundeth the curse of the prophet, *Pluet super eos laqueos*, of multitude of penal laws, which are worse than the showers of hail or tempest upon cattle, for they fall upon men.

There are some penal laws fit to be retained, but their penalty too great; and it is ever a rule, that any over-great penalty (besides the acerbity of it) deads the execution of the law.

There is further inconvenience, of penal laws obsolete and out of use; for that it brings a gangrene, neglect, and habit of disobedience upon other wholsale laws that are fit to be continued in practice and execution; so that our laws endure the torment of Mezentius:

> *The living die in the arms of the dead.*

*   *   *   *

The work itself; and the way to reduce and recompile the Laws of England.

This work is to be done (to use some few words, which is the language of action and effect,) in this manner.

It consisteth of two parts; the digest or recompiling of the common laws, and that of the statutes.

In the first of these, three things are to be done:

1. The compiling of a book *De antiquitatibus juris.*
2. The reducing or perfecting of the course or corps of the common laws.
3. The composing of certain introductive and auxiliary books touching the study of the laws.

For the first of these. All ancient records in your Tower or elsewhere, containing acts of parliament, letters patents, commissions, and judgments, and the like, are to be searched, perused, and weighed. And out of these are to be selected those that are of most worth and weight; and in order of time, not of titles, (for the more conformity with the Year-books,) to be set down and registred; rarely in *haec verba*; but summed with judgment, not omitting any material part. There are to be used for reverend precedents, but not for binding authorities.

For the second, which is the main; There is to be made a perfect course of the law *in serie temporis*, or Year-books (as we call them), from Edward the First to this day. In the compiling of this course of law, or Year-books, the points following are to be observed.

First, in all cases which are at this day clearly no law, but constantly ruled to the contrary, are to be left out; they do but fill the volumes, and season the wits of students in a contrary sense of law. And so likewise all cases wherein that is solemnly and long debated, whereof there is now no question at all, are to be entered as judgments only, and resolutions, but without the arguments, which are now become but frivolous. Yet for the observation of the deeper sort of lawyers, that they may see how the law hath altered, out of which they may pick sometimes good use, I do advise that upon the first in time of those obsolete cases there were a *memorandum* set, that at that time the law was thus taken, until such a time, *etc.*

Secondly, *Homonymiae*, (as Justinian calleth them,) that is, cases merely of iteration and repitition, are to be purged away: and the cases of identity which are best reported and argued to be retained instead of the rest; the judgments nevertheless to be set down, every one in time as they are, but with a quotation or reference to the case where the point is argued at large: but if the case consist part of repitition, part of new matter, the repitition is only to be omitted.

Thirdly, as to the *Antinomiae*, cases judged to the contrary, it were too great a trust to refer to the judgment of the composers of this work, to decide the law either way, except there be a current stream of judgments of later times; and then I reckon the contrary cases amongst cases obsolete, of which I have spoken before: Nevertheless this diligence would be used, that such cases of contradiction be specially noted and collected, to the end those doubts that have been so long militant may, either by assembling all the Judges in the Exchequer Chamber, or by Parliament, be put into certainty. For to do it by bringing them in question under feigned parties is to be disliked. *Nil habeat forum ex scena.*

Fourthly, all idle queries, which are but seminaries of doubts and incertainties, are to be left out and omitted, and no queries set down but of great doubts well debated and left undecided for difficulty; but no doubting or upstarting queries; which though they be touched in argument for explanation, yet were better to die than to be put into the books.

Lastly, cases reported with too great prolixity would be drawn into a more compendious report; not in the nature of an abridgment; but tautologies and impertinencies to be cut off. As for misprinting, and insensible reporting, which many times confound the students, that will be *obiter* amended; but more principally, if there be any thing in the report which is not well warranted by the record, that is also to be rectified. The course being thus compiled, then it resteth but for your Majesty to appoint some grave and sound lawyers, with some honourable stipend, to be reporters for the time to come; and then this is settled for all times.

For the auxiliary books that conduce to the study and science of the law, they are three: Institutions; a treatise *De regulis juris*; and a better book *De verborum significationibus*, or terms of the law. For the Institutions, I know well there be books of introductions (wherewith students begin) of good worth, specially Littleton and Fitzherbert; *Natura brevium*; but they are no ways of the nature of an *Institutions*; the office whereof is to be a key and general preparation to the reading of the course. And principally it ought to have two properties; the one a perspicuous and clear order or method; and the other, an universal latitude or comprehension, that the students may have a little prenotion of every thing, like a model towards a great building. For the treatise *De regulis juris*, I hold it of all other things the most important to the health, as I may term it, and good institutions of any laws: it is indeed like the ballast of a ship, to keep all upright and stable; but I have seen little in this kind, either in our law or other laws, that satisfieth me. The naked rule or maxim doth not the effect. It must be made useful by good differences, ampliations, and limitations, warranted by good authorities; and this not by raising up of quotations and references, but by discourse and deducement in a just tractate. In this I have travelled myself, at the first more cursorily, since with more diligence, and will go on with it, if God and your Majesty will give me leave. And I do assure your Majesty, I am in good hope, that when Sir Edward Coke's Reports and my Rules and Decisions shall come to posterity, there will be (whatsoever is now thought,) question who was the greater lawyer? For the books of the Terms of the Law, there is a poor one; but I wish a diligent one, wherein should be comprised not only the exposition of the terms of law, but of the words of all ancient records and precedents.

For the Abridgements, I could wish, if it were possible, that none might use them but such as had read the course first; that they might serve for repertories to learned lawyers, and not to make a lawyer in haste: but since that cannot be, I wish there were a good abridgment composed of the two that are extant, and in better order. So much for the Common Law.

Statute Law.

For the reforming and recompiling of the Statute Law, it consisteth of four parts.

1. The first, to discharge the books of those statutes whereas the case by alteration of time is vanished; as Lombard Jews, Gauls half-pence, etc. Those may nevertheless remain in the libraries for antiquities, but no reprinting of them. The like of statutes long since expired and clearly repealed; for if the repeal be doubtful, it must be so propounded to the Parliament.

2. The next is, to repeal all statutes which are sleeping and not of use, but yet snaring and in force. In some of those it will perhaps be requisite to substitute some more reasonable law instead of them, agreeable to the time; in others a simple repeal may suffice.

3. The third, that the greviousness of the penalty in many statutes be mitigated, though the ordinance stand.

4. The last is, the reducing of concurrent statutes, heaped one upon another, to one clear and uniform law. Towards this there hath been already, upon my motion and your Majesty's direction, a great deal of good pains taken; my Lord Hobart, myself, Serjeant Finch, Mr. Heneage Finch, Mr. Noye, Mr. Hackwell, and others; whose labours being of a great bulk, it is not fit now to trouble your Majesty with any further particularity therein; only by this you may perceive the work is already advanced: but because this part of the work, which concerneth the Statute Laws, must of necessity come to Parliament, and the houses will best like that which themselves guide, and the persons that themselves employ, the way were to imitate the precedent of the commissioners for the Canon Laws in 27 Hen. VIII, and 4 Edw. VI, and the commissioners for the Union of the two realms, *primo* of your Majesty, and so to have the commissioners named by both houses; but not with a precedent power to conclude, but only to prepare and propound to Parliament.

This is the best way, I conceive, to accomplish this excellent work, of honour to your Majesty's times, and of good to all times; which I submit to your Majesty's better judgment.

JOHN ADAMS AS ROMAN LAWYER

Note: John Adams (1735–1826) was, of course, a great patriot and second President of the United States. As a young law student, however, he could be a bit compulsive, competitive and arrogant. He was trained as a lawyer by the "apprentice system"—there being no American law schools, at least of a professional type, in his day. What follows are excerpts from his diary. He made a great effort to study Roman law, as you can see. Later, this was to become very valuable to him. Not only did he litigate cases in the Vice Admiralty courts, where the civil law was used, but he also negotiated loans with the Dutch for the new Republic, and helped draft the Constitution. All of the above made use of Roman law. See D.R. Coquillette, "Justinian in Braintree: John Adams, Civilian Learning, and Legal Elitism, 1758–1775" in *Law in Colonial Massachusetts* (eds. Coquillette, Brink, Menaud, 1984), 359–418. Adams' tutor, Jeremiah Gridley, told the young lawyer that classical legal writers and texts "ought to be the study of our whole lives." *Id.*, 418. Do you think law should be taught as a humanity? Do you study as hard as John Adams did?

Diary of John Adams

Reprinted by permission of the publisher from *The Diary and Autobiography of John Adams,* edited by L.H. Butterfield, Leonard C. Faber, Wendell D. Garrett, Cambridge, Mass.: Harvard University Press, Copyright © 1961 by the Massachusetts Historical Society. (Vol 1, pp. 44–45.)

23 Monday.

Came to Mr. Putnams and began Law. And studied not very closely this Week.

29 Sunday.
Braintree Octr. 5th. 1758

Yesterday arrived here from Worcester. I am this Day about beginning Justinians Institutions with Arnold Vinnius's Notes. I took it out of the Library at Colledge [Harvard]. It is intituled, D. Justiniani Sacratissimi Principis Institutionum sive Elementorum Libri quatuor, Notis perpetuis multo, quam hucusque, dilligentius illustrati, Cura & Studio, Arnoldi Vinnii J.C. Editio novissima priori Progressu Juris civilis Romani, Fragmentis XII. Tabularum & Rerum Nominumque Indice Auctior, ut ex Præfatione nostra patet.—Now I shall have an opportunity of judging of a dutch Commentator whom the Dedicat[ion] calls celeberrimus sua Etate in hac Academia Doctor.—Let me read with Attention, Deliberation, Distinction. Let me admire with Knowledge. It is low to admire a Dutch Commentator m[erely] because he uses latin, and greek Phraseology. Let me be able to draw the True Character both of the Text of Justinian, and of the Notes of his Commentator, when I have finished the Book. Few of my Contemporary Beginners, in the Study of the Law, have the Resolution, to aim at much Knowledge in the Civil Law. Let me therefore distinguish myself from them, by the Study of the Civil Law, in its native languages, those of Greece and Rome. I shall gain the Consideration and perhaps favour of Mr. Gridley and Mr. Pratt by this means.—As a stimulus let me insert in this Place Justinians Adhortationem

Illustration 1-6   This is Arnold Vinnius's commentary on *Justinian's Institutes*. See John Adams' diary for Sunday, October 5th, 1758, *supra*. [Author's Collection.]

ad Studium Juris. "Summa itaque ope et alacri Studio has Leges nostras accipite: et vosmet ipsos sic eruditos ostendite, ut Spes vos pulcherrima foveat, toto legitimo Opere perfecto, posse etiam nostram Rem publicam in Partibus ejus vobis credendis gubernari." Data Constantinopoli XI. Kalendas Decembris, Domino Justiniano, perpetuo Augsusto tertium Consule.—Cic. I. de Orat.—Pergite, ut facitis, Adolescentes, atque in id Studium in quo estis incumbite ut et vobis honori, et Amicis Utilitati, et Reipublicae emolumento esse possitis.—Arnoldus Vinnius in Academia Leidensi Juris Professor fuit celeberrimus.

[Note: Compare the last section of Adams' notes with *Justinian's Institutes*, *PROCEMIUM*, sec. 7, set out above.]

I have read about 10 Pages in Justinian and Translated about 4 Pages into English. This is the whole of my Days Work. I have smoaked, chatted, trifled, loitered away this whole day almost. By much the greatest Part of this day has been spent, in unloading a Cart, in cutting oven Wood, in making and recruiting my own fire, in eating nuts and apples, in drinking Tea, cutting and smoaking Tobacco and in chatting with the Doctor's Wife at their House and at this. Chores, Chatt, Tobacco, Tea, Steal away Time. But I am resolved to translate Justinian and his Commentators Notes by day light and read Gilberts Tenures by Night til I am master of both, and I will meddle with no other Book in this Chamber on a Week day. On a Sunday I will read the Inquiry into the Nature of the human Soul, and for Amusement I will sometimes read Ovids Art of Love to Mrs. Savel.—This shall be my Method.—I have read Gilberts 1st Section, of feuds, this evening but am not a Master of it.

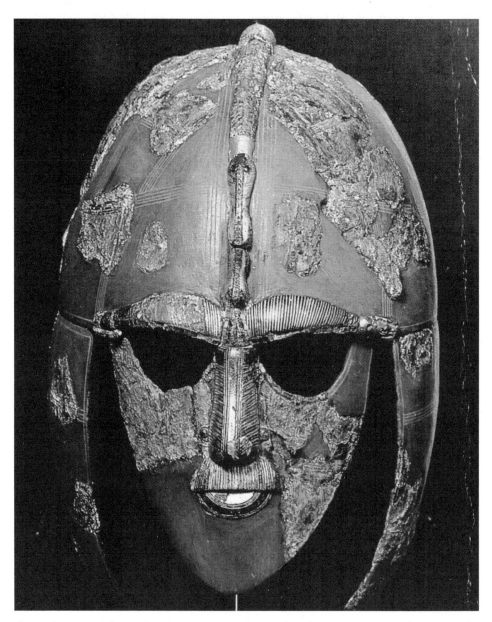

Illustration 2-1   This is the "Sutton Hoo Helmet," found in a massive royal grave on the East Anglian Coast. (*circa* 620 A.D.) Courtesy British Museum. © The British Museum, British Museum Press.

II

THE ANGLO-SAXON PERIOD

A. "PRIMITIVE" ORIGINS

True cultural "darkness" fell over England a generation after the Roman departure. Savage invasions wiped the remaining "Romanized" peoples away. By the time St. Augustine arrived as a Christian missionary in 597 A.D., he reported that Saxon tribes were literally living in the Roman ruins at Canterbury and elsewhere. True, there were romantic legends of stout resistance by Romanized Britons. These even may have been the foundation of the tales of King Arthur. In cold reality, however, the land was divided among invading tribes, who constantly warred with each other and with new invaders. Except for the work of a handful of Christian priests, who were in frequent danger, there was no writing, and almost no written record. Indeed, the number of Anglo-Saxon records, even just before the Norman invasion, remains minuscule compared to all other historical periods, including the Roman. This, in itself, makes it hard to know enough about this period, which lasted from the famous letter of Emperor Honorius of 410 A.D., abandoning the Romanized Britons, to the Norman Invasion of 1066 A.D., a period of more than six centuries.

We do know some things. The first invaders were Angles and Saxons from Germany who came, not as a united people, but as a group of separate tribes. These tribes were called "kin" and their leaders were called "chief kin" or "kings." Anglo-Saxon "kingdoms" were little more than tribal territories, and there were dozens of them.

During the period from 600 to 800 A.D., some of the more powerful "kings" were able to consolidate their kingdoms into fairly big units, such as the kingdom of Wessex in the south, Mercia and East Anglia in the Midlands, and Northumbria in the north. Christian missionaries, such as St. Germanus and St. Augustine, also visited at this time, and succeeded in converting most of the tribes to a fairly rude form of Christianity, although some evidence of paganism persisted for centuries alongside the new religion. In the period 800 A.D. to 900 A.D. there were even more invasions, this time by Vikings and Danes. The Danes drove the Anglo-Saxons out of much of the North and also settled down, creating a region still known as the "Danelaw." Anglo-Saxon kingdoms in the South united under the leadership of Alfred, King of Wessex (878–900 A.D.), "Alfred the Great," who succeeded in reaching a truce with the Danish in 879 A.D. which included the conversion of the Danish leaders to Christianity. Later, under King Cnut (1016–1035 A.D.), large areas of England were actually united with Norway and Denmark, and many Scandinavian cultural traditions took root. The word "law" itself is of Danish origin.

From Alfred's death in 900 A.D. to the Reign of Cnut in 1016–35 A.D., England was divided into two customary areas, English and Danish, and there was constant struggle between the two regions. It is truly ironic that a Dane, King Cnut, was the first to unite the country, following major military victories over Wessex and Mercia, assisted by treason in the English court. But Cnut recognized the integrity of the English customs. A treaty at Oxford in 1018 A.D. began a long period of peace between the two groups, now under a national "king." When Cnut died in 1035 A.D., however, warring nobles of his Court again divided the country. Cnut's succession was disputed. Eventually the kingdom was inherited by one of the sons of the last English King, Ethelread. This son was Edward "the Confessor" (1042–66 A.D.). Edward succeeded in restoring unity, but his death in 1066 A.D. once again left the country disorganized and divided, ripe for the Norman Conquest.

B. ANGLO-SAXON "LAW"

The warring tribes of the English and the Danes all had customs and traditions for resolving disputes, but we know very little about them. There were almost no written records. Only as the English and Danes were able to consolidate their tribes into larger "kingdoms," from about 880 A.D. to the end of the period in 1066 A.D., do we get better information.

Anglo-Saxon records fall into roughly three categories: 1) *dooms* or "laws" of particular kings; 2) customary oaths; and 3) *bocs*, or grants to land. Almost all of these were written by clerics, and many, particularly the *bocs*, were kept in churches. Not surprisingly, many of the surviving *bocs* involved grants of land to the Church itself or to ecclesiastical foundations. Each of these different types of records tells us something about the evolution of law.

Dooms, or "laws," were promulgated by Anglo-Saxon and Danish kings. The earliest surviving example is from Ethelbert of Kent (c. 601–604 A.D.), but the most famous and best preserved are those issued by the great unifying kings, Alfred (between 890 and 901 A.D.) and Cnut (between 1016 and 1035 A.D.). Included in this Chapter are sections from the "laws" or *"dooms"* of Alfred. *"Doom"* referred to a judgment, hence our current usage of "Doomsday" for "Judgment Day." Most of Alfred's "laws" or *"dooms"* were formulas for settling disputes, and they were often very graphic and technical, i.e., "44. For a wound in the head if both bones are pierced, 30 shillings shall be given to the injured man." They also focus almost exclusively on reimbursement to victims, except for specific provisions relating to the Church or the King himself.

There is a good reason for this. Most disputes involved tribal squabbles between rival kin groups. The King was often powerless beyond the immediate vicinity of his own stronghold, and there was no regular system of police, jails, or professional judges. Most cases involved direct injury and were resolved by settlements negotiated between kin groups. The King's "laws" or "*dooms*" were little more than guidelines for such settlements.

But why would tribal kin groups settle such disputes in the absence of any official force? The answer lay in the central role of the blood feud. Like many "primitive" people—i.e., peoples without much formal government—Anglo-Saxon clans, or extended families, felt a strong moral duty to retaliate for any wrong done to one of their own. The revenge could be directly to the perpetrator, or to a member of the perpetrator's clan who was "equivalent" in value to the victim. "Value" was determined by custom, and was expressed as the *wergeld*, or the "man price" of an individual, usually in shillings (e.g., "a 1200 shilling man").

Family members subject to blood revenge, or required to administer such revenge, might be less enthusiastic than say, the perpetrator. It is one thing to seek revenge in your own quarrel, but what about having to fight because of a stupid act by your dim nephew? In addition, blood feuds could go on and on, and use up time and energy. There was a clear incentive to resolve them peacefully, by making the payments set out in the *dooms*.

The occasions for these negotiations were the customary "courts," which met regularly at local sites, often a "Law Rock." These were called "*moots*," and it was an obligation of all freemen in a particular neighborhood to attend ("moot worthy"). The most local of these courts, the courts of the "hundred" or, in the Danelaw, the "*wapentake*," met every four weeks. (A "hundred" or "*wapentake*" was a group of villages—whether consisting of a hundred families or a hundred hides of land remains unclear. A hundred court was convened by a deputy of the sheriff.) There were also *shire* moots, run by the King's representative in the shire, the "shire-reeve" or sheriff, and—at the top—moots convened by the King himself.

At these *moots*, the freemen attending—the so-called *doomsmen* ("judgment men")—would discuss cases and suggest resolution of problems. In extreme cases, individuals would be declared "outlaws," and could be killed by anyone without any duty by kin to retaliate. Usually, however, kin were able to control the renegade relations and to hold them to settlements reached with the victim's kin.

While we are not sure exactly how these sessions proceeded, the *dooms* of the kings do give us some hints. In addition, there are descriptions of "Law Rock" meetings in some *bocs*, such as the *boc* written at Aegelnoth's Stone in 1036 A.D. and included in the *Materials* at the end of this chapter. Finally, traditional *moots* persisted in some remote parts of Scandinavia, particularly Iceland, until after writing was more common. *Njal's Saga*, written by an unknown Icelandic author in about 1280 A.D., contains many descriptions of "Law Rock" negotiations, and of blood feuds when such negotiation failed. Although these Icelandic proceedings occurred long after the Anglo-Saxon period, they seem to fit closely the evidence left by the *Dooms* of Alfred and Cnut as to how proceedings occurred in Anglo-Saxon England.

Finally, we have written records of "customary oaths," taken by accusers and by defendants alike at the Law Rock. Moots were often attended by the local priest and, as will be seen, ordeals arranged by the priest were sometimes used to establish the truth of a statement. In general, however, it was "your word against mine," although fear of lying under a holy oath may have been very real. Fear of blood feud, however, led to serious efforts to arrange victim compensation, even when oaths clashed, as the passages in *Njal's Saga* indicate.

C. "CIVILIZING INFLUENCES"

Two factors gradually led to a change in this rudimentary system of victim compensation through fear of revenge. First, as the Kings developed more power, there were offenses which could not be discharged by paying a blood price, or *bot*. These were originally offenses against the King's own peace, the "King's Peace," or against the Church. They were called *botless* offenses, and required paying a fine directly to the King or Church, as well as paying victim compensation. For serious offenses, people could be executed. The "King's Peace" originally just extended to his own hall, or to the market places or roads under his protection. Later, the concept expanded to include violent acts almost anywhere. This was, of course, the birth of our criminal law.

The Church had no kin. It relied, therefore, on the King for retaliation of harm to its priests and nuns. The Church also was the only institution where many people could read and write. The Anglo-Saxon *bocs* (hence our term "book") were probably invented by the Church to prove grants of land to itself and to provide "a record" to gain royal support if someone tried to steal Church property or land.

Thus the growing power of the King and the Church led to more *botless* "crimes" and more written records. Still, the *moot* system had no trained judges or lawyers. Much of its effectiveness rested on local negotiations, sometimes guided by the King's *dooms*. This was true right up to the Conquest, and even afterward.

D. WAS THIS A "LEGAL" SYSTEM AT ALL?

Assume that the so-called Anglo-Saxon "law" consisted of customary norms that were followed by tribal groups as an alternative to blood feuds. Is this "law" properly so called?[1] Certainly there were no police, no institutional jails, no professional lawyers or judges, very little writing of any kind, and a high degree of informality of process. Those written laws that did exist, *dooms*, customary oaths, and *bocs*, or land grants, were not really rules backed by official sanctions, i.e., such as modern criminal codes. They were more like statements of customary norms, effective because of voluntary acceptance.

Of course, the growing power of the King led to fines and *botless* offenses that began to resemble modern criminal rules. In addition, the Church—standing as it did outside the protection of the "kin"—gradually encouraged centralized royal power and written records for its own purposes. But were the negotiations at the "Law Rock" really a legal process?

One thing is certain. The Anglo-Saxons themselves called the customary system "law." In fact, it is the actual origin of our word. Secondly, we can recognize in it incipient elements of a formal legal system, including the regularly scheduled *moots* and the oath process. Most importantly, it was a system that defined and protected the value of each person in an increasingly formal way. It was, indeed, from the Anglo-Saxon *folc riht* that we derive our notion of "rights," and the word itself.

---

1. For a good summary of the Academic controversy around this question, see Robert Redfield's "Primitive Law" set out in the *Materials, infra*, p. 51.

As we have mentioned before, to an Anglo-Saxon every person had a value, usually defined by the *wergeld* or blood price. The value might differ greatly from King to slave, but even slaves had value recognized by the "law." Secondly, every person had a personal "space" or "peace." The King's "peace" was quite large, and was expanded to include roads and markets, but even a slave or laboring *coerl* had a defined "space." The custom defining this "space" and value was called the "*folc riht.*" From this idea we get both the concept of personal "rights" and of "freedom" itself. Indeed, these are all Anglo-Saxon words. If we owe to the Romans the ideas and words for "justice," "legal," "codification," "judge," "equity," and "constitution," we owe to the Anglo-Saxon the concepts of "rights" and "freedom." As we shall see, the *folc riht* of the Anglo-Saxons was so important that the Norman conquerors, from William on, swore to uphold it.

If we deny the title "law" to such a system, we must do the same for much that we call "law," especially, "international law."[2] "International law," like Anglo-Saxon law, is largely consensual, and survives because the alternative is risk of combat. There are often no genuinely effective "international jails," or "police," but we perceive the system as at least using the terminology and symbols of a state legal system. When international punishments are administered for human rights violations, it is usually when a state is overthrown, defeated, or coerced by other sanctions. Those proceedings often are described as "legal" if they follow the customary norms.[3]

Of course, some elements of the Anglo-Saxon system are also compatible with any total vacuum of orderly government. Conditions in Albania before World War I led to a blood feud system, as documented in the article below by Margaret Hasluck. Indeed, whenever there is no credible police power, or where parties cannot make use of the formal system of sanctions, the same patterns emerge. Thus, even today the "families" of organized crime negotiate to avoid bloody retaliation in ways sharply reminiscent of the *dooms* of Alfred! Perhaps the best example is our own "Wild West," where the Anglo-Saxon sanction of "*outlawry*" was also found, and where "*shire reeves*" or sheriffs administered a rough justice. Even the words were the same as in Anglo-Saxon England! Whether called "law" or "no law," the dynamics of incipient legalism are very much worth studying, because they reoccur with regularity throughout time.

E. ANGLO-SAXON ISSUES

It has been said that legal history is merely a specialized form of comparative law. Instead of comparing different existing systems, i.e., a "horizontal" comparison, legal historians make "vertical" comparisons, i.e., between systems separated by time, rather than by space. Anthropologists, such as Margaret Mead

---

2. As Redfield observed: "The road to the right recognizes law to exist only where there are courts and codes supported by the fully politically organized state. This road quickly becomes a blind alley, for only a few preliterate societies have law in this sense." *Materials, infra,* p. 51.

3. See Telford Taylor, *Nuremburg and Vietnam* (New York, 1971), 76–94, 154–182.

and A.S. Diamond, have made extensive studies of "primitive" legal systems existing today among remote peoples. See their works cited in "For Further Reading," below. But these systems, instructive as they may be, can never tell us as much about ourselves as the study of *our* own special primitive system, the ancestral forebear of our present legal science. Whether we discuss "murder," "moots," "shires," "books," "shire-reeves," etc., we are still using the language of the Anglo-Saxon law, just as our system of county government in many states has many features inherited directly from the Anglo-Saxons.

The crucial questions with regard to the Anglo-Saxon Period, however, are fundamentally "comparative," i.e., they concern differences and not similarities. How could a non-compulsory criminal process work? How did the early communism of "the hundred," so romanticized by Marxist writers, actually operate and why did it disappear? What lessons of effectiveness and justice can our society learn from a system whose principal sanctions were blood feud and outlawry? But are all "primitive" systems inherently inferior, and what do we mean by "primitive" anyway? This is a good time to consider the questions concerning the quality and effectiveness of dispute resolution raised by Karl Llewellyn in his essay "Law and Civilization," from *The Bramble Bush*, set out in the *Materials*, below.

It should not take a Karl Llewellyn to remind us that neither an Anglo-Saxon nor a Roman would be entirely impressed by the present operation of our system of dispute resolution, whether it be criminal or civil. How would a Roman or an Anglo-Saxon react to our system? Should we judge the "operation" of a legal system by its efficiency—i.e., social ordering—or its moral legitimacy, i.e., "justice?"

FOR FURTHER READING

I. Original Texts

The classic sources of early Anglo-Saxon texts are William Stubbs, *Select Charters and Other Illustration of English Constitutional History* (Oxford, 8th ed. 1895), pp. 60 ff, and F.L. Attenborough, *The Laws of the Earliest English Kings* (Cambridge, 1922). See also Dorothy Whitelock, *English Historical Documents, 500-1042* (2ed., London, 1979), part ii, and H.G. Richardson and G.O. Sayles, *Law and Legislation from Aethelberht to Magna Carta* (London, 1966), and C. Stephenson and F.G. Marcham, *Sources of English Constitutional History* (1937). There have also been some very elegant special printings of Anglo-Saxon *bocs* and wills. Of particular interest is *The Will of Aethelgifre*, a tenth-century will of an extraordinarily wealthy Anglo-Saxon woman. The text, translated and edited by Dorothy Whitelock, is not only interesting as an early legal record, but it also sheds much light on Anglo-Saxon society, the status of Anglo-Saxon women, and the concept of *rihts*. See *The Will of Aethelgifre* (trans. Dorothy Whitlock, Oxford, 1968).

As for contemporary historical accounts, the obvious choice is the Venerable Bede's *The Ecclesiastical History of the English Nation*. Bede was a priest who lived from 673 to 735 A.D., mostly teaching Latin, Greek, and Hebrew at Jarrow. His history, written in Latin, is a unique account of the growing consciousness of

England as a nation, beyond warring tribes, and of the civilizing role of the Church. A good translation is that of John Stevens, *Bede, The Ecclesiastical History of the English Nation* (trans. John Stevens, London, 1951). As for the blow by blow account of events at an Icelandic "Law Rock," discussed above, see *Njal's Saga* (trans. Magnus Magnusson, Hermann Palasson, Baltimore, 1976).

II. Helpful Introductions

There is an excellent short introduction in J.H. Baker, *An Introduction to English Legal History* 3ed. (London, 1990), 1–13. Dorothy Whitelock's *The Beginning of English Society* (London, 2d ed., 1954) is now available in paperback. See also Peter Hunter Blair, *An Introduction to Anglo-Saxon England* (Cambridge, 1962); Peter Hunter Blair, *Roman Britain and Early England 55 B.C.–A.D. 871* (London, 1963); and Christopher Brooke, *From Alfred to Henry III, 871–1272* (London, 1961), all available in paperback. There is also a classic account, magnificently written as usual, in Frederick Pollock, F.W. Maitland, *The History of English Law Before The Time of Edward I* (2d ed., reissued by S.F.C. Milsom, 1968) vol. 1, 1–63. For a fine account of one of the earliest *dooms*, see A.W.B. Simpson, "The Laws of Ethelbert," in A.W.B. Simpson, *Legal Theory and Legal History* (London, 1987), 1–15.

III. "Primitive Law"

On the significance of the word "primitive" and its application in the study of law, see *Cooperation and Competition Among Primitive Peoples* (ed. Margaret Mead, Boston, 1961); A.S. Diamond, *The Comparative Study of Primitive Law* (London, 1963) and *Law and Warfare* (Bohannon, ed. 1967), which is also excerpted in the following chapter.

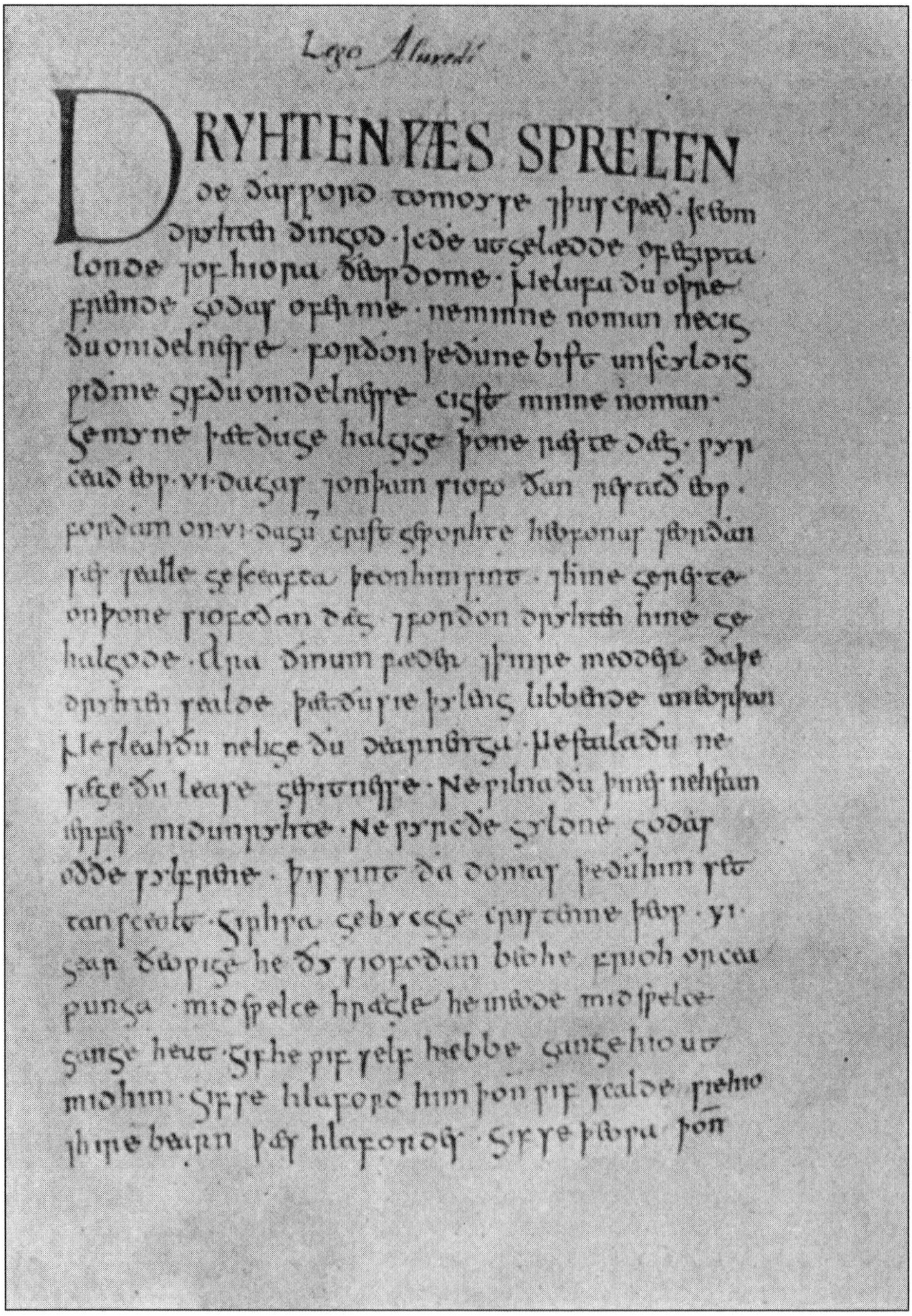
Lego Aluredi

DRYHTEN WÆS SPRECEN

Illustration 2-2 *Alfred's Laws* (890–901 A.D.) at Corpus Christi College, Cambridge. *Social England* (1901), *supra*, vol. 1, 243.

MATERIALS

DOOMS

Laws of Alfred (between 890 and 901 A.D.).

I, Alfred king of the West Saxons, showed the following laws to all of my *Witan* and they declared that all of them are satisfied that they be observed....

4. If anyone plots against the life of the king, either on his own account or by harboring outlaws...he shall forfeit his life and all he possesses...

7. If anyone fights or draws his weapon in the king's hall and is for this arrested, it is for the king to decide on his death or on his life in the event the king wishes to grant him life...

8. If anyone takes a nun from the cloister without the permission of the king or the bishop, he shall give 120 shillings, half to the king and half to the bishop or to the lord of the church in whose charge the nun is...

10. If anyone lies with the wife of a 1200 man [i.e., a man whose *wergeld* is 1200 shillings], he shall pay the man 120 shillings, to a 600 man he shall pay 100 shillings, to a common free man 40 shillings....

12. If a man burns or cuts down the trees of another without permission, he shall pay 5 shillings for each big tree and 5 pence for each of the rest no matter how many there may be; and 30 shillings as a fine.

13. If one kills another unintentionally while they are engaged in common work by a blow from a falling tree, the tree shall be given to the dead man's kindred and they shall remove it from the land within 30 nights; otherwise the owner of the wood shall take it....

19. If one lent to another his weapon, by which he kills another, they may if they wish combine to pay the *wergeld*.

    1. If they do not combine, he who lends the weapon shall pay one-third of the *wergeld* and one-third of the fine.

    2. If he wishes to purge himself by swearing that in lending he knew nothing evil, he may do so....

24. If a cow or bull injures a man, its owner must hand it over to the injured person or settle with him for payment....

44. For a wound in the head if both bones are pierced, 30 shillings shall be given to the injured man.

    1. If the outer bone [only] is pierced, 15 shillings shall be given.

45. If a wound an inch long is made under the hair, one shilling shall be paid.

46. If an ear is cut off, 30 shillings shall be paid....

47. If one knocks out another's eye, he shall pay 66 shillings, 6 ⅓ pence.

    1. If the eye is still in the head but the injured person can see nothing with it, one-third of the payment shall be withheld....

Note: The *Dooms, Oaths* and *Bocs* are from C. Stephenson and F.G. Marcham, *Sources of English Constitutional History* (Harper Brothers, 1937), pp. 10–12, 30–32, with some additional editing by John P. Dawson. [Reproduced courtesy Addison Wesley Educational Publishers Inc.]

OATHS

14. CUSTOMARY OATHS

(A) Oath of a Man to His Lord

By the Lord before whom this holy thing is holy, I will to N. be faithful and true, loving all that he loves and shunning all that he shuns, according to the law of God and the custom of the world; and never by will or by force, in word or in deed, will I do anything that is hateful to him; on condition that he will hold me as I deserve and will furnish all that was agreed between us when I bowed myself before him and submitted to his will.

(B) Oath of an Accuser

By the Lord before whom this holy thing is holy, I thus bring my charge with full folkright, without deceit and without malice, and without any guile whatsoever, that stolen from me was this property, N., which I claim and which I seized in the possession of N.

(C) Oath of One Thus Accused

By the Lord...neither by counsel nor by deed had I knowledge of or part in this, that the property, N., was carried off. On the contrary, I possess the property for this reason, that I lawfully inherited it....that *he*, having the lawful right to sell it, sold it to me....that it is the offspring of my own animals, my private property raised under my care.

(D) Oath of One Seizing Property

By the Lord...I seize N. neither through hate nor hostility, nor through unrighteous greed, and I know nothing truer than what my spokesman has said for me, and what I now myself state as truth, that *he* was the thief of my property.

(E) Oath in Reply to Such Seizure

By the Lord...I am guiltless, both in thought and in deed, of the accusation made against me by N.

(F) Oath of an Oath-Helper

By the Lord...the oath which N. has sworn is clean and without falsehood.

* * * * *

BOCS

(E) Canute: Grant to St. Paul's, London (1036)

I, King Canute, give friendly greetings to my bishops, my earls, and all my thegns in the shires where my priests of St. Paul's monastery hold land. And I make known to you my will that they shall enjoy their *sac* and *soc*, *toll* and *team*, within tide and without tide, as fully and continuously as they best had them in

Illustration 2-3   This is from an 11th-century Anglo-Saxon manuscript of the *Old Testament*, paraphrased by Aelfric. While it purports to show the execution of the Pharoah's baker (Gen. 40.22), it really is a picture of an Anglo-Saxon king with his *Witan*, or chief advisors. The king clearly has the power to execute for *botless* crimes. See *Dooms of Alfred*, 4, *supra*. See *Social England* (1894), *supra*, vol. 1, xviii. Illustration reproduced from *Social England* (1894), *supra*, vol. 1, 201.

any king's day, in all things, in borough and out of borough. And I will not permit any man in any way to do them wrong. And of this the witnesses are Aegelnoth, archbishop; Aelfric, archbishop; Aelwi, bishop; Aelwine, bishop; Dudoc, bishop; Godwine, earl; Leofric, earl; Osgod Clapa, Thored, and many others.

May God curse him who shall pervert this [grant]!

(Anglo-Saxon) Thorpe, *Diplomatarium*, pp. 319 f.

(F) Confirmation of a Title to Land in the Shire Court of Hereford (1036)

Here, in this writing, it is made known that a shire court sat at Aegelnoth's Stone in the time of King Canute. There sat Aethelstan, bishop; Ranig, alderman; Edwin, [son] of the alderman; Leofwine, son of Wulfsige; and Thurcil the White (*Hwita*). And thither came Tofig the Proud (*Pruda*) on the king's errand. And there were Bryning the sheriff, Aegelweard of Frome, Leofwine of Frome, Godric of Stoke, and all the thegns of Herefordshire. Then came faring to the court Edwin, son of Eanwen, and there claimed as against his own mother a portion of land, namely, Wellington and Cradley. Then the bishop asked who would speak for his mother. Then Thurcil the White answered, saying that he would if he knew the defence [that she cared to make]. Since he did not know the defence, three thegns were chosen from the court [to ride to the place] where she was, and that was Fawley. These [thegns] were Leofwine of Frome, Aegelsige the Red (*Reada*), and Winsige Sceagthman. And when they had come to her, they asked her about the land which her son claimed. Then she said that she had no land which in aught belonged to him, and she burst into a noble rage against her son. Then she called thither her kinswoman Leoflaed, Thurcil's wife, and before those [present] thus addressed her: "Here sits Leoflaed, my kinswoman, to whom, after my day, I give both my lands and my gold, both gear and garments, and all that I possess." After which she said to the thegns: "Do nobly and well. Announce my message to the court before all good men, telling them to whom I have given my land and all my belongings; and [that] to my own son [I have] never [given] anything. And bid them be witness of this [gift]." And they then did so, riding to the court and declaring to all the good men what she had directed them [to say]. Then Thurcil the White stood up in the court and prayed all the thegns to grant his wife a clean title to all the lands which her kinswoman had given her, and they did so. And Thurcil then rode to St. Aethelberht's monastery, with the leave and witness of all folk, and caused this [grant] to be set forth in a Christ's book.

(Anglo-Saxon) *Id.*, pp. 336 f.

NJAL'S SAGA

Note: Written in Iceland by an unknown author, *circa* 1280 A.D. The relevance to Anglo-Saxon law 400 years earlier is striking. [Trans. M. Magnusson, H. Palsson, Penguin, 1960, pp. 112–113, 298–299. Reproduced courtesy Penguin Press.]

When the messenger came to the Althing to tell Gunnar about the killing, Gunnar said, 'This is terrible news; I do not think I could ever hear worse. Now we must go at once to see Njal; I am sure that he will not fail us, even though he is tried so severely.'

They went to see Njal and called him out to talk. Njal came out at once, and he and Gunnar talked. There was no one else present at first except Kolskegg.

'I have harsh news to tell you,' said Gunnar. 'Thord Freedmansson has been killed. I want to offer you the right to assess your own compensation.'

Njal was silent for a while, and then said, 'It is a generous offer, and I shall accept it, even though I am sure to be reproached by my wife and my sons for doing so, as they will disapprove strongly. But I shall take that risk, for I know that I am dealing with a man of honour, and I do not want to be the cause of any breach of friendship.'

'Do you want to have your sons present at all?' asked Gunnar.

'No,' said Njal, 'for they will not break any settlement that I make. But if they were present, they would refuse to be party to it.'

'Very well,' said Gunnar. 'Do this on your own.'

They shook hands, and agreed to make a prompt and full settlement. Then Njal said, 'I assess the compensation at 200 ounces of silver; and you will think it high.'

'I do not think it too high,' said Gunnar, and went back to his booth.

Njal's sons returned to the booth, and Skarp-Hedin asked where all that good silver his father was holding had come from.

Njal said, 'I have to tell you that your foster-father Thord has been killed. Gunnar and I have come to a settlement over it, and he has paid double compensation for the killing.'

'Who killed him?' asked Skarp-Hedin.

'Sigmund and Skjold did it,' replied Njal. 'But Thrain Sigfussen was also present.'

'They were not taking any risks,' said Skarp-Hedin. 'But how far must matters go before we can take things into our own hands?'

'It will not be very long now,' replied Njal, 'and nothing will be able to hold you back then. But it is of the greatest importance to me that you do not break this settlement.'

'Then we shall not do so,' said Skarp-Hedin. 'But if there is any further trouble, we shall remember what they have already done to us.'

'In that case I would not try to hold you back,' said Njal.

* * * * *

One day when everyone was at the Law Rock, the chieftains were ranged as follows: Asgrim Ellida-Grimsson, Gizur the White, Gudmund the Powerful, and Snorri the Priest were standing close up to the Law Rock, while the men from the Eastfjords stood further below.

Mord Valgardsson stood beside his father-in-law Gizur the White. Mord was an extremely fine speaker. Gizur told him that he should now give notice of the manslaughter actions, and asked him to speak loudly and clearly so that all might hear him.

Mord named witnesses — 'to testify that I give notice of an action against Flosi Thordarson for unlawful assault, inasmuch as he assaulted Helgi Njalsson at the place where he assaulted Helgi and inflicted on him an internal wound, brain wound, or marrow wound, which did cause Helgi's death. I demand that Flosi be sentenced to full outlawry on this charge, not to be fed nor forwarded nor helped nor harboured. I claim that all his possessions be forfeit, half to me and half to those men in the Quarter who have lawful right to receive his confiscated goods. I refer this manslaughter action to the proper Quarter Court. I give lawful notice of it, in public, at the Law Rock. I give notice of an action, to be heard at this session, for full outlawry against Flosi Thordarson, as assigned to me by Thorgeir Thorisson.'

There was loud approval at the Law Rock for the eloquent and forceful way Mord had spoken.

Mord continued: 'I call upon you to testify that I give notice of an action against Flosi Thordarson, inasmuch as he inflicted on Helgi Njalsson an internal wound, brain wound, or marrow wound, which did cause Helgi's death, at a place where Flosi had previously made an unlawful assault on Helgi. I demand that you be sentenced to full outlawry on this charge, Flosi, not to be fed nor forwarded nor helped nor harboured. I claim that all your possessions be forfeit, half to me and half to those men in the Quarter who have lawful right to receive your confiscated goods. I refer this action to the proper Quarter Court. I give lawful notice of it, in public, at the Law Rock. I give notice of an action, to be heard at this session, for full outlawry against Flosi Thordarson, as assigned to me by Thorgeir Thorisson.'

With that, Mord sat down. Flosi had given him a good hearing, and never uttered a word throughout.

Thorgeir Skorar-Geir then stood up and named witnesses — 'to testify that I give notice of an action against Glum Hildisson, inasmuch as he took fire and kindled it and applied it to the buildings at Bergthorsknoll on the occasion when they burned to death Njal Thorgeirsson and Bergthora Skarp-Hedin's daughter and all those people who died therein. I demand that he be sentenced to full outlawry on this charge, not to be fed nor forwarded nor helped nor harboured. I claim that all his possessions be forfeit, half to me and half to those men in the Quarter who have a lawful right to receive his confiscated goods. I refer this action to the proper Quarter Court. I give lawful notice of it, in public, at the Law Rock. I give notice of an action, to be heard at this session, for full outlawry against Glum Hildisson.'

Karl Solmundarson raised actions against Kol Thorsteinsson, Gunnar Lambason, and Grani Gunnarsson, and everyone commented that he spoke remarkably well. Thorleif Crow raised actions against all the Sigfussons, while his brother Thorgrim the Mighty raised actions against Modolf Ketilsson, Lambi Sigurdarson, and Hroar Hamundarson (the brother of Leidolf the Strong). Asgrim Ellida-Grimsson raised actions against Leidolf, Thorstein Geirleifsson, Arni Kolsson, and Grim the Red.

They all spoke well. After that, other men gave notice of their actions, and this occupied most of the day. Then people went back to their booths.

COMMENTARY

Note: The following short excerpts are from leading writers about "primitive" law: Pollock and Maitland, Robert Redfield, Margaret Hasluck, and Karl Llewellyn. They each represent points of view about what constitutes "law," or is a source of "law." What is your view? For that matter, how should we define "primitive?" If the utility of a system of "law" is measured by social order and efficiency, some "primitive" systems may far exceed more formal and "sophisticated" regimes. Are there other ways of measuring the "sophistication" of a legal system? Should the word "primitive" connote a value judgment?

Pollock and Maitland, *History of English Law*, I 46–50 (2d ed., 1898, Cambridge University Press).

...An Anglo-Saxon court, whether of public or private justice, was not surrounded with such visible majesty of the law as in our own time, nor furnished with any obvious means of compelling obedience. It is the feebleness of executive power that explains the large space occupied in archaic law by provisions for the conduct of suits when parties make default. In like manner the solemn prohibition of taking the law into one's own hands without having demanded one's right in the proper court shows that law is only just becoming the rule of life. Such provisions occur as early as the dooms of Ine of Wessex, and perhaps preserve the tradition of a time when there was no jurisdiction save by consent of the parties.

*　*　*　*

Imprisonment occurs in the Anglo-Saxon laws only as a means of temporary security. Slaves were liable to capital and other corporal punishment, and generally without redemption. The details have no material bearing on the general history of the law, and may be left to students of semi-barbarous manners. Outlawry, at first a declaration of war by the commonwealth against an offending member, became a regular means of compelling submission to the authority of the courts, as in form it continued so to be down to modern times. In criminal proceedings, however, it was used as a substantive penalty for violent resistance to a legal process or persistent contempt of court. Before the Conquest, outlawry involved not only forfeiture of goods to the king, but liability to be killed with impunity. It was no offence to the king to kill his enemy, and the kindred might not claim the wergild. It was thought, indeed, down to the latter part of the sixteenth century, that the same reason applied to persons under the penalties appointed by the statutes of *praemunire*, which expressly included being put out of the king's protection.

It would appear that great difficulty was found both in obtaining specific evidence of offences, and in compelling accused and suspected persons to submit themselves to justice, and pay their fines if convicted. This may serve to explain the severe provisions of the later Anglo-Saxon period against a kind of persons described as 'frequently accused,' 'of no credit.' One who had been several times charged (with theft, it seems we must understand), and kept away from three courts running, might be pursued and arrested as a thief, and treated as an outlaw if he failed to give security to answer his accusers. A man of evil repute is already half condemned, and if he evades justice it is all but conclusive proof of guilt. In communities where an honest man's neighbours knew pretty well what he was doing every day and most of the day, this probably did not work much injustice. And English criminal procedure still held to this point of view two centuries after the Conquest. It may be said to linger even now-a-days in the theoretical power of grand juries to present offences of their own knowledge.

Robert Redfield, "Primitive Law," excerpted from 33 *University of Cincinnati Law Review*, No. 1, Winter, 1964, 1–22. [Reproduced courtesy University of Cincinnati Law Review.]

One who sets out to talk about primitive law has a choice of three roads. The road to the right recognizes law to exist only where there are courts and codes supported by the fully politically organized state. This road quickly becomes a blind alley, for only a few preliterate societies have law in this sense, and these few are not characteristically primitive. Making this choice amounts to saying that there is no law in truly primitive society and that therefore there is nothing for one to talk about.

The road to the left has been recently opened with a great flourish by B. Malinowski (1926; 1934) and is apparently preferred by Julius Lips (1938). He who takes this road does not identify law with courts and codes. To Malinowski law consists of "the rules which curb human inclinations, passions or instinctive drives; rules which protect the rights of one citizen against the concupiscence, cupidity or malice of the other; rules which pertain to sex, property and safety." These rules are of course found everywhere, and in this sense law exists in the most primitive society. Malinowski (1938: lxii) notes that primitive people, like other people, are kept from doing what their neighbors do not want them to do chiefly not because of courts and policemen, but for many other personal and social reasons. In effect he bids us investigate the ways in which social control is brought about in the simpler societies, or at least the mechanisms whereby the individual is induced to do what people expect of him even of law as they are variously represented in very various societies. Only at the end of this paper shall I say something in general terms about what the rudimentary law found in primitive societies tends typically to be. The paper is chiefly devoted to pointing out that the beginnings of law are diverse, not unified, and to citing some instances of some of the principal elementary juridical, or proto-legal, institutions. The subject might be stated to be "rudimentary law as represented in some of the simpler societies." Rudimentary law might also be studied in such groups within the modern state as clubs, gangs and families. The highly developed state with its powerful law looms so large that perhaps we do not always see that within it are many little societies, each in some ways a little primitive society, enforcing its own special regulations with a little primitive law of its own. But here I stand as an anthropologist, and speak to the subject from what are sometimes called the "savage societies."

Margaret Hasluck, "The Albanian Blood Feud," from *Law and Warfare* (Paul Bohannan ed., Natural History Press, 1967), pp. 381–82. [Reproduced courtesy Cambridge University Press.]

Family Vengeance and Collective Vengeance

Till after the 1914–18 war communications in Albania were so bad, government centers so few and the gendarmerie so ill-organized that communities were largely self-governing. These communities consisted in the narrower sense of the family, and in the wider sense of the tribe. If a person was injured, the family in most cases, and the tribe in a few cases, by the law of self-government punished the wrongdoer. Since the individual was almost completely submerged in the family, an injury to him was an injury to the whole family and might be punished by any of its members. When the tribal community was involved, the injury might again be avenged by any of its members. When the injury took the form of murder, vengeance generally took the Mosaic form of a life for a life, but sometimes was achieved by the exaction of blood money or the imposition of exile.

When the family of a murdered man, in default of government action, took the punishment of the murderer into its own hands and killed him or one of his male relatives, the head of his family might admit that both sides were equal and make peace. On the other hand, while still admitting that both sides were equal he might prefer to continue the feud by killing a second male from the avenging family; that done, a second life was forfeit on his side. In this way the feud might rage backwards and forwards for years or even generations, each family being in turn murderer and victim, hunter and hunted. 'To take vengeance' was 'to take the blood' (that is, of the man already killed, not of him who was to make atonement); the criminal was called 'the bloodstained,' and avenger and criminal thought of each other as the 'enemy.' In north Albania the criminal was also called the 'agent' and the avenger the 'master of the blood of the victim,' i.e., the master of the house in which the victim lived. 'To incur a feud' was 'to fall into blood' or 'enmity.'

A murdered man found his most natural avenger in his brother, especially if they had not separated. If his father was not too old, and his son too young, to bear arms, they shared the brother's obligation. In slightly less degree so did his father's brother and cousin in the male line, and their sons and grandsons, that is to say, all the other males who were in the collective sense his 'father,' 'brother' and 'son,' through being at the time, or having recently been, members of his household. If his son was in the cradle, the child's mother and the neighbors told him of the crime as he grew up and urged him, failing another avenger, not to rest till he had done his duty. No matter which of these relatives took revenge, his 'rifle could be hung up' and 'go to sleep,' to quote the picturesque phrases of Dibër and the North. The lawful representative of his murdered kinsman because he belonged to the same household, he had only made the two sides equal, with one of two results; either peace could be made or the feud continued between the same two families.

A man might kill his enemy where and when he could—in a chance encounter, in a meeting deliberately sought or in a carefully laid ambush. If he was 'strong' with plenty of good shots in his house, he and his family went alone on set expeditions. If he was weak he was probably accompanied by friends, who included friends in the ordinary sense, relatives by marriage, dependents, and servants. They came, not for pay, but on his invitation or of their own accord. Invitations, always verbal, requested the recipients to come with so many rifles to such-and-such a place by such-and-such a day and hour. Those invited were bound to come; those who volunteered were praised by the public...

Karl Llewellyn, "Law and Civilization," from *The Bramble Bush* (1930), 107–108. [Reproduced courtesy of Oceana Publishing Inc.]

When one turns his eyes from law outward, the first effect is to make law shrink into seeming insignificance. There is so much outside. And it so obviously bears in upon and changes and remodels law itself. After a further while—so to speak as the eyes grow adjusted to the glare—one attains a truer picture. One perceives an interplay of causation between law and the world outside. One begins to suspect something of the nature of the interplay. It may have value for you, it may shorten the period of refocussing, it may indeed stir you to break the surface tension of the law and take a slow look around, if I sketch here some outline of what I think one comes to see when he sets out to survey law's relation to civilization.

By *civilization* I mean what anthropologists call *culture*, the whole set-up of society, including the ways in which we act and the ways in which we are organized, including our material and intellectual equipment and our ways of using both. As to law, you know roughly what I mean. But it is not workable to tie to a single meaning when dealing with primitive times and with our own as well. You would not have me deny the presence of law in a society merely because there were no state officials. There was an international law before League or U.N. Both law and state have grown, and grown gradually, and at times quite independently of each other. If we are to watch law's relation to civilization we must therefore watch law's development in civilization—and what we watch will be a different thing from time to time and place to place. The sole inescapable common element is dealing with disputes. The sole inescapable common focus is the relation between the *ways* of dealing with disputes and the other ways of living. Hence, when I am talking of a ruder culture, before the state and the state's courts, I shall be thinking in the first instance of established ways for settling disputes without resort to violence by the contending parties, or even for settling them by violence, but by violence bridled and curb-bitted. As the state of culture concerned grows more advanced I shall be introducing other ideas commonly associated with this symbol *law*: e.g., the regular tribunal. As soon as a state appears upon the scene, the idea of action about disputes by the officials of the state will of course appear, and will be contrasted, say with the settlement of a strike by the mediation of a prominent citizen. And that other aspect of law, regulation by officials for greater convenience and safety and prevention of disputes, will play a part. And there will come in from the beginning the notion of some considerable regularity in anything that is done, some recurrence and predictability, and some conception that there ought to be recurrence and predictability: the ideas of precedent and rules—for these are aspects of any institution, legal or other.

Illustration 3-1 A scene from the famous Bayeux Tapestry, showing Norman Knights charging Anglo-Saxon foot soldiers. The tapestry was created about 1082 A.D. to give the Norman account of the victory. As such, it is an early example of propaganda. See David M. Wilson, *The Bayeux Tapestry* (London, 1985). (The Bayeux Tapestry—11th century. By special permission of the City of Bayeux.)

III

THE NORMAN-ANGEVIN ADMINISTRATORS: BIRTH OF THE MODERN STATE
(WILLIAM "THE CONQUEROR" THROUGH HENRY II, 1066–1216 A.D.)

On October 14, 1066 a French war lord, Duke William of Normandy, with only 6,000 men, defeated the English forces under King Edward's successor, Harold, at the Battle of Hastings. This astonishing invasion and victory, the last successful invasion in English history, was possible largely because Harold's forces were exhausted after defeating powerful Norwegian forces on September 25 in the far north of England. They had marched the entire length of the country in two weeks.[1]

Debates have long raged about the historical significance of the Norman Conquest and the so-called "Norman administrators." One thing is certain. During the reign of Henry II, institutions emerged that have dominated our legal process ever since. In particular, a central court system, a professional judiciary, the jury trial, and a pleading system utilizing articulated forms of action all originated in England at this time. No modern Anglo-American lawyer can fully understand the conceptual framework in which he or she operates without some familiarity with this period. To put it another way, if Henry II walked into your law office, you could easily explain your professional world to him in terms of developments from, or reactions to, thirteenth-century ideas.

There are, however, two other reasons for concentrating study here. First, when the Norman conquerors consolidated a government over the English, they overcame administrative and conceptual challenges of extraordinary difficulty. We will examine each of the legal problems they faced, and their resolutions. The

---

1. For exciting accounts, see Doris A. Stenton, *English Society in the Early Middle Ages* (4th ed., 1965 London), 11–59; Winston S. Churchill, *The Birth of Britain, A History of English Speaking Peoples*, vol. 1. (London, 1956), 112–130.

Norman experience remains relevant to the situations currently existing in a large part of the world today, particularly where a central administration attempts to establish a common legal order in an underdeveloped country. It is truly ironic that modern British imperialism, the legal "heir" of the Normans, has left many former colonies with a Norman style "common law" system, including central courts, juries, and writ pleading.[2]

Secondly, this period introduced to England the "science of law," or "jurisprudence," which in turn underpins much of our constitutional doctrine. While the origin of modern constitutionalism will be discussed at length in the next section, it is not too early to begin to consider what it means to resolve human conflicts through use of a formal "process" or a "system." This "legal" mentality is clearly opposed to the kind of simplistic "eye for an eye" rule making which marks some of the written endeavors of the Anglo-Saxons. In the Norman legal treatises called *Glanvill* and *Bracton*, we not only meet the first truly articulate written legal scholarship in our Anglo-American heritage, we also encounter, for the first time, notions of procedural rule-making and due process of law.

The English monarchs before Henry II, i.e., William I, William II, Henry I and Stephen (1066–1154), are usually described as "Norman," while Henry II (1154–1189) and later kings are called "Plantagenet" or "Angevin." This is because Henry II was the son of the Holy Roman Emperor Henry V, a powerful European sovereign, and Matilda, Henry I's daughter, rather than descending in a direct male lineage from William I. Through his father, Henry II held vast French lands, including Aquitaine and Anjou, as well as Normandy. But, Henry II was also a true heir of his great grandfather, William I. His style, talents, and character were in the Norman tradition, and his rule of England saw the continuing, gradual synthesis of Norman and English political and legal institutions. In truth, the "Norman-Angevins" were a fairly consistent dynasty right through the reign of Richard II and up to the dislocation of the War of the Roses in the fifteenth century.

A. THE NORMAN-ANGEVIN BUREAUCRACY

The Normans were great bureaucrats. We should begin our study by looking at their superb administrative tools and skills. William's challenge was to control a vast land and a hostile, conquered native population. By 1086 A.D., his bureaucrats had compiled the tax collector's dream, a compilation of all the taxable assets in the kingdom and their owners. This was known as the "Doomsday Book," because only God on Doomsday would have a comparable record.

---

2. English imperialism certainly had a problematic history. Nevertheless, recent English legal history conferences have included scholars from India, New Zealand, Nigeria, Ghana, Kenya, South Africa, Australia, Pakistan, Hong Kong, Malaysia, Canada, Jamaica and, of course, from that other former colony, the United States.

Illustration 3-2 (A.F. Kersting) This is Dover Castle, built by Henry II (1133–1189) in the years between 1180 and 1188 A.D., about the time of the first English law treatise, *Glanvill* (*circa* 1187–1189 A.D.). Courtesy, A.F. Kersting.

This extraordinary record was made possible by dividing the country into administrative districts, controlled by Normans loyal to the Crown, and anchored by powerful military garrisons in local castles. But William was too wise to create a totally new system. Like all shrewd conquerors, he claimed from the beginning that he intended to change nothing. Indeed, William claimed that he had been promised the Crown by Edward and that Harold was the true usurper! His Court followers even produced a vast tapestry to this effect, the Bayeux Tapestry, surely an early example of "media" propaganda. His new administrative districts, therefore, incorporated the old English shire boundaries, and the ancient courts of the shire and the hundred continued to function. Indeed, the Normans used the ancient systems to strengthen their own bureaucracy, as Henry I's "Ordinance on Local Courts," set out in the *Materials, infra*, demonstrates.

In addition, the Norman bureaucrats developed new written records, and also new ways to communicate in writing. The latter were called "writs." At first, these "writs" were simply for administrative purposes, but they soon developed legal significance.

For our purposes, however, the most important contributions of the Normans and their immediate Angevin successors took two forms: a new system of "royal" or national courts, and the emergence of a constitutional order, reflected in early forms of legislation and restatement of ancient rights, including the famous *Magna Carta*. In the next two chapters, we will look at two other important Norman contributions: 1) a sophisticated feudal system and, 2) a system of legal pleading.

B. ORIGIN OF THE CENTRAL COURTS

The Anglo-Saxon courts were hierarchical, going from the local courts of the "Hundred," to the courts of the "Shire," where the King's representative, the "shire reeve" or sheriff, was present. Extraordinary cases, however, could come up directly to the King himself, as advised by his immediate court, called the "Witan." See Illustration 3-7, *infra*. The Normans made no immediate change in this system, but saw in the "Witan"—called by them the *Curia Regis* (King's Court)—a potential administrative vehicle of great value. From this *Curia Regis* developed the first professional central courts of England, called the "common law" courts because they administered a law "common" throughout the Kingdom, as opposed to the local law of the shires and the hundreds. The original "royal" or "central" common law courts derived from the King's personal jurisdiction. Thus they were originally held at the King's court. This "court," or royal household, actually moved frequently. The early Norman and Angevin Kings not only traveled from house to house through England, but through their French lands as well. We know from *Bracton*, the first great treatise of English Law, that the King increasingly delegated his legal responsibilities to trained "justiciars" or judges. These traveled with him, hearing cases.

From the beginning, the royal courts were not open to all people, nor did they hear all matters. For example, matters involving unfree tenancies in land were left to the local courts, and cases of petty criminal misdemeanors, or cases involving small sums of money, were also left to local courts. But all disputes involving free tenancies in land, and all major crimes or "felonies," were heard by the royal courts. One possible reason is that cases involving title to freeholds or serious crimes could involve potential Crown revenues. As we will see in the next chapter, Crown revenues came in part from feudal dues collected on real property interests and from escheat, or forfeiture of property interests, upon the owner's conviction of a serious crime. Norman monarchs, ever eager to get more revenue, found it convenient to have real property cases tried in royal courts, with records of property ownership kept in writing by their own people.

At least by the time of the *Magna Carta* (1215 A.D.), royal justice was becoming popular. This was doubtless because it had written records. It was also professional, uniform, and not subject to further appeals. But the mobile nature of the court, following the King's travels, was a nuisance. Thus Section 17 of the *Magna Carta* provided that "Common pleas shall not follow our [the King's] court, but shall be held in some definite place." This resulted in the royal court being divided into three parts. One section was called the Court of Common Pleas. It was always held in one place, at the King's Palace at Westminister in the great Westminister Hall, an astonishing room built by the Norman kings and still surviving today. Another section was called the Court of King's Bench. It followed the King on his travels. A third court, specializing only in taxation, was called the Court of Exchequer. (The name comes from a large chequerboard table where accounts were figured by moving tokens on the squares.) The Court of Exchequer, too, stayed in one place; at Westminister Hall.

Eventually the King's Bench stopped following the King, and all three royal courts found a permanent home at Westminister Hall. Due to its historical proximity with the King's own person, however, the King's Bench became regarded as the senior court. This fact became important when the court later developed an appellate jurisdiction. For the same reason, the King's Bench always had a special jurisdiction over serious crimes, or "Pleas of the Crown." Its proceedings were recorded in the *Coram Rege Rolls*.

The Common Pleas court at Westminister became the general court of civil jurisdiction, doubtless because its permanent, central location aided litigants and the emerging class of professional lawyers. From 1272 on, it had its own Chief Justice and kept its records in a separate set of *De Banco* rolls. Eventually, it developed a monopoly on real property actions and the old personal actions of debt, detinue account, and covenant, which we will discuss at length later.

The Court of Exchequer had a monopoly on all cases involving money owed to the Crown. By around 1250 A.D., it had its own chief judge, called the Chief Baron of the Exchequer. Originally, its jurisdiction was very narrow. But later, by a fiction called *quominus*, it was expanded to almost all personal actions. *Quominus* alleged that a plaintiff was "less able" (*quominus sufficiens existit*) to pay tax to the Crown because the defendant owed money to him. It followed, at least arguably, that the Crown had an interest in the action.

All three of these courts had important things in common. The law they applied was the same throughout the Kingdom, i.e., it was the "common law." Their judges were also all trained professionals. These judges were not only literate, but were educated in the law. This was very different from relying on local freemen with long memories, as in the ancient local courts. Such educated, professional judges developed the first uniform procedures, based on the "writ," and soon began to develop the substantive doctrines of civil and criminal law that we will be examining in the next two chapters.

C. THE ORIGINS OF CONSTITUTIONAL LAW

The Anglo-Saxons gave us some fundamental legal concepts. Every time we speak of "rights" or "freedom" we are using Anglo-Saxon words, referring to the customary *folc riht* that gave each English person, including women and slaves, some individual "space" that was their own. True, that "space," as defined by customary *riht*, varied greatly from class to class and person to person, just as your "blood price," or *wergeld*, would depend on your station, but everybody had some *riht*. Unlike American race slavery, no person was without any rights. But these customary rights and freedoms were not part of any treatise or master document. No one "enacted" them, or even necessarily wrote them down. Except for the *bocs*, the oaths, and the *dooms*, there were no legal documents, and there was certainly no theory.

The first examples of a self-conscious, written tradition of constitutionalism in Anglo-American law were the records by the trained justiciars of the Norman royal courts. Some of these judges were also quite familiar with at least some Roman law. While the official language of the law courts was Norman French, the judges all knew Latin. In addition, Roman law was being taught in the English university town of Oxford at least as early as Vacarius' *Summa Pauperum de Legibus* or *Liber Pauperum*, a little book written between 1143–1149 A.D. to assist poor English students in learning Roman law.

Norman legislation was certainly a great step ahead of the *dooms* of the Anglo-Saxon Kings. The legislative body for both the Anglo-Saxons and the Normans was technically the same, the King surrounded by his chief nobles. This was called the "witan" (Anglo-Saxon) or "curia regis" (Norman). But Anglo-Saxon "laws" were almost exclusively in the form of hopeful restatements of existing custom, with unclear enforcement. Norman legislation, such as the Assise (or Assize) of Clarendon (1166)[3] included in your *Materials*, established new legal procedures and had real "teeth," including provisions for remedy and defined responsibility for compliance.

Perhaps the most important constitutional document of the Norman-Angevin period, however, purported to be just a restatement of past customs and "rights," although it did contain some very specific, and innovative, "enforcement clauses." This was the famous *Magna Carta*, of 1215 A.D.

The *Magna Carta* was a set of assurances agreed to by King John, under duress. King John was the younger son of Henry II and the brother of the popular Richard I, "The Lionhearted." He reigned from 1199 to 1216 A.D., and had a reputation of abusing feudal customs to enrich himself and his followers. As we shall see in the next chapter, the feudal system was a complex reciprocal set of rights and duties, running both from governed to ruler, and ruler to governed. This idea of customary reciprocity, which was a basis of legitimacy for Norman-Angevin government, was a key source of our modern theories of constitutionalism. John apparently ignored a number of these customs.

Eventually, John's chief nobles became fed up with his sharp practices and, at Runnymede Meadow by the River Thames on June 12th, 1215 A.D., John was forced to acknowledge an elaborate list of feudal customs, and to promise not to subvert them for personal power and gain. This written statement of the rights of the governed and the government was our first great constitutional document. (When we study feudalism in the next chapter, we will return to its text again and again, and its provisions should eventually all make sense to you.) Mind you, the *Magna Carta* was not an enacted "Constitution" in a modern sense. It was hardly even a piece of legislation in the Norman sense. It was more like a title deed, or Anglo-Saxon *boc*, confirming a title to rights and privileges already yours by ancient custom. Nevertheless, it was of the greatest importance. In addition, as we shall see, it had many later symbolic roles in vastly different times, and continues to be cited as an authority to this day. Even if the historical context of its famous provisions has been widely misunderstood, the document remains a great symbol of the rule of law and of limitations on arbitrary executive power.

Each section of the *Magna Carta* should be read with care. How many can you understand? What do you think of the provisions defining the rights of women, of Jews? Why is this document of interest to environmentalists? Is it a radical or conservative document?

---

3. The term "assize" comes from the Norman-French "assise" or "sit at." It is another one of these historical legal terms, like "common law," which has many meanings. "Assise" can refer 1) to the "sitting down" or meeting of the King and nobles, 2) to the legislation enacted at such a meeting, such as the "Assise of Clarendon," 3) to royal court proceedings where judges and others have a "sitting down," particularly in shire towns, as in "justices of assize" and 4) to remedies applied by such "assize" justices, using an "assize" of twelve jurors, such as the "Assise of Novel Disseisen" or the "Assise of Mort d'Ancestor," which we will study later, in Chapter V, *infra*.

D. BRACTON

By the beginning of the thirteenth century, the Normans had developed: 1) a trained, professional bureaucracy and judiciary, 2) a system of central courts, and 3) the rudimentary emergence of a "theory" of government, or constitutional law. Their fourth achievement resulted from all three of these. It was the development of a truly professional "legal" literature.

The Anglo-Saxon courts were held by laymen and were governed by local customs and self-help. Except for efforts to record outcomes in *bocs*, or to set guidelines for settlements in *dooms*, there was no purpose to be served by written records, and no one to write them. It is a telling fact that our best accounts of how these courts worked in practice came from the poets and bards, as in *Njal's Saga*.

The emergence of a trained, professional judiciary, of central courts with written records, and of "constitutional" charters created a new legal environment. This led, in turn, to the first true law books. Their purpose was education of practitioners and judges. The first great treatise is one that we will revisit later, because it contains some of the earliest references to the emerging legal profession. It was called *Glanvill*, and was written in Latin between 1187–1189 during the reign of Henry II. The author may have been Henry II's chief justice, Ranulph de Glanvill, who at least gave it his name. *Glanvill* focused on the procedure in the new central, royal courts, and contained over eighty writs and pleadings. *Glanvill* was a practitioner's book, pure and simple. What is truly amazing is that it has been circulated, first as a manuscript and then in print, ever since. There have been editions in every century, and one was even brought to America by one of the first settlers of Massachusetts, Richard Bellingham (1592–1672). It is astonishing to think that a Norman law book could have a 800 year life span, and that tells us something about the importance of the Norman period to our legal system today.[4]

Even more important, however, was the second great treatise in Anglo-American law, *Bracton*. *Bracton* was also written in Latin and named for a royal judge, Henry de Bracton (d. 1268), although it was apparently written by more than one person and over a period of years around 1220–1230 A.D. Its author was familiar with Roman Law, and with *Justinian's Institutes* in particular, but *Bracton* was a thoroughly English book. Although never finished, it has been rightly called "the flower and crown of English jurisprudence."[5]

What makes *Bracton* so remarkable is that it goes far beyond what is needed as a practitioner's guide. While *Glanvill* could be explained by the first two Norman developments: the professional bureaucracy and the central courts, *Bracton* required and emphasized the third: a genuine development of constitutional and legal theory. In this sense, it was a true offspring of Runnymede and the *Magna Carta* (1215) of a few years before.

We will be returning to sections of *Bracton* throughout these *Materials*. While written to educate and train Norman judges, *Bracton's* impact on the common law and constitutional doctrine extends to this very day. It was even cited by the

---

4. There were other, earlier Norman law books. Some, such as the *Leges Henrici Primi*, predated *Glanvill*. See *Leges Henrici Primi* (L.J. Downes, ed., trans. Oxford, 1972), 1–7. The *Leges* had clear Anglo-Saxon antecedents.

5. See T.F.T. Plucknett, *A Concise History of the Common Law* (5th ed., Boston, 1956).

Supreme Court of the United States in *Roe v. Wade.*[6] As we shall see, *Bracton* took on a "second life" during the epic constitutional struggles of the seventeenth century, and great figures, such as Edward Coke, cited its pages—both in context and out of context.

For our purposes now, however, *Bracton* helps us in four ways. First, its passages make very clear the growing sophistication of the new "common" law and the royal Norman courts, and of the professionals who served them as both judges and lawyers. Second, its sections on the source of the legitimacy of the laws and the power of the Crown help us to understand the political thought of the Angevin rulers and its influence on legal doctrine. Third, in its pages we begin to recognize the development of the doctrines of both criminal and civil law that we still employ today. Good examples include early examples of environmental protection, through nuisance doctrine, and a development of better contract remedies. Finally, *Bracton* was written, in part, by reference to a notebook of decided law cases, kept by Henry de Bracton himself. This notebook has actually been found and edited by two of the great English historians, Vinogradoff and Maitland.[7] In *Bracton's* pages we not only see the beginning of common law jurisprudence, but also the advent of judge-made law.

FOR FURTHER READING

I.   Original Texts

There are excellent translations of *Leges Henrici Primi* (L.J. Downes, Oxford, 1972); *Glanvill (Tractatus de legibus et consuetudinibus regni Anglie qui Glanvilla vocatur)* (G.D.B. Hall, London, 1965); and *Bracton (De Legibus et Consuetudinibus Angliae)* (S.E. Thorne, Cambridge, Mass, 1968). I particularly recommend reading the opening passages of each treatise and comparing them. The majesty of the opening sections of *Bracton* represents one of the great heights of Anglo-American legal literature, still moving and impressive after more than 700 years.

II.   Helpful Introductions

For a general historical context, see the ever helpful *Oxford History of Britain* (ed. Kenneth O. Morgan, Oxford, 1988), John Gillinghaus, "The Early Middle Ages" (1066–1290), 120–191. See also Doris Mary Stenton, *English Society in the Early Middle Ages* (Penguin Books, 4th ed., London, 1965); and Christopher Brooke, *From Alfred to Henry III, 871–1272* (London, 1969).

As for an excellent, concise summary of Norman-Angevin legal history, see J.H. Baker, *An Introduction to English Legal History* (3d ed., London, 1990), 14–62. See also R.C. Van Caenegem's classical study *The Birth of the English*

---

6. *Roe v. Wade*, 410 U.S. 113, 134–136 (1973).

7. See W.S. Maitland, *Bracton's Note-Book*, (Cambridge, 1887) and *Select Passages from Bracton and Azo* (1874, Selden Society, vol. 8). The latter work attempted to trace the influence of Roman law on *Bracton's* authors, a contentious subject for scholars. See the sources in "Further Reading," *infra*, p. 63, under "III."

Common Law (Cambridge, 1973), 1–28. The account in T.F.T. Plucknett's *A Concise History of the Common Law* (Boston, 1956), 11–26, 139–156, 252–266, also contains very concise and lucid summaries, although somewhat out-of-date.

III.   Special Topics: Bracton

Bracton exerts a special fascination as a "window" into the early English common law. For excellent general accounts see David J. Seipp, "Bracton, the Year Books, and the Transformation of Elementary Legal Ideas in the Early Common Law," 7 *Law and History Review* (Spring, 1989), 175; and S.E. Thorne, "The Text of Bracton's 'De Legibus Angliae,'" *Atti del il Congresso Internazionale della Societa' Italiana di Storia del Dritto* (Florence, 1971), 803–820. (The latter article gives a fine summary of the problems of *Bracton* scholarship, but has been surpassed in part by Thorne's own new edition and translation, *supra*.) See also Percy H. Winfield, *The Chief Sources of English Legal History* (New York, 1925), 256–262.

MATERIALS

THE DOMESDAY BOOK

In 1085 A.D., William the Conqueror undertook a massive inventory of almost every asset in England, at least every real property asset and most livestock. The results were compiled in two volumes, "Great" and "Little" *Domesday*, the smaller containing Essex, Norfolk and Suffolk, and the larger everything else. Note how William collected information.

RETURN FROM THE DOMESDAY INQUEST (1086)

Here is written down the inquisition of the lands [of Cambridgeshire] as made by the king's barons: namely, by the oath of the sheriff of the shire; of all the barons, their Frenchmen, and the whole hundred [court]; of the priest, the reeve, and six villeins of each vill. Then [is set down] how the manor is called, who held it in the time of king Edward, who holds it now, how many hides there are, how many ploughs in demesne, how many ploughs of the men, how many men, how many villeins, how many cotters, how many serfs, how many freemen, how many sokemen, how much woods, how much meadow, how many pastures, how many mills, how many fishponds, how much has been added or taken away, how much it was worth altogether and how much now, and how much each freeman or sokeman had or has there. All this [information is given] three times over:

Illustration 3-3 *Great and Little Domesday* from Public Record Office Museum Pamphlet No. 10 (HMSO, 1981, intro. A. Nicol), 2. Crown copyright material in the Public Record Office is reproduced by permission of the Controller of Her Majesty's Stationery Office.

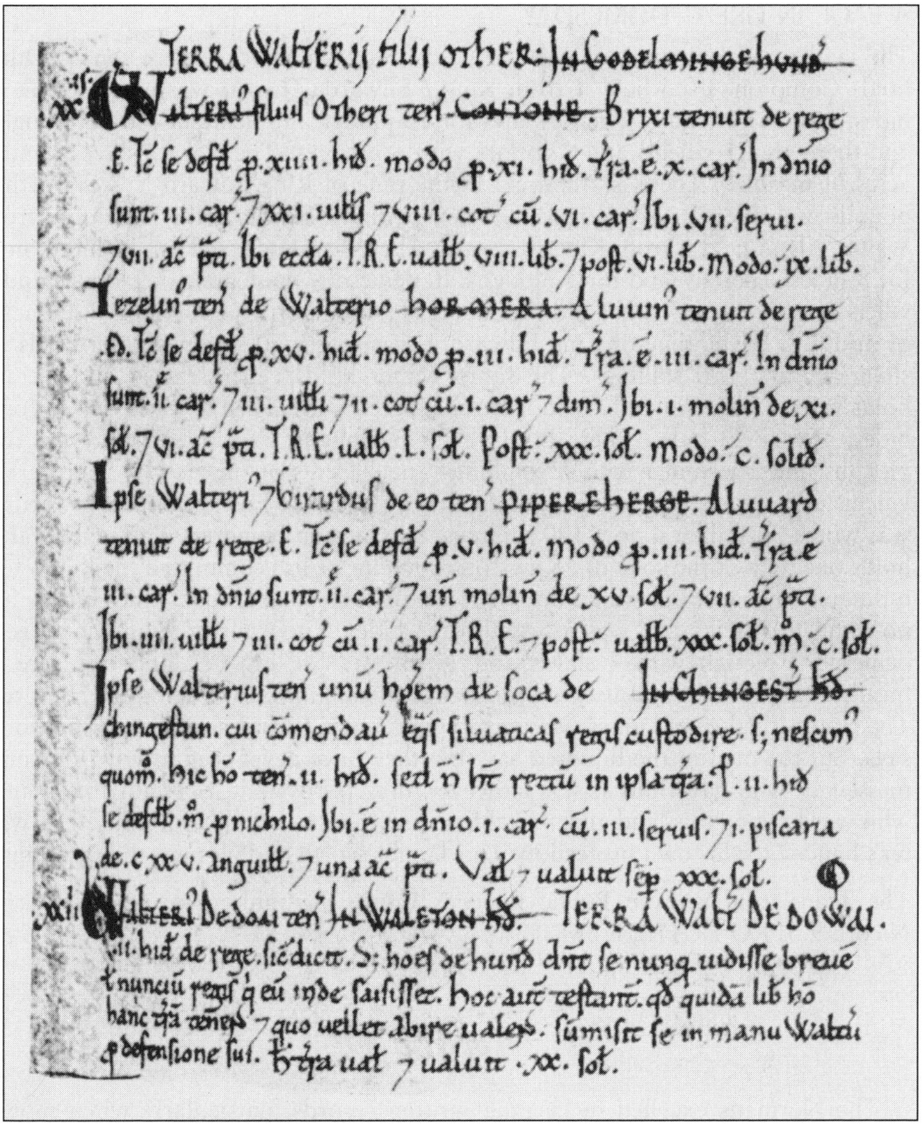

Illustration 3-4 A Page in Great Domesday (1086 A.D.). In custody Public Records Office, PRO E 31/2, E 36R. Reproduced with agreement. This page is translated on the next page of these *Materials*.

namely, in the time of King Edward, when King William gave it out, and how it is now—and whether more can be had [from it] than is being had.

These men swore....

From C. Stephenson, F.G. Marcham, *supra*, *Sources of English Constitutional History* (Harper Brothers, 1937), 40.

Note: "Juror" is from the Latin *jurare*, "to swear." Note how the Normans collected facts by assembling groups of neighbors and putting them under oath. This would later be adapted to legal proceedings in court.

A PAGE IN GREAT DOMESDAY

The land of Walter son of Other. In Godalming Hundred. Walter son of Other holds Compton. Brixi held it from King / Edward. Then it was assessed for 14 hides, now for 11 hides. There is land for 10 ploughs. In demesne / are 3 ploughs, and there are 21 villeins and 8 cottars with 6 ploughs. There are 7 slaves / and 7 acres of meadow. There is a church. In the time of King Edward it was worth 8 pounds and afterwards 6 pounds; now 9 pounds. Tezelin holds Hurtmore from Walter. Alwin held it from King / Edward. Then it was assessed for 15 hides, now for 3 hides. There is land for 3 ploughs. In demesne / there are two ploughs and 3 villeins and 2 cottars with 1 plough. There is 1 mill worth 11 shillings and 6 acres of meadow. In the time of King Edward it was worth 50 shillings; afterwards 30 shillings; now 100 shillings. The same Walter holds Peper Harow and Gerard holds it from him. Alward / held it from King Edward. Then it was assessed for 5 hides, now for 3 hides. There is land / for 3 ploughs. In demesne there are two ploughs and one mill worth 15 shillings and 7 acres of meadow. / There are 4 villeins and 3 cottars with 1 plough. In the time of King Edward and afterwards it was worth 30 shillings; now 100 shillings. In Kingston Hundred. The same Walter holds one man of the soke of / Kingston to whom he has committed the king's forest mares to guard. But we do not know / how. This man holds 2 hides but he has no right in that land. It was assessed for 2 hides, / now for nothing. There is in demesne 1 plough with 3 slaves and 1 fishery / for 125 eels and one acre of meadow. It is worth and was always worth 30 shillings. In Wallington Hundred. The land of Walter of Douai. Walter of Douai holds / 2 hides from the king, so he says. But the men of the hundred say that they have never seen a writ / or king's messenger who gave him seisin. However, they testify that a certain free man, / who was holding this land and was able to go where he would, put himself in Walter's hands / for his own protection. This land is worth and was worth 20 shillings.

The Translation is from Public Records Office, Pamphlet No. 10, *supra*, (A. Nicol), 9. (PRO E 3112, E 36R.)

ROLLS

The Normans excelled in keeping written records, particularly when money was involved—or administration. These were kept on long rolls of membrane, made of vellum stitched together. See Illustration 3-5. Many of these have survived, and are an extraordinary source of information. In Illustration 3-6, showing the King's Bench court, note the court scribes with the rolls before them. The Normans knew that control of information was power.

PIPE ROLL 31 HENRY I (1130 A.D.)

Henry I: Ordinance on Local Courts

Henry, king of the English, to Samson, bishop [of Worcester], Urse d'Abetot, and all his barons of Worcestershire, French and English, greeting. Know that I grant and command that henceforth [the courts of] my counties and hundreds shall meet in the same places and at the same times as they did in the time of King

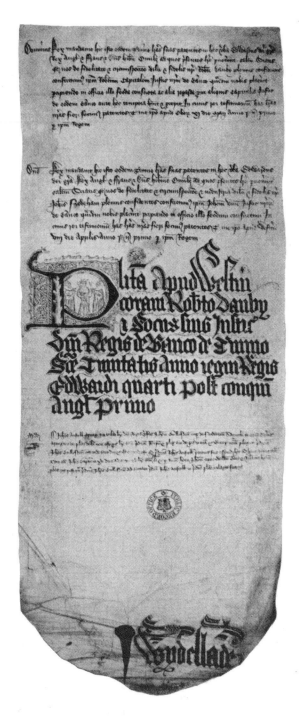

Illustration 3-5 First Membrane of Plea Roll of Trinity Term, I Edward IV. (CP 40/801, m1) Courtesy Public Record Office. Crown Copyright Material in the Public Record Office is reproduced by permission of the Controller of Her Majesty's Stationery Office.

Edward, and not otherwise. And I am unwilling that my sheriff, on account of any business that peculiarly concerns him, should have them meet in any other way. For I, when I please and on my own decision, will have them adequately summoned for the sake of my royal needs (*dominica necessaria*). And henceforth, if a plea arises concerning the division or occupation of lands, and if it is between my own barons (*dominicos barones meos*), let it be tried in my court. And if it is between vassals of some baron who holds an honour of me, let the plea be tried in the court of their lord. And if it is between vassals of two lords, let it be tried in the county [court]. And this [trial] shall be by combat unless it is given up through their own fault (*nisi remanserit in eis*). Also I will and command that all men of the county shall attend the county [court] and the hundred [courts] as they did in the time of King Edward, and no peace or quittance of mine shall excuse them from following my pleas and judgments according to the usage of that time.

Witnesses: R [ichard], Bishop of London; Roger, Bishop [of Salisbury]; Ralph the Chamberlain; Robert, Count of Meulan. At Reading.

From: Stephenson and F.C. Marcham, *supra*, 49–50. [Reproduced courtesy Addison Wesley Educational Publishers, Inc.]

Excerpts, Pipe Roll 31 Henry I (1130 A.D.)

Geoffrey de Clinton renders account of 44*s*. 8*d*. blanch from the old farm. He has paid it into the treasury. And he is quit.

And the same man [renders account] of the new farm. In the treasury £100. 4*s*. 4*d*. by weight. And he owes £32. 9*s*. 4*d*. blanch.

And the same Geoffrey renders account of 310*m*. of silver for an office in the treasury at Winchester. In the treasury 100*m*. of silver. And he owes 210*m*. of silver.

And the same man owes 40*m*. of silver on behalf of the earl of Leicester for the debt of Ernald de Vétheuil.

And the same man owes 20*m*. of silver and 1*m*. of gold that the king will confirm in a charter for his church of Arden everything that the earl of Warwick gave him for the benefit of the said church.

And the same man owes £7. 13*s*. 8*d*. from the old farm of the land of William de Roumare.

And the same man owes 40*m*. of silver with which he should acquit Nicholas Fitz-Gundewin of Rouen.

Geoffrey Lovet owes £9. 13s. 4d. for the security that he unjustly took from a certain man; of which [money] the pledges are Geoffrey de Clinton and Robert de Neufbourg.

Osbert of Arden renders account of £10 for the pleas of William Hubold. In the treasury 40s. And he owes £8.

And the same sheriff renders account of 100s. from old pleas and murders. In pardon by the king's writ to the earl of Warwick 100s. And he is quit.

Hugh Fitz-Richard renders account of 200*m*. of silver and one valuable horse (equo de pretio) and two war-horses (dextrariis) for the land that Geoffrey de Lovet holds of him. In the treasury £30. And by the witness of Miles of Gloucester he has acquitted himself toward the king of the valuable war-horse (dextrario pretioso). And he owes 155*m*. of silver and two horses. And thereof [these men] are pledges: the earl of Warwick, 60*m*. of silver; Henry de Sai, 20*m*. of silver; Henry d'Armentières, 20*m*. of silver.

From: C. Stephenson and F.C. Marcham, *supra*, 49–50. (Reproduced courtesy Addison Wesley Educational Publishers, Inc.) The word "blanch" refers to a rent payable in high quality silver.

ASSIZES

The Assize of Clarendon (1166)

From: C. Stephenson, F.G. Marcham, *supra*, *Sources of English Constitutional History* (Harper Brothers, 1937), 77–79. (Reproduced courtesy Addison Wesley Educational Publishers, Inc.) Translations from the Latin notes omitted.

Note: This is an "assize" in the sense of an ordinance. See n. 3, in the preceding introduction. References to trial by ordeal or by "oath helping," sometimes called "making their law," are fully discussed in Chapter 5, *infra*.

Here begins the Assize of Clarendon made by King Henry, namely the second, with the assent of the archbishops, bishops, abbots, earls, and barons of all England.

1. In the first place the aforesaid King Henry, by the counsel of all his barons, has ordained that, for the preservation of peace and the enforcement of justice, inquiry shall be made in every county and in every hundred through twelve of the more lawful men of the hundred and through four of the more lawful men of each vill, [put] on oath to tell the truth, whether in their hundred or in their vill there is any man accused or publicly known as a robber or murderer or thief, or any one who has been a receiver of robbers or murderers or thieves, since the lord king has been king. And let the justices make this investigation in their presence and the sheriffs in their presence.

2. And whoever is found by the oath of the aforesaid men to have been accused or publicly known as a robber or murderer or thief, or as a receiver of them since the lord king has been king, shall be seized; and he shall go to the ordeal of water and swear that, to the value of 5s., so far as he knows, he has not been a robber or murderer or thief, or a receiver of them, since the lord king has been king.

3. And if the lord of the man who has been seized or his steward or his men seek [to free] him under pledge, within the third day after he has been seized, let him and his chattels be remanded under pledge until he has made his law.

4. And when robbers or murderers or thieves, or receivers of them, are seized in consequence of the aforesaid oath, if the justices are not soon to come into that county where they were seized, the sheriff shall, through some intelligent man, notify the nearest justices that he has seized such men; and the justices shall send back word to the sheriff that those [accused] are to be brought before them, wherever they please. The sheriff shall then take those [accused] before the justices, and with him he shall take two lawful men from the hundred or the vill where they were seized, to bring the record of the county and hundred as to why they were seized; and there before the justices they shall make their law.

5. And with regard to those seized in consequence of the aforesaid oath of this assize, no one shall have jurisdiction or judgment or [forfeiture of] chattels but the lord king in his court and in the presence of his justices; and the lord king shall have all their chattels. With respect, however, to those seized otherwise than through this oath, let whatever is customary and right be done.

6. And the sheriffs who have seized them shall take them before the justice without other summons than shall be had from him. And when robbers or murderers or thieves, or receivers of them, whether seized in consequence of the oath or otherwise, are delivered to the sheriffs, the latter shall take them immediately and without delay.

7. And in every county where there are no jails let them be made within a borough or some castle of the king — with the king's money and with his wood if that is near at hand, or with some other wood close by, and by view of the king's serjeants — so that the sheriffs may have the seized men guarded in those [jails] by the officials accustomed to do so and by their serjeants.

8. The lord king also wills that all should come to the county [court] for the making of this oath; so that no one, on account of any liberty that he has, or on account of any jurisdiction or soke that he may enjoy, shall abstain from attendance for the making of this oath.

9. And let there be no one, in castle or out of castle, or even in the honour of Wallingford, who forbids the sheriffs to enter upon his jurisdiction or his land for view of frankpledge; and let all men be placed under sureties, and let them be sent before the sheriffs under frankpledge. ["Frankpledge" referred to groups of ten persons who were required to act as sureties for each other's good behavior. This was a tool to ensure public orderliness by collective responsibility.]

10. And within cities or boroughs no one shall have men, or shall receive [men] within his house or his land or his soke for whom he will not be sponsor, [guaranteeing] that he will bring them before the justice, should they be summoned, or that they are under frankpledge.

11. And let there be no persons, either in a city or a borough or a castle, or outside them, or even in the honour of Wallingford, who forbid the sheriffs to enter upon their land or their soke for the purpose of seizing those who have been accused or publicly known as robbers or murderers or thieves, or receivers of them, or outlaws, or those accused under forest [law], on the contrary, [the king] commands them to give assistance in seizing those [suspects].

12. And if any one is seized who possesses [the proceeds] of robbery or theft, should he be a notorious person and have a bad reputation, and should he not have a warrantor, let him not have his law. And if he is not notorious, let him, on account of his [suspicious] possessions, go to the [ordeal of] water.

13. And if any one, in the presence of lawful men or of a hundred [court], has confessed robbery or murder or theft, or the reception of those [who have committed such crimes], and should he then wish to deny it, let him not have his law.

14. The lord king also wills that those who make their law and are cleared by the law, if they are of very bad reputation, being publicly and shamefully denounced by the testimony of many lawful men, shall abjure the lands of the king, so that they shall cross the sea within eight days unless they are detained by the wind; then, with the first [favourable] wind that they have, they shall cross the sea and thenceforth not return to England, except at the mercy of the lord king; [so that] they shall there be outlaws and shall be seized as outlaws if they return.

15. And the lord king forbids that any waif (*vaivus*) — that is to say, one wandering or unknown — shall be given lodging anywhere except in a borough; and he should not be given lodging there for more than one night unless he or his horse becomes ill there, so that he can show evident excuse [for his delay].

6. And if [otherwise] he stays there for more than one night, let him be seized and held until his lord may come to give pledge for him, or until he himself may find good sureties; and let him who provided the lodging be likewise seized.

17. And if any sheriff has notified another sheriff that men have fled from his county into the other county as the consequence of robbery or murder or theft, or of receiving those [who have committed such crimes], or of outlawry, or of accusation under the king's forest [law], let the latter [sheriff] seize them. Also, if he knows of himself or through others, that such men have fled into his county, let him seize them and guard them until he has good sureties for them.

18. And all sheriffs shall have the names of all fugitives who have fled from their counties written down, and this they shall do before [the courts of] their counties. And the names of those men, [thus] written down, they shall bring before the justices when first they report to those [justices], so that the latter may make inquiry throughout all England and may seize the chattels [of the fugitives] for the use of the king.

19. And the lord king wills that, as soon as the sheriffs have received the summons of the itinerant justices to come before the latter together with [the courts of] their counties, they shall bring together [the courts of] their counties and make inquiry concerning all who recently, after this assize, have come into their counties; and they shall put those [newcomers] under pledge to appear before the justices, or they shall guard those [newcomers] until the justices come to them, and then they shall bring [the newcomers] before the justices.

20. The lord king also forbids monks or canons or any religious community to receive any one from the lower classes (*de minuto populo*) as a monk or a canon or a brother until it is known of what reputation he may be, unless he is sick unto death.

21. The lord king also forbids that any one in all England shall receive under him within his land or his soke or his house any from the sect of those renegades branded and placed under ex-communication at Oxford. And if any one does receive them, he shall be in the mercy of the lord king; and the house in which they resided shall be taken outside the vill and burned. And every sheriff shall take an oath to obey this [command]; and he shall have this sworn by all his officials, by the stewards of barons, and by all knights and freeholders of the county.

22. And the lord king wills that, during his pleasure, this assize shall be observed in the kingdom.

COURTS

S.F.C. Milsom, *Historical Foundation of the Common Law* (2d Ed., Butterworth, 1981) 25–36. Excerpt from Chapter 1, "The Centralization of Justice."

Note: Professor S.F.C. Milsom of St. John's College, Cambridge, is one of the greatest modern English legal historians. [Reproduced courtesy Lexis Law Publishing.]

"The Pattern of Centralization"

The pattern of centralisation from local institutions is clear to hindsight. People were first governed by the courts of county and hundred, those courts by the king. Government in the upper tier was largely a matter of accounting for what had become due to the king from the lower. Certain wrongs, for example, entailed a forfeiture to the king of the wrongdoer's goods; local institutions must therefore produce what was in effect a balance-sheet of wrongs and goods, and would be penalised for any failure. The earliest method of control appears to have been a system of local agents, local justiciars, who were to take part in the determination of any matter involving royal rights. This gave way to a system of periodic audit by commissioners sent out from the centre, the justices in eyre, supplemented by a permanent local accountant, the coroner, whose records provided a check on the accounts given by the local institutions themselves. Seen from another angle, the system of eyres, journeys by the king's commissioners and the king himself, represents a system of governing the kingdom bit by bit, checking on one county after another; and within each county the sheriff would similarly make periodic tours of the hundreds. But there was an inevitable tendency for matters to be drawn up from the lower tier of the old structure, for the king to govern people directly and for people to seek justice from the king directly. As this happened in more and more matters, the realm became the important community. Instead of the king coming to the counties one after another, the counties sent representatives to treat together with the king and to become the house of commons. And as more and more kinds of dispute were brought to royal judges, visitations at a frequency suitable for the old audit were less and less appropriate. Litigants sought royal justice wherever they could find royal power, which was most often in the exchequer; there a permanent central court was established. Centralisation and specialisation proceeded together.

But the pattern which hindsight can see was not being consciously drawn at the time. Institutions begin in expedients. An immediate problem arises: an immediate solution is found. Nobody can know that the solution will later be seen as the origin of something, or the problem as the effective end of something else. There was never a time at which the county was consciously reduced from its position as the most important court for ordinary people. Indeed, attempts were made to stem or reverse the tide of centralisation and send some matters back there. Nor were eyres consciously abolished, or the central courts adjusted to their new function. With legal institutions as with the law itself, change was until the nineteenth century an almost sedimentary deposit of expedients.

Illustration 3-6 Court of King's Bench from a manuscript (*circa* 1420 A.D.). While this picture comes long after the Norman-Angevins, it emphasizes the court records or "rolls," which were so important. The jury is on the left. Below are the prisoners. The ushers carry a white staff of office. The figures in the gowns are lawyers wearing their "coifs." This head dress showed that the lawyers had the rank of Serjeants of Law. We will return to this distinctive group of professionals in Chapter IX, *infra*. Does your law school have an "Order of the Coif?" From Archaeologia XXXXIX (1863), p. 367. (Whaddon Folio, Inner Temple).

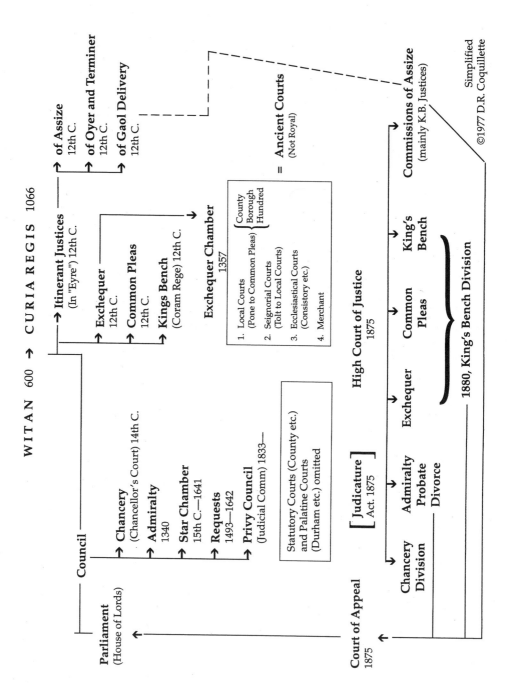

Illustration 3-7: Evolution of the English Courts. We will be returning to this chart many times. The bottom line shows courts in existence in England in 1977, when this chart was first prepared. Others have also survived. In particular, the Norman itinerant judges, the justices "in eyre," are still to be found as royal judges with "commission of assize," who visit county towns to hold courts. See text, note 3. This chart was prepared with the kind help of Ann McDonald, together with Illustrations 4-2, 4-4, 5-4, 5-6, 7-2, 8-2, and 14-5. I am most grateful for her skilled assistance.

The Eyre System

Of the earliest eyres the only official traces are entries of the proceeds in the pipe rolls, the great central accounts, from which the personnel and the circuits of some commissions can be reconstructed. But from the late twelfth century we have records made for the commissioners themselves, eyre rolls; and for some fourteenth-century eyres these are supplemented by year book reports, made for the technical purposes of lawyers. In all this we can see not judges on circuit but a whole system of government. The coming of the justices in eyre was the coming of royal power, and before them would appear the fullest assembly of the county. The ordinary governmental authorities stopped working, and they themselves came to judgment. The catastrophic nature of the visitation can be seen in events at the opening of the eyre. For example machinery had to be set up to regulate more minutely than in ordinary times the prices of food, and special arrangements had to be made about accommodation for the crowds who were to come. And the sheriff surrendered to the justices his wand of office and received it back at their hands: they were the king and he was to act at their command and to hold office at their will.

The conduct of business at an eyre epitomised its historical role. The work was divided into two parts, and sometimes at least the commissioners formed themselves into two groups to deal with them. The first part, the pleas of the crown, represents the system of itinerant government, the first stage in institutional centralisation. At its core was a list of questions, the articles of the eyre, about all matters of possible profit to the king. Some of these were about the feudal rights of the crown, wardships and the like, which will later be discussed for their own sake. Some were about such arbitrary oddities as wreck and treasure trove; and the coroner's inquest into treasure trove survives today to remind us that the enforcement of rules, and not the refinement of their content, was the first achievement. The coroner's inquest into unexplained deaths reminds us even more clearly that law and order on the national scale were first expressed in terms of revenue. When in 1221 a Worcestershire hundred jury, answering the articles of the eyre, said that Roger's wife Emma had been drowned in the Avon, it turned out that she had really been killed by Roger. Roger had already been hanged for it, and he had no chattels to be forfeited to the king; but if the untruth had passed unchecked, two other communal imposts would have been saved. Roger had not been in a tithing, one of the groups into which the population of each area was required to be divided, and upon which was cast the responsibility of producing such of their members as should be called to justice. And upon Emma's death Englishry had not been presented, a requirement dating from the time when the Normans were in the position of an occupying army, protected by a fine levied upon any community in which one of their number, or anyone not proved to be English, was found dead. But of course we misunderstand the eyre if we imagine some distinction between the financial motive and the aims of government; this was how government was conducted. And other articles of the eyre asked questions more obviously governemental in character, for example concerning franchises, the controlled market in cloth and wine, or the misdeeds of sheriffs and other royal officers.

The other part of the eyre's business was the common pleas, ordinary litigation between ordinary people. And since almost all our evidence comes from a time when there existed also the central court which came to be known as the court of common pleas, and since that court became the ordinary forum for such litigation, it is important to emphasise that it was in the eyre that such pleas could first come to royal justice as a matter of routine. It was the central court that was at first the exceptional thing, in that cases were begun there for special reason, sometimes for special payment by a litigant unwilling to wait for the next eyre; and it always needed the special authorisation of a writ.

Particularly in connection with the personal actions, this exchange between the ordinary and the exceptional is a source of misunderstanding. Seemingly avoidable difficulties arose, for example, because modes of proof which depended upon a litigant's standing with his neighbours were transplanted from local courts to Westminster Hall. But it was not in Westminster that they were first accepted by the king's judges: it was in the county town with the neighbours present.

Misunderstanding has gone deeper than that. The first scholar to investigate the eyre, assuming that what the court of common pleas did was and always had been the essence of the common law, was surprised to find personal actions begun without writ, and even more surprised to find complaints of kinds of wrong which never appeared in the court of common pleas at all. These last were in fact cases so humdrum that normally they would be settled at an ordinary session of the county and never reach royal justice. But they and the procedure by more bill of complaint were taken as evidence of a power to override the rules of the common law, and the eyre was identified as the first home of English equity. What matters is not the particular misapprehension about the eyre, or even the larger misapprehension about the nature of early equity: it is an underlying misconception of the early common law itself, to be considered at the end of this chapter and from time to time throughout this book.

More numerous than personal actions on the common pleas section of an eyre roll are actions concerning land; and in any court these required a writ for a reason which was not purely administrative, and which will be explained together with the actions themselves. It seems to flow from a feature of the actions which is relevant to their place in the overall pattern of centralisation. The two most frequently brought were legislative creations of the late twelfth century, the 'possessory assizes' of novel disseisin and mort d'ancestor. And these have been seen by historians as alternatives to remedies in feudal courts, so that their part in centralisation was just to expand the demand for royal justice by competitive attraction. But their original function turns out to have been more integral to that of the eyre. They began as measures for the control of feudal jurisdictions themselves; and it is even possible that novel disseisin was first a matter for the presentment of the countryside like the pleas of the crown.

The judicial functions of the eyre may be seen as having ultimately been inherited partly by the court of common pleas and partly by itinerant justices commissioned more frequently but with restricted rather than general powers. Both of course were in use long before the eyre began to decline from being the regular arm of central government to its last state in the fourteenth century as an occasional means of extortion. Visitations at intervals of seven years or so, which became accepted as the minimum, were appropriate for an auditing function, for checking what local men had done; but for the actual conduct of business, for the dispensation of royal justice when that was in common demand, other machinery had to be found. The two matters in which this first happened both followed from changes made under Henry II. The introduction of the possessory assizes brought great numbers of small disputes about property to be settled by royal inquest. And the elaboration of the indictment system, which we see as the beginning of crime as a separate branch of the law, replaced royal supervision by royal action in the case of most serious wrongs. Local communities were increasingly concerned not merely to account for what had happened about wrongs from which profit might come to the king, but to accuse the wrongdoers before royal justices.

For both these purposes frequent local sessions of royal justices were needed. But the business was trivial in comparison with that of the eyre, and did not require great men for its settlement. The commissioners to whom it was entrusted might therefore be persons of no more than local importance; and in the case of pleas of the crown this feature came to be accepted by the establishment in the fourteenth century of permanent commissioners for each county, the justices of the peace, who were to act at regular intervals without further instruction. But the regular dispatch from the centre of royal officers never ceased, and the name and business of those assizes which lasted until our own day went back to a time when their usual commission was to hear possessory assizes and to deliver the jails. To these there came to be added a new class of what we should call civil business, the taking from local juries of verdicts in cases depending before the central courts; and it was partly for this reason that the commissioners sent on circuit nearly always included professional judges from those courts. But when we speak of professional judges, we are speaking of a time at which the law has become distinct from government in general, something to which a man can devote his life; and this was by far the most important result of the rise of the central courts themselves.

Rise of the Central Courts

The process had its beginnings in itinerant government, which had two centres. There was first the king himself, constantly on the move within his kingdom and in his other possessions, having with him a court in all the institutional senses of that word. From this court *coram rege* there slowly developed the king's bench, a regular court of law separate from the king's person and separate from his council, which was in time to engross much ordinary civil litigation. But it could not be a regular channel for royal justice so long as it was in constant motion, and in the thirteenth century to commence an action there seems to have been one way of harassing an enemy.

The second centre of itinerant government was the exchequer, brought to rest by the weight of its financial apparatus, but playing a much larger part in the kingdom than that of a modern financial department of state. We have seen that central government took the form of accountancy, and consisted in the enforcement by financial sanctions of the financial rights of the crown. The eyres can be seen as local audits by officers sent out from the centre; and that centre was the exchequer. If the will of government was with the king, this was its mind; and the frequent absences of the king assured it the control of all necessary routines and the services of those who made government their profession. At the head of this machine, the embodiment of all these factors, was the chief justiciar, the regent in the king's absence and the centre around which royal justice first grew.

By a process of specialisation of which the details may be beyond recovery, not one but two regular courts of law grew from this centre. There was the court of exchequer itself, which had for its special business the legal disputes arising out of revenue. This court was later to justify a large concern with purely private causes by colour of a fictitious revenue interest; but in fact it seems never to have quite given up the wide jurisdiction of the old undifferentiated body from which it grew. The other offspring of that body was the common bench or court of common pleas, whose name, happily preserved in many American jurisdictions, was allowed to disappear from the English legal system in 1880. Here the common law was made.

The common bench had to establish an identity distinct not only from the exchequer, but also from the court *coram rege*. A single body of justices served the common and the king's bench, and they merged when the king was out of the country or was an infant. And that is why, although the Great Charter of 1215 was only confirming the practice of many years when it required that possessory assizes should be heard locally at frequent intervals and that other common pleas should be held in some fixed place, the court emerges as a distinct and permanent institution only after the majority of Henry III, who had succeeded John as a child in the year after the Charter was issued.

Ninety years later, when Henry III's son died, the three central courts of common pleas, exchequer and king's bench were settled institutions. Eyres would occasionally be commissioned for a few decades longer, but they were no longer integral to either government or judicature. What were integral were lesser commissions by which justices on circuit took the possessory assizes and took also verdicts in cases in which jury issues had been reached in the central courts. And many disputes, especially in what we should call contract and tort, were still heard in local courts. The system was to make some sense until the sixteenth century, to last until the nineteenth, and to leave its imprint in every common law jurisdiction today. But it was not devised as a national system of civil judicature. It was an accumulation of expedients as more and more kinds of dispute were drawn first to a jurisdictional and then also to a geographical centre. One result was to invest the machinery which controlled jurisdiction with an importance that was to outlive and to overshadow its reason.

The Writ System

That machinery was the system of writs, and in principle it was no more than a part of the administrative routine made necessary by centralisation. In the ancient jurisdiction of the county court, for example, a law-suit was started by simple complaint, and the only preliminary required was that the plaintiff should give security to pursue it before the defendant would be summoned to answer. But when matters arose which it was convenient to refer to the county but which were not within its accepted jurisdiction, the sheriff was given royal authority to act by what is called a viscontiel writ. This probably came to happen most often when the royal courts themselves began to hear private disputes as a regular thing. Lines of demarcation emerged between local and royal jurisdictions, depending upon the amount at stake or upon some royal interest; and if a plaintiff preferred to sue in the county on a matter lying on the royal side of the boundary, the sheriff could not act without the authority of a viscontiel writ. But the earliest writs seem to have dealt with matters properly within the jurisdiction not of the king but of some lord, but in which the lord was unable to act. His inability was itself sometimes a result of royal control; and royal writs interfered with feudal jurisdiction, originally as self-sufficient as that of the county, in fundamental ways to be considered later in this book.

More important for the later development of the common law was the part played by writs in the king's courts themselves. The plaintiff makes his first complaint to a secretariat, the chancery. The writ is in form just an order telling the sheriff—again only if the plaintiff gives security to prosecute his claim—to bring the defendant to answer. But since it has to specify the court to which the defendant is to come it operates also as that court's warrant to proceed. In some situations, however, the plaintiff could be heard without going through the secretariat at all. Take first the eyre. Like the county court, the eyre was older than the writ system. The commission under which the judges went out gave them almost unlimited jurisdiction in the county concerned; and as for the other function of writs, that of securing the presence of defendants, the sheriff attended on the judges and was directly under their orders. Direct complaint to the eyre was then a normal routine for seeking royal justice, and it was the later development of the writ system that was to make it look exceptional. Much the same is true of the king's bench. The king's own court needed no warrant to give it jurisdiction, and if it would entertain a dispute at all, it could do so directly at the instance of the plaintiff as well as on a formal reference by writ. But the court in fact came to restrict the cases it would hear by plaint to those arising in the county in which it was sitting; and this is probably because the sheriff of that county was in attendance upon the court, so that there was no difficulty about securing the presence of the defendant. The result was like that reached in the eyre, but reflected the practical function performed by writs in getting the defendant, rather than a theoretical limit on jurisdiction. In the sixteenth century, as will appear, this procedure by bill in the king's bench, under the name of the Bill of Middlesex since that was the county in which the court then always sat, was used to subvert the jurisdictional order whose establishment is now being described.

That order hinged upon the position of the common bench. This court had come into being to provide royal justice in ordinary disputes between subject and subject, and its emergence had been compelled by a demand for this on a scale beyond the capacity of the eyre system. But the demand was, to begin with, for a luxury. The plaintiff seeking to begin a case there was asking not just for royal rather than local justice, but also for royal justice at once: his right, if such it can be called, was to have it in the eyre. The most regular institution of the middle ages therefore started, not as part of the regular routine of government, but as a provision for exceptional cases. One could not apply directly to the court for justice, because the court had no inherent power to act. Its nature was that of a committee to which cases were individually referred by writ; and, except for matters involving the court's own staff and practitioners, bills came to play no part in its jurisdiction.

The need for a writ in the common pleas as the court's warrant to act, an accidental result of its earliest business being outside the ordinary course of things, was to have many consequences. It explains a great deal of what looks like captiousness in the early common law: a plaintiff who brought a writ for £20 and claimed £19 was not making the claim the court was authorised to hear. And it explains a great deal of inflexibility in the scope of the law, the kinds of matters with which it could deal at all. However much royal and central justice had started as something exceptional, as it became more and more the regular thing, the court slowly established a monopoly. It was not merely the body to which private disputes could conveniently be sent; they could not normally be sent to any other central court, for example the king's bench. Partly this was the familiar hardening of practice into right, but partly it was a matter of 'due process.'

When the Great Charter required common pleas to be held in some fixed place, it was perhaps mainly concerned with the need of the plaintiff to have access to justice. But there was also the defendant to consider. Litigation in a traveling court could be intolerable; and even when the king's bench came increasingly to rest, great men and great corporations, who retained standing attorneys in the common pleas, could argue that they should not be forced elsewhere. The paradoxical result was that the regular court to which ordinary disputes had to go was a court which could not act without special authority in each case, namely a writ from the chancery.

This jurisdictional accident was to be of growing consequence. In the middle ages it hampered the expansion of the common law by restricting the kinds of claim that could be brought before the court. If ordinary private disputes had continued to come before a jurisdiction like that of the eyre, to which plaintiffs had direct access, the common law could have reacted directly to changing needs; and in particular it could have continued to admit kinds of claim familiar in local courts but at first regarded as inappropriate for royal judges. But plaintiffs could not get to the court without a chancery writ, and the formulae of the writs, most of which were highly practical responses to the needs of thirteenth-century litigants, became an authoritative canon which could not easily be altered or added to. Important areas, some new but many older than the king's courts themselves, were in this way cut off from legal regulation; and they could later be reached only be devious ingenuity in the common law courts, or by resorting to the chancellor's equitable jurisdiction, to which once more the litigant could directly complain.

All this was no more than the constriction of red tape. But so complete did it become that in the eighteenth century it engendered a purely formalistic view of the law and of its development which has lasted until our own day. The common law writs came to be seen as somehow basic, almost like the Ten Commandments or the Twelve Tables, the data from which the law itself was derived. And since the mechanism of change within the common law had been to allow one writ to do the work formerly done by another, the whole process came to be seen as an irrational interplay between 'the forms of action.' It was not. It was the product of men thinking.

MAGNA CARTA (1215)

Text from C. Stephenson & F.G. Marcham, *Sources of English Constitutional History, supra* (Harper Brothers, 1937). (Reproduced courtesy Addison Wesley Educational Publishers, Inc.)

Note: The italics indicate words only found in the 1215 original. The rest is the text reissued under Henry III in 1216 and confirmed in 1225, the so-called "official" text. For more background, see J.C. Holt, *Magna Carta* (Cambridge 1965). For a complete annotated bibliography, see *Magna Carta in America* (D.V. Stimson, ed., 1993), 118–179.

MAGNA CARTA (1215)

John, by the grace of God king of England, lord of Ireland, duke of Normandy and of Aquitaine, and count of Anjou, to his archbishops, bishops, ab-

Illustration 3-8   Runnymede. Here the Magna Carta was signed in 1215 A.D. In 1965, a plot of this meadow was given to the American people as a memorial to John F. Kennedy. Photograph by kind permission of Bruce Kennett.

bots, earls, barons, justiciars, foresters, sheriffs, reeves, ministers, and all his bailiffs and faithful men, greeting. Know that, through the inspiration of God, for the health of our soul and [the souls] of all our ancestors and heirs, for the honour of God and the exaltation of Holy Church, and for the betterment of our realm, by the counsel of our venerable fathers [here eleven ecclesiastics], of our nobles [here sixteen lay "barons"], and our other faithful men—

1. We have in the first place granted to God and by this our present charter have confirmed, for us and our heirs forever, that the English Church shall be free and shall have its rights entire and its liberties inviolate. *And how we wish [that freedom] to be observed appears from this, that of our own pure and free will, before the conflict that arose between us and our barons, we granted and by our charter confirmed the liberty of election that is considered of prime importance and necessity for the English Church, and we obtained confirmation of it from the lord pope Innocent III—which [charter] we will observe ourself and we wish to be observed in good faith by our heirs forever.* We have also granted to all freemen of our kingdom, for us and our heirs forever, all the liberties hereinunder written, to be had and held by them and their heirs of us and our heirs.

2. If any one of our earls or barons or other men holding of us in chief dies, and if when he dies his heir is of full age and owes relief, [that heir] shall have his

inheritance for the ancient relief: namely, the heir or heirs of an earl £100 for the whole barony of an earl; the heir or heirs of a baron £100 for a whole barony; the heir or heirs of a knight 100s. at most for a whole knight's fee. And let whoever owes less give less, according to the ancient custom of fiefs.

3. If, however, the heir of any such person is under age and is in wardship, he shall, when he comes of age, have his inheritance without relief and without fine.

4. The guardian of the land of such an heir who is under age shall not take from the land of the heir more than reasonable issues and reasonable customs and reasonable services, and this without destruction and waste of men or things. And if we entrust the wardship of any such land to a sheriff or to any one else who is to answer to us for its issues, and if he causes destruction or waste of [what is under] wardship, we will exact compensation from him; and the land shall be entrusted to two discreet and lawful men of that fief, who shall answer for the issues to us or the man to whom we may assign them. And if we give or sell the wardship of any such land to any one, and if he causes destruction or waste of it, he shall forfeit that wardship and it shall be given to two discreet and lawful men of that fief, who likewise shall answer to us as aforesaid.

5. Moreover, the guardian, so long as he has wardship of the land, shall from the issues of that same land keep up the houses, parks, preserves, fish-ponds, mills, and other things belonging to that land. And to the heir, when he comes of full age, [the guardian] shall give all his land, stocked with ploughs *and produce, according to what crops may be seasonable and to what the issues of the land can reasonably permit.*

6. Heirs shall be married without disparagement; *yet so that, before the marriage is contracted, it shall be announced to the blood-relatives of the said heir.*

7. A widow shall have her marriage portion and inheritance immediately after the death of her husband and without difficulty; nor shall she give anything for her dowry or for her marriage portion or for her inheritance — which inheritance she and her husband were holding on the day of that husband's death. And after his death she shall remain in the house of her husband for forty days, within which her dowry shall be assigned to her.

8. No widow shall be forced to marry so long as she wishes to live without a husband; yet so that she shall give security against marrying without our consent if she holds of us, or without the consent of her lord if she holds of another.

9. Neither we nor our bailiffs will seize any land or revenue for any debt, so long as the chattels of the debtor are sufficient to repay the debt; nor shall the sureties of that debtor be distrained so long as the chief debtor is himself able to pay the debt. And if the chief debtor, having nothing with which to pay, defaults in payment of the debt, the sureties shall be responsible for the debt; and, if they wish, they shall have the lands and revenues of the debtor until satisfaction is made to them for the debt which they previously paid on his behalf, unless the chief debtor proves that he is quit of such responsibility toward the said sureties.

10. *If any one has taken anything, whether much or little, by way of loan from Jews, and if he dies before that debt is paid, the debt shall not carry usury so long as the heir is under age, from whomsoever he may hold. And if that debt falls into our hands, we will take only the principal contained in the note.*

11. *And if any one dies owing a debt to Jews, his wife shall have her dowry and shall pay nothing on that debt. And if the said deceased is survived by chil-*

dren who are under age, necessities shall be provided for them in proportion to the tenement that belonged to the deceased; and the debt shall be paid from the remainder, saving the service of the lords. In the same way let action be taken with regard to debts owed to others besides Jews.

12. *Scutage or aid shall be levied in our kingdom only by the common counsel of our kingdom, except for ransoming our body, for knighting our eldest son, and for once marrying our eldest daughter; and for these [purposes] only a reasonable aid shall be taken. The same provision shall hold with regard to the aids of the city of London.*

13. And the city of London shall have all its ancient liberties and free customs, *both by land and by water.* Besides we will and grant that all the other cities, boroughs, towns, and ports shall have all their liberties and free customs.

14. *And in order to have the common counsel of the kingdom for assessing aid other than in the three cases aforesaid, or for assessing scutage, we will cause the archbishops, bishops, abbots, earls, and greater barons to be summoned by our letters individually; and besides we will cause to be summoned in general, through our sheriffs and bailiffs, all those who hold of us in chief—for a certain day, namely, at the end of forty days at least, and to a certain place. And in all such letters of summons we will state the cause of the summons; and when the summons has thus been made, the business assigned for the day shall proceed according to the counsel of those who are present, although all those summoned may not come.*

15. *In the future we will not grant to any one that he may take aid from his freemen, except for ransoming his body, for knighting his eldest son, and for once marrying his eldest daughter; and for these [purposes] only a reasonable aid shall be taken.*

16. No one shall be distrained to render greater service from a knight's fee, or from any other free tenement, than is thence owed.

17. Common pleas shall not follow our court, but shall be held in some definite place.

18. Assizes of novel disseisin, of mort d'ancestor, *and of darrein presentment* shall be held only in their counties [of origin] and in this way: we, or our chief justice if we are of the kingdom, will send two justices through each county *four times a year; and they, together with four knights of each county elected by the county [court], shall hold the aforesaid assizes in the county, on the day and at the place [set for the meeting] of the county [court].*

19. *And if within the day [set for the meeting] of the county [court] the aforesaid assizes cannot be held, as many knights and free tenants shall remain of those present at the county [court] on that day as may be needed for holding the trials, according as the business is greater or less.*

20. A freeman shall be amerced for a small offence only according to the degree of the offence; and for a grave offence he shall be amerced according to the gravity of the offence, saving his contentment. And a merchant shall be amerced in the same way, saving his merchandise; and a villein in the same way, saving his wainage—should they fall into our mercy. And none of the aforesaid amercements shall be imposed except by the oaths of good men from the neighbourhood.

21. Earls and barons shall be amerced only by their peers, and only according to the degree of the misdeed.

22. No clergyman shall be amerced with respect to his lay tenement except in the manner of those aforesaid, not according to the value of his ecclesiastical benefice.

23. Neither vill nor man shall be distrained to make bridges on river-banks, except such as by right and ancient custom ought to do so.

24. No sheriff, constable, coroner, or other bailiff of ours shall hold the pleas of our crown.

25. *All counties, hundreds, wapentakes, and tithings shall remain at the ancient farms without any increment, with the exception of our demesne manors.*

26. If any one holding a lay fee of us dies, and if our sheriff or bailiff shows our letters patent of summons concerning a debt that the deceased owed to us, our sheriff or bailiff shall be permitted, by view of lawful men, to attach and record such chattels of the deceased as are found on the lay fief to the value of that debt; so that, moreover, nothing shall thence be removed until a debt that is manifestly owed shall be paid to us. And the residue shall be left to the executors for carrying out the will of the deceased. And if nothing is owed us from it, all the chattels shall be yielded to [disposition by] the deceased, saving to his wife and children their reasonable portions.

27. If any freeman dies intestate, his chattels, under ecclesiastical inspection, shall be distributed by the hands of his near relatives and friends, saving to each [creditor] the debts that the deceased owed him.

28. No constable or other bailiff of ours shall take grain or other chattels of any one without immediate payment therefor in money, unless by the will of the seller he may secure postponement of that [payment].

29. No constable shall distrain any knight to pay money for castleguard when he is willing to perform that service himself, or through another good man if for reasonable cause he is unable to perform it himself. And if we lead or send him on a military expedition, he shall be quit of [castle-]guard for so long a time as he shall be with the army *at our command.*

30. No sheriff or bailiff of ours, nor any other person, shall take the horses or carts of any freeman for carrying service, *except by the will of that freeman.*

31. Neither we nor our bailiffs will take some one else's wood for [repairing] castles or for doing any other work of ours, except by the will of him to whom the wood belongs.

32. We will hold the lands of those convicted of felony only for a year and a day, and the lands shall then be given to the lords of the fiefs [concerned].

33. All fish-weirs shall henceforth be entirely removed from the Thames and the Medway and throughout all England except along the sea-coasts.

34. Henceforth the writ called praecipe shall not be issued for any one concerning any tenement whereby a freeman may lose his court.

35. There shall be one measure of wine throughout our entire kingdom, and one measure of ale; also one measure of grain, namely the quarter of London; and one width of dyed cloth, russet [cloth], and hauberk [cloth], namely, two yards between the borders. With weights, moreover, it shall be as with measures.

36. Nothing henceforth shall be taken or given for the writ of inquisition concerning life and limbs, but it shall be issued gratis and shall not be denied.

37. If any one holding of us by fee-farm or by socage or by burgage holds land of some one else by military service, on account of that fee-farm or socage or burgage we are not to have the wardship of the heir or of the land that is another's fee, unless the said [land held by] fee-farm owes military service. By virtue of some little serjeanty held of us by the service of rendering knives or arrows or

something of the sort, we are not to have wardship of any one's heir or of land that he holds of another military service.

38. No bailiff shall henceforth put any one to his law by merely bringing suit [against him]without trustworthy witnesses presented for this purpose.

39. No freeman shall be captured or imprisoned or disseised or outlawed or exiled or in any way destroyed, nor will we go against him or send against him, except by the lawful judgment of his peers or by the law of the land.

40. To no one will we sell, to no one will we deny or delay right or justice.

41. All merchants may safely and securely go away from England, come to England, stay in and go through England, by land or by water, for buying and selling under right and ancient customs and without any evil exactions, except in time of war if they are from the land at war with us. And if such persons are found in our land at the beginning of a war, they shall be arrested without injury to their bodies or goods until we or our chief justice can ascertain how the merchants of our land who may then be found in the land at war with us are to be treated. And if our men are to be safe, the others shall be safe in our land.

42. *Every one shall henceforth be permitted, saving our fealty, to leave our kingdom and to return in safety and security, by land, or by water, except in the common interest of the realm for a brief period during wartime, and excepting [always] men imprisoned or outlawed according to the law of the kingdom and people from a land at war with us and merchants, who are be treated as aforesaid.*

43. If any one holds of any escheat—such as the honour of Wallingford, Nottingham, Boulogne, Lancaster, or the other escheats that are in our hands and are baronies—and if he dies, his heir shall give only such relief and shall render us only such service as would be due to the baron if that barony were in the hands of the baron; and we shall hold it in the same way that the baron held it.

44. *Men dwelling outside the forest shall no longer, in consequence of a general summons, come before our justices of the forest, unless they are [involved] in a plea [of the forest] or are sureties of some person or persons who have been arrested for [offences against] the forest.*

45. *We will appoint as justiciars, constables, sheriffs, or bailiffs only such men as know the law of the kingdom and well desire to observe it.*

46. All barons who have founded abbeys, concerning which they have charters from kings of England or [enjoy] ancient tenures, shall have the custody of those [abbeys] during vacancies, as they ought to have.

47. *All forests that have been afforested in our time shall at once be disafforested; and the same shall be done with regard to riverbanks which in our time we have placed under ban.*

48. *Concerning all bad customs of forest and warrens, of foresters and warreners, of sheriffs and their officers, and of river-banks and their wardens, inquisition shall at once be made in each county through twelve knights of that same county placed under oath, who ought to be elected by the good men of the same county. And within forty days after the inquisition has been made, they shall be utterly abolished by the same [knights], so that they shall never be restored; in such fashion [however] that we may have prior notice, or our justiciar [may] if we are not in England.*

49. *We will immediately restore all hostages and charters which were delivered to us by Englishmen as security for the peace or for faithful service.*

50. *We will utterly remove from their offices the relatives of Gerard d'Athée, Engelard de Cigogné, Peter and Guy and Andrew de Chanceaux, Guy de Cigogné, Geoffrey de Martigny and his brothers, Philip Marc and his brothers and his nephew Geoffrey, together with all their adherents, so that henceforth they shall have no office in England.*

51. *And immediately after the restoration of peace we will remove from the kingdom all alien knights, crossbowmen, serjeants, and mercenaries, who have come with horses and arms to the injury of the kingdom.*

52. *If any one, without the lawful judgment of his peers, has been disseised or deprived by us of his lands, castles, liberties, or rights, we will at once restore them to him. And if a dispute arises in this connection, then let the matter be decided by the judgment of the twenty-five barons, concerning whom provision is made below in [the article on] security for the peace. With regard, however, to all those [possessions] of which any one, without lawful judgment of his peers, was disseised or deprived by King Henry, our father, or by King Richard, our brother -which possessions we have in our hands or which are held by others whose possession we are bound to warrant—we are to have respite for the ordinary term of crusaders, except those [possessions] concerning which suit was brought or inquest was made by our precept before we took the cross. Moreover, when we return from our journey, or if perchance we abandon our journey, we will at once administer full justice in such matters.*

53. *Moreover, we are to have similar respite and in the same way with regard to the disafforestation or retention of the forests which Henry, our father, or Richard, our brother, afforested; with regard to wardships over lands of another's fee, which sort of wardships we have hitherto enjoyed on account of a fee that any one holds of us by military service, and with regard to abbeys which were founded in a fee other than our own, and over which the lord of the fee has asserted that he has the right. And when we return, or if we abandon our journey, we will at once give full justice to those making complaints in such matters.*

54. *No one shall be seized or imprisoned on the appeal of a woman for the death of any one but her husband.*

55. *All fines which have been made with us unjustly and contrary to the law of the land, and all amercements made unjustly and contrary to the law of the land, are to be entirely pardoned; or decision is thereon to be made by the judgment of the twenty-five barons concerning whom provision is made below in [the article on] security for the peace, or by the judgment of the majority of them, together with the aforesaid Stephen, archbishop of Canterbury, if he can be present, and other men whom he may wish to associate with himself for this purpose—and if he cannot be present, the business shall nevertheless proceed without him; yet so that, if any one or more of the twenty-five barons aforesaid are [involved] in a dispute of this kind, they shall be removed so far as this judgment is concerned, and others, elected and sworn for this purpose, shall be substituted in their places by the rest of the twenty-five.*

56. *If, without the lawful judgment of their peers, we have disseised or deprived Welshmen of their lands, liberties, or other things in England or in Wales, [the same] shall be immediately restored to them. And if a dispute arises in this connection, then decision is thereon to be made in the [Welsh] march by the judgment of their peers—according to the law of England for their tenements in*

England, according to the law of Wales for their tenements in Wales, and according to the law of the march for their tenements in the march. Welshmen shall act in the same way toward us and our men.

57. *Moreover, with regard to those [possessions] of which any Welshman, without the lawful judgment of his peers, was disseised or deprived by King Henry, our father, or King Richard, our brother.*

58. *We will at once restore the son of Llewelyn and all the [other] hostages of Wales, together with the charters that were given us as security for the peace.*

59. *We will act toward Alexander, king of the Scots, in the matter of restoring his sisters and the [other] hostages, together with his liberties and rights in the same way as we act toward our other barons of England, unless by the charters which we have from his father William, one time king of the Scots, the action ought to be otherwise—and this shall be [determined] by the judgment of his peers in our court.*

60. Now all these aforesaid customs and liberties, which we have granted, in so far as concerns us, to be observed in our kingdom toward our men, all men of our kingdom, both clergy and laity, shall, in so far as concerns them, observe toward their men.

61. *Since moreover for [the love of] God, for the improvement of our kingdom, and for the better allayment of the conflict that has arisen between us and our barons, we have granted all these [liberties] aforesaid, wishing them to enjoy those [liberties] by full and firm establishment forever, we have made and granted them the following security: namely, that the barons shall elect twenty-five barons of the kingdom, whomsoever they please, who to the best of their ability should observe, hold, and cause to be observed the peace and liberties that we have granted to them and have confirmed by this our present charter; so that, specifically, if we or our justiciar or our bailiffs or any of our ministers are in any respect delinquent toward any one or transgress any article of the peace or the security, and if the delinquency is shown to four barons of the aforesaid twenty-five barons, those four barons shall come to us, or to our justiciar if we are out of the kingdom, to explain to us the wrong, asking that without delay we cause this wrong to be redressed. And if within a period of forty days, counted from the time that notification is made to us, or to our justiciar if we are out of the kingdom, we do not redress the wrong, or, if we are out of the kingdom, our justiciar does not redress it, the four barons aforesaid shall refer that case to the rest of the twenty-five barons, and those twenty-five barons, together with the community of the entire country, shall distress and injure us in all ways possible— namely, by capturing our castles, lands, and possessions and in all ways that they can—until they secure redress according to their own decision, saving our person and [the person] of our queen and [the persons] of our children. And when redress has been made, they shall be obedient to us as they were before. And any one in the land who wishes shall swear that, for carrying out the aforesaid matters, he will obey the commands of the twenty-five barons aforesaid and that he, with his men, will injure us to the best of his ability; and we publicly and freely give licence of [thus] swearing to every one who wishes to do so, and to no one will we ever prohibit [such] swearing. Moreover, all those of the land who of themselves and by their own free will are unwilling to take the oath for the twenty-five barons, with them to distress and injure us, we will by our mandate cause to swear [such an oath] as aforesaid. And if any one of the twenty-five*

barons dies or departs from the land, or in any other way is prevented from carrying out these aforesaid matters, the rest of the twenty-five barons aforesaid shall by their own decision choose another in his place, who is to be sworn in the same way as the others. Moreover, in all the matters entrusted to those twenty-five barons for execution, if perchance the same twenty-five are present and disagree among themselves in some respect, or if certain of those summoned are unwilling or unable to be present, that which the majority of those present may provide or command shall be held as settled and established, just as if all twenty-five had agreed to it. And the aforesaid twenty-five shall swear that they will faithfully observe all that has been set forth above. And neither of ourself nor through others will we procure from any one anything whereby any of these concessions and liberties may be revoked or diminished; and should anything of the sort be procured, it shall be null and void, and we will never make use of it either of ourself or through others.

62. And to all we freely pardon and condone all the ill-will, indignation, and rancour that from the beginning of the conflict have arisen between us and our men, both clergy and laity. Furthermore, to all, whether clergy or laity, we fully pardon and condone, in so far as pertains to us, all trespasses committed on account of the said conflict since Easter in the sixteenth year of our reign until the reestablishment of peace. And besides we have caused to be drawn up for them letters patent of the lord Stephen, archbishop of Canterbury, of the lord Henry, archbishop of Dublin, of the bishops aforesaid, and of Master Pandulf, in witness of that security and the concessions aforesaid.

63. Wherefore we wish and straitly enjoin that the English Church shall be free and that the men in our kingdom shall have and hold all the aforesaid liberties, rights, and grants well and in peace, freely and quietly, fully and completely, for themselves and their heirs from us and our heirs, in all things and in all places forever, as aforesaid. Moreover, it has been sworn both on our part and on the part of the barons that all the aforesaid [provisions] shall be observed in good faith and without malicious intent.

By the witness of the aforesaid men and of many others. Given by our hand in the meadow that is called Runnymede between Windsor and Staines, June 15, in the seventeenth year of our reign.

BRACTON

Bracton (circa 1230 A.D.) from the Samuel E. Thorne translation, *Bracton on the Laws and Customs of England* (Harvard, 1968). (Notes omitted). [Courtesy Harvard University Press.]

INTRODUCTION

The needs of a king.

To rule well a king requires two things, arms and laws, that by them both times of war and of peace may rightly be ordered. For each stands in need of the other, that the achievement of arms be conserved [by the laws], the laws themselves

Illustration 3-9 Perhaps the greatest of the "classics" of the Anglo-American legal literature is "*Bracton*" (*Bracton De Legibus Et Consuetudinibus Angliae*). It was "created" over
a period of time but is usually dated circa 1230 A.D. The illustration above is the illustrated
border on one of the earliest manuscripts. (MS. Add 11353) from *Social England, supra,*
vol. 1, 410. Note the symbolism, with the men "at arms" on the left, the ruler in the middle,
and his judges and legal counselors on the right. The text says, "[t]o rule well, a king requires two things, arms and laws." This parallels *Justinian's Institutes* and *Glanvill.* We will
be returning to Thorne's great text of *Bracton* at many points in the course.

preserved by the support of arms. If arms fail against hostile and unsubdued enemies, then will the realm be without defence; if laws fail, justice will be extir-
pated; nor will there be any man to render just judgment.

[*England alone uses within her boundaries unwritten law and custom*].

Though in almost all lands use is made of the *leges* and the *jus scriptum*, England
alone uses unwritten law and custom. There law derives from nothing written
[but] from what usage has approved. Nevertheless, it will not be absurd to call
English laws *leges*, though they are unwritten, since whatever has been rightly
decided and approved with the counsel and consent of the magnates and the general agreement of the *res publica*, the authority of the king or prince having first
been added thereto, has the force of law. England has as well many local customs, varying from place to place, for the English have many things by custom
which they do not have by law, as in the various counties, cities, boroughs and
vills, where it will always be necessary to learn what the custom of the place is
and how those who allege it use it.

If an unwise and unlearned man ascends the judgment seat.

Since these laws and customs are often misapplied by the unwise and unlearned
who ascend the judgment seat before they have learned the laws and stand

amid doubts and the confusion of opinions, and frequently subverted by the greater [judges] who decide cases according to their own will rather than by the authority of the laws, I, Henry de Bracton, to instruct the lesser judges, if no one else, have turned my mind to the ancient judgments of just men, examining diligently, not without working long into the night watches, their decisions, *consilia* and *responsa*, and have collected whatever I found therein worthy of note *into a summa*, putting it in the form of titles and paragraphs, without prejudice to any better system, by the aid of writing to be preserved to posterity forever.

[Fol. 1, Thorne 19]

I ask the reader, if he finds in this work anything superfluous or erroneous, to correct and amend it, or pass it over with eyes half closed, for to keep all in mind and err in nothing is divine rather than human.

The author's preamble.

In this tractate, as in others, these must be considered: the matter with which it deals, its intention, its utility, the end it serves and the division of learning into which it falls.

The matter with which it deals.

Its matter consists of the judgments and the cases that daily arise and come to pass in the realm of England.

The intention of the author.

The intention of the author is to treat of such matters and to instruct and teach all who desire to be taught what action lies and what writ, [and], according as the plea is real or personal, how and by what procedure, [by suing and proving, defending and excepting, replicating and the like,] suits and pleas are decided according to English laws and customs, and [the art] of preparing records and enrollments according to what is alleged and denied, and to treat of these so that those who err may be instructed and set right and those who obstinately do otherwise punished. The general intention is to treat of law that the unskilled may be made expert, the expert more expert, the bad good and the good better, as well by the fear of punishment as by the hope of reward, according to this [verse]:

> Good men hate to err from love of virtue;
> The wicked from fear of pain.

The utility.

The utility [of this work] is that it ennobles apprentices and doubles their honours and profits and enables them to rule in the realm and sit in the royal chamber, on the very seat of the king, on the throne of God, so to speak, judging tribes and nations, plaintiffs and defendants, in lordly order, in the place of the king, as though in the place of Jesus Christ, since the king is God's vicar. For judgments are not made by man but by God, which is why the heart of a king who rules well is said to be in the hand of God.

The end served.

The end of this work is to quiet disputes and avert wrongdoing, that peace and justice may be preserved in the realm. It must be set under ethics, moral science, as it were, since it treats of customary principles of behaviour.

[Fol. 1 [b], Thorne 20]

* * * *

The king has no peer in the realm, because then he would lose [the power of] command.... Much less does he have a superior or one more powerful because then he would be inferior to his subjects and those who are inferior cannot be peers of the more powerful. But the king must not be under man but under God and the law, for the law makes him king (*Ipse autem rex non debet esse sub homine sed sub Deo et lege quia lex facit regem*). Therefore the king attributes to the law what the law attributes to him, namely domination and power. For he is not king where the will controls and not the laws.

[Fol. 5b] Dawson Translation

* * * *

Of liberties and who may grant liberties and which belong to the king.

We have explained above how rights and incorporeal things are transferred and *quasi*-transferred, how they are possessed or *quasi*-possessed, and how retained by actual use. Now we must turn to liberties [and see] who can grant liberties, and to whom, and how they are transferred, how possessed or *quasi*-possessed, and how they are retained by use. Who then? It is clear that the lord king [has all] dignities, [It is the lord king] himself who has ordinary jurisdiction and power over all who are within his realm. For he has in his hand all the rights belonging to the crown and the secular power and the material sword pertaining to the governance of the realm. Also justice and judgment [and everything] connected with jurisdiction, that, as minister and vicar of God, he may render to each his due. Also everything connected with the peace, that the people entrusted to his care may live in quiet and repose, that none beat, wound or mistreat another, [or] steal, take and carry off by force and robbery another's property, or maim or kill anyone. Also coercion, that he may punish and compel wrongdoers, [He in whose power it is to cause the laws, customs, and assises provided, approved and sworn in his realm to be observed by his people, ought himself to observe them in his own person.] for it is useless to establish laws unless there is someone to enforce them.] rights or jurisdictions in his hand. He also has, in preference to all others in his realm, privileges by virtue of the *jus gentium*. [By the *jus gentium*]

[Fol. 55b, Thorne translation, 166]

Of the oath the king must swear at his coronation.

In the first place, that to the utmost of his power he will employ his might to secure and will enjoin that true peace shall be maintained for the church of God and all Christian people throughout his reign. Secondly, that he will forbid rapacity to his subjects of all degrees. Thirdly, that he will cause all judgments to be given with equity and mercy, so that he may himself be shown the mercy of a clement and merciful God, in order that by his justice all men may enjoy unbroken peace.

For what purpose a king is created; of ordinary jurisdiction.

To this end a king made and chosen, that he do justice to all men [that the Lord may dwell in him, and he by His judgments may separate] and sustain and uphold what he has rightly adjudged, for if there were no one to do justice peace might easily be driven away and it would be to no purpose to establish laws (and do justice) were there no one to enforce them. The king, since he is the vicar of God on earth, must distinguish *jus* from *injuria*, equity from iniquity, that all his subjects may live uprightly, none injure another, and by a just award each be restored to that which is his own. He must surpass in power all those subjected to him, [He ought to have no peer, much less a superior, especially in the doing of justice, that it may truly be said of him, 'Great is our lord and great is his virtue etc.,' though in suing for justice he ought not to rank above the lowliest in his kingdom.] nevertheless, since the heart of a king ought to be in the hand of God, let him, that he be not unbridled, put on the bridle of temperance and the reins of moderation, lest being unbridled, he be drawn toward injustice. For the king, since he is the minister and vicar of God on earth, can do nothing save what he can do *de jure*, [despite the statement that the will of the prince has the force of law, because there follows at the end of the *lex* the words 'since by the *lex regia*, which was made with respect to his sovereignty'; nor is that anything rashly put forward of his own will, but what has been rightly decided with the counsel of his magnates, deliberation and consultation having been had thereon, the king giving it *auctoritas*.] His power is that of *jus*, not *injuria* [and since it is he from whom *jus* proceeds, from the source whence *jus* takes its origin no instance of *injuria* ought to arise, and also, what one is bound by virtue of his office to forbid to others, he ought not to do himself.] as vicar and minister of God on earth, for that power only is from God, [the power of *injuria* however, is from the devil, not from God, and the king will be the minister of him whose work he performs,] whose work he performs. Therefore as long as he does justice he is the vicar of the Eternal King, but the devil's minister when he deviates into injustice. For he is called *rex* not from reigning but from ruling well, since he is a king as long as he rules well but a tyrant when he oppresses by violent domination the people entrusted to his care. Let him, therefore, temper his power by law, which is the bridle of power, that he may live according to the laws, for the law of mankind has decreed that his own laws bind the lawgiver, and elsewhere in the same source, it is a saying worthy of the majesty of a ruler that the prince acknowledge himself bound by the laws. Nothing is more fitting for a sovereign than to live by the laws, nor is there any greater sovereignty than to govern according to law, and he ought properly to yield to the law what the law has bestowed upon him, for the law makes him king.

* * * *

[Fol. 107–107b, Thorne translation, 304–307]

THE CORONATION OATH OF EDWARD II

C. Stephenson & F.G. Marcham, *Sources of English Constitutional History, supra,* vol. 1, 192 (Harper Brothers, 1937).

EDWARD II: CORONATION OATH (1308)

"Sire, will you grant and keep and by your oath confirm to the people of England the laws and customs given to them by the previous just and god-fearing kings, your ancestors, and especially the laws, customs, and liberties granted to the clergy and people by the glorious king, the sainted Edward, your predecessor?" "I grant and promise them."

"Sire, will you in all your judgments, so far as in you lies, preserve to God and Holy Church, and to the people and clergy, entire peace and concord before God?" "I will preserve them."

"Sire will you so far as in you lies, cause justice to be rendered rightly, impartially, and wisely, in compassion and in truth?" "I will do so."
"Sire, do you grant to be held and observed the just laws and customs that the community of your realm shall determine, and will you, so far as in you lies, defend and strengthen them to the honour of God?" "I grant and promise them."

CONSTITUTION OF NEW HAMPSHIRE

(1937–Manual of the General Court, p. 11)

[ART.] 10th. Government being instituted for the common benefit, protection and security, of the whole community, and not for the private interest or emolument of any one man, family, or class of men; therefore, whenever the ends of government are perverted, and public liberty manifestly endangered, and all other means of redress are ineffectual, the people may, and of right ought, to reform the old, or establish a new government. The doctrine of nonresistance against arbitrary power, and oppression, is absurd, slavish, and destructive of the good and happiness of mankind.

Note: This is an excellent example of a modern "reciprocity" clause—permitting the governed to rise if their rights are revoked. See the similar, but more complete, clause 61 of the *Magna Carta, supra.*

Illustration 4-1 This is Bamburgh Castle in Northumbria, a twelfth-century Norman stronghold built on the site of an earlier Saxon fort. Courtesy M. Scott Weightman.

IV

A BRIEF INTRODUCTION TO ENGLISH FEUDALISM

A. FEUDALISM

"Feudalism" is an immensely difficult concept, in part because the word itself is an invention of modern historians, and was unknown to the Norman-Angevins. In addition, "feudalism" is not just a legal idea, but a term which also has military, economic, political, social, and philosophical aspects, and which can be discussed from many different points of view. Finally, while it can be said that the Normans were masters of "feudalism," in the same way that they were remarkable warriors, bureaucrats, lawyers, and judges, "feudalism" itself was not unique to Norman England. Far from it. There were feudal elements to Anglo-Saxon society and law, particularly in the later years before the Conquest, and feudalism was found throughout Western Europe. Indeed, historians have described "feudal" periods in the history of China and Japan. American land was even held by "feudal" tenures along the Hudson River during the Dutch rule of New York. Thus, English feudalism was not just a "Norman" development. It was part of a vast historical context.

All this makes feudalism hard to discuss in a concrete fashion. Let us begin by focusing just on England, and on the legal structure of the English land law—which was both the conceptual "backbone" of feudalism and of fundamental importance to the future development of the common law.

I. THE STRUCTURE

"Feudalism" comes from the Latin word *feudum*, "used in medieval times to designate the fee."[1] A "fee" was an interest in land. Originally, it was often held

---

1. See J.M.W. Bean, *The Decline of English Feudalism: 1215–1540* (Manchester, 1968), 1–6.

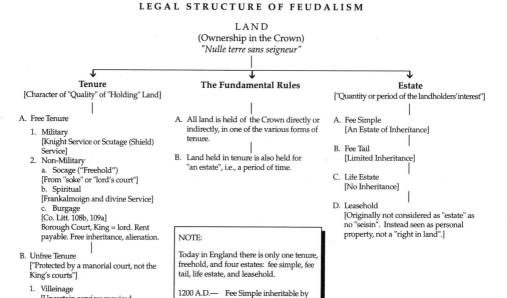

Illustration 4-2

in exchange for military service. When William conquered England, a large part of his tiny army were mercenaries, and were sent home. He determined that he needed at least 6,000 knights to control the country. At a highly symbolic meeting with his chief supporters at Salisbury, William claimed all the land of England for himself. He then proceeded to carefully grant "fees" in the land to his loyal supporters on condition that they supply him on demand with so many knights, armed men, or—probably even from the very beginning—"shield money" or "scutage," a money equivalent of the actual manpower. These top supporters were called "tenants-in-chief" or tenants "*in capite*" because they "held" their fees directly for the Crown.

Note that the "fee" was not the ultimate ownership of the land. Only the Crown held that. The "fee" was a conditional right to occupy and exploit the land, subject to the "feudal" incidents required, i.e., knights, armed men, or money. In a feudal system, the sovereign is the only entity capable of absolute ownership, as when the Crown holds land without a tenant.

Top supporters, "tenants-in-chief" were said to "hold" the land by "knight-service," as their feudal "incidents" required the production of military support. The Norman French word for "hold" was "*tenire*." The way you "held" your land was, therefore, called "*tenure*."

The tenants-in-chief were almost exclusively Norman, and they could hardly produce the required knights on their own. They needed farmers, crafts people, and others to work their land and produce the revenue needed to support the military establishment. Thus they regranted much of the land they received from the King to others, the so-called "mesne lords" ("mesne" = "in the middle"). The "mesne lords" were often Norman, but also could be powerful Anglo-Saxons who decided to cooperate. They were a "manager" class, usually living in manors, or fortified farms, throughout the countryside.

Some "mesne lords" also held by "military" tenure, i.e., knight-service or knight-service equivalents in money ("scutage" or "shield money"). These were usually Normans. Others held by "non-military" tenures that just involved paying with crops, animals or money. This kind of tenure was called a "free and common socage" from "soke," a reference to the lord's court. Some "mesne lords" also regranted the land to others, usually yeomen farmers. The "free yeomen" were often English and usually "held" by free and common socage. Their cottages frequently clustered near the manors for protection. The manors, in turn, looked to the castles of the tenants-in-chief for ultimate military security. These castles were usually built by the Normans in or near the old Anglo-Saxon shire towns.

Originally, this system was established by what is called "sub-infeudation," another term invented by historians. It meant that each level created another level below itself, and feudal "incidents" passed up the hierarchy of holdings, ultimately to the king—who was the ultimate "legal" owner. For example, take a plot of earth near thirteenth-century Warwick. You could ask a local farmer, "who owns this plot?" His answer would be complicated. Technically, only the King "owned" the land, but our farmer, Cedric the Saxon, would probably tell you that he "held" the land of Sir Richard Dubois for so much cash or vegetables per year. Dubois would be a Norman knight who was lord of the manor of Little Dimple, and Cedric would be one of "his" free yeomen farmers. Sir Richard, in turn, held the manor of Little Dimple, a tract of several hundred acres including Cedric's plot, from the Earl of Warwick, either for direct military service—he could be one knight himself—or for "scutage" ("shield money"), or a combination of the two. Let us say Sir Richard held the manor of Little Dimple in knight service for two knights. He would have to support himself and one other professional soldier, or pay the "scutage" money equivalent, and be at the call of the Earl.

The Earl would almost certainly be a tenant-in-chief, i.e., *in capite*, holding his "domain," or lands, of the Crown for knight service. He would, at first, certainly be a Norman in ancestry, and would be trusted by the King as an administrator and military leader. (Disloyal tenants-in-chief were highly dangerous, as King John discovered.) The Earl's seat would be Warwick Castle, a stronghold held by a permanent garrison. His "tenure" might include the "incidents" of "castle guard," to support the castle, plus many knights with supporting troops, and other military support, all at the call of the King. One of the Earl's many sources of money and men would be Sir Richard.

The Normans brought a highly developed version of this "feudal" hierarchy with them from Normandy, but it worked well in England for another reason. Despite romantic myths about the "free" Anglo-Saxon yeomen and their "communal" villages, the Anglo-Saxons themselves had developed a rough version of feudal systems before the Conquest as a way of organizing protection more efficiently than through the ancient *fyrd*, or draft. The Normans simply removed the top layers, and replaced the English earls and knights with Normans. Many English yeomen were already used to the system.

There were always three classes of people that fitted into the "tenure" system in a special way. The first was the Church and its priests, monks, nuns, and charitable institutions. Sometimes, they held by ordinary "scutage" or "socage" tenure, and paid money for defense. Frequently, however, they held the land by "spiritual tenure" ("frankalmoign" or "divine service") where they were only obliged to say masses or pray for the donor. As we will see, if the Church got too much land like this, it could be a problem for the King's tax base, because you cannot pay troops with prayers.

Less problematic were those who lived in towns and cities, a fairly small, but important group in early feudal England. The towns and cities were called "boroughs" and their free residents were called "burgesses." They often made a living of craftsmanship, trade or fishing. They held land in "burgage" tenure, which was a non-military tenure like socage—a simple payment of money or goods to the feudal lord above.

Finally, at the bottom, were the descendants of the Anglo-Saxon slaves or "serfs," also known by their French name, "villeins." (We still use these terms in a derogatory way.) They "held" land in "unfree" tenure or *villeinage*. In an odd way, they were "invisible," as the royal courts took no notice of "unfree" tenure until the seventeenth century. Instead, the "unfree" tenure of the serfs was protected by the Lord of the Manor, often according to a written book kept at the manor. From this book, unfree tenure got its other name, "copyhold" tenure.

Initially, the big difference between free and unfree tenure was that free tenure was always for precisely defined services or money, i.e., so many knights or so many silver shillings. Unfree tenure was for "uncertain services." This could be brutally oppressive in practice. Lords could, and did, force serfs to work limitless hours on the lord's own land in exchange for hovels and a subsistence diet. But serfs had it better than American slaves, for example. Due to the old Anglo-Saxon protections, observed by the Norman conquerors, they could not be moved from their land—unlike "chattel" slaves—nor could they be physically harmed. Further, the terrible "Black Death" and plagues of the period led to a shortage of agricultural labor. "Good" lords kept their serfs, while cruel lords saw their serfs "disappear" to the lands of better masters, who would carefully fail to report their presence.

Thus the lords of the manor had good reasons to treat their serfs well, particularly after the "Black Death" of 1349 and 1361, and the Peasant's Revolt of 1381. "Uncertain" services became replaced by services more precisely defined in the "copyhold" book of the manor. This more defined unfree service was called "villein socage," to distinguish it from "pure villeinage." In addition, the Church, through the parish priests, would pressure a lord of the manor to be charitable to "his" unfree tenants. They were, after all, Christian "souls." Eventually, many serfs held their land on fair and reliable terms, but legal protection still lay with the manor court, not the royal courts, until the seventeenth century.

Here is how these three "special classes" would look in our example. We are still talking to our friend Cedric, the yeoman farmer. We point to the small parish church, beyond his plot and close to the manor house. "Oh," he'd say, "that is held by the Parish Church from Sir Richard by the terms of a grant made by his grandfather in 'free alms' or 'frankalmoign'." The young priest, Father Boniface, was appointed to the "living" by Sir Richard, with the Bishop's consent. In addition to the Church and a parsonage, there would be "glebe" lands to support the priest, and he would collect tithes from the villagers. Father Boniface's only obligation in "free alms" or "frankalmoign" tenure would be a general duty to perform divine services. If he held some of the land in more specific spiritual "divine service," his duties also could be more specific, such as his saying Mass each Thursday for the soul of Sir Richard's grandfather, "Dick The Cruel," who gave the supporting land in spiritual tenure to atone for his many sins.

You ask where the little road goes. It goes to Dimpleton, a small town, close to the Earl's castle on the River Chin. Dimpleton-on-Chin's residents all hold directly of the Earl in "burgage" tenure. It is a non-military tenure, and they pay in cash. They are very valuable to the Earl, and they, in turn, look to him to protect their highways, wharfs, and shops. The Earl also sponsors a regular, and lucrative, trade fair in the town. They have also developed their own city government to provide service within the borough. The Earl is sometimes uncomfortable with this independence, but he needs their cooperation. Indeed, he is in debt to some of the burgers.

Finally, you ask Cedric about the little family that just walked down the road, bent with fatigue. They are Garth and his wife Matilda, and their two sons. They are returning from working in Sir Richard's fields to their small cottage by the road. Behind the cottage is a tiny garden and a fenced "paddock" for a cow. Only men and unmarried women can "hold" land, so Cedric would call the plot "Garth's croft." In exchange for his land, Garth must work directly for Sir Richard. In the days of "Dick the Cruel," Garth's grandparents would be worked to exhaustion. Today, the Lord's bailiff has a book that indicates that Garth and his family must do four days labor a week on Sir Richard's land. The other two working days they can spend on their "unfree" plot. This is "copyhold." Only Sir Richard himself "protects" this arrangement, but Garth and his family would run away if things got bad again. Besides, Father Boniface visits their cottage regularly, and, when he is with Sir Richard and his wife Lady Elaine, Father Boniface frequently points out how tired the serfs are, and how God's judgment will come on the likes of "Dick the Cruel," at least unless masses are said for their soul. Besides, Sir Richard needs Garth's cheerful effort, and down the valley there are other feudal lords, who would ask few questions to pick up some more help. Even worse, Sir Richard knows of stories about disgruntled serfs who took to the woods, and about lords of the manor found with an arrow shaft in their backs, even outside their very doors. All in all, it's worth listening to Father Boniface, and having a relatively happy manor.

The system of collective security that underlay a feudal society was a "two way street." Ideally, the upper rungs provided security and good government, and the bottom rungs provided resources and loyalty. Absolute ownership, with its modern prerogatives, was unknown when it came to the chief source of income and power: land. As for Cedric's plot, it had at least four "owners," or, more accurately, four separate individuals had a "fee" or interest in it, all conditional on reciprocal rights and duties. Of course, Cedric "occupied" it, in the sense of managing it day to day. But it was also part of Sir Richard's manor which was, in turn, part of the lands of the Earl and, ultimately, the King's kingdom. Each "occupied" their "fee," in that they held their interest legally and "in occupation." To Cedric, it would be perfectly natural. Indeed, it would be far more natural for his people than the idea of a rich person in modern Beverly

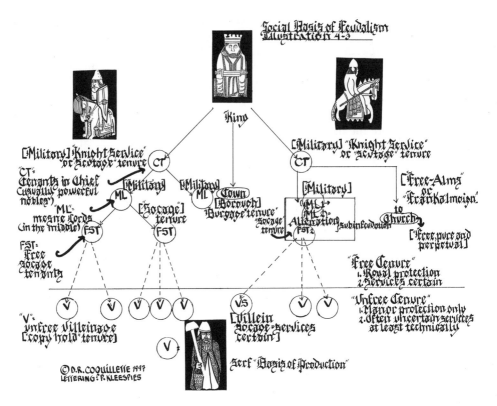

Illustration 4-3   I am most grateful to my dear friend, Penelope Kleespies, for this chart.

Hills, who owned an estate absolutely, and who felt no responsibility for the poor of Los Angeles. With real property interests came, automatically, reciprocal duty. Such a system was as far removed from our system of "absolute" marketable title as Native American ideas of collective ownership are today.

English feudalism had two fundamental rules. The first was that all land was "held" from the Crown, directly or indirectly, in one of the various forms of tenure we have just discussed. The second rule was that all land "held" in a tenure was also held for an "estate," i.e., a period of time. There were only three estates possible at English common law: 1) "life estate" (for the tenant's life only, no inheritance); 2) "fee simple" (inheritance by the tenant's heirs); and 3) "fee tail" (limited inheritance). Ironically, "leasehold," the only form of real property estate where we still use the feudal terms "land lord" and "tenant," was not recognized as a true estate at common law. It was viewed as merely a personal contract, as opposed to a "right in land."

At first, all estates were life estates, with the land reverting to the feudal lord on death of the tenant. At least by 1200 A.D., and maybe much earlier, this was supplanted by a presumption that the tenant's heir inherits on death, with a payment (called "relief") to the feudal lord. An estate which was automatically inheritable was called a "fee simple," even as it is today. Finally, as we shall see, there were always efforts to restrict inheritance further, by "cutting down" a fee. ("Tail" comes from the low French "*tailler*," "to carve.") After the statute *De Donis* (1285), this could be done effectively, and it was usually used to restrict inheritance to male heirs. (All land held by women automatically was controlled by their husbands on marriage. Thus, there was a major incentive to keep land in the family control by having only male heirs.) An inheritance thus "chopped down" (*taillatum*) by restriction was called a "fee tail." A typical example would be an "entail male," where only males to be heirs could inherit. With an "entail male," having many daughters could result in the inheritance of great estates by remote uncles or male cousins, a fairly frequent occurrence, and one that interested Jane Austin as late as the nineteenth century.

Thus our friend Cedric would not only know the "tenure" for each piece of land in the village, he would probably know the "estate" as well. Most humble lands were held in the estate "fee simple." A combination of "free and common socage" (or "freehold") tenure with a "fee simple" estate was the direct ancestor of our most common way to hold land today, "freehold" in "fee simple." The lands of the Earl and Sir Richard, however, might well have been entailed by their lawyers.

Finally, under the rules of English feudalism there were only two ways to transmit land: 1) "sub-infeudation" and 2) "substitution." Sub-infeudation resulted in another level in the feudal hierarchy. For example, Cedric wishes to raise money to set his children up as apprentices in town. He could convey some of the land he holds of Sir Richard to Garth, who aspires to "free" status and who has saved some money. Garth would hold of Cedric in free and common socage and in the estate fee simple. Garth's feudal dues to Cedric might be set to help Cedric meet his payments to Sir Richard or, if Garth paid enough "up front" in purchase money, the incidents could be nominal, like "a rose at midsummer's night," with Cedric looking to his remaining land to meet his obligations to his lord. Theoretically, Sir Richard need not care as long as Cedric remains his direct tenant and is responsible for the incidents owed to Sir Richard. Thus, Sir Richard's consent would not be required for subinfeudation. As we shall see, however, subinfeudation in practice began to remove actual control of the land from the person who owed the lord the feudal tax, and this became a serious problem.

The other way to convey interests in land was by "substitution." Here Garth would simply take Cedric's place, or "fee," in the feudal ladder. Thus, Garth then would become a free tenant, in free and common socage, of Sir Richard, for a fee simple estate. (Many serfs, incidentally, were able to buy such freehold land interests and become "free" yeomen, even if they continued to hold some lands by "unfree" tenure.) But because Sir Richard had not chosen Garth as a tenant directly beneath him, Sir Richard's consent was required. In addition, Cedric had to pay Sir Richard a tax on transfer, called a "fine."

Thus, initially, all land in England was held directly or indirectly from the Crown by a form of tenure and for the duration of an estate. It could only be conveyed during the grantor's lifetime by subinfeudation or substitution. Initially, land was not freely alienable by substitution without the lord's consent, nor could it be left by will. On death, the land descended automatically to the common law heir, regardless of the will. In other words, land was neither freely alienable nor devisable.

B. TWO VERY HARD IDEAS: SEISIN AND COMMUNAL OWNERSHIP

I. SEISIN

We are used to exclusive ownership which vests all rights in the owner. When we ask if someone "owns" a house, we assume that there is an "owner" who can sell that house freely on the open market at any time. Feudalism simply did not recognize such ownership. As we have seen, there were at least four "owners" of different fees in Cedric's land, all occupying different levels in the feudal chain, and all exercising some controls or demands on the land. The expression actually used at the time to describe such control of interests in land was "seisin," from *seising*, the same root as "to seize." Cedric would say that he was "seised" of a socage tenure, fee simple, in his little plot. At the same time, Sir Richard could be "seised" of the same land by scutage tenure in fee simple estate from the Earl and the Earl could be "seised" in knight service tenure with an "entail male" estate from the Crown. All were "seised" of their "fee." None "owned" absolutely.

Maitland has described what he called "the mystery of seisin." See *Materials, infra.* As a concept, "seisin" is far closer to "possession" than ownership. While Sir Richard might not be "possessed" of Cedric's plot directly, he was "possessed" of the fee of the manor. As we shall see, this distinction has important consequences. In a troubled kingdom, Norman rulers put a premium on "quiet possession." Whoever was "seised" was treated as controlling the fee legally, even if he or she had no right to the "seisin," but had just taken the interest in land by force—say if someone stole the manor from Sir Richard. The courts could put you back into "seisin" if you were wrongly "disseised," but until you regained "seisin," the person with "seisin" was treated as having legal control. The English feudal system had no place for ownership in the abstract. What interested it was actual possession of a fee, i.e., "seisin."

2. COMMUNAL OWNERSHIP

Equally difficult for modern minds was medieval communal ownership. This was largely an inheritance from Anglo-Saxon England. Most villages were surrounded by unused land. The major limitation on agricultural production was, for centuries, a shortage of laborers, not a shortage of land. Some of these lands were held by the King as hunting forests, and others were held by the lord. Important tracts, however, were held by all the freemen of the manor or village "in common," a "tenure by the commonalty" which descended collectively in fee simple from generation to generation.

The most usual surviving examples are common pastures, like the great Port Meadow at Oxford or even Boston Common and Cambridge Common in Massachusetts, or wood lots, many of which still exist on Cape Cod. In early feudal time, however, great fields were also farmed in common by the "open field system," whereby each villager was entitled to a particular furrow of the plow in every open field. This meant that each shared equally in the good and bad fields, and in the success or failure of particular crops. See Illustration 4-8, *Materials, infra.*

We live in an age dominated by risk, property, and individual entrepreneurship. The middle ages were different. The feudal system was a reciprocal security system which did not know absolute ownership divorced from responsibility. And it incorporated an even older form of collective ownership in the "commons," the communally held fields or pastures of the village. There everyone shared by the rules and divided the produce of the land. Even today some natural resources, such as beaches or rivers, are better managed as *res communes*, or resources owned in common, rather than as exclusive, private property.[2]

II. SOME FEUDAL PROBLEMS AND THEIR "SOLUTIONS": THE GREAT STATUTES OF EDWARD I, DE DONIS (1285) AND QUIA EMPTORES (1290)

A. THREE PROBLEMS

The feudal system was hardly perfect. Initially, there were three intrinsic problems. The first involved inheritance. Originally, land in the feudal system could descend on death only to the common law heirs. The tenant "seised" could not change this by will. Nor could the tenant sell the land during his or her lifetime without the lord's consent. Put in technical terms, land was neither freely alienable nor freely devisable.

The only way to transfer land was during your lifetime (*inter vivos*) and, unless your lord consented, it had to be by subinfeudation, creating another feudal "layer." But, for reasons explored in Shakespeare's *King Lear*, parents were reluctant to give away their land while they were alive, and subinfeudation could also cause serious problems, as we shall see.

Finally, "feudalism" itself was rapidly changing as the King and the chief nobles relied on standing armies of mercenaries, rather than calling on their feudal tenants to serve in person. (Paid mercenaries tended to be more loyal!) Once the feudal system became a "cash" only system of taxation, the reason for many of the restrictions on free alienation and devisibility disappeared. At the same time, however, certain wealthy English families began to try to limit free alienation for an entirely different purpose, i.e., to keep land in the same family for eternity. This is the story of how their three problems were "solved" by one of England's great legislators, King Edward I.

B. THE CANONS OF DESCENT

To understand these problems, we must understand the traditional common law rules governing inheritance of land on death. There were many local customs as to inheritance, but the dominant system was called "primogeniture." Under this system, the eldest son took all the land on his father's death. If there was no son, the land was divided equally among the daughters ("coparcenage"). On failure of all issue, the land would go back to "collateral" heirs, siblings, cousins

---

2. See D.R. Coquillette, "Mosses from an Old Manse: Another Look at Some Historic Property Cases About the Environment," 64 *Cornell L. Rev.* 761, 799–821.

etc., with those on the father's side preferred to those on the mother's, however remote, unless the land descended through the mother.[3]

Males were always preferred to females in the same degree. For example, a brother was always preferred as heir to his sisters, even if they were much older. But lineal heirs were preferred to collateral heirs, so daughters would take before an uncle. Finally, a deceased person was "represented" by his issue. Thus, if a father had two sons, and the elder son died before the father but left a grandson, the grandson took over the younger son. These rules put dark temptation before uncles appointed as guardians of their deceased elder brother's children, and tales were told of "accidents" to innocent young nieces or nephews. Some were true, as the modern discovery of the skeletons of two young princes in the Tower of London, almost certainly done to death by their uncle, Richard III, demonstrated.

Primogeniture was, in practice, a pretty harsh system. A heavy burden fell on younger sons. They would inherit no land, so they would be dependent on whatever their father would give them before his death. Otherwise, even if they were gentry, they would have to earn a living. The only acceptable occupations for gentry were the Church, the Army, and the Law. Younger sons, disinherited by primogeniture, also became leaders in the colonies. As adventurers and explorers, they sought the fortune their eldest brother achieved effortlessly. The literature and history of England is filled with stories of estranged eldest sons, waiting for the death of a father, or of younger brothers going to bed as poverty stricken soldiers or adventurers, and waking up the lord of a vast estate, due to an elder brother's death.

The effect on women was worse. Daughters had to be married to men of inheritance, or become dependent on the charity of their eldest brother. Even if they had no brother, and inherited their father's land equally, they lost control of all the land to their husband if they chose to marry. Their sole ultimate protection was the doctrine of dower. On their husband's death, their eldest son would inherit the land, but the widow would retain a life estate in a third of the land to provide for a protected old age. Even today, "dower" houses can be seen on the great English estates, usually built a bit away from the great house itself. These might have been built for a "dowager" countess or duchess—whose often problematic relationship with her eldest son's wife in the "great" house was a regular source of interest in English song and story.

For English upper class women, the laws of marriage and inheritance constantly impinged on their "freedom" and legal personality. Even as late as Jane Austin's novels, the tyranny was quite evident. Ironically, women of the lower classes, whose labor was valuable, made more progress toward legal rights. In some cities, such women began to run and own businesses. But the women of the aristocracy had no such leverage. Indeed, as claims of illegitimacy were one of the greatest threats to orderly inheritance of great estates, their personal lives were always closely curtailed. Men had no such constraints. It might have been a gilded cage, but it was a true cage—one that forced many into convents and forced one English Queen, Elizabeth I, never to marry.

It is easy to see the original reasons for primogeniture. The feudal lord wanted loyal warriors holding the land beneath him, and clarity as to who owed what feudal duties. Primogeniture meant that the tenant below was usually a direct

---

3. For the rules of the *jus recadentiae*, exclusion of collaterals of the half-blood, and other more technical matters, see J.H. Baker, *Introduction, supra*, 304 ff.

Illustration 4-4

CANON OF DESCENT

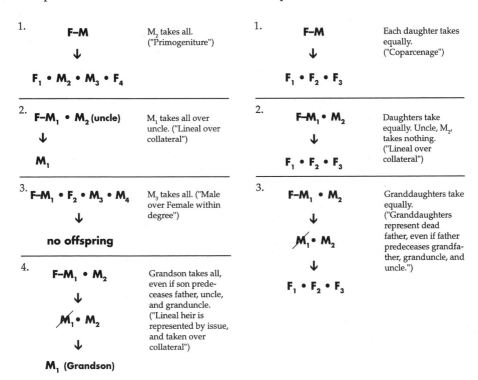

| **F** | = Female | **F–M** | = Marriage |
| **M** | = Male | **1,2, etc.** = | Order of Birth |

A. Examples of Male Inheritance

1.

F–M

↓

F₁ • M₂ • M₃ • F₄

M₂ takes all. ("Primogeniture")

2. **F–M₁ • M₂ (uncle)**

↓

M₁

M₁ takes all over uncle. ("Lineal over collateral")

3. **F–M₁ • F₂ • M₃ • M₄**

↓

no offspring

M₃ takes all. ("Male over Female within degree")

4.

F–M₁ • M₂

↓

M̸₁ • M₂

↓

M₁ (Grandson)

Grandson takes all, even if son predeceases father, uncle, and granduncle. ("Lineal heir is represented by issue, and taken over collateral")

B. Examples of Female Inheritance

1.

F–M

↓

F₁ • F₂ • F₃

Each daughter takes equally. ("Coparcenage")

2. **F–M₁ • M₂**

↓

F₁ • F₂ • F₃

Daughters take equally. Uncle, M₂, takes nothing. ("Lineal over collateral")

3. **F–M₁ • M₂**

↓

M̸₁ • M₂

↓

F₁ • F₂ • F₃

Granddaughters take equally. ("Granddaughters represent dead father, even if father predeceases grandfather, granduncle, and uncle.")

male descendent of an ally holding an undivided tract of land charged with specific numbers of men or of money. If all the sons inherited equally, estates would be soon divided into small tracts, and feudal dues could become impossible to manage: i.e., "1/16 of a knight etc." Inheritance by women was worse, because they might marry the sons of rival nobles, who would then control the land. If there were only daughters, the rule of equal division at least meant that no one rival husband would control all the land.

The rationale of the need for personal loyalty from feudal tenants neatly explains the other major legal rules, as well. Bars on changing the automatic rules of inheritance by individual will and on transfer of land *inter vivos* without the lord's consent (except by subinfeudation) served the same purposes. The feudal lord could be assured that the immediate layer of tenants below was largely male and largely loyal.

C. THE FORMALITIES OF FEUDALISM: HOMAGE AND FEALTY

This picture is also consistent with the formalities of feudalism. The relationship between a feudal lord and a tenant (one "holding" by a tenure from that lord) was established by a public ceremony. During the ceremony, the lord invested the tenant with the lands by a symbolic delivery of the "seisin". This was called the "livery of seisin," and could actually include the delivery of a clump of earth, some twigs, or some other concrete part of the land. Then the tenant did "homage" to the lord, and became the lord's "man" (Norman French *homme*). "Homage" usually consisted of the tenant placing his two hands between those of his lord which, according to *Bracton*, "symbolized protection, defense and warranty (of good seisin) on the part of the lord and subjection and reverence on that of the tenant." See Illustration 4-6, *Materials, infra*. The tenant than usually stated that " I become your man...and I will bear you fealty (loyalty) in life and limb and earthly honor." Following this ceremony, the tenant took an oath of fealty, usually putting his or her right hand on a bible or sacred relics, saying "Hear this lord, that I will bear you fealty in life and limb, in body, goods and earthy honor, so help me God and these sacred relics."[4] From these rituals comes a picture of a relationship in which personal loyalty of the tenant was crucial.

D. ANOTHER PICTURE

There is only one problem with this vision of a feudal past. Most modern economic and political studies paint a very different picture.[5] According to J.M.W. Bean and others, the King very quickly abandoned the idea of an army based on men and knights provided through feudal incidents.[6] Far more reliable was an army of mercenaries, paid in cash and beholden to the King alone. Tenants-in-chief, particularly after the first generation, were no longer old friends. They could be dangerous. The Norman Kings soon learned to never grant too much land to any powerful follower in one area. Small tracts scattered throughout the country were much safer than one large area in the hands of an ambitious earl. According to Bean, feudalism rapidly became a fiscal system of taxation, rather than a military system. "Tenants-in-chief in the thirteenth century sent only a fraction of the *servitium debitum* to the field, paying scutage (cash) on the rest of their fees."[7] Increasingly, women did homage like men, although they would never fight in person. Why, then, were not the old rules and ceremonies changed?

To start, the ceremony of homage and fealty helped keep track, in the public memory, of who held from whom and for how much, a vital matter for both tax and civil litigation. As *Bracton* observed, "Homage ought not to be done in pri-

---

4. See *Materials, infra*, p. 118–119, for a sample oath from *Bracton* and an illustration of the rites of homage from the *Sachsenspiegel Curia* (1320 A.D.).

5. See *Materials, infra*, 131 ff.

6. See J.M.W. Bean, *supra* note 1, at p. 1–6.

7. *Id.*

vate, but in a public place and openly, in the presence of many, in the county or hundred court or the court of the lord so that if, through malice, the tenant should wish to deny his homage, the lord could more readily produce proof...."[8] Even today, one of our remaining "feudal" ceremonies, marriage, involves a legal necessity of public vows before witnesses, and for the same reason. Documents could be forged or lost, and frequently were. Public witnesses, however, had long memories, particularly because such ceremonies, homage and fealty and marriage, would be the talk of the village for months.

Secondly, the old military reasons for subordinating women and preventing the break up of large lands came to be replaced by a new reason: the desire of the great noble families to ensure the survival of their power. Free alienation or devisability of land meant that each generation could split the inheritance into smaller pieces, or sell it. Concentrating the land in the hands of the eldest son kept the great estates, and thus the family power and honor, intact. It also aided the King and chief tenants in collecting taxes.

Yet countervailing forces were also developing. Wealthy new classes of merchants were eager to buy respectability and land. Profligate land holders needed to sell. Others, such as concerned fathers, wished to provide security for their daughters in lands or dowry, or to provide for their younger sons. Finally, a new class of lawyers began to develop ways to use the subinfeudation process to evade taxes, rather than to make them easier to collect. The tension between these forces came to a head during the reign of Edward I (1239–1307).

E. THE "ENGLISH JUSTINIAN" AND HIS GREAT STATUTES

Edward I reigned from 1272–1307. He has been widely regarded as one of the greatest of all English Kings. He was a great soldier. During the years 1267–1283 he conquered Wales, and he made a good effort at conquering Scotland and Ireland, thus his nick name, "Hammer of the Scots." He was constantly fighting to secure his French lands, as well. This required money, as Edward relied heavily on mercenaries.

Fortunately, Edward was also a fine administrator. He early recognized the importance of trade, and he prospered from taxes on the merchants.[9] He also saw the need to tax land as efficiently as possible. Finally, he understood, like the Roman emperor Justinian, that a sound legal system not only ensures loyalty, but leads to prosperity. Indeed, during his reign an "imitation" of *Bracton* appeared in the exact form of *Justinian's Institutes*, with Edward "speaking the law." Like Justinian, Edward declared that "peace cannot be duly maintained without laws."[10] But Edward was confronted with a nagging legal problem. Clever members of the newly emerging legal profession had discovered a way to enable some of their wealthier clients to avoid feudal incidents. Here is how it worked.

---

8. *Materials, infra*, pp. 118–119.

9. See generally T.F.T. Plucknet, *Legislation of Edward I* (Oxford, 1949), 136–161.

10. This "imitation" was written about 1290 A.D. and was called *Britton*, possibly after John Le Breton, Bishop of Hereford.

F. FEUDAL TAX EVASION

Feudal "incidents" had one wonderful quality as taxes. They were due automatically on the occasion of certain events which were hard to deny or fake. There were six common types:

    1. *"Aids."* These were payments due to assist the lord in meeting specific financial obligations. By the *Magna Carta,* they became limited to reasonable payments on the occasion of only three events: (a) money to ransom the lord from captivity, (b) money to knight his eldest son, (c) money to provide a dowry on the first marriage for his eldest daughter. As of 1275, the two last were fixed at 20 shillings per knight fee or 5% of the value of socage land.

    2. *Fines on Alienation.* These were payable to obtain the consent of the lord for direct sale of a fee by the tenant below. They were usually fixed at ⅓ the annual value of the land.

    3. *Relief.* In theory, on the death of a tenant the land "reverted" to the lord. Obviously, a life estate would then terminate and the lord could regrant the land. If the estate were "fee simple," the lord had to regrant the land to the tenant's heir, but he was entitled to a fee, called "relief." For socage tenure, for example, a "reasonable" relief could be a year's profit from the land. The lord could also claim the profits from the land until the new tenant performed the ceremony of homage. This was called "primer seisin."[11]

    4. *Wardship.* If a tenant left an underage heir, the land came back to the lord until the heir was of age. (This was 21 for military tenure and 14 for socage tenure). During this time, the lord was expected to look after the ward and his or her training, and could help himself to the land's income. This was subject to much abuse, as the *Magna Carta, supra, secs. 3 and 4,* attests. In particular, the lord could not commit "waste," i.e., destroy the capital value of the land.

    5. *Marriage.* A lord could arrange a marriage for his ward. This could be very profitable. The ward had to consent, but if he or she refused, the lord could recoup the value of the marriage. If the ward married without the lord's consent, he would double the value of the marriage. Technically, the lord's marriage arrangements had to be "suitable" socially to the ward, but the *Magna Carta* again testifies to widespread abuse. Needless to say, harsh abuse of wards and romantic elopements fill our literature, and even our fairy tales.

    6. *Escheat.* If a tenant was convicted of a felony or died without an heir, the land came back to the lord. Treason was the only exception. Then, the land reverted to the King. This was doubtless one reason that the King's Bench took jurisdiction over felonies.

Again, all of these incidents had one common feature. The tax became automatically due on the occurrence of an event. Tax evasion consisted of either

---

    11. See the excellent summary in J.H. Baker, *An Introduction to English Legal History,* (3d ed., London, 1990), 272–275.

keeping the events to a minimum, or by making it hard for the lord to keep track of who owed what to whom.

An example of the former device, keeping taxable events to a minimum, was to grant your land to an institution, like the Church. A corporation never died, never got married, never left underage heirs, etc. If you granted your land to, say, a monastery, they could then subinfeudate the land back to you, doubtless for a reward. The interposition of the religious corporation could greatly reduce dues. Both the *Magna Carta* and Edward I tackled this problem, preventing such alienations. Under Edward's statute of 1279, all alienations to the "dead hand" (*"mortmain"*) of such charitable corporations were prohibited without special license.

An example of the latter device, making it hard for the tax collector to collect, was to create so many levels through subinfeudation that the actual occupant of valuable land was greatly removed legally from the lord. Lawyers put in "men of straw" in these intermediary positions, usually persons hard to locate or impecunious. It was not unlike the modern levels of interlocking incorporation that hide the true ownership of New York taxi cabs and Caribbean casinos.

G. QUIA EMPTORES (1290)

Edward I tackled this problem by legislative reform. This, in itself, was an extraordinary development in a world that still thought of the law as a relatively permanent body of custom, and where great charters, like the *Magna Carta*, purported just to restate existing principles. The notion of the law as a tool to obtain political and economic results, the so-called "instrumentalist" view of law, was very novel. Edward I was certainly unusual in the scope and daring of his statutes. Of course, there was not yet a "parliament" in the modern sense. There were no democratic elections, for example. A "parliament," from the Norman French *"parler,"* "to talk," was just a meeting of the king and his chief lords and advisors. Thus Edward's great statutes were promulgated by "our lord the King in his parliament," meaning simply the King sitting with his chief lords and advisors.

Edward's chief "reform" statute was called *Quia Emptores* from its first words, "Forasmuch as purchasers…" or *"Quia Emptores …"* It is also designated "18 Edward I, c.1" meaning simply the first chapter of the statutes of the 18th year of Edward's reign (1290 A.D.).

At this point it is helpful to turn to *Materials* page 131 and just look at the text of the statute, here translated into English by K.E. Digby. There are three sections. The first contains a long recitation of the policy reasons for the statute. ("For as much as purchasers of lands and tenements of the fees of great men… have many times heretofore entered into their fees whereby the same chief lords have many times lost their escheats, marriages, and wardships…which thing seems very hard and extreme….") This "policy" section is sometimes called the "preamble."

Next is the "action" section of the statute. This almost always starts by an account of the place of the parliamentary actions and the date. "[O]ur lord the King in his parliament at Westminster [place] after Easter in the eighteenth year of his reign [date, i.e., 1290 A.D.] at the instance of the great men of the realm granted, provided, and ordained that...." There follows the "action items" of the statute. Most old statutes follow this form.

Quia Emptores has three "action items." Chapter 1 declares that all land will be freely alienable without the feudal lord's consent, a monumental departure. But purchase and sale must be by "substitution." "Subinfeudation" is prohibited. In other words, the purchaser "steps into the shoes" of the seller and has exactly the same feudal relationship with the lord as the seller. From henceforth, no new layers of feudalism could be created, i.e., the seller could not make the purchaser the seller's feudal tenant. This would prevent evasion of feudal tax by creating a confusing maze of sub-tenancies.

Chapter 2 made sure the purchaser took a fair share of the feudal tax to the lord. If a seller sold less than all the land, the buyer's feudal services would be apportioned exactly like the split in the land. For example, if A held by military tenure of one knight and sold half the land to B, B would hold by 1/2 a knight... doubtless reduced to a sum of money or scrutage payments. This made sure that the burden of the services was on all the land.

Finally, Chapter 3 limited the statute to grants in fee simple, set out that the statute should be prospective only, commencing at "the Feast of St. Andrew... next coming," and restated the policy against tax evasion by gifts to the Church with a gift back, i.e., *"mortmain"* gifts. ("And it is understood that by the said sales...such lands...shall in no wise come into Mortmain.")

Here is the amazing fact about *Quia Emptores*. Today land is still freely alienable, and all land must be purchased by substitution, not subinfeudation. In short, *Quia Emptores* is still the law, 700 years later.

It is certainly easy to see why the King wanted *Quia Emptores*. As the top rung of the feudal ladder, he was the only feudal lord who did not benefit by feudal tax evasion. Eliminating subinfeudation was pure benefit for him. But how did he get the leading nobles to concur? In particular, how did he get them to agree to free alienation of land without their consent? Would this not weaken the great land of families? The answer lies in the fact that *Quia Emptores* occurred just after another major statutory initiative, a statute called *De Donis*, which gave English landowners a way to tie up their land despite free alienation.

H. DE DONIS (1285)

We mentioned before that the common law recognized three different durations for "holding" land by a "tenure." These were called "estates:" 1) life estate (for life only); 2) fee simple estate (hereditable by your heirs forever); and 3) fee tail. Again, the "fee tail" was a limited or "chopped down" fee, from the Law French *"tailler,"* to carve or chop. The most common "fee tail" was one that limited the grant of a fee to inheritance by males only, "entail male." Originally, such grants were frequently made on the marriage of a daughter. "To A and B and the heirs male of their body." Thus, if A and B did not give birth to a male heir, the land "reverted" to the father's family, and could go to the daughter's brother or uncle. This prevented the land going to the husband's family. Before *De Donis*, however, it was only necessary to give birth to a male heir—the so-called "cry within four walls." At that point the land vested in fee simple estate, even if the son died soon after. Most important, once a son was born, his parents could sell or give away the land.

The "Preamble" of *De Donis* stated that this situation was "very hard" on donors, as recipients of the gift "after issue begotten and born between them" could "aliene the land so given, and to disinherit their issue of land, contrary to the minds of the givers and contrary to the form expressed in the gift." The "action" clause stated that "wherefore our lord the king, perceiving how necessary and expedient it should be to provide remedy on the aforesaid cases, hath ordained..." that "the will of the giver...shall be henceforth observed, so that they to whom the land was given under such condition shall have no power to aliene the land so given, but that it shall remain unto the issue of them to whom it was given after their death, or shall revert unto the giver or his heirs if issue fail...."

De Donis clearly prevented the recipients of the grant from selling it and thus disinheriting their children, once there was a "cry within four walls." But there was to be far more. It was eventually held that the statute would protect entails beyond the donees' generation, through the entire series of their issues. Thus, one who held land for an estate of "fee tail" could alienate the land, but never more than a life estate, because on his or her death the land descended to the heir as defined by the entail, or reverted to the heirs of the donor. This effectively "locked in" family land forever.

Here is an example. Guilbert de Boef's beloved daughter Hilda is to marry Hubert, the son of Herbert Fitzroy. The de Boefs and the Fitzroys have always been rivals for influence in the shire, and do not particularly trust each other, but this marriage is uniting the families, and de Boef wants to do the right thing by Hilda. Beside he likes the idea of little de Boef-Fitzroy grandchildren playing at his knee. So he is going to grant to Hilda and Hubert two manors. But de Boef has a clever lawyer from London who writes for him. The lawyer asks, "what will happen if Hilda sickens and dies in childbirth, and there is no surviving heir? Do you then want the Fitzroys to have the manors to strengthen their forces in the shire?" So when de Boef proudly presents the grant of the manors to his daughter and son-in-law there is a catch. The grant is not to "Hilda and Hubert and their heirs" (words of "purchase" establishing a fee simple), but to "Hilda and Hubert and the heirs male of their body." The words "heirs male of their body" are words of limitation. This is an estate of fee tail.

Assume that before *De Donis*, Hilda and Hubert gave birth to a son. Hubert, who controlled the land as husband, could then sell or give it outright to anyone. This would be true even if the son died at birth. After *De Donis*, neither Hilda nor Hubert could ever sell more than a life estate. If their son survived, he would get the land, but under the same conditions. If there ever was a "failure of male issue" descending from Hilda and Hubert, the land would revert to Hilda's father and the de Boef heirs. It would never go to Fitzroys who were not born of the marriage. Incidentally, the heirs of de Boef always had an interest in the land called a "possibility of reverter," if the male issue failed. These heirs were called reversioners. Equally, the descendants of Hilda and Hubert also always had an interest to prevent sale, even before they were seised of the estate. This was called a "remainder" interest, and they were called "remaindermen." Both reversioners and remaindermen could stop the sale of entailed land by bringing a writ called a writ of formedon (from *forma doni*, or "form of the gift.") Here is how an entail would look:

Chart 4-1

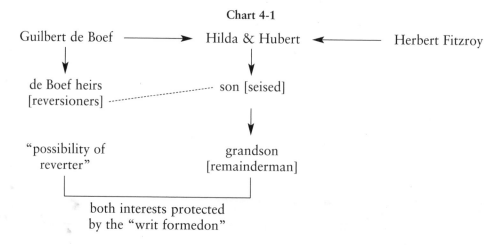

For many years it was unclear if the royal courts would actually enforce the *De Donis* entails after the first generation, or for more than several generations.[12] As we shall see, the curious outcome was that the courts elected to theoretically enforce the entails forever, but permitted a bizarre fiction, the "fine and recovery" to permit a tenant in occupation to break entails under certain circumstances. In any event, for centuries entailed land became a feature of the great English families, and their ability to pass great estates intact from eldest son to eldest son was quite astonishing. Indeed, some estates are in the hands of such eldest sons at this very day.

I. EDWARD'S STATUTES: "REACTIONARY AND CONSERVATIVE" OR "RADICAL AND REVOLUTIONARY"?

Edward's two great property statutes, *De Donis* and *Quia Emptores*, transformed English feudalism. After *Quia Emptores* (1290), anyone holding fee simple estates in free tenure could alienate them freely by substitution, without the lord's consent, exactly as land is bought and sold today. Equally important, new feudal relationships could no longer be created, except as they existed before 1290, because sub-infeudation was prohibited. Inevitably, old feudal layers would be forgotten or made meaningless by inflation. No new ones could be created to take their place. Thus the system would gradually atrophy, until the Tenure Abolition Act of 1660 converted all tenures into free and common socage, with the exception of frankalmoign and copyhold, and abolished most feudal incidents. The ultimate irony was that the lost revenue to the Crown was replaced by a tax on beer! As Megarry and Wade observed: "After 1290 the feudal pyramid began to crumble. The number of mesne lordships could not be in-

---

12. Beresford, C.J., writing in 1311, claimed that "He that made the statute meant to bind the issue in fee tail, as well as the feeoffees, until the tail had reached the fourth degree, and it was only through negligence that he omitted to insert express words to that effect in the statute; therefore we shall not abate this writ." See Plucknett, *supra*, 331–332, 553 (Y.B.B. Edward II, (Selden Society), xi 170–177).

creased, evidence of existing lordships disappeared with the passing of time, and so most land came to be held directly from the Crown."[13]

Quia Emptores also marked the end of any notion of feudalism as a system of personal military service. From Edward's perspective, it must have been a system of taxation, pure and simple. But to the extent feudalism was a social system of hierarchical classes, existing in mutual dependence and exploitation and founded in customary inheritance and "status" relationships, this system continued for centuries.[14] Its characteristics not only survived into the nineteenth century but, many would argue, it still remains in certain parts of England.

One reason for this was certainly the fact that *Quia Emptores* was immediately preceded by *De Donis*. The free alienation provided by the former was curtailed by the latter. But there was a big change. Bars against free alienation before Edward's statutes were inherent in the customary law of the reign and were automatic. After *Quia Emptores* and *De Donis*, if you wished to tie up your land, you needed legal documents. What began Edward's reign as a system of customary feudalism, emerged as a system of free alienation curbed only by carefully contrived individual legal schemes. This was a big difference. After 1290 A.D., you needed a lawyer.

This leaves us with one large question. Did Edward I's "reforms" save feudalism, or did they seal its fate? Edward and his legal advisors would certainly have said the former. As a military system, feudalism was dead. As a fiscal system, it could only survive if further subinfeudation were prohibited. At the top of the pyramid, Edward had only one incentive, preventing evasion of feudal taxes— taxes that he was entitled to without having to convene parliaments for special supplements. He would say his statutes saved the only thing worth saving, the feudal system as a system of tax.

But there was always more to feudalism than its military and legal aspects. It was a social and political system, where the great lords held power transferred automatically from generation to generation, and the classes below worked the countryside, each in its proper place. This system was threatened by *Quia Emptores*, but ultimately saved by the application of *De Donis* and other methods of "strict settlement" to tie up land from generation to generation.

J. THE SEQUEL: BREAKING THE ENTAIL

Quia Emptores is the law in most common law jurisdictions today. Aspects of *De Donis* survived until the law of Property Act of 1925, and even later.[15]

Long before, however, *De Donis* was widely evaded by the use of a legal fiction, the "fine and recovery." Here is how it worked. Suppose A was the tenant "in fee tail" of land he wished to sell to B. Under *De Donis*, all he could convey was a life estate. If he tried to convey more, the reversioners (the donor and

---

13. *Materials, infra,* p. 134.

14. Maine described the "progress" of law as proceeding from "status" to "contract," i.e., that individual will and the ability to change your place in society by voluntary agreements was inherently more advanced than "status" systems where your place is fixed, largely by birth, such as by primogeniture. Do you agree?

15. See *Materials, infra,* pp. 133–134.

donor's heirs) and the remaindermen (his own heirs), could bring a legal action by writ of "formedon" (from *forma doni* referring to the form of the original gift establishing the entail).

So A did something very different. He had B sue him in a royal court, claiming that A's land actually belonged to B. Such an action, know as a "recovery," was voidable as collusive. But the lawyers hit on a bizarre addition. A, in defense of the suit, would call a witness to warrant under oath that he, A, was the true owner, a so-called "voucher." This witness would be "C," in real life the court usher or other "man of straw." At the crucial time, C would ask permission to "talk things over" with B out of court (i.e., "crave leave to emparl"). C would then just fail to reappear, in contempt of court.[16] The court would award B the judgment, and require A to convey a fee simple to B—free of any entail. (Of course, this is what they wanted all along). The court would also award a judgment for A against C for equal lands, for violating his duty of warranty. But what about the reversioners and remaindermen? In theory, they were protected by the judgment for equal lands against C.

This was, of course, a ridiculous fraud. In later years, C was the Common Plea's crier, who got fourpence for every fictitious "fine and recovery."[17] This fiction simply drove an immense hole through *De Donis*.

So why did not all entailed land soon disappear? The secret lay in another technicality. A "recovery" was a real action, so that a fine and recovery could only be brought against a tenant in possession. Those simply waiting to inherit entails could do nothing, and an eldest son could not do so until he reached his majority. Between 1640 and 1700 the so-called "strict settlement" was devised, which basically gave only a life estate to the owner of land at any given time. Before his heir was in a position to break the settlement by reaching majority, his father would persuade him to resettle the land so that he would in turn have only a life estate. This was often in return for the father giving his son immediate income, so he wouldn't have to wait until his father died to enjoy some of the benefit of his inheritance. When his son reached his majority, he would have become wise enough to do the same thing with *his* son.[18] This way, no owner in possession would have more than a life interest. Thus was much of the spirit of *De Donis* preserved.

One might have asked why Parliament, in all these years, would never simply repeal *De Donis*. Apparently Parliament was frequently asked to do so, but could never take the final step. One explanation, advanced by Sir Edward Coke in 1606, seems as reasonable as any:

> But the truth was, That the Lords and Commons, knowing that the estates tail were not to be forfeited for Felony or Treason; as their estates of Inheritance were before the said Act...and finding that they were not answerable for the debts or Incumbrances of their Ancestors, nor did the sales, leases or alienations of their Ancestors, did bind them for the Lands which were entailed to their Ancestors; always rejected such bills.[19]

---

16. *Materials, infra,* pp. 137–138.

17. "Fine" referred to the compromised action, from "*finalis concordice,*" and "recovery" referred to B's fictitious "recovery" of his allegedly "lost" lands.

18. For a complete description, see Baker, *supra,* 332–335.

19. *Mildmay's Case* (1606), 6 Co. Rep. at f. 40b.

Thus *Quia Emptores* and *De Donis* have shaped the Anglo-American land law, and English society, for seven centuries.

FOR FURTHER READING

I. Historical Introduction

For a good historical setting, including social, political and economic factors, see George Holmes, *The Later Middle Ages 1272–1485* (New York, 1962); Sir Maurice Powicke, *The Thirteenth Century 1216–1307* (Oxford, 2d ed., 1962); and J.M.W. Bean, *The Decline of English Feudalism, 1215–1540* (Manchester, 1968).

II. The Legal Basis of Feudalism

As usual, the first recommendation for a concise introduction is J.H. Baker's *An Introduction to English Legal History* (3d ed., London, 1990), 255–315. The great classic is K.E. Digby's *An Introduction to the History of the Law of Real Property* (5th ed., Oxford, 1987) 62–239. More up to date is A.W.B. Simpson, *A History of the Land Law* (2d ed., Oxford, 1426), 1–102. See also Pollock & Maitland, *supra*, vol. 1, 229–356; R.C. Palmer, "The Feudal Framework of English Law" 79 *Michigan Law Review* (1981), 1130–1164, and S.D. White, "English Feudalism and Its Origins" 19 *Amer. J. Legal History* (1975), 138–155.

III. The "Reforms" of Edward I

The classic account of Edward's great legislation is T.F.T. Plucknett, *Legislation of Edward I* (Oxford, 1949). For a highly readable account, see W.S. Holdsworth, *Some Makers of English Law* (Cambridge, 1966), 25–45. For Edward's efforts in other areas of the law, see T.F.T. Plucknett, *Edward I and Criminal Law* (Cambridge, 1960).

The feudal system

Illustration 4-5   From Terry Deary, *The Measly Middle Ages*, Scholastic Ltd., 1996 (Illustrator, Martin Brown). Text © Terry Dreary, 1996, illustrations © Martin Brown, 1996. First published by Scholastic Ltd. Reproduced by permission.

MATERIALS

FEUDAL WRITS

C. Stephenson and F.G. Marcham, *Sources of English Constitutional History* (Harper Bros., 1937), 58–59. [Courtesy Addison Wesley Educational Publishers, Inc.]

Writs Concerning Feudal Tenures

(A) William I: Grant in Free Alms (1070–71)

William, king of England, to Baldwin, sheriff of Devonshire, and to all his barons and ministers of the province, greeting. Know that I have granted to my monks of Battle [Abbey] the church of St. Olave in Exeter, with all the lands of Sherford and Kenbury, and with all other lands and things belonging to that church. Wherefore I will and command that they shall hold it freely and peacefully, and that, as my royal alms (*elemosina dominica*), it shall be exempt from all custom of earthly service: [namely,] from all pleas and plaints and shires and hundreds, and from all geld, scot, aid, gift, Danegeld, and army [service], with *sac* and *soc*, toll and *infangenetheof*, and all work on castles and bridges.

Witnesses: Thomas, archbishop of York; William Fitz-Osbert. At Winchester.

(Latin) Oliver, *Monasticon Dioecesis Exoniensis*, p. 117.

(B) William I: Summons for Military Service (1072)

William, king of the English, to Aethelwig, abbot of Evesham, greeting. I command you to summon all those who are under your charge and administration that they shall have ready before me at Clarendon on the octave of Pentecost all the knights that they owe me. Come to me likewise yourself on that day, and bring ready with you those five knights that you owe me from your abbey.

Witness, Eudo the Steward. At Winchester.

(Latin) Round, *Feudal England*, p. 304.

(C) William II: Writ for the Collection of Relief (1095–96)

William, king of the English, to all French and English who hold free lands of the bishopric of Worcester, greeting. Know that, since the bishop has died, the honour has reverted into my own hand. It is now my will that from your lands you give me as much relief as I have assessed through my barons: [namely,] Hugh de Lacy £20; Walter Punther £20; Gilbert Fitz-Turnold £5; Robert, bishop [of Hereford], £10; the abbot of Evesham £30; Walter of Gloucester £20; Roger Fitz-Durand £10.... And if any one refuses to do this, Urse and Bernard are to take both his lands and his chattels into my hand.

Witnesses: Renulf the Chaplain, Odo the Steward, Urse d'Abetot.

(Latin) *Ibid.*, p. 309.

(D) Henry I: Grant Concerning Scutage (1127)

Henry, king of the English, to his archbishops, bishops, abbots, earls, etc., greeting. Know that to the church of St. Aetheldreda of Ely, for the love of God, for the souls of my father and mother, for the redemption of my sins, and on petition of Hervey, bishop of the same church, I have forgiven £40 of those £100 which the aforesaid church was accustomed to give for scutage whenever scutage was as-sessed throughout my land of England; so that henceforth forever the church shall on that account give no more than £60 when scutage is levied throughout the land. And so let the aforesaid church be quit in perpetuity of the aforesaid [40] pounds.

Witnesses: Roger, bishop of Salisbury; Geoffrey, my chancellor; Robert, [keeper] of the seal; William de Tancarville; William d'Aubigny, steward; Ralph Basset, Geoffrey de Clinton, William de Pont-de-l'Arche. At Eling during my crossing.

(Latin) *Ibid.*, p. 268.

"HOMAGE AND FEALTY"

Bracton (*circa* 1236) Thorne trans. (1968) *supra*, vol. 2. [Courtesy Harvard University Press.]

What homage is.

What is homage? Homage is a legal bond by which one is bound and con-strained to warrant, defend, and acquit his tenant in his seisin against all persons for a service certain, described and expressed in the gift, and also, conversely, whereby the tenant is bound and constrained in return to keep faith to his lord

Illustration 4-6   The rite of homage is depicted above, with the lord holding the tenant's hand, and the affected land being clearly indicated. The importance of witnesses and cere-mony in establishing and recording vital relationships continues today, in the widespread legal requirement of a marriage ceremony before witnesses. The illustration is from *Sachsen-spiegel, LX* (Heidelberg, *circa* 1320), courtesy Akademie Verlag, GmbH, Berlin.

and perform the service due. {Homage is contracted by the will of both, the lord and the tenant, [and] is to be dissolved by the contrary will of both, if both so wish, for it does not suffice if one alone wishes, because nothing is more in conformity with natural equity etc.} The *nexus* between a lord and his tenant through homage is thus so great and of such quality that the lord owes as much to the tenant as the tenant to the lord, reverence alone excepted.

*   *   *   *

By what persons.

By what persons? Homage may be done neither by procurators nor by letters, but must be taken and done personally by both lord and tenant, for wherever personal participation is necessary the matter cannot be concluded by a procurator or letters.

How and by what words.

How and by what words ought homage to be done? It is clear that he who ought to do homage {In view of the reverence which he owes his lord, he ought to wait upon him no matter where he is in the realm, or (if it can be done without great difficulty) outside it; a lord is not bound to seek out his tenant.} ought to do it thus: he ought to place both his hands between the two hands of his lord, by which there is symbolized protection, defense and warranty on the part of the lord and subjection and reverence on that of the tenant, and say these words: 'I become your man with respect to the tenement which I hold of you (or 'which I ought to hold of you') and I will bear you fealty in life and limb and earthly honour (according to some, but according to others, 'in body and goods and earthly honour') and I will bear you fealty against all men (or 'all mortal men,' according to some) saving the faith owed the lord king and his heirs.' And immediately after this let him swear an oath of fealty to his lord in these words:

The oath of fealty.

'Hear this, lord N., that I will bear you fealty in life and limb, in body, goods, and earthly honour, so help me God and these sacred [relics].' And some add the following to the oath, and properly, that at the agreed terms he shall do his service to his lord and his heirs faithfully and without diminution, contradiction, impediment, or wrongful delay. Homage ought not to be done in private, but in a public place and openly, in presence of many, in the county or hundred court or the court of the lord, so that if, through malice, the tenant should wish to deny his homage the lord could more readily produce proof of the homage done and the service acknowledged.

[What should be ascertained before homage is done].

Diligent inquiry ought to precede the performance of homage [in order to ascertain] whether he who claims as heir is the natural [and legitimate] son of him whose heir he claims to be; a right and near heir with respect to the right of possession, and not merely a right and near heir but a nearer heir with respect to the proprietary right. Every nearer heir ought to have both rights, possession and property, though another has a greater right than he. Inquiry ought also to be made concerning the kind of tenement for which and from which he is bound to do homage, and how much he holds. What in demesne and what in service, whether he holds the entire tenement in demesne or in service or part in demesne and part in service. And by what service, and how the inheritance descends to him so that he may be the heir, lest in taking his homage the lord be deceived through negligence or error.

What the effect of homage is.

The effect of homage is this, that if one has done homage to another, his true lord or a non-lord, he cannot withdraw from such lord or his homage without judgment, as long as he holds the tenement, either in demesne or in service, by which he is bound to homage. Because of the bond of homage the tenant may do nothing to the disherison of his lord or his severe injury, nor conversely may the lord so act toward the tenant. If either so acts homage is completely dissolved and extinguished, [and the *nexus* and obligation of homage,] since they act contrary to homage and the oath of fealty, and it will be a just judgment <that they be punished with respect to that in which they offend, that is, [if] it is the lord, that he lose his lordship; [if] the tenant, his tenement, as will be explained more fully below. In this way homage may be dissolved.>

WOMEN

Note: *Status of Women.* As Maitland observed in the following excerpt "we have yet to speak of half the inhabitants of England." In some ways, women had full legal personalities by *Bracton's* time (*circa* 1236). They could sue and be sued, and could stand seized of any feudal "fee." They could, and did, act as powerful legal guardians of their children or their tenants' children. But they were excluded from almost all public functions, including the jury—except in certain "sensitive cases," where a "jury of matrons" was employed. (Those cases tended to involve pregnancy or other "women's issues." A good example can be found in the next chapter (V), Peter of Melton's case (*Bracton's Note Book Case No. 1503, Materials, infra*)).

The biggest legal disadvantage suffered by women was marriage. For a good account of the law, see Catherine M.A. McCauliff, "The Medieval Origin of the Doctrine of Estates in Land: Substantive Property Law, Family Considerations, and the Interests of Women," 66 *Tulane L. Rev.* 919 (1992). On marriage, all of a woman's property and rights essentially fell under the guardianship of her husband, who became her legal representative. In addition, many women were married by arrangement of their parents and guardians, sometimes—if they were heiresses—for substantial payment. Finally, in a "status" society where birth meant a great deal, illegitimacy was a major threat to social stability. Upper class women lived cloistered and guarded lives "to prevent doubts about the parentage of the heir (*Id.*, 921)," while their men had no such constraints. Even to this day, the English monarchy ensures legitimacy by attempting to curtail women, but not men (*Id.*, 921).

Ironically, women of the working classes of both town and country had more leverage under such a system than the upper class women in their gilded cages. For the former, their labor made them valuable, and they could insist on better legal treatment. Particularly in the town and cities, such women ran shops and businesses, and developed independence. For the wealthy, such independence

Illustration 4-7   Pictures from the *Luttrell Psalter* of the different lives of medieval women, both the working poor and the aristocratic. From *Social England, supra,* (Cassell and Co., 1894), vol. 11, 141, 173.

only occurred if you survived your husband. English history and literature are full of powerful widows, such as Bess of Hardwicke, who survived four husbands to become one of England's most powerful women, and Chaucer's great character, the Wife of Bath, "housbondes at chirche dore she hadde fyve." See *The Works of Geoffrey Chaucer* (F.N. Robinson, ed., 2d ed., 1957), 21.

But such women were the exception. Most wealthy women lived closely curtailed lives, and some were even forced into convents to avoid loveless marriages. Where even the best upper class marriages were respectful, but arranged, partnerships, "courtly love" was a natural, romantic escape. Passionate but chaste, a "true love" manifested only by the tip of a helmet, or a tiny token of secret affection pinned to a spear or glove, these tales of chivalry and love were favorites in the closely guarded world of the English aristocracy. Chaucer's works are full of them. See, for example, the "Knight's Tale," "The Romaunt of the Rose," "Troilus and

Criseyde," and the "Legend of Good Women," in *The Works of Geoffrey Chaucer* (F.N. Robinson, ed., 2d ed., 1957), 25–46, 385–479, 480–518, 564–640. We will return to further discussions of the legal history of women in later chapters.

Pollock and Maitland, *History of English Law*, *supra* (2d ed., 1898), vol. I, 465–468, "Women."

§ 11. Women.

We have been rapidly diminishing the number of 'normal persons,' of free and lawful men. We have yet to speak of half the inhabitants of England. No text-writer, no statute, ever makes any general statement as to the position of women. This is treated as obvious, and we believe that it can be defined with some accuracy by one brief phrase:—private law with few exceptions puts women on a par with men; public law gives a woman no rights and exacts from her no duties, save that of paying taxes and performing such services as can be performed by deputy.

A very different doctrine is suggested by one ancient rule. A woman can never be outlawed, for a woman is never in law. We may well suppose this to come from a very remote time. But in Bracton's day it means nothing, for a woman, though she cannot be outlawed, can be 'waived,' declared a 'waif,' and 'waiver' seems to have all the effects of outlawry. Women are now 'in' all private law, and are the equals of men. The law of inheritance, it is true, shows a preference for males over females; but not a very strong preference, for a daughter will exclude a brother of the dead man, and the law of wardship and marriage, though it makes some difference between the male and the female ward, is almost equally severe for both. But the woman can hold land, even by military tenure, can own chattels, make a will, make a contract, can sue and be sued. She sues and is sued in person without the interposition of a guardian; she can plead with her own voice if she pleases; indeed—and this is a strong case— a married woman will sometimes appear as her husband's attorney. A widow will often be the guardian of her own children; a lady will often be the guardian of the children of her tenants.

The other half of our proposition, that which excludes women from all public functions, was subject to few if any real exceptions. In the thirteenth century the question whether a woman could inherit the crown of England must have been extremely doubtful, for the Empress had never been queen of England. Queens-consort and queens-dowager had acted as regents during the absence of their husbands or sons and presided in court and council. The line between office and property cannot always be exactly marked; it has been difficult to prevent the shrievalties from becoming hereditary; if a woman may be a *comitissa*, why not a *vice-comitissa*? Ornamental offices, hereditary grand serjeanties, women are allowed to carry to their husbands and to transmit to their heirs. So also, when the constitution of the House of Lords takes shape, the husbands of peeresses are summoned to sit there as 'tenants by the curtesy,' but peeresses are not summoned. 'The nearest approach to such a summons,' says Dr Stubbs, 'is that of four abbesses, who in 1306 were cited to a great council held to grant an aid on the knighting of the prince of Wales.'

In the nineteenth century our courts have more than once considered the question whether women did suit to the local moots, more especially to the county court, and have come to what we think is the right conclusion. Undoubtedly a woman might owe suit to the hundred or the county, or rather (for this we think to be the truer phrase) the land that she held might owe suit. Also it is certain that some sheriffs in the latter part of Henry III.'s reign had insisted on the personal attendance of women, not indeed at the county courts, but at those plenary meetings of the hundred courts that were known as the sheriff's turns. But it is equally certain that this exaction was regarded as an abuse and forbidden. We cannot doubt, though the evidence on this point is tacit rather than express, that women did the suit due from their land by deputy. Again, we never find women as jurors, except when, as not infrequently happened, some expectant heir alleged that there was a plot to supplant him by the production of a suppostitious child, in which case a jury of matrons was employed. To say that women could not be jurors is, in this period, almost equivalent to saying that they could not give evidence, but their names sometimes appear among the witnesses of charters. In all actions a plaintiff had to produce a suit (*secta*) of persons who in theory were prepared to testify on his behalf; we cannot find that he ever brought women. One of the actions in which such 'suitors' were of importance was the action of deciding whether a person was free or villein, and here Britton expressly tells us that a woman's testimony was not received, 'for the blood of a man shall not be tried by women'; the word of women, we are elsewhere told, cannot be admitted as proof, 'because of their frailty.' In the ecclesiastical courts the rule seems to have been that a woman's compurgators ought to be women, just as a man's compurgators ought to be men, but apparently in the king's court a woman had to find male oath-helpers. In one respect a woman's capacity of suing was curtailed by her inability to fight. A rule older than, but sanctioned by, the Great Charter prevented her from bringing an appeal of felony unless the crime of which she complained was violence to her person or the slaughter of her husband. In these excepted cases the accused must submit to trial by jury; at an earlier time one or the other of the parties would have been sent to the ordeal. In the thirteenth century this limitation of the right to make criminal charges was already becoming of little importance, since the procedure by way of appeal (that is, of private accusation) was giving place to the indictment.

On the whole we may say that, though it has no formulated theory about the position of women, a sure instinct has already guided the law to a general rule which will endure until our own time. As regards private rights women are on the same level as men, though postponed in the canons of inheritance; but public functions they have none. In the camp, at the council board, on the bench, in the jury box there is no place for them.

We have been speaking of women who are sole, who are spinsters or widows. Women who have husbands are in a different position. This, however, can be best discussed as part of family law, and under that title we shall also say what has to be said of infants. But here it may be well to observe that the main idea which governs the law of husband and wife is not that of an 'unity of person,' but that of guardianship, the *mund*, the profitable guardianship, which the husband has over the wife and over her property.

Note: What do you think of Pollock and Maitland's view of women's legal status as of 1898?

SEISIN

Pollock & Maitland, *The History of English Law* (2d ed, 1898, Cambridge) vol. 11, 29, 33, "Seisin."

§ 2. Seisin

In the history of our law there is no idea more cardinal than that of seisin. Even in the law of the present day it plays a part which must be studied by every lawyer; but in the past it was so important that we may almost say that the whole system of our land law was law about seisin and its consequences.

Seisin is possession. A few, but only a few words about etymology may be ventured. The inference has been too hastily drawn that this word speaks to us of a time of violence, when he who seized land was seised of it, when seizing land was the normal mode of acquiring possession. Now doubtless there is an etymological connexion between 'seizing' and being 'seised,' but the nature of that connexion is not very certain. If on the one hand 'seisin' is connected with 'to seize,' on the other hand it is connected with 'to sit' and 'to set':—the man who is seised is the man who is sitting on land; when he was put in seisin he was set there and made to sit there. Thus seisin seems to have the same root as the German *Besitz* and the Latin *possessio*. To our medieval lawyers the word *sesina* suggested the very opposite of violence; it suggested peace and quiet. It did so to Coke. 'And so it was said as *possessio* is derived *a pos et sedeo*, because he who is in possession may sit down in rest and quiet; so *seisina* also is derived *a sedendo*, for till he hath seisin all is *labor et dolor et vexatio spiritus*; but when he has obtained seisin, he may *sedere et acquiescere*.

*   *   *   *

When we say that seisin is possession, we use the latter term in the sense in which lawyers use it, a sense in which possession is quite distinct from, and may be sharply opposed to, proprietary right. In common talk we constantly speak as though possession were much the same thing as ownership. When a man says, 'I possess a watch,' he generally means, 'I own a watch.' Suppose that he has left his watch with a watchmaker for repair, and is asked whether he still possesses a watch, whether the watch is not in the watchmaker's possession, and if so whether both he and the watchmaker have possession of the same watch at the same time, he is perhaps a little puzzled and resents our questions as lawyers' impertinences. Even if the watch has been stolen, he is not very willing to admit that he no longer possesses a watch. This is instructive:—in our non-professional moments the term *possession* seems much nearer to our lips than the term *ownership*. Often however we do slur over the gulf by means of the conveniently ambiguous verbs 'have' and 'have got'—I have a watch, the watchmaker has it—I have a watch, but some one else has got it. But so soon as there is any law worthy of the name right and possession must emerge and be contrasted:—so soon as any one has said 'You have got what belongs to me,' the germs of these two notions have appeared and can be opposed to each other. Bracton is never tired of emphasizing the contrast; in so doing he constantly makes use of the Roman terms, *possessio* on the one hand, *proprietas* or *dominium* on the other. These are not the technical terms of English law; but it has terms which answer a like purpose, *seisina* on the one hand, *ius* on the other; the person who has right may not be seised, the person who is seised may not be seised of right.

W. S. Holdsworth, *An Historical Introduction to Land Law* (Oxford, 1927), 121–123, 127–128.

§ 8. Seisin and Possession.

We have seen that feudalism had two aspects. It was a branch of public law in so far as it placed governmental rights and duties on the owners of land. It was a branch of private law in so far as it defined the forms and modes of landowning. Our feudalized land law, therefore, had these two aspects. The theory of tenure, and the elaboration of its different forms, with which I have already dealt, were intimately related to the public aspect of the land law. They supplied this aspect of the land law with its background of principle. On the other hand, the theory of seisin and possession supplied the background of principle to the land law regarded as a branch of the private law of property; and, as the public aspect of the land law diminished, and its aspect as a branch of the law of property increased in importance, as the learning which centered round estates and interests in or over the land became more important than the learning which centred round the forms of tenure and their incidents, the theory of seisin and possession naturally began to be of much greater importance than the theory of tenure. In fact it still supplies the background of principle to many parts of the modern land law.

Let us begin by defining our terms. Seisin means possession. It is derived from the same root as the Roman *possessio* and the German *besitz*. 'The man who is seised is the man who is sitting on the land; when he was put in seisin he was set there and made to sit there.' During the medieval period the terms seisin and possession were used convertibly. One could talk of the seisin of chattels, or the possession of freehold interests in land. But, in the latter part of the fifteenth century, when Littleton was writing his book on Tenures, the term seisin came to be appropriated to describe the possession of freehold estates in the land, while the term possession was appropriated to chattels real or personal. It became definitely wrong to use the term possession in connexion with chattels. This change in terminology is due to the fact that the incidents of the seisin protected by the real actions, particularly the conditions under which it could be recovered by these actions, came to differ from the incidents of the possession protected by personal actions. It is true that, fundamentally, the main principles applicable to the seisin of freehold estates were then and always have been the same as those applicable to the possession of chattels. But, for all that, differences had arisen, owing to the development of these two allied conceptions in the sphere of different classes of actions, which could be aptly represented by this differentiation in terminology.

So much for terminology. Let us now endeavour to describe the theory of seisin which the medieval common lawyers worked out. It is necessary to grasp it, because, with some modifications with which I shall deal in a subsequent chapter, it dominates our modern land law.

This general theory is, of course, a generalization from the rules of mature systems of law. Primitive systems of law have not yet attained these abstract conceptions of ownership and possession. They are concerned rather with the invention and maintenance of rules for the settlement of disputes. Since this is their point of view, they naturally regard the man in possession of land as the owner. If his possession is disputed the plaintiff must prove his case. Till he has proved his case he has no right at all to the land. This was the point of view of the common law in the twelfth and thirteenth centuries. In the writ of right the plaintiff must show that he or his ancestors had a better right than the defendant to the land of which the defendant was seised. This he could do by showing that he or his ancestors had been in possession, or that he or they had done such acts—e.g. collected the rents—as only a possessor could do, and that he or they had been wrongfully deprived of possession by the defendant or his ancestors. The defendant must deny the plaintiff's claim and prove any facts which he has alleged to show that he has the better right to possession. But he could not say to the plaintiff, 'You have not proved your case because X, a third person, through whom neither of us claims, has a better right than either of us, and this I am prepared to prove.' Seeing that the plaintiff need only prove a better right to possession, and not an absolute *dominium*, the defendant could not rely upon a *jus tertii* through which he did not claim. The question at issue was the better right of the parties to possession; and, if this be the issue, such a *jus tertii* is merely irrelevant.

In this respect English and Roman law differ fundamentally. Roman law recognized an absolute *dominium*, so that in Roman law *dominium* and *possessio* can be and are sharply contrasted. In English law we can only compare seisin with seisin, the seisin protected by the writ of right with that protected by the writ of entry, the seisin protected by the writ of entry with that protected by the novel disseisin—the older, in short, with the more recent. English law protects seisin and various rights to seisin of varying dates by different forms of action.

English law, therefore, regarded the person seised as the owner. It gave facilities to the man wrongfully disseised to recover his seisin. But, till he recovered it, he had no more right to the land than any stranger. It is to the man seised that the law gives all the advantages and privileges of ownership. The man disseised has no single one of these advantages and privileges.

*   *   *   *

But it is obvious that some parts of this theory will gradually come to look anomalous in a more orderly state of society, and in a more developed system of law. It will seem anomalous to regard only the rights of the person seised— seised rightfully or wrongfully, and to disregard the rights of the man who is wrongfully disseised. This changed point of view is apparent at the latter part of the medieval period. In most cases the man wrongfully disseised had been given a right of entry; and the omission to pass statutes of limitation extended his rights of action. One or two cases, indeed, were left till 1833, in which the disseised owner had no right of entry—but they remained only as anomalous survivals. The result of this development was not to curtail the advantages possessed by the man seised as against the world at large, nor to give the greater powers of disposition to the man disseised—the man seised could still alienate, and the man disseised was still unable to alienate. The result was to make the seisin the wrongdoer, and his acts done while wrongfully seised, more easily defeasible by the man who had a better right to get seisin. Moreover, it was still true in the Middle Ages and much later, that the law did not recognize an abstract right of ownership, but only seisin and rights to get seisin. We shall see that it was not till the eighteenth century, and under the influence of ideas which grew up round the action of ejectment, that the disseised owner, who was seeking to recover on the strength of a right to seisin, must prove not merely a better right than the man seised, but an absolutely good right. It is not till then that it can be said that English law recognized an abstract right of ownership; and, even then, it did not depart from its original conception that the man seised, whether rightfully or wrongfully, is prima facie owner, and has therefore all the rights of an owner. No doubt his rights, and his dealings with the land in the exercise of these rights, are defeasible if his prima facie ownership is disproved; but, till it is disproved, he has these rights.

"OPEN FIELDS" AND RIGHTS OF COMMON

C.S. Orwin, *The Open Fields*, 36, 39–41, 61–62 (1954). [Courtesy Oxford University Press]

The origin of the [open field] system is lost in the days of prehistory, and any attempt to describe it can be based only upon conjecture and upon the interpretation of its earliest manifestations in recorded times. It must be remembered that communal systems of cultivation were not peculiar to Britain and to neighbouring European countries from which Britain was colonized. Farming in Open Fields under conditions resembling our own was general all over the plains of Europe and central Asia and it persists today over large areas in some countries....

It must be remembered that in those early days, whenever they were, and indeed for long centuries after, life was a pretty grim business. The task of keeping body and soul together was hazardous, quite apart from the possibility of misadventures with hostile neighbours or wild beasts. Men had to support themselves and their families by the work of their hands, and in the earliest days much of their time was occupied in rendering services in lieu of rent. Unequipped as they were with anything beyond the simplest aids to manual labour, the extent of land which they were able to handle gave them no more than a bare subsistence in a normal season and very short commons in a bad one. It follows that every minute of their own time was needed for productive work, and their farming system had to dispense with much that in an age of large-scale operations conducted with the aid of machinery and mechanical power is regarded as indispensable. For instance, the subdivision of the reclaimed land into fields grouped together to form separate farms was never contemplated by them before the period in which modern history begins. To make and maintain hedges and gates would have meant so much time taken from the cultivation of the land or the tending of live stock; to group fields thus created into farms would have given some members of the village community the advantage of holdings near their homes while entailing upon others the disadvantage of having to walk varying distances to reach theirs. In those days such handicaps could not be compensated. To secure protection, shelter, and water the people herded together in the village; there were no homesteads built on or near the remoter parts of the cleared area. With the development in modern times of commercial farming, inequalities in convenience or in productivity between the compact holdings which came to be created could be, and they were, adjusted by differences in rent. No such equalization was possible in the days when farmers were self-sufficient.

And so we get the origin of the Open Fields. They were the clearings in the natural woods and waste made by communities of tillage farmers and occupied by them in large areas, as cleared, without any attempt at subdivision by a process of inclosure. But how was the land in these fields allotted between man and man? We know what was done, but we can only conjecture how and why it was done, and the most probable explanation is to be found *in the action of the plough*. When every one was farming for subsistence, every one would follow, naturally enough, the same farming system. The land first cleared for cultivation would be that immediately adjacent to the settlement, and upon this the men of the community would go to work, setting out a day's ploughing for each team, side by side. By the end of the working-day each would have ploughed one or more 'lands,' according to the nature of the soil and the length of the 'lands'. Next day the village husbandmen would move on, to set out and then to plough the section of the field next beyond the first day's work, and thus they would proceed throughout the ploughing season. So, at the finish, every man would have land ready for sowing which consisted not of a compact field or group of fields but of a number of narrow strips, each consisting of one or more 'lands' making up a day's plough-work, and each of them divided from the next by those of his neighbours.

An allocation of the Open Field in this way was the natural consequence of a self-sufficient community following the same farming system for the same purpose, and cultivating the soil with the plough. Incidentally, also, it was the fairest, for it gave to each member an equal share of the near and of the remoter land, and of the good and of the less good parts of the field if it were not uniform in every part....

This, then, was the economy of the open-field land system as it developed in England. Remembering the equal need of all to extract their subsistence from the soil, its balance and fitness are at once apparent. Each of the village farmers had so much land as his own hands and implements could cultivate in the year. Each one followed the same system of husbandry. The method by which the holdings were distributed followed upon the simultaneous employment of every one upon the same task in the same season of the year, both in the arable fields and in the meadows. It resulted in holdings divided into strips of a day's work each, scattered evenly over the whole of the land, giving to every one, incidentally, but only incidentally, an equal share in the advantages and in the disadvantages of soils and situation.

Further, the farming system thus evolved spread the work evenly through the seasons. Autumn sowing on the fallow was followed by winter cultivation of the stubble and spring sowing, after which fallow cultivation and hay-making occupied the farmer until the corn harvest finished the farming year. The livestock fitted naturally into this system, the commons and the aftermath of the meadows providing their summer and autumn keep, which was supplemented after harvest by the stubbles and sikes of the Open Fields, while the hay and straw kept them through the winter, until, in springtime, the grass on the commons began to grow again.

The system of farming in Open Fields was common in England by the time that historical records of land-tenure begin; and from thence onward through the centuries, until their enclosure was virtually complete, say, a hundred years ago, its fundamental characteristics had undergone no change. The essence of the system was that it demanded the rigid adherence of every member of the village community. The right, jealousy guarded, of a common grazing on the stubbles made it impossible for anyone to grow a crop which would still be unharvested when his

Illustration 4-8   Ancient Open Field systems. Laxton (below) and Crimscote (above). Note the ridge and furrow plough marks. Laxton still retains a medieval Open Field system today. Courtesy AeroFilms, Ltd.

neighbours had gathered their corn. It was this rigidity in the system which killed it, ultimately, as knowledge of new crops and more productive methods developed, while at the same time the pace of change was that of the slowest.

Statute of Westminster II, 13 Edward I, c. 46. (1285)

Whereas in a statute made at Merton it was granted that lords of wastes, woods, and pastures might approve [improve] the said wastes, woods, and pastures, notwithstanding the contradiction of their tenants, so that the tenants had sufficient pasture to their tenements, with free egress and regress to the same; and, forasmuch as no mention was made between neighbours and neighbours, many lords of wastes, woods, and pastures have been hindered heretofore by the contradiction of neighbours having sufficient pasture; and because foreign tenants have no more right to common in the wastes, woods, or pastures of any lord, than the lord's own tenants; It is ordained that the statute of Merton, provided between the lord and his tenants, from henceforth shall hold place between lords of wastes, woods, and pastures and their neighbours, saving sufficient pasture to their tenants and neighbours, so that the lords of such wastes, woods, and pastures may make approvement of the residue. And this shall be observed for such as claim pasture as appurtenant to their tenements. But if any do claim common by special feoffment or grant for a certain number of beasts, or otherwise, which he ought to have a common right, whereas covenant barreth the law, he shall have such recovery as he ought to have had, by form of the grant made unto him. By occasion of a windmill, sheepcote, deyry, enlarging of a court necessary, or courtelage, from henceforth no man shall be grieved by assise of novel disseisin for common of pasture. And where sometime it chanceth, that one having right to approve doth then levy a dyke or an hedge, and some by night or at another season when they suppose not to be espied do overthrow the hedge or dyke, and it cannot be known by verdict of the assise or jury who did overthrow the hedge or dyke, and men of the towns near will not indict such as be guilty of the fact, the towns near adjoining shall be distrained to levy the hedge or dyke at their own cost, and to yield damages. And where one, having no right to common, usurpeth common, what time an heir is within age, or a woman is covert, or while the pasture is in the hands of the tenants in dower, by the courtesy, or otherwise, for term of life or years, or in fee tail, and have long time used the pasture, many hold opinion that such pastures ought to be said to belong to the freehold, and that the possessor ought to have action by writ of novel disseisin if he be deforced of such pasture; but from henceforth this must be holden that such as have entered within the time that an assise of mortdauncester hath lien, if they had no common before, shall have no recovery by a writ of novel disseisin if they be deforced.

[Trans. K.E. Digby, from *An Introduction to the History of the Law of Real Property* (Oxford, 5th ed., 1897), 232–233.]

Bracton's Notebook, No. 835

(Common Pleas, 1234). The Abbot Reginald complains (*queritur*) that Unfrid of Gravele, William of Norwych of Acle, Nicholas the picker and all the others named in the writ, as appears in the record of Trinity term on the morrow if St.

John's, with force and arms and against the peace of the lord king fished in the fishery of the said Abbot between the bridge of Weybridge and the bridge of Frogham were they should not and are not accustomed to fish and took away the stakes of the said Abbot, and he says that his church was seised from the conquest of England, as of a fishery that always belonged exclusively to his church, and thereby he is worse off, etc.

And Unfrid and all the others came on another day and said that they fished in that fishery through Roger and Earl Bigod and they call him to warranty. And he now comes and warrants that they are his men and villeins and that they fished through him.

[Earl Roger then asserts immemorial rights of common in the fishery, on which his land abuts, and denies that the rights of the Abbot's church are exclusive; as to this issue he places himself on the country. The Abbot reasserts an immemorial and exclusive right to the fishery.]

And the Earl denies all this and places himself on the grand assize of the lord king and asks a recognition [by the assize] whether he has a right to fish in that fishery together with the said Abbot, or whether the said Abbot [has a right] to hold the fishery exclusively within the above limits and without rights of common in the Earl....and in the meantime the Earl to remain in seisin of the common. (*Bracton's Notebook*, no. 835.) (J.P. Dawson, ed.)

THE STATUTES OF EDWARD I

The Statute "*Quia Emptores*" 18 Edward I, c.1. (1290) (trans., K.E. Digby, *supra*, 237–238.)

c. i. Forasmuch as purchasers of lands and tenements of the fees of great men and other lords have many times heretofore entered into their fees, to the prejudice of the lords, to whom the freeholders of such great men have sold their lands and tenements to be holden in fee of their feoffors and not of the chief lords of the fees, whereby the same chief lords have many times lost their escheats, marriages, and wardships of lands and tenements belonging to their fees, which thing seems very hard and extreme unto those lords and other great men, and moreover in this case manifest disinheritance, our lord the King in his parliament at Westminster after Easter the eighteenth year of his reign, that is to wit in the quinzine of Saint John Baptist, at the instance of the great men of the realm granted, provided, and ordained, that from henceforth it should be lawful to every freeman to sell at his own pleasure his lands and tenements or part of them, so that the feoffee shall hold the same lands or tenements of the chief lord of the same fee, by such service and customs as his feoffer held before.

c. ii. And if he sell any part of such lands or tenements to any, the feoffee shall immediately hold it of the chief lord, and shall be forthwith charged with the services for so much as pertaineth or ought to pertain to the said chief lord, for the same parcel, according to the quantity of the land or tenement so sold; and so in this case the same part of the service shall remain to the lord, to be taken by the hands of the feoffee, for the which he ought to be attendant and answerable to the same chief lord according to the quantity of the land or tenement sold for the parcel of the service so due.

Illustration 4-9   The Parliament of Edward I. The ecclesiastical lords are to the left, the secular lords to the right, and the judges are on woolsacks to the middle. To this day, the Lord Chancellor sits on a wool sack. (Courtesy Royal Collection Enterprises Ltd. © Her Majesty Queen Elizabeth II. Windsor Royal Library, Heraldic MS. 2, Fol. 8v.)

c. iii. And it is to be understood that by the said sales or purchases of lands or tenements, or any parcel of them, such lands or tenements shall in no wise come into mortmain, either in part or in whole, neither by policy nor craft, contrary to the form of the statute made thereupon of late. And it is to wit that this statute extendeth but only to lands holden in fee simple, and that it extendeth to the time coming. And it shall begin to take effect at the Feast of Saint Andrew the Apostle next coming.

"The Statute Quia Emptores, 1290" from R.E. Megarry, H.W.R. Wade, *The Law of Real Property* (4th ed.), 1975, 30–32. [Courtesy Sweet & Maxwell.]

(a) The statute. Magna Carta, 1217, c. 39, had attempted to meet the lords' objections by prohibiting alienations which left insufficient security for the services. But dissatisfaction continued until a revolutionary settlement was made by the statute *Quia Emptores*, 1290. The effect of this was as follows:

(i)   Alienation by subinfeudation was prohibited (c. 1).
(ii) All free tenants were authorised to alienate the whole or part of their land by substitution, without the lord's consent, the new tenant to hold by the same services as the old (c. 1).
(iii) On alienation of part of the land by substitution, the feudal services were to be apportioned (c. 2).
(iv) The statute applied only to grants in fee simple (c. 3).

(b) Effect of the statute. Quia Emptores marked the victory of the modern concept of land as alienable property over the more restrictive principles of feudalism. For no new tenures in fee simple could thenceforth be created except by the Crown. Existing tenures could be freely transferred from hand to hand, and they could be extinguished as before by escheat or forfeiture. The network of tenures could therefore no longer grow; it could only contract. Every conveyance of land in fee simple by a subject after 1290 was bound to be an out-and-out transfer and could not create the relationship of lord and tenant between the parties. On such a conveyance no services could be reserved; any rights reserved, such as a rent, must be rights existing independently of the relationship of lord and tenant. Nor could any fines for alienation be lawfully demanded by any subject.

(c) Limits of statute. Since the statute was expressly confined to alienations in fee simple, it did not prevent a tenant in fee simple from granting a life estate or a fee tail to another to hold of him as lord. Further, as it did not mention the Crown either expressly or by necessary implication, the Crown was not bound by it. Consequently the statute conferred no right of free alienation upon tenants in chief, and an Ordinance of 1256 forbidding them to alienate without a royal licence remained effective. However, in 1327 tenants in chief were given a right of free alienation, subject only to the payment of a reasonable fine in some cases, and the Tenures Abolition Act, 1660, abolished this fine. Nor did the Statute prevent the Crown from granting land to be held of the Crown; but the Tenures Abolition Act, 1660, provided that such grants could be made only in common socage.

(d) Effect today. Quia Emptores, 1290, is still in force today and may be regarded as one of the pillars of the law of real property. It operates every time that a conveyance in fee simple is executed, automatically shifting that status of tenant from grantor to grantee and fulfilling the rule that all land held by a subject shall be held in tenure of the Crown either mediately or immediately. The lord of the fee is the successor in title to the person who was lord in 1290, for there can have been no change in the tenure since then. But it is rare for records of a mesne lordship to have been preserved for so long, except in the case of manors where mesne tenure remained of importance until 1925 and later. Other cases are governed by the presumption that, if no mesne lord appears, the land is held immediately of the Crown. Innumerable mesne lordships came to be forgotten as, with the passage of time and the inflation of the cur-

rency, the ancient services or commutation rents ceased to be worth collecting. After 1290 the feudal pyramid began to crumble. The number of mesne lordships could not be increased, evidence of existing mesne lordships gradually disappeared with the passing of time, and so most land came to be held directly from the Crown.

Sect. 2. The Tenures Abolition Act, 1660

1. Tenures. The system of landholding in return for services fell into decay long before the most onerous incidents of tenure were legally abolished. In particular, the incidents of military tenure, such as wardships, marriages and aids, were zealously preserved by the Crown for the sake of revenue. The King, who was always lord and never tenant, was the only proprietor who had all to gain and nothing to lose by preserving these feudal imposts. But, like certain other items of unparliamentary revenue, they were swept away in the seventeenth century. The Tenures Abolition Act, 1660, confirming a resolution of the Long Parliament of 1646, converted all tenures into free and common socage with the exceptions of frankalmoign and copyhold.

2. Incidents. The statute also abolished many burdensome incidents, including aids for the knighting of the lord's eldest son and the marriage of his eldest daughter, wardships, marriages, primer seisin, *ouster le main*, and most fines for alienation; and it abolished the Court of Wards and Liveries which the Crown had set up to enforce some of these incidents against tenants *in capite*. The Crown was compensated for its loss of revenue by the imposition of a tax on beer and other beverages. Fixed rents, heriots and suit of court were expressly saved, and reliefs were restricted to those payable for land of socage tenure, *i.e.*, one year's rent. Since it was uncommon for military tenure to be subject to rent, relief in effect disappeared with the other incidents.

3. Summary. The principal results of the Act may be summarised thus:

> (a) Nearly all burdensome incidents were abolished for all land of free tenure. Escheat and forfeiture survived as the only important incidents of free tenure. Fealty survived, but was of no importance.
>
> (b) All free tenures were converted into free and common socage and no other type of tenure might be created in future. But the Act preserved, *inter alia*, (i) copyhold, (ii) frankalmoign, (iii) the honorary incidents of grand sergeanty, and (iv) services incident to socage (*e.g.*, those of petty sergeanty). Customs such as gavelkind and borough English, and the peculiarities of ancient demesne, continued unaltered.

[Note: When English law was "received" in America, the real property system in England remained pretty much as left by the Tenures Abolition Act, 1660. As we will see, there were a few abortive attempts at "copyhold", but free and common socage ("freehold") held the day. In 1922, the English finally "enfranchised" all copyhold land, i.e., made it land of freehold (socage) tenure, by the Law of Property Act, 1922. Frankalmoign, long obsolete because it could not survive any alienation after 1290 (*Quia Emptores*), was formally abolished. Gavelkind, borough English, and all other special customs of inheritance, were replaced by a new system of intestate succession. Now all land is held in freehold—i.e., free and common socage.]

The Statute *"De Donis"* (Statute of Westminster II, c.1.) 13 Edw. I, c.1. (1285) (Excerpted)

First, concerning lands that many times are given upon condition, that is, to wit, where any giveth his land to any man and his wife, and to the heirs begotten of the bodies of the same man and his wife, with such condition expressed that if the same man and his wife die without heir of their bodies between them begotten, the land so given shall revert to the giver or his heir; in case also where one giveth lands in free marriage, which gift hath a condition annexed, though it be not expressed in the deed of the gift, which is this, that if the husband and wife die without heir of their bodies begotten, the land so given shall revert to the giver or his heir; in case also where one giveth land to another and the heirs of his body issuing, it seemed very hard and yet seemeth to the givers and their heirs, that their will being expressed in the gift was not heretofore nor yet is observed. In all the cases aforesaid after issue begotten and born between them, to whom the lands were given under such condition, heretofore such feoffees had power to aliene the land so given, and to disinherit their issue of the land, contrary to the minds of the givers, and contrary to the form expressed in the gift. And further, when the issue of such feoffee is failing, the land so given ought to return to the giver or his heir by form of gift expressed in the deed, though the issue, if any were, had died; yet by the deed and feoffment of them, to whom land was so given upon condition, the donors have heretofore been barred of their reversion of the same tenements which was directly repugnant to the form of the gift: wherefore our lord the king, perceiving how necessary and expedient it should be to provide remedy in the aforesaid cases, hath ordained, that the will of the giver according to the form in the deed of gift manifestly expressed shall be from henceforth observed, so that they to whom the land was given under such condition shall have no power to aliene the land so given, but that it shall remain unto the issue of them to whom it was given after their death, or shall revert unto the giver or his heirs if issue fail, either by reason that there is no issue at all, or if any issue be, it fail by death, the heir of such issue failing. * * * *

[Translation, K.E. Digby, *An Introduction to the History of the Law of Real Property, supra,* 1897, 5th ed., Oxford, 229–230.]

Note: The Statute *De Donis,* as judicially construed, permitted great English landed families to "lock-in" their land for generations. Was this good or bad? Almost all great English estates were entailed, with some remaining intact to the present day.

As the following note describes, lawyers eventually evaded the Act by use of an outrageous legal fiction, the "fine and recovery."

W.S. Holdsworth, *An Historical Introduction to the Land Law* (Oxford, 1927), pp. 55–60.

"The Estate Tail"

(ii) *The estate tail.* Before 1285 a gift to a man and the heirs of his body created a fee simple conditional. That is, it was construed as a gift to a man and his heirs (i.e., a fee simple) conditionally upon his having an heir of his body. Thus, if an heir were born alive (whether he survived or not) the condition was ful-

COUNTRY LIFE

Vol. CLXXXIX No. 11   *MARCH 16, 1995*

THE EARL AND COUNTESS HOWE WITH THEIR FAMILY

The Earl and Countess Howe, of Penn House, Penn, Buckinghamshire, at the christening
of their son, Viscount Curzon, in the parish church at Penn, where many of his ancestors
have been christened since the 15th century. With them are their daughters *(from left)*,
Lady Anne Curzon, Lady Flora Curzon and Lady Lucinda Curzon.

Illustration 4-10   A distinguished English family at the christening of their fourth child and
first son, Viscount Curzon. (Courtesy June Buck/Country Life Picture Library, March 16,
1995, frontis.)

filled, and the donee got a fee simple, which he could alienate, which would be forfeited if he committed treason, or would escheat if he committed felony. If, on the other hand, the donee had never had an heir, or if he had had an heir who had predeceased him and he had not alienated the estate, the land reverted to the donor. This interpretation disappointed the intentions of the donors, and so the great landowners procured the passing, in 1285, of the statute De Donis Conditionalibus, which created the estate tail. It was so called because it was an estate the descent of which was cut down (*talliatum*) to the heirs of the body of the donee.

The statute provided that, for the future, the land should descend according to the terms of the gift (*secundum formam in carta expressam*), and that donees should have no power to deprive their issue, or persons entitled in reversion or remainder, of the land given to them. The donee in tail could alienate the property, but the estate which he created could not last for a longer period than his own life; for the statute gave to the issue, the reversioners, and the remaindermen writs of formedon (*forma doni*), by means of which they could recover their interests when they fell into possession. It was ultimately held that the words of the statute must be interpreted to mean that, not only the first donee in tail, but also the whole series of his issue, could thus be restrained from alienating the estate for a longer period than their own lives.

The restrictions placed by the statute, as thus interpreted, upon tenants in tail were soon found to be not only irksome, but productive of great injustice. Parliament was petitioned for its repeal, but these petitions were always rejected.

> 'The truth was that the lords and commons, knowing that their estates tail were not to be forfeited for felony or treason; as their estates of inheritance were before the said Act...and finding that they were not answerable for the debts or incumbrances of their ancestors, nor did the sales, alienations, or leases of their ancestors bind them for the lands which were entailed to their ancestors, they always rejected such bills.'
>
> [Mildmay's Case, 1606, 6 Co. Rep. at F. 40b.]

In default of Parliamentary aid the ingenuity of the legal profession set itself to work to evade the statute.

The expedients which were ultimately adopted to effect this purpose were the fictitious legal proceedings known as recoveries and fines.

A recovery was a fictitious real action, pursued through all its stages to final judgement. But a recovery by itself would not have been efficacious, since these collusive recoveries were voidable. But the machinery of a recovery was made efficacious by combining it with the doctrine of warranty. If A had given land to B and his heirs, and had bound himself and his heirs to warrant B's title, and X claimed the land from B, B could call on A to fulfil his duty of warranting the title—he vouched A to warranty. If A admitted his duty to warrant the title, X's action went on against A. If X succeeded in his action, the court gave judgement that X do recover the land from B, and that A convey lands to B of equal value. These rules were applied to the estate tail as follows: X, a friend of A the tenant in tail, brought a writ of right in the court of Common Pleas claiming the land from A for an estate in fee simple. A vouched to warranty Y—a man of straw. Y admitted the duty to warrant, asked to be allowed to talk the matter over out of the court with X, "crave leave to impart," and then departed in contempt of the court. X therefore recovered the land from A for an estate in fee simple—which he at once conveyed to A; and A got judgement against Y ordering him to convey to A lands of equal value. This judgement Y was wholly unable to satisfy; but this fact the courts regarded as quite immaterial—they had done their best. If, however, lands had been conveyed by Y to A in accordance with the judgement, all the persons interested in the entailed lands would have been compensated. It was for this reason that a recovery barred all those interested in the entailed lands—issue, remainder-men, and reversioners.[1] In later law all this elaborate process was not gone through. The steps in the fictitious action were merely enrolled on the records of the court. The part of Y was played by the crier of the court of Common Pleas, who received for his services the sum of 4d. for each occasion on which he acted. He was known as the common vouchee, because he was vouched to warranty by all those who suffered a recovery.[2]

A fine was a fictitious personal action which was compromised—hence the name *finalis concordia*. The statute De Donis had enacted that a fine should have no effect on an estate tail. But, by virtue of statutes of the reigns of Henry VII and VIII, a fine was allowed to bar the issue, but not the reversioners or remainder-men.[1] Thus the person in whose favour the fine was levied got an estate which was like a fee simple in that it descended to his heirs general. But it was unlike a fee simple in that it was cut short if the issue of the tenant in tail failed. The estate was known as a base fee.

It was therefore only a recovery which completely barred the estate tail. But, because a recovery was a real action, it must be begun against the man in possession of the first estate of freehold. Now estates tail were usually created by family settlements, under the limitations of which the father had an estate for life, and his son the first estate tail. Since the action must be begun against the father, the son could not completely bar the estate tail without his father's consent. That consent was not required for a fine, because, being a personal action, it could be begun against the tenant in tail; but, by the levy of a fine, only a base fee could be created; and that was not a marketable commodity. The result of this procedural rule was therefore beneficial. It is for this reason that it has outlived the old processes to which it owed its origin.

Fines and recoveries were abolished in 1833;[2] and the Act, while retaining the substance of the old law, substituted, as Blackstone had suggested,[3] the simple machinery of a deed enrolled, formerly in the court of Chancery, and later in the Central Office of the Supreme Court. A tenant in tail of full age, whose interest was in possession, could in this way completely bar his estate tail, and turn it into an estate in fee simple. But if the tenant in tail's estate was not in possession, he could not effect a complete bar without the consent of the protector of the settlement, who was usually the man in possession of the first estate of freehold. If he tried to bar the estate tail without the consent of the protector, he could only cre-

---

1. Exactly when this expedient for barring an estate tail was introduced is not certain, Holdsworth, H. E. L. (3rd ed.), iii. 118–19; *Taltarum's Case* (1472), Y.B. 12 Ed. IV, Mich. pl. 25 shows that the expedient of a common recovery was then well known.

2. As Sir F. Pollock has said (The Land Laws, 84) the crier of the court of Common Pleas thus 'passed his life cheerfully and not ungainfully in perpetual contempt of the court of Common Pleas and liability to be fined at the king's discretion'.

1. 4 Henry VII, c. 24; 32 Henry VIII, c. 36.

2. 3, 4, William IV, c. 74

3. Comm. ii. 361.

Illustration 4-11   The Seal of Edward I, *Social England, supra*, vol. 121, 5. (Cassell & Co., 1894.)

ate a base fee. The Law of Property Act 1925 has retained the substance of the old law as to barring estates tail; but it has modified it in two ways. In the first place, the disentailing deed need not be enrolled. In the second place, an estate tail can be barred by will, if the property entailed, the instrument under which it was acquired, or entailed property generally, is referred to specifically in the will.

ROBIN HOOD

Note: Students frequently ask why, as a practical matter, feudal lords met their duties under feudal custom to their tenants or, even more remarkably, to the powerless unfree serfs. One simple answer is that the "good lord" saw these duties as dictated by good moral conduct and by religious obligation. Good feudal conduct could also be in the lord's long term best economic interest. Actual uprisings, such as were experienced by King John from his chief tenants or in the Peasant Revolt of 1381, were rare. But there could be labor shortages caused by disease and other factors. Outbreaks of the plague in 1349 (the "Black Death"), 1360–2, 1369 and 1375 caused such shortages. A loyal peasantry would be inclined to stay on the land, but an abused peasantry could be lured away, legally or illegally, by rival lords.

There was also a more sinister inducement to good conduct. Peasants who were pressed too hard sometimes simply gave up, and retreated to the forests. These "outlaws" could be dangerous, living by poaching and robbery. It is interesting that today we romanticize these figures. For example, take "Robin Hood" and his "Merrie Men." If such desperation was caused by a "hard" lord, "outlaws" could easily have had secret support among the populace. Thus must have begun the legends of "good" outlaws, like "Robin Hood."

Robert Louis Stevenson was a great student of history, and his novel, *The Black Arrow*, paints a compelling, and largely accurate, picture of why a feudal lord had to behave, or "watch his back." It also paints a largely correct picture of life in a feudal manor during the Wars of the Roses.

You will also note, in the following passages, references to how Sir Daniel Brackley cheated on his legal obligation to preserve the property of his underage ward, Richard Shelton. This was something King John and his followers also did to their wards, and it was prohibited explicitly by the *Magna Carta*, chapters 3 and 4, set out in Chapter 3, *supra*.

For a good account of the legends of "William Robenhod," which date back to 1262, and the accompanying "culture of protest," see Edmund King, *Medieval England* (Oxford, 1988), 206–207.

Robert Louis Stevenson, *The Black Arrow* (1888, Charles Scribners' Sons), pp. 3–11.

PROLOGUE

JOHN AMEND-ALL

On a certain afternoon, in the late springtime, the bell upon Tunstall Moat House was heard ringing at an unaccustomed hour. Far and near, in the forest and in the fields along the river, people began to desert their labours and hurry towards the sound; and in Tunstall hamlet a group of poor countryfolk stood wondering at the summons.

Tunstall hamlet at that period, in the reign of old King Henry VI, wore much the same appearance as it wears today. A score or so of houses, heavily framed with oak, stood scattered in a long green valley ascending from the river. At the foot, the road crossed a bridge, and mounting on the other side, disappeared into the fringes of the forest on its way to the Moat House, and further forth to Holywood Abbey. Half-way up the village, the church stood among yews. On every side the slopes were crowned and the view bounded by green elms and greening oak-trees of the forest.

Hard by the bridge, there was a stone cross upon a knoll, and here the group had collected—half-a-dozen women and one tall fellow in a russet smock—discussing what the bell betided. An express had gone through the hamlet half an hour before, and drunk a pot of ale in the saddle, not daring to dismount for the hurry of his errand; but he had been ignorant himself of what was forward, and only bore sealed letters from Sir Daniel Brackley to Sir Oliver Oates, the parson, who kept the Moat House in the master's absence.

But now there was the noise of a horse; and soon, out of the edge of the wood and over the echoing bridge, there rode up young Master Richard Shelton, Sir Daniel's ward. He, at the least, would know, and they hailed him and begged him to explain. He drew bridle willingly enough—a young fellow not yet eighteen, sunbrowned and grey-eyed, in a jacket of deer's leather, with a black velvet collar, a green hood upon his head, and a steel cross-bow at his back. The express, it appeared, had brought great news. A battle was impending. Sir Daniel had sent for every man that could draw a bow or carry a bill to go post-haste to Kettley, under pain of his severe displeasure; but for whom they were to fight, or of where the battle was expected, Dick knew nothing. Sir Oliver would come shortly himself, and Bennet Hatch was arming at that moment, for he it was who should lead the party.

"It is the ruin of this kind land," a woman said. "If the barons live at war, ploughfolk must eat roots."

"Nay," said Dick, "every man that follows shall have sixpence a day, and archers twelve."

"If they live," returned the woman, "that may very well be; but how if they die, my master?"

"They cannot better die than for their natural lord," said Dick.

"No natural lord of mine," said the man in the smock. "I followed the Walsinghams; so we all did down Brierly way, till two years ago, come Candlemas. And now I must side with Brackley! It was the law that did it; call ye that natural? But now, what with Sir Daniel and what with Sir Oliver—that knows more of the law than honesty—I have no natural lord but poor King Harry the Sixt, God bless him!—the poor innocent that cannot tell his right hand from his left."

"Ye speak with an ill tongue, friend," answered Dick, "to miscall your good master and my lord the king in the same libel. But King Harry—praised be the saints!—has come again into his right mind, and will have all things peaceably ordained. And as for Sir Daniel, y' are very brave behind his back. But I will be no tale-bearer; and let that suffice."

"I say no harm of you, Master Richard," returned the peasant. "Y' are a lad; but when ye come to a man's inches, ye will find ye have an empty pocket. I say no more: the saints help Sir Daniel's neighbours, and the Blessed Maid protect his wards!"

"Clipsby," said Richard, "you speak what I cannot hear with honour. Sir Daniel is my good master, and my guardian."

"Come, now, will ye read me a riddle?" returned Clipsby. "On whose side is Sir Daniel?"

"I know not," said Dick, colouring a little; for his guardian had changed sides continually in the troubles of that period, and every change had brought him some increase of fortune.

"Ay," returned Clipsby, "you, nor no man. For, indeed, he is one that goes to bed Lancaster and gets up York."

Just then the bridge rang under horse-shoe iron, and the party turned and saw Bennet Hatch come galloping—a brown-faced, grizzled fellow, heavy of hand and grim of mien, armed with sword and spear, a steel salet on his head, a leather jack upon his body. He was a great man in these parts; Sir Daniel's right hand in peace and war, and at that time, by his master's interest, bailiff of the hundred.

"Clipsby," he shouted, "off to the Moat House, and send all other laggards the same gate. Bowyer will give you jack and salet. We must ride before curfew. Look to it: he that is last at the lych-gate Sir Daniel shall reward. Look to it right well! I know you for a man of naught. Nance," he added, to one of the women, "is old Appleyard up town?"

"I'll warrant you," replied the woman. "In his field, for sure."

So the group dispersed, and while Clipsby walked leisurely over the bridge, Bennet and young Shelton rode up the road together, through the village and past the church.

"Ye will see the old shrew," said Bennet. "He will waste more time grumbling and prating of Harry the fift than would serve a man to shoe a horse. And all because he has been to the French wars!"

The house to which they were bound was the last in the village, standing alone among lilacs; and beyond it, on three sides, there was open meadow rising towards the borders of the wood.

Hatch dismounted, threw his rein over the fence, and walked down the field, Dick keeping close at his elbow, to where the old soldier was digging, knee-deep in his cabbages, and now and again, in a cracked voice, singing a snatch of song. He was all dressed in leather, only his hood and tippet were of black frieze, and tied with scarlet; his face was like a walnut-shell, both for colour and wrinkles; but his old grey eye was still clear enough, and his sight unabated. Perhaps he was deaf; perhaps he thought it unworthy of an old archer of Agincourt to pay any heed to such disturbances; but neither the surly notes of the alarm bell, nor the near approach of Bennet and the lad, appeared at all to move him; and he continued obstinately digging, and piped up, very thin and shaky:

"Now, dear lady, if thy will be, I pray you that you will rue on me."

"Nick Appleyard," said Hatch, "Sir Oliver commends him to you, and bids that ye shall come within this hour to the Moat House, there to take command."

The old fellow looked up.

"Save you, my masters!" he said, grinning. "And where goeth Master Hatch?"

"Master Hatch is off to Kettley, with every man that we can horse," returned Bennet. "There is a fight toward, it seems, and my lord stays a reinforcement."

"Ay, verily," returned Appleyard. "And what will ye leave me to garrison withal?"

"I leave you six good men, and Sir Oliver to boot," answered Hatch.

"It'll not hold the place," said Appleyard; "the number sufficeth not. It would take two-score to make it good."

"Why, it's for that we came to you, old shrew!" replied the other. "Who else is there but you that could do aught in such a house with such a garrison?"

"Ay! when the pinch comes, ye remember the old shoe," returned Nick. "There is not a man of you can back a horse or hold a bill; and as for archery — St. Michael! if old Harry the Fift were back again, he would stand and let ye shoot at him for a farthen a shoot!"

"Nay, Nick, there's some can draw a good bow yet," said Bennet.

"Draw a good bow!" cried Appleyard. "Yes! But who'll shoot me a good shoot? It's there the eye comes in, and the head between your shoulders. Now, what might you call a long shoot, Bennet Hatch?"

"Well," said Bennet, looking about him, "it would be a long shoot from here into the forest."

"Ay, it would be a longish shoot," said the old fellow, turning to look over his shoulder; and then he put up his hand over his eyes, and stood staring.

"Why, what are you looking at?" asked Bennet, with a chuckle. "Do you see Harry the Fift?"

The veteran continued looking up the hill in silence. The sun shone broadly over the shelving meadows; a few white sheep wandered browsing; all was still but the distant jangle of the bell.

"What is it, Appleyard?" asked Dick.

"Why, the birds," said Appleyard.

And, sure enough, over the top of the forest, where it ran down in a tongue among the meadows, and ended in a pair of goodly green elms, about a bowshot from the field where they were standing, a flight of birds was skimming to and fro, in evident disorder.

"What of the birds?" said Bennet.

"Ay!" returned Appleyard, "y' are a wise man to go to war, Master Bennet. Birds are a good sentry; in forest places they be the first line of battle. Look you, now, if we lay here in camp, there might be archers skulking down to get the wind of us; and here would you be, none the wiser!"

"Why, old shrew," said Hatch, "there be no men nearer us than Sir Daniel's, at Kettley; y' are as safe as in London Tower; and ye raise scares upon a man for a few chaffinches and sparrows!"

"Hear him!" grinned Appleyard. "How many a rogue would give his two crop ears to have a shoot at either of us? St. Michael, man! they hate us like two polecats!"

"Well, sooth it is, they hate Sir Daniel," answered Hatch, a little sobered.

"Ay, they hate Sir Daniel, and they hate every man that serves with him," said Appleyard; "and in the first order of hating, they hate Bennet Hatch and old Nicholas the bowman. See ye here: if there was a stout fellow yonder in the wood-edge, and you and I stood fair for him—as, by St. George, we stand!—which, think ye, would he choose?"

"You, for a good wager," answered Hatch.

"My surcoat to a leather belt, it would be you!" cried the old archer. "Ye burned Grimstone, Bennet—they'll ne'er forgive you that, my master. And as for me, I'll soon be in a good place, God grant, and out of bow-shoot—ay, and cannon-shoot—of all their malices. I am an old man, and draw fast to homeward, where the bed is ready. But for you, Bennet, y' are to remain behind here at your own peril, and if ye come to my years unhanged, the old true-blue English spirit will be dead."

"Y' are the shrewishest old dolt in Tunstall Forest," returned Hatch, visibly ruffled by these threats. "Get ye to your arms before Sir Oliver come, and leave prating for one good while. An' ye had talked so much with Harry the Fift, his ears would ha' been richer than his pocket."

An arrow sang in the air, like a huge hornet; it struck old Appleyard between the shoulder blades, and pierced him clean through, and he fell forward on his face among the cabbages. Hatch, with a broken cry, leapt into the air; then, stooping double, he ran for the cover of the house. And in the meanwhile Dick Shelton had dropped behind a lilac, and had his cross-bow bent and shouldered, covering the point of the forest.

Not a leaf stirred. The sheep were patiently browsing; the birds had settled. But there lay the old man, with a cloth-yard arrow standing in his back; and there were Hatch holding to the gable, and Dick crouching and ready behind the lilac bush.

"D' ye see aught?" cried Hatch.

"Not a twig stirs," said Dick.

"I think shame to leave him lying," said Bennet, coming forward once more with hesitating steps and a very pale countenance. "Keep a good eye on the wood, Master Shelton—keep a clear eye on the wood. The saints assail us! Here was a good shoot!"

Bennet raised the old archer on his knee. He was not yet dead; his face worked, and his eyes shut and opened like machinery, and he had a most horrible, ugly look of one in pain.

"Can ye hear, old Nick?" asked Hatch. "Have ye a last wish before ye wend, old brother?"

"Pluck out the shaft, and let me pass, a' Mary's name!" gasped Appleyard. "I be done with Old England. Pluck it out!"

"Master Dick," said Bennet, "come hither, and pull me a good pull upon the arrow. He would fain pass, the poor sinner."

Dick laid down his cross-bow, and pulling hard upon the arrow, drew it forth. A gush of blood followed; the old archer scrambled half upon his feet, called once upon the name of God, and then fell dead. Hatch, upon his knees among the cabbages, prayed fervently for the welfare of the passing spirit. But even as he prayed, it was plain that his mind was still divided, and he kept ever an eye upon the corner of the wood from which the shot had come. When he had done, he got to his feet again, drew off one of his mailed gauntlets, and wiped his pale face, which was all wet with terror.

"Ay," he said, "it'll be my turn next."

*   *   *   *   *

CONCLUSION

From **W. S. Holdsworth**, *An Historical Introduction to the Land Law* (Oxford, 1927), 136–138.

§ 10. General Conclusions.

Throughout the Middle Ages the land law was the principal branch of the common law. Its main outlines had been drawn by the lawyers and statesmen of the twelfth and thirteenth centuries, and by the legislation of the reign of Edward I. In the fourteenth and fifteenth centuries these outlines had been elaborated by the legal profession; and the rules which they evolved contain some of the oldest and most permanent parts of the law. Though many of them have been modified by the Property Acts, they have not been wholly swept away; and they are still the foundations of large parts of the law. We have seen, for instance, that a few of the consequences of tenure, much of the law as to estates in the land, and much of the law as to seisin and possession, have survived these Acts.

The medieval land law was summed up at the close of this period in Littleton's Tenures. We can see from his summary, that, though the work of the lawyers had been skillfully done, though some of that work has been very permanent, it suffered from two grave defects.

In the first place, it was so rigid and narrow a system of law that it did not meet the needs of land-owners. As the land law came to be more and more purely property law, the incidents and consequences of tenure tended to become burdensome anachronisms; and the restrictions placed by the common law on the landowner's powers of disposition, especially the denial of the power to devise, and the inconvenience of the modes by which he could give effect to his limited powers of disposition, were felt to be irksome and unreasonable. In the second place, the land law was made unreasonably technical by the intricacies of the procedure of the real actions. The age was at once lawless and litigious; and the procedure of the real actions was so technical that it afforded abundant opportunities to the lawless to defeat just claims, and made litigation a useful alternative to violence. That it was largely this system of procedure, as used and misused by the legal profession at the bidding of their clients, which was at fault, is, I think, demonstrated by the fact that the contingent remainder was hardly yet recognized, and that uses were in their infancy. These two topics, which, in the following period, were destined to introduce many complications into the land law, could be neglected by a writer upon tenures in the fifteenth century; and yet the law was then almost as complex as it has ever been.

We shall see in the following chapter that it was the development of uses by the Chancellor which helped to meet the first of these defects. This development introduced many new doctrines into the legal system; and when the Statute of Uses incorporated much of this into the common law, and when the Chancellor, starting from the basis of a liberalized common law, introduced new equitable ideas into the land law, we get the conditions in which the modern land law will be constructed upon its medieval basis.

But these developments would not have produced their full effect if the second of these defects—the intricacy of the procedure of the real actions—had not been remedied. At the end of this period we can see the source from which the remedy for this defect will come. Rivalry with the Chancery was inducing the common lawyers to expand the actions of trespass and trespass on the case. The effects of this expansion were almost as notable in the land law as in the law of contract and tort. It was through a development in one of the forms of the action of trespass—the action of ejectment—that the lessee for years and the copyholder had got full protection. In the following period this action of ejectment will, by a series of fictions, be used to do the work of the real actions; and it will be adapted so successfully to this new sphere of activity that it will gradually reduce the real actions to the rank of antiquarian curiosities.

Note: In Chapter IX, *infra*, we will investigate at length how the Lord Chancellor "introduced new equitable ideas into the land law," through the "use," thus leading, as Holdsworth indicates, to modern land law.

From **T.F.T. Plucknett, *A Concise History of the Common Law*,** (5th Ed., 1956) pp. 533–534. [Courtesy Aspen Publishers Inc.]

THE EFFECTS OF TENURE

Occasionally attempts have been made to estimate the effects of tenure upon English law, but it is curious that the subject has been so little explored. A comparison between English and continental law in this respect should be fruitful, for on the continent the feudal lawyers admitted that tenure divided the ownership of the land between the lord and the tenant. English law refused to admit this proposition. Instead of regarding the lord and tenant as dividing between them the ownership of one thing, it looked upon each of them as a complete owner of two different things, the tenant being the owner of the land in demesne and the lord being owner of a seignory, which, although incorporeal, was treated in every way as property. One result, therefore, of the doctrine of tenure as it was developed in England, was not to divide ownership between lord and tenant but to add the lord's seignory to the growing list of incorporeal hereditaments which medieval law was particularly fond of handling on exactly the same lines as real property.

*   *   *   *   *

The burden of the feudal incidents bore so heavily on tenants that the history of real property law is largely concerned with attempts to evade them. On the one hand lay the possibility of separating the enjoyment of land from the legal title to it—hence the long history of the use. On the other lay various devices to ensure that he who was really the heir should take not as heir but as purchaser, so avoiding the relief; this gave us the contingent remainder and the *Rule in Shelley's Case*. In short, the persistence of a system which had long ceased to correspond with the real social structure of the country, although it continued to be an important source of revenue to large numbers of landowners as well as to the Crown, inevitably drove tenants to devise evasions, with the result that the law was warped beyond endurance.

Note: In subsequent chapters, particularly Chapter IX, *infra*, and Chapter X, *infra*, we will investigate how the feudal system eventually became simply a system of taxation.

V

COURTS OF RECORD

The *Doomsday Book*, the *Magna Carta*, the statutes of Henry II and Edward I, the evolution of Parliament, and the "reform" of English feudalism into a modern fiscal system, were all major achievements of the Norman-Angevins. But it could be argued that their greatest achievements were none of these. For perhaps the most lasting monuments of the English medieval state were the direct result of the central royal courts that they founded, the two great ideas of a systematic and predictable legal procedure and of an evolving judge-made law.

Of course, these ideas developed slowly. Early English judges certainly did not have an articulated view of either law or legal procedure as a dynamic tool or "instrument" of social policy. On the contrary, they perceived themselves as administering the just application of a relatively static body of customary law— static, that is, except for the royal statutes. But the vital prerequisites of judicial process and judicial law making were, none the less, being assembled.

First, as we will see in the excerpts from Van Caenegem and Pollock & Maitland, the English courts developed a superb tool for defining and developing court jurisdiction and doctrine, the "writ." This tool began as a creature of bureaucratic administration, a brief piece of writing (hence "writ") directed to a particular official, commanding certain action, and authenticated by seals and counter-signatures. But its potential was seen by the Norman justiciars, and "formulary" justice and pleading was born. No longer did an oral tradition address every grievance on its own terms at a Law Rock or in a throne room. Now grievances had to be expressed in a written form cognizable by a court. This required not only lawyers, but a "legal" approach to problems.

The second ingredient was written record keeping. The Norman royal courts kept detailed records on the so-called great "rolls," rolls of sheepskin sewn together. Royal scribes can be seen writing their rolls in the manuscript illustration of the Court of Common Pleas in the *Materials*, *supra*, and there is also an illustration of a Plea Roll itself. See Illustrations 3-5 and 3-6, *supra*. Of course these rolls were not modern law reports. To start with, they rarely recorded reasons for decisions. In addition, they were carefully guarded, and available to only a few judges and privileged lawyers. But they were the basis for private notebooks and treatises, including Bracton's famous *Notebook* discussed early in Chapter III. In particular, they often indicated the appropriate or inappropriate use of initial writs. Not until 1270, at the earliest, did accounts of judicial reasoning begin to be kept,

Illustration 5-1   An English king with his legal advisors and judges. Note the "coifs" on the left—the white cap designating a Sergeant at Law. This woodcut was first used by the printer Pynson in London, 1496–1508. [From the Author's Collection.]

almost certainly by law students attending court for education. These records, called "Year Books" because they were kept by chronological court years in an almost unbroken series until 1535, will be discussed at length in Chapter IX. But the rolls and the judges' own notebooks were records enough to develop a body of law about the use of writs, which in turn led to a judge-made jurisprudence both of procedure and of substantive doctrine, called the "forms of action."

There were two more crucial ingredients to the flourishing of the royal courts. The first, the development of a legal profession, will be discussed at great length in Chapter IX. The growth of the use of writs, the keeping of records, and the development of formulary pleading all required professional, literate judges and trained advocates to appear before them. By 1292, Edward I required that "learners" in the professions should be directly supervised by the royal justices themselves.

The second was the jury. The old Norman administrative device of gathering neighbors together under oath to answer questions, called "juries" from the Norman French "*juror*," to swear, was brilliantly adapted by Henry II and his advisors to provide a superior method of judicial fact finding. It was certainly far superior to customary ordeals and battle...and superior enough to last to this very day.

For now, let us take a closer look at both the "writ" and the "jury."

A. THE WRIT

The first fact about a judicial writ, surprising even to this day to lay people, is that a writ is both "official" and "private." A writ is "official" in that it is in the form of an official letter from a public official—usually the King himself—to another official—usually the King's official representative in the shire, the "shire reeve" or sheriff.

It directs the sheriff to do something to a private person, usually pending resolution of a dispute in court. For example, a Writ of Covenant starts off:

> "The King to the sheriff of L greeting. Command A (a private party) that justly and without delay he keep to B the Covenant between them made for a certain granary to be newly constructed at N at the charge of him the said B. And unless he will do this, and if the aforesaid A shall give you security to prosecute his claim, then summon by good summoners the aforesaid B that he be before our justices at Westminster (i.e., Common Pleas Court) [on such a day] to show wherefore he hath not done it. And have these the summoners and this writ."

But here is the twist. No royal officer is actually involved in issuing this document, except the sheriff who serves it on B. This document is actually purchased by A's lawyer from the King's secretariat, called The Chancery. The writ is just a way for a private party to start a law suit. The same is true today. A complaint usually comes, ostensibly, from a public authority, such as "Clerk of the Court, U.S. District Court, Massachusetts." In fact, these complaints are bought from legal printers and kept in drawers by the thousands in private law firms. They are used at will to start law suits, with only some rough controls over frivolousness, such as Rule 11 of the Federal Rules of Civil Procedure. See the modern examples in the *Materials, Illustration 5-4, infra*. (Sometimes lay persons are so intimidated by the "official" complaint that they concede at once, a fact well known by unscrupulous debt collection agencies.) The idea of a technically "public" document used at the behest of private parties to initiate law suits was a fundamental idea of early English royal justice—and one that has survived seven hundred years.

The crucial question about "writs" was whether you could obtain a writ to remedy any wrong, or whether only certain writs could be obtained and, thus, only certain wrongs remedied by royal justice. It is certainly clear that the royal courts never aspired to a universal jurisdiction. Royal justices were happy to

Illustration 5-2   The Seal of Henry II on a Writ of 1173/74 [Reproduced by permission of the Selden Society and the British Library]. See *Royal Writs in England from the Conquest to Glanvill* (R.C. Van Caenegem, ed., 1959), vol. 77 Selden Society, plate 6. This was an administrative writ. Common law writs were more modest. See Illustration 5-3, *infra.*

leave minor crimes ("misdemeanors") and minor wrongs to the ancient local and feudal courts, and to leave disputes about divorce, libel, and spiritual offenses to the church courts. Only serious crimes (felonies) and serious wrongs were appropriate for the royal courts, just as federal courts in America have a limited jurisdiction by design. Serious crimes were called the "Pleas of the Crown," and soon became defined. Serious civil wrongs included all disputes over freehold land and all disputes involving more than a defined sum of money. These were addressed by a royal writ. We know from Chapter 34 of the *Magna Carta* that some feudal lords feared that they might lose their feudal courts to royal writs, but it appears that, in fact, there was little incentive for hard-pressed royal judges to take on too much.

The clerks in Chancery kept model writs to be copied as requested by individual plaintiffs. These model writs collectively became known as the "Register of Writs," and very early on lawyers wrote up their own collection of model writs, reflecting those available in the "Register." *Glanvill* (1187) contained more than eighty model writs, and we know that there were many early collections.[1] The crucial issue of remedy was confronted when you wished to buy a writ to remedy a wrong, but no such writ was in the "Register." *Bracton* (*circa* 1235) took the view that established forms of writs (*brevia formata*), which were in ordinary form, i.e., "*de cursu*," are granted and approved by the common counsel of all the reign and cannot be changed in any way without their will and consent...."[2] In addition, "there are as many forms of writs as there are kinds of actions and no one can sue without a writ, since the other party is not bound to answer without a writ unless he wishes to do so...."[3] But *Bracton* made one large exception. A new writ could issue "without warrant of law" if "it is consonant with reason and not contrary to the law, provided it has been granted by the King and approved by his council. Such a writ must be personal and must be granted only as a special favor...for it pertains to the King to provide a competent remedy for the suppression of every wrong."[4]

The first two rules in *Bracton*: (1) that writs *de cursu* could not be changed at will and (2) that no one need answer in royal courts without a writ, are, in a sense, still rules today under modern "notice pleading." But the exception permitting the execution of new writs did not persist. "Personal" discretionary writs, creating novel new royal remedies to any problem, eventually ceased to exist, and "the Register of writs was closed," i.e., no new legal remedies could be created.

In 1285, a different solution was attempted. Edward I's Statute of Westminster II, Chapter 24, stated:

> And whensoever henceforth it shall happen in the chancery that a writ is found in one case, but none is found in a similar case falling under the same law and requiring a similar remedy, let the clerks of the chancery agree in making a writ; or let them adjourn the plaintiffs into the next parliament, and write down the cases in which they could not agree and refer them to the next parliament, and let a writ be made by those learned in the law so that for the future it shall not befall that the court fail in doing justice to complainants.[5]

But even this solution, referred to as the rule *in consimili casu* ("in a similar case"), did not prevent the gradual "closing of the Register." By 1300, "the categories became more or less closed." As Baker observed: "The effect was momen-

---

1. See *Early Registers of Writs* (ed. E. de Haas, G.D.G. Hall, London, 1970). Seldon Society Vol. 87.
2. *Materials, infra*, pp. 167–168.
3. *Id.*
4. *Materials, infra*, p. 168.
5. *Materials, infra*, p. 168.

tous. Finding the right formula was no longer simply a matter of consistency and routine. If a would-be plaintiff could not find a writ in the register he was without remedy as far as the two benches (King's Bench and Common Pleas) were concerned."[6]

B. THE WRIT "FAMILIES:" THE ANCIENT PRAECIPE CLAN

After the Register was "closed," you had to find an existing form of a writ to fit your client's case or you were out of the royal court. (You could still try the local courts, the feudal courts, or the Church courts!) This "formulary" system of pleading is, of course, exactly what lawyers still do today. We do not simply take a client's sad story to court. We attempt to translate those grievances into legally actionable wrongs. The "forms of action" were the origin of today's legal doctrines, and they, in turn, grew from types of writs. Each form of action was founded on a particular writ in the Register.

From the beginning, lawyers grouped these writs into "families," doubtless as a learning aid. The oldest and most dignified of the "families" were the "*Praecipe*" writs, because they began with the words "*Praecipe* X" or "Command X (the defendant) that justly and without delay he sends to A (the plaintiff)..." etc. Seniority in the Register was very important, because it became a rule that if an older, more senior writ was available, you could not employ a more junior or more modern writ.

The "*Praecipe*" writs included the great writ to determine title to land, the "Writ of Right" (*Breve de Recto*) and the "Writ of Right" for "Chief Tenants" holding directly by the King, "*tenere de nobis in capite*," the so called "Writ *Praecipe in Capite*." Also in the family were the early "personal actions" (i.e., action not involving land) called "Covenant," "Debt" and "Detinue." Samples of all of these writs, taken from a famous manual on writs called Fitzherbert's *Natura Brevium*, are set out at *Materials, infra*. You should read them all carefully.

The original "*Praecipe*" writs were very primitive. They only offered one remedy, return of the thing taken, be it land (writ of right), money (debt) or chattel (detinue), or the specific performance of something promised (covenant). As to the latter, such performance was only ordered if there was a deed under seal (i.e., a "covenant") which specifically indicated what was agreed between the parties. This was because the "*Praecipe*" writs came before jury trial. Disputed facts were resolved by battle (writs of right) or by "oath helping" (covenant, debt, detinue, etc.). "Oath helping," also called "wager of law" or "compurgation," involved the defendant denying the plaintiff's charges under an oath, using certain exact words. The defendant would then have to get a set number of supporters, usually eleven, to then take an oath as to his or her innocence. The supporters did not take an oath as to the facts of the case, but to the fact that the defendant's oath was "clean," i.e., true and honorable. If any of them slipped on the words of the oath, it was a sign from God that the defendant was guilty.

Thirteenth century people did not take holy oaths lightly, and this system may have worked better than it might seem today. Indeed, as Professor Simp-

---

6. Baker, *Introduction, supra,* 66.

son has observed, "even today, I suppose, it would be difficult to collect eleven perjurers in order to resist an action for breach of contract..."[7] But there could be no sophisticated findings of fact or quantities of damages using this approach. The old "*Praecipe*" writs, and their form of action, had to address just "yes" or "no" questions. If it was your cow, it should be returned. If not, it should be kept by the defendant (the "detinue" questions). If it was your signature and your seal on the covenant, you were bound to its terms exactly. If not, you were not bound at all (the "covenant" questions).

C. THE "QUESTUS EST NOBIS" WRITS AND THE "POSSESSORY ASSIZES"

Henry II (1133–89) reigned from 1154 to 1189. He was a great Norman-Angevin King, rivaled only by his grandson, Edward I, as a law maker. His greatest contribution to English law was a new family of legal remedies called the "Possessory Assizes." These took the form of a new set of writs which all used the words "*Questus est Nobis A*" or "A hath complained unto us (the King)" at the beginning. A typical example was the writ of "*Novel Disseisin*," set out at *Materials, infra*.

Henry's problem was that the old *Praecipe* writs were too cumbersome, and their methods of proof too unreliable, to protect against bad people simply "seizing" the seisin of fees belonging to others. As a good king, he wished to stop "self help" on both sides, and get people to use royal courts instead. His new actions were called "possessory" because they were designed to protect peaceful possession, or seisin, until a court could determine ultimate right.

The two important features of these new writs were: 1) they would automatically restore possession to anyone who had something taken from their possession during a fairly short period before the action—usually about six months; and 2) factual issues would be resolved by the jury. The question of whether a seizure of possession, or "disseisin," actually occurred was decided—not by battle or wager of law—but by a jury of twelve neighbors. Notice that the question asked and remedy offered is still very simple. Did the plaintiff have possession within six months? If so, the possession should be restored. But now there is a potentially far better fact finder, the jury.

There were four "possessory assizes," each with its own writ. The most important was "*novel disseisin*" (i.e., "new" disseisin) which remedied any seizure of land which occurred fairly recently, say "after the last return of our lord the King from Brittany." If the plaintiff was in possession, and recently removed by the defendant (a simple factual issue), the remedy was to return the plaintiff to possession. The more complex issue, whether the plaintiff had ultimate good title versus the defendant, could be decided later through a writ of right. There is a sample writ of novel disseisin set out in the *Materials, infra*.

Also important was the writ of "*mort d'ancestor*," established by Henry II at the Assize of Northhampton in 1176. This protected a particular weak point in the feudal chain of possession—the period between the death of an ancestor (*mort d'ancestor*) and the seisin of the heir. An unscrupulous baron, hungry for

---

7. A.W.B. Simpson, *History of the Common Law of Contract* (Oxford, 1975), 139.

land, would strike just after the death of a landowner and before the heir even heard of the death. Before anyone could react, the manor house would be occupied, charters and deeds destroyed, and the new "owner" would claim inheritance "of right," backed by a band of armed retainers.

In such a case, the heir would obtain a writ of *mort d'ancestor*. All that would have to be proved is: 1) that the plaintiff was the legal heir of the dead owner—usually proved by a routine application of the canons of descent—and 2) that the dead owner died seized of the property, a clear issue of fact. If the answers of the jury to both questions were "yes," then the plaintiff was restored to possession by the king's sheriff (who had his own soldiers).

The purpose in both the cases of *novel disseisin* and *mort d'ancestor* was to prevent the plaintiff from simply counter-attacking with his or her own armed friends and retainers. These writs were designed to replace "self-help" with legal order.[8]

In all of these "possessory assizes" the emphasis was on quick action to regain seisin, or "possession." But there was also the idea of the "assize." We have seen that the word "assize" has many meanings—all relating to the idea of people "sitting" together for some purpose. Here the reference of "assize" is to the twelve men jury, the "assize of twelve," required by the *Questus est nobis* writ.[9] Take the *"novel disseisin"* writ as an example. It states that, once the plaintiff has "made you secure to prosecute his claim," the land should be "reseised" and delivered to the plaintiff:

> ...and the same tenement with the chattels to be in peace until the first assize when our justices shall come into those parts. And in the mean time you shall cause twelve free and lawful men of that venue to view that tenement and their names to be put into the writ. And summon them by good summoners that they be before the justices afores at the assize afores, ready to make recognizance thereupon. And put by gages and safe pledges the affores X or, if he shall not be found, his bailiff, that he be then there to hear that recognizance. And have there the (names of the) summoners, the pledges, and this writ.

Here the "twelve free and lawful men of that venue" i.e., the jury, are the "assize of twelve" of the "possessory assize."

But there is yet another use of the word "assize," as in "the first assize when our justices shall come into those parts." This is a reference to the machinery established to make sure the possessory assizes, and other royal remedies, were effective. Approximately every six months, some of the royal justices of the central courts traveled to the chief shire towns of each shire, or county, and there held

---

8. There were two other "possessory writs" that began "*questus est nobis*": 1) the writ of *darrein presentment* and at the writ of *utrum*. These both involved the Church. Ability to "present" a parson to a "living," or a parish church, was like a political patronage job in modern America—except the Bishop had to concur. It had value, i.e., the annual salary, and was "a job for the boys." The issue in *darrein presentment* was simply whether the plaintiff was the last (*darrein*) person to make such an appointment (*presentment*). If so, the plaintiff was seized and could make the next one. *Utrum* only involved the issue of whether the land in question was held in spiritual tenure, like *frankalmoin*, or was held by lay tenure. It was chiefly used by clerics seeking to recover land belonging to their churches.

9. See T.F.T. Plucknett, *Concise History*, *supra*, 112.

court. These courts were also called "assizes" and their judges were called "justices of assize" or "justices in eyre." ("Eyre" comes from the Norman French "*eire*" or "journey" and the Latin "*in itenere*." This is the same root as "itinerary.") These "assize" justices, or "justices in eyre" usually had three royal commissions: 1) of "assize," which would include all civil pleas cognizable before royal courts; 2) of "*oyer and terminer*" (to "hear and determine"), which directed the justices to enquire about certain crimes; and 3) of "gaol delivery," which was to deliver the local county gaol of all its prisoners awaiting trial, and to try every such prisoner. These justices "of assize" would inevitably call assize juries from the neighbors to assist their task.

This idea of traveling "circuit" judges "in eyre" trying local cases, and then rejoining their colleagues in central courts, should be familiar to us. Indeed, we owe to the Norman assize judges the origins of our federal "circuit" courts of appeals. Originally, U.S. Supreme Court justices also "rode circuit." Massachusetts Superior Court judges do so to this day.

D. THE OSTENSURUS QUARE FAMILY: THE "MOTHER" WRIT OF TRESPASS AND HER CHILDREN

The Statute of Westminster II (1285) further improved the ingenious "assize" system of traveling justices by adding another idea. It occurred to the royal judges that it would save time and expense if cases commenced in London, at the King's Bench or Court of Common Pleas in Westminster, could be tried in the locality where the events occurred, before knowledgeable juries. The Statute provided that a day and place should be set aside on the assizes to try all such cases, and that the case should not be tried in London unless the assize judges "had not previously" (*nisi prius*) tried them on the appointed day in the county town. This system, called the *nisi prius* system, permitted inexpensive and knowledgeable trials before local juries.

The *nisi prius* system gave rise to our last great family of writs, the famous "trespass" writs, which featured jury trial. These writs were also called "*ostensurus quare*" writs, because they always used the words "*ostensurus quare*" i.e., "to show wherefore." These words were usually coupled with two other "characteristic" trespass phrases: *vi et armis* ("force and arms") and "*contra pacem nostram*" ("against our (the King's) peace"). Here's how a typical trespass writ would read:

> The King to the Sheriff of S greeting. If A shall make you secure to prosecute his claim, then put by gages and safe pledges B that he be before us on the octave of St. Michael, wheresoever we shall then be in England to show wherefore (*ostensurus quare*) with force and arms (*vi et armis*) he made an assault upon him the said A to N and beat, wounded and ill treated him, so that his life was despaired of, and other enormous things to him did, to the great damage of him the said A and against our peace (*contra pacem nostram*). And have there the names of the pledges and this writ.

Trespass writs were originally designed to give victims of violent attacks "with force and arms" (*vi et armis*) a special civil remedy. These were the particular business of the King's Bench, the central royal court with criminal jurisdiction, because such attacks, like serious crimes, were "against our [the King's] peace" (*contra pacem nostram*). Like crimes, these were also tried to a jury.

Now it is impossible to "restore" the victim of a violent attack to his or her previous well-being, like the way you can "restore" a cow in response to a writ in detinue. Who can "put back" a smashed nose, or broken arm? Even after the wound has healed, there is the pain and suffering endured, and the fear. For this reason, the juries in such actions were not only asked to determine who was at fault, but also to determine fair monetary damages for the harm, a harm that, by its nature, could not just be "put back."

These materials include a series of examples of trespass writs, showing how—eventually—the attraction of jury trial and damages persuaded both lawyers and judges to treat the requirement of an attack with "force and arms" as a fiction. See *Materials, infra*. By the 16th century, trespass writs were being used to substitute for what today would be unintentional negligence and even contractual nonfeasance. This was all because of the jury and its ability to award damages.[10]

The expansion began with straight trespass writs like number "VII" in *Materials, infra*, entitled "writ of trespass *vi et armis*." This writ alleges a physical attack *vi et armis* ("force and arms") *contra pacem nostram* ("against our [the King's] peace"). There may have been such a physical attack. Or, increasingly, the writ could have been used for a simple tort of unintentional, carelessness injury, with the words of the pleading "taken loosely." A good example would be hitting the plaintiff accidentally with a wagon. The next writ, number "VIII" or the "writ of ejectment," was clearly to protect the plaintiff's leasehold. As we have seen, leaseholds were not considered true forms of property seisin, but were considered just contractual rights. Thus they were not protected by the "real" possessory actions. The "writ of ejectment" certainly uses the same words as the old trespass writ, including an allegation of an attack *vi et armis* and *contra pacem nostram*, but it certainly looks as if these words were not literally construed. The important thing was to create a new remedy, triable by jury, that gave money damages for interfering with a leasehold.

There was another factor at work here as well. The King's Bench was always the venue for trying serious crimes "against the King's peace" because it had traditionally been "closest to the King," i.e., it was the court that traveled with the King while the Common Pleas remained fixed at Westminster. The Common Pleas, on the other hand, had a special jurisdiction over cases involving the old real actions, including the possessory assizes to protect land, and also the old writs of convenant, debt, detinue and account. Because the original trespass writs were designed to remedy violent behavior against the King's peace, it was a King's Bench action. As the writ was expanded, it gave the King's Bench, and the legal practitioners who worked there, a way to move legal business into their court and away from the Common Pleas, a powerful incentive for change!

Writ number IX at *Materials, infra*, shows the next step. This writ is still called a "writ of trespass," although the words *vi et armis* and *contra pacem nostram* are

---

10. See *Materials, infra*, pp. 171–172.

now gone. Instead, there is a factual description in the writ itself of an act that is clearly not intentional physical violence, but that has the same effect, such as putting a nail carelessly into a horse's hoof. Such a physical injury cannot just be made right by restitution. The horse's hoof cannot be instantly "restored!" Damages are needed. This type of writ is called an "action on the case" because it sets out the case itself in the writ. (Note that the old words "*Ostensurus quare*" are still used.) This writ is obviously the ancestor of our modern negligence action.

The final evolution of the "trespass" writ is illustrated by writs number "X" and number "XI" in *Materials, infra*. These writs still use the words "*ostensurus quare*," but now contain the new word "*assumpsit*." They are called "writs of assumpsit," or actions on the case in assumpsit. Writ number "X" still involves physical damage. B had "assumed" safely and securely to carry a "pipe of wine" (a kind of barrel) from town S to town F, but had cracked it. The damage may seem the same as a physical harm done deliberately, i.e., B cracking the barrel with an ax on purpose, but it is clear that B did not do this on purpose. Indeed, he had specifically agreed to do just the opposite. The damage was a mistake. If A and B had entered into a covenant under seal to convey the barrel safely, A would have an action in covenant, and B would be able to rely on oath helpers in the trial of fact. But most such business transactions were done more informally, and there was usually no written covenant. Here, the old trespass action is being stretched to provide a remedy similar to modern contract actions.

The final step is evident in writ number "XI," "writ of *assumpsit* for nonfeasance." Now the defendant—far from committing a violent act—has simply "assumed" to construct a cross of stones and done nothing. By the time the courts permitted an *ostensurus quare* writ to be effective here, as a remedy for no act at all, the old basis for trespass writs in deliberate violent acts was long in the past.

Why did not the flexible *ostensurus quare* trespass writ and its progeny just take over at this point? It certainly offered better mode of proof—jury trial rather than wager of law—and better remedies—damages rather than just restitution. The answer lay in the old idea that where a "senior" or earlier writ lay, like covenant or debt, the "new" writ of trespass or an action on the case would be barred. This rule kept the old writs "alive" in a marginal role for many years. (Plaintiffs almost always tried to use the more effective trespass writs, while defendants insisted that older writs, with wager of law, were appropriate.) As we will see, this tension finally came to an end through the use of another legal fiction, called *indebitatus assumpsit* ("being indebted, he undertook"). Put roughly, this fiction assumed a subsequent "assumpsit" wherever an old action would have been appropriate: i.e., you and I had a written covenant, and then I later made an oral "assumption" of duties. The idea was that the later oral assumpsit permitted a trespass remedy. Soon that later *assumpsit* itself became alleged, even when it clearly never happened. It was a pure "fiction." We will discuss this bizarre development, and, indeed, the entire strange idea of making law by these "legal fictions," in Chapter VIII.

The extraordinary expansion of the original trespass writ, through its *ostensurus quare* "progeny," gave it the title of "Mother Writ." The success of the trespass writ was due to the fact it offered that most important of legal breakthroughs—trial by jury with damages to be awarded by the jury. We will return to this great breakthrough in a moment.

E. COMMON LAW ACTIONS WITHOUT WRITS: "PLAINTS" AND "QUERELAS"

Research has demonstrated that, despite our admiration for the formulary system developed by the medieval English jurists, they sometimes ignored it in practice. In particular, once royal justices were visiting the chief shire towns regularly in their "assizes," the temptation to hear informal pleas for help was occasionally irresistible.[11] These pleas were called "*plaints*" (i.e., complaints) or "*querelas*," or "bills." The theory was that the King was ultimately a source of remedy for all wrongs, and the King's representative was the royal assize justice. Examine the sample case edited by Professor Dawson and set out at *Materials, infra.* Why was this not actionable by writ? Why did Muriel desperately wish to be pregnant by Peter? Later, we will see cases like this dealt with by a "bill" in equity jurisdictions, such as the Chancery. As common law justice became closely constrained by the form of writs, "safety valves" had to be found to do justice in extraordinary cases. The "*plaint*" or "*querela*" was such a safety valve. The "bill" in equity was another. This type of "justice" will be discussed at length in the next chapter, Chapter VI, "Equity."

F. "PRIMITIVE" MODES OF PROOF

The earliest forms of "proof" always took the form of an appeal to God. This had two distinct advantages. First, God was inscrutable. There was no hope of threatening God, or seeking revenge on God, or cross-examining God. Imagine a lonely royal assize judge in a remote shire town, caught in a bitter dispute between two powerful families about a murder. The judge needed a credible fact finder who was *someone else*, or that judge might not return safely to London. Also, there was no appeal from God's decision. Once God had spoken, the matter was over.

The three common methods of appealing to God were the oath, the ordeal, and battle. We have already discussed "wager of law" and "oath helpers," where God would make a guilty party slip on the oath, or make one of the "oath helpers" falter.[12] Again, hell and damnation were taken quite seriously. Perjury was not lightly undertaken, so there was some element of rationality to the use of oaths.

Recent research has shown that the "ordeal" too, was more rational than would first appear.[13] The "ordeal" was most commonly used for alleged crimes, particularly where a suspect was unable to produce oath helpers, had been guilty

---

11. See G.O. Sayles, "The Evolution of the King's Bench Before 1272," (1936) 55 Selden Society lxviii–lxx, *Select Cases in the Court of King's Bench Under Edward I* (1936).

12. See *Materials, infra,* pp. 176–177.

13. See R. Bartlett, *Trials by Fire and Water* (1986); P.H. Blair, *An Introduction to Anglo-Saxon England* (2d ed., Cambridge, 1977) Chapter 4; C. Brooke, *From Alfred to Henry III, 871–1272* (London, 1961), 69–70; P. Hyams, "Trial by Ordeal, the Key to Proof in Early Common Law," *Laws and Customs* (1981), 90–126. For wonderful macabre details, see F.J. Snell, *The Customs of Old England* (New York, 1911), 144–172.

of lying under oath before, or was a serf. Suspects caught "red-handed" were also obliged to do the ordeal. The most common ordeals were that of "water" (the innocent was "accepted" by the water and sank), "hot iron" or "boiling water" (burns healed quickly if the suspect was innocent) and the "cursed morsel" (a piece of bread with a feather in it — the guilty choked). It has now been established that many accused confessed instead of suffering the ordeal — usually after much discussion with the local priest. (Of course, a "confession" was ideal... even loyal kinsmen could not be too irate if their bad nephew actually admitted his guilt.) For those who didn't confess, but were believed guilty, particularly tough ordeals could be arranged.

Ordeals and oaths were known to the Anglo-Saxons, but battle was introduced from the continent by the Normans. The idea was that God would not permit the party in the right to lose. Early on, women, infants and old people could employ champions. Eventually, nearly everyone did, except when the accuser was bringing a private "appeal" of a felony. The champions were covered with pads or armor and given matching weapons.[14] Eventually these weapons were limited to staffs with pads which looked like huge "Q-tips." The champions fought in a circle or enclosure in front of the royal justices. They could not hurt each other very easily. The objective was to get the opponent to give up from exhaustion. If the stars came out while both champions were still fighting, the defendant won. Baker has observed that battle was never popular, and was discouraged by judges as early as the thirteenth century.[15]

The most common form of appeal to God was oath-helping. As we have seen, it was the mode of proof for most of the old "*praecipe*" writs, like covenant, detinue, and debt. As we will see, both the old writs and wager of law fell into disuse after the introduction of fact finding juries and trespass writs.

"Ordeal" required the active participation of priests. This was forbidden by the Fourth Lateran Council in 1215, and ordeal quickly disappeared to be replaced by criminal "petty" or "petit" juries. "Battle" was the original mode of proof for the writ of right. It also fell from favor after the Fourth Lateran Council (1215). Battle, like oaths, technically survived into the 19th century. Indeed, it was only abolished in 1819 by statute after a party tried to use it to bring an appeal of felony in the case *Ashford v. Thornton* (1818), 1 B. & Ald. 405.[16]

As a practical matter, however, "appeals to God" were replaced by the evolution of jury trial, particularly after 1200. Juries — like God — were inscrutable and were impossible for neighbors to effectively challenge. Eventually, however, juries were triumphant because they could do more than answer "yes" or "no" to a question. In particular, they could calculate money damages... something God failed to do. As we have seen, the "appeals" to God were, in fact, more rational than might appear at first, but it was the jury which was — from the beginning — openly rational.

---

14. One of my legal history classes actually "staged" a trial by battle, complete with armor and costumes based on early illustrations. The dramatic video tape is available from Boston College Audio Visual Services, Newton, MA, 02159.

15. See Baker, *supra*, 87, 575.

16. See Baker, *Introduction*, *supra*, 87, n.10. Baker observes that "In 1985 a defendant in the High Court of Justiciary in Scotland tried unsuccessfully to wage battle against the lord advocate, claiming the 1819 statute applied only to England." *Id.*

G. THE JURY

In legal fact finding there were always two pressing concerns: 1) legitimacy and 2) rationality. The "primitive" vehicles of battle, ordeal and oaths were focused on the need for legitimacy. In a land where central power, or any legal power, was inherently suspect, appeal to God's judgment was necessary. Although there was more rationality in the process than might appear on the surface, it was not the primary concern.

The jury, on the other hand, was a classic compromise between legitimacy and rationality. It has now survived a thousand years as our paramount method of resolving factual disputes "legally." The legitimacy of the jury comes from two sources. First, each juror was put under oath to give a true answer to a question. Indeed, that is the origin of the name "jury," from the Norman French "juree" or "oath" and the Latin jurare, "to swear." Thus, in a sense, the jury incorporated part of the power and fear associated with the oath. Second, the jury had legitimacy because it did not consist of professional judges, but of local people from the neighborhood, "peers" of the accused. A royal justice sitting in an assize court in a remote shire town, unsure—perhaps—even of the support of the sheriff, might be delighted to pass over to a local group the ultimate test of innocence or guilt.

On the other hand, a jury was inherently more rational than the earlier forms of proof. Jurors were originally sworn to find the truth of their own knowledge, and, as "good men and true of the vicinage," they often had first-hand knowledge, or good second-hand sources about what really took place. Norman administrative juries, like the ones that were used to compile the *Doomsday Book*, and the early assize juries, were both expected to have direct knowledge, and to get it. Juries that were chosen for "impartiality," in the sense of being ignorant of the true facts, were still far in the future.

Great scholarly games have been played about the origins of the jury. The Normans certainly knew that putting a group of neighbors under oath was a good way to get information. But juries predated the Conquest on both sides of the Channel. By at least 997 A.D. Ethelred II was using a group of "xii senior thegns" in each wapentake or hundred to present, under oath, all those they believed had committed a crime. This is like the Grand Jury of today, the so-called "jury of presentment," because the "xii senior thegns" merely accused. Guilt or innocence was still decided by God through the use of the ordeal. Meanwhile, across the Channel, Charlemagne's son, Louis "the Pious," was using a "Frankish" jury of inquiry for administrative purposes. "Royal right ascertained by the sworn statement of the best and most credible people of the district," was found as early as 829 A.D. Doubtless, the Normans were influenced by such Frankish juries, and they probably grafted their continental ideas on to the pre-existing Anglo-Saxon traditions, just as they did with so many institutions of their government.

The unique contribution of early English law, however, was integrating the jury into the central royal court system. From the Norman administrative "fact finding" jury for administration were derived three separate tools for resolving three different legal needs. These were: 1) the "jury of accusation"—the so-called "Grand Jury"; 2) the jury of criminal trial—the so-called "Petite" or "Petty Jury"; and 3) the jury of civil trial or the "Petite" or "Petty" assise jury. The "grand jury" was simply "bigger" than the "little" or "petite jury." A grand jury usually had twenty-three under oath. A "petite jury" always had the magical number of twelve, as it does to this day.

These three "types" of juries had a common root, but evolved separately. The earliest to appear was the jury of accusation, which dates from the Assize of Clarendon (1166). (There, however, the number was twelve, not twenty three.)[17] The criminal trial "Petty Jury" appeared following the Fourth Lateran Council of 1215, when the Church essentially abolished the ordeal by prohibiting clerical involvement. As we have seen, the civil trial jury, 12 "legales homines," was an inherent part of Henry II's "Possessory Assizes," and was established by about 1179 A.D.[18]

Of course these juries were quite different from their modern offspring. In particular, modern juries are said to have five characteristics. They are: 1) "inscrutable," 2) "mandatory," 3) "impartial," 4) "representative," and, in criminal matters, 5) "unanimous." An "inscrutable" jury is one where the judge must accept their conclusions, and cannot cross-examine jurors individually, a feature not unlike the "divine" inscrutability of the ordeal. We know from passages in *Bracton*, that royal judges were still cross-examining jurors and rejecting jury verdicts in 1235 A.D. See *Materials, infra*. Even today, the judgment "n.o.v." provides some check on civil jury inscrutability, but there is no check on criminal acquittals!

A "mandatory" jury is one where the parties must accept jury trial. This was slow in coming, and gave rise to one of the cruelest aspects of English law, the "*peine forte et dure*" ("pain hard and strong"). According to the Statute of Westminster c. 12 (1275), criminal defendants couldn't be tried by jury without their consent—a continuing legacy of the old ordeal as appeal to God. But defendants could be locked in a "*prison forte et dure*" until that consent was given. An extraordinary misreading substituted "peine," or "pain," for "prison." This led to "pressing." "Pressing" was placing weights on to a prisoner until the prisoner "pleaded" and submitted to trial by jury. "Mandatory" jury trial without the coercive "consent" of pressing was not finally achieved until pressing was formally abolished in 1772. The last English pressing was in 1741. After 1827, a plea of not guilty was automatically entered if a prisoner chose not to plead. From then on, jury trial could not be avoided. It was completely "mandatory."

There was a macabre sidelight. Before 1772 some prisoners bravely refused to consent to jury trial as a way of avoiding conviction of felonies and subsequent loss of their properties for their heirs and families by escheat. They were crushed to death. One of the Salem witchcraft defendants was crushed to death in Massachusetts as late as 1692.[19]

"Impartial" juries, in the sense of juries without personal knowledge of the truth, and "representative" juries, in the sense of juries whose composition reflected the locality, race, and class of the accused, were also slow in coming.

---

17. By Statute 25 Edw. III, St. 5, c. 4 (1350) "no one shall be taken by petition or suggestion to our lord the King...unless it be by indictment or presentment of good and lawful people of the neighborhood where such acts were done..." See *Materials, infra*.

18. See the chart at *Materials, infra*, p. 178.

19. See sources cited at D.R. Coquillette, "Introduction," *Law in Colonial Massachusetts* (Coquillette, Brink, Menand eds., Boston, 1984), xxxviii–xxxix, n.2.

Only in the late 1460s was there a full shift to juries as judges, rather than as witnesses. Finally, "unanimity" was also a slow development, and even today it is only required in criminal cases. In 1290, *Britton* simply provided that "if they [the jury] cannot all agree in one mind, let them be separated and examined why they cannot agree, and if the greater part of them know the truth and the other part do not, judgment shall be according to the greater part."[20] By 1310, a judge locked up a civil assize jury without food or water until they agreed.[21] By 1367, unanimity was required, and the jury finally shifted from being individual witnesses to a collective, judicial role.

Ironically, the modern criminal jury—inscrutable, mandatory, impartial, representative and unanimous—remains surprisingly free from judicial scrutiny. In some ways, it more resembles the inscrutable divine will of the ordeal than the rational tool of inquiry described by *Britton*. Thus has the balance between legitimacy and rationality been readjusted, for both moral and political purposes. The glory of the jury remains that it, of all legal fact finding methods, has been the most able to make such crucial adjustments over time. If this were the only gift of the Norman-Angevins to our modern justice systems, it would be a great one indeed.

H. THE WARS OF THE ROSES

In 1399 Richard II died in a most suspicious way, almost certainly murdered. From then until 1485, when Henry VII established the Tudor dynasty by killing Richard III at the Battle of Bosworth Field, England was preoccupied by both foreign wars and by bitter internal conflicts. The culmination of the internal fighting, from 1460 to 1487, was called the Wars of the Roses. The two chief protagonists were the House of York (symbolized by a white rose) and the House of Lancaster (symbolized by a red rose). It is simply impossible to even begin to describe here the elaborate intrigues and feuds, except to say that this was largely a series of military conflicts between chief lords, involving relatively few soldiers. In fact, most ordinary burgers and farmers did everything possible to stay out of the way. See the quite accurate picture in Stevenson's *The Black Arrow*, Chapter IV, *supra*.

From the perspective of a legal historian, there is also a kind of mystery here. This was a period of turmoil and several relatively weak kings, but it was also a period of genuine legal innovation and advancement. The development of a strong Parliament is beyond the scope of this course, but the so-called "Lancas-

---

20. See *Britton* (ed., F.M. Nichols, 1865), vol. 1, 31.

21. See *Materials, infra*, p. 180.

22. As Jolliffe observed "It is to the reigns of the three Edwards that we owe the creation of parliament, and the peaceful and almost unnoticed growth of its most essential principles." See George L. Haskins, *The Growth of English Representative Government* (New York, 1960) quoting Jolliffe's *Constitutional History*, 405. For accounts of this "almost unnoticed growth" and what Maitland called the "Lancastrian view of the Constitution," see F.W. Maitland, *The Constitutional History of England* (Cambridge, 1908), 197–200, A.R. Myers, *England in the Late Middle Ages* (8th ed., London, 1971), 37–53; T.F.T. Plucknett, *A Concise History of the Common Law* (5th ed., Boston, 1956), 35–36.

Shortage of money for the many military expeditions during this period may well have been one reason for the development of the Parliament. As we shall see, English monarchs until the middle of the seventeenth century attempted to retain fiscal independence by col-

trian Constitution" was a step in that direction.[22] We have already seen that the formulary systems of pleading and jury trial slowly advanced through this period—although trial by jury did suffer in practice when local nobles were too strong. In the next chapter we will study equitable remedies, another development that began during this period.

One explanation for this progress during a "bad" time is that old, feudal baronies effectively destroyed themselves by fighting, leaving a strengthened middle-class and a Crown which, when peace resumed under the Tudors, was more powerful than ever. Indeed, the Tudors were noted for their skill in controlling powerful nobles, while forging alliances with middle-class interests. The "Tudor" Parliament was an important part of this equation, but so was a system of royal justice that made sense to ordinary people. The roots of such a system, based on jury trial and the "notice" pleading of the writs and the forms of action, were quietly reinforced during the turmoil of the previous century. Perhaps one lesson is that the slow evolution of legal doctrines and institutions can continue in bad times "from the bottom up," even when there is little or no leadership from "the top down." In fact, during this time of dislocation and confusion, the legal profession prospered, as we will see in Chapter IX.

Charles Ross described "[t]he years from 1460 to 1487" as "the first truly revolutionary period in English history."[23] Ross was referring to the systematic attempts to overthrow the sitting monarchs and the violent deaths of Henry VI, Edward V and Richard III. But legal historians also have been studying the late English medieval period as the source of revolutionary legal ideas. The Wars of the Roses left the chief protagonists decimated: the factions of Lancaster and York both lost their direct male line. Yet, even as the medieval barony fought itself to exhaustion, the seeds were planted for a new social, political, religious and legal order, the Tudor dynasty and the English Renaissance.

FOR FURTHER READING

I. Writs and the "Forms of Action"

The classic account of writs and forms of action is a very slim volume, only 81 pages with an appendix, by the great legal historian F.W. Maitland. This is Maitland's *The Forms of Action at Common Law* (Cambridge, 1909). As usual, the best updated summary is in J.H. Baker, *An Introduction to English Legal History* (3d ed., London, 1990), 63–83, 612–627. See also the lucid, if somewhat outdated, account in T.F.T. Plucknett, *A Concise History of the Common Law* (5th ed., Boston, 1956), 353–378. Once again, R.C. Van Caenegem's *The*

---

lecting feudal incidents and developing their own fortunes. This was a hopeless cause when at war. "Defense spending" deficits, so familiar in our modern world, drove English sovereigns to legislative democracy. Only with the cooperation of the Commons could special subsidies be enacted and, most importantly, be effectively collected. Ironically, unsettled times not only saw the evolution of better legal systems and prosperity for lawyers, but may also have improved the position of Parliament.

23. Charles Ross, *The Wars of the Roses* (New York, 1976), 43.

Birth of the English Common Law (Cambridge, 1973) provides a fine overview at pages 1–61. For a full account of real property actions and for an extended discussion of the "Possessory Assizes," see A.W.B. Simpson, *A History of the Land Law* (2d ed., Oxford, 1986). Simpson also provides an extensive introduction to the early personal actions in A.W.B. Simpson, *A History of the Common Law of Contract: The Rise of the Action of Assumpsit* (Oxford, 1975), 3–196. The best discussion of the earliest history of writs remains *Early Registers of Writs* (ed. E. de Haas, G.D.G. Hall, London, 1970), Selden Society vol. 87 (1970). This volume also contains many helpful early examples of writs carefully translated.

II. Early Modes of Proof and the Evolution of the Jury

There is a fine summary in J.H. Baker, *An Introduction to English Legal History, supra*, 84–90. See also R.C. Van Caenegem, *The Birth of the English Common Law, supra*, 62–84; J.M. Mitnick, "From Neighbor-Witness to Judge of Proofs: The Transformation of the English Civil Juror" (1988) 32 *Amer. J. of Legal History*, 201–235; and John P. Dawson, *A History of Lay Judges* (Cambridge, Mass., 1960), 118–129.

For good accounts of "assize" justice in medieval England, and the relationship between royal and local courts, see Alan Harding, *The Law Courts of Medieval England* (London, 1973) and Robert C. Palmer, *The County Courts of Medieval England* (Princeton, 1982).

III. The Wars of the Roses

For the standard introduction, again see *The Oxford History of Britain* (K.O. Morgan, ed., Oxford, 1988), Chap. 3, Ralph A. Griffith's "The Later Middle Ages" (1290–1485), 192–256. For a gripping, dramatic account, reflecting the drama of Shakespeare's plays about the period, see Winston S. Churchill's account in *A History of English Speaking Peoples* (London, 1956), 312–368. See also A.R. Myers, *England in the Late Middle Ages* (8th ed., London, 1971), 115–210, which gives a complete picture of the political, economic and religious elements of the time. For an excellent account of daily life during the period, including the system of law and government at all levels, see Paul M. Kendall, *The Yorkist Age* (New York, 1962). Finally, Charles Ross' *The Wars of the Roses* (New York, 1977) is vividly illustrated, and gives a full account of the origins of the civil war and military strategy. There is also the highly detailed, scholarly account of E.F. Jacob, *The Fifteenth Century 1399–1485* (Oxford, 1961).

IV. Evolution of Parliamentary Government

In a manageable introductory course on legal history, the emphasis has to be on the evolution of "private" law, as opposed to "public"or "constitutional" law. But there are some good introductions to the evolution of the Parliament and English constitutional history. See, for example, George L. Haskins, *The Growth of English Representative Government* (New York, 1960) and S.B. Chrimes, *English Constitutional History* (4th ed., Oxford 1967). The best classic account is, of course, F.W. Maitland, *The Constitutional History of England* (Cambridge, 1908).

MATERIALS

A FORMULARY SYSTEM

R.C. Van Caenegem, *Royal Writs in England from the Conquest to Glanvill*, 177–179. (Vol. 77 Selden Society, for 1958–1959). [Courtesy Selden Society].

It has long been recognised that the growth of administration and government was the chief characteristic of the reigns following 1066. The all-perceiving eye and the autocratic hand of the Anglo-Norman and Angevin kings built up a powerful system of all-pervading royal government that is one of the most remarkable spectacles of world history. It was not in legislation or in the declaration of principles, nor in attempts at long-term improvement of human society that their genius expressed itself, but in the everyday business of governing the realm, in solving problems as they came, on practical lines. They had the power to govern and they used it with great skill. No aspect of the nation's life escaped their impact. Wherever order had to be restored, they acted and a writ went out, whether it were concerned with grave matters of state or with trivial occasions, such as people fishing in the Thames to the detriment of the fisheries of the monks of Rochester. The instrument *par excellence* to convey their will, to notify some decision, to express some order or to prohibit some action, was the royal writ. If anything is typical of royal government in the eleventh and twelfth centuries in England, it is this scrappy little strip of sealed parchment. It contained only the essentials: *intitulatio*, address and *dispositio*, as well as a date of place, a witness for internal control and a seal for external authentication.... The terseness and curtness of the writ are proverbial. There was no trace of a *proemium* or other solemnities, no justification or explanation. The age saw the decay of the old solemn charter. Efficiency was the only consideration in writ and writ-charter. The writ was an instrument adequate for its purpose, nothing more, nothing less. It was parsimonious, no more than a tiny strip of parchment and written with numerous abbreviations. That was because so many left the chancery, dealing with such a wide variety of subjects. The writ was in fact a most protean document. The number of matters in which the king was liable to intervene was unlimited and so was the number of sorts of writs which conveyed these interventions. Differentiation was slow to take place. Originally there was only one vast class of undifferentiated writs, which we have called the "old executive writ," because of their executive, authoritative, commanding or forbidding aspect. Out of this common group, various classes with well-defined functions and formulae took shape, by the same process of division and specialization by which the original undifferentiated activities of king and council developed into Exchequer, Common Pleas, Wardrobe, Council, and so on. In the same way some writs became exchequer writs, some common law writs, some letters close. Within these great classes various functions were performed by writs with appropriate formulae.

It is in this diffuse mass of royal orders and notifications, cast in the diplomatic mould of the writ, that we best see royalty at work kneading the soft clay of the kingdom, regulating, commanding, forbidding. The time would come when these old executive writs, products of a real outburst of powerful government, would be dammed and confined into the channels of fixed

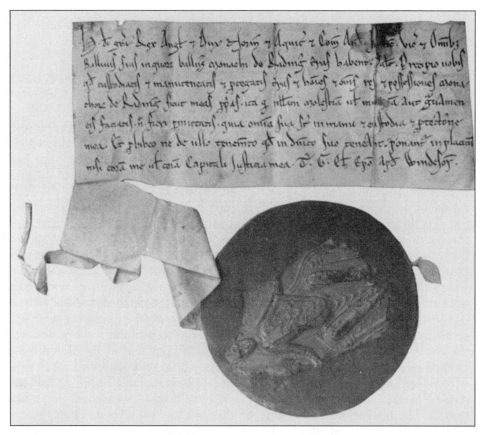

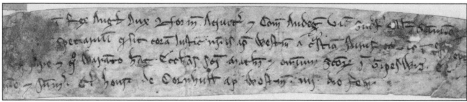

Illustration 5-3   Examples of Writs, 1173, 1190 A.D.

Top: "Writ of Henry II to his justices, sheriffs and bailiffs." 1173/74 [Courtesy the Selden Society and the British Museum].

Bottom: "Writ of Richard I to the sheriff of Suffolk (1190 A.D.). Earliest returned common law writ." (KB 136/1/1, no. 1). Crown copyright material in the Public Records Office is reproduced by permission of the Controller of Her Majesty's Stationery Office.

See *Royal Writs in England From the Conquest to Glanvill* (R.C. Van Caenegem ed., 1959), vol. 77 Selden Society, plate 6, 7.

chancery formulae. There was to be a special writ for every action (administrative, judicial, financial). There would be fixed forms for fixed purposes, order, systematisation, classification and the naming of writs by technical terms....

F. Pollock and F.W. Maitland, *The History of English Law Before the Time of Edward I* (2d ed., 1898) II 558–559, 561–565.

....[W]e have yet to speak of the most distinctively English trait of our medieval law, its 'formulary system' of actions. We call it distinctively English; but it is also in a certain sense very Roman. While the other nations of Western Europe were beginning to adopt as their own the ultimate results of Roman legal history, England was unconsciously reproducing that history; it was developing a formulary system which in the ages that were coming would be the strongest bulwark against Romanism and sever our English law from all her sisters.

The phenomenon that is before us cannot be traced to any exceptional formalism which prevailed in the England of the eleventh century. All ancient procedure is formal enough, and in all probability neither the victors nor the vanquished on the field at Hastings knew any one legal formula or legal formality that was not well known throughout many lands. No, the English peculiarity is this, that in the middle of the twelfth century the old, oral and traditional formalism is in part supplanted and in part reinforced by a new, written and authoritative formalism, for the like of which we shall look in vain elsewhere, unless we go back to a remote stage of Roman history. Our *legis actiones* give way to a formulary system. Our law passes under the dominion of a system of writs which flow from the royal chancery. What has made this possible is the exceptional vigour of the English kingship, or, if we look at the other side of the facts, the exceptional malleableness of a thoroughly conquered and compactly united kingdom....

Our forms of action are not mere rubrics nor dead categories; they are not the outcome of a classificatory process that has been applied to pre-existing materials. They are institutes of the law; they are—we say it without scruple—living things. Each of them lives its own life, has its own adventures, enjoys a longer or shorter day of vigour, usefulness and popularity, and then sinks perhaps into a decrepit and friendless old age. A few are still-born, some are sterile, others live to see their children and children's children in high places. The struggle for life is keen among them and only the fittest survive.

Bracton (*circa* 1236 A.D.) J.P. Dawson, trans.

Bracton, De Legibus et Consuetudinibus Regni Angliae, fol. 413b.

No one can bring an action without a writ, for the other party is not bound to answer without a writ unless he wishes to do so.

Bracton, De Legibus et Consuetudinibus Regni Angliae, fol. 413b, 414b.

There are some formed writs (*brevia formata*) in certain cases which are *de cursu* and which are granted and approved by the common counsel of all the realm and cannot be changed in any way without their will and consent.... There are as many forms of writs as there are kinds of actions and no one can sue without a writ unless he wishes to do so....

A writ will abate if it has been brought against the law and custom of the realm, especially against the charter of liberties, such as the writ which is called *praecipe* by which a free man may lose his court. If a writ is brought without warrant of the law, it shall be sustained as long as it is consonant with reason and not contrary to the law, provided it has been granted by the king and approved by his council. Such a writ must be personal and must be granted only as a special favor, and it does not matter that the magnates have not given their assent expressly, so long as they have not expressly dissented and no sufficient reason is shown why it should not be valid; for it pertains to the king to provide a competent remedy for the suppression of every wrong.

Statute of Westminster II, c.24 (1285 A.D.) (trans. Plucknett, 31 *Col. L. Rev.* 789).

In cases where a writ is granted in chancery concerning an act done by one person, let not the plaintiffs depart from the king's court without remedy merely because the tenement has been transferred from that person to another, and no writ fitting that special case is to be found in the register of chancery. For example, a writ is granted against one who levies a house, wall or market; but if the house, wall, market or the like is transferred to another person, the writ is denied. Henceforth, therefore, when a writ is granted in one case, but a corresponding remedy is lacking in a similar case (as above said) let there be a writ. [Thus] "A has complained to us that B unjustly, etc., levied a house, wall, market, etc., to the nuisance, etc.;" but if the things so levied are transferred to another person, then the writ henceforward shall be thus: "A has complained to us that B and C have levied, etc."

Likewise, just as a parson of a church can recover common of pasture by a writ of *novel disseisin*, so henceforth let his successor against the disseisor or his heir by a writ of *quod permittat*, although such a writ has not been granted heretofore by the chancery.

Likewise, where a writ is granted to enquire whether (*utrum*) a tenement is the free alms of a church or the lay fee of a certain person, henceforth let there be a writ to enquire whether it is the free alms of one church or of another church, in cases where the free alms of one church have been transferred into the possession of another church.

And whensoever henceforth it shall happen in the chancery that a writ is found in one case, but none is found in a similar case falling under the same law and requiring a similar remedy, let the clerks of the chancery agree in making a writ; or let them adjourn the plaintiffs into the next parliament, and write down the cases in which they could not agree and refer them to the next parliament, and let a writ be made by those learned in the law so that for the future it shall not befall that the court fail in doing justice to complainants.

SAMPLE WRITS

Note: Medieval law students knew that writs were very important in pursuing a successful cause of action in the royal courts. Both they, and practicing lawyers, kept their own "Registers of Writs," with sample forms of writs organized into categories. Imagine that what follows is your own "Register." (It is actually based on excerpts from a student text, Fitzherbert's *Natura Brevium* (1794 ed.), together with a few of F.W. Maitland's samples from his *The Forms of Action at Common Law* (Cambridge, 1909), 82–84, and excerpts from the *Registrum Omnium Brevium* (London, 1531), translated and edited by J.H. Baker. See Baker, *An Introduction, supra*, 440–444. I have emphasized certain words. This list contains both medieval and more modern writs, and contains writs that developed long after the Norman-Angevins. The later writs are included to demonstrate how the writs evolved.

All of these writs are organized in the characteristic way, with the "oldest" writs first, followed by the "youngest." What does this tell us about the development of common law?

"PRAECIPE WRITS"

Writ I.   Writ of right. ["*Praecipe in Capite*," for tenants in chief]

The King to the sheriff greeting. Command X that justly and without delay he render to A one messuage with the appurtenances in Trumpington which he claims to be his right and inheritance, and to hold of us in chief and whereof he complains that the aforesaid X unjustly deforceth him. And unless he will do this, and (if) the aforesaid A shall give you security to prosecute his claim, then summon by good summoners the afores X that he be before our justices at Westminster [on such a day] to show wherefore he hath not done it. And have there the summoners and this writ.

Rex vicecomiti salutem. Praecipe X quod juste et sine dilatione reddat A unum mesuagium cum pertinentiis in Trumpingtone quod clamat esse jus et haereditatem suam et tenere de nobis in capite et unde queritur quod praedictus X ei injuste deforciat ut dicit. Et nisi fecerit, et praedictus A fecerit te securum de clamore suo prosequendo, tunc summone eum per bonos summonitores quod sit coram justiciariis nostris apud Westmonasterium [tali die] ostensurus quare non fecerit. Et habeas ibi summonitores et hoc breve.

Writ II.   Writ of right.

The King to K greeting. We command you that without delay you do full right to A of one messuage with the appurtenances in Trumpington which he claims to hold of you by free service of [so much] *per annum* for all service, of which X deforceth him. And unless you will do this, let the sheriff of Cambridge do it that we may hear no more clamour thereupon for want of right.

Rex K salutem. Praecipimus tibi quod sine dilatione plenum rectum teneas A de uno mesuagio cum pertinentiis in Trumpingtone qoud clamat tenere de te per liberum servitium [unius denarii per annum] pro omni servitio, et quod X ei deforciat. Et nisi feceris, vicecomes de Cantabrigia faciat, ne amplius inde clamorem audiamus pro defectu recti.

Writ III.   Writ of debt.

The King to the Sheriff of N greeting. Command A that justly and without delay he render to B one hundred shillings, which he owes to him, and unjustly detains, as it is said. And unless he will do this *etc.*

Rex Vicecomiti N salutem. Praecipe A quod juste et sine dilatione reddat B centum solidos quos ei debet et injuste detinet ut dicit. Et nisi fecerit etc.

Writ IV.   Writ of covenant.

The King to the Sheriff of L greeting. Command A that justly and without delay he keep to B the covenant between them made for a certain granary to be newly constructed at N at the charges of him the said B. And unless he will do this *etc.*

Rex Vicecomiti L salutem. Praecipe A quod juste et sine dilatione teneat B conventionem inter eos factam de quodam granario sumptibus ipsius B apud N de novo construendo. Et nisi fecerit etc.

"POSSESSORY WRITS"

("*Questus est Nobis*")

Writ V.   Assize of *novel disseisin.*

The King to the sheriff greeting. A hath complained unto us that X unjustly and without judgment hath disseised him of his freehold in Trumpington after (the last return of our lord the king from Brittany into England). And therefore we command you that, if the afores A shall make you secure to prosecute his claim, then cause that tenement to be reseised and the chattels which were taken in it and the same tenement with the chattels to be in peace until the first assize when our justices shall come into those parts. And in the meantime you shall cause twelve free and lawful men of that venue to view that tenement and their names to be put into the writ. And summon them by good summoners that they be before the justices afores at the assize afores, ready to make recognizance thereupon. And put by gages and safe pledges the afores X or, if he shall not be found his bailiff, that he be then there to hear that recognizance. And have there the (names of the) summoners, the pledges, and this writ.

Rex vicecomiti salutem. Questus est nobis A quod X injuste et sine judicio disseisivit eum de libero tenemento suo in Trumpingtone post [ultimum reditum domini regis de Brittannia in Angliam] (or other period of limitation). Et ideo tibi praecipimus quod, si praedictus A fecerit te securum de clamore suo prosequendo, tunc facias tenementum illud reseisiri de catallis quae in ipso capta fuerint et ipsum tenementum cum catallis esse in pace usque ad primam assisam cum justiciarii nostri ad partes illas venerint. Et interim facias xij liberos et legales homines de visneto illo videre tenementum illud et nomina illorum imbreviari. Et summoneas eos per bonos summonitores quod sint ad primam assisam coram prefatis justiciariis nostris, parati inde facere recognitionem. Et pone per vadium et salvos plegios praedictum X vel ballivum suum, si ipse inventus non fuerit, quod tunc sit ibi auditurus recognitionem illam. Et habeas ibi summonitorum nomina, plegios et hoc breve.

Writ VI.   Assize of *mort d'ancestor.*

The King to the sheriff greeting. If A shall make you secure, &c. then summon, &c. twelve free and lawful men of the neighbourhood of Trumpington that they be before our justices at the first assize when they shall come into those parts, ready to recognize by oath if B father [mother, brother, sister, uncle, aunt,] of the afores A was seised in his demesne as of fee, of one messuage with the appurtenances in Trumpington the day wherein he died, and if he died after [the period of limitation] and if the same A be his next heir; and in the mean time let them view the messuage, and cause their names to be put in the writ, and summon by good summoners X who now holds the afores messuage, that he may be there to hear that recognizance; and have there the summoners and this writ.

Rex vicecomiti salutem. Si A fecerit te securum de clamore suo prosequendo tunc summoneas per bonos summonitores xij liberos et legales homines de vis-

neto de Trumpingtone quod sint coram justiciariis nostris ad orimam assisam cum in partes illas venerint, parati sacramento recognoscere si B pater, [mater, frater, soror, avunculus, amita] praedicti A fuit seisitus in dominico suo ut de feodo de uno mesuagio cum pertinentiis in Trumpingtone die quo obiit, et si obiit post [period of limitation]. Et si idem A ejus haeres propinquior sit. Et interim praedictum mesuagium videant et nomina eorum inbreviari facias. Et summone per bonos summonitores X qui mesuagium praedictum tenet quod tunc sit ibi auditurus illam recognitionem. Et habeas ibi summonitores et hoc breve.

"TRESPASS" WRITS

["*Ostensurus Quare*"]

Writ VII.   Writ of trespass *vi et armis* (for battery).

[*Vi et armis, contra pacem nostram*]

The King to the Sheriff of S greeting. If A shall make you secure to prosecute his claim, then put by gages and safe pledges B that he be before us on the octave of St. Michael, wheresoever we shall then be in England to show wherefore with force and arms he made an assault upon him the said A at N and beat, wounded and ill treated him, so that his life was despaired of, and other enormous things to him did, to the great damage of him the said A and against our peace. And have there the names of the pledges and this writ.

Rex Vicecomiti S salutem. Si A fecerit te securum de clamore suo prosequendo, tunc pone per vadios et salvos plegios B quod sit coram nobis in octavis Sancti Michaelis ubicunque fuerimus tunc in Anglia ostensurus quare vi et armis in ipsum A apud N insultum fecit, et ipsum verberavit, vulneravit et male tractavit, ita quod de vita ejus desperabatur, et alia enormia ei intulit, ad grave damnum ipsius A et contra pacem nostram. Et habeas ibi nomina plegiorum et hoc breve. Teste etc.

Writ VIII.   Writ of ejectment.

[*Vi et armis, contra pacem nostram*]

The King to the Sheriff of N greeting. If A shall make you secure to prosecute his claim, then put by gages and safe pledges B that he be before our Justices at Westminster [on such a day] to show wherefore with force and arms he entered into the manor of I which T demised to the said A for a term which is not yet passed, and the goods and chattels of him the said A to the value of etc. found in the same manor, took and carried away, and ejected him the said A from his farm aforesaid, and other wrongs to him did, to the great damage of him the said A and against our peace. And have the names of the pledges and this writ.

Rex Vicecomiti N salutem. Si A fecerit te securum de clamore suo prosequendo, tunc pone per vadios et salvos plegios B quod sit coram Justiciariis nostris apud Westmonasterium [tali die] ostensurus quare vi et armis manerium de I quod T praefato A dimisit ad terminum quod nondum praeteriit, intravit, et bona et catalla ejusdem A ad valentiam etc. in eodem manerio inventa cepit et asportavit, et ipsum A a firma sua praedicta ejecit, et alia enormia ei intulit ad grave damnum ipsius A et pacem nostram. Et habeas ibi nomina plegiorum et hoc breve.

Writ IX.   Writ of trespass on the case for negligence.

["Case"]

The King to the Sheriff of L greeting. If John S shall make you secure to prosecute his claim, then put by gages and safe pledges R that he be, etc., to show wherefore whereas the same John had delivered a certain horse to the said R at N, well and sufficiently to shoe; the same R fixed a certain nail in the quick of the foot of the aforesaid horse in such a manner that the horse was in many ways made worse, to the damage of him the said John one hundred shillings, as he saith. And have the names of the pledges and this writ.

Rex Vicecomiti L salutem. Si Johannes S fecerit te securum de clamore suo prosequendo, tunc pone per vadios et salvos plegios R quod sit etc. ostensurus quare cum idem Johannes quendam equum prefato R ad bene et competenter ferrandum apud N tradidisset: idem R quendam clavum in vivo pedis equi predicti intantum infixit, quod equus ille multipliciter deterioratus fuit, ad damnum ipsius Johannis centum solidorum ut dicit. Et habeas ibi nomina plegiorum et hoc breve.

Writ X.   Writ of assumpsit for negligence by a carrier.

["Case"]; ["*Assumpsit*"]

The King to the Sheriff of L greeting. If Nicholas A shall make you secure to prosecute his claim, then put by gages and safe pledges Thomas B that he be, etc., to show wherefore whereas the same Thomas at the town of S had assumed safely and securely to carry a certain pipe of wine of him the said Nicholas from the [aforesaid] town of S to the town of F; the aforesaid Thomas carried the pipe so negligently and carelessly that in default of him the said Thomas the pipe was cracked, so that the same Nicholas lost the great part of the aforesaid wine, to the damage of him the said Nicholas ten marks, as he saith. And have there the names of the pledges and this writ.

Rex Vicecomiti L salutem. Si Nicolas A fecerit te securum de clamore suo prosequendo, tunc pone per vadios et salvos plegios Thomas B quod sit etc. ostensurus quare cum idem Thomas ad quandam pipam vini ipsius Nicolai a villa de S usque villam de F salvo et secure cariandum apud praedictum villam de S assumpsit: praedictus Thomas pipam illam tam negligenter et impovide cariavit, quod pipa illa in defectu ipsius Thomae confracta fuit, sicque idem Nicolas magnam partem vini praedicti amisit, ad damnum ipsius Nicolai decem marcarum ut dicit. Et habeas ibi nomia plegiorum et hoc breve.

Illustration 5-4

Federal Rules of Civil Procedure (December 1, 1995)
Appendix of Forms

Form 1. Summons

To the above-named Defendant:

   You are hereby summoned and required to serve upon _____, plaintiff's attorney, whose address is _____ an answer to the complaint which is herewith served upon you, within 20 days after service of this summons upon you, exclusive of the day of service. If you fail to do so, judgment by default will be taken against you for the relief demanded in the complaint.

_____
Clerk of Court.

[Seal of the U.S. District Court]
Dated _____

Form 3. Complaint on a Promissory Note

   1. Allegation of jurisdiction.
   2. Defendant on or about June 1, 1935, executed and delivered to plaintiff a promissory note [in the following words and figures: (here set out the note verbatim)]; [a copy of which is hereto annexed as Exhibit A]; [whereby defendant promised to pay to plaintiff or order on June 1, 1936 the sum of _____ dollars with interest thereon at the rate of six percent. per annum].
   3. Defendant owes to plaintiff the amount of said note and interest.
      Wherefore plaintiff demands judgment against defendant for the sum of _____ dollars, interest, and cost.

   Signed: _____
Attorney for Plaintiff.

SUMMONS

COMPLAINT

I. All Writs from *Registrum Omnium Brevium* (1531), trans. J.H. Baker, *Introdution*, 1st ed., supra, 440, 443.

1. Writ of covenant
   The King to the Sheriff of *L* greeting. Command *A* that justly and without delay he keep to *B* the covenant between them made for a certain granary to be newly constructed at *N* at the charges of him the said *B*. And unless he will do this *etc.*

NOTE:
The "Forms" Appendix at the back of the Federal Rules of Civil Procedure is centuries removed from the Register of Writs, but the essence of formulary pleading is still there.

©1998 D.R. Coquillette

Form 8. Complaint for Money Had and Received

1. Allegation of jurisdiction.
2. Defendant owes plaintiff _____ dollars for money had and received from one G.H. on June 1, 1936, to be paid by defendant to plaintiff.
   Wherefore (etc. as in Form 3).

Form 11. Complaint for Conversion

1. Allegation of jurisdiction.
2. On or about December 1, 1936, defendant converted to his own use ten bonds of the _____ Company (here insert brief identification as by number and issue) of the value of _____ dollars, the property of plaintiff.
   Wherefore plaintiff demands judgment against defendant in the sum of _____ dollars, interest and costs.

Form 9. Complaint for Negligence

1. Allegation of jurisdiction.
2. On June 1, 1936, in a public highway called Boylston Steet in Boston, Massachusetts, defendant negligently drove a motor vehicle against plaintiff who was then crossing said highway.
3. As a result plaintiff was thrown down and had his leg broken and was otherwise injured, was prevented from transacting his business, suffered great pain of body and mind, and incurred expenses for medical attention and hospitalization in the sum of one thousand dollars.
   Wherefore plaintiff demands judgment against defendant in the sum of _____ dollars and costs.

2. Writ of debt

The King to the Sheriff of N greeting. Command A that justly and without delay he render to B one hundred shillings, which he owes to him and unjustly detains, as it is said. And unless he will do this *etc.*

DEBT →

DETINUE →

II. A "Trespass on the Case" Writ

Writ of trespass on the case for negligence

The King to the Sheriff of L greeting. If John S shall make you secure to prosecute his claim, then put by gages and safe pledges R that he be, *etc.*, to show wherefore whereas the same John had delivered a certain horse to the said R at N, well and sufficiently to shoe; the same R fixed a certain nail in the quick of the foot and the aforesaid horse in such manner that the horse was in many ways made worse, to the damage of him the said John one hundred shillings, as he saith. And have there the names of the pledges and this writ.

Writ XI.   Writ of *assumpsit* for nonfeasance.

["Case"]; ["*Assumpsit*"]

The King to the Sheriff of L greeting. If WH shall make you secure to prosecute his claim, then put by gages and safe pledges JP that he be, etc., to show
wherefore whereas the same J, for a certain sum of money paid to him in
hand by the aforesaid W, had assumed [at R] newly to construct a cross of
stones at R within a certain term; the aforesaid John did not take care to construct the said cross within the aforesaid term, to the damage of him the said
W twenty pounds, as he saith. And have there the names of the pledges and
this writ.

Rex Vicecomiti L salutem. Si WH fecerit te securem de clamore suo prose-
quendo, tunc pone per tadios et salvos plegios JP quod sit etc. ostensurus quare
cum idem J pro quadam pecuniae summa sibi per praefatum W prae manibus so-
luta, quandam crucem de iapidibus apud R infra certum terminum de novo con-
struere ibidem assumpsisset: praedictum Johannes crucem illam infra terminum
praedictum construere non curavit, ad damnum ipsius W viginti librarum ut
dicit. Et habeas ibi nomina plegiorum et hoc breve.

AN ACTION WITHOUT A WRIT

(*Bracton's Note Book, Case No. 1503*, J.P. Dawson, ed. and trans.)

(Court of Common Pleas, 1220–1221) Peter of Melton complained (*questus fuit*)
that Muriel, who was the wife of William of Melton [Peter's brother] and who made
out that she was pregnant by William her husband, was not pregnant by him but
made out she is pregnant to the disinheritance of Peter. On the petition of Muriel it
was ordered that the sheriff [of Norfolk] make an inquest by lawful women to see
whether she was pregnant or not. The inquest was made and sent to Westminster.

But in the meantime she came before the justices of the Bench and offered herself and showed them that she was pregnant and offered to prove this and prayed
that she be examined. By order of the justices she was examined by 14 lawful
and discreet ladies of London chosen by the mayor and sheriff of London and it
appeared to them that she was pregnant, so it was said to her that she should go
thence without day until someone made complaint thereof.

But later the said Peter came and showed himself and again complained
(*questus fuit*) that she was not pregnant by his brother, so that by his complaint
(*per querelam suam*) she was resummoned. And when asked when her husband
died and when she last saw him, she said in truth she last saw him on Wednesday after the feast of the Holy Trinity [May 24, 1220] and that he died on the
day of the Apostles Peter and Paul [June 29, 1220] so that she never saw him
after that Wednesday. And Peter confessed this and said clearly that she was not
pregnant by his brother and prayed that she be committed into custody, so that
by the judgment of the court she was committed to the custody of Saer, mayor of
London. And four lawful ladies were assigned to view her often and guard her.

Later Peter came and showed that the period for delivery had passed if she
was pregnant by his brother and prayed that justice be done to him; so that the
said Muriel came before the justices of the Bench by their order on the Wednesday before the feast of the Apostles Philip and James in the next year [May 1,

1221] and said the same, that is, that she was pregnant by the said William and she knew well that her time for delivery had passed and she awaited the grace of God. And Peter similarly said that the time [for delivery] had passed and prayed that this be allowed to him. And on this it was found that 48 weeks had passed since the Wednesday on which she confessed that her husband last saw her.

Later she confessed that she was not pregnant but that hitherto she felt so heavy with disease that she thought she was pregnant. And therefore it is considered that Peter recover as heir of the said William, etc., notwithstanding, etc.

And on this the said Peter came and prayed judgment whether she should have her dower, since in order to disinherit him she falsely made herself out to be pregnant. (*Bracton's Notebook*, no. 1503; also published in the *Curia Regis Rolls*, X 36.)

THE JURY

J.P. Dawson, "The Introduction of the Jury," from *A History of Lay Judges* (Cambridge, 1960), Harvard University Press, 125–128. [Courtesy Harvard University Press.]

Through the first centuries of its history...the common law jury was a crude instrument, however superior it undoubtedly was to the modes of proof it supplanted. Its crudity was not due simply to a requirement of unanimity; indeed unanimity was not established as a firm requirement until the second half of the fourteenth century. Whether the verdict was unanimous or by simple majority or by some intermediate fraction, the insistence on a collective or group verdict mingled indiscriminately the informed and the ignorant jurors. The remedy was simple and Bracton recommended it: let the judge interrogate the individual jurors and find out how much they really knew. If it then turned out that the jurors were ignorant or unreliable, it would not have been a very great step to assemble individual witnesses who were better informed; for in certain limited types of civil litigation proof by witnesses presented by the parties was quite well known to the thirteenth century common law and there were also some examples of criminal proceedings begun by interrogation of individual witnesses rather than collective accusation by presentment jury. Suggestions like these were most seductive but there was only one direction in which they could lead—toward the adoption in England of the canonist inquest. It seems clear that the road was open, just as open in England as it was in France. What was needed was extra zeal or sustained curiosity on the part of the English judges, inspired by a conviction that determination of the facts on which the judgment must rest was an essential part of the judge's task. But zeal and curiosity were both repressed. The whole drive was strongly in the other direction. Proof by individual witnesses was restricted, not expanded. Dissent by individual jurors, which had been both tolerated and recorded in early cases, was suppressed in the records and discouraged in fact. The pressure for unanimous verdicts grew constantly stronger. The judges in effect divested themselves of any duty to assemble or appraise the evidence. The fact-finding function was imposed instead on groups of laymen, whose ignorance was disguised by a group verdict and whose sources of knowledge the judges refused to examine. We need not consider the long process by which methods of inform-

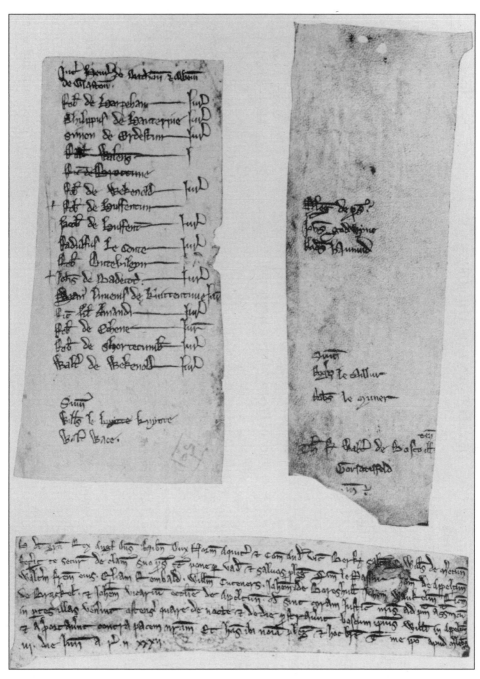

Illustration 5-5 Examples of a jury panel and writs of 1248. See *The Roll and Writ File of the Berkshire Eyre of 1248* (M.T. Clanchy, ed., 1973), vol. 90 Selden Society, frontispiece. [By permission, Selden Society and the Controller of H.M. Stationery Office.]

DEVELOPMENT OF THE JURY

Illustration 5-6

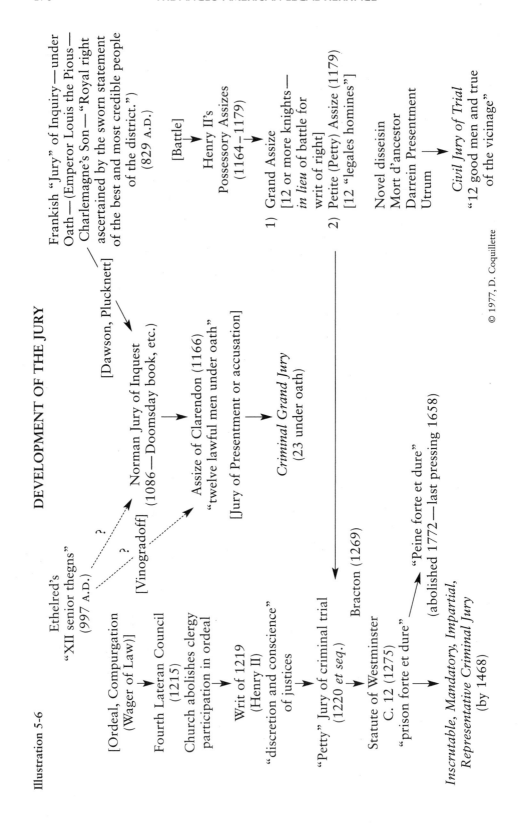

Frankish "Jury" of Inquiry—under Oath—(Emperor Louis the Pious—Charlemagne's Son—"Royal right ascertained by the sworn statement of the best and most credible people of the district." (829 A.D.)

[Dawson, Plucknett]

Norman Jury of Inquest (1086—Doomsday book, etc.)

Assize of Clarendon (1166) "twelve lawful men under oath"

[Jury of Presentment or accusation]

Criminal Grand Jury (23 under oath)

[Battle]

Henry II's Possessory Assizes (1164–1179)

1) Grand Assize [12 or more knights—*in lieu* of battle for writ of right]

2) Petite (Petty) Assize (1179) [12 "legales homines"]

Novel disseisin
Mort d'ancestor
Darrein Presentment
Utrum

Civil Jury of Trial "12 good men and true of the vicinage"

Ethelred's "XII senior thegns" (997 A.D.)

[Ordeal, Compurgation (Wager of Law)]

Fourth Lateran Council (1215)
Church abolishes clergy participation in ordeal

Writ of 1219 (Henry II)

"discretion and conscience" of justices

"Petty" Jury of criminal trial (1220 *et seq.*)

[Vinogradoff]

Bracton (1269)

Statute of Westminster C. 12 (1275) "prison forte et dure"

"Peine forte et dure" (abolished 1772—last pressing 1658)

Inscrutable, Mandatory, Impartial, Representative Criminal Jury (by 1468)

© 1977, D. Coquillette

ing juries were slowly developed, documentary and witness proof were reinstated, and trial juries were finally transformed into judges of the facts, so that their ignorance became a virtue. The final transformation came late. For a full 500 years from its organization in the thirteenth century the trial jury of the common law courts retained its mixture of elements. It was both source and judge of evidence, in proportions that were never completely defined and that changed gradually through the centuries. So long as this confusion remained, a critic from the continent might well have described the common law jury as a twelve-headed monster, wholly uncanonized. To rely on it for establishing truth on disputed issues of fact and to leave it as free from judicial controls as the English did for centuries, would have seemed to a well-trained lawyer from Paris a judicial abdication.

Various reasons have been suggested to explain why the English royal judges followed the course they did. Their main choice was between the group inquest, with some form of collective verdict, and the Roman-canonist examination of individual witnesses conducted by the judge. The specific question, therefore, is why group verdicts were accepted and then insisted upon, instead of treating the jurors truly as witnesses and examining them individually. From Maitland comes the suggestion that group verdicts were accepted because the thirteenth century trial jury was commonly used with the consent of the parties; since the parties had agreed to submit to a jury neither party could contest a result that he had in advance accepted. But this seems to be less a statement of cause than rationalization of a result, since consent could be used, as it was in France, to confer on the judge a power to examine individual witnesses by means of the canonist inquest. Another suggestion by Maitland seems again to do no more than describe a result, when he asserts that the verdict of a jury was a verdict of a neighborhood, "the voice of the countryside." It is true that modern eyes cannot readily detect the spirit of community that pervaded these medieval societies. But even though it be true that the jurors were sometimes viewed as spokesmen for a larger group, the question remains why the English crown laid upon local neighborhoods so onerous a duty.

The answer seems to be that at the outset the crown had no choice. When large-scale use of juries began in 1166 there were scarcely enough experienced men merely to direct the new court system. If, where facts were disputed, the judges were to take on the fact-finding job and interrogate individual witnesses, whether the witnesses were members of juries or not would be relatively unimportant. The judges would have been drawn irresistibly, as they were in France, into examining the testimony, determining credibility and relative weight, and making the ultimate difficult findings on contradictory evidence. It is no wonder that the English royal judges in the twelfth and early thirteenth centuries resisted the temptation to start on this long road. Crude and clumsy as it was, the early common law jury was an essential means of conserving trained manpower in a government that had taken on new tasks of immense scope and complexity.

* * * *

Bracton, De Legibus et Consuetudinibus Angliae, fol. 185b. (Trans. J.P. Dawson) [discussing the assize of *novel disseisin*]

When the oath has thus been taken, let the jurors retire to some secret place and have a conversation between themselves concerning what they have been enjoined to do and let no one have access to them or conversation with them until they have said their verdict nor let them by sign or word manifest to anyone what will be said by them. It happens often that the jurors in saying the truth are contrary to one another, so that they cannot come to one opinion. In this case by the advice of the court let the assize be afforced so that others may be added to the larger group of those who disagreed, or at least four or six, and let them be added to the others or even let them by themselves without the others discuss and decide the truth and reply by themselves, and their verdict shall be allowed and shall hold good with [the verdict of] those with whom they agree, but the others [i.e., the minority] shall not be convicted [by attaint] but shall be amerced as if for trespass, because it still may be that they spoke the truth and the others falsehood so that [the others] may be convicted of perjury.

NOTE (J.P. Dawson)

In two other passages (fol. 179b and 184b) Bracton stated that in the assize of novel disseisin (though not in the assize of mort d'ancestor) a verdict by a majority of seven was enough.

Bracton, De Legibus et Consuetudinibus Regni Angliae, fol. 143–143b. (Trans. J.P. Dawson)

When on account of fame and suspicion it is necessary to inquire into the truth as to whether the person indicted of crime is guilty or not, the king's justice if he is discreet should first inquire, if he has doubts of the case and the jury is suspected, from whence or from whom the twelve have derived what they offer in their verdict concerning the accused, and after their answers have been heard he will be able readily to determine whether there has been fraud or iniquity. If one or even a majority of the jurors should say that what they offer in their verdict was derived from one of the co-jurors and each one when interrogated says that he derived it from another, thus the questions and answers may lead from one person to another till they come to a vile and abject person such that no credence whatever is to be placed in him. The judge should inquire in this manner so that his reputation and honor may be increased and so that it will not be said that Jesus was crucified and Barabas set free.

Year Book Mich. 4 Edward II (1310), 74 Anon., Year Books of Edward II, vol. IV, 3 & 4 Edward II, A.D. 1309–1311 (ed. F.W. Maitland, G.J. Turner), vol. 22 Selden Society, London, 1907, 188.

In a writ of entry sur disseisin an inquest was joined. And after the inquest was sworn, they could not agree.

STANTON, J. "Good people, you cannot agree?"

STANTON, J., to John Allen [keeper of the rolls]. "Go and put them in a house until Monday, and let them not eat or drink."

On that commandment John put them in a house without [food or drink]. At length on the same day about vesper time they agreed. And John went to Sir Hervey [Stanton] and told him that they were agreed. Then Stanton, J., gave them leave to eat. Then on Monday the inquest came and wanted to give a verdict in gross. And Stanton, J., said that he wanted the story told. So the inquest told the story etc.

Statute 25 Edw. III, st. 5, c.4 (1351). (Trans. J.P. Dawson)

Whereas it is contained in the great charter of the franchises of England, that none shall be imprisoned or put out of his freehold or of his franchises or free customs except by the law of the land, it is accorded, assented and established that from henceforth no one shall be taken by petition or suggestion made to our lord the king or to his council, unless it be by indictment or presentment of good and lawful people of the neighborhood where such actes were done and in due manner or by process made by writ original at the common law and that no one shall be ousted of his franchises or freehold if he has not been duly put to answer and forejudged of the same by course of the law and if anything be done against the same it shall be redressed and held to be void.

Statute 42 Edw. III, c.3 (1368). (Trans. J.P. Dawson)

Item, at the request of the commons by their petitions put forth in this parliament, to eschew the mischiefs and damages done to divers of his commons by false accusers, which oftentimes have made their accusations more for revenge and singular benefit, than for the profit of the King, or of his people, which accused persons, some have been taken, and sometime caused to come before the King's council by writ, and otherwise upon grievous pain against the law: it is assented and accorded, for the good governance of the commons, that no man be put to answer without presentment before justices, or matter of record, or by due process and writ original, according to the old law of the land: and if any thing from henceforth be done to the contrary, it shall be void in the law, and holden for error.

[Above excerpts edited by J.P. Dawson.]

Illustration 6-1 Lord Hailsham of St. Maryleborne, Lord Chancellor from 1970–1974. Note the mace, symbol of royal authority, and the purse (in his hand), which was used to contain the Matrix of the Great Seal of the Realm. [From M. Bond, D. Beamish, *The Lord Chancellor*, London, Her Royal Majesty's Stationery Office, 1977, p. 33. Crown copyright is reproduced with the permission of the Controller of Her Majesty's Stationery Office.]

VI

EQUITY

We noted earlier that the royal common law courts were not an exclusive source of legal remedies. From the beginning, they coexisted with the old Anglo-Saxon local courts of the hundred and shire, as well as with the feudal courts of the manor, the so-called "seignorial" courts that had jurisdiction over copy-hold and other forms of unfree tenure. Later, we will also discuss special courts that sprung up in the towns and cities, or during trade fairs. These heard the claims of merchants and were called "mercantile courts," or courts "piepoudre."[1] Yet, the most important courts outside of the royal common law courts were none of the above. They were the courts of the Church.

A. CHURCH COURTS AND THE CANON LAW

Even before the Norman Conquest, the Church exercised a parallel governance of England, with a system of dioceses and parishes that reflected the shires, towns and manors of civil authority. While this parallel system could result in trouble—such as the infamous split between Henry II and Thomas Beckett— usually spiritual and civil authority reinforced each other, both symbolically and practically.

As we have seen, priests actually participated in the old forms of judicial proof, particularly the ordeal, until this was prohibited by the Fourth Lateran Council (1215). By the thirteenth and fourteenth centuries, however, the Church in England had developed a complementary jurisdiction. This encompassed not only matters involving Church lands and priests, but also many disputes that today would be regarded as purely secular matters, including divorce, defamation, grants of probate, important issues of legitimacy, supervision of executors and administrators of personal property. Also included were abrogation of certain undertakings, "breaches of faith," even though the undertakings were unsupported by formal covenants, i.e., in writing and under seal. Of course, spiri-

---

1. "Piepoudre" probably refers to the dusty feet, or "pied poudre" of the merchants. Simple Simon's "pieman going to a fair" was, in fact, a "pie poudre" man.

tual courts often could only enforce their judgments by spiritual sanctions, but excommunication and other such punishments could have profound consequences, even for the most secular.

The Church courts looked to Rome and the Continent for their procedures and doctrines, a feature that would later lead to criticism by opponents. The Canon Law was, however, a rich source of juristic ideas, drawing in turn from the Roman Law. The famous books of the Canon Law were the *Decretum* of Gratian (1140), the *Decretals* of Gregory IX (1234) and *The Liber Sextus* (1298) of Boniface VIII, together forming the so-called *Corpus Juris Canonici*. These books were full of both procedural ideas and important doctrines, including many of the notions of good faith that we will discuss in the context of commercial law and the equity courts.

B. THE ORIGIN OF EQUITY

It would be easy to attribute the introduction of "equity," and equitable doctrines, to the Canon Law. In this we would not be entirely wrong, for Canon Law and Christian theology were central to many fundamental principles of equity including protection of the weak and vulnerable, enforcement of good faith bargains, mitigation of harsh terms or technical "traps," and mercy for those whose conduct deserved mercy. But the idea of "equity" predates Christianity, and derives from Greek and Roman theory. Indeed, as we will see, the greatest century for equitable jurisdictions in English history was the same that saw a renaissance of classical learning, the sixteenth century. Indeed, equity's roots in classical humanism proved important when the Catholic Church was expelled from England, also in the sixteenth century.

The linguistic origins of equity were the Greek *epieikeia* and the Latin *aequitas*. The original classical meaning was "fairness," but the Romans added a related notion, the ideal of a "fairness" that transcends that strict positive law in those individual situations where a mechanical application of a rule of law would be unjust. This "fairness" would also be available to plug the inevitable gaps in enacted positive law, or to construe and apply statutes in a commonsense way, a notion later to be called "equity of the statute." Aristotle defined equity as that which corrects "the error that is generated by the unqualified language in which absolute justice must be stated." *Nichomachean Ethics*, 5.10.

Here is a common example. Even the best drafted set of parking ordinances should not always be enforced. You should not park in front of a hydrant, and in 99.9% of all cases you should be towed away and fined. But suppose you stopped to rescue an infant who had run away from home? Equity would say you should not be punished. Equity is the fair (rather than equal) application of positive law, a principle that may demand that positive laws be applied by exception and exemption, rather than by "blind obedience." See *Materials, infra*. Almost by definition, then, "equity" should be applied on an individual case by case basis, and one case should not necessarily be "precedent" for the next. Thus, as a process, equity is very different from the development of the common law by case precedent.

C. THE SPECIAL ROLE OF THE LORD CHANCELLOR AND THE CHANCERY

Catholic philosophers, such as Thomas Aquinas, were strongly influenced by the work of Aristotle. Aquinas' *Summa*, and other leading theological and philosophical works, seized on the idea of "legalism ruled by equity" and saw in it the essence of divine will and God's mercy. Not surprisingly, therefore, the Church courts and the Canon Law were hospitable to the idea.

"Equity" was also advanced by another factor, the medieval belief that the King had a residual power, and a duty, to right any wrong that came before him for which there was no regular remedy. Medieval monarchs swore "to do equal and right justice and discretion in mercy and truth." See Baker, *Introduction, supra*, 113 quoting the Coronation Oath of Edward II.

The religious and royal components of equity met in the office and person of the King's Confessor, the Lord Chancellor. He was the cleric who was responsible for running the royal secretariat, housed in the King's Chapel, and staffed originally by other literate clerics. (This office was, among other functions, the source of the common law writs.) He was also the custodian of the Great Seal of the Realm, symbol of royal authority, used to authenticate important documents. Finally, he was the King's official Confessor, the "King's Conscience," and had a special duty to advise the King in moral and legal matters.

By the fourteenth century, special pleas to the King for "equity" were routinely referred to the Lord Chancellor. The court where the Lord Chancellor heard these pleas became known as the "Chancery."[2] As a judge, the Lord Chancellor had extraordinary powers, but he usually chose not to use them if there was an adequate common law remedy. This was an early notion of "exhaustion of remedies." But if the common law either could not, or would not, do the right thing, the Lord Chancellor had the discretion, in appropriate circumstances, to put things right.

There were three major differences between this court and the common law courts. First, remedies at equity were always discretionary. At law, you were entitled to your remedy, no matter who you were. At equity, you would have to impress the Chancellor with your "clean hands" (and heart!). At equity, precedents were not binding. Every case was individual and personal. Second, the Chancellor had a fearsome power, the *subpoena*, to summon individuals before him. Equitable jurisdiction focused on the person, not on land or things. It was *in personam*. The Chancellor could, and did, imprison individuals for contempt if they disobeyed his orders. Such orders were often for specific performance of agreements or restitution of unjust enrichment. Finally, there was no jury at equity. The Chancellor was both judge of law and trier of fact. To obtain facts he used procedures similar to those developed in the canon law, including written interrogatories and inquisitorial procedures. There were also no formal writs, only informal "bills" and even "word of mouth" complaints. Thus, there were no formulary restrictions on either remedies or modes of trial.

---

2. This was technically called the "English" side of the Chancery, as the pleas were usually in English, to distinguish itself from the "Latin" side which was responsible for administration and record keeping, usually done in Latin.

Given the differences between the Chancery and the common law courts, it might be expected that there would be conflicts between them. In fact, the record shows remarkable cooperation between a system of vested legal rights and remedies and a complementary system of discretionary relief. One reason may be that, despite the Canon Law influences, the Chancery was not a Church court, but another royal court. As we will see, many of its practitioners were common lawyers, trained in the same institutions as those practicing in the common law courts. Another reason may be that the Chancery permitted the common law courts to adhere to strict forms and rules without worrying about the "hard case" which would make poor precedent if decided compassionately.

A typical example, which occurred regularly, was the debtor who repaid a debt without insisting on canceling the sealed bond. See Baker, *Introduction, supra,* 118. At law, the sealed bond was conclusive proof of the debt, and the creditor could sue and be paid again. The advantage of a strict and reliable rule for proof of debt was obvious in 99% of all cases, and the common law felt no obligation to protect fools. If exceptions were permitted, they would quickly become precedents that every debtor would use to avoid payment. But what about a debtor who was inexperienced, or feeble minded, or under age, or senile? These cases would be taken care of by the Chancellor's mercy.

As we will see later, this mutual cooperation did not persist under all conditions. In particular, the Lord Chancellor served at the immediate pleasure of the King, and was the King's confidant. When the Stuarts come to the throne in the seventeenth century, and divisions began between the King and Parliament, the Chancellor and his court were naturally seen as royal instruments, while the common law courts—particularly under the leadership of Chief Justice Edward Coke—were seen as bastions of the "rule of law."

It is the danger of any form of discretionary justice that it can quickly look arbitrary and corrupt under the wrong circumstances. Thomas More, a saint, martyr, and, ironically, one of the first non-clerics to become Chancellor, was executed by Henry VIII when he failed to comply with the royal will. At the other extreme, Francis Bacon, another great Chancellor, was a fervent advocate of the royal cause of James I. For this, he was impeached by Parliament for corruption.[3] These episodes, however, were the reflection of great political and philosophical struggles that divided England. The dichotomy of common law courts and equitable jurisdiction, when given a chance, worked surprisingly well under normal conditions, and the system lasted for centuries.[4]

Incidentally, there were other courts of equity besides the Chancery. We will discuss some of them in Chapter VII, "Specialized Courts."

D. HENRY VIII, ST. GERMAN, AND "SECULAR EQUITY"

We have already seen that some of the roots of equity were in the medieval notions of kingship, while others were rooted in classical humanism. This is not

---

3. See the electrifying account in D.R. Coquillette, *Francis Bacon* (Stanford and Edinburgh, 1992), 219–223.

4. Indeed, we will discuss its modern developments in Chapter XIII, *infra.*

a bad simile for the early English Renaissance in general, during which equitable jurisdiction flourished. Following the death of Richard III at Bosworth Field, Henry Tudor (Henry VII) took the Crown. When Henry married Elizabeth of York, the heiress of the rival house, the red and white roses were at last reunited into the familiar Tudor Rose.

The Tudors ruled England from 1485 to 1603, and provided three of England's greatest leaders, Henry VII, Henry VIII, and Henry VIII's extraordinary daughter by Anne Boleyn, Elizabeth I. During this century, the full cultural Renaissance came to England. The later Tudor years saw an outpouring of poetry, drama, prose, scientific and political thought, and humanistic study that has not been exceeded by any period since. There was national pride in holding Continental enemies at bay, excitement in the discovery of the New World, commercial prosperity based on trade, and a strong, wise leadership. For centuries to come, this period was to symbolize the best of the English language and the English culture.

One of the most traumatic events of this century was the Reformation and Henry VIII's ultimate decision, effective in January, 1534, to take England out of the Catholic Church. The immediate reason was Henry's desire for a legitimate male heir, and, therefore, a legitimate divorce, which the Pope refused to grant. This was a conventional wish, but full of irony, given the great strength of his ultimate heir, Elizabeth. (But Elizabeth could never marry without risk to her legal power, thus ending the dynasty.) Another reason for Henry's action was consolidation of royal power. Both spiritual and secular authority were united for the first time in one person. There were also vast rewards to Henry's supporters. The dissolution of vast Church holdings and their distribution among Henry's trusted lieutenants created a new nobility, directly indebted to the King.

The new commercial wealth of the Kingdom, and the self-destruction of the old aristocracy in the Wars of the Roses, also strengthened the Parliament. As we will see, Henry VIII was a master at winning parliamentary support without relinquishing royal power, a trait inherited by Elizabeth. See *Materials*, Chapter IX.

In particular, Henry VIII understood the need to divide the power bases of his rivals, and to consolidate his own. With the abolition of the Catholic Church in England, English Canon Law no longer came from Rome. Henry, however, saw the need for retaining the ecclesiastical courts under his control. He also saw the advantages of a Chancery responsive directly to his wishes. He encouraged Roman law based "civil law" in England, and strengthened "specialty courts" which used that law exclusively. This was done, in part, because he understood the power of the common lawyers as a profession and the common law courts. Thus, he sought to balance the common law's power with other jurisdictions closely linked to his council, including the Chancellor's Chancery, and with civil law practitioners, whose work we will discuss in the next chapter.

But the abolition of the Catholic Church in England left equity without one of its best theoretical foundations. The execution of Thomas More, Henry's great Lord Chancellor, was symbolic of this break. Fortunately for the English law, an extraordinary book had been published only a few years before More's execution in 1535. It was by Christopher St. German (1460?-1540) and was called the *Doctor and Student*.[5]

---

5. Thomas More was a saint. St. German was not. Both were common lawyers, and they actually debated each other on a number of topics during their lives.

The *Doctor and Student* was first published in Latin in 1523 ("Dialogue I") and then in English with a second "Dialogue" in 1530. It was the first major law book published in English. This in itself was an extraordinary and symbolic break, as all prior law books had been in Latin or Norman "Law French." It was also the first purely analytical English law book. In the true Renaissance spirit, it examined candidly and scientifically "the principles or grounds of the laws of England," an unthinkable exercise only a few years before.[6]

The great achievement of this small book was to establish a secular basis for English equity, just as Henry VIII jeopardized its religious basis by suppressing the Catholic Church. This substitution of analytical theology and philosophy for the unquestioned authority of the Church was not only typical of both the Reformation and Counter-Reformation, it also laid the groundwork for modern jurisprudence.

The "method" of the book was ingenious and a fairly typical genre for the period: a dialogue.[7] The two participants were a "A Doctoure of Dyvynytie" who "had great desyre of longetyme to know wherupon the lawe of Englande is grounded" and his friend "of great acquayntaunce," a "student in the Lawes of England." The "Doctor" was not conversant in Law French, the professional language of the lawyer since Norman times, "in that tonge I am no thynge experte." The Student was probably more conversant in Law French than the "Doctor's" Latin. English was an obvious compromise, and the *Doctor and the Student* was one of the first legal treatises widely circulated in English.

Key sections of the dialogues are set out in the *Materials* that follow, so there will be no attempt to summarize them here. St. German was a clear and compelling writer. His "bottom" line, sometimes implicit from necessity, was that the common law will be effective only if it is firmly based on a moral foundation, and that its continuing health requires careful and critical examination of its fundamental assumptions. This was a proposition striking in its modernity. Indeed, St. German was, in 1523, in many ways a modern man writing a modern book. Such was the miracle of the Renaissance.[8]

FOR FURTHER READING

I.   Original Texts

The scholarly edition of St. German's great treatise is *St. German's Doctor and Student* (eds. T.F.T. Plucknett, J.L. Barton, London, 1974), vol. 91 Selden Society. A classic collection of original Chancery records is *Select Cases in Chancery 1364-*

---

6. The "common law" was, to the medieval mind, based on the ancient customs of the land, manifesting God's will. It was simply *there*.

7. Dialogues were safer in days when it was risky to take an overt political position in print. It could be argued that neither character necessarily represented the author's actual views.

8. For a full discussion of St. German's *Doctor and Student* see "Introduction," *St. German's Doctor and Student* (eds. T.F.T. Plucknett, J.L. Barton, London, 1974), Selden Society vol. 91, xi–lxvii. See also D.R. Coquillette, *The Civilian Writers of Doctors' Commons, London* (Berlin, 1988), 48–59.

1471 (ed. J.F. Baldwin, London, 1896), vol. 10 Selden Society. See also, J. A. Guy, *Christopher St. German on Chancery and Statute* (London, 1985), which contains the text of St. German's *A Little Treatise Concerning Writs of Subpoena*, 106 ff.

II.   Origins of Equity

See William W. Buckland *Equity in Roman Law* (London, 1911); George B. Adams "The Origin of English Equity," the *Columbia Law Review* (1916), 16, and other sources cited at *Materials, infra*. For an excellent account of the influence of Canon Law on English law generally, see R.H. Helmholz, *Canon Law and The Law of England* (London, 1987). See also Charles Donahue's brilliant "Roman Canon Law in the Medieval English Church," 72 *Michigan Law Rev.* (1974), 647–716. There is a very concise account in T.F.T. Plucknett, *Concise History, supra*, 301–306, and a good summary in J.H. Baker, *Introduction, supra*, 146–154.

III.   The Chancellor and the Court of Chancery

For an excellent concise account, see J.H. Baker, *Introduction, supra*, 112–134. See also J.L. Barton, "Equity in the Medieval Common Law," *Equity in the World's Legal Systems* (R.O. Newman, ed., 1973), 139–155; W.J. Jones, *The Elizabethan Court of Chancery* (1967); L.A. Knafla, *Law and Politics in Jacobean England* (1977). There is an excellent theoretical discussion of equity in C.K. Allen, *Law in the Making* (7th ed., 1964), 383–425.

IV.   The Tudors and the English renaissance

For an excellent historical summary, see John Guy, "The Tudor Age (1485–1603)" in *The Oxford History of Britain* (Oxford, 1986), 257–326. For extended accounts of daily life and political conditions, see S.T. Bindoff, *Tudor England* (London, 1950) and for an account of the Tudor world view, see E.M.W. Tillyard, *The Elizabethan World Picture* (New York, 1957). For an account focused on the religious changes, see T.M. Parker, *The English Reformation to 1558* (New York, 1966). Perhaps the most interesting achievement of the Tudors was a stable domestic government, founded on a careful balance of royal and parliamentarian interests, with particular attention to means of public finance, good local government, and careful foreign relations. The Tudor dynasty has been described as the origin of the "modern national state," but the truth is more complex. See S.B. Chrimes, *English Constitutional History* (Oxford), 87–120, and *The Tudor Constitution: Documents and Commentary* (2d ed., G.R. Elton, Cambridge, 1960).

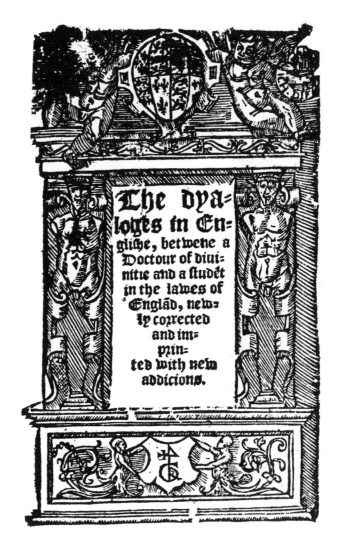

Illustration 6-2   The title page of an early St. German *Doctor and Student,* in English. (London, 1554). [Author's Collection.]

MATERIALS

Bracton (*circa* 1236 A.D.) (S.E. Thorne, trans.) fol. 3a – 3b.

What equity is.

Equity is the bringing together of things, that which desires like right in like cases and puts all like things on an equality. Equity is, so to speak, uniformity, and turns upon matters of fact, that is, the words and acts of men. Justice, [on the other hand,] lies in the minds of the just. Hence it is that if we wish to speak properly we will call a judgment equitable, not just, and a man just, not equitable. But using these terms improperly, we call the man equitable and the judgment just. Jurisprudence therefore differs in many ways from justice. For jurisprudence [discerns,] justice awards to each his due. Justice is a virtue, jurisprudence a science. Justice is a certain *summum bonum*; jurisprudence a *medium.*

Daniel R. Coquillette, "Equity," from *Dictionary of the Middle Ages*, American Council of Learned Societies, 1981, 501. [Courtesy American Council of Learned Societies].

EQUITY. Derived from the Greek *epieikeia* and the Latin *aequitas*, the medieval concept of equity incorporated a variety of legal, philosophical, and institutional ideas. The basic meaning of *aequitas* in classical law was "fairness" or, in Ciceronian formulation, "that which demands like law in like cases." A second related Roman idea was that of *aequitas* as an abstract ideal that transcended positive law (*jus*) and confirmed such rights as that of a child to inherit, or that of a landowner to retain any treasure found on his land—whether or not these rights were expressed in written law. The classical texts called on this concept of *aequitas* to offer guidance in filling the inevitable gaps in the established positive law. It was also used to test, by contrast or comparison, the "just spirit" of the enacted rules, the "correspondence between a legal rule or institution and the spirit of civil or natural law" (J.B. Moyle, *Imperatoris Iustiniani Institutionum*, 29, 5th ed. [1964]). See *Digest* 1.1. pr.; 1.1.7.1; 1.1.17; 1.3.25; 2.14.1 pr.; 4.1.7 pr.; 15.1.32 pr.; 16.3.31.1; 37.5.1 pr.; 44.4 pr.; 47.4.1.1; 50.17.90. A final and very distinct, element of classical equity jurisprudence was Aristotle's definition of equity as that which corrects "the error that is generated by the unqualified language in which absolute justice must be stated" (*Nicomachean Ethics*, 5.10). In other words, equity is the fair (rather than equal) application of positive law, a principle that may demand that positive laws be applied by exception and exemption rather than by blind obedience. Thus, there were these basic classical ideas about equity: first, the *aequitas* of Cicero that demanded that all laws be justly, in the sense of equally, applied; second, the *aequitas naturalis* of the *Digest* and the *Institutes*, that spirit of natural justice that stands apart from the positive law (*jus*) and guides the discretion of the praetor; and third, the Aristotelian *epieikeia* which, by modification and exception in the light of particular circumstances, corrects the error generated by the unqualified language in which all positive law inevitably must be expressed.

Classical *aequitas* exerted a strong influence on Christian ethical doctrines. Thomas Aquinas particularly seized on both Aristotle's teachings and the classical notion of *aequitas* as an abstract spirit of justice apart from positive law, thus facilitating his great effort to reconcile the law of God, the law of the church, and temporal law. Aquinas thoroughly understood Aristotle's principle of "equitable" construction: "A man who follows the lawmaker's intention is not interpreting the law simply speaking, as it stands, but setting it in a real situation; there, from the prospect of the damage that would follow, it is evident that the lawmaker would have him act otherwise" (*Summa Theologiae*, la2ae.96.6). The notion that "legalism should be ruled by equity" was a fundamental idea of Aquinas. "It seems that human law does not set up an obligation in the court of conscience. An inferior power has no jurisdiction in a superior court" (*Summa Theologiae*, la2ae.96.4, 6). It was also largely Aquinas' influence, not classical doctrine, that introduced to Europe the "equity" of Henry Maine's famous definition: "Any body of rules existing by the side of the original civil law, founded on distinct principles and claiming incidentally to supersede the civil law in virtue of a superior sanctity inherent in those principles" (*Ancient Law,* 2nd ed. [1864], 27).

But "distinct principles" more specific than Christian theology itself were slow to emerge. As early as the Frankish kings, and in England after the Conquest, it was accepted that the responsibility for "equity," in the sense of a kind of roughhewn extraordinary justice, lay with the king and his council. In England, the royal council had discretionary powers that enabled it to promote equity, but this discretion was regarded as part and parcel of the common law and the legal constitution, not as a separate system with distinct principles. (See *Glanvill* II, 7, G. D. G. Hall, ed. [1965], 28. See also *Bracton,* vol. 2, 23–24 [fol. 3]; 304 [fol. 107]; 307 [fol. 108], S. E. Thorne, trans. [1968].) Indeed *Bracton* (*ca.* 1230) included the obligation to render decisions "with equity and mercy" as part of the coronation oath of the king, and spoke of the "countenance" from which comes "forth the judgment of equity" when describing the judges who "represent the king's person...as they sit in justice" (*Bracton,* 304 [fol. 107]; 307 [fol. 108]).

The king's peculiar responsibility for "equity" was surely assisted by the civil jurists of developing continental and English university law schools and by the canon lawyers of the church. One of the first teachers of law in England was Vacarius, who was teaching at the infant Oxford University, probably earlier than 1149. Vacarius was a follower of continental jurists, such as Irnerius, who regarded the sovereign as both legislatively omnipotent and capable of interpreting and modifying legal rules in specific cases, as he himself could hardly be bound by what was a creation of his own will. According to Vacarius, the king and council could give weight to considerations of "equity," whereas a lower judge was bound by the law. These theories were the seeds of the later special equity jurisdictions of the English conciliar courts.

The growth of humanism among civil law jurists and churchmen during the fourteenth and fifteenth centuries tended to promote the concept of *aequitas*. Jurists such as Lucas de Penna (*d. ca.* 1390) wrote of equity as, first, the source of law, the abstract principle of justice; second, the principle that decides cases concerning which the positive law is silent (*casus omissi*); and third, the criterion of interpretation that safeguards "against the mechanical, literal interpretation of law." The first idea was certainly found in medieval England and known to common lawyers as "reason," the traditional sense of right and wrong that preserved the law from legalistic inconsistency or absurdity. The third idea, the criterion of statutory construction, became equally familiar to English common lawyers as the "equity of statute." Furthermore, through the ecclesiastical courts and through the royal secretariats that they dominated, canonists in England and on the Continent sought to define equity as including Christian ethics—in effect a higher law to be enforced by the sovereign.

In England, the focus of these ideas became the King's Chancellor. Traditionally a cleric and "keeper of the king's conscience," the Chancellor was also a natural representative of the king and council before extraordinary pleas for justice, when ordinary judges and officers either could not or would not "do right." Around this figure developed one of several special courts of equity, together with a distinct and highly developed body of equity law that for centuries was unique to these courts.

There is no doubt that common law and equity originated together: the king ensured justice for all by means of his own prerogative power and his prerogative legal machinery. But differentiations between the royal prerogative powers and the law of equity did eventually occur, and in ways neither required nor anticipated by the classical writers of medieval jurisprudence. This particularly English phenomenon was to have a profound and lasting effect on Anglo-American jurisprudence.

The rationale for this development was more institutional than theoretical, and it is largely explained by the history of English royal courts, particularly the King's Council and the Chancellor. By the time of Edward I, the king's court had gradually evolved into three tribunals: a Common Bench (which sat in Westminster Hall), a King's Bench (which was supposed to follow the king's travels), and a higher court, which in the days of Edward I we may indifferently call the King in Council or the King in Parliament. The Chancery, by contrast, was not originally a court at all, but a great secretarial bureaucracy and a ministry of justice. As such, it was somewhat similar to the King's Exchequer, an office that was already a curia by the thirteenth century, in that it called the king's debtors before it, issued process, and judged controversies. Both of these royal bureaus were to develop jurisdictions apart from the royal common law courts of Common Bench and King's Bench. Their claim to distinction would be their particular closeness to the King in Council, the "fountainhead" of justice.

At first these institutions did not spawn separate doctrines or bodies of rules. There was, after all, no complete body of written law in England. No one can be absolutely certain when the Chancellor, in addition to his many other duties, began to hear petitions regularly on the "English side" of the Chancery, directed to the King's special justice or equity. Suggestive petitions survive from the latter half of the fourteenth century. Decrees were first issued in the name of the King in Council, but by 1473 at the latest the Chancellor issued decrees in his own name.

At least initially, there were four critical differences between this "equity" jurisdiction and the process of the "law" courts. First, the petition was in the form of a simple "bill," not a formal legal writ, alleging some reason why extraordinary justice was required, that is, why the petitioner considered his case to be beyond ordinary procedures. Second, the Chancellor issued a subpoena to the individual defendant, which commenced the action *in personam* and was good in all counties—a clear advantage over the more restricted common-law process. Third, there was no jury—on the theory that a jury could be misled more easily by faulty pleading than the Chancellor. Fourth, until the 1440s the defendant was verbally examined under oath by the Chancellor, a practice replaced by written answers serving the same purpose. The parties could both testify and be examined.

With time, English equity evolved special remedies as well as special procedures: the enforcement of "uses," or medieval trusts, wherein the formal legal title of the owner is held to the "use" of a beneficiary; the recognition of copyhold title; the recognition of assignment as a chose in action; relief against inequitable penalties and forfeitures; and specific performance of agreements and injunctive orders, a type of legal remedy that could be substantially more flexible and adaptive than the common-law forms of action.

There is no doubt that these procedures and remedies were derived in part from the procedures of the church courts and the canon law. They were familiar to the Chancellors, who were clerics and trained in the civil and canon law traditions of a cosmopolitan church. But as H. D. Hazeltine has shown, many if not most of these special features were borrowed from the older English practices of the justices in eyre and other courts: "The new tribunal... simply carried on the work of the older courts by developing in greater fullness and with a different machinery the equity inherent in royal justice" (Hazeltine, in Paul Vinogradoff, ed., *Essays in Legal History* [1913], 285).

Thus the other so-called conciliar courts that split off from the King's Council could be, and were, "courts of equity." One of the most important examples was the Court of Requests, which originated with the official of the King's Council who had the responsibility of dealing with the requests and petitions of the poor. By Tudor times the Court of Requests was a court of conscience that also had many of the "equitable" procedural features of the Chancellor's court. All of these courts, at various times, employed "equitable" procedures and had functions similar to the court of the Chancellor himself. Equity was not the monopoly of the Chancellor. Neither was English equity the special domain of canonists and clerics. Had it been otherwise, the Reformation, Henry VIII's Act of Settlement or Supremacy (1534), and the concurrent suppression of canon-law study in England would have had a disastrous effect.

The ultimate survival and even flourishing of equitable ideas in England, despite the laicization of the Chancery, was due in large part to the intellectual influence of one man, Christopher St. German, an English common lawyer. St. German's great book, *Doctor and Student,* appeared first in a Latin version in 1523. It bridged the gap from a clerical to a lay Chancery with intellectual brilliance. *Doctor and Student's* success in preserving and reconciling the role of equity in modern English law was one of the first examples of a printed book substantially influencing the course of the law.

Thus, "equitable" law, developed in part from classical and medieval roots, became a permanent part of English law. As such, equity took special notice of fiduciary relationships; gave special relief from fraud or unconscionable dealing; gave relief from strict legal obligation where, through unforeseen events and pure accident, a party was unreasonably prejudiced; and gave special attention to the intentions of parties in the interpretation of wills, settlements, and other formal documents, where a strict legal reading would have perverted the common understanding. Finally, equity took "tutelary jurisdiction" over those who, "through special circumstances, are particularly in need of protection: infants, married women, mariners, borrowers, those who are subject to harsh penalties, and formerly the poor and the insane" (Carleton K. Allen, *Law in the Making*, 2nd ed. [1930], 236). To all these concerns were brought, in principle, the special evidentiary procedures and the special remedies of equitable doctrine, a lasting heritage of classical and medieval thought.

BIBLIOGRAPHY

Equity in medieval jurisprudence. George B. Adams, "The Origin of English Equity," in *Columbia Law Review*, 16 (1916); J. L. Barton, "Equity in the Medieval Common Law," in Ralph A. Newman, ed., *Equity in the World's Legal System* (1973); Charles S. Brice, "Roman *Aequitas* and English Equity," in *Georgetown Law Review*, 2 (1913); William W. Buckland, *Equity in Roman Law* (1911); Frederic W. Maitland, "Canon Law in England," in his *Collected Papers*, III (1911); Frederick Pollock and Frederic W. Maitland, *The History of English Law Before the Time of Edward I*, 2nd ed. by S. F. C. Milsom, I (1968), 189–197, 286–296; S. E. Thorne, "The Equity of a Statute and Heydon's Case," in *Illinois Law Review*, 31 (1936); Paul Vinogradoff, *Roman Law in Mediaeval Europe*, 2nd ed. (1909), 54–58; Walter Ullmann, *The Medieval Idea of Law* (1946, repr. 1969), 41–44; H. E. Yntema, "Equity in the Civil Law and the Common Law," in *The American Journal of Comparative Law*, 15 (1967).

The special English courts and law of equity. Margaret E. Avery, "The History of the Equitable Jurisdiction of the Chancery Before 1460," in *Bulletin of the Institute of Historical Research*, 42 (1969), and "An Evaluation of the Effectiveness of the Court of Chancery Under the Lancastrian Kings," in *Law Quarterly Review*, 86 (1970); William P. Baildon, ed., *Select Cases in Chancery*, A.D. 1364 to 1471, Selden Society, X (I 896); John H. Baker, *An Introduction to English Legal History*, 2nd ed. (1979), 83–100; Willard T. Barbour, *The History of Contract in Early English Equity*, Oxford Studies in Social and Legal History, IV (1914); Edgar Bodenheimer, *Jurisprudence*, rev. ed. (1974), 249–251, 363–367; William H. Bryson, *The Equity Side of the Exchequer* (1975); A. D. Hargreaves, "Equity and the Latin Side of the Chances," in *Law Quarterly Review*, 68 (1952); H. D. Hazeltine, "The Early History of English Equity," in Paul Vinogradoff, ed., *Essays in Legal History* (1913); William S. Holdsworth, *A History of English Law*, I, *History of the Chancery* (1903), 194–263; IV, *Canon Law and Equity*, 3rd ed. (1945), 275–283; and V, *Rules of Equity in the Fifteenth and Sixteenth Centuries*, 3rd ed. (1945), 278–338; Frederic W. Maitland, *Equity* (1909); S. F. C. Milsom, *Historical Foundations of the Common Law* (1969), 74–87; T. F. T . Plucknett, *A Concise History of the Common Law*, 5th ed. (1956), 178–181, 675–694.

DANIEL COQUILLETTE

St. German's *Doctor and Student* (1523, 1530) (ed. T.F.T. Plucknett, J.L. Barton, 1974), vol. 91, Selden Society 3, 7, 95–101, 228–231.[Courtesy Selden Society].

¶HERE AFTER FOLOWETH THE FYRSTE DYALOGE IN ENGLYSSHE/ BYTWYXT A DOCTOURE OF DYUYNYTE/ AND A STUDENT IN THE LAWES OF ENGLANDE: OF THE GROUNDES OF THE SAYD LAWES, AND OF CONSCYENCE/ NEWLY CORRECTYD: AND EFTSONES EMPRYNTED: WITH NEWE ADDYCYONS.

* * * * * * * * * * * * *

¶THE INTRODUCCYON.

A Doctoure of Dyuynytie that was of great acquayntaunce/ and famylyarytie with a Student in the Lawes of Englande sayde thus vnto him/ I haue had great desyre of longe tyme to knowe wherupon the lawe of Englande is grounded/ but because moche part of the lawe of Englande is wryten in the frenche tonge/ Therfore I can not through myne owne studye atteygne to the knowlege therof: for in that tonge I am no thynge experte. And bycause I haue alwayes founde the a faythfull frende to me in all my busynes. Therfore I am bolde to come to the by-fore any other to know thy mynde what be the very groundes of the lawe of Eng-lande as thou thynkest.

¶STUDENT) that wolde aske a great leasure/ and it is also aboue my cun-nynge to do it. Neuerthelesse y thou shalt not thynke that I wold wylfully refuse to fulfyll thy desyre: I shall with good wyll do that in me is to satysfye thy mynde/ but I pray the that thou wylte fyrste shewe me somwhat of other lawes that pertayne most to this mater: [and that Doctoures treate of howe lawes haue bygon.] [2b] And then I wyll gladly shewe the as me thynketh what be the groundes of the lawe of Englande.

¶DOCTOURE) I wyll with good wyll do as thou sayste: wherfor thou shalt vnderstande that Doctours treate of foure lawes the whiche [as me semyth] per-tayne moste to this mater. The fyrste is the lawe eternall. The seconde is the lawe of nature [of reasonable creature] the which as I haue harde saye is called by them that be lernyd in the lawe of Englande the lawe of reason. *And so under that name " law of reason " I shall treat of it in this work.* The thyrde is the lawe of god. The fourth is the lawe of man. And therfore I wyll fyrste treate of the lawe eternall.

* * * * *

¶WHAT IS EQUYTIE.

The .xvi. chapytre.

DOCTOURE) Equytye is a [ryghtwysenes] that consideryth all the pertyculer cyrcumstaunces of the dede/ the whiche also is temperyd with the swetnes of mer-cye. And [suche an equytye] must alway be obscruyd in euery lawe of man/ and in euery generall rewle therof/ & that knewe he wel that sayd thus. Lawes couet to be rewlyd by equytye. And the wyse man sayth: be not [36b] ouer moch ryghtwyse for the extreme ryghtwysenes is extreme wronge/ [as who sayth yf thou take all that the wordes of the law gyueth the thou shalte somtyme do agaynst the lawe.] And for the playner declaracyon what equytie is thou shalt vnderstande that syth the dedes and acts of men/ for whiche lawes ben ordayned happen in dyuers man-

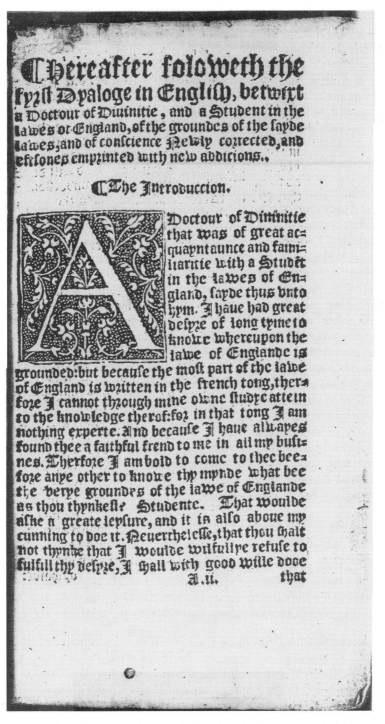

Illustration 6-3 The first page of an early St. German, *Doctor and Student*, (London, 1554) in English. [Author's Collection.]

ers infynytlye. It is not possyble to make any generall rewle of the lawe/ but that it shall fayle in some case. And therfore makers of lawes take hede to suche thynges as may often come and not to euery particular case/ for they coulde not though they wolde And therfore to folowe the wordes of the lawe/ were in some case both agaynst Iustyce & the common welth: wherfore in some cases it is *good and even necessary* to leue the wordis of the lawe/ & to folowe that reason and Justyce requyreth/ & to that intent equytie is ordeyned/ that is to say to tempre and mytty-gate the rygoure of the lawe. And it is called also by some men epicaia. The whiche is no other thynge but an excepcyon of the lawe of god/ or of the lawe of reason/ from the generall rewles of the lawe of man: when they by reason of theyr genera-lytye wolde [37a] in any partyculer case Iuge agaynste the lawe of god/ or the lawe of reason/ the whiche excepcion is secretely vnderstande in euery generall rewle of euery posytyue lawe. And so it apperyth that equytie taketh not away the very ryght/ but only that that [semyth to be ryght by the generall wordes of the lawe/] nor is it not ordayned agaynst the cruelnes of the lawe for the law in such case gen-erallye taken is good in hym selfe/ but equytye folowyth the lawe [in al partyculer cases where ryght and Iustyce requyreth/ notwythstandynge that a general rewle of the lawe be to the contrary/ wherfore it apperyth that] yf any lawe were made by man without any suche excepcyon expressyd or implyed it were manyfestly vnres-onable & were not to be sufferyd for suche cases myght come that he that wolde obserue that lawe shuld breke both the lawe of god and the lawe of reason. As yf a man make auowe that he wyll neuer eate whyte meate/ & after it happenyth hym to come there where he can gette none other meate. In this case it behouyth hym to breke his auowe for that partyculer case is excepted secretly from his general auowe by this equy[37b]tie or epykay as it is sayd byfore. Also yf a law were made in a cytie that no man vnder the payn of deth shuld open the gates of the cytie by-fore the sonne rysynge/ yet yf the Cytyzens byfore that houre fleynge from theyr en-emyes come to the gates of the cytie & one for sauynge of the cytyzens openyth the gates [byfore the houre appoynted by the lawe:] yet he offendyth not the law/ for that case is exceptyd from the sayd general law by equytie as is sayd byfore/ and so it apperytb that equytie rather foloweth the intent of the lawe/ then the wordes of the lawe. *And because I have now acceded to your wish, I beg you to delay no longer in answering my question.*

At this point the Latin begins a new chapter with the heading "The answer to the Doctor's first question."

¶STUDENT. *I gladly take in hand the answering of your question, reverend doctor, for you have shown me a broad and straight way; indeed it seems that you yourself have fully discussed it, so that it only remains for me to show how your question should be understood according to the true law of England.*

The answer, so long delayed by the Latin text, was anticipated by the transla-tor and will be found above at pages 77–79 together with another question pro-voked by the student's explanation—whether equity is administered in the same or a different court. In the Latin an answer is given immediately; the old transla-tions omit it altogether.

Besides transposing the above portion to an earlier stage of the work, the translator interjects at this point some new material (on the equity of a statute) which is introduced by a new termination to the speech of the Doctor last given, which, after the words "then the wordes of the lawe" is amended to continue thus:-

[And I suppose that there be in lykewyse some lyke equyties groundyd vpon the generall rewles of the lawe of the realme.

¶STUDENT) ye veryly wherof one is this. There is a generall prohibycyon in the lawes of Englande: that it shal not be lawfull to no man to entre in to the freholde of another without auctorytie of the owner or of the law/ but yet it is exceptyd from the sayde prohybycyon by the lawe of reason: that yf a man dryue beestes by the hyghe way & the beestes happen to escape in to the corne of his neyghbour. And he to brynge out his beestes that they shuld do no hurte gothe in [38a] to the grounde and fetteth out the beestis there he shall Iustyfie that entre in to the grounde by the lawe. Also notwithstandyng the statute of Edwarde the thyrde made the .xxiii. yere of his reygn/ wherby it is ordayned that no man vpon payne of imprysonement shuld gyue any almesse to any valyant begger/ that is well able to laboure: yet yf a man mete with suche a valyant begger in so colde a wether and so lyght apparell/ that yf he haue no clothes he shall not be able to com to no towne to haue succour: but is lykely rather to dye by the waye/ & he therfor gyueth hym apparell to saue his lyfe he shall be excused of the sayde statute] [by suche an excepcyon of the lawe of reason as I haue spoken of.

¶DOCTOURE) I knowe well that as thou sayst he shall be exceptyd of the sayd statute by conscyence/ and ouer that y he shall haue great rewarde of god/ for his good dede/ but I wolde wytte whether the partie shal be also dischargyd in the common lawe by suche an excepcyon of the lawe of reason or not/ for though ygnoraunce inuyncyble of a statute excuse the partie agaynst god/ yet as I haue herde it excusyth not in the lawes of the realme/ ne yet [38b] in the Chauncerye as some say all though the case be so that the partie to whom the forfayture is gyuen may not with conscyence leuye it.

¶STUDENT) Veryly by thy questyon thou haste put me in a great doute/ wherfore I pray the gyue me a respyte therin to make the an answere but I suppose for the tyme how be it I wyll not fully afferme it to be as I saye/ but it shuld seme that he shulde wele plede it for his dyscharge at the common lawe/ bycause it shall be taken that it was the intent of the makers of the statute to excepte suche cases. And the Iuges may many tymes Iuge after the mynde of the makers as farre as the lettre maye suffre and so it semyth they may in this case And dyuers other excepcyons there be also from other generall groundes of the lawe of the realme by suche equyties as thou hast remembred byfore that were to longe to reherce nowe.]

[¶DOCTOURE) but yet I pray the shewe me shortlye somewhat more of thy mynde vnder what maner a man may be holpen in this Realme by suche equytie.

¶STUDENT) I wyll with good wyll shewe the somewhat therin. [39a]

*   *   *   *   *

¶WHAT IS A NUDE CONTRACTE OR A NAKED PROMYSE AFTER THE LAWES OF ENGLANDE/ AND WHETHER ANY ACCYON MAY LYE THERE VPON.

The.xxiiii. Chapytre. (Second Dialogue)

¶STUDENT) Fyrst it is to be vnderstande that contractes be grounded vpon a custome of the realme and by the lawe that is called (Jus gencium) and not dyrectly by the lawe of reason/ for whan all thynges were in comon: yt neded not to haue contractes/ but after property was broughte in: they were ryght expedyent to all people/ so that a man myght haue of his neyghbour that he had not of his owne/ & that could not be lawfully but by hys gyfte/ by waye of [62a] lendynge/ concord/ or by som lease/ bargeyn/ or sale/ and suche bargaynes and sales be called contractes/ & be made by assent of the partyes vppon agrement betwene theym of goodes or landes for money or for other recompence/ but of money vsuell/ for money vsuall is no contracte. Also a concorde is proprely vppon an agrement bytwene the partyes with dyuers artycles therin/ some rysynge on the one parte & some on the other/ as yf Johan at style letteth a chambre to Henry herte & it is ferther agreed bytwene theym that the sayd Henry herte shall goo to borde with the sayd Johan at style/ and the sayde Henry herte to paye for the chambre & bordynge a certayne summe .&c. thys is properly called a concorde/ but yt ys also a contracte & a good accyon lyeth vppon yt/ howe be it yt ys not moche argued in the lawes of Englande what dyuersyty is bytwene a contracte/ a promyse/ a gyfte/ a lone/ a bargeyne/ a couenant/ or suche other/ for the intente of the lawe ys to haue the effecte of the mater argued and not the termes/ and a nude contracte is where a man maketh a bargayne or a sale of his goodes or landes wythout any [62b] recompence appoynted for yt. As yf I saye to a nother I sell the all my lande or all my goodes & nothynge is assygned that the other shall gyue or paye for yt/ that ys a nude contracte/ and as I take yt: it ys voyde in the lawe and conscyence/ and a nude or a naked promyse ys where a man promyseth an other to gyue hym certayne money suche a daye or to buylde hym an house/ or to doo hym suche certeyne seruyce/ and nothynge is assygned for the money/ for the buyldyng/ nor for the seruyce/ these be called naked promyses bycause there ys nothynge assygned why they shold be made/ and I thynke no accyon lyeth in those cases thoughe they be not perfourmed. Also yf I promyse to a nother to kepe hym suche certayne goodes safely to such a tyme/ & after I refuse to take theym there lyeth no accyon agaynst me for yt/ but yf I take theym and after they be loste or empeyred throughe my neclygent kepynge/ there an accyon lyeth.

¶DOCTOURE) But what oppynyon holde they that be lerned in the lawe of Englande in such promyses that be called naked or nude promyses/ whether doo they holde that they that make the promyse be bounden in [63a] conscyence to perfourme theyr promyse though they can not be compelled therto by the lawe or not.

¶STUDENT) The bookes of the lawe of Englande treate lytell therof/ for yt ys lefte to the determynacyon of doctours/ and therfore I pray the shew me somwhat now of thy mynde therin/ and then I shal shew the therein somwhat of the myndes of dyuers that be lerned in the lawe of the realme.

¶DOCTOUR) To declare that matter playnly after the sayenge of doctours: yt wolde aske a longe tyme and therfore I wyll touche yt bryefly to gyue the occasyon to desyre to here more therin hereafter.

¶Fyrste thou shalte vnderstande that there ys a promyse that ys called an aduowe/ and that ys a promyse made to god/ & he that doth make suche auowe vppon a delyberate mynde entendynge to perfourme yt ys bounde in conscyence to doo yt/ thoughe yt be onely made in the herte withoute pronounsynge of wordes/ and of other promyses made to man vpon a certayne consyderacyon/ yf the promyse be not agaynst the lawe. As yf A. promyse to gyue .B..xx. li. bycause he bathe made hym suche a house or hath lente hym suche a thynge or [63b] suche other lyke/ I thynke hym bounde to kepe hys promyse. But yf hys promyse be so naked that there is no maner of consyderacyon why yt sholde be made/ than I thynke hym not bounde to perfourme it/ for it is to suppose that there was som errour in the makyng of the promyse/ but yf suche a promyse be made to an vnyuersytye/ to a Cytye/ to the chyrche/ to the clergy/ or to pore men of suche a place/ & to the honoure of god or suche other cause lyke/ as for mayntenaunce of lernynge/ of the comon welth/ of the seruyce of god/ or in relyef of pouerty or suche other/ than I thynke that he is bounden in conscyence to perfourme it thoughe there be no consyderacyon of worldly profyte that the grauntour hath had or intended to haue for it/ & in all suche promyses it must be vnderstand that he that made the promyse intended to be bounde by his promyse/ for els comonly after all doctours he is not bounde/ oneles he were bounde to it before his promyse. As yf a man promyse to gyue his fader a gowne that hath nede of yt to kepe hym fro colde/ and yet thynketh not to gyue it hym/ neuertheles he is bounde to gyue it for he was bounde therto before. Also after [64a] some doctours a man may be excusyd of suche a promyse in conscyence by a casueltye that cometh after the promyse if yt be so that yf he had knowen of that ca-sueltye at the makynge of the promyse he wolde not haue made yt. And also suche promyses yf they shall bynde they muste be honest/ lawfull/ and possyble/ and elles they are not to be holden in conscyence though there be a cause. &c. And yf the promyse be good and with a cause thoughe no worldely profyte shall growe therby to hym that maketh the promyse but onely a spyrytuall profyte as in the case before rehercyd of a promyse made to a vnyuersytye/ to a cytye/ to the chyrche/ or suche other and with a cause/ as the honoure of god or suche other/ there yt ys moost comonly holden that an accyon vpon those promyses lyeth in the lawe canon.

¶STUDENT) whether doste thou meane in suche promyses made to a vniuer-sytye/ to a cytye/ or to suche other as thou hast reherced before/ and with a cause/ as to the honour of god or suche other. That the partye shall be bounde by hys promyse yf he intendyd not to be bounden thereby ye or naye.

¶DOCTOURE) I thynke nay noo more then vpon pro[64b]myses made vnto comon persones.

¶STUDENT) And than me thynketh clerely that no accyon can lye agaynste hym vpon suche promyses/ for yt ys secrete in hys owne conscyence whether he entendyd for to be bounde or naye. And of the entent inwarde in the herte: mannes lawe can not Juge/ and that ys one of the causes why the lawe of god ys necessary (that is to saye) to Juge inwarde thynges/ and yf an accyon sholde lye in that case in the law Canon: than sholde the lawe Canon Juge vppon the in-warde intente of the herte/ whyche can not be as me semeth. And therfore after dyuers that be lerned in the lawes of the realme: all promyses shall be taken in this maner. That ys to saye. Yf he to whome the promyse ys made: haue a charge by reason of the promyse whyche he hathe also perfourmed: than in that case he shall haue an accyon for that thyng that was promysed thoughe he that made the promyse haue no worldely profyte by yt. As yf a man saye to an other (heele suche a poore man of hys dyssease/ or make suche an hyghewaye/ and I shall gyue the thus moche/ and yf he do yt I thynke an accyon lyeth at the co[65a]mon lawe. And more ouer though the thynge that he shall doo be all spyrytuall: Yet yf he perfourme yt I thynke an accyon lyeth at the comon lawe. As yf a man saye to an other (fast for me all the next Lent & I shal gyue the . &c. And he per-fourmeth yt/ I thynke an accyon lyeth at the comon lawe. And in lyke wyse yf a man saye to another mary my doughter and I wyll gyue the .xx. li. Vppon thys promyse an accyon lyeth yf he mary hys doughter/ and in this case he can not dyscharge the promyse thoughe he thought not to be bounde therby/ for yt ys a good contracte/ and he maye haue quid pro quo/ that is to saye/ the preferment of hys doughter for hys money/ But in those promyses made to an vnyuersytye or suche other as thou haste remembred before/ wyth suche causes as thou haste shewed/ that ys to saye/ to the honour of god/ or to the encrease of lernynge/ or such other lyke/ where the party to whome the promyse was made is bounde to no newe charge by reason of the promyse made to hym but as he was bounde to before/ there they thynke that no accyon lyeth agaynst hym thoughe he perfourme not hys promyse/ for yt is no [65b] contracte/ and hys owne conscyence must be his Juge whether he intended to be bounde by hys promyse or not. And yf he intendyd yt not: than he offended for hys dyssymulacyon onely/ but yf he intended to be bounde: than if he perfourme it not: vntrouth is in hym/ and he proueth hym selfe to be a lyer which is prohybyted as well by the lawe of god as by the lawe of reason/ and ferthermore many of theym that be lerned in the lawe of Englande holde that a man is as moche bounden in conscyence by a promyse made to a comon person yf he intended to be bounde by hys promyse as he ys in the other cases that thou haste remembred of a promyse made to the chyrche/ or to the clergye/ or suche other/ for they say that as moche vntrouth ys in the brekynge of the one as of the other/ and they say that the vntrouthe ys more to be pondered than the persone to whome the promyses be made.

¶DOCTOUR) But what hold they yf the promyse be made for a thyng past/ as I promyse the .xl. pounde for that thou hast buylded me such a house/ lyeth an accyon there.

¶STUDENT) They suppose nay/ but he shall be bounde in conscyence to perfourme it after hys entent [66a] as ys before sayd.

PETITIONS IN CHANCERY

From W.T. Barbour, "The History of Contract in Early English Equity," *Oxford Studies in Social and Legal History*, (Oxford, 1914) vol. IV, pp. 182, 221, 231. See also the valuable editing and analysis in C.H.S. Fifoot, *History and Sources of the Common Law* (Steven & Sons, London, 1949), 298–307, 321–329.

CASE I

Bundle IX, No. 335.
Bellers' Case, circa A.D. 1432
(Barbour, p. 182)

To hise fulgracius Lord the Chaunceller of England

Rightmekely besechith Rauf Bellers that, for as moche as William Harper of Mancestre and Richard Barbour weren endetted to the seyde Rauf in certain sumes of mone withoute specialte to be payed unto the seyde Rauf or to hise certain attorne at certain dayes past, at the wheche dayes and longe aftir the seyde William and Richard weren required by the seyde Rauf to make hym payment of the seyde sumes, the wheche request the seyde William and Richard wolde not

obeye in any wyse, soo that the seyde Rauf, consideryng that the seyde William
and Richard wolde make hor lawe in that partie agens faithe and good conscience, sued to the Archebisshop of Yorke, at that tyme chaunceller of England,
for remedie in that caas; apon the wheche suggestion the seyde chaunceller
graunted under certain payne writtes severally direct unto the seyde William and
Richard to apere afore hym in the chauncery, there to be examyned apon the
seyde matere; by force of that oon of the seyde writtes the seyd Richard apered in
the seyde chauncerie and there agreed with the seyd suppliant, and the seyde
William myght nat be founde, soo that the writ direct unto hym stode in none effect: wherefore liketh to youre gracious lordeship to graunte a writ under a certain payn direct to the seyd William to aper afore yowe in the chauncerie, there
to be examyned upon the matere aforesayd for goddis luf and in werk of charite.

CASE II

Bundle XXXIX, No. 55.
The Case of the University of Cambridge, circa A.D. 1433
(Barbour, p. 221)

To the full reverent Fader in god the Bisshop of Bathe, Chaunceller of England

Besecheth lowely your pore oratour John Langton, Chaunceller of the universite
of Cantebrigge, that, where the seyd Chaunceller and universite by the assent and
graunte of our soverain lord the Kyng have late ordeyned to founde and stablisse a
college in the same toun, it to be called the universite college, and to endowe it
with diverse possessions in relevyng of the said universite and encresing of clergie
thereof, And how late acorde took bytwix oon Sir William Bingham that the seyd
Chaunceller and scolers shuld have a place of the seyd Sir William adjoyning on
every side to the ground of the seyd Chaunceller and universite that they have
ordeyned to bild her seyd college upon for the augmencacion and enlargeyng of her
seyd college and to edifie upon certain scoles of Civill and other faculteez, and for
to gif the seyd Sir William a noder place therfor, lyeng in the sayd toun betwix the
Whit Freres and seint Johns Chirch, and do it to be amorteysed suerly after the intent of the seyd Sir William at the cost of the seyd Chaunceller and universite, as
the ful reverent fader in god, the bisshop of Lincoln, in whose presence this
covenaunt and acorde was made, wole recorde: And it is so, reverent lord, that the
seyd Chaunceller and universite according to this covenaunt have ordeyned the
seyd Sir William a sufficeant place lyeing in the seyd toun of Canterbrigge bytwix
the said Whit Freres and seint Johns Chirch and extendyng doun to the Ryver of
the same toun wyth a garden therto, which place is of better value then this other
place is, and profred to amorteyse it at her own cost acordyng to the covenaunt
forseyd, and therupon diverse costes and grete labores have made and doon late
therfor: And also required diverses tymes the seyd Sir William to kepe and performe on his parte these seyd covenauntz, the seid Sir William now of self wille and
wythoute any cause refusith it and will not doo it in noo wise:

Plese it to your gracious lordship to consider thes premisses and therupon to
graunt to your seyd besechers a writ sub pena direct to the seyd Sir William to
appere afore yow in the Chauncery of our lord kyng at a certain day upon a certain peyne by yow to be limited, to be examened of these materes forseid and

therupon to ordeyne by your gracious lordship that the said Sir William may be compelled to do what trowth, good faith and consciens requiren in this caas, considering that, in alsomich as there is no writing betwix your seyd besechers and the seyd Sir William, thei may have noon accion at the comyn lawe, and that for god and in wey of charite.

CASE III

Bundle LIX, No. 227.
Godemond's Case, A.D. 1480–1481
(Barbour, p. 231)

To the right reverend Fader in god and my gode lorde
the Bisshope of Lyncoln Chauncellar of Englonde

Mekely besecheth your gode and gracious lordshipp youre Poure Oratour Roger Godemond, that, where he afore this tyme upon a X yere past and more was bounde to one Alice Reme, Wedowe, by his syngle Obligacion in X marke sterlyng paiable at a certeyn day in the said Obligacion specified, and afterward the same Alice made her executours John Hale and one Thomas Plane and died, after whos dethe youre seid Oratour truely paied and full contented the seid executours of the dewete of the seid Obligacion, trustyng by that payment to be discharged of the seid Obligacion, and lefte the same Obligacion in the handys of the seid executours, trustyng that the seid executours wolde have delyvered the seid Obligacion to your seid besecher at all tymes when they hadde ben therto requyred; And afterward the seid John Hale died, after whos dethe the seid Thomas Plane as executour of the seid Alice, not withstandyng the seid payment hadde and contentacion of the Obligacion made, suethe an accion of dette nowe late afore the kyngis Justice of the Comen Place upon the seid Obligacion agenst your seid besecher, not dredyng god ne th' offens of his owne consciens, intendyng bi the same accion shortly to condempne your seid besecher in the seid X marke, because the seid payment can make no barr at the comen lawe, and so to be twys satisfied upon the same Obligacion for one dewte, contrary to all reason and gode conscience, whereof your seid besecher is withoute remedy be the Comen lawe without your gode and gracious lordship to him be shewed in this behalf:

Please it therfor your gode and gracious lordship the premysses tenderly to consyder and to graunte a writte Suppena to be directe to the seid Thomas Plane, comaundyng hym bi the same to appere afore the kyng in his Court of Chauncerie at a certeyn day and upon a certeyn peyn by your lordshipp to be lemette, there to answer to the premysses and to bryng afore your seid lordshipp the seid Obligacion to be cancelled, and ferthermore that he may have ynyongcion no further to procede in the seid accion at Comen lawe till your seid lordshipp have examyned the premysses and sett such rewle and direction in the same as shall accorde with reason and gode consciens, and this for the love of god and in the Wey of Charite.

Plegii de prosequendo: Ricardus Somer de London, Gentilman. Thomas Mey de London, Gent'.

VII

THE SPECIALIZED COURTS AND THE "CIVILIANS"

A. THE CONCILIAR COURTS: THE ADMIRALTY AND THE COURT OF THE CONSTABLE AND THE MARSHAL

The common law was an inherently *national* legal system. It could not try causes of action "arising outside the realm, because...an issue of fact had to be tried by a jury from the place where it was 'laid'; a jury could not be summoned from outside an English county. Ordinary justice ended where the power of the sheriff ended."[1] This left a theoretical "gap" where international commercial and maritime disputes were concerned.

This gap was filled by courts created roughly in the same way as the Court of Chancery. The King "in" his Council was the residual sovereignty in the State. When pleas for extraordinary equitable relief, beyond the common law, were directed to the "King in Council," they were referred to a powerful member of that Council. This was the Lord Chancellor, because of his role as the "King's Conscience." This "referral" led to the formation of the Lord Chancellor's own equitable Court of Chancery. A similar process occurred with international cases. Those that involved ships and merchants were directed to the Lord High Admiral, who eventually established his own court, the High Court of Admiralty. The other prominent international cases came from military expeditions, and included issues of treason, ransom, contracts for foreign supplies and the right to coats of arms and other distinctions. All of these cases, including domestic disputes over military honors, were referred to the Earl Marshal, who established the Court of the Lord High Constable and the Marshal to hear them. The Court of the Admiral, the Court of the Lord High Constable and the Marshal, and the

---

1. J.H. Baker, *Introduction, supra*, 141.

205

Illustration 7-1 The Court Room at Doctors' Commons in 1808, from *The Microcosm of London* (1808) vol. I, facing p. 224 (pub. Rudolph Ackermann). Court is in session. To the immediate right is the door to the Hall and Library, where a Proctor and a Doctor can be seen enjoying a drink. Doctors are sitting in the highest tier around the Judge, while Proctors, who served a role similar to common law solicitors, are sitting at the table below. In the foreground, a Doctor and a Proctor are seen consulting with clients. The figures are executed by Thomas Rowlandson (1756–1827), a famous draughtsman and caricaturist. [Author's Collection.]

other courts created in this way, the Court of Star Chamber, the Court of Requests, and eventually, the Judicial Committee of the Privy Council, were called "Conciliar Courts," because they were formed out of the King's Council.

B. THE COURT OF STAR CHAMBER

The inherent authority of the "King in Council" to fill "gaps" with these so-called "Conciliar Courts" was not just limited to foreign cases. There were domestic cases that, in their own way, were also beyond "the power of the sheriff." In particular, some cases involved such powerful political figures, or political issues so explosive, that an ordinary jury trial and legal process could not be expected to work. These cases the Council took over collectively. Sitting together, the King's Privy Council formed the "Court of Star Chamber," probably named for the stars on the ceiling of the room in the Westminster Palace where they

Illustration 7-2 "Conciliar Courts"

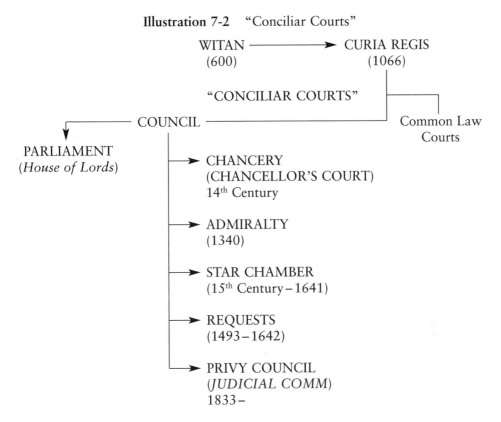

Note: Of the "Conciliar Courts," only the Judicial Committee of the Privy Council still survives, exercising a jurisdiction over appeals from Crown colonies. See the discussion in Section F, *infra*.

met.[2] Until nearly 1540, there was no real distinction between this Court and the King's Privy Council. The Court was really just a special Council meeting in a particular place dealing with both pleas for justice and other matters of state, as well. While the Star Chamber handled both civil and criminal cases, its later history was focused on crimes threatening the welfare of the state, such as sedition and conspiracy.

Of all English "special" courts, the Star Chamber is now the most infamous. It has been portrayed as a bastion of tyranny. It sometimes used torture, and there was no jury trial. While it could not execute a defendant (only the common law courts could do that), it could, and did, mutilate and brand. (One such punishment was cutting off the ears.) Complaints could be brought directly by "informations" from state officers. There was no need for indictments by juries of presentment, and none of the safeguards such juries represented.

---

2. The room may also have been named for "estarre," Jewish mortgages that had been stored in that room when the King had the right to such mortgages on the lender's death. Coke mentioned that "the roof of the Court is garnished with golden stars" and that is "the true cause of the name." See Edward Coke, *The Fourth Part of the Institute of the Laws of England* (6th ed., London, 1681), 65–66.

But the Star Chamber was, for more than a century, a relatively popular court, even with the general populace. The reasons are of great interest to us today. In some ways, the Star Chamber was the "equity" court of criminal law, ready to address crimes, in an innovative way, that could not be handled properly in routine proceedings. But, as Baker points out, "in this instance 'equity' was an integral part of the common law, because the offenses cultivated in the Star Chamber could be prosecuted on indictment in the regular courts."[3]

Two specialties of the Star Chamber were cases that raised major issues for the security of the state, or cases involving powerful subjects. This was, perhaps, one of the reasons for the court's early popularity, as average subjects could see justice done to local magistrates who might otherwise have defied normal controls. If we reflect on some of the more spectacular cases of our day, say the Watergate scandal or the Rodney King beating in Los Angeles, we can see that they might place extraordinary demands on the system that the usual courts and juries find hard to handle. The Star Chamber was the Tudor answer.

The deterioration of relations between the Crown and Parliament, and the forces that caused friction between the Common law courts and the Chancery proved fatal to the Star Chamber. It became too closely associated with the Stuart Monarchy and its unpopular prosecutions, and was abolished by Parliament in 1641.

C. THE COURT OF REQUESTS

Poor people also flocked to the King's presence seeking the justice they could not afford in other courts. These petitions literally came to the "back door" of the palace, and by 1483 a Royal official was named to receive the "bill, requests and supplications of poor persons."[4] Originally, this was a special responsibility of the King's Almoner and Dean of the Chapel Royal, but it eventually became a court of the Lord President of the Privy Seal, who managed the King's personal affairs.

This court was particularly interesting because it, too, was a court of equity, like the Chancery. It used the same simple pleading by bill and, like the Chancery, had flexible remedies. These were administered by two "Masters of Requests." The irony of this "small-claims" type court was that it became so popular that it attracted litigation among the wealthy. This, in turn, attracted the jealousy of the common law courts. The Court of Requests, like the Star Chamber, was effectively destroyed in 1641.

Other courts of equity existed. The most important were the Courts of the Council in the North and the Council of Wales. These were regional councils designed to assist with royal authority in the dangerous border regions. These "regional" conciliar courts exercised much the same powers as the Star Chamber and the Chancery in their regions, and were regarded with suspicion by common lawyers. Equity was also practiced in the Tudor Exchequer "on the equity side"

---

3. Baker, *Introduction, supra,* 137.
4. Baker, *Introduction, supra,* 138.

until 1842.[5] Finally, there were many local courts throughout England, some dating from before the conquest. These included the powerful so-called "Palatine" courts of Durham, Lancaster and Chester, which often operated like royal courts, and on occasion used equitable remedies and procedures. Some lasted for many years. The Court of Chancery of Durham lasted until 1971.

Among the customary local courts were courts that particularly served merchants. These courts, called "courts pied poudre" because of the "dusty feet" of the commercial travelers, were located at major cities and ports, and also could be found at major trade fairs for the duration of the fair. Later, the Statute of Staples (1353) provided for statutory "staple courts" in key cities. Some of these local courts, particularly the Court of the Lord Warden of the Cinque Ports (Dover, Sandwich, Rommey, Hastings and Hythe), also exercised some maritime jurisdiction. All of these courts looked to the international practices of merchants in resolving cases, and they certainly had expedited process. It is, however, doubtful that they administered a different substantive law from the royal courts. We will return to this issue when we examine the question of "incorporation" of the law merchant into the common law in Chapter XII, *infra.*[6]

D. THE "CIVILIANS" OF DOCTORS' COMMONS

When Henry VIII broke with the Catholic Church, he removed, at a stroke, one of the great sources of cosmopolitanism in Tudor England. Characteristically, Henry not only saw the need to replace the Catholic canon lawyers, but also saw clearly the dangers of simply handing over a new jurisdiction to the already powerful common lawyers. The answer was to develop and encourage the study of Roman law, or "civil" law, within the Universities. There the study of Roman laws had been pursued, with that of canon law, for centuries. (It was not until the eighteenth century that common law began to be taught at Oxford or Cambridge.) Henry abolished canon law study at Oxford and Cambridge, and established a new "Regius" (or "royal") professorship in Roman Law. More important, he confirmed that the graduates of these programs at the doctoral levels, the "Doctors of Civil Law," should have special monopolies, including valuable monopolies in the conciliar Courts of Admiralty, the Court of the Constable and Marshal, and in the new ecclesiastical courts that replaced the old Catholic system. The "Doctors" also could appear in the Court of Requests, a court which they shared with common lawyers. The "Doctors" were also active as Masters in Chancery and in some of the regional conciliar courts, such as that of the Council of the North.

The primary function of the "Doctors of Civil Law," or "civilians" as they were called, was to assist where English national law met foreign systems. This was certainly the case with the Court of the Admiralty and the Court of the Constable and the Marshal. Because Continental systems were based on the Roman law, English civilians were the best trained to make the connections. For the same

---

5. See T.F.T. Plucknett, *Concise History, supra,* 185–186.
6. See also C.H.S. Fifoot, *History and Sources of the Common Law* (London, 1949), 289–301.

reason, they were frequently used by the King as special envoys and for diplomatic posts.

Transferring the former Church jurisdictions to the civilians also made common sense. The laws of marriage, divorce, and executorship of personal property, as opposed to real estate, were all previously governed by the Roman law influenced canon law. The civilians were expert in this area. The civilians practiced these monopolies in their London headquarters, called "Doctors' Commons." This was where the Admiralty Court was actually held. (Doctors' Commons was conveniently located exactly between St. Paul's Cathedral, the symbolic center of ecclesiastical jurisdictions, and the wharves at Paul's Wharf, the center of maritime trade.) Dickens attended cases in Doctors' Commons as a newspaper reporter. (He had a particular interest in the divorces!) He observed in *David Copperfield* that Doctors' Commons was "a place that has an ancient monopoly in suits about people's wills and people's marriages, and disputes among ships and boats."[7] See Illustration 7-1, supra.

Later, people would reflect on how both shipwrecks and divorces got to be handled by the same specialty bar! The answer is simple, both were originally governed by Roman-based legal rules. The Admiralty looked to the international maritime law of Europe, and the divorce law grew from the old international law of the Church of Rome. Both looked, ultimately, to Roman based law. This historical fact led to a continuing linkage of these disparate subjects when the royal courts were reorganized by statue in 1875. Thus there was an Admiralty, Probate and Divorce Division of the new High Court of Justice. Such is the influence of the past on the present!

It has been said that Henry VIII encouraged the "civilians" because they were better disposed toward centralized executive power—due to their Roman antecedents—than were the Common lawyers with their heritage of the *Magna Carta* and *Bracton*.[8] By the seventeenth century, such tales of civilian totalitarianism were certainly being told by common lawyers with an eye to driving the civilians out of the London practice and seizing valuable civilian monopolies. Even the great Chief Justice Edward Coke was not above implying that civilian experts in "foreign" law had secret "foreign" loyalties, and were even Catholics![9]

As it happened, the English Civil War, which so fiercely set royalists against parliamentarians, saw civilians active in both camps. Doctors' Commons survived that war, and even flourished as British sea power increased the lucrative Admiralty prize business, but the civilian practice was narrowed to the core of their traditional monopolies. Finally, in 1858, a statute was passed that permitted the remaining Doctors to sell Doctors' Commons, including its invaluable library of international and comparative law, and divide the profits among themselves. Several members unselfishly resisted, but in the end greed won out, and the only independent English "specialty" bar ceased to exist.[10]

---

7. See *Materials, infra,* p. 217.

8. See Daniel R. Coquillette, *The Civilian Writers of Doctors' Commons, London* (Berlin, 1988) 15–96.

9. *Id.,* 92.

10. *Id.,* 22–24. Each of the remaining twenty-six advocates received £4,000, a small fortune at the time.

E. "SPECIALTY" CONCILIAR COURTS IN AMERICAN HISTORY

The conciliar courts were not just significant in England. While America never developed a separate branch of the bar that specialized in civil law, like the "Doctors" of Doctors' Commons, separate legal specialties have existed, and continue to exist. Of course, we are all aware that separate "Chancery" courts were established in some colonies, and that they were retained for many years, together with a special field of "equitable" remedies.[11] Admiralty courts were also established by the British in the American colonies, in part to avoid the bias of local juries, and Admiralty practice has continued to be a specialty in America, long after the courts were abolished.[12] For Colonial lawyers, like John Adams, knowledge of the Roman-based civil law and of the Admiralty practice was no intellectual affectation, but rather a vital part of Adams' practice in the Vice Admiralty courts, as the cases described in the *Materials, infra*, demonstrate.

F. THE "NATIONALISM" OF THE COMMON LAW AND THE ROLE OF PROFESSIONAL SPECIALISTS

In the end, the specialized conciliar courts in England were all abolished, or absorbed into the common law courts. Today they are just as extinct as the Doctors' Commons. The only exception is the last conciliar court of all, the Judicial Committee of the Privy Council, which still can hear appeals from Commonwealth countries and colonies, but which has no direct binding authority on any English court. (Even this court has lost much of its past glory, as most of the major former colonies have abolished appeals to the Privy Council.)[13]

Most common lawyers still have a view of history that would regard these developments as progressive. After all, the common law courts and their common law practitioners regard themselves as the historic defenders of jury trial and the rule of law against despotism at home and abroad. Specialized civilian courts had no juries, and were suspiciously cosmopolitan. But today we live in a more sophisticated world, and "international" and "Europe" are no longer such ugly

---

11. Delaware has a separate Chancery court to this day, and New Jersey did not abolish its separate Chancery jurisdiction until 1947. See Lawrence M. Friedman, *A History of American Law* (NY ed., New York, 1973), 23

12. See *id.*, 45–47, 228–231, 482–484; F.L. Wiswall, *The Development of Admiralty Jurisdiction and Practice Since 1800* (Cambridge, 1970), 17–18, 53–54, 164–165, 188–190, 193–194, 202–207.

13. High Court of Chivalry may still be in existence. In 1954 it sat for the first time in two centuries in the case of *Manchester Corporation v. Manchester Palace of Varieties, Ltd.* [1955] p. 133, [1955] 1 All E.R. 387, a case which grappled with the epic question of whether a "variety" theater could use the coat of arms of Manchester above the main theater curtain. See *Materials, infra,* and G. Squibb, The High Court of Chivalry (1959, Oxford, 123).

Church courts certainly continue, and frequently hear cases as diverse as disputes about proper church furniture to the sexual misconduct of the vicar. See, for example, "Dean Tried to have Sex with Me Twice, Verger Tells Church Court," and "Powers from the Middle Ages," both in *The Daily Telegraph*, July 6, 1995, 3.

words to the English, much less so to the Nigerians, Pakistanis, Indians, Ghana-
ians, Canadians, Australians, New Zealanders, Kenyans and others who, like
ourselves, "inherited" a common law system through colonialism. Was it really a
good thing that international and comparative specialists were abolished as a
separate professional group, and that their specialized jurisdiction was lost?

This gets us to a major historical controversy called the "incorporation" dispute. Common lawyers would argue that the best of the comparative legal ideas
represented by the conciliar courts and Doctors' Commons have been "incorporated" into common law doctrine, just as "equitable" remedies are now usually
administered by courts of law.[14] All that has been lost were the ill suited, or even
dangerous, foreign doctrines. The best was preserved.

Needless to say, continental jurists have had a different view. The English
common law was an island legal system, separated by sea from the transnational legal culture of Church and Holy Roman Empire. English law was regarded as both literally and figuratively insular.[15] This is now believed true of
the common law of the United States as well. Practicing lawyers in the United
States know little, if anything, about comparative legal systems and, unlike
even England, no comparative law study is required. Even more remarkable,
since colonial days the residual sovereignty has rested in the individual states
and the District of Columbia, which still control bar examination and admission. Despite efforts at uniform state laws and unified federal rules, most
American lawyers know little about the law of other states, much less other
countries. It is one of the ironies of history that John Adams, as a practicing
lawyer in Boston before Independence, was conversant in the Roman law and
civilian doctrine.[16] Today few American lawyers could match Adams for
breadth of knowledge and cosmopolitanism, strengths Adams used for the
new republic in crucial foreign negotiations.[17]

If the United States is to be a leader in a new world order based on commerce
and a rule of law, there is still a lesson to be learned from the extinct civilians of
Doctors' Commons. As Francis Bacon observed, there will be no hope of a systematic improvement in the law without a comparative study of first principles.[18] That
requires more than just the existence of isolated specialists in international and
comparative legal systems. There needs to be an exchange of experience and
knowledge among the leaders of the bar and the judiciary. Despite the great size
and diversity of the United States, the challenges of common law insularity and the
limited "incorporation" of new legal ideas remain formidable obstacles to
progress.

---

14. See Daniel R. Coquillette, "Legal Ideology and Incorporation IV: The Nature of
Civilian Influence on Modern Anglo-American Commercial Law," 67 *Boston Univ. L. Rev.*
(1987) 877–970, also included in *The Civilian Writers, supra*, 149–303.

15. *Id.,* 94–96, 255–303.

16. See Daniel R. Coquillette, "Justinian in Braintree: John Adams, Civilian Learning,
and Legal Elitism, 1758–1775" in *Law in Colonial Massachusetts* (eds. Coquillette, Brink,
Menand, Boston, 1984), 359–418.

17. For example, Adams was the man sent in 1784 to negotiate the vital five million
guilder loan from the Dutch. *Id.,* 368–369.

18. Daniel R. Coquillette, *Francis Bacon* (Stanford and Edinburgh, 1992), 219–297.

FOR FURTHER READING

I.   The Conciliar Courts

For an excellent brief account, see J.H. Baker, *Introduction, supra,* 135–145. See also *The Tudor Constitution* (ed. G.R. Elton, 2d ed., London, 198) 163–217. For a more detailed analysis of the development of the Admiralty Court, see T.J. Runyan, "The Rolls of Oleron and the Admiralty Court in 14th Century England" 19 *Amer J. of Legal History* (1975) 95–111; *Hale and Fleetwood on Admiralty Jurisdiction* (eds. M.J. Prichard, D.E.C. Yale London, 1993) vol. 108, Selden Society; and F.L. Wiswall, Jr., *The Development of Admiralty Jurisdiction Since 1800* (Cambridge, 1970). For the Court of Requests, see *The Ancient State, Authoritie, and Proceedings of the Court of Requests by Sir Julius Caesar* (ed. with introduction, L.M. Hill, Cambridge, 1975) and for the Court of the Constable and Marshal, see G.D. Squibb, *The High Court of Chivalry* (Oxford, 1959) which includes an analysis of the astonishing *Manchester Corporation Case* in 1955. As for the Star Chamber, see J.A. Guy, *The Court of Star Chamber and its Records to the Reign of Elizabeth I* (1985) and T.G. Barnes, "Star Chamber and the Sophistication of the Criminal Law," *Criminal Law Review* [1977] 316–326. For a full account of the history of the English ecclesiastical jurisdiction after 1532, see G.I.O. Duncan, *The High Court of Delegates* (Cambridge, 1971).

II.   The Civilians and Doctors' Commons

See the excellent short accounts by F. Donald Logan, "Doctors' Common in the Early Sixteenth Century: A Society of Many Talents" in vol. 61 *Historical Research* (June, 1988) 151–165 and by Brian P. Levack "The English Civilians, 1500–1750" in *Lawyers in Early Modern Europe and America* (ed. W. Prest, New York, 1981), 108–128. See also Levack's authoritative political study, *The Civil Lawyers in England* 1603–1641 (Oxford, 1973). The best account of the institutional history of Doctors' Commons is G.D. Squibb, *Doctors' Commons* (Oxford, 1977). For the jurisprudence of the English civilians, see Daniel R. Coquillette, *The Civilian Writers of Doctors' Common, London* (Berlin, 1988).

For general accounts of the "civilian" heritage, see Alan Watson, *The Making of the Civil Law* (Cambridge, Mass, 1981) and Paul Vinogradoff's classic lectures, *Roman Law in Medieval Europe* (Oxford, 1961).

THE
CHARGE OF
SIR FRANCIS

Bacon KNIGHT, HIS

Maiesties Attourney generall,

touching *Duells*, vpon an information in the St *ar-chamber* again*ſt*
Prie*ſt* and Wright.

WIT H

The Decree of the Star-chamber in
the ſame cauſe.

Printed for *Robert Wilſon*, and are to be ſold at Graies
Inne Gate, and in Paules Churchyard at the ſigne
of the Bible. 1 6 1 4.

Illustration 7-3   This is the title page of the first printing of Bacon's argument before the Star Chamber, set out in full in the *Materials* following. See D.R. Coquillette, *Francis Bacon*, Edinburgh, Stanford, 1992, 167–170, 333. [Author's Collection.]

MATERIALS

THE "CIVILIAN" LAWYERS IN ENGLAND

Legal Ideology and Incorporation I: The English Civilian Writers, 1523–1607, Daniel R. Coquillette

Note: This article originally appeared in 61 *Boston Univ. L. Rev.* 1 (1981), as the first in a four part series, later published together in amended form as Daniel R. Coquillette, *The Civilian Writers of Doctors' Commons, London* (Berlin, 1988). The notes are omitted. © 1980 by Daniel R. Coquillette.

> "And sure I am that no man can either bring over those bookes of late written (which I have seene) from Rome or Romanists, or read them, and justifie them, or deliver them over to any other with a liking and allowance of the same (as the author's end and desire is they should) but they runne into desperate dangers and downefals.... These bookes have glorious and goodly titles, which promise directions for the conscience, and remedies for the soul, but there is *mors in olla*: They are like to Apothecaries boxes... whose titles promise remedies, but the boxes themselves containe poyson."
>
> Sir Edward Coke

> "A strange justice that is bounded by a river! Truth on this side of the Pyrenees, error on the other side."
>
> Blaise Pascal

I. INTRODUCTION

Two years ago, a group of Russian jurists visited Boston as part of the exchanges made possible by the Prague Accords. It was their first trip out of Russia. They had prepared certain lines of questions, hoping to surmount both the language and cultural barriers.

I was part of a small group of nervous American lawyers assigned to be their guides. The initial questions of the Russians all concerned what they hoped would be our common bond as lawyers and jurists, namely, our university programs in Roman and foreign legal systems, comparison of our legal procedures with those of Roman and other civil law systems, and our notions of *ius gentium* and universal principles of law. Owing to our narrow professional training as common lawyers, it was most difficult for us to respond in any meaningful way.

There is danger in a limited, provincial view of what a lawyer should know, and what legal principles can do. This danger was a basic concern of the early English specialists in civil and Roman law, the so-called English "civilians." These English civilians were dedicated to legal science as a transnational force and as a critical source of principles of universal application.

Harold Berman has emphasized that "the growth of nationalism in modern times has made inroads into the transnational character of Western legal education and the links between law and other university disciplines have been substantially weakened." The insular professionalism of legal education in America today would be striking to English civilians such as Alberico Gentili, William Fulbecke, or John Cowell. They believed that ideas about law were eminently suitable for transplanting. It made no difference to them whether the source was university scholarship, legal practice, or a foreign system. They were committed to the transnational character of Western legal science, and to the nature of law as a universal discipline inviting comparative study and innovative thought. As Fulbecke observed, "[T]he common lawe cannot otherwise bee divided from these twain [canon and civil law], then the flower from the roote and the stalke."

It has been too easy to forget that not all "English lawyers" were "common lawyers." The English civilians played an important role in the development of English legal science. Stereotypical views of these civilians, often invented by their enemies, have greatly obscured the extent and quality of their contribution. The critical distinguishing feature of English civilians was their specific legal ideology—their ideas about law. "The community of civil law systems consists more in a unity of formal technique than of content." Although particular substantive legal rules can be characterized as "civilian" because of their Roman origins, the most critical contributions of the Roman jurists and their civilian followers have been in the nature of legal ideas and legal methods; not so much the formulation of specific substantive rules of law, but "the basic principles underlying the rule and the methodology used to arrive at that rule."

The writings of the English civilians in the sixteenth and early seventeenth centuries support this thesis. Their important contribution to English jurisprudence was not a system of specific rules, but a professional "world view" that was distinctly different from that of the common lawyers. In particular, these civilians were the pioneers of English comparative legal studies, the study of public international law in England, and the development of a private international law of commerce—all at a time when the intellectual efforts of the common lawyers were narrowly focused on the centralized national law courts in London. Furthermore, these early English civilians had a distinctive view of the study of law as a kind of humanistic study. Accordingly, they cultivated ties between civilian legal practitioners in London and law teachers in the English universities. By contrast, throughout the sixteenth century, legal study at the common law Inns of Court remained practical and insular.

*   *   *   *

II. THE ENGLISH CIVILIANS

A. *The Institutional and Educational Setting: Doctors' Commons and the Ancient Universities*

The English civilians are extinct. As one of their contemporaries put it, "[They] will ere long be as extinct as the dodo." Extinction occurred on January 15, 1858, when a majority of the last twenty-six surviving English civilians voted to distribute the considerable assets of their professional organization, the College of Advocates, to themselves. There was about £4,000 for each: a lot of money at the time. This distribution entailed the breakup of their great library and the sale of their armorial relics and portraits. Ultimately, it also meant the destruction of the quadrangle and buildings of Doctors' Commons, for nearly two hundred years the home of civilians and the College of Advocates, and one of the great centers of cosmopolitan legal learning in the world. Much of the site is now under Queen Victoria Street. The remainder is a modern office block. Such institutional mass suicide, using as a weapon an enabling clause in the 1857

Court of Probate Act designed for that purpose by their rivals, the common lawyers, hardly speaks well of the civilians' idealism or the vigor of their intellectual allegiances.

Charles Dickens, at sixteen, covered Doctors' Commons as a freelance reporter. He candidly observed that Doctors' Commons was, if not in fact dead, at least suffering advanced senility by 1828. It was "a little out-of-the-way place where they administer what is called ecclesiastical law, and play all kinds of tricks with obsolete old monsters of acts of parliament, which three-fourths of the world know nothing about, and the fourth suppose to have been dug up, in a fossil state, in the days of the Edwards. It is a place that has an ancient monopoly in suits about people's wills and people's marriages, and disputes among ships and boats." Dickens' great character, David Copperfield, visited Doctors' Commons shortly before its dissolution. It was like a nursing home:

> The languid stillness of the place was only broken by the chirping of this fire and by the voice of one of the Doctors...[a]ltogether, I have never, on any occasion, made...[a stop] at such a cosey, dosey, old-fashioned, time-forgotten, sleepy-headed little family-party in all my life; and I felt it would be quite a soothing opiate to belong to it in any character—except perhaps as a suitor.

How could this geriatric ward symbolize a vital option in the development of English law? By Dickens' day, the ideological juices at Doctors' Commons had almost ceased to flow. The civilian jurisdictions had been pared away, and there was corruption among the staff. The scent of decay hung in the air.

But three hundred years earlier the picture was very different. The renaissance of humanist legal study on the continent, closely related to the English civilian scholarship, could have made the English common law institutions appear isolated, parochial, and old-fashioned in a Europe of new national states. The triumph of the Tudor monarchy over the Church had largely eliminated the canonical lawyers as a distinct class, and powerful royal patronage was being exerted to see to it that the common lawyers, hardly more trusted by Henry VIII, would not exclusively benefit. Instead, favor fell on the civilians.

The civilians enjoyed nearly exclusive monopolies of university teaching in law at Oxford and Cambridge. Between 1540 and 1546 Henry VIII had assisted in the establishment of the regius professorships in Civil Law. These positions would provide prestigious leadership for the civilian cause. By 1568, the civilians had also obtained a new and luxurious professional headquarters at Mountjoy House in Knightrider Street, London. In addition, the powerful Sir Thomas Gresham, chief financial advisor to the Queen, had established Gresham College, which had a special mandate to provide civil law instruction, in London in 1597. Blessed with royal favor, and directly tied to a great renaissance of continental jurisprudence, the civilian prospect in England was at least hopeful. To some contemporaries, common lawyers and civilians alike, it seemed filled with exciting opportunity.

At the heart of this opportunity was the civilians' unique chance to unite university legal education, specialized practice, and government service. Unlike the common lawyers, whose powerful professional establishments, the Inns of Court, had cut off legal training from the study of the humanities, the civilians—alone among English lawyers—required a university education. Admission to the Doctors' Commons and the civilian College of Advocates effectively required a university doctorate in civil law (D.C.L.)—hence the name "Doctors' Commons." The English civilians also recognized appropriate doctorates from foreign universities as meeting these requirements, a true and early form of interjurisdictional legal certification. The College of Advocates was thus the first English professional society to have direct, formal ties to higher education; its particularly close relationship to All Souls College at Oxford and Trinity Hall at Cambridge, as well as to the regius professorships, was a source of great potential influence.

Furthermore, the civilian "Roman law" curriculum came to dominate law instruction at Oxford and Cambridge. After the Act of Supremacy of 1534 and the expurgation of canon law instruction by Henry VIII, the civilians enjoyed a complete monopoly over the teaching of law in the universities. Despite the efforts of Blackstone, this monopoly was not broken until 1839, and then at the "new" University of London. During the critical periods of the sixteenth and seventeenth centuries, the civilian university monopoly was fully intact. University fellowships and professorships were occupied by powerful spokesmen for the civilian cause, including Thomas Smith, Alberico Gentili, Thomas Ridley, John Cowell, Richard Zouche, and Arthur Duck.

The civilian specialties of international public law, admiralty law, and the international law of commercial transactions made the civilians natural candidates for governmental preferment in the developing renaissance nation-state, particularly in regard to foreign relations. Many English civilians became devoted civil servants of the Tudor Crown and its expanding bureaucracies. It was even suggested that the zeal of the civilians for humanistic learning and imperial authority was seen by Henry VIII as an excellent substitute for the influence of the clerics and canonists of the Roman Church, which he was rapidly dismembering and integrating into his government.

In all events, the late sixteenth century saw a great strengthening of Doctors' Commons. The physical facilities continued to improve, and the Court of Admiralty and lesser ecclesiastical courts began to meet in the hall itself. The library grew steadily. It included not only the "classical" Roman law texts, but also many of the best continental commentaries. Many books about international law, law of trade, the "customary" or "common" law of continental countries, and ecclesiastical law were acquired, making Doctors' Commons one of the centers of cosmopolitan learning in London and Europe. The civilians' expertise in many fields of law was well recognized by the Tudor government. The members of the College of Advocates came to regard themselves as a professional elite, equal at least to the Serjeant's Order of common lawyers, and unequaled in their unique ties to university legal studies at Oxford and Cambridge.

B. *The English Civilians as Specialist Legal Practitioners:*
The "Civilian Monopolies"

Nearly as important as the civilian monopolies in the university legal education were their monopolies in certain specialist areas of legal practice. The civilians had a complete monopoly over actions in the High Court of Admiralty, which included not only the law of prize and shipwreck, but many overseas commercial transactions as well. Equally significant—as well as lucrative—was the civilians' stronghold on the central ecclesiastical courts. These courts represented a far more important practice than the church courts of today, and heard probate, matrimonial, and estate matters. All wills in the Archdiocese of London were actually stored at Doctors' Commons until the Court of Probate Act of 1857 and the Matrimonial Causes Act of 1857. Other less significant civilian monopolies included proceedings in the ancient court of the Constable and Marshal, and the High Court of Chivalry. The latter court was still active in the seventeenth century and, indeed, had a case in 1954.

Also important were the civilian "specialties" in areas in which they did not have exclusive privileges. These areas included (1) legal positions in the provincial church bureaucracies, such as commissaries or prebendaries for archdeacons and bishops, and as deans; (2) positions as legal deputies of vice-admirals, and judges of local admiralty courts; or (3) positions as commissioners and members for various conciliar courts, including the High Court of Delegates and the King's Council of the North. In addition, civilians traditionally held positions as Masters in Chancery and had active practices in the busy and popular Court of Requests, although common lawyers could also practice in that court. Finally, Levack's research has shown that a substantial number of civilians held important diplomatic positions, as well as some high academic posts at Oxford, Cambridge, and Gresham College.

In short, civilian legal practice and civilian careers were not narrowly confined during the renaissance. Their law practices spread from their valuable monopolies into many other fields. An Elizabethan man of affairs who needed a will, or had troubles with his wife, or suffered a shipwreck, or wished a coat of arms, or sought to import wine from France, or wanted to complain about his vicar's behavior, or sought advice about a sensitive foreign transaction, or wished to consult about the special equitable relief and procedures available in the Chancery or the Court of Requests, might find his steps leading past St. Paul's Cathedral and down Great Knightrider Street to consult with a civilian at Doctors' Commons.

The activities of the civilians did not escape the jealous attention of common lawyers. The number of civilians was small. There were roughly 200 during the period from 1603 to 1641, as contrasted to approximately 2,000 common lawyers. It is not clear that civilians ever constituted a serious economic threat to their more numerous and powerful brethren. Nevertheless, there is evidence that the common law writ of prohibition was used by common lawyers to keep the civilian courts strictly within their "proper" spheres. One common lawyer was moved to write of prohibition, "Blest Writ! By which their [civilians] fees are stay'd and briefs into our bags conveyed." Particularly, however, in the years prior to the serious political problems which led to the Civil War, there is evidence of practical cooperation between civilian and common lawyers, not unlike the relationship between general practicing lawyers and specialists today. The internecine jurisdictional battles between the common law courts themselves, particularly between the Common Pleas and Kings Bench, were far more pronounced than any early tension between civilians and common lawyers. Moreover, the common lawyers of the central courts also attacked their own minor common law courts, such as the Court of the Marshalsea, with relish. When serious hostility did develop between certain common lawyers and civilians, intellectual and juristic differences were as serious a focus as any economic competition.

C. *The English Civilians as Jurists: The "Bartolist Cause"*

There was no question but that the English civilians did have important ideological differences with the common lawyers. The rapid change of English society in the late sixteenth century began to provoke and draw out these differences. At first the conflicts were literary only, and the purpose of the writers conciliatory. But then the lines hardened into jurisdictional battles between common law and civilian courts. These battles ultimately destroyed any possibility of coexistence.

1. The Proper Source of Law: The *Ius Gentium* and *Ius Naturale*

The first, and most profound, category of disagreement between the civilians and common lawyers concerned the proper sources of law. The English civilian, like the English canonist, looked—and often traveled—to foreign sources to find and study the "best law." Common lawyers would later accuse civilians of doing this out of subordination to foreign religious or political authority, but the true reason was intellectual, and rooted in Roman jurisprudence. As the Digest and Institutes of Justinian demonstrate, the Roman law taught the notions of *ius gentium* and *ius naturale*. These terms roughly stood for the idea that legal systems can be tested for validity by natural reason, and that some legal precepts are universally valid.

The Romans themselves used these notions, through the different periods in their own legal history, in at least three different ways. First there was the *ius gentium* as the product of natural reason, *naturalis ratio*. This was closely related to, but not identical with the Greek notions of natural law. As the classical jurist Gaius said, "[T]hose rules prescribed by natural reason [*naturalis ratio*] for all men are observed by all peoples alike, and are called the law of nations [*ius gentium*]." In this usage, the *ius gentium*, later known as *ius omnium gentium* to distinguish it from narrower usages, was included as a part of the law of each nation—for example, in the Roman *ius civile* proper. Thus, it could be regarded as "incorporated" into the *ius civile* of each nation. It could not by its definition *conflict* with the *ius civile*, because it was *part* of the *ius civile*. The *ius gentium*, in other words, was that part of each national legal system that was demanded by natural reason.

2. The *Aequitas Mercatoria* and Conflict of Law Doctrine

There was also a second usage of the phrase *ius gentium* which, though narrower, was no less important. This usage involved specific, factual questions as to existing foreign and mercantile law. As the Roman state expanded, its contacts with foreign territories and its commercial relations with these territories likewise increased. There is some evidence that the *praetor peregrinus*, the Roman magistrate [*praetor*] with authority over a foreigner [*peregrinus*], had power to resolve disputes involving foreign transactions not governed by the *ius civile* of the Roman state, applying instead the custom of traders. Thus, this narrower *ius gentium* would also lead civilians to examine foreign sources to find the best rule.

The narrower usage of *ius gentium* gave rise in medieval times to two concepts of critical importance to English civilians. First was the notion of a "law merchant" which applied especially to mercantile transactions, according to mercantile custom. This was called the *aequitas mercatoria*. Many disputes in later years between common lawyers and civilians turned, in part, on whether the law merchant was a "special" law for merchants, separate from the national law. The later English civilians argued that this law was *ius gentium* in the sense of being a special transnational law for merchants and it should, therefore, be handled by specialist jurists—i.e., themselves—rather than by common lawyers.

A second concept that developed from the narrower *ius gentium* of the *praetor peregrinus* was conflict of law doctrine. English common lawyers had long regarded "conflict of law" as simply a matter of jurisdiction. If the matter was appropriately in the court's jurisdictions, the law of the forum [*lex fori*] applied. Thus choice of law would depend on which court established jurisdiction: the common law courts applied common law, the Admiralty court applied maritime and civil law, and the ecclesiastical courts applied canonical law. In England, therefore, issues that may best have been resolved by deciding which set of legal principles would be the most practical or appropriate were instead resolved by mechanical rules dividing jurisdiction. By contrast, the civilians argued the need for an intelligent application of foreign legal principles when appropriate. This led to conflict between the common lawyers and the civilians, with the common lawyers permitting nontraversable fictions to expand common law jurisdiction, particularly *vis-à-vis* the Admiralty, and the civilians arguing for the appropriate application of foreign legal principles, on which they were the best English experts.

3. The *Ius Inter Gentes*: Public International Law

The term *ius gentium* had a final usage that was even more specialized, and of great interest to renaissance civilians. It was the *ius gentium* that governed the relations of Rome with other states. The civilians sometimes called this *"ius gentium"* by the name *"ius inter gentes"*; i.e., the law (*"ius"*) *between* nation-tribes (*"gentes"*) as opposed to *"ius gentium"* ("the law of *all* nation-tribes). This usage included the law of war, *iura belli*, the law of diplomats, *iura legati*, and the law of the special early courts of treaties and relations between Romans *peregrini*. The expertise of the English civilians in these "public" international law subjects was unchallenged by practicing common lawyers until a relatively late date. But the disputes between the civilians themselves, both in England and externally, were fierce. Was this *ius gentium* to be determined by natural reason, as with the law "common to all" [*ius omni gentes*]? Was it predetermined by the "natural law" [*ius naturale*]? Or was it a matter not of ideals, but merely of the actual custom and behavior of nations?

Each of the various aspects of *ius gentium* and *ratio naturalis* firmly directed the English civilian's mind to foreign sources of law. Only through extensive study of comparative rules and systems could the merits and demerits of any law be ascertained. The development of scientific methods of inquiry in the renaissance strengthened these civilians' notions. It was even irrelevant to the civilian whether a particular "system" of law presently existed. Led by the inquiries of Lodowick Lloyd, Gentili, Fulbecke, Wiseman and others, English civilians pioneered in crude comparative legal history. If the *ratio scripta* of historical systems of law could be discovered and deciphered, their lessons could be learned. The common lawyers were certainly familiar with the use of historical records, but hardly with the notion of the study of *foreign* legal history. And it was one thing to use the past to legitimize and then to establish the present order, as the common lawyers often did, and something else to use it as an ideological gold mine of "external" ideas and standards against which the present order could be tested and thus improved. This, to a large extent, was the way of the civilians.

4. The *Ratio Scripta* and the Flaws of the Common Law

The outgrowths of the civilian intellectual traditions of *ius gentium, ratio naturalis,* and *ratio scripta* could threaten the common lawyers in a most fundamental way. For by the tests of "external" reason and universality, it was clear at least to some English civilians that the common law was flawed.

Juries, for example, may have been competent "memories for fact," but as arbitrators of customary rules they were clearly without qualification. The civilians doubtless suspected that juries were devices for saving common law judges labor — and possibly for saving the common law judges from the responsibility of open and principled decisionmaking as well. Would not law be best made and best applied by the most intelligent and educated? Except for the "collective witnesses of fact" rationale, the basis for jury trial seemed to be posited in terms of negatives: the common law courts lacked money, skilled manpower, and power on the part of the judge to enforce a decision without "community participation." Worst of all, residual superstition may have required an inscrutable factfinder as a substitute for the newly disallowed ordeal and oath-helping. Thus, English civilian courts used inquisitorial procedures, written interrogatories, and depositions. They subpoenaed witnesses, cross-examined the parties themselves, and requested the advice of experts on relevant subjects, such as the Elder Brethren of Trinity House on maritime questions. With rare exception, they did not use juries.

Furthermore, to the civilians the "common law" method of "shaping legal doctrine by incremental decisionmaking could hardly have appeared ideal. What kind of notice did that method give the average citizen of changes in the rules, and what opportunity did it give anyone for building a systematized, harmonious legal system? Of course one could try to force the raw dross of the common law, *ex post facto,* into some elegant jurisprudential mold — as Englishmen from Bracton to Cowell had done — but it would be like "crushing an Ugly sister's foot, bunions and all, into Cinderella's glass slipper." As one civilian said of the Lombard customary law, "*[N]on lex, sed faex.*"

One solution, of course, would be to develop a written, systematic, codified body of law, setting out the rules clearly and publicizing them widely, on the model of the *Institutes.* The fragmented structure of common law courts, with the Common Pleas and the King's Bench in rivalry and with a complex substructure of local and feudal courts still in existence, would have been to the civilian mind, primitive. Such a system lacked the virtues of clarity, consistency, and structure, those virtues that were at least in theory paramount to Justinian and — centuries later — to the Benthamite radicals.

Short of codification, the English civilians considered other possibilities for reform of the English legal system. For example, the civilians attempted to use specialized courts and special commissioners, such as the Court of the Arches and the Admiralty, to remedy some abuses of the common law. This was a stop-gap measure, but it was, for civilians, better than nothing. It was particularly useful in those legal areas where English merchants and diplomats had to deal with foreigners who were accustomed to the more cosmopolitan legal culture of Europe. Such transactions, at least, could be isolated from the rest through the special jurisdictions of the King, the Admiral, and the Marshal. At least in those areas, as in the university, learned men could still treat the law as a science and a humanity.

5. Relations with the Crown: *Quod Principi Placuit*

Codification and specialized courts, both areas of particular civilian involve-ment, required close association with the Crown. Major "law reform" legislation remained a Crown prerogative throughout the Tudor period, and those special courts that dealt with foreign trade and shipping were obviously related to Crown diplomacy and Crown revenues. Indeed, civilian officials of these courts regularly took on diplomatic missions for the Crown in which their cosmopoli-tan legal learning proved important.

Proud of such expertise, the English civilians must have regarded themselves as the modern equivalent of the great Roman jurists—men who achieved au-thority not through public office or judicial power, but through the force of their learning and argument. This self-image may have been comforting for a group of men who held few judicial positions in the growing common law system. It also drew them closer to the Crown. After all, in light of the Byzantine texts, the most important audience of the Roman jurists appeared to have been the Emperor. Would not enlightened English monarchs similarly be the civilians' best avenue to power?

Whig historians, following the lead of Edward Coke, have long tarred the civilians with the brush of royal absolutism. The famous *Digest* motto, *quod principi placuit legis habet vigorem* (what the Prince determines, has the force of law), became an accusatory challenge to the civilians from men who understood its qualifications not at all—or chose not to. Civilian legal science no more pos-tulated absolutism than did the common law. Indeed, the civilians' dedication to known abstract principles of justice, written laws, and expert jurists was an obvi-ous bar to tyranny. Some English civilians might have favored a powerful royal executive over an entrenched squirearchy served by the common lawyers. Yet, other civilians, such as Isaac Dorislaus, Walter Walker, Calibute Downing, and John Godolphin, were fervent Parliamentarians, and some later civilians, such as John Ayliffe, were loyal Whigs.

The vice most civilians would have feared was ministerial weakness and inef-fectiveness, for it could make a mockery of any "scientific" improvements in the law. From the civilian viewpoint, arguments for decentralized private power could too often masquerade as appeals for "freedom." Progress, to the civilians, demanded faith in human nature and the human intellect. The enlightenment of humanist learning showed the way. The object was a strong central system that would give every citizen "his due," efficiently and certainly. This, to some civil-ians' minds, was the precondition of real freedom.

6. Bartolism

The English civilians were much aware of continental "advances" in political theory, culminating in the writing of Jean Bodin. The laicization of English and French society was important in promoting the civilian cause over that of the canonists. The rise of the national state and the Reformation did not diminish the idealism or the zeal of the civil lawyers, and continental writers quickly found converts among the English civilians. Bodin was especially popular, possibly because his view of an effective, rationalist, central state closely coincided with civilian convictions and self-interest.

The practical need for English civilians to accommodate themselves to what was, in their view, a parochial and backward legal system was aided, ironically, by developments in Italy in the study of Roman law, particularly the spread of the so-called "Bartolist School." Bartolism was a reaction to the results of early civilian scholarship. The early civilians had regarded the Byzantine text of the *Corpus Juris Civilis* with awe. They limited themselves to the glossing of its passages — hence they were called "glossators." Like early biblical students, the glossators considered it their duty to "explain and expound" the text, not to suggest that the text could be revised, or even worse, that the text was imperfect. As Dawson has observed, however, "[t]he intellectual environment in which the glossator worked was greatly altered by the effects of his own teaching." The success of their students in attaining positions of power, particularly in Italy, ensured a "reception" of Roman law there, at least in part. Following this "reception," a new breed of scholars led by Bartolo di Sassoferrato (Bartolus) addressed themselves to the inherent challenges of applying an ancient law to practical, contemporary problems. The Bartolists began openly to use the *Corpus Juris* as an instrument for organizing a modern system of Italian law.

In the attempt to organize current Italian law according to the *Corpus Juris*, the Bartolists developed important attitudes toward customary law. Some glossators had assumed that the *Corpus Juris* was still law in medieval Italy. But obviously it was inconsistent with the customary law of many Italian principalities. Which should prevail? After considerable intellectual agony, it became accepted that, when there was no conflict between the *Corpus Juris* and custom, the custom could take on the validity of law, particularly when not prohibited by the state. Even when there was a possibility of conflict, "special custom" could be established by common consent of the users. The Bartolists thus opened the way to compromise with customary legal systems and greatly increased the attraction of "applied" Roman law. In England, the writings of the Bartolists were found in major libraries, and were obviously studied. Jean Bodin himself was an acknowledged Bartolist, as were such English civilians as the great Alberico Gentili, Regius Professor of Civil Law at Oxford, and his eccentric disciple William Fulbecke.

It is most striking that these English civilians, led by the great Gentili, rejected the attempts by the Frenchman Cujas and the new continental "humanist" movement to return to the study of the "pure" classical Roman texts. Cujas and his colleagues had brilliantly introduced modern linguistics and techniques of textual criticism to isolate and reject "interpolations" and impurities in Byzantine compilations. This permitted, for the first time, a knowledge of what the classical Romans' texts actually said. It was a great achievement of the European renaissance. Yet, most English civilians stoutly resisted this movement. For

Gentili and English civilian followers, the civilian cause in England was best served by Bartolism. The time was hardly right for them to retreat to the ivory tower of the *Corpus Juris*. Their struggle was to reconcile civilian enlightenment with the growing challenge of the common law. The Bartolist dialectic, a constructive dialogue between customary law and Roman legal science, provided a way....

THE HIGH COURT OF THE ADMIRALTY

Note: This court, centered around the office of the Lord High Admiral of England, was a civilian stronghold, i.e., its practitioners were all trained in the Roman based civil law, not the common law. As the following case illustrates, there were frequent jurisdictional tussles with common law courts. In the next chapter, Chapter VIII "Appeals," we will discuss the writ of prohibition, which gave the common lawyers an advantage in these disputes. The following case, *Palmer v. Pope* was also set out and analyzed in A.K.R. Kiralfy, *A Source Book of English Law* (London, Sweet & Maxwell, 1957), 372–374.

Palmer v. Pope (A.D. 1611)

The Record
High Court of Admiralty. P.R.O. ref. H.C.A. 24/74

LIBEL

In the name of God, before you, the venerable and excellent Master Richard Trevor, Doctor of Law, Judge of H.M. Supreme Court of Admiralty of England, or your surrogate or other judge competent thereto:

The plaintiff, the honest man, William Palmer, merchant of the City of London, against

The ship called "Blessing" of the Longstone, and its apparel, belonging to George Wood and Thomas Pope or one of them and against the said Wood and Pope and against any other persons lawfully intervening therein,

Says alleges and proposes in law by articles as follows:

(1) Throughout March 1608–February 1609, and March 1609 to July 1609, &c George Wood and Thomas Pope were owners and possessors of the said ship, the "Blessing" of Longstone, and its apparel, ornament and accessories, and were so generally known &c.

(2) During those months George Wood and Thomas Pope, or one of them with the consent and authority of the other, leased and let the ship, for a commercial voyage to carry goods and merchandise of the said William Palmer to foreign parts and back to England, upon the high seas and within the jurisdiction of the Admiralty of England.

(3) Thomas Pope was then master of the said vessel and in charge thereof for the said voyage.

(4) During the said time William Palmer, on the high seas and within the jurisdiction of the Supreme Court of Admiralty of England, loaded and placed aboard the said ship certain goods and merchandise to be taken and traded in the Azores.

(5) On March 18 last, or thereabouts, on the high seas &c, it was concluded and agreed between William Palmer and Thomas Pope, that, since the said William Palmer, in regard of a lawsuit pending betwixt the said Palmer and one John Rivett in the town of Punta Delgada in the island of St. Michael, so that the said Palmer could not have and receive his goods and merchandises to relade the said ship back from thence to London within the time limited and agreed upon, the said Thomas Pope and company should stay with the said ship in the seas near the said town of Punta Delgada until 26 March last past, to take to the said ship the goods and merchandise which Palmer should lade on board the said ship within the said time, to be transported for England in the ship for the use and account of Palmer.

(6) At the same time and at the said bargain and agreement made as aforesaid Palmer did deliver and pay to Thomas Pope or to his use and the use of Wood, or one of them, the full sum of £5.16.9, in full payment and satisfaction of the stay and demurrage of the said days for the said ship and company, and that Pope, or some other for him, did there and then receive and take the said sum of £5.16.9 in full content for the same stay and demurrage, and undertake there and then, to and with the said William Palmer, to abide there with the said ship and company till 26 March aforesaid and two days after and over and above that day, to receive and take in the goods of the said Palmer, as aforesaid to be laden on the said ship.

(7) Before 26 March, or at least before 28 March, William Palmer had made ready and provided according to the said agreement 500 quintals of goods, sufficient to relade the said ship, together with a chest of sugar &c.

(8) Thomas Pope, together with the said ship and company, contrary to the said promise and agreement, departed on 23 March, or thereabouts, before 26 March, from the said port and left the goods behind and received no part thereof.

(9) William Palmer, by reason of Pope's departure could not provide or have any other ship or vessel to transport the said goods for England, but was afterwards forced to ship and lade the same for Flanders or some other place beyond the seas.

(10) By reason of the departure of the ship within and before the time agreed upon, and by the leaving of the said goods behind, Palmer hath sustained loss and damage by the means of the said Pope in the sum of £500 of lawful money of England.

(11) In the said voyage and in the time aforesaid, before the coming of the said ship to Punta Delgada, or before the agreement aforesaid, Palmer delivered or caused to be delivered, brought and laden into the said ship, upon the high seas &c, all and singular the sugars, ready money, goods and apparel, specified and set down in the Schedule hereunto annexed, safe and well-conditioned, to be transported and carried in the said ship to the port of London or some other place or port agreed upon between Thomas Pope and William Palmer, designed or appointed by them, for the use and account of the said William Palmer, and there to be safely delivered to him.

(12) The several moneys, apparel, goods, chests of sugar, at the time of the lading thereof, were of the several prices, worths and weights set down in the said Schedule.

(13) William Palmer claims £200 damages for non-delivery of the said goods &c.

(14) William Palmer, having no other hope of recovering the said goods mentioned in the Schedule annexed to this libel, save by arrest of the said Wood and

Pope and the said ship, caused Wood and Pope to be arrested or at least caused his action to be brought in the said Court and George Wood appeared and undertook to reply to the said action.

(15) Wood and Pope were asked to deliver the goods and compound the said damages but have always refused and denied to do so, and still refuse to do so.

(16) Wood and Pope are subjects of this realm and subject to the jurisdiction of this court.

(B) The Report
Hob. 212. In the Common Pleas

Mich. 9 Jac. Palmer libelled against Pope, for that it was agreed between them on the high seas, that Pope should carry certain sugars, and that the agreement was after put in writing in the Port of Gado, in the coast of Barbary, and shews, that Pope suffered the sugars to be spoiled at sea by salt water.

Houghton Serjeant suggested, that the charter party was made in the Port of Gado, upon the continent of Barbary, whereupon the Court resolved, that a prohibition lay, because the original contract, though it were made at sea, yet was changed when it was put in writing sealed, which being at land changed the jurisdiction as to that point; but if it had been a writing only without seal, it had made no change. If the contract were at land, though the breach be at sea, which are two several acts, yet because these two must concur to make the cause of the suit which is entire, the party shall be forced to sue in the King's Court, because that and the common law must prevail against other Courts and laws....

Note, that every libel in the Admiralty doth, and must lay the cause of suit "on the high seas," which argues that this is a necessary point; for the jurisdiction there groweth not from the cause, as of tithes and testaments in the Spiritual Court, but from the place. Therefore I am of opinion, that if a Contract were made in truth at sea, and a suit upon that in the Admiral's Court, and there the contract is laid generally, without saying "at sea," a Prohibition will lie, for the libel must warrant the suit itself, though you may on the contrary part surmise, that the contract was made at land, against the libel that lays it on the sea. And I hold it also not sufficient for the libel to lay it "within the maritime jurisdiction" generally, but it must be so laid as it may appear to the King's Court to be so indeed.

THE COURT OF REQUESTS

Note: This equitable jurisdiction, established first around the personage of the King's almoner and later the Lord Privy Seal, was originally for royal servants or for those too poor to go through the usual legal channels. (See the case below.) It soon became popular with the rich as well "as men of substance sought to take advantage of the simple procedure." Baker, *supra*, 139. It was abolished, for practical purposes, in 1641.

In the Court of Requests "Anno 7 E.6" (1554)

26 April. Whereas sute and contention hath bene mooved in the Queenes Majesties Court of Requests by Rafe Kingston, plaintiff, against Richard Sampford the older etc., defendant, for a certaine lease for terme of yeres etc. It is seen to her Majesties honourable counsell of her said court, that the matter is deter-

minable at the Common lawe, and that the sayde parties be men of wealth and abilitie to sue and prosecute the same there, and neither of them the Queenes Majesties servant; wherefore the said counsell have dismissed the sayd parties out of this court etc. [Req. 2/17/101]

From Sir Julius Caesar, *The Ancient State Authoritie and Proceedings of the Court of Requests* (1596), now edited by L.M. Hill in an excellent new edition *The Ancient State Authoritie, and Proceedings of the Court of Requests* by Sir Julius Caesar (Cambridge, 1975), 166.

COURT OF THE CONSTABLE AND MARSHAL

Note: The court of the Constable and Marshal, established around the personage of the Lord High Constable and Earl Marshal, had jurisdiction over military matters, including the law of coats of arms. Incredibly, the following case took place in 1954. It involved the unauthorized use of the arms of the city of Manchester in the auditorium of a theater, the "Manchester Palace of Varieties." The case does not indicate what kind of "shows" took place, but the city clearly did not wish to be associated. The case contains a more learned account of the jurisdiction of this ancient, and previously important, specialized court.

Manchester Corporation v. Manchester Palace of Varieties, Ltd.

[Court of Chivalry (Duke of Norfolk (Earl Marshal) and
Lord Goddard, C.J. (Surrogate), with Officers of Arms in attendance),
December 21, 1954, January 21, 1955.]
[Excerpts] (Notes omitted.)
1955 *All England Reports*, Feb. 10, 1955, vol. 1 387.

*   *   *   *

It is not contended that this court, however long a period may have elapsed since it last sat, is no longer known to the law. It was originally the Court of the Constable and Marshal and has probably existed since the Conquest. At least it had been in existence for very many years before the reign of Richard II, who reigned from 1377 to 1399, and during his time the famous case of *Scroop v. Grosvenor* was heard before it. The hereditary office of Lord High Constable was abolished on the attainder of the Duke of Buckingham in 1521, since when the court has always been held before the Earl Marshal or his surrogate alone and his right to hold the court and to adjudicate at least on heraldic matters was recognised and confirmed by Letters Patent of James I in 1622 and those of Charles II, which were read at the opening of this court. Its records show that frequent sittings have taken place and judgments have been given by the Earl Marshal alone acting through his surrogate. In origin, no doubt, the court was essentially a military tribunal, the forerunner of courts martial, which in later years were established under articles of war issued by the Sovereign from time to time, and now are established and regulated by the Army Act. As the origin of armorial bearings was, or, at least, is commonly believed to have been, a method of identifying knights clothed in armour, it was natural that disputes with regard to the right to display a particular achievement on a shield should have fallen within the cognisance of this court. The power to grant armorial bearings is, as I understand it, delegated by the Sovereign to the Kings of Arms who with their officers were incorporated as a College of Arms in the reign of William and Mary. The Earl Marshal is the head and, I think, the visitor of the college. The right to bear arms is, in my opinion, to be regarded as a dignity and not as property within the true sense of that term. It is conferred by a direct grant or by descent from an ancestor to whom the arms had been originally granted. There is authority that a dignity which descends to heirs general or to heirs of the body is an incorporeal hereditament whether or not the dignity concerns lands: see *Re Rivett-Carnac's Will* which related to a baronetcy. It was not contended before me that armorial bearings were an incorporeal hereditament, and in any case it is clear that the right to bear arms is not a matter cognisable by the common law which seems to show that there is no property in arms in the legal sense, otherwise the courts of law would protect them.

Counsel for the defendant, in the course of a careful and learned argument, submitted that the powers of the court were defined by the statutes of Richard II referred to above, since repealed by the Statute Law Revision and Civil Procedure Act, 1881. He argued that the effect of those statutes was that the court had power to act in relation to armorial bearings only when carried to war outside the realm or displayed at a tournament within the realm and, possibly, if carried in an army engaged in suppressing rebellion, that is to say, in a civil war. In my opinion, however, the statutes of Richard were intended, or, at least, have been regarded as intended to confine this court to matters of dignity and arms and to prevent it from entertaining matters cognisable by the ordinary courts of the kingdom. The common law courts have always been vigilant and jealous of any attempt to usurp or encroach on their jurisdiction. Many instances are to be found in the books of prohibitions to the Court of Admiralty and to the spiritual courts, and the liability of the latter to writs of prohibition, though not of certiorari, was fully discussed in the recent case of *R. v. St. Edmundsbury & Ipswich Diocese (Chancellor), Ex p. White*. But that the Court of Chivalry has jurisdiction in matters relating to armorial bearings has been recognised by the highest authorities. *Coke*, C.J., deals with the Court of Chivalry at length in 4 *Coke's Institutes*, ch. 17. In *Comyn's Digest*, tit. Courts, E 2, it is said:

> "...the Court [of Chivalry] has an absolute jurisdiction, by prescription, in matters of honour, pedigree, descent, and coat armour."

*   *   *   *

To deal, then, with the present complaint, two matters are alleged: the display of the arms in the auditorium of the theatre, and the use of the arms of the City of Manchester as the common seal of the defendant company. The latter does seem to me to be a legitimate subject of complaint. The corporation of a great city can properly object to their arms being used on any seal but their own. A deed sealed with an armorial device is thereby authenticated as the act and deed of the person entitled to bear the arms. It is, indeed, the seal which makes a document a deed and enabled an action of covenant to be maintained, a form of action far older in English law than assumpsit. For the defendant company to use the arms of the city as its seal looks very much like an attempt to identify the company with the Corporation. With regard to the display in the auditorium, if that were the only complaint, I should have felt it raised a matter of some difficulty. I am by no means satisfied that nowadays it would be right for this court to be put in motion merely because some arms, whether of a corporation or of a family, have been displayed by way of decoration or embellishment. Whatever may have been the case 250 years ago, one must, I think, take into account practices and usages which have for so many years prevailed without any interference. It is common knowledge that armorial bearings are widely used as a decoration or embellishment without complaint. To take one instance, hundreds, if not thousands, of inns and licensed premises throughout the land are known as the so-and-so Arms, and the achievements of a nobleman or landowner are displayed as their sign. It may be and frequently is the case that the family whose arms are those displayed have parted with their lands in the neighbourhood and perhaps have never owned the inn or, at least, do so no longer. The arms of universities, colleges or dioceses displayed on tobacco jars, ash trays, teapots and other articles of domestic use are to be found in shops all over the country and are dear to the heart of souvenir hunters, tourists, American and others, as well as sea-side visitors. In strictness, I suppose none of these people have any right to use or display articles thus emblazoned. Then again, at the present day, many a gracious ancient house bears over its porch the arms of the family who built but no longer lives in it. It may be that the line is extinct; it may be that necessity has compelled a sale to another who has recently made a fortune as ample as that of the original builder, amassed perhaps in Cotswold wool, the slave trade, or just as an acquisitive landowner. Could this court be asked to deface the fabric by ordering the removal of the original achievement which has adorned the house, it may be for hundreds of years? The vendor would not complain if he sold the house without first removing the device, nor can I conceive of the Attorney-General, in whom is vested such of the powers and duties of the former King's Advocate as may still remain, emulating the activities of Dr. Duck or Dr. Oldys in the seventeenth and early eighteenth centuries and seeking to have the new owner declared to be "no gentleman and disentitled to bear arms," or, at least, the arms thus displayed. Let me quote from *Bacon's Essay on Judicature*:

> "...let penal laws, if they have been sleepers of long, or if they be grown
> unfit for the present time, be by wise judges confined in the execution."

Where, then, is one to draw the line? It can, I think, only be done by the exercise of common sense and by saying that use or display in such circumstance would not be a ground for intervention by this court. In view, however, of the use by the defendant of the arms of the City of Manchester as its common seal, and the contentions which it has set up in this case, I think the court may properly inhibit and enjoin it from any display of the Corporation's arms, and, accordingly, I pronounce the sentence porrected [sic] by the plaintiffs, except that, subject to further argument, I should propose to delete the words "without the leave and licence of the [Corporation]." These words appear to assume that a grantee of arms can himself authorise and permit another to bear them. I am not at present satisfied that this is permissible by the law of arms, as it seems to me it would infringe the rights of the Officers of Arms who alone can make grants and might deprive them of revenue.

*   *   *   *

THE COURT OF STAR CHAMBER

Note: This court was the ultimate "conciliar" court, as it consisted of the entire Privy Council meeting in a judicial capacity. Its special concern by the latter part of its history, was as "an extraordinary or supplementary court of law, particularly for cases with a criminal element." Baker, *Introduction, supra*, 137. Obviously appropriate kinds of cases were sedition and conspiracy, or other acts that directly threatened the welfare of the entire realm. Others were cases which, for one reason or another, could not be tried by regular courts, perhaps because the defendant was a powerful political figure, or because a jury would not convict for other reasons. (There was no jury trial in the Star Chamber.) Not surprisingly, the Star Chamber became seen as a symbol of central power. Yet, through most of its life it was highly popular with the common people. Why would that be? Why was the following case about dueling particularly appropriate for the Star Chamber? Some commentators have described the later role of the Star Chamber as "the equitable function of developing the criminal laws to meet new circumstances." *Id.,* 137. What do you think of that kind of "equity?" From what you know of Francis Bacon from Chapter I, why do you think he prosecuted this case?

A Decree of the Star Chamber "In Camera Stellata," January 26, 1614

From Francis Bacon, *The Charge of Sir Francis Bacon Touching Duells* (London, 1614) 37–61. See discussion in D.R. Coquillette, *Francis Bacon* (Edinbugh, Stanford, 1992) 167–170.

This day was heard and debated at large, the severall matters of Informations here exhibited by Sir *Francis Bacon* Knight, his Majesties Attourney Generall, th'one against *William Priest* Gentleman, for writing and sending a Letter of challenge, together with a stick which should bee the length of the weapon, And th'other against *Richard Wright* Esquire for carrying and delivering the said letter and stick unto the partie challenged, and for other contemptuous and insolent behaviour used before the Justices of Peace in *Surrey* at their Sessions, before whom he was convented. Upon the opening of which cause his Highnes said Attourney generall did first give his reason to the Court why in a case which he intended should be a leading case, for the repressing of so great a mischiefe in the commonwealth, and concerning an offence which raigneth chiefly amongst persons of honor and qualitie, he should begin with a cause which had passed betweene so meane persons as the defendants seemed to be; which he said was done because hee found this cause ready published and in so growing an evill, he thought good to lose no time, whereunto he added, that it was not amisse sometimes to beate the dogge, before the Lyon, saying further, that hee thought it would be some motive for persons of birth & countenance to leave it, when they saw it was taken up by base and mechanicall fellowes, but concluded; That hee resolved to proceed

THE DECREE
OF THE STAR-
CHAMBER IN THE
SAME CAVSE.

In camerâ ſtellatâ coram concilio ibidem
26°. die Ianuarij anno ʋndecimo
Iacobi regis.

The Prefence.

Tho: Lo: Ellefmere Lord Chancellor of England.	Geor: Lo: Arch-biſhop of Canter-bury.
Hen: Earl of North: L: Priuie Seale	Iohn Lo: Biſhop of London.
Charles Earle of Notting: Lo: high Admiral of England.	Sir Edvvard Cooke Knight, L: chiefe Iuſtice of England.
	Tho:

Illustration 7-4 From Francis Bacon, *The Charge of Sir Francis Bacon Touching Duells*, London, 1614, 37. [Author's Collection.]

without respect of persons for the time to come, and for the present to supply the meannesse of this particular Case by insisting the longer upon the generall point.

Wherein he did first expresse unto the Court, at large, the greatnes & danger-ous consequence of this presumptuous offence, which extorted revenge out of the Magistrates hand, and gave boldnes to private men to bee lawe-givers to them-selves, the rather because it is an offence that doth justifie itselfe against the lawe,

38

Tʜo: Earle of Suffolke   *Sir* Hᴇɴ: Hobart
Lord Chamberlaine.   knight Lord chiefe
   Eᴅ: Lord Zouche.   Iuſtice of the com-
                         mon-pleas.

Wɪʟʟɪᴀᴍ: Lo. Knolles, Treaſuror of the
Houſhold.

Eᴅ ᴠʏ ᴀʀ ᴅ Lo. Wotton Controwler.

Iᴏʜ: Lo: Stanhop, Vicechamberlaine.

Sir Iᴠ ʟ ɪ ᴠ s *Cæſar* knight, Chancellor of the
Exchequer:

His day was heard and de-
bated at large, the ſeuerall
matters of Informations
here exhibited by Sir *Fran-
cis Bacon* Knight, his Maieſties Attourney Generall, th'one againſt *William
Prieſt* Gentleman, for writing and
ſending a Letter of challenge, together with a ſtick which ſhould bee the
length of the weapon, And th'other
againſt *Richard Wright* Eſquire for carrying

Illustration 7-5   From Francis Bacon, *The Charge of Sir Francis Bacon Touching Duells*, London, 1614, 38. [Author's Collection.]

and plainely gives the law an affront; describing also the miserable effect which it draweth upon private families by cutting off yong men, otherwise of good hope, and cheifely the losse of the King and Common-wealth, by the casting a-way of much good blood, which being spent in the field upon occasion of service were able to continew the renowne, which this Kingdome hath obtained in all ages, of being esteemed victorious.

Secondly his Majesties said Atturney generall did discourse touching the causes and remedies of this mischefe, that prevaileth so in these times, shewing the ground thereof to bee a false and erroneous imagination of honor and credit, according to the terme which was given unto those *Duells*, by a former proclamation of his Majesties, which called them *bewitching Duells*, for that it is no better then a kind of sorcery, which enchanteth the spirits of young men, which beare great minds with a shew of honor in that which is no honor indeed, beeing against religion, law, morall vertue, and against the presidents and examples of the best times, and valiantest Nations of the world, which though they excelled for prowesse and millitary vertue in a publique quarrell, yet knew not what these private *Duells* ment: saying further, that there was too much way and countenance given unto these *Duells* by the course that is held by noblemen and gentle-men in compounding of quarrells, who use to stand too punctually uppon conceipts of satisfactions and distinctions, what is before hand and what behind hand, which doe but feed the humor; Adding likewise that it was no fortitude to shew vallour in a quarrell, except there were a just and worthy ground of the quarell; but that it was weakenesse to sette a mans life at so meane a rate as to bestowe it uppon trifling occasions, which ought to bee rather offered up and sacrificed to honourable services, publique merrits, good causes, and noble adventures. And as concerning the Remedies, hee concluded: That the onely way was, that the State would declare a constant and settled resolution to master and put downe this presumption in private men, of what-soever degree of righting their owne wrongs, and this to doe at once; For that then every perticuler man would think himselfe acquitted in his reputation, when that he shal see that the State takes his honor into their hands, and standeth betweene him and any Interest, or prejudice, which he might receive in his reputation for obeying; whereunto he added likewise, that the wisest and mildest way to suppresse these *Duells* was rather to punish in this Court all the acts of preparation, which did in any wise tend to the *Duells*, (as this of Challenges and the like) and so to prevent the Capitall punishment, and to vexe the roote in the branches, then to suffer them to run on to the execution, and then to punish them Capitally, after the manner of *France*, where of late times Gentlemen of great quality, that had killed others in *Duell*, were carried to the Gibbet with their woundes bleeding, least a naturall death should keepe them from the example of Justice.

Thirdly his Majesties said Atturney generall did by many reasons, which hee brought and alledged, free the Law of *England* from certaine vaine and childish exceptions, which are taken by these *Duellists*: The one, because the Law makes noe difference in punishment betweene an insidious and foule murther, and the killing of a man upon Challenge and faire tearmes, as they call it, Th'other for that the Law hath not provided sufficient punishment, and reparation for contumelie of wordes, as the *lye*, and the like: wherein his Majesties said Atturney generall did Shew, by many waighty arguments and examples: That the Law of *England* did consent with the Law of *God*, and the Law of *Nations* in both those pointes, and that this distinction in murther betweene Foule and Fayre, and this grounding of mortall quarrells upon uncivill and reproachfull words, or the like disgraces, was never authorised by any law, or ancient examples, but it is a late vanity crept in from the practice of the *French*, who themselves since have beene so weary of it, as they have beene forced to put it downe with all security.

Fourthly, his Majesties said Attourney Generall did proove unto the Court by rules of law and presidents; that this Court hath capacity to punish sending and accepting of Challenges, though they were never acted nor executed; taking for a ground infallible, that wheresoever an offence is capitall or matter of fellony, if it be acted and performed, there the conspiracy, combination, or practice tending to the same offence is punishable as a high misdemeanor, although they never were performed. And therefore that practice to impoyson though it tooke no effect, and the like, have beene punished in this Court: and cyted the president in *Garnons* case, wherein a crime of a much interiour nature, the suborning and preparing of witnesses though they never were deposed, or deposed nothing materiall, was censured in this Court, whereupon hee concluded, that forasmuch as every appoyntment of the field is in law but a combination of plotting of a murther, howsoever men might guilde it: That therefore it was a case fit for the censure of this Court; and therein he vouched a president in the very point, that in a case betwene *Wharton* plaintife and *Elerker* and *Acklam*, defendants. *Acklam* beeing a follower of *Elerker* had carried a challenge unto *Wharton*, and although it were by word of mouth, and not by writing, yet it was severely sensured by the Court; the Decree having wordes, that such Chalenges doe tend to the subversion of government: And therefore his Majesties Atturney willed the standerds by to take notice that it was noe innovation that he brought in, but a proceeding, according to former presidents of the Court, although he purposed to follow it more throughly then had been done ever heeretofore, because the times did more & more require it. Lastly, his Majeesties said Attorney generall did declare and publish to the Court in severall Articles his purpose and resolution in what cases hee did intend to prosecute offences of that nature in this Court, That is to say, That if any man shall appoynt the field, although the fight bee not acted or performed. If any man shall send any challenge in writing, or message of challenge: If any man shall carry or deliver any writing or message of challenge, If any man shall accept or returne a challenge, If any man shall accept to bee a second in a challenge of eyther part: If any man shall depart the Realme with intention and agreement to performe the fight beyond the seas: If any man shall revive a quarrell by any scandalous bruites or writings contrary to a former Proclamation, published by his Majesty in that behalfe, that in all these cases his Majesties Atturney generall, in discharge of his duety by the favour and assistance of his Majesty and the Court, would bring the offenders of what state or degree soever to the justice of this Court, leaving the Lords Comissioners Marshall to the more exact remedies, adding further, that hee heard there were certaine Councell learned of *Duells*, that tell yong men when they are before hand and when they are otherwise, and did incense and incite them to the *Duell*, and made an art of it, who likewise should not be forgotten, and so concluded with two petitions, the one in perticuler to the Lord Chancellor, that in case advertisement were given of a purpose in any to goe beyond the seas to fight, there might bee granted his Majesties writte of *Ne exeat regno* against him: and the other to the Lords in generall, that hee might bee assisted and countenanced in this service.

After which opening and declaration of the generall cause, his Majesties said Atturney did proceed to set forth the proofes of this perticuler challendge and offence now in hand and brought to the judgment and censure of this honorable Court; whereupon it appeared to this honorable Court by the confession of the said defendant *Priest* himselfe, that hee having received some wrong and disgrace at the hands of one *Hutchest*, did thereupon in revenge thereof writ a letter to the said *Hutchest* containing a challenge to fight with him at single rapier, which letter the said *Priest* did deliver to the said defendent *Wright*, together with a sticke containing the length of the rapier, wherewith the said *Priest* ment to performe the fight; whereupon the said *Wright* did deliver the said letter to the said *Hutchest*, and did read the same unto him and after the reading thereof did also deliver to the said *Hutchest* the saide sticke, saying, that the same was the length of the weapon mentioned in the saide Letter. But the saide *Hutchest*, (dutifully respecting the preservation of his Majesties peace) did refuse the said Challeng, whereby noe further mischeefe did ensue thereupon. This honorable Court, and all the honorable presence this day fitting, upon grave and mature deliberation , pondering the quality of these offences, they generally approved the spech and observations of his Majesties saide Atturney generall, and highly commended his great care and good service in bringing a cause of this nature to publique punishment and example, and in professing a constant purpose to goe on in the like course with others; letting him knowe, that hee might expect from the Court all concurrence and assistance in so good a worke. And thereupon the Courte did by theire severall oppinions and sentences declare how much it imported the peace and prosperous estate of his Majestie and his kingdome to nippe this practise and offence of *Duells* in the head, which now did overspread and grow universall, even among meane persons, and was not onely entertayned in practise and custome, but was framed into a kinde of Art and Preceptes; so that according to the saying of the Scripture, *Mischeefe is imagined like a lawe.* And the Court with one consent did declare their opinions. That by the ancient law of the land al Inceptions, preparations, & Combinatios to execute unlawful acts, though they never be performed as they be not to be punished capitally, except it bee in case of treason, and some other perticuler cases of statute law: So yet they are punishable as misdemeanors and contempts: And that this Court was proper for offences of such nature, specially in this case, where the bravery and insolency of the times are such as the ordinary Magistrates and Justices, that are trusted with the preservation of the Peace, are not able to master and represse these offences, which were by the Court at large set forth, to bee not only against the law of God, to whom, and his substitutes all revenge belongeth as part of his prerogative, but also against the oath and duety of every subject unto his Majesty, for that the subject doth sweare unto him, by the ancient law, allegeance of life and member, whereby it is plainely inferred that the subject hath no disposing power over himselfe of life and member to bee spent or ventured according to his owne passions and fancies, in-so-much as the very practise of Chivalry in Justs and Turneys, which are but images of Martiall actions, appeare by ancient presidents not to be lawfull without the Kings lycence obtained. The Court also noted, that these private *Duells* or Combats were of another nature from the Combats which have beene allowed by the law aswell of this land as of other nations for the tryall of rightes or appeales. For that those Combats receive direction & authority from the law, wheras these contrariwise spring only from the unbrideled humors of private men. And as for the pretence of honor, the Court much misliking the confusion of degrees which is growne of late (every man assuming unto himself the tearme and attribute of honor) did utterly reject and condemne the opinion that the private *Duell*, in any person whatsoever, had any groundes of honor, aswell because nothing can be honorable that is not lawfull, and that it is no magnanimity or greatnes of mind, but a swelling & tumor of the minde, where there faileth a right and sound Judgement; as also for that it was rather justly to be esteemed a weaknes, and a conscence of smale value in a mans selfe to be dejected, so with a word or trifling disgrace as to thinke there is no recure of it, but by hazard of life, whereas true honour in persons that know their owne, worth is not of any such brittle substance but of a more strong composition. And finally, the Court shewing a firme and setled resolution to proceede with all severity against these *Duells* gave warning to all young noble-men and gentlemen that they should not expect the like connyuence or tolleration as formerly have beene, but that justice should have a full passage without protection or interruption; Adding that after a straight inhibition, whosoever should attempt a challenge or combatte, in case where the other party was restrayned to answere him (as now all good subjects are) did by their owne principles receive the dishonor and disgrace uppon himselfe. And for the present cause, The Court hath ordered, adjudged, and decreed, that the said *William Priest*, and *Richard Wright*, bee committed to the prison of the *Fleete*, and the said *Priest* to pay five hundred pound, and the said *Wright* five hundred markes for their severall fines to his Majesties use. And to the end that some more publique example may bee made heereof amongst his Majesties people, The Court hath further ordered and decreed, That the said *Priest* and *Wright* shall at the next Assises to bee houlden in the County of *Surrey* publiquely in face of the Court, the Judges sitting, acknowledge their high contempt and offence against God, his Majesty, and his lawes, and shew themselves penitent for the same. Moreover the wisdome of this high and honourable Court thought it meete and necessary that all sorts of his Majesties subjects should understand and take notice of that which hath beene said and handled this day touching this matter, aswell by his highnesse Atturney generall, as by the Lords, Judges, touching the law in such cases. And therefore the Court hath enjoyned Majster Atturney to have speciall care to the penning of this decree, for the setting forth in the same summarily the matters and reasons which have beene opened and delivered by the Court touching the same, and never-thelesse also at some time convenient to publish the perticulers of his speeche and declaration, as very meete and worthy to bee remembred, and made known to the world, as these times are: And this decree, being in such sort carefully drawne & penned, the whole Court thought it meete, and so have ordered and decreed, that the same bee not onely read and published at the next Assises for *Surrey* at such time as the said *Priest* and *Wright* are to acknowledge their offences as aforesaid; But that the same be likewise published and made knowne in all Shires of this Kingdome. And to that end Justices of Assize are required by this honorable Court to cause this decree to bee solemnly read and published in all the places and sittings of their severall Circuits, and in the greatest assembly, to the end that all his Majesties subjects may take knowledge and understand the opinion of this honorable Court in this case, and in what measure, his Majesty, and this honorable Court purposeth to punish such as shall fall into the like contempt and offences hereafter. Lastly this honorable Court, much approving that which the right honorable Sir *Edward Coke* knight, Lord Chiefe Justice of *England* did now deliver touching the law in this case of *Duells*, hath enjoyned his Lordship to report the same in print, as hee hath formerly done divers other Cases, that, such as understand not the law in that behalfe, and all others may better direct themselves, and prevent the danger thereof hereafter.

FINIS.

THE ADMIRALTY PRACTICE OF JOHN ADAMS

Note: John Adams (1735–1826) became the second President of the United states (1796–1800). As a young lawyer practicing in colonial Boston, he frequently found himself in the Vice-Admiralty Court, where cases involving maritime law were heard, as well as other "civilian" specialties, including divorces and wills of chattel. See D.R. Coquillette, "Justinian in Braintree: John Adams, Civilian Learning, and Legal Elitism, 1758–1775" in *Law in Colonial Massachusetts 1630–1800* (Coquillette, Brink, Menand eds. 1984), 359, 382–395. The following case descriptions come from that article. The "Case of the Whale" is obviously a maritime case, but note the "Case of the Harpoon" which follows. Why would the prosecutor prefer a Vice-Admiralty Court to try Michael Corbet? In writing this article, I was most indebted to L.K. Wroth and Judge H.B. Zobel, editors of the *Legal Papers of John Adams* (Cambridge, Mass. 1965). Notes in the original, omitted here, contained many acknowledgements to them.

A. The Case of the Whale: *Doane v. Gage* (1766–1769)

The colonial vice-admiralty courts were "primarily to provide a forum for enforcement of the Acts of Trade and Navigation, with which England sought to control colonial commerce for the benefit of the Mother Country." Most admiralty cases in Adams' Massachusetts were smuggling and revenue cases. But Adams did have one classic civil jurisdiction (i.e. non-revenue or non-criminal) admiralty case, *Doane v. Gage*, the "Case of the Whale."

This was a truly fabulous squabble over which whale ship was entitled to a dead whale. The whale had been hit by a harpoon from a boat launched by a ship captained by Adams' client, a Captain Doane. The whale, quite sensibly, took off for the bottom. At some later point he returned to the surface and was hit by another harpoon. This harpoon came from a boat launched by a rival ship, commanded by a Captain Gage. At some other point—either before or after Gage's "iron" hit—Doane's boat's line came free. Under the custom of the whalers, a whale "belonged" to the boat that first struck it, even if another stuck it later, *if* the first harpoon's line was attached to its boat at the time of the second hit. But "if the whale became 'loose' without having been struck a second time," the new harpoon gained full possession.

So the key issue was simply whether Doane's boat was attached to the whale when Gage struck it, or whether the whale was a "loose" whale. No less than seventy-four witnesses, thirty-four for Doane and forty for Gage, would testify. John Adams represented Captain Doane and Robert Treat Paine and James Otis represented Captain Gage. Never was a dead whale given such posthumous dignity. He was fought over by seventy-four eyewitnesses, two signers of the Declaration of Independence—one a future President of the United States—and the great James Otis!

For this case Adams prepared a truly remarkable "Notes of authorities," with lengthy quotations on ownership of wild animals from Grotius' *De Jure Belli ac Pacis* and Justinian's *Institutes*. Adams' key point—rather contrary to the whalers' custom—was that once a wild animal was acquired by possession (presumably by being hit with his client's harpoon) that "Property acquired by Possession does not cease with the Loss of Possession." This proposition came directly from Grotius. But Adams' notes contained a contrary rule from the Roman law sources themselves. "*Ferae igitur Bestiae et Volucres, et Pisces, et omnia animalia, quae mari, Coelo, et Terra nascuntur: simulatque ab aliquo capta fuerint, jure gentium, statim illius esse incipiunt. Quod enim ante nullius est, id, naturali Ratione, occupanti conceditur.*" "Wild animals, birds, and fish, that is to say all the creatures which the land, the sea, and the sky produce, as soon as they are caught by any one become at once the property of their captor by the law of nations; for natural reason admits the title of the first occupant to that which previously had no owner." (Justinian's *Institutes*, 2:1:12). But the *Institutes* add: "*[c]um vero tuam evaserit Custodiam, et in Libertatem naturalem sese receperit, tuum esse definit, et rursus occupantis fit,*" "An animal thus caught by you is deemed your property so long as it is completely under your control; but so soon as it has escaped from your control, and recovered its natural liberty, it ceases to be yours, and belongs to the first person who subsequently catches it." This, of course, was a rule more in keeping with the whalers' custom.

Adams did not leave it there. He checked the *Institutes'* passage against the *Digest*, thus demonstrating both a degree of sophistication about the Roman law and access to a copy of the entire *Corpus Juris Civilis*. There he located the section (*Digest* 41:1:5) describing a contoversy between Trebatius and Justinian's compilers. Trebatius was of the opinion that one who wounded a wild beast immediately became owner, and that "he must be held to retain the ownership so long as he kept on following the animal up, but that, if he relinquished the pursuit, his ownership ceased...so that if, at any moment while the pursuit lasted, some other person should capture it...he must be held to have committed a theft on the person first mentioned." This was certainly a view which would appeal to Captain Doane. Justinian's compilers, however, indicated that "[a] good many authorities hold that the party does not become owner unless he captures it, because there is a considerable chance of the capture not being made; and this is a better view to take." Here was a view that would surely appeal to Captain Gage!

Regrettably, no one seems to have recorded who won. There is only Paine's cryptic note on 27 October 1769, "Whale case finished." Lengthy depositions survive, however, and they tend to indicate more concern with whalers' customs, such as "mateship," than with Roman law. There is no indication that Adams' classical learning was ever brought to bear. This result would have amused Herman Melville—who described the unwritten law of whaling as "a system which for terse comprehensiveness surpasses Justinian's Pandects and the By-laws of the Chinese Society for the Suppression of Meddling with other People's Business...

I. A Fast-fish belongs to the party fast to it.
II. A Loose-fish is fair game for anybody who can soonest catch it."

But Adams certainly did get his Roman law books out for the case, and doubtless would have tried to see if the Court of Vice Admiralty would have listened to those arguments, even in Boston in 1768. This would have been particularly true if the Roman law had clearly cut his way. Equally significant, the lengthy testimony and depositions that definitely did take place were all in the form of written interrogatories, a civilian practice adopted "in deference to the civil law procedure followed in the High Court of Admiralty in England, or for convenience in a hearing four years after the event...."

The Case of the Harpoon (1769)

Even more striking examples of applied civilian learning were provided by Adams' cases on the criminal side of the Admiralty. The statute of 28 Hen. 8. c. 15 (1536) established a "criminal jurisdiction" for the Admiralty, encompassing various criminal offenses committed at sea. Provision was included for jury trial. During the days of Adams' practice in Massachusetts, such trials were held before a Special Court of the Admiralty under a commission issued on 14 January 1762.

On 22 April 1769 the British warship, H.M. frigate *Rose*, intercepted the brig *Pitt Packet* off Marblehead. The brig was boarded, apparently to press sailors. The crew hid in the forepeak, and, when confronted by the British lieutenant, Henry Panton, one sailor, Michael Corbet, drew back a harpoon and impaled the British officer, killing him instantly. [Corbet apparently had drawn a line on the deck with the harpoon, and had said he would kill the first Englishman to cross the line. Panton, taking a pinch of snuff, crossed the line, to his death.] Lieutenant Panton is now in a King's Chapel, Boston, grave.

Adams, with James Otis, was hired to represent the seaman. The key issue was whether the killing was justifiable homicide and, if so, was there any appropriate punishment at civil law. In his preparation for the case Adams scoured the civil law authorities on self-defense and provocation. Among the sources listed in his "notes of Authorities" and/or quoted in his "Argument and Report:" are John Calvin's *Magnum Lexicon Juridicum*, title "culpa" (Geneva, 1734); Jean Domat's *The Civil Law in its Natural Order: Together with the Public Law* (1st ed. Strahan trans., 1722); Thomas Wood's *A New Institute of the Imperial, or Civil Law* (3d ed., 1721); Robertus Maranta's *Praxis, sive de ordine judiciorum...vulgo speculum aureum et lumen advocatorum* (Cologne, 1614); and Andreas Gail's *Practicarum observationum tam ad processum judiciarum praesertim imperialis camerae quam causarum decisiones pertinentium* (Cologne, 1721).

At trial, on 14 June 1769, Adams came prepared to argue that the homicide was a justified response to the threat presented by press gang officers to an innocent seaman, who only wished to stay with his ship:

> In these Circumstances what could he do? But defend himself, as he did?
> In these Circumstances what was his Duty? He had an undoubted Right, not merely to make a push at Lt. Panton, but to have darted an Harpoon, a dagger thro the heart of every Man in the whole Gang.

Adams invoked the *Codex*, 9:16:2, for the right to kill in self-defense. " '*De eo, qui salutem suam defendit. Is qui aggressorem vel quemcunque alium, in dubio vitae discrimine constitutus occiderit, nullum ob id factum, calumniam metuere debet.*' " He also invoked the Scottish civil law authority, Barrington's *Observation upon the Statutes* (London, 2nd ed., 1766). " 'By the Law of Scotland there is no such Thing as Man Slaughter, nor by the civil Law; and therefore a criminal indicted for Murder, under the Statute of Henry the Eighth, where the judges proceed by the Rules of the civil Law, must either be found guilty of the Murder or acquitted.' "

Furthermore, reasoned Adams, if the governing law was civil law, then the killing was punishable by death only if it were murder, there being no civil law death penalty for unjustifiable homicide without malice. The equivalent common law crime of manslaughter was more risky, as it might be argued that the seamen were not entitled to benefit of clergy before a Special Admiralty Court. Adams also discovered a statute forbidding impressment of American seamen and moved for jury trial.

The result was dramatic. Adams had only just begun his closing argument to the Special Court of Admiralty when, suddenly, Lieutenant Governor Hutchinson called for an adjournment. Four hours later the Special Court returned. A verdict of justifiable homicide was announced. The seamen were set free.

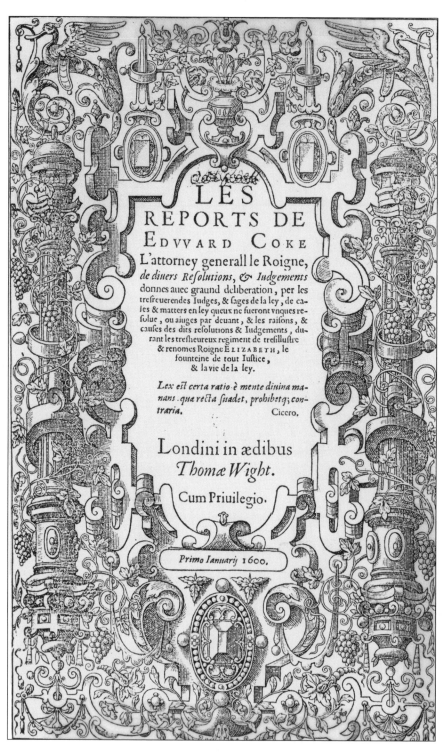

LES REPORTS DE EDVVARD COKE

L'attorney generall le Roigne,
de diuers Resolutions, & Iudgements
donnes auec graund deliberation, per les
tresreuerendes Iudges, & sages de la ley, de cases & matters en ley queux ne fueront vnques re-
solue, ou aiuges par deuant, & les raisons, &
causes des dits resolutions & Iudgements, du-
rant les tresheureux regiment de tresillustre
& renomes Roigne ELIZABETH, le
founteine de tout Iustice,
& la vie de la ley.

Lex est certa ratio è mente diuina ma-
nans, quæ recta suadet, prohibetq; con-
traria.   Cicero.

Londini in ædibus
Thomæ Wight.

Cum Priuilegio.

Primo Ianuarij 1600.

Illustration 8-1 First edition of the first installment of *Coke's Reports* (1600). [Author's Collection.]

VIII

APPEAL

American law students are usually introduced to "the law" through the "case method," which focuses almost exclusively on appellate cases. It is thus hard for American lawyers to accept that the whole idea of "appeal" is a relatively new one in the history of Anglo-American law.[1] Compared to other fundamental ideas, like centralized courts, formulary pleading, jury trial, and statutory law reform, "appeal" represents "the new kid on the block."

On reflection, it is easy to understand why. As Baker put it, "[t]here was no possibility of error in a judgment supported by divine intervention." *Introduction, supra,* 155. The ordeal, the wager of law, and the trial by battle—the basis of all the old *praecipe* writs—represented trial by the will of God. There was nothing to "appeal." Introduction of jury trial made little difference at the outset. It, too, was somewhat "inscrutable." Further, the judges of the three royal courts were equal in rank, and all three courts represented the King. Every decision was by the whole court. There was no "higher" court, except the residual authority of the King in Council or the King in Parliament. Equity was available as a complementary, not superior, system when common law remedies were inadequate. In the last resort, there was the collateral power of the Star Chamber, when the common law system could not work effectively. But these were complementary institutions, not appellate courts.

In addition, individual trial judges, sitting as "assize" judges in the *nisi prius* system away from Westminster, would bring back verdicts for review by the full court before entering final judgment. This was a kind of "review," in that legal issues could be raised by the other judges or, within strict limits, by the losing party. This process was called "arrest of judgment." In theory, however, this was not a true appeal, because no judgment had been entered. It was a procedure followed *before* the court entered its judgment, which was always collective. The

---

1. Incidentally, in this Chapter we are using the term "appeal" in its most common modern sense, i.e., judicial review of decisions by lower courts. There are other uses of the word in legal history, i.e., "appeal of felony." See Baker, *Introduction, supra,* 574–576. In addition, there is a very long tradition of judicial review in the canon and civil law, as my valuable colleague and friend, Mary Bilder, reminds me. See, for example, J.H. Baker, *Introduction, supra,* 146–154; G.I.O. Duncan, *The High Court of Delegates* (Cambridge, 1971), 1–80; W.W. Buckland, *A Text Book of Roman Law* (Cambridge, 3d. ed., P. Stein ed. 1966), 670–673.

judge who conducted the trial participated in all stages of this "review," so there was certainly no "appeal" in the sense of superior judges reviewing courts "below."

A. ERROR

The first vehicle at common law for regular supervision of one court by another was the writ of error, which was well established by the sixteenth century. This was an extremely narrow remedy that was limited to a manifest error on the formal record (i.e., the plea roll), or some plain fact, proven by the plaintiff in error, that was clearly inconsistent with that record, and which directed a different result. The latter category was extremely restrictive in practice, and was limited to facts like the death of a party. The former category was also very narrow, as very little actually appeared on the plea roll. For example, as long as a jury verdict was properly recorded, there was nothing on the record to indicate anything more, so there was no basis of review.

The "bottom line" was that the law could tolerate an unjust result, but not an obvious technical mistake reflected on the formal record. A classic example would be the use of the wrong writ or cause of action, say an action in debt to recover, not money, but possession of land. To prevent this kind of mistake, the King's Bench was given general supervision over local courts of record and the Common Pleas. There was also an attempt to give the King's Bench a general supervision in error over the Exchequer, but this failed.[2] Instead, a statutory court of error was established consisting of the Chancellor, two royal judges, and the Treasurer, the so-called "Council Chamber." As far as supervision of the King's Bench, another statutory court of error was established, consisting of all of the judges of The Common Pleas and the Exchequer. This was called the statutory "Exchequer Chamber." From all these courts, final review in error was to the House of Lords.

This "last step" was rarely used, at least initially. The House of Lords consisted primarily of untrained lay peers. Of course, they could, and did, invite judges to attend and, eventually, some judges were made peers. But for centuries lay peers could outvote their learned brethren. A final solution was reached only in 1876, by the Appellate Jurisdiction Act. This provided for Lords of Appeal in Ordinary who were experienced judges. (First there were two such peers; now there are eleven.) These peers were given life peerages. Today, they are the only peers to decide the strictly legal business of the House.

B. ALDRED'S CASE (1611)

An interesting example of *nisi prius* "arrest of judgment" procedure was *William Aldred's Case*, in *Coke's Reports* 57b., 77 *English Reports* 816 (1611).[3]

---

2. See Baker, *Introduction, supra*, 157–158.

3. See *Materials, infra*, p. 257. We will be discussing Sir Edward Coke's reports at length in *Materials*, Chapter X. The original pagination is in "folio" form, in which each page had one number, say "57," plus an "a" side and a "b" side. The second citation is to the *English Reports*, a modern reprinting of the old "name" reporters.

The issue was whether Aldred could have a remedy to prevent "corrupted air," stench from a neighbor's hog sty, from destroying the enjoyment of his property in Norfolk. While we may laugh today at this kind of case, it was an important pioneer precedent in environmental protection. In the absence of railroads and refrigeration, fresh meat had to come from immediately around population centers. Piggeries were a major industry, and the defendant, Thomas Benton, emphatically argued "that the building of the house for hogs was necessary for the sustenance of man."[4] He also argued the "one ought not to have so delicate a nose, that he cannot bear the smell of hogs."[5]

The plaintiff brought a regular action on the case at the royal assizes in Norfolk. The jury found his allegation to be true, and assessed damages. Following the standard *nisi prius* procedure, the trial judge reserved judgment for his brethren of The Common Pleas in London. There the defendant's lawyers moved in arrest of judgment that "the building of said house for hoggs was necessary for the sustenance of man, and no one ought to be so delicate nosed, that he cannot endure the scent of hoggs," but the Common Pleas held that the action was maintainable, and entered judgments.[6] Note, again, that the original action of the assize court had been "reviewed," but *before* final judgment was entered.

Why did not the defendant then proceed in error to the King's Bench? A classic allegation of error would be that a "nuisance" action like this should not be brought by an "action on the case," but by the old possessory nuisance action, *novel disseisin ad nocumentum liberi tenementi*, which was analogous to the possessory assizes—particularly novel disseisin. (Depriving you of your enjoyment of land by actions off the land, "nuisance," had long been regarded as equivalent to disseisin.) But, of course, possessory actions merely restored the appropriate *status quo*. Here, the plaintiff wanted damages, and this required an action on the case. Was this not an error, as the possessory action was older?

Unfortunately for the defendant, this issue had been decided on a writ of error eight years before by the Exchequer Chamber in *Cantrel v. Church, Cro. Eliz.* 845, 78 *English Reports* 1672 (Ex. Chamber, 1601). This case held that a nuisance plaintiff could have his election of action on the case or the old assize of nuisance.[7] Thus, there was no legal error presented by the record in *Aldred's Case.*

---

4. See Daniel R. Coquillette, "Mosses from an Old Manse: Another Look at Some Historic Property Cases About the Environment," 64 *Cornell Law Review* 761, 772–781 (1979). As Professor Dawson noted: "hundreds of folio pages of jury orders relate to swine alone and their numerous misdeeds and nuisances." J. Dawson, *A History of Lay Judges*, 268–69 (1900).

5. 9 *Coke's Report* at 58a, 77 *English Reports*, at 817.

6. See *Materials, infra*, p. 257.

7. In *Cantrel v. Church*, the issue involved a nuisance action for interference with a right of way. The court observed that the decision was required because such an interference could be perpetuated by someone with no interest in land or by a lease holder. In both cases, the possessory action would be inappropriate "especially as this Case is, where it appears not, that the stopping was made him, who is the Tenant of the Free-hold; but it might be done by a stranger, who hath nothing to do with the Land; or by one who hath but a Term therein." *Cro. Eliz, supra*, 845. This left open an interesting issue of what would happen where it was clear on the record that the interference was caused by a tenant of a free-hold. Would the action on the case be barred by the availability of the possessory action? Coke's

C. PREROGATIVE WRITS

The writ of error was not the only writ by which the King's Bench supervised other courts. While appellate review of another court on the merits was an idea late in coming, it was another matter when a court exceeded its jurisdiction or used the wrong procedures. Indeed, this was just a specific application of a more general principle that governed everyone acting under the "countenance of authority," including Crown officers. If official jurisdictions were exceeded or the wrong procedure used, the King's Courts should provide a remedy.

The tools for this judicial supervision were called the "prerogative writs." These included some of the most famous of all judicial writs, whose names have become synonymous with protection of civil liberty. These writs were called "prerogative" writs because they were inherently discretionary and were, theoretically, based on the King's "royal prerogative." They were even "technically brought in the King's name." This, as Baker has observed, was quite ironic, as the prerogative writs earned their place in history largely by curbing the power of the King's officers and conciliar courts, often to the intense displeasure of monarchs such as James I and Charles I.[8] In fact, these writs were never issued by the King, but almost solely by the King's Bench, in its capacity as the "senior" common law court, closest to the King. As we will see later in the *Materials*, James I actually tried to sit in the King's Bench during the constitutional crisis of the early seventeenth century, only to be told by Chief Justice Coke that the King's Bench exercised an abstract sovereignty quite apart from the King's person, a suggestion that gave great offense to the King. The "prerogative writs" evolved, not as a vehicle for royal prerogative in the sense of the King's executive discretion, but rather a check on the arbitrariness of the Crown and the King's officers and councilors. We will now review the most important of these writs.

I. WRIT OF PROHIBITION

The prerogative writ called "prohibition" was the oldest. It was available at the request of a private party to halt a judicial or quasi-judicial action against that party in a court or tribunal. This writ originally evolved to keep Church courts out of secular business, but it was extended to control all inferior judicial entities by the sixteenth century. There was extensive use of prohibition writs against civilian jurisdictions, such as the Admiralty or the Court of the Marshal, and even attempts to curtail Chancery. The latter use of prohibition led to a fierce struggle between Lord Chancellor Ellesmere and Chief Justice Coke in the early seventeenth century, a struggle that had to be resolved by the direct intervention of the King.[9] In addition, aggressive use of the prohibition writ curtailed the development of mercantile courts, and aided in the "incorporation" of mercantile law into the common law by effectively destroying the finality of commer-

---

report on *Aldred's Case* says that the defendant was "possessed" of the adjoining parcel, but does not say how. 9 *Coke's Reports, supra*, 57b.

8. J.H. Baker, *Introduction, supra*, 164–166.

9. See J.P. Dawson, "Coke and Ellesmere Disinterred, the Attack on the Chancery in 1616," (1941) 36 *Illinois Law Review* 127–152.

cial judgments in the specialized courts.[10] Whether the prohibition writ was a noble instrument to protect the rule of law, or a selfish vehicle to promote the common law and the common lawyers over professional rivals, depended on your point of view. In fact, both occurred. For a good example of the use of a writ of prohibition against an admiralty proceeding, see *Palmer v. Pope* (1611), set out in Chapter VII, *supra*.

2. WRIT OF QUO WARRANTO

The "Quo Warranto" writ differed from "prohibition" because it went to the underlying authority of any court or tribunal—thus its name "*quo warranto?*" (or "by what authority?"). The prohibition writ lay solely to determine the appropriateness of just a single action involving the petitioner. The "*quo warranto*" writ, on the other hand, went to the whole picture. It asked the sheriff to determine "by what authority" someone was holding a court. The writ evolved as one that was usually brought "by information" of the Attorney General or other royal officers, but it now appears that many such "informations" were in fact brought by private suitors, usually in the name of the master of the Crown office.[11]

3. WRIT OF MANDAMUS

The writ *Mandamus* (from "we command") was basically the collateral remedy to *quo warranto*. Like *quo warranto*, it was always directed at an inferior public authority or tribunal. While *quo warranto* would challenge the basis of an official act, *mandamus* would require or "command" a local authority to act, or else to show cause why it should not act. Traditionally, the writ was used to restore legitimately appointed officials to public office and to protect those entitled to other public benefits (private benefits being protected by contractual actions). Today, *mandamus,* in the form of an order available from the modern Queen's Bench, is still the primary remedy for enforcing a public duty—although, unlike private contractual remedies at law, it remains discretionary.

Because *mandamus* was a general remedy for lack of relief from inferior tribunals and public bodies, it is important to note that it never served as a true appeal on the merits. It lay when a public authority wrongly failed to exercise jurisdiction or used the wrong procedures, not where that authority has simply come to the wrong decision on the merits.

---

10. See D.R. Coquillette, *The Civilian Writers of Doctors' Commons* (Berlin, 1988) 97–148.

11. See J.H. Baker, *Introduction, supra,*167–168. An analogous procedure, based on the writ of *scire facias* ("that you caused him to know") was used to enforce judgements, letters, patents and other legal records by requiring the defendant to show cause why the plaintiff should not have the benefit of what was shown by the record. It was used, for example, to vacate a provincial charter of Massachusetts in 1684 for ostensibly encroaching on the royal prerogative in founding Harvard College. *Ibid,* 167.

4. WRIT OF CERTIORARI

The writ of *certiorari* (from the Latin *certiorare*, "inform") is used today in the United States as a general vehicle of discretionary appeal. Historically, however, the writ had a much narrower function. It lay only to inferior courts and only to demand that the record be "certified" and sent to the King's Bench to see if that court had exceeded its power in a particular case. It was most frequently used to review criminal indictments and local administrative orders, and was often used to examine the statutory authority for acts of administrative bodies created by statute. But, like *mandamus, certiorari* was, at least originally, not a basis for a true appellate review on the merits. All that could be reviewed was the formal record. There could be no *new* trial in the King's Bench, or a reexamination of the case on the merits, although *certiorari* eventually could be used to remove a case into the King's Bench before trial. If it appeared on the face of the record that an inferior court lacked jurisdiction, *certiorari* would lie, but "not on the ground that it had misconceived a point of law if it had jurisdiction and the proceedings are *ex facie* regular, nor on the ground that its decision is wrong in fact. It is accordingly not an appeal."[12]

Nevertheless, *certiorari* did evolve in England as a constitutional remedy. If a judicial authority below used procedures that, on their face, violated the "rules of natural justice," this became the equivalent of exceeding jurisdiction or making a clear error of procedure.[13] Of course, the most conspicuous use of *certiorari* in America today is the writ of *certiorari* to the Supreme Court of the United States, to test the constitutionality of decisions by courts below. It remains, like the old prerogative writ, a highly discretionary remedy. While the original *certiorari* writ, like the *mandamus* writ, was abolished in England by the Administration of Justice Act of 1938, the High Court now has the statutory power to make an order of *certiorari* in appropriate cases, just as it can make a statutory order of *mandamus*.

It is worth noting here another writ that was frequently included with prerogative writs like *certiorari*. This was the writ of "*procedendo*." As with *certiorari*, *procedendo* was addressed solely to inferior courts. It commanded an inferior court to "proceed" to judgment promptly, without specifying what the judgment should be. *Procedendo* basically addressed the fact that "justice delayed is justice denied." If a judgment is erroneous, it could be challenged by writ of error, or, if it is *ultra vires*, by prerogative writ. But if no judgment at all is forthcoming, these writs are useless. Thus the need for the writ of *procedendo*. Otherwise, the parties are without remedy. In a sense, *procedendo* was a *mandamus* type remedy solely directed at urging inferior courts to make a judgment.

5. WRIT OF HABEAS CORPUS

The most famous of the prerogative writs, "*habeas corpus*" ("that you have the body") developed very slowly. In its earliest forms, it was far from the all-purpose civil liberties remedy that it is today. As Baker observed: "It is not a little

---

12. David M. Walker, *The Oxford Companion to Law* (Oxford, 1980), 198.
13. See Earl Jowitt, *The Dictionary of English Law* (ed. C. Walsh, London, 1959), 335.

ironic...that its original purpose was not to release people from prison but to secure their presence in custody."[14] By the sixteenth century, however, the King's
Bench had begun to use the writ to challenge any unauthorized imprisonment by
royal officers.

The writ was directed to the jailer, and required producing the prisoner in person before the court, together with the reason for imprisonment. By the time of
Chief Justice Coke, the writ had become a powerful weapon against royal absolutism, and—in addition—a formidable tool for common law supremacy. Coke
issued *habeas corpus* against inferior courts, as well as royal officers, and even
released prisoners ordered held by the Chancery. After Coke's dismissal by James
I, matters finally came to a head. The new King, Charles I, attempted to raise
money by forced loans, without Parliamentary consent. Those who didn't comply, were imprisoned. Five "brought their *habeas corpus*" in the *Five Knight
Case* (1627), set out in Chapter X of the *Materials, infra*. The jailer could only
produce a royal order, and an intimidated King's Bench said only that "[t]he
King hath done it, and we trust him in great matters." *Id.*

This weak decision resulted in a crisis the next year when, because of financial
pressure, Parliament finally had to be called. The Parliament unanimously voted
for a "Petition of Right," providing "[t]hat the Writ of Habeas Corpus may not
be denied...." See Chapter X, *infra*. The Habeas Corpus Act of 1640 followed.
After a bloody civil war, fought in large part over the issues symbolized by the
Five Knights Case, the *habeas corpus* remedy was made even more effective by
the guaranteed procedures under the *Habeas Corpus Amendment Act* of 1679.
By that time, the King's Bench had extended the remedy to a wide range of
wrongs. These grew to include more than just criminal cases. Prisoners held for
contempt of Parliament, women held by their husbands, abused children, those
held in England as slaves, those detained in hospitals or mental institutes, and
those threatened with extradition all turned to the remedy. By the *Habeas Corpus Act* of 1816, the remedy was extended to non-criminal matters, and the
judges were given statutory authority to review the truth of the facts in the answer defending the custody.

For most of its history, however, *habeas corpus* was a true prerogative writ,
and not a form of appeal. As Baker observed: "Even in its widest application...it
does not enable an appeal on the merits of a decision to imprison. Its function is
to question the lawfulness, not the inherent correctness, of an imprisonment."[15]
Nevertheless, it was, and is, one of the great cornerstones of the rule of law, and
is now incorporated into Article I, Section 9, of the Constitution of the United
States.

D. THE SLOW EVOLUTION OF TRUE "APPEAL"

We have already seen how a common law trial judge would never enter final
judgment in the *nisi prius* system. Rather, this was done by the whole bench of
the court back in London. The delay provided a natural opportunity for the

---

14. J.H. Baker, *Introduction, supra*, 168.
15. J.H. Baker, *Introduction, supra*, 169.

judge to discuss tough issues with colleagues before final action. An obvious next step occurred fairly early in the middle ages – assize judges began "reserving" tough issues encountered on assize for *en banc* argument before the whole Common Pleas in London, with a similar procedure being used after verdict, but before sentencing, in criminal cases.

This "adjournment for difficulty" led to another informal proceeding for cases of great difficulty or importance. Not only could such a case be heard *en banc* before final judgment, but discussion could be arranged with all the royal judges from all three courts participating. As Baker observed, those judges together "were not acting as a court of record, but as an advisory assembly; nevertheless their opinion was always acted on, and (if reported) would serve as a precedent for the future."[16]

To make matters complicated for law students, this informal assembly was called by the same name as the statutory court of error, the "Exchequer Chamber," probably because the judges often met in that room.[17] The informal "Exchequer Chamber" was, however, much more like a modern court of appeal, because it was not limited to narrow legal errors, but could, and did, address broad changes in the law.

The very informality of those proceedings was important. It meant that outcomes, on the record, were simply the entered judgment, or an order for new trial. This left little or nothing to attack by writ of error.

An excellent example of such a process, and a highly important case, was *Slade's Case*, set out in the *Materials, infra*. The case was simple. The plaintiff, John Slade, had sold the defendant, Humphrey Morley, "all the ears of wheat and corn which did then grow" on a certain eight acres called Rack Park. Morley promised to pay £16 on a specific day ("the feast of St. John the Baptist the next following"). It was a standard futures contract. Morley did not pay, perhaps because the price of grain fell, and Slade sued Morley in the King's (Queen's) Bench. What was interesting was his choice of writ, action of the case in *assumpsit*. Slade's lawyer doubtless did this for two reasons: 1) to get a jury trial and 2) to get damages. Indeed, Slade won a jury verdict and asked for £40 damages. But Morley's lawyer said that the case should have been brought on a writ of debt.

> And against the maintenance of this action divers objections were made by *John Doddridge*, of Counsel with the defendant. 1. That the plaintiff upon this bargain might have ordinary remedy by action of Debt, which is an action formed in the Register, and therefore he should not have an Action on the Case, which is an extraordinary action and not limited within any certain form in the Register.... The second objection was, That the maintenance of this action takes away the defendant's benefit of Wager of Law and so bereaves him of the benefit which the Law gives him, which is his birthright. For peradventure the defendant has paid or satisfied the plaintiff in private betwixt them, of which payment or satisfaction he has no witness, and therefore it would be mischievous if he should not wage his Law in such case... The defendant shall not be

---

16. J.H. Baker, *Introduction, supra*, 160.
17. The Exchequer Chamber discussions also occurred in other venues, such as Serjeants' Inn. Royal courts would also seek advice from each other during deliberations.

charged in an action in which he shall be ousted of his Law, when he may charge him in an action in which he may have the benefit of it. *Materials, infra.*

Obviously, as a defendant, Morley would prefer the absence of damages and availability of the archaic defense by oath helping, or "wager of law," which came with the old writ of debt.

According to Coke's account, the Common Pleas—which had a monopoly on the old actions like debt—insisted on a writ of debt in this kind of case. The King's Bench, on the other hand, had a monopoly on the trespass actions and their progeny such as action on the case in *assumpsit*. It preferred the new form of action.

> And as to these objections the Courts of King's Bench and Common Pleas were divided; for the Justices of the King's Bench held that the action (notwithstanding such objections) was maintainable, and the Court of Common Pleas held the contrary. And for the honour of the Law and for the quiet of the subject in the appeasing of such diversity of opinions (quia nil in lege intolerabilius est eandem rem diverso jure censeri), the case was openly argued before all the Justices of England and Barons of the Exchequer, sc., Sir John POPHAM, Kt. C.J. of England, Sir Edm. ANDERSON, Kt. C.J. of the Common Pleas, Sir W. PERIAM, Chief Baron of the Exchequer, CLARK, GAWDY, WALMESLEY, FENNER, KINGSMILL, SAVIL, WARBUTON and YELVERTON, in the Exchequer Chamber, by the Queen's Attorney-General for the Plaintiff and by *John Dodderidge* for the Defendant, and at another time the case was argued at Serjeant's Inn by the Attorney General [Edward Coke himself] for the Plaintiff and by *Francis Bacon* for the Defendant. And after many conferences between the Justices and Barons it was resolved that the action was maintainable and that the plaintiff should have Judgment.
>
> And in this case these points were resolved.
>
> 1. That altho' an action of Debt lies upon the contract, yet the bargainor may have an Action on the Case or an action of Debt at his election; and that...in respect of infinite precedents (which *George Kemp*, Esq., Secondary of the Prothonotaries of the King's Bench shew'd me) as well in the Court of Common Pleas as in the Court of King's Bench..., to which precedents and judgments, being of so great number in so many successions of ages and in the several times of so many revered Judges, the Justices in this case gave great regard... So that in the case at Bar it was resolved that the multitude of the said judicial precedents in so may successions of ages well prove that in the case at Bar the action was maintainable. *Materials, infra.*

There were two special arguments by counsel before the Exchequer Chamber. Among the distinguished lawyers involved were Edward Coke (then the Queen's Attorney General) for the plaintiff and Francis Bacon, Coke's great rival and future Lord Chancellor, for the defendant.[18] (At the time, government attorneys

---

18. See Daniel R. Coquillette, *Francis Bacon* (Edinburgh, Stanford, 1992).

could argue for private parties in cases not involving the Crown.) The decision, "that the plaintiff should have Judgment," indicates that this was probably all argued before formal entry of judgment by the King's Bench, a good example of why this was not technically an appeal. Indeed, it is possible that this case was first argued before a jury in Devon on assize, the verdict taken, and then reported back to the King's Bench in London, the so-called *nisi prius* system.

As we will see, Coke frequently reported cases where he was an advocate or a judge, and he did not stick strictly to the truth. He reported *Slade's Case* as deciding, once and for all, that a plaintiff could choose either the older writ or a new trespass based action upon the case. Indeed, after *Slade's Case*, the action on the case superseded the old actions and their archaic modes of proof. This was a very good thing, at least in Coke's opinion.

> It was said, That an Action on the Case on *Assumpsit* is as well a formed action, and contained in the Register, as an action of Debt, for there is its Form. Also it appears in divers other cases in the Register that an Action on the Case will lie, altho' the plaintiff may have another formed action in the Register...And therefore it was concluded that in all cases when the Register has two writs for one and the same case it is in the party's election to take either. But the Register has two several actions, *sc.* Action upon the Case upon *Assumpsit* and also an Action of Debt, and therefore the party may elect either.
>
> And as to the objection which has been made, that it would be mischievous to the defendant that he should not wage his Law, forasmuch as he might pay it in secret: to that it was answered that it should be accounted his folly that he did not take sufficient witness with him to prove the payment he made. But the mischief would be rather on the other party; for now experience proves that men's conscience grow so large that the respect of their private advantage rather induces men (and chiefly those who have declining estates) to Perjury...; and therefore in Debt, or other action where Wager of Law is admitted by the Law, the Judges without good admonition and due examination of the party do not admit him to it...And I am supriz'd that in these days so little consideration is made of an oath, as I daily observe... (*Materials, infra,* 263).

Whether the actual decision was so clear cut has been much discussed.[19] In all events, *Slade's Case* was certainly an excellent example of the informal "Exchequer Chamber" as an antecedent of a genuine appellate system.

E. THE APPEARANCE OF FORMAL APPELLATE SYSTEMS

True formal "appeal" proceedings were very late in coming. The first involved the jurisdiction of the King's Council in reviewing foreign colonial judgments

---

19. See J.H. Baker, "New Light on Slade's Case," in *The Legal Profession and the Common Law* (London, 1986), 393–432.

Chart 8-1   Appeals (Before the Legislation of 1854 and 1875)

1. *Reservation of Judgment*
   Not a true "appeal," but merely a delay in entering judgment while legal issues
are discussed with other judges on same court as trial judge.

2. *Writ of Error*
   (only blatant error of law on face of plea roll record, i.e., wrong writ altogether)

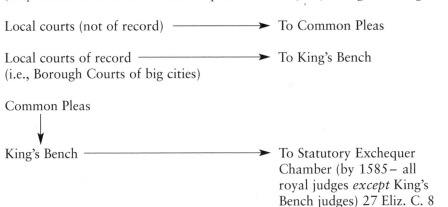

Local courts (not of record) ──────────────▶ To Common Pleas

Local courts of record ──────────────▶ To King's Bench
(i.e., Borough Courts of big cities)

Common Pleas
  │
  ▼
King's Bench ──────────────────────────▶ To Statutory Exchequer
                                           Chamber (by 1585– all
                                           royal judges *except* King's
                                           Bench judges) 27 Eliz. C. 8

3. *Prerogative Writs*
   (Prohibition, Quo Warranto, Habeas Corpus, Mandamus, Certiorari) all = super-
visory power of king's bench over lower courts.

4. *Reference to the "Informal" (i.e., non-statutory) Court of Exchequer Chamber*
   Cases reargued before all the royal judges at Westminster. Could be a "true"
form of appeals or arguments could take place before any formal entry of judgment, as probably occurred in *Slade's Case.* See *Materials, infra.*

through the so-called Judicial Committee of the Privy Council. See the discussion
in Chapter VII. This jurisdiction was established by 1833. A similar development
occurred in reviewing the Chancery. By 1675, the House of Lords decided that it
could review regular "English Side" Chancery proceedings. Since these equitable
proceedings had, officially, no record and no jury, this was a true appeal, a "re-
hearing on the merits."[20] The House of Lords was initially a poor body for professional review, due to the participation of lay members. By 1851, however, professional "Justices of Appeal in Chancery" were appointed.
   The appellate jurisdiction of the Privy Council, established in 1833 for colonial
appeals, and the "Justices of Appeal in Chancery" provided the models for the ultimate reform of common appeal. By legislation in 1854, true appeal was allowed
from a court *en banc* to a court of error, and by 1875 all proceedings in error and
the statutory Exchequer Chamber were replaced entirely by a new Court of Appeal, consisting of professional "Lords Justices of Appeal." In the next year, 1876,
the Appellate Jurisdiction Act provided for life peerages for the "Lords of Appeal
in Ordinary." A professional three-tier appellate system was, at last, established.

───────────

20. J.H. Baker, *Introduction, supra,* 162.

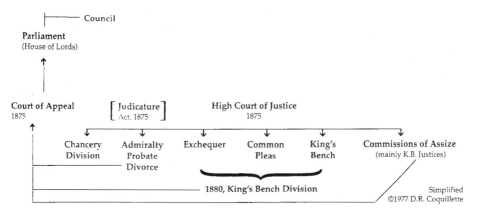

Illustration 8-2   The English courts after the nineteenth-century legislation.

It certainly is a striking fact that an appellate system came so late in England. Doubtless the success of the informal process of the *nisi prius* system and the "advisory" Exchequer Chamber was one reason. Another may be a different conception of how law is ultimately "made" and how it should be evaluated. As we will see in Chapter XIII, American nineteenth-century courts had a more "instrumentalist" view of law than the early English common law courts. In other words, in nineteenth-century America the law was perceived as a "tool" or "instrument" to particular social and political ends.[21] The medieval common lawyer hardly saw it this way. For them the law was the everlasting and constant *folc riht* of the nation. Even after the Tudor Renaissance, only a few advanced and radical English thinkers, including Hobbes and Bacon, dared describe the legal establishment in instrumentalist terms. For this, they were attacked by the prevalent Whig political establishment of eighteenth-century England.[22] Even in today's United States, where jurisprudence is now dominated by theories of legal instrumentalism, there has been a reaction by "judicial conservatives" back to earlier, more static, theories of juridical law making. Doubtless, such factors govern the rate of evolution of appellate systems.

FOR FURTHER READING

I.   Appeal

By far the best short summary of the evolution of appellate review in English legal history is J.H. Baker, *Introduction, supra,* 155–176. See also J.H. Baker, "The Stay and Reversal of Judgments" in *The Reports of Sir John Spelman* (London, 1978) 94 Selden Society, 116–123. For the role of "appeal" in the canoni-

---

21. See, for an excellent discussion, Morton T. Horwitz, *The Transformation of American Law* (Cambridge, Mass, 1972), 17–30.

22. See Daniel R. Coquillette, *Francis Bacon* (Edinburgh, Stanford, 1992), 277–297.

cal and civil law traditions, see G.I.O. Duncan, *The High Court of Delegates* (Cambridge, 1971) 1–80; W.W. Buckland, *A Text-Book of Roman Law* (3d. ed., P. Stein ed., Cambridge, 1966), 670–673.

II.   Prerogative Remedies

See L.L. Jaffe and E.G. Henderson, "Judicial Review of the Rule of Law: Historical Origins" (1956) 72 *Law Quarterly Review*, 345–364, and E.G. Henderson, *Foundations of English Administrative Law* (Cambridge, Mass, 1963) 46–159.

III.   *Aldred's Case* and *Slade's Case*

On *Aldred's Case*, see Daniel R. Coquillette, "Mosses from an Old Manse: Another Look at Some Historic Property Cases About the Environment," 64 *Cornell Law Review* (1979), 761, 765–781. On *Slade's Case* see the excellent analysis in J.H. Baker, "New Light on Slade's Case" in *The Legal Profession and the Common Law* (London, 1986) 393–432. See also A.W.B. Simpson, "The Place of Slade's Case in the History of Contract" (1958) 74 *Law Quarterly Review* 381. For a discussion of Bacon's argument in the case, see Daniel R. Coquillette, *Frances Bacon*, supra, 136–193.

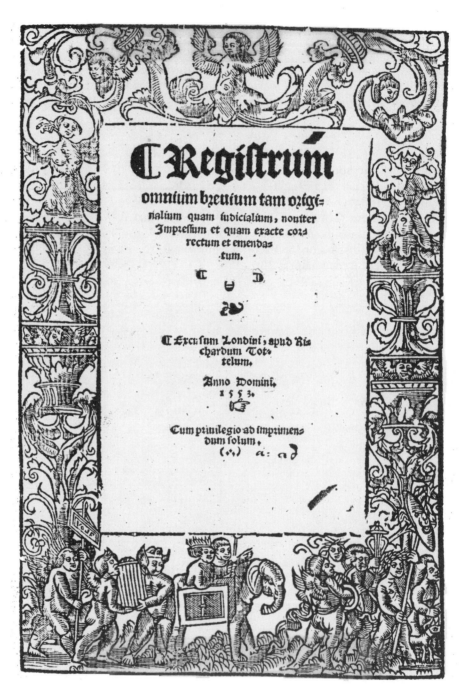

Illustration 8-3   First printed edition of a *Register of Writs* (1553) containing, among the judicial writs, a writ of *habeas corpus*. See Illustration 8-3. [Author's Collection.]

MATERIALS

NISI PRIUS - ARREST OF JUDGEMENT

From: *The Reports of Sir Edward Coke* (London, 1658), an early English translation, p. 862–864, with editing assistance from C.H.S. Fifoot, *History and Sources of the Common Law* (London, 1949) 99–101. For a full discussion, see Daniel R. Coquillette, "Mosses from an Old Manse: Another Look at Some Historic Property Cases About the Environment," 64 *Cornell Law Rev.* 761, 765–781.

Mich. 8 Jac. In the Common Pleas (1611)
William Aldred's Case
Part IX, *Coke Reports* 57(b)

William Aldred brought an action on the case against Thomas Benton. That whereas the plaintiff...was seised of a house and a parcel of land in length 31 feet and in breadth 2 feet and a half next to the hall and parlour of the plaintiff of his house aforesaid in Harleston in the county of Norfolk in fee; and whereas the defendant was possessed of a small orchard on the east part of the said parcel of land,...And the defendant pleaded not guilty, and at the assises in Norfolk he was found guilty of both the said nuisances, and damages assessed. And now it was moved in arrest of judgment, that the building of the house for hogs was necessary for the sustenance of man, and one ought not to have so delicate a nose that he cannot bear the smell of hogs: for *lex non favet delicatorum votis*. But it was resolved that the action for it is (as this case is) well maintainable. For in a house four things are desired, *habitatio hominis, delectatio inhabitantis, necessitas luminis et salubritas aeris*; and for nuisance done to three of them an action lies, *sc.* (1) To the habitation of a man, for that is the principal end of a house. (2) For hindrance of the light, for the ancient form of an action on the case was significant,...

[In a prior case, *Bland v. Moseley*, concerning hindrance of light, the defendant pleaded in bar "a custom of York entitling him so it build].

And it was adjudged [in *Bland v. Moseley*] by Sir Christopher Wray, Chief Justice, and the whole Court of King's Bench that the bar was insufficient in law to bar the plaintiff of his actions, for two reasons:

1. When a man has a lawful easement or profit by prescription from time whereof, etc., another custom, which is also from time whereof, etc., cannot take it away, for the one custom is as ancient as the other: as if one has a way over the land of A. to his freehold by prescription from time whereof, etc., A. cannot allege a prescription or custom to stop and said way.

2. It may be that before time of memory the owner of the said piece of land has granted to the owner of the said house to have the said windows without any stopping of them, and so the prescription may have a lawful beginning: And Wray, C.J. then said [in *Bland v. Moseley*] that for stopping as well of the wholesome air as of light an action lies, and damages shall be recovered for them, for both are necessary; for it is said *et vescitur aura ætherea*; and the said words *horrida tenebritate*, etc. are significant and imply the benefit of the

light. But he said that for prospect, which is a matter only of delight and not of
necessity, no action lies for stopping thereof and yet it is a great commendation
of a house if it has a long and large prospect, *unde dicitur, laudaturque domus
longos qui prospicit agros*. But he does not give an action for such things of delight. And Solomon says, Ecclesiast. 11. 7, *Dulce lumen est et delectabile oculis
videre solem...*; and if the stopping of the wholesome air, etc. gives cause of
action, a *fortiori* an action lies in the case at Bar for infecting and corrupting
the air. And the building of a lime-kiln is good and profitable; but if it be built
so near a house that when it burns the smoke thereof enters into the house so
that none can dwell there an action lies for it. So if a man has a watercourse
running in a ditch from the river to his house for his necessary use, and if a
glover sets up a lime-pit for calve-skins and sheep-skins so near the said watercourse that the corruption of the lime-poit has corrupted it, for which cause his
tenants leave the said house, an action on the case lies for it, as it is adjudged
in 13 Hen. 7, 26,b., and this stands with the Rule of Law and Reason, sc. *Pro-
hibetur ne quis faciat in suo quod nocere possit alieno, et sic utere tuo ut
alienum non lædas*....So in the case at Bar, forasmuch as the declaration is
that the defendant, maliciously intending to deprive the plaintiff of the use and
profit of his house, erected a swine stye....To which declaration the defendant
pleaded not guilty and was found guilty of the matter in the declaration. It was
adjudged that the plaintiff should recover.

PREROGATIVE WRITS

1. *Writ of Error*

   The Lord the king hath given in charge to his trusty and beloved sir
John Willes, knight, his writ closed in these words: GEORGE the second
by the grace of God of Great Britain, France, and Ireland king, defender
of the faith, and so forth; to our trusty and beloved sir John Willes,
knight, greeting. Because in the record, and process , and also in the giving of judgment, of the plaint which was in our court before you, and
your fellows, our justices of the bench, by our writ, between William
Burton, gentleman, and Charles Long, late of Burford in the county of
Oxford, gentleman, of a certain debt of two hundred pounds, which the
said William demands of the said Charles, manifest error hath intervened, to the great damage of him the said William, as we from his complaint are informed: we, being willing that the error, if any there be,
should be corrected in due manner, and that full and speedy justice
should be done to the parties aforesaid in this behalf, do command you,
that, if judgment thereof be given, then under your seal you do distinctly
and openly send the record and process of the plaint aforesaid, with all
things concerning them, and this writ; so that we may have them from
the day of Easter in fifteen days, wheresoever we shall then be in England: that, the record and process aforesaid being inspected, we may
cause to be done thereupon, for correcting that error, what of right and
according to the law and custom of our realm of England ought to be

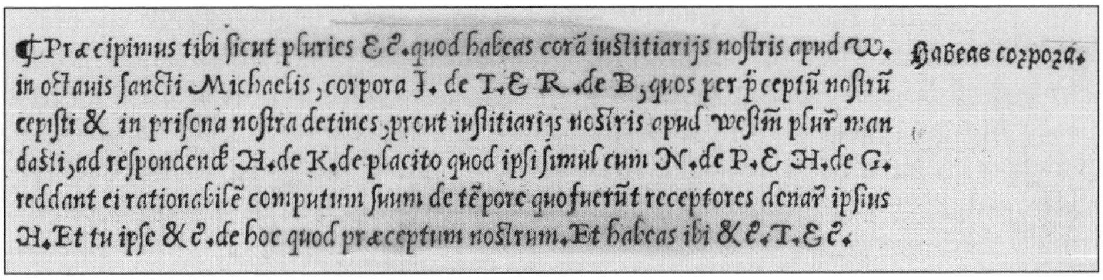
¶ Præcipimus tibi sicut pluries &c. quod habeas corã iustitiarijs nostris apud W. in octavis sancti Michaelis, corpora J. de T. & R. de B, quos per p̃ceptũ nostrũ cepisti & in prisona nostra detines, prout iustitiarijs nostris apud westm̃ plur̃ mandasti, ad respondend̃ H. de K. de placito quod ipsi simul cum N. de P. & H. de G. reddant ei rationabilẽ computum suum de tẽpore quo fuerũt receptores denar̃ ipsius H. Et tu ipse &c. de hoc quod præceptum nostrum. Et habeas ibi &c. T. &c.

Habeas corpora.

Illustration 8-4 A writ of *habeas corpus* set out in the judicial writ addition to the *Register of Writs* (1553) in Illustration 8-3. [Author's Collection.]

> done. Witness ourself at Westminster, the twelfth day of February, in the twenty ninth year of our reign.

From: William Blackstone, *Commentaries on the Laws of England* (Oxford, 1768), Vol. 3, Appendix XXI.

2. Writ of *Habeas Corpus*

> The king to J.L., knight, warden of our prison of the Fleet, greeting. We command you that you have the body of W.E., knight, who (as it is said) is detained in our prison under your custody, by whatever name the aforesaid W.E. is charged, before us [at such a day] wheresover we shall then be in England, together with the day and the cause of his detention, to undergo and receive whatever our court should then and there happen to order concerning him in this behalf. And this in no wise omit, upon the peril that may befall. And have there this writ. Witness etc.

From: 3 State Trial II (1628), as edited in J.H. Baker, *supra*, 626.

BLACKSTONE ON HABEAS CORPUS

From: William Blackstone, *Commentaries on the Laws of England* (Oxford, 1768), Vol. 3, 131–133.

But the great and efficacious writ in all manner of illegal confinement, is that of *habeas corpus ad subjiciendum*; directed to the person detaining another, and commanding him to produce the body of the prisoner with the day and cause of his caption and detention, *ad faciendum, subjiciendum, et recipiendum*, to do, submit to, and receive, whatsoever the judge or court awarding such writ shall consider in that behalf. This is a high prerogative writ, and therefore by the common law issuing out of the court of king's bench not only in term-time, but also during the vacation, by a fiat from the chief justice or any other of the judges, and running into all parts of the king's dominions: for the king is at all times intitled to have an account, why the liberty of any of his subjects is restrained, wherever that restraint may be inflicted. If it issues in vacation, it is usually returnable before the judge himself who awarded it, and he proceeds by himself thereon; unless the term should intervene, and then it may be returned in court. Indeed, if the party were privileged in the courts of common pleas and exchequer, as being an officer or suitor of the court, an *habeas corpus ad subjiciendum* might also have been awarded from thence: and, if the cause of imprisonment were palpably illegal, they might have discharged him; but, if he were committed for any criminal matter, they could only have remanded him, or taken bail for his appearance in the court of king's bench; which occasioned the common pleas to discountenance such applications. It hath also been said, and by very respectable authorities, that the like *habeas corpus* may issue out of the court of chancery in vacation: but, upon the famous application to lord Nottingham by Jenks, notwithstanding the most diligent searches, no precedent could be found where the chancellor had issued such a writ in vacation, and therefore his lordship refused it.

In the court of king's bench it was, and is still, necessary to apply for it by motion to the court, as in the case of all other prerogative writs (*certiorari*, prohibition, *mandamus*, etc.) which do not issue as of mere course, without shewing some probable cause why the extraordinary power of the crown is called into the party's assistance. For, as was argued by lord chief justice Vaughn, "it is granted on motion, because it cannot be had of "course; and there is therefore no *necessity* to grant it: for the "court ought to be satisfied that the party hath a probable cause "to be delivered." And this seems the more reasonable, because (when once granted) the person to whom it is directed can return no satisfactory excuse for not bringing up the body of the prisoner. So that, if it issued of mere course, without shewing to the court or judge some reasonable ground for awarding it, a traitor or felon under sentence of death, a soldier or mariner in the king's service, a wife, a child, a relation, or a domestic, confined for insanity or other prudential reasons, might obtain a temporary enlargement by suing out an *habeas corpus*, though sure to be remanded as soon as brought up to the court. And therefore sir Edward Coke, when chief justice, did not scruple in 13 Jac. 1. to deny a *habeas corpus* to one confined by the court of admiralty for piracy; there appearing, upon his own shewing, sufficient grounds to confine him. On the other hand, if a probable ground be shewn, that the party is imprisoned without just cause, and therefore hath a right to be delivered, the writ of habeas corpus is then a writ of right, which "may not be denied, but ought to be granted to every man that is committed, or detained in prison, or otherwise restrained, though it be by the command of the king, the privy council, or any other."

In a former part of these commentaries we expatiated at large on the personal liberty of the subject. It was shewn to be a natural inherent right, which could not be surrendered or forfeited unless by the commission of some great and atrocious crime, nor ought to be abridged in any case without the special permission of law. A doctrine co-eval with the first rudiments of the English constitution; and handed down to us from our Saxon ancestors, notwithstanding all their struggles with the Danes, and the violence of the Norman conquest: asserted afterwards and confirmed by the conqueror himself and his descendants: and though sometimes a little impaired by the ferocity of the times, and the occasional despotism of jealous or usurping princes, yet established on the firmest basis by the provisions of *magna carta*, and a long succession of statutes enacted under Edward III. To assert an absolute exemption from imprisonment in all cases, is inconsistent with every idea of law and political society: and in the end would destroy all civil liberty, by rendering it's protection impossible: but the glory of the English law consists in clearly defining the times, the causes, and the extent, when, wherefore, and to what degree, the imprisonment of the subject may be lawful. This induces an absolute necessity of expressing upon every commitment the reason for which it is made; that the court upon an *habeas corpus* may examine into it's validity; and according to the circumstances of the case may discharge, admit to bail, or remand the prisoner.

Note: As we shall see in Chapter XI, *infra*, Blackstone's *Commentaries* were widely read in America before the revolution. Blackstone continued the discussion above by attacking the decision in *The Five Knights Case*, 3 State Trials 1 (1627), which denied habeas corpus at the onset of the English Civil War. 3 *Commentaries, supra*, 134. *The Five Knights Case* is set out in Chapter X, *infra*. There is no doubt that Blackstone's views influenced the new American Republic and its notions of constitutional rights.

THE EXCHEQUER CHAMBER

From: *The Reports of Sir Edward Coke* (London, 1658), an early English translation, pp. 307–310, with editing assistance from C.H.S. Fifoot, *History and Sources of the Common Law* (London, 1949) 372–374.

Trin. 44 Eliz. (1602)
Slade's Case
Part IV, *Coke's Reports* 92(b)

John Slade brought an Action on the Case in the King's Bench against Humfrey Morley...and declared that...the defendant, in consideration that the plaintiff, at the special instance and request of the said Humfrey, had bargained and sold to him the said blades of wheat and rye growing upon the said close..., assumed and promised the plaintiff to pay him £16 at the Feast of St. John the Baptist then to come; and for non-payment thereof...the plaintiff brought the said action. The defendant pleaded *Non assumpsit modo et forma*; and on the trial of this issue the Jurors gave a special verdict, *sc.*:

> That the defendant bought of the plaintiff the wheat and rye in blades growing upon the said close as is aforesaid, *prout* in the said Declaration is alleged, and further found that between the plaintiff and the defendant there was no other promise or assumption, but only the said bargain.

And against the maintenance of this action divers objections were made by *John Doddridge*, of Counsel with the defendant. 1. That the plaintiff upon this bargain might have ordinary remedy by action of Debt, which is an action formed in the Register, and therefore he should not have an Action on the Case, which is an extraordinary action and not limited within any certain form in the Register.... The second objection was, That the maintenance of this action takes away the defendant's benefit of Wager of Law and so bereaves him of the benefit which the Law gives him, which is his birthright. For peradventure the defendant has paid or satisfied the plaintiff in private betwixt them, of which payment or satisfaction he has no witness, and therefore it would be mischievous if he should not wage his Law in such case.... The defendant shall not be charged in an action in which he shall be ousted of his Law, when he may charge him in an action in which he may have the benefit of it.

And as to these objections the Courts of King's Bench and Common Pleas were divided; for the Justices of the King's Bench held that the action (notwithstanding such objections) was maintainable, and the Court of Common Pleas held the contrary. And for the honour of the Law and for the quiet of the subject in the appeasing of such diversity of opinions (*quia nil in lege intolerabilius est eandem rem diverso jure censeri*), the case was openly argued before all the Justices of England and Barons of the Exchequer, sc., Sir John POPHAM, Kt. C.J. of England, Sir Edm. ANDERSON, Kt. C.J. of the Common Pleas, Sir W. PERIAM, Chief Baron of the Exchequer, CLARK, GAWDY, WALMESLEY, FENNER, KINGSMILL, SAVIL, WARBURTON and YELVERTON, in the Exchequer Chamber, by the Queen's Attorney-General [Edward Coke] for the Plaintiff and by *John Dodderidge* for the Defendant; and at another time the case was argued at Serjeant's Inn by the Attorney-General [Edward Coke] for the Plaintiff and by *Francis Bacon* for the Defendant. And after many conferences between the Justices and Barons it was resolved that the action was maintainable and that the plaintiff should have Judgment.

And in this case these points were resolved.

1. That altho' an action of Debt lies upon the contract, yet the bargainor may have an Action on the Case or an action of Debt at his election; and that... in respect of infinite precedents (which *George Kemp*, Esq., Secondary of the Prothonotaries of the King's Bench shew'd me) as well in the Court of Common Pleas as in the Court of King's Bench..., to which precedents and judgments, being of so great number in so many successions of ages and in the several times of so many reverend Judges, the Justices in this case gave great regard.... So that in the case at Bar it was resolved that the multitude of the said judicial precedents in so many successions of ages well prove that in the case at Bar the action was maintainable.

2. The second cause of their Resolution was divers judgments and cases resolved in our books where such Action on the Case on *Assumpsit* has been maintainable, when the party might have had an action of Debt...

3. It was resolved, That every contract executory imports in itself an *Assumpsit*, for when one agrees to pay money or to deliver any thing, thereby he assumes or promises to pay or deliver it; and therefore, when one sells any goods to another and agrees to deliver them at a day to come, and the other in consideration thereof agrees to pay so much money at such a day, in that case both parties may have an action of Debt or an Action on the Case on Assumpsit, for the mutual executory agreement of both parties imports in itself reciprocal Actions on the Case as well as Actions of Debt; and therewith agrees the judgment in *Read* and *Norwood's* Case.

4. It was resolved, That the plaintiff in this Action on the Case in *Assumpsit* should not recover only damages for the special loss (if any be) which he had, but also for the whole debt, so that a recovery or bar in this action would be a good bar in an action of Debt brought upon the same contract. So, *vice versa*, a recovery or bar in an action of Debt is a good bar in an Action on the Case on Assumpsit....

5. In some cases it would be mischievous if an action of Debt should be only brought, and not an Action on the Case; as in the case *inter Redman* and *Peck*, [where] they bargained together that for a certain consideration Redman should deliver to Peck 20 quarters of barley yearly during his life, and for non-delivery in one year it was adjudged that an action well lies, for otherwise it would be mischievous to *Peck*; for, if he should be driven to his action of Debt, then he himself could never have it, but his executors and administrators; for Debt does not lie in such case 'till all the days are incurred, and that would be contrary to the bargain and intent of the parties.... Also it is good in these days in as many cases as may be done by the Law to oust the defendant of his Law and to try it be the Country, for otherwise it would be occasion of much perjury.

6. It was said, That an Action on the Case on *Assumpsit* is as well a formed action, and contained in the Register, as an action of Debt, for there is its Form. Also it appears in divers other cases in the Register that an Action on the Case will lie, altho' the plaintiff may have another formed action in the Register.... And therefore it was concluded that in all cases when the Register has two writs for one and the same case it is in the party's election to take either. But the Register has two several actions, *sc.* Action upon the Case upon *Assumpsit* and also an Action of Debt, and therefore the party may elect either.

And as to the objection which has been made, that it would be mischievous to the defendant that he should not wage his Law, forasmuch as he might pay it in secret: to that it was answered that it should be accounted his folly that he did not take sufficient witnesses with him to prove the payment he made. But the mischief would be rather on the other party; for now experience proves that men's consciences grow so large that the respect of their private advantage rather induces men (and chiefly those who have declining estates) to Perjury...; and therefore in Debt, or other action where Wager of Law is admitted by the Law, the Judges without good admonition and due examination of the party do not admit him to it.... And I am surpriz'd that in these days so little consideration is made of an oath, as I daily observe....

Note: Consider the last sentence of the report, above. The "I" is, of course, Coke himself. What kind of case reporting is this?

Illustration 9-1 Sir Thomas Littleton (1402–1481), a Serjeant of the Law and a Justice of the Common Pleas. Note the characteristic white hat, or "coif," of the Serjeants. From a frontispiece to early editions of Edward Coke's *First Institutes* "Coke on Littleton," (1628) fol. 3. [Author's Collection.]

IX

THE BIRTH OF THE ENGLISH LEGAL PROFESSION AND ENGLISH LEGAL EDUCATION

A. LEGAL PROFESSIONALISM

We have just completed an overview of how the common law courts and remedies worked, including formulary pleading, the jury, equity, special courts and systems of appellate review. We now should step back a moment and look at the "big picture," because all of these developments occurred against a particular back drop. This was the development of the English legal profession.

Despite the great diversity of the American legal profession, being "a lawyer" today has a fairly specific meaning. Most lawyers attend an accredited law school, often associated with a university. Almost all are licensed by their state of practice, and are usually supervised by the highest court of that state. Many are also members of the bar of federal courts, as well.

The past was very different. The first "lawyers," in the sense of persons who represented others in legal proceedings, were called "attorneys," from the medieval Latin "*attornatus*," ("substituted") and the Norman French "*attorner*" ("to transfer or assign"). They probably were no more than particularly articulate and bright kinsmen, or assistants, who were "assigned" by a party to speak on the party's behalf, not unlike the "eloquent and forceful" Mord at the Law Rock in *Njal's Saga*. See Chapter II, *Materials, supra*. These "attornies" literally "stood in the shoes" of a litigant, very much the way a power of attorney operates today. As Edward Coke observed, attorney "signifies one that is set in the turne, stead, or place of another." *Coke on Littleton*, fol. 128a.

Along with the role of the "attorney" there was the ancient idea of the "counselor." This also derived from an old French term, "*conseiller,*" and ultimately came from the Latin "*consilium*" (referring to the giving of "advice" or "counsel"). This term also appeared very early, usually in reference to the King's advisors who were learned in the law. These he would consult ("*pur conseiller*") in legal matters. Originally, such learned advisors were available in both a public and private capacity, but by the twelfth century a clear distinction was developing between "counselors" to the Crown, who increasingly acted as judges in disputes, and "counselors" to private persons, who acted as "attorneys." After the development of the centralized Norman courts in the thirteenth century, the "justicars" to the Crown were a well defined elite group. This division between the function of the private representative, the "attorney," and the representative of the state, the "judge," still persists today.

It is not an accident, therefore, that our two oldest models of legal professionalism, the "counselor" and the "attorney," have Norman French names. They were products of the new Norman-Angevin bureaucracy and court systems. Although the function of legal advisor and legal advocate clearly go back to the "Law Rock" of the Anglo-Saxons, as does the word "law" in "lawyer" itself, the Normans brought an entirely new dimension of training and expertise. They introduced the idea of the "professional," the judge or advocate who was more than just a learned and talented amateur, rather one who had a permanent identity and business with the law. As early as the treatise *Glanvill*[1] (*circa* 1187 A.D.), the word "attorney" appears to be used in a way that implies a professional representative, not just a kinsman or a volunteer to stand in "your shoes." See *Materials, infra*. This coincided with the evolution of a formulary system and, indeed, *Glanvill* is basically a collection of legal forms, clearly designed for use by such a practitioner. By the time of *Bracton* (*circa* 1236 A.D.), there was a clearly understood office of royal "justicar." Indeed, *Bracton's* purpose was to instruct "the unwise and unlearned who ascend the judgment seat before they have learned the laws."[2] The evolving formulary system, the growing central royal courts, and assize system, and the sophisticated new modes of trial and remedies, including Henry II's possessory assizes, all required experts to function properly.

As we have seen, the reign of Edward I brought even more sophistication, including the major statutes of *De Donis,* and *Quia Emptores.* The complexity of these statutes—and the list of abuses set out in their prologues—testified to a growing class of legal professionals.[3] By 1292, the professional judges of the royal courts began to take responsibility for "lawful and ready learners" who "shall attend the court, enter into a business, and no other."[4] Eventually, lawyers trained directly by the royal courts to be advocates in these courts became known as "barristers," because they could plead at the "bar" of the court. The term first appears in 1455, but the idea of a litigation specialist directly under the supervision of the royal judges was, as we have seen, much older. Not surprisingly, it became customary to choose royal judges from the ranks of these "barrister" specialists.

---

1. See *Materials, infra,* p. 287.
2. *Materials, supra,* Chapter III.
3. See *Materials,* Chapter IV, *supra.*
4. In 1292, the following royal writ [*Rot. Parl.* i, 84] was sent to the Common Pleas: "Concerning attorneys and learners ('apprentices') the lord King enjoined Mettingham and his fellows to provide and ordain at their discretion a certain number, from every country, of the better, worthier and more promising students..., and that those so chosen should follow the court and take part in its business; and no others."

See the discussion at T.F.T. Plucknett, *Concise History, supra,* 217–218.

Another distinct group continued in the "attorney" tradition of managing their client's affairs day to day. They also became regulated directly by the bench and were subject to professional oaths, but their close association with their clients created a contrast with the barrister elite, who were more identified with the courts themselves. Eventually, the attorneys became known as "solicitors," and no client could employ a barrister directly, but only through a solicitor. This "bifurcated" legal profession, split between barristers and solicitors, still exists in England. It reflects a division of legal skills many centuries old.

It originally represented more. Younger sons disinherited by primogeniture needed a way to make a living, but trade was beneath them. The "honorable" professions were three: the Church, the Army, and the Bar, to which was later added colonial governance. The "barrister class" reflected a social aristocracy, while the busy solicitors became a symbol of middle class advancement. When I studied law in England in the 1960s, these class distinctions still persisted. Even today, it is considered rude to discuss legal fees directly with a barrister, rather than the barrister's "clerk."

Above the barristers was an even older class, dating from at least the fourteenth century. These "serjeants at law" had a monopoly in the Common Pleas, and—until the sixteenth century—were the exclusive source of new royal judges. With their characteristic hoods and "coifs," or head coverings, serjeants at law were certainly an admired elite, "leaders of the bar by natural, judicial, and royal selection."[5] Perhaps their greatest importance was as a "bridge" between the judiciary and the private advocates. In other legal culture, such as that of Germany and France, the private bar and the judiciary came to be trained separately, and were really different professions. It is of great importance, even today, that a different tradition arose in England, and spread to all common law countries. Serjeants at law not only represented private clients, but took on royal commissions as assize judges when there was a shortage of judicial labor.

Chaucer left us a wonderful picture of this elite professional in "The Prologue" to *Canterbury Tales* (*circa* 1390 A.D.). Chaucer's serjeant at law "often had been justice of Assize, by letters patent, and in full commission," and "[h]is fame and learning and his high positions, had won him many a robe and many a fee." But Chaucer had it in for this pompous lawyer. "Discreet he was, a man to reverence, *or so he seemed*, his sayings were so wise...Nowhere there was so busy a man as he; *But was less busy than he seemed to be.*"[6] Busy or not, the serjeants gradually declined in influence, and became extinct in 1921. Today their memory survives in American law schools through an honorary society, the "Order of the Coif."

Even today, the dominant norm of the legal profession reflects this past. Although there is no bifurcated bar in America, the division between litigation and business specialties certainly persists—as does the practice of choosing new judges primarily from the ranks of experienced litigators. Perhaps most important, the "attorney" ideal of "stepping in the shoes" of your client for legal purposes—with its associated values of loyalty and confidentiality—dominates the American profession. But this "attorney" role also continues to be checked by

5. J.H. Baker, *Introduction, supra,* 180.
6. *Materials, infra,* p. 289 (emphasis added).

the "counselor" role of cautious advice and by "officer of the court" duties to the supervising courts of the jurisdiction, and to the justice system generally.

B. PROFESSIONAL EDUCATION: THE INNS OF COURT

There is one additional "professional" norm besides loyalty to the client and to the court. That norm is loyalty to the profession itself as a guild with some very pronounced ethical and political values. The "legal" guild has always defined itself by its special education. This was first achieved in England by the Inns of Court.

The earliest legal study in England was associated with the ancient Universities of Oxford and Cambridge, where teachers taught Roman law as early as 1149 A.D. As seen before, canon law was also taught in the universities before the suppression by Henry VIII.[7] But the common law of the royal courts was not a university subject until the eighteenth century and Blackstone's lectures.[8] So the model of legal education so familiar to us today, the university law school, had very little to do with the common law for nearly six centuries.

One of the major reasons for this extraordinary fact was the Inns of Court. Located conveniently in London, between the law courts at Westminster and the commercial districts of the city proper, this center of legal education combined the characteristics of a powerful trade guild with that of a university. All common law barristers, serjeants, and judges were "graduates" and members. As an Elizabethan observer remarked, the Inns of Court were "a whole university...of students, practices or pleaders, and judges of the laws of this realm, not living of common stipends, as in other universities...but of their own private maintenance...for that the younger sort are either gentlemen, or the sons of gentlemen, or of other most wealthy persons..."[9] By 1600, one of the distinctions between a barrister or a serjeant and a plain "attorney" was that the former were trained in the Inns of Court, and—increasingly—the latter were barred from the premises. As mentioned before, this legal elite was an acceptable occupation for gentry—particularly the younger sons disinherited by primogeniture—and the distinction between serjeants and barristers, as opposed to attorneys or "solicitors," became one of function reinforced by class.

The early history of the Inns is still somewhat mysterious. The name, "inns," probably comes from the hospices that filled western London for the benefit of government officials, supplicants, agents and, during term time, lawyers and clients. By 1350 some of these hospices had hit on the idea of housing apprentices at law, perhaps the apprentices mentioned in Edward I's royal writ of 1292 as under the supervision of the courts.[10] This provided tenants for the "slack" periods when the courts were out of session, and also business for experienced lawyers at these slow times—as teachers and supervisors. Some of the students stayed in the large homes of prominent lawyers, or occupied the under-utilized

---

7. See *Materials, supra*, Chap. VII.
8. See *Materials, infra*, Chap. XII.
9. This was John Stow. See Alan Harding, *A Social History of English Law* (London, 1960) 185–186.
10. See *Materials, infra*, p. 293 ff.

city mansions of nobles who rarely come to London.[11] Other students stayed in the houses of Chancery clerks, which became collectively known as "Inns of Chancery," although there was no direct connection with the Court of Chancery itself. Perhaps these students learned the drafting of legal writs from these clerks, a valuable skill for a common lawyer.

By 1400, four "inns" began to establish a dominant position. Two were named from nobles who either owned or sponsored the original houses: "Gray's Inn," a house of the Lords Grey, and "Lincoln's Inn," which either was named for Henry de Lacy, Earl of Lincoln, or Thomas de Lincoln, a prominent serjeant at law.[12] Two others were founded in the defunct London premises of the powerful Knights Templar, and became known as "Middle Temple" and "Inner Temple." By 1450, these four "inns" were professional schools, with the exclusive right to train common law barristers and serjeants, and the Inns of Chancery—of which there were nine or more—became "feeders," or schools for young students who wished to enter one of the four Inns of Court. Finally, for the very elite who became serjeants, there were two "Serjeant's Inns," although these were more like small clubs than educational institutions. Over time, the Inns of Chancery diminished and disappeared, and the Serjeant's Inns died with that order at the end of the 19th century. The four Inns of Court, however, not only remain, but are among the wealthiest and most powerful institutions in London. Although they have now coordinated their educational and regulatory functions into the Consolidated Inns of Court, they are still four separate entities, with magnificent libraries, gardens, dining halls, and common rooms. Three, the Inner and Middle Temple and Lincoln's Inn, also house the "chambers," or offices, of most practicing London barristers. (The fourth, Gray's Inn, is largely filled with solicitors' offices.) Despite heavy bomb damage during the war, many sixteenth- and seventeenth-century features survive.[13]

In the sixteenth and seventeenth centuries, the Inns of Court not only trained young lawyers, but were centers of political influence, literature, and even art. Some of Shakespeare's plays were first performed in the dining halls of Gray's Inn and Middle Temple, and Francis Bacon composed poetry for magnificent "masques," which featured lovely costumes and stage settings—and attracted the grandest people in the kingdom, including the sovereign personally.[14] The quadrangles were familiar to Ben Johnson, Oliver Goldsmith and Charles Dickens alike, and former students routinely occupied the greatest political positions in the land.

One of our best contemporary pictures of this extraordinary "legal university" comes from Sir John Fortescue (?1394–?1476). Fortescue became Chief Justice of the King's Bench in 1442, but followed the exiled House of Lancaster to

---

11. See J.H. Baker, "Introduction," *Readings and Moots at the Inns of Court in the Fifteenth Century*, vol. 2 (eds. S.E. Thorne, J.H. Baker) (London, 1990), Selden Society vol. 105, xxv–xxxi; Samuel E. Thorne "The Early History of the Inns of Court," (1959) 50 *Graya* 79–96, reprinted S.E. Thorne, *Essays in English Legal History* (1985) 137–154.

12. Baker believes it was the latter, despite tradition favoring the Earl. See Baker, *Introduction, supra*, 183.

13. Parts of two "Inns of Chancery" also can still be seen, Barnard's Inn and Staples Inn. The latter, close to Gray's Inn on High Holborn, has been heavily, but beautifully, restored, and today houses the Society of Actuaries.

14. See Daniel R. Coquillette, *Francis Bacon, supra*, 31–35.

France, where he was a tutor to Edward, Prince of Wales. In exile, he apparently had the office of Lord Chancellor to the Lancastrian monarchs. See Illustration 9-5. Fortescue's efforts to explain to the Prince differences between the French and English legal system resulted in a little book, *De laudibus legum angliae*, written about 1470, and first printed in 1545–46.[15] It is very significant that, along with trial by jury, precedent justice, and lack of torture, Fortescue emphasized the importance of the professional training of lawyers in the independent Inns of Court.[16]

Of course, the mode of legal training changed across the centuries. In the sixteenth century, promising students like Thomas More would either go directly into the Inns of Chancery, at age fifteen or less, or would spend a few years at Oxford and Cambridge, and then enroll. After about two or three years in the Inns of Chancery, one would enter one of the four Inns of Court as a student. After three or four years, the student would be admitted as "utter barrister," and by six or seven years, at about age twenty-two or twenty-three, could be "called to the bar."[17]

The nature of legal education within the Inns has only recently received careful study.[18] Its three most important characteristics certainly make an interesting contrast with modern legal education. First, the faculty were almost exclusively practicing lawyers. They had been trained as common lawyers themselves through the same system. Providing "readings" on statutes and supervising the exercises within the Inn were part of the duties of those seeking advancement from barrister to benches. The benchers were also expected to sit on "the bench" at moot court exercises, and to critique the student participants.

The second important characteristic of this educational system was the required exercises, the "moots," or public pleading exercises, and the "bolts," similar exercises held in private. These combined learning by rote and "learning by doing," under close personal supervision. The moots and bolts encouraged "thinking on your feet" and the kind of quick ingenuity that was the essence of the pleader's skill. This skill remains important to litigators today.

The final characteristic was the most important. The Inns were a compulsory society, where keeping commons with your colleagues was required. To this day

---

15. See S.B. Chrimes, "General Preface," *Sir John Fortescue. De Laudibus Legum Angliae* (Cambridge, 1942), ix–liii.

16. See *Materials, infra*, p. 293 ff.

17. Francis Bacon (1561–1626) was a good example of a very bright young man on a "fast track." He matriculated at Trinity College, Cambridge, at age 12 (1573), left Trinity at age 14 (1575) and was admitted at Gray's Inn, Inns of Court, at age 15 (1576). (By this time, the Inns of Chancery were in abeyance. A century earlier, they might have substituted for Cambridge.) At age 21 (1582), he was admitted "utter barrister," and by age 25 (1586) he was made "bencher" at Gray's Inn, and began reading to students. In 1594, at age 33, he reached the highest standard levels within the bar, being called "within the bar" and named "Queen's Counsel, Extraordinary" at age 34 (1595), a position at least equivalent to serjeant in precedence. By 1607, at age 46, he was Solicitor General; at age 52 (1613) he was Attorney General, and at age 57 (1618), he was finally appointed Lord Chancellor. By 1621 (age 60), he was impeached, and disgraced. Altogether, the entire process of "higher" education leading to a professional law certification was about seven to eight years, not that far from the typical American "path" through the B.A. to the J.D., although in the past, the process started at an earlier age.

18. See, for example, J.H. Baker, "Introduction" to *Readings and Moots at the Inns of Court in the Fifteenth Century* (ed. S.E. Thorne, J.H. Baker, London, 1990) vol. II, Selden Society, vol. 105.

eating a substantial number of dinners at your Inn of Court is required to be called to the bar. I would have regarded this compulsory collegiality as trivial had I not undergone it myself for over three years at Gray's Inn. I can still recall the moots argued in Hall, after dinner, before demanding benchers. Then there were "name games," such as the compulsory toasts, naming all in the "messes" below and above at the table. Missing a name resulted in a "fine" of a bottle of port. And then there were the debates, where quick minds were praised, and the reflective, but awkward, student assisted. To say this "society" built a sense of professional identity and value was certainly true, even in the more democratic and diverse days of 1966–1969. There is every evidence that in the sixteenth century this was true with a vengeance, a fact that had both juristic and political consequences. Even today, the "cultural" and "social" values of legal education are more significant than we like to acknowledge, and there is even an "American Inns of Court" organization which seeks to restore some of the advantages of past centuries.

After the English Civil War, the educational function of the Inns deteriorated. Only recently has the Consolidated Inns of Court revived serious educational programs. Today, most students at the Inns of Court will also get university degrees. As we have seen, this was not uncommon, even in the fifteenth and sixteenth centuries. More remarkable, however, to an American law student is the fact that many of those students will not take a university law degree, but will study "greats" (classics), "P.P.E." (politics, philosophy, and economics) or English literature. Law, likewise, is taught routinely as an undergraduate degree, and many with this degree do not become professional lawyers at all. While many young English barristers today do have university law degrees, the technical separation between university legal study and professional legal qualification continues.

It is important to emphasize the historical importance of this separation. As Baker has observed,

> "The strength and unity of this profession explain how the reasoning of a small group of men in Westminster Hall grew into one of the world's two greatest systems of law. For this peculiarly English professional structure was wholly independent of the university law faculties, where only Canon law and Roman Civil law were taught, and this factor as much as any other ensured the autonomous character of English law and its isolation from the influence of Continental jurisprudence."[19]

It could be argued that legal education in America, with powerful university law faculties as early as the mid-nineteenth century, presents a different picture. In fact, the separation of the legal curriculum from the humanities, which isolates legal study in graduate schools, has created a very similar situation. Law is taught as a professional subject, primarily for future practitioners. The study is not well integrated with economics, philosophy, politics, history, or cultural comparative work. The result is a highly provincial approach to most legal problems, and a lack of knowledge of the comparative or international context. Interestingly enough, American law schools are accredited by a professional organiza-

---

19. Baker, *Introduction, supra*, 177.

tion of lawyers, the American Bar Association, as well as by an academic group, the American Association of Law Schools. Such accreditation is a delegated power of the state supreme courts, which largely regulate the bar. Thus, ultimate supervision by the practicing bench and bar, similar to that of the Inns of Court, has persisted in most American states. This "professionalism" of legal education in America is directly related to attitudes that can be traced back to the Inns of Court themselves.[20]

C. PROFESSIONAL LITERATURE: YEARBOOKS AND ABRIDGEMENTS

Most lawyers have heard of "Yearbooks," but few know what they are. The common perception is that they are a kind of antique law report. This is only partly correct. "Yearbooks" do consist of accounts of court proceedings, but their historical origins and functions are very different from modern reports. Indeed, they were closely tied to the developments in legal education just discussed, rather than to any "official" reporting system.

We know that, besides attending the "readings" or lectures and participating in the "moots" and "bolts," law students in the fifteenth and sixteenth centuries frequently attended the courts themselves. This was one of the obvious reasons for studying law in London. Beginning in the thirteenth century, manuscript accounts of arguments in the royal courts appeared. These were very different from the plea rolls, because they frequently omitted important formal facts about the case, including—on occasion—who won. On the other hand, they contained much more detail about what was said and done in the courtroom than a plea roll. By the end of the thirteenth century, these manuscripts appeared regularly. Because they were identified by the regnal year of the court proceedings described, they began to be called "Yearbooks." Thus a typical "Yearbook" citation, say to the case *Jankyn v. Anon.* reproduced in the *Materials, infra*, would be "Mich. 2 Ric. II pl. 7." This meant that the case was in the Michaelmas court term of the second regnal year of Richard II (i.e., 1378) and that the "pl." or *placitum* (case-number) was seven. Some cases also referred to the "f" or folio page in the earliest printed editions.

These cases were certainly recorded for educational purposes, probably both for students and their practitioner teachers. What interested those practical professionals was not who won a case, but how a case was handled by the lawyers involved—including even corrections or personal observations which were clearly "off the record" and useless for the formal plea rolls—but fascinating to eager, nervous new advocates.

Let us take a look at our sample case in the *Materials, infra*. This would be "Mich. 2 Ric. II, pl. 7," otherwise called "*Jankyn v. Anon.*" Like many yearbook cases, it was in the King's Bench, and the plaintiff used a writ of trespass, which, as we have seen, was a writ restricted to the King's Bench. The facts of the case were

---

20. See Daniel R. Coquillette, "Introduction: The 'Countenance of Authorite'" in *Law in Colonial Massachusetts* (eds. Coquillette, Brink, Menand, Boston, 1984) xxvi–lxii, 359–418.

that the plaintiff Jankyn owned a house in Rochester which was damaged when, in the defendant's words, "building stone and timber fell, unintentionally and nonwilfully," while the defendant was repairing his house, which was next door. The defendant's lawyer is identified as "Clopton" and his argument is that "as for coming with force and arms (*vi et armis*)...we plead not guilty." In short, Clopton argued that Jankyn should not have used a trespass writ, with its "force and arms" *vi et armis* formula, when the harm was completely involuntary and was, at worst, merely negligent. "Burgh," the plaintiff's lawyer, demands "judgment" and "damages"—jury trial and damages certainly being the reasons why he used a trespass writ. See our discussion of the trespass writ at *Materials*, Chapter IV, *supra*.

We never find out who won. We do, however, get an "off the record" conversation, between the bench and the defendant's lawyer about settlement offers:

> "PERCY J. to *Clopton*. You have not alleged on the defendant's behalf that you offered the plaintiff, as between neighbors, any compensation for his home since this was done nonwilfully. *Clopton*. Certainly, sir, to speak off the record, we offered him four pence as compensation for his home, and as I am informed he was not damaged a single penny. And even if the defendant were held legally liable for this act he will not be amerced, nor will he make fine in such a case.
> KIRTON, J. denied that.[21]

And here the case record simply ended. What good was this? No good at all as a legal record, or even as a "holding" in the later sense of a "legal precedent." But it was all very informative to a young apprentice pleader or practitioner who wants to know what's "really going on" and "what to do in court."

Yearbooks survive, with some gaps, from 1250 to after 1535, nearly three centuries. As the years passed, their function slowly changed. While there was still no attempt to have "official" records apart from the plea rolls, the yearbooks became much more uniform, and there were practically no gaps. Individual reporters, some now identified, clearly had defined responsibility of some sort for particular years. The reports were also more complete. But in certain ways they remained like the earlier yearbooks. The language was still not Latin, or English, but the Law French of the courts, and the cases were still arranged by regnal year and chronological order. There was no organization by topic, no way to find a "precedent."

The development of "Abridgements" is our first hint that written reports are being used in modern ways, i.e., as precedent. The first, known as *Statham's Abridgement*, appeared in 1490. It was followed by two "great" Abridgements containing summaries of tens of thousands of yearbook cases, organized under alphabetical topics. These were *Fitzherbert's Graunde Abridgement* (1514–16) and *Brooke's Graunde Abridgement* (1513).

These books were doubtless composed by combining "common place" books of many judges and students, organizing useful cases under captions. They symbolize three big changes: 1) the impact of printing, for sets of yearbooks were among the first printing projects in England, and an almost complete set was

---

21. *Materials, infra*, p. 296. The editor of this case, Morris S. Arnold, points out a similar case, the *Case of the Thorns*, Y.B. 6 Edw. 4, f. 7, pl. 18. See *Year Books of Richard II, 2 Richard II 1378–1379* (ed. M.S. Arnold), Ames Foundation, 1975, 70.

available by 1558; 2) the use of these newly uniform and accessible yearbooks for a different purpose—authority for judicial decision, rather than education; and 3) an early attempt to form a *corpus juris*, not of statutes or formulary pleadings, but of decided cases.

In his great, little book, *Precedent in English Law*, Rupert Cross describes the slow evolution of the "doctrine of precedent." This evolution had two elements: 1) the idea of a *ratio decidendi* (the "rule" of a case, as opposed to simply the views of a judge, *obiter dictum*) and 2) the idea that judicial precedent should be binding in future cases. For centuries, English judges saw themselves as recognizing and "speaking" an existing law, not "making" law.[22] Without a means to preserve, much less publish, the *ratio decidendi*, and no method to retrieve relevant earlier precedents, a modern precedent system would have been hardly possible in any case.

The impact of printing and the "discovery" of America by Europeans occurred almost at the same time. The Abridgements make it clear that a revolution was afoot in how judges "made" law, and how they saw their role in the public order, just as the voyages of discovery permanently changed the horizon of the common law. In both cases, it took a century for the impact to be fully manifested. But most surely the new printed Yearbooks and their "keys," the printed Abridgements, were the special professional literature, the tools of what was to become the modern legal profession.

D. THE SAGA OF THE STATUTE OF USES (1536)

Yet it is not to the nascent "case law" that we turn to fully appreciate the "new" state of the Tudor dynasty, but to a series of statutes. These statutes were the direct achievement of one of England's most extraordinary rulers—a man who still captures the public imagination in books, TV serials, and movies—Henry VIII. As powerful as Henry was, the story of these statutes tells of another rival power—the emerging political influence of the common lawyers themselves and their clients, a new commercial and land-holding bourgeoisie.

In some ways, it was an old story. Edward I, in order to protect his feudal revenues, revolutionized the feudal law through the statutes *De Donis* and *Quia Emptores*. The same issues were at the core of the great Statute of Uses. Henry VIII was a canny operator of the so-called "Tudor Compromise." He knew how to accommodate the increasingly powerful House of Commons, while constantly seeking to increase his own feudal revenues—which were independent of parliamentary control. As with Edward I, the enemies were the same, ingenious lawyers bent on evading the taxes due from their clients. This time, the vehicle the lawyers had discovered was a particularly brilliant series of adaptations of a very old idea, the "use."

---

22. Rupert Cross, *Precedent in English Law* (2d ed., Oxford, 1968) 35–47. As we will see, Francis Bacon defined the judge's role as "*ius dicere*," i.e., to state the law, not make it. See *Materials*, Chap. XI, *infra*.

I. THE "USE"

The origins of the "use" go back to the thirteenth century, and at least one tradition would attribute it to the Crusades. Basically, the idea was that sometimes a legal owner of land was bound in conscience to use the land to "benefit" another. Indeed, the word "use" comes from the Latin "*ad opus*" (to the benefit). We are very familiar with the idea today, for it is the essence of the modern "trust," where a "trustee" holds a legal title for the benefit of a "beneficiary." As we will see, the "use" was the ancestor of the "trust."

The classic example usually given of a "use" would be a crusader who transfers his land legally to a friend to safeguard it until he returns. If the crusader returned, his friend would be under a moral obligation to convey it back. If he died, his friend would hold it "to the use" of the crusader's heirs.

While this is a very attractive theoretical example, in actuality the most common early "uses" were probably ways to transfer land to religious groups. As we have seen in Chapter IV, gifts of land to religious institutions were widely prohibited by the *mortmain* statutes unless a license was obtained. Pending the license, the gift could be held "to the use" of the institution. This temporary "use" could be extended to be a permanent arrangement if the license were not given.

Establishing settlements under the Statute *De Donis* also often involved re-granting land, under condition of entails, from yourself back to yourself and your heirs under the terms of the settlement. This could be done by granting to a "man of straw," who then regrants the land back. As Baker points out, the "man of straw," usually a lawyer, would hold "to the use" of the original grantor.[23]

"Uses" were initially not legal titles. They were enforced as equitable matters in Chancery. We have already discussed equitable procedures, and how the Chancellor could interrogate witnesses and parties under the power of the *subpoena* and could imprison them for contempt. The essence of equity was to look beyond the legal form to see the substance of the matter, and then to "treat as done what ought to be done." Once "uses" were recognized by Chancery, they became almost as good as legal title.

Indeed, in some ways, they were better. As we have seen, legal "seisin" was a matter of public record, based on a public ceremony. But being a beneficiary of a "use" could be secret. This could be useful in evading feudal dues. In the days of Edward I, layers of subinfeudation were created to evade feudal dues, leading to the prohibition of subinfeudation by the statute *Quia Emptores*. See *Materials*, Chapter IV, *supra*. Similar results could be obtained by having public seisin in the hands of "strawmen," often lawyers, holding to undisclosed uses.

Even more important, "uses" could be "used" to do things prohibited at common law. For example, as discussed in Chapter IV, land could not be devised on death. It all went automatically to the deceased's heir under the canons of descent, i.e., all to the eldest son or, if there were only daughters, to each daughter equally. But suppose a landowner wished to make provisions on death for younger sons or daughters who might not otherwise inherit—but was unwilling to grant them land *inter vivos* (i.e., before death)? (The natural reluctance to

---

23. J.H. Baker, *Introduction, supra*, 284.

make transfers before death, thus defeating the canons, has been called the "Lear" complex, from Shakespeare's play where the father did make *inter vivos* transfers, only to have his children spurn him.) The landowner's lawyer might suggest that land be granted to the lawyer *inter vivos*, to be held to the "use" of the landowner for life, and then to the "use of his or her children according to instructions, which might be quite different from ordinary rules of inheritance. For example, the land could be held to the "use" of all sons equally. The legal title would descend according to the strict rules of inheritance, i.e., to the lawyer's eldest son if he had one, etc. But this made little difference if the land were held to the "use" of others and that use was enforceable at Chancery. In short, uses could be used to devise land, despite the common law prohibition.

This could have bad effects on old safeguards, such as dower. The wife of a deceased landowner was entitled to life estate in one third of her late husband's land, but if most of the land had been transferred before death to another legal owner, the dower rights could be evaded. More important to the royal coffers, legal "men of straw" could also be chosen to minimize the dangers of leaving un-deraged heirs, or escheat by treason, or other windfalls to the King and other feudal lords. Again, alone among all subjects of the realm, the King could not benefit by schemes of evasion of feudal dues. As the top of the feudal pyramid, he could only lose by these schemes.

2. THE "STATUTE OF USES," 27 HENRY VIII, CAP. 10 (1536)

By 1529, Henry VIII needed money badly, and wished to remain independent of Parliament. Like Edward I, before him, he saw restoration of feudal dues as one answer. His first idea was truly radical, a statute that would prohibit all estates in land except the fee simple for all subjects except peers of the realm, who could still entail their land. "[U]ses were to be valid only if registered in the Court of Common Pleas, and elaborate provisions were drafted to ensure utmost publicity."[24] At one stroke, real property seisin would become both public and simple, a tax collector's dream, and the peers could still have their great family settlements protected.

Such a measure might have had a chance in Parliament at an earlier day, but not by Henry's time. Two very powerful groups got nothing except more exposure to tax from this proposal. The first group was the growing class of untitled landowners, some spending monies made in trade to buy land to enjoy the status of landed estates. The second was the common lawyers who represented them. The lawyers saw "in this arrangement the ruin of their profession; it left them with no more interesting topic of study than a fee simple, save in the very few cases of peers, and at this moment there were but fifty peers of the realm."[25] And it was not just exposure to more tax which concerned these groups. "Uses" had become the *de facto* way to devise land. To the new landholding classes and their lawyers, this was too important a power to lose. The net result was that the King's reforms met great opposition, largely in the House of Commons.

Henry was nothing, if not a quick learner. In 1536 he tried a new approach, but this time there was a substantial benefit to the common lawyers. The strategy

---

24. T. F. T. Plucknett, *A Concise History, supra*, 583.
25. *Id.*, 584.

was simple. Common lawyers in the Common Pleas had lost much business to the Chancery, because "uses" were only recognized in equity. Why not just "execute" all "uses," i.e., just make them into interests at law? If, at the same time, provisions were made to record these new legal interests, the King's revenue goals could be promoted, and the common lawyers would once again have the nation's land law back in the Common Pleas.[26]

This is exactly what was done. The "Statute of Uses" was passed, to "execute" all uses, and, at the same time, the Statute of Enrolments was passed to keep a record of these interests.[27] It was a brilliant legislative scheme. See the text of the statute at *Materials, infra*. Once again, the Statute begins with a "propaganda" statement as a "Preamble." Note the attack on something perceived as akin to today's "ambulance chasing." The villains were "greedy and covetous persons" who exploited those "in extreme agonies and pains," i.e., got them to dispose of land by uses rather than through the canons of inheritance. There were also those scoundrels that make "assurances craftily made to secret uses, intents and trust" to evade tax.

> ...Whereby the common laws of this realm, lands, tenements, and hereditaments be not devisable by testament, nor ought to be transferred from one to another, but by solemn livery and seisin, matter of record, writing sufficient made *bona fide*, without covin or fraud, yet nevertheless divers and sundry imaginations, subtle inventions, and practices have been used, whereby the hereditaments of this realm have been conveyed from one to another by fraudulent feoffments, fines, recoveries, and other assurances craftily made to secret uses, intents, and trusts, and also by wills and testaments, sometimes made by *nude parolx* and words, sometimes by signs and tokens, and sometimes by writing, and for the most part made by such persons as be visited with sickness, in their extreme agonies and pains, or at such time as they have had scantly any good memory or remembrance; at which times they being provoked by greedy and covetous persons lying in wait about them, do many times dispose indiscreetly and unadvisedly their lands and inheritances; by reason whereof, and by occasion of which fraudulent feoffments, fines, recoveries, and other like assurances to uses, confidences, and trusts, divers and many heirs have been unjustly at sundry times disinherited, the lords have lost their wards, marriages, reliefs, harriots, escheats, aids, *pur fair fitz chivalier* [knighthood] and *pur file marier* [marriage], and scantly any person can be certainly assured of any lands by them purchased, nor know surely against whom they shall use their actions or execution for their rights, titles, and duties; also men married have lost their tenancies by the curtesy, women their dowers; manifest perjuries by trial of such secret wills and uses have been committed; the king's highness hath lost the profits and advantages of the lands of persons attainted, and of the lands craftily put in feoffment to the uses of aliens born, and also the

---

26. As Baker observed, the other logical alternative, abolishing uses outright, would leave most of the land in England in the legal seisin of lawyers acting as strawmen! See Baker, *Concise History, supra*, 292.

27. 27 Henry VIII, chap. 16 (1536)

profits of waste for a year and a day of lands of felons attainted, and the lords their escheats thereof; and many other inconveniences have happened, and daily do increase among the king's subjects, to their great trouble and inquietness, and to the utter subversion of the ancient common laws of this realm; for the extirping and extinguishment of all such subtle practised feoffments, fines, recoveries, abuses, and errors heretofore used and accustomed in this realm, to the subversion of the good and ancient laws of the same, and to the intent that the king's highness or any other his subjects of this realm, shall not in any wise hereafter, by any means or inventions be deceived, damaged or hurt, by reason of such treats, uses, or confidences: It may please the King's most royal Majesty, that it may be enacted by his Highness, by the assent of the Lords Spiritual and Temporal, and the Commons, in this present parliament assembled, and by the authority of the same, in manner and form following:

Compared to this great piece of rhetoric, the "action" part of the statute is short and sweet: everyone seised of any freehold interest to the use of anyone else will lose legal title, which will vest in the beneficiary. Thus the effect of a grant to "A to the use of B," is simply to vest the freehold in B.

Chart 9-1

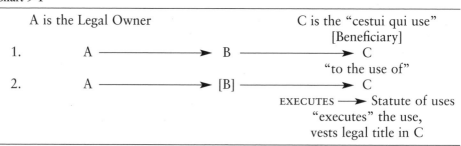

The immediate effect of the Statute of Uses was that it aggravated political unrest already building as a result of Henry's religious policies. A rebellion, called the "Pilgrimage of Grace" broke out, and many land-holding gentry were involved. One of their major complaints was that "execution" of uses took away the *de facto* power to devise the land which they had previously enjoyed. Henry realized he had gone too far and, by the Wills Act of 1540, all land held in fee simple by common socage tenure was made devisable, as was two-thirds of all land held in fee simple by Knight tenure.[28] In the same year, however, he was able to consolidate his new revenue gains by the establishment of a new court, the Court of Wards, which specialized in collecting his increased feudal dues.

---

28. Pressure to find means to evade the Statute of Uses would have been intense without this compromise. "The fears of evasion were doubtless more effective than the wails of the Pilgrims of Grace, or of younger brothers, in bringing about the establishment of the Court of Wards." J.H. Baker, "Introduction," *The Report of John Spellman* Vol II, (London, 1978), 203 (Selden Society Vol. 94).

3. THE FATE OF THE "STATUTE OF USES"

It all seemed like a brilliant compromise. The King had restored public conveyancing and more efficient tax collections through his Statute of Enrolments (1536) and the Court of Wards (1540). The landowners could devise their land freely, thanks to the Statute of Wills (1540). The common lawyers recaptured their land business from Chancery thanks to the magical transformation of the equitable "use" to a legal interest by the Statute of Uses (1536) itself. Indeed, the scheme succeeded for a generation. Yet by 1600, Francis Bacon could deliver a "reading" on the Statute of Uses before students at Gray's Inn and say that the statute was "a law whereupon the inheritance of this realm are tossed at this day, like a ship upon the sea."[29] What went wrong?

In the seventy years between the adoption of the Statute of Uses and Bacon's day, the most ingenious legal minds in England were bent to evading the Statute's provisions. There were a few narrow holes left by the draftsman, but ultimately it was the courts that circumvented the law through legal fictions. In so doing, they actually turned the statute into a tool to achieve results that had been legally impossible before. Henry Sumner Maine once observed that there were three "Agencies by which Law is brought into harmony with society...Legal Fictions, Equity, and Legislation."[30] The history of "Uses" and the Statute illustrates all three. "Uses" were creatures of equity. They were curtailed by statute, and then resurrected by legal fiction.

First, let us take a look at how the Statute was supposed to work and, indeed, did work for a generation. The two goals of the Statute were to eliminate secret conveyances of land and to eliminate *de facto* devises of land by "use." Before the Statute, secret conveyances were usually achieved by "bargain and sale."

If someone had "bargained and sold" a freehold to another, equity would enforce the sale by specific performance. Thus, the "bargain and sale" was said to leave the seller with a legal title held to "the use" of the buyer, although there had been no formal livery of seisin, no fealty and homage ceremony. After 1535 this use was "executed" by the statute, and the seller had legal title by reason of the bargain and sale. This was not a secret conveyance, however, because the transaction had to be recorded under the statute of Enrollments (1536).

Chart 9-2

GOAL:	Bargain & Sale of Land
EVASION	A "bargain and sale" = $\longrightarrow$ B = "use" for B.
FEALTY &	Executed by Statute of Uses (1535) = Legal Title in B,
HOMAGE	But enrolled, Statute of Enrollments (1536)
CEREMONY	

Likewise, the common law did not permit devise of land, but only inheritance through the canons of descent. This was achieved by granting land to straw man "B" *inter vivos*, to the use of the donor for life, and then to the use of specified

---

29. See *Materials, infra,* p. 300.
30. Henry Sumner Maine, *Ancient Law* (Pollock ed., 1963), 24.

heirs, at the donor's discretion. The legal title would descend by the regular canons of descent to B's heirs, but that made little difference as it was a "bare" legal title. (B was probably the donor's lawyer.) After the Statute, the legal title would vest in the donor, defeating the whole exercise. The Statute of Wills (1540), however, made such devises legal at common law, except for ⅓ of a "knight tenure" freehold.

Chart 9-3

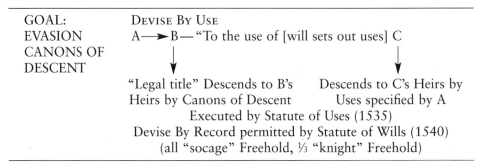

GOAL: EVASION CANONS OF DESCENT	DEVISE BY USE

A——▶B— "To the use of [will sets out uses] C

"Legal title" Descends to B's Heirs by Canons of Descent   Descends to C's Heirs by Uses specified by A
Executed by Statute of Uses (1535)
Devise By Record permitted by Statute of Wills (1540)
(all "socage" Freehold, ⅓ "knight" Freehold)

The first "hole" in the Statute was the fact that it was not intended to abolish all "uses." The Statute used the term "seised" to the use of another. "Seisin" referred solely to real hereditaments. It was also early decided that "active" uses, where the legal owner had real duties to perform, were not covered by the Statute. These kinds of "active" uses, not executed by the Statute, became known as "trusts." Finally, a covenant to stand seised by consideration of marriage or of "natural love" also raised a use before the Statute, and this use was executed by the Statute. But the Statute of Enrollments did not catch the transaction, because there was no "bargain and sale." Thus, private family settlements were still possible.

These "holes" may have been foreseeable, but the next set of developments were surely not the fault of any draftsmen. By Bacon's day, vendors routinely "bargained and sold" long leasehold terms rather than freeholds.

> "The Statute of Enrolments did not affect bargains for a term, and so these were left to the combined operation of the Chancery rule and the Statute of Uses; the bargainor is therefore seised to the use of the termor, and the termor acquires the legal term under the statute, without having to enter. Hence it was possible to convey secretly by using two deeds--a bargain and sale for a term, followed by a release of the fee to the termor. Neither had to be enrolled, and neither needed actual entry for its completion. This ingenious device is ascribed to Sir Francis Moore, and was sanctioned by the courts in 1621. By the end of the century, in spite of some doubts, it was in general use, for besides its secrecy it had the additional advantage over the bargain and sale enrolled, that uses could be limited in the deed of release.[31]

This defeated a principal goal of the Statute. It would have been easy for the courts to have prevented this blatant manipulation, or for Parliament to close the

---

31. T. F. T. Plucknett, *Concise History, supra,* 616.

gap. But the "fiction" clearly served political and economic purposes, and Henry was long dead. Indeed, the fiction lasted until 1845, when the Real Property Act of that year recognized that land could be transferred by deed of grant.[32]

But worse was to come. The Statute, designed to simplify the law, was actually used to create new and complex legal interests never before permitted at law.

Legal estates had always been governed by two strict rules:

1. "A remainder has to be supported by a prior estate, and vest when it ends—no sooner and no later."
2. "Remainders cannot cut short a prior estate."

For example, suppose a donor wished to make the following grant: "to B until C turns 21, and then to C." This would be a convenient way to be sure land did not fall into the hands of an underaged person, but it violates Rule 1, because B might die before C turns 21, or might live after C turns 21. Since the only legal estates were life estates, entails or fee simple—and the first two would be for B's life and the latter would be an unqualified gift to B—the gift over to C would not be supported by a recognized legal estate in B.

Another typical attempt would be an effort to prevent someone from getting married, or holding land after marriage. (If the recipient were a woman, she would lose legal control of the land to her husband after a marriage. The donor might not want this.) A grant might say "to B, unless B marries, and then to C." But this grant violates Rule 2, as the only possible legal estates B could have would be an unqualified fee simple or a life estate. Either way, the gift over cuts short the prior estate.

Chart 9-4

Rules of Feudal Estates	1. A remainder has to be supported by a prior estate, and vest when it ends—no sooner and no later.
	2. Remainder cannot cut short a prior estate.
Examples:	*Violation Rule 1*
	Donor A gives "to B until C turns 21 and then to C"
	Violation Rule 2
	Donor A gives "to B unless B marries; if so, to C"

Before the Statute, efforts were made to make these grants by uses, by having legal title vested in a straw man, subject to "uses." A use that shifted from one beneficiary to another on the happening of a contingency cutting short what would otherwise have been a legal estate, was called a "shifting use." (Say if in our second example B decided to get married.) A use that attempted to come into being after a pre-existing use had terminated, say in our first example if B had died before C turned 21, was called a "springing use," because it "sprung" out of nowhere.

---

32. Baker, *Introduction, supra,* 346.

Chart 9-5

("Shifting" and "Springing" uses)
1. "A To S (Straw), to the use of B until C turns 21, and then to C."
2. "A To S (Straw), to the use of B, unless B marries, remainder to C."

But did not the Statute end this? If the Statute "executed" the interests in the above examples, and made them legal interests, surely the gifts over or remainders were in violation of the common law rules and should be void, vesting a fee simple in B! But exactly the opposite was decided. To start, take the simple grant "to S, for the use of B for life, and then to C." Since the Statute only executed interests seised to the use of another, and B was not seized to the use of C, what happened when B died? The Courts solved this by saying that the straw, S, still had a "spark of title," a "*scintilla juris*," which could leap out and ignite C's remainder when B died.

This extraordinary fiction led to an argument that springing and shifting uses could also be "executed" into future legal interests in the same way. "[B]ut did this make them subject to the legal rules about remainders? Strict logic at first denied it. There had been no restriction on future interests before 1536: 'uses are not directed by the rules of the common law but by the will of the owner of the lands; for the use is in his hands as clay is in the hands of the potter, which he in whose hands it may put into whatever form he pleases...' "[33] As Baker observed: "The Courts therefore drew the conclusion that, however the clay was moulded, the legislation fired it into legal solidarity. Seisin could be made to skip and jump as never it could before..."[34]

There was an even more bizarre final chapter, the "use on a use." This began by means of simple errors by conveyancers. Suppose a widow, A, bargained and sold her lands to her son B in fee simple to her own use for life, remainder over to B.

Chart 9-6

A ⟶ B	⟶ A (for life)	⟶ B
(Bargain and sale)	use of	remainder

The effect was not at all what the conveyance or the widow wanted, because the "bargain and sale" created a use, which was executed by the Statute giving the son a fee simple outright. The use to the life of the widow was a second use, a "use on a use." What if the son ignored the second use, and threw his mother on the sidewalk? This actually came about, in a sense, in *Jane Tyrrel's Case* (1557), and the mother went to equity.

The first reaction of the Chancellor was not to protect the second use, because he knew that the result would be a deliberate evasion of the Statute by conveyancers putting a "use on a use." Eventually, however, the pressure to protect

---

33. J.H. Baker, *Introduction, supra*, 324, quoting Manwood J. in *Brent's Case* (1575), B.&M. 135, at 137. See also D.R. Coquillette, *Francis Bacon, supra* 128–135.

34. J.H. Baker, *Introduction, supra*, 324. Common law courts eventually realized their error and began to cut back on this rationale. *Id.*, 324–325.

the innocent victims of such blunders became too great, and it was held that the second use was not necessarily executed by the statute. These valid second uses were called "trusts," and the formula "to A to the use of B upon trust for C" became widely employed in the eighteenth century. Thus were the Statute's limitations slowly defeated, and the modern law of trusts gradually born.[35]

What is the lesson here?

The "*scintilla juris*" fiction and its progeny eventually led to an extraordinary system of illogic. As Maitland put it, "Springing and shifting uses and executory devises...thus took their place besides entails and remainders to make the common law of future interests the most elaborate folly ever built by logic."[36] All this from a statutory scheme that was designed to reduce the law to simplicity and clarity.

The lesson, put simply, was that Maine was correct about how law develops. "Legal Fiction, Equity, and Legislation" all work as molding forces of the law, each in their own way. No statutory scheme will remain untouched by equity or fictions, over time, nor will any rule survive with full effectiveness after the context or culture that created it has been changed. Part of the richness of legal history is how these forces work on each other. The Statute of Uses was a great success in its day. As its original context changed, its legal significance changed as well.

One question remains. Would not explicit statutory amendment or reform always be better than change through the operation of equity or fictions? Not necessarily. Equity, as we have seen before, operates in an individual, *ad hoc* way. It prevents the cruel or unfair application of a statutory scheme where the statute itself is as perfect as possible—it being impossible to create any rule that can always be fairly applied. Equity does not change the statute or create a precedent. It merely creates an exemption. Thus, "hard cases" do not create "bad law" at equity.

The value of legal fiction is harder to define, because it rests deep in the human psyche. Legal fictions are usually not deceptions—everyone usually knows the truth. But human beings resist change. We often prefer to pretend that something has stayed the same, when it has actually changed a great deal. The English monarchy is a legal fiction. So is the idea that the Constitution of the United States is unchanging. Fictions permit useful incremental reform, when wide scale reform is too threatening. These are the profound lessons of the history of the Statute of Uses.

FOR FURTHER READING

I.   Development of the English Legal Profession

The best summary is once again in J.H. Baker's *Introduction, supra,* 177–199. See also Alan Harding, *A Social History of English Law* (London, 1960),

---

35. See A.W.B. Simpson, *A History of the Land Law* (2d ed., Oxford, 1986), 194–207. It was, however, to be a long process, of which the "use on a use" played only a small part. See T.F.T. Plucknett, *Concise History, supra,* 602.

36. See S.F.C. Milsom, *Historical Foundations of the Common Law* (2d, ed., Toronto 1981), 226.

167–193. For more detailed accounts, see E.W. Ives, *The Common Lawyers of Pre-Reformation England* (Cambridge, 1983); W.R. Prest, *The Rise of the Barristers* (Oxford, 1986); Robert Robson, *The Attorney in Eighteenth-Century England* (Cambridge, 1959); and J.H. Baker's excellent study, *The Order of Serjeants at Law* (London, 1984) Selden Society Supp. Series, Vol 5. See also, E.W. Ives, "The Common Lawyers" in *Profession, Vocation, and Culture in Later Medieval England* (C.H. Clough ed., Liverpool, 1982) and the fine selection of essays by J.H. Baker collected in *The Legal Profession and the Common Law* (London, 1980), particularly "The English Legal Profession, 1450–1550," "Counsellors and Barristers," and "Solicitors and the Law of Maintenance, 1590–1640." *Id.* at 75, 99, and 125 respectively.

For accounts of the parallel civilian system, see C.T. Allmand, "The Civil Lawyers," *Profession, Vocation, and Culture in Later Medieval England* (C.H. Clough, ed., Liverpool, 1982); Brian P. Levack, *The Civil Lawyers in England, 1103–1641* (Oxford, 1973); and Daniel R. Coquillette, *The Civilian Writers of Doctors' Commons, London* (Berlin, 1988).

II. "Professional" Legal Education and the Inns of Court

For a fine introduction, see Sir Robert Megarry, *Inns Ancient and Modern* (London, 1972), Selden Society Lecture for 1971. See also, Wilfred R. Prest, *The Inns of Court under Elizabeth I and the Early Stuarts 1590–1640* (London, 1972); David Lemmings, *Gentlemen and Barristers, The Inns of Court and the English Bar 1680–1730* (Oxford, 1990); and the excellent essays collected in J.H. Baker *The Legal Profession and the Common Law Historical Essays* (London, 1980), particularly "The Inns of Court in 1388" and "Learning Exercises in the Medieval Inns of Courts and Chancery," *Id.*, at 3 and 7, respectively. Sir Cecil Carr's "Introduction" to *Pension Book of Clement's Inn* (ed. C. Carr, London, 1960), xvi–xvii, provides a fine view of the rise and fall of the Inns of Chancery. There is a fine, detailed bibliography of this subject, now a bit outdated. See D.S. Bland, *A Bibliography of the Inns of Court and Chancery* (London, 1965), Selden Society Supp. Series, 3.

For a perspective of the rival systems of Roman and canon law studies in the ancient universities, see Francis de Zulueta, Peter Stein, *The Teaching of Roman Law in England Around 1200* (London, 1990), Selden Society Supp. Series Vol. 8 and B.P. Levack, "The English Civilians, 1500–1750" in *Lawyers in Early Modern Europe and America* (ed. W. Prest, New York, 1981).

For further background on that great observer of the English legal system in the early Renaissance, see S.B. Chrimes, *Sir John Fortescue, De Laudibus Legum Angliae* (Cambridge, 1942), ix–cviii.

III. Professional Literature: Yearbooks and Abridgements

The best short account remains John P. Dawson, *The Oracles of The Law* (Ann Arbor, 1968), 1–99. The two classic sources are Percy H. Winfield, *The Chief Sources of English Legal History* (Cambridge, 1925), 145–251; and W.S. Holdsworth, *Sources and Literature of English Law* (Oxford, 1925), 74–111. For a detailed analysis of each relevant Abridgement, see John D. Cowley, *A Bibliography of Abridgements, Digests, Dictionaries and Indexes of English Law to the Year 1800* (London, 1932). See also L.W. Abbot's definitive study, *Law Re-*

porting in England 1485–1585 (London, 1973) and J.H. Baker, "Law Reporting" in *The Reports of Sir John Spelman* (London, 1978), Vol. 2, 164–178, Selden Society Vol. 94.

IV. The "Statute of Uses"

The best concise modern study is A.W.B. Simpson, *A History of the Land Law* (2d, ed., Oxford, 1986), 173–207. See also, S.F.C. Milsom, *Historical Foundation of the Common Law* (2d, ed., Toronto, 1981), 200–239; and T.F.T. Pluckett, *A Concise History, supra*, 515–602. The two classic older accounts also remain useful, W.S. Holdsworth, *An Historical Introduction to the Land Law* (Oxford, 1927), 153 and K.E. Digby, *An Introduction to the History of the Law of Real Property* (Oxford, 1897), 344–376. For a lucid account of the effect of the statute on modern law, see Sir Robert Megarry and H.W.R. Wade, *The Law of Real Property* (4th ed., London, 1975), 152–172. See also R.H. Helmholz, *Canon Law and the Law of England* (London, 1987), 341–353; and J.H. Baker, *The Reports of Sir John Spelman, Vol. 2* (London, 1978), Selden Society Vol. 94, "Uses and Wills," 192–208.

For the early history of uses, including the important suggestion that uses were enforced by Church Courts prior to the Chancellor, see R.H. Helmholz, *Canon Law and the Church of England* (London, 1987), 341–353.

Accion sur le case Fol. 4

9 Nota p Littleton arguend in fine casus q̄ le roy et le party greve poient aũ premunire & ex hoc videtur q̄ cest accion nest populer pro omnibus, car nul ceo auera mes le roye ou le party greve, vide hic inde Titulo Premunire in 13. Anno 7. E. 4. fol. 2. et auters que ne sont greues nauera cest accion. (7. E. 4. f. 2. Preminire.

Accion sur le case.

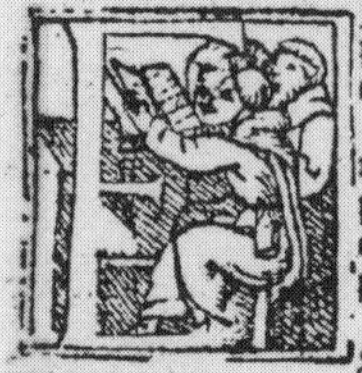

N &c. fuit agree p Cur̄ q̄ si home q̄ ad charter de exemption q̄ il ne ser̄ im panel sur nul Jure et mõstre ceo al vic. et vncor̄ il luy retorñ q̄ il auera accion sur le case vers le vic. (18. H. 8. 5. Vers vicount.

2 Nota p Fitzherb. & Shelley cleremẽt q̄ accion sur le case ne gist al comẽ ley pur appell̄ hõe heritike, ou avowterer, mes en le spiritual ley, mez pur appell̄ de traytour ou felon, accion gist al comẽ ley, mes en le aut̄ case ceux del comẽ ley ne poient discuss. quid est heresy ou avowtery, mz pur appeller Bawde, accion gist in lun court ou laut̄, et hic 115. (27. H. 8. 14. Pur defamiacion ×

3 Nota acciõ sur le case pur appell̄ le pl̄ thief & q̄ il eble ij. barbits d̄ J. S. le defẽd dit q̄ le pl̄ steale m̄ les barbits p q̄ il luy appel̄ thiefe cõe biẽ luy list & bõ p cur̄, sãz exprest. le value, q̄r silz ne vault xij. d. issint q̄ ne soit q̄ petit larceny & nul feloñ de mort, vnc. ceo ẽ felony ẽ s natur̄, & eadẽ lex 28. H. 8. int̄ Awsten & Thom Leues pur appell̄ luy false & piured il iustify pur ceo q̄ le pl̄ fuit pariure in camera stell̄ in tiel mat̄ &c. & bon pl̄ per cur̄. (27. H. 8. 22. Thiefe piured.

4 Nota q̄ lou fuit rule in banco reg̃ sur br̄ det̄ p deliberatiõ 12. H. 8. hic 106. q̄ acc. sur l̄ case gist biẽ vs execut̄ sur lassũpsit del testator sils ont assets. Fitzherb. Justice dit cleremẽt q̄ ceo nest pas ley et q̄ nul tiel accion gist. Ideo quere, car 37. H. 8. concord, cum Fitzh. (27. H. 8. 23 Vers executours Vide hic. 106.

5 Accio sur le case q̄ le def. assumpsit al pl̄ q̄ si le pl̄ discharge J. T. de tiel &c. in q̄ il ẽ al suit le pl̄ q̄ donq̃ si le dit J. T. ne satisfie le pl̄ p tiel iour q̄ donq̃ le defend ceo ferra, et count accordãt et fuer̄ a issue sur non assumpsit, et leuidẽce al Jure in proofe del assumpsit et le veritie del matter auci fuit q̄ le def. assumpsit al fẽe le pl̄ en absence le pl̄, et quant il vient a sã feme il agree a ceo & discharg̃ J. T. sans plee oue le pl̄ et p totam curiam sur bon argumt laccion sur le case gist, car feoffemt ou done de byens fait al feme est bõ si le bar̄ ne disagree et optima opiñ, car il aũa acc. sur s̄ case et nemy br̄ de dett. Et p ascũ il poit eslier lũ ou laut̄, et la fuit dit q̄ en multz cases hõe aũa acciõ sur le case qñt il poit bñ aũ aut̄ remedy, tamẽ hoc videtur q̄ ceo est ẽ aut̄ degree cõe ou hõe est endetted a moy et il pmes de payer deuãt Michelmas ieo puis auer accion de det sur le contract ou accion del case sur le promise et issint ceo est in diuers respects, car sur le promyse ne gist acc. de det. Et hec in banco Regis. (27. H. 8. 24. 25. Sur assũpc. al fem Lou aut acc. gist.

6 Nota p Baldwine chiefe Justice si home estop le haut chemin roial issint q̄ ieo ne puisse aler de mõ measõ a mõ close, ideo naũa acciõ sur l̄ case, car lestopper de comẽ chemin roial serra puny p le leete et chescũ home greue naũa acciõ de ceo contra Fitzherbert Justice et q̄ lou vne ad plus graũd dañ q̄ aut̄ (vt hic) il aũa acciõ sur case. Eadem lex ou home fait fosse vltra haut chemin et ieo et mõ chiual chie la en le nuite ieo auera acciõ sur case, et 93. (27. H. 8. 26. 27 Pur estop chimin

7 Trñs sur le case port vers vn milmaker pur ceo q̄ il imprist pur faire vn molin p vn iour & ne fist. Et optima opinio q̄ il doit declare quid le miller averoit pur sõ labor. Et p Martine, ceo mat̄ sound en couenant et de couenãt nient fait hõe nauera acciõ sur case, mes de couenaunte malemt fait, cõe si il misfait le molin. Acciõ sur le case gist. Tamen p Babb. & Cokein, tout est vn & si ne soit ascũ specialty, accion sur case gist en lũ case et laut̄ cleremt et sic vtitur a ceo iour in bãco regis en Lõdon per q̄ Rolfe pas oustre et dit q̄ le defend fist le molin et ceo offer al pl̄ & il refuse et luy eant discharge. Straunge, ne discharga pas prist, et alii econtra. Et ibidẽ concordatur si ne soit expresse quid il aũa pur son labor q̄ le bargaine est voide, et ratio videtur eo quod aliter il est nude pacte vnde non oritur accio quod nota, car si il assumpsit pro nichillo il nest lye p cest assumpt̄ quod nota in chescũ declaracion. (3. H. 6. 36. Pur non fesant molin. Sans especialty. Nudũ pact̄ ×

Illustration 9-2 Part of a page from Sir Robert Brooke's *La Grande Abridgement* (London, 1576). Note the many yearbook cases, designated by regnal year (i.e., "18.h.8.5"—or 18th year of Henry the 8th, case 5) arranged under the subject heading "Accion sur le case," or "Action on the case." [Author's Collection.]

MATERIALS

THE LEGAL PROFESSION

Glanvill (*circa* 1187) (trans. G.D.G. Hall, Nelson & Selden Society, 1965), 132–135. [Reprinted by permission of the Selden Society and Oxford University Press].

[BOOK XI]

Appointing of attornies in court in place of principals

The pleas so far discussed concern the right and property in any thing, and one may prosecute them, and all other civil pleas, either in person or by an attorney put in his place to gain or to lose. He who thus puts another in his place must, however, be present in court then, and it is generally done before the justices of the lord king sitting on the bench. No-one ought to be received as an attorney unless it is done by his principal, present in court; but the other litigant need not be present for the purpose, nor even need he who is put in the principal's place, if he is known to the court. It may be one person only who is thus put in the place of another: or it may be two or more jointly, or severally, so that, if one of them is not able to attend, the other or others can prosecute that plea. The plea can be tried and determined, by judgment or final concord, as fully and finally by such an attorney as by his principal. It should, however, be known that the appointment of a man as bailiff or steward with power to dispose of lands and goods, even where this is known to the court, will not entitle him to be received in court in place of his principal in any plea; for this there must be a special authority, and he must be expressly put in the place of his principal in the manner set out above, to gain or to lose for him in that plea.

It should further be noted that anyone may, in the court of the lord king, put another in his place to gain or to lose for him even in a plea which he has in some other court; and the following writ shall order that he be received in that court in place of his principal:

The writ for receiving an attorney in place of his principal

The king to the sheriff (or to another who presides over such-and-such a court), greeting. Know that N. has, before me or my justices, put R. in his place to gain or to lose in the plea which is between him and M. concerning one carucate of land in such-and-such a vill (or concerning some other named thing). And therefore I command you to receive the aforesaid R. in place of N., to gain or to lose for him in that plea. Witness, etc.

Whether an essoin cast by the principal or by the attorney will excuse the attorney

When anyone is put in the place of another in any plea in the manner set out above, are essoins allowable in respect only of the attorney's person, or only of his principal's, or both? The answer is that only the essoins of the representative are allowable in such a case, until his appointment is revoked.

Furthermore, when anyone is thus put in the place of another and answers or does what is appropriate in court concerning that plea, may his principal remove him at his pleasure and appoint another as representative, particularly if deadly

Illustration 9-3   DEVELOPMENT OF THE ENGLISH LEGAL PROFESSION

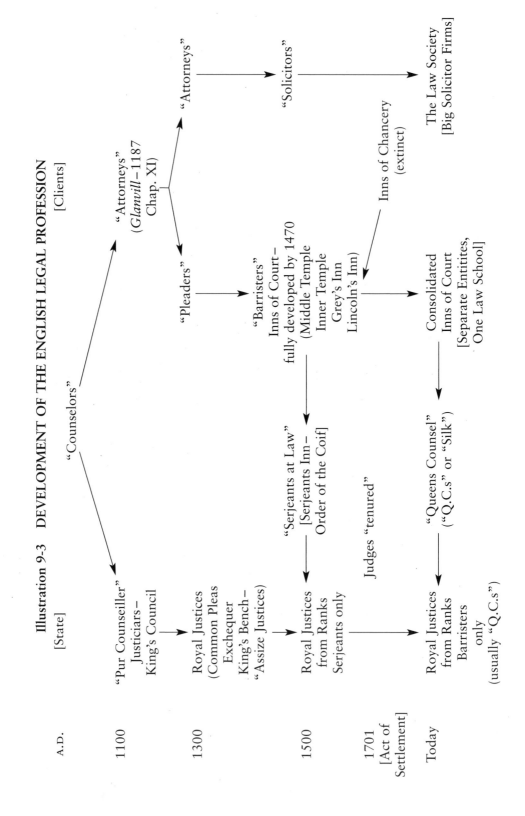

enmity has supervened? Now there is no doubt that a principal may remove his attorney and prosecute his own plea, for he puts another in his place only because he cannot be present in person; but, furthermore, the principal may remove such a representative at any stage of the case and may, in court, in the manner set out above, put another to act for him in the place of that one.

A father may in this way put his son in his place and *vice versa*, one stranger may put another, and a wife may put her husband. When a husband put in place of his wife in a plea concerning the wife's marriage-portion or dower loses or releases any of the wife's right, whether by judgment or by concord, may the woman reopen the plea, or is she wholly bound by the act of her husband after his death? It does not seem that the woman ought in such a case to lose any right by her husband's act, for while she was in the power of her husband she could not contradict him in any matter nor act against his will, and thus could not, if her husband were unwilling, take care for her own right. Yet, on the other hand, it is proper that things done in the court of the lord king should be settled and inviolable.

The principal must be distrained to abide by whatever was done in the court by his attorney, whether it was a judgment or a concord. But what if the principal is insolvent and has nothing that can be distrained, and the attorney has? Even then the attorney must not be distrained.

Geoffrey Chaucer, Excerpts from "The Prologue," *The Canterbury Tales* (*circa* 1387) Translated by Nevill Coghill (Penguin Classics 1951, Fourth revised edition, 1977) Copyright © Nevil Coghill 1977. [Courtesy Penguin Books Ltd.]

A *Serjeant at the Law* who paid his calls
Wary and wise, for clients at St. Paul's
There was also, of noted excellence.
Discreet he was, a man to reverence,
Or so he seemed, his sayings were so wise.
He often had been Justice of Assize
By letters patent, and in full commission.
His fame and learning and his high position
Had won him many a robe and many a fee.
There was no such conveyancer as he;
All was fee-simple to his strong digestion,
Not one conveyance could be called in question.
Nowhere there was so busy a man as he;
But was less busy than he seemed to be.
He knew of every judgement, case and crime
Recorded, ever since King William's time.
He could dictate defences or draft deeds;
No one could pinch a comma from his screeds,
And he knew every statute off by rote.
He wore a homely parti-coloured coat
Girt with a silken belt of pin-stripe stuff;
Of his appearance I have said enough.

*   *   *   *

Illustration 9-4 "The Serjeant at the Law" from Chaucer's *Canterbury Tales*. Note again the "coif" of the serjeant (the little white cap). This illustration comes from the famous Ellesmere Manuscript (*circa* 1410) courtesy the Huntington Library, San Marino, California. See James Thorpe, *Chaucer's Canterbury Tales: The Ellesmere Manuscript* (1978, San Marino, Cal.), 18.

The *Manciple* came from the Inner Temple;
All caterers might follow his example
In buying victuals; he was never rash
Whether he bought on credit or paid cash.
He used to watch the market most precisely
And got in first, and so he did quite nicely.
Now isn't it a marvel of God's grace
That an illiterate fellow can outpace
The wisdom of a heap of learned men?
His masters — he had more than thirty then —
All versed in the abstrusest legal knowledge,
Could have produced a dozen from their College
Fit to be stewards in land and rents and game
To any Peer in England you could name,
And show him how to live on what he had
Debt-free (unless of course the Peer was mad)
Or be as frugal as he might desire,
And they were fit to help about the Shire
In any legal case there was to try;
And yet this Manciple could wipe their eye.

Note: Chaucer's writings are full of information. From the description of the Serjeant at Law we learn: where serjeants met their clients — St. Paul's Church, London; that serjeants served as justices of assize, doubtless to save the time of royal judges; that this serjeant could break entails resulting from the *Statute De Donis*, described in Chapter IV, "all was fee-simple to his strong digestion;" and that he wished he had more work "But was less busy than he seemed to be."

We learn much from the description of the "Manciple" as well. He was a kind of steward for an Inn of Court. Since Chaucer tells us there were 30 in his Inn, Inner Temple, we can estimate the number of law students in 1387 as about 120 in the Inns of Court (4 × 30), not counting students in the Inns of Chancery. Like some old law school cafeterias, the "Manciple" made money on his charges by supplying cheap food, and otherwise cheating them.

Sir John Fortescue, *De Laudibus Legum Anglie* (translation S.B. Chrimes, Cambridge, 1942), 115 – 121. [Reprinted with the permission of Cambridge University Press.]

Chapter XLVIII

*Herein the chancellor shows why the laws of
England are not taught in the Universities*

The chancellor: 'In the Universities of England the sciences are not taught unless in the Latin language. But the laws of that land are learned in three languages, namely English, French, and Latin; in English, because among the English the law is deeply rooted; in French, because after the French had, by duke William the Conqueror of England, obtained the land, they would not permit the advocates to plead their cause unless in the language that they themselves knew, which all advocates do in France, even in the court of parliament there. Similarly,

Chancellor Fortefcue *following King* Henry's *Fortune, and attending his Son* Edward *into* France *wrote this Book to recommend the Laws of* England *to the Esteem and Protection of that Young Prince*

Illustration 9-5 This is the frontispiece of the 1737 edition of Sir John Fortescue's *De Laudibus Legum Angliae* (written *circa* 1470 and first printed in 1545–6). It shows Fortescue, on the left, explaining the English legal system to the exiled Lancastrian Prince of Wales, Edward. Behind Fortescue are the symbols of the office of Lord Chancellor, the mace and the purse for the Great Seal. See *Materials*, Chapter VI, *supra*. [Author's Collection.]

after their arrival in England, the French did not accept accounts of their revenues, unless in their own idiom, lest they should be deceived thereby. They took
no pleasure in hunting, nor in other recreations, such as games of dice or ball,
unless carried on in their own language. So the English contracted the same habit
from frequenting such company, so that they to this day speak the French language in such games and accounting, and were used to pleading in that tongue,
until the custom was much restricted by force of a certain statute; even so, it has
been impossible hitherto to abolish this custom in its entirety, partly because of
certain terms which pleaders express more accurately in French than in English,
partly because declarations upon original writs cannot be stated so closely to the
form of these writs as they can in French, in which tongue the formulas of such
declarations are learned. Again, what is pleaded, disputed, and decided in the
royal courts is reported and put into book form, for future reference, always in
the French speech. Also, very many statutes of the realm are written in French.
Hence it happens that the language of the people in France now current does not
accord with and is not the same as the French used among the experts in the law
of England, but is commonly corrupted by a certain rudeness. That cannot happen with the French speech used in England, since that language is there more
often written than spoken. In the third language above mentioned, in Latin, are
written all original and judicial writs, and likewise all records of pleas in the
king's courts, are also certain statutes. Thus, since the laws of England are
learned in these three languages, they could not be conveniently learned or studied in the Universities, where the Latin language alone is used. But those laws are
taught and learned in a certain public academy, more convenient and suitable for
their apprehension than any University. For this academy is situated near the
king's courts, where these laws are pleaded and disputed from day to day, and
judgements are rendered in accordance with them by the judges, who are grave
men, mature, expert and trained in these laws. So those laws are read and taught
in these courts as if in public schools, to which students of the law flock every
day in term-time. That academy, also, is situated between the site of those courts
and the City of London, which is the richest of all the cities and towns of that
realm in all the necessaries of life. And that academy is not situated in the city,
where the tumult of the crowd could disturb the students' quiet, but it is a little
isolated in a suburb of the city, and nearer to the aforesaid courts, so that the
students are able to attend them daily at pleasure without the inconvenience of
fatigue.'

CHAPTER XLIX

Here he shows the general organisation of the academy of the laws of England

'But, prince, in order that the form and arrangement of this academy may be
clear to you, I will now describe it as far as I can. For there are in this academy
ten lesser inns, and sometimes more, which are called Inns of Chancery. To each
of them at least a hundred students belong, and to some of them a much greater
number, though they do not always gather in them all at the same time. These
students are, indeed, for the most part, young men, learning the originals and
something of the elements of law, who, becoming proficient therein as they mature, are absorbed into the greater inns of the academy, which are called the Inns
of Court. Of these greater inns there are four in number, and some two hundred

LINCOLN'S INN HALL & CHAPEL.

Illustration 9-6 Lincoln's Inn Hall & Chapel. From W. Herbert, *Antiquities of the Inns of Court and Chancery* (London, 1804), facing 296. [Author's collection.] Both buildings are still standing today.

students belong in the aforementioned form to the least of them. In these greater inns, no student could be maintained on less expense than £13. 6s. 8d. a year, and if he had servants to himself alone, as the majority have, then he will by so much the more bear expenses. Because of this costliness, there are not many who learn the laws in the inns except the sons of nobles. For poor and common people cannot bear so much cost for the maintenance of their sons. And merchants rarely desire to reduce their stock by such annual burdens. Hence it comes about that there is scarcely a man learned in the laws to be found in the realm, who is not noble or sprung of noble lineage. So they care more for their nobility and for the preservation of their honour and reputation than others of like estate. In these greater inns, indeed, and also in the lesser, there is, besides a school of law, a kind of academy of all the manners that the nobles learn. There they learn to sing and to exercise themselves in every kind of harmonics. They are also taught there to practise dancing and all games proper for nobles, as those brought up in the king's household are accustomed to practice. In the vacations most of them apply themselves to the study of legal science, and at festivals to the reading, after the divine services, of Holy Scripture and of chronicles. This is indeed a cultivation of virtues and a banishment of all vice. So for the sake of the acquisition of virtue and the discouragement of vice, knights, barons, and also other magnates, and the nobles of the realm place their sons in these inns, although they do not desire them to be trained in the science of the laws, nor to live by its practice, but only by their patrimonies. Scarcely any turbulence, quarrels, or disturbance ever occur there, but delinquents are punished with no other punishment than expulsion from communion with their society, which is a penalty they fear more than criminals elsewhere fear imprisonment and fetters. For a man once expelled from one of these societies is never received into the fellowship of any other of those societies. Hence the peace is unbroken and the conversation of all of them is as the friendship of united folk. It is not, forsooth, necessary to relate here the manner in which the laws are learned in these inns, for, prince, you are not to experience it. But be assured that it is pleasant, and in every way suited to the study of that law, and also worthy of every regard. But I want you to know one point—that in neither Orléans, where the canon as well as the civil laws are studied, and whither students resort from all parts, nor Angers, nor Caen, nor any other University of France, except only Paris, are so many students of mature age to be found as in this academy, though all the students there are of English birth alone.'

Illustration 9-7   Benchers, barristers and students in Inner Temple Hall, July 3, 1990. From J.H. Baker, *The Inner Temple: A Brief Historical Description* (London, 1991, Hon. Society of the Inner Temple), page 15. Courtesy Hon. Society of the Inner Temple. Copyright held by the Hon. Society of the Inner Temple.

YEARBOOKS

From: *Year Books of Richard II, 2 Richard II (1378–1379)* (ed. Morris S. Arnold), Ames Foundation, 1975, 69. [Courtesy Ames Foundation.]

Michaelmas Term, 2 Richard II (1378)
7.—Jankyn v. Anon.

Query whether a defendant in trespass may plead that he committed the act complained of unintentionally and nonwilfully; in any event, however, the normal sanctions of amercement and making fine will follow upon a finding of liability.

Thomas Jankyn brought a writ of trespass complaining of the breaking of his house and of his door posts and rafters taken and carried away with force and arms at Rochester.

Clopton. As for coming with force and arms and carrying away the rafters and door posts we plead not guilty. And as for the breaking of his house, we tell you that we have a house in Rochester abutting on his, which house was dilapidated and needed repair. So we hired masons and carpenters to repair our house, and, as we were tearing it down to repair and remodel it, a small piece of building stone and timber fell on the plaintiff's house, unintentionally and nonwilfully and without any malice on our part. So we demand judgment whether you can assign any wrong in our person for any such breaking.

Burgh. We are complaining about our house being broken, which fact he neither admitted, denied, nor justified for any reason; he has therefore given us no answer. So we demand judgment and pray our damages.

PERCY, J. to *Clopton.* You have not alleged on the defendant's behalf that you offered the plaintiff, as between neighbors, any compensation for his home since this was done nonwilfully.

Clopton. Certainly, sir, to speak off the record, we offered him four pence as compensation for his home, and as I am informed he was not damaged a single penny. And even if the defendant were held legally liable for this act he will not be amerced, nor will he make fine in such a case.

KIRTON, J. denied that.

THE STATUTE OF USES (1536), 27 HEN. 8, C.10

Section 1 of "The Statute of Uses," 27 Hen. 8, Cap. 10, sec.1. An Act Concerning Uses and Wills. From K.E. Digby, *An Introduction to the History of the Law of Real Property* (Oxford, 1897), 347–349.

27 Henry VIII, Cap. 10. An Act Concerning Uses and Wills.

Where by the common laws of this realm, lands, tenements, and hereditaments be not devisable by testament, nor ought to be transferred from one to another, but by solemn livery and seisin, matter of record, writing sufficient made *bona fide*, without covin or fraud, yet nevertheless divers and sundry imaginations, subtle inventions, and practices have been used, whereby the hereditaments of this realm have been conveyed from one to another by fraudulent feoffments,

Anno · xxxix · E · tercii. fo · i ·

De termino Hillarii Anno regni Regis Edwardi tercii, post conquestum xxxix.

N brefe de Crespas le playntyfe **Jugement.**
counta q le defend batist son seruaut certein
iour, a force et armes lan xxxvii a ses da
mages etc. Et pleda de rien coulpable. Du
troue fuit p verdit q il luy batist a vn au
ter iour lan xxxvi. Et nient contristeaunt
q il se a autre iour et auter an, le pl auoit
iugement de recouer ses damages etc.

Johan de H. executour del testament de R. de E. pt vn bir de **Variance.**
Dette vers N. de S. et mia vn testament q luy proua ex
ecutour p tielz polz. Facio et constituo Iohannem fratrem
meum executorem meum. Et pour cel cause Cavn. Demaunde
iugement del variaunce entre le brefe et le testament. Belk.
Il nest pas le peire, tout ne soit il mpe accordaunt en parolz,
depuis que vous ne redites pas, que il nest mesme le person.
Fynch. En cas que home mette auaunt vn obligacyon / et
le brefe ne soit mpe accordaunt al obligacyon le brefe est abata
ble/mes en cas de testament le brefe nest pas abatable sil soit
mesme le persone. Cavn. Si est: quar le court ne post au
ternent sauer que il doit auer actyon come executour, sil ne
soit p le testament/et quant il y ad variaunce entre le brefe et
le testament del surnosme, il appiert al court q il ne pas exe
cutour. Knyuet: Sil soit nosme par vn auter surnosme en
le testament, il couiendra de faire le bir accordaunt/ mes icy ne
il pas nosme par surnosme en le testament/eins Iohannem fra
trem meum, quel est vn chose materiel/par q il moy semble q
le brefe est assetz bon etc. Ideo quere etc. Voyes semble in ater
Anno iii H iiii placito primo.

Belk. vient al barre et voillet auer treте vn tyne par tielz **Fyne.**
parolz. Le baron et sa feme grauntont et redont vn mees
a Johan etc. quel ilz teignont pur terme del vie la feme re
dant a eux viii s de rent etc oue clause de distres / et fuit re
fuse. Et puis ilz grauntont et rendont come deuaunt/ pur quel
graunt, Johan graunta arere viii s hors de mesme le mees
etc et fuit refuse, quere causam etc. Et puis ilz grauntont et re
dont a Johan et ceo relesscount et quiteclaymout a luy et a ses
heires pur terme del vie la feme/ pur q Johan grauta viii s.
J t etc oue

fines, recoveries, and other assurances craftily made to secret uses, intents, and trusts, and also by wills and testaments, sometimes made by *nude parolx* and words, sometimes by signs and tokens, and sometimes by writing, and for the most part made by such persons as be visited with sickness, in their extreme agonies and pains, or at such time as they have had scantly any good memory or remembrance; at which times they being provoked by greedy and covetous persons lying in wait about them, do many times dispose indiscreetly and unadvisedly their lands and inheritances; by reason whereof, and by occasion of which fraudulent feoffments, fines, recoveries, and other like assurances to uses, confidences, and trusts, divers and many heirs have been unjustly at sundry times disinherited, the lords have lost their wards, marriages, reliefs, harriots, escheats, aids, *pur fair*

Illustration 9-9   Henry the Eighth. From a painting by an unknown artist in the National Portrait Gallery. By courtesy of the National Portrait Gallery.

fitz chivalier and *pur file marier*, and scantly any person can be certainly assured of any lands by them purchased, nor know surely against whom they shall use their actions or execution for their rights, titles, and duties; also men married have lost their tenancies by the curtesy, women their dowers; manifest perjuries by trial of such secret wills and uses have been committed; the king's highness hath lost the profits and advantages of the lands of persons attained, and of the lands craftily put in feoffment to the uses of aliens born, and also the profits of waste for a year and a day of lands of felons attained, and the lords their escheats thereof; and many other inconveniences have happened, and daily do increase among the king's subjects, to their great trouble and inquietness, and to the utter subversion of the ancient common laws of this realm; for the extirping and extinguishment of all such subtle practised feoffments, fines, recoveries, abuses, and errors heretofore used and accustomed in this realm, to the subversion of the good and ancient laws of the same, and to the intent that the king's highness or any other his subjects of this realm, shall not in any wise hereafter, by any means or inventions be deceived, damaged, or hurt, by reason of such trusts, uses, or confidences: It may please the King's most royal Majesty, that it may be enacted by his Highness, by the assent of the Lords Spiritual and Temporal, and the Commons, in this present parliament assembled, and by the authority of the same, in manner and form following: that is to say, that where any person or persons stand, or be seised, or at any time hereafter shall happen to be seised of and in any honours, castles, manors, lands, tenements, rents, services, reversions, remainders, or other hereditaments, to the use, confidence, or trust of any other person or persons, or of any body politick, by reason of any bargain, sale, feoffment, fine, recovery, covenant, contract, agreement, will, or otherwise, by any manner means whatsoever it be; that in every such case, all and every such person and persons, and bodies politick, that have or hereafter shall have any such use, confidence, or trust, in fee simple, fee tail, for term of life, or for years, or otherwise; or any use, confidence, or trust, in remainder or reverter, shall from henceforth stand and be seised, deemed, and adjudged in lawful seisin, estate, and possession of and in the same honours, castles, manors, lands, tenements, rents, services, reversions, remainders, and hereditaments, with their appurtenances, to all intents, constructions, and purposes in the law, of and in such like estates, as they had or shall have in use, trust, or confidence of or in the same; and that the estate, title, right, and possession that was in such person or persons that were or hereafter shall be seised of any lands, tenements, or heritaments, to the use, confidence, or trust of any such person or persons, or of any body politick, be from henceforth clearly deemed and adjudged to be be in him or them that have, or hereafter shall have such use, confidence, or trust, after such quality, manner, form, and condition as they had before, in or to the use, confidence, or trust that was in them.

Francis Bacon, *Reading on the Statute of Uses* (Lent Vacation, 1600), excerpts, from Francis Bacon, *The Learned Reading... Upon the Statute of Uses* (London, 1642), 1–3. See D.R. Coquillette, *Francis Bacon, supra,* 48–59.

The LEARNED READING
of
MR. FRANCIS BACON,
One of Her Majesty's Council at Law, Upon
THE STATUTE OF USES.
Being His Double Reading to the Honourable Society
of Gray's Inn. 42.Eliz.

I have chosen to read upon the Statute of Uses, made 27 H. VIII. ch. 10, a law whereupon the inheritances of this realm are tossed at this day, like a ship upon the sea, in such sort, that it is hard to say which bark will sink, and which will get to the haven; that is not to say, what assurances will stand good, and what will not. Neither is this any lack or default in the pilots, the grave and learned judges; but the tides and currents of received error, and unwarranted and abusive experience have been so strong, as they were not able to keep a right course according to the law, so as this statute is in great part as a law made in the parliament, held 35 Reginae; for, in 37 Reginae, by the notable judgment given upon solemn arguments of all the judges assembled in the exchequer chamber, in the famous case between Dillon and Freine, concerning an assurance made by Chudleigh, this law began to be reduced to a true and sound exposition, and the false and perverted exposition, which had continued for so many years, but never countenanced by any rule or authority of weight, but only entertained in a popular conceit, and put in practice at adventure, grew to be controled; since which time (as it cometh to pass always upon the first reforming of inveterate errors) many doubts and perplexed questions have risen, which are not yet resolved, nor the law thereupon settled: the consideration whereof moved me to take the occasion of performing this particular duty to the house, to see if I could, by my travel, bring the exposition thereof to a more general good of the commonwealth.

Herein, though I could not be ignorant either of the difficulty of the matter, which he that taketh in hand shall soon find, or much less of my own unableness, which I had continual sense and feeling of; yet, because I had more means of absolution than the younger sort, and more leisure than the greater sort, I did think it not impossible to work some profitable effect; the rather because where an inferior wit is bent and constant upon one subject, he shall many times, with patience and meditation, dissolve and undo many of the knots, which a greater wit, distracted with many matters, would rather cut in two than unknit: and, at the least, if my invention or judgment be too barren or too weak, yet, by the benefit of other arts, I did hope to dispose or digest the authorities and opinions which are in cases of uses in such order and method, as they should take light from another, though they took no light from me. And like to the matter of my reading shall my manner be, for my meaning is to revive and recontinue the ancient form of reading, which you may see in Mr. Frowicke's upon the prerogative, and all other readings of ancient time, being of less ostentation, and more fruit than the manner lately accustomed: for the use then was, substantially to expound the statutes by grounds and diversities; as you shall find the readings still to run upon cases of like law and contrary law; whereof the one includes the learning of a ground, the other the learning of a difference; and not to stir conceits and subtle doubts, or to contrive a multitude of tedious and intricate cases, whereof all, saving one, are buried, and the greater part of that one case which is taken, is commonly nothing to the matter in hand; but my labour shall be in the ancient course, to open the law upon doubts, and not to open doubts upon the law.

S.F.C. Milsom, ***Historical Foundations of the Common Law*** (2d ed. 1981, Butterworth's), 225–226. [Notes omitted.] [Courtesy Lexis Law Publishing. All rights reserved.]

LEGAL EXECUTORY INTERESTS

...[T]he draftsman of the Statute of Uses perhaps ought to have foreseen that he was supplying lawyers with a magical force which they could harness. The matter is usually put in this way. At common law settlements of land had to obey certain rules, especially those governing contingent remainders. A remainder had always to be supported by a prior estate, and had to take effect as soon as that prior estate came to an end; this was because there had always to be somebody seised. But equally a remainder could not intervene and cut short the prior estate; and this was to prevent conditions being used to create indestructible settlements. Then it is said that in equity before the Statute of Uses, with a fee simple continuously in the hands of the feoffees and continuously obeying the law, interests could be made to spring, that is to break the first of these rules, or to shift, to break the second. Then lastly it is said that when the Statute of Uses brought such interests into the law, it was decided after hesitation that they should retain the plastic quality they had enjoyed in equity and not in general be subjected to the rigid legal rules. The undoubted result was a new and distinct class of legal future interests, shifting and springing uses. They were brought into being by a conveyance expressed as granting the land to feoffees to uses; and the uses, being at once exposed like magic ink to the rays of the Statute, were transmuted into legal interests. For example a grant to feoffees to the use of one person in fee simple, but upon the happening of some event to the use of another in fee simple, produced a legal fee simple which the event would simply transfer from the one to the other. The feoffees were real people, but in the nature of a fiction: no real title ever lodged in them, although in order to explain events after the first vesting it became necessary to postulate a *scintilla juris* always existing in their persons. In the case of devises even this measure of intellectual satisfaction was denied to the audience. The Statute of Wills was understood by its language to have enabled testators to produce these results even though the devise was expressed as conveying the land directly to the beneficiaries and not nominally to others to their use. Springing and shifting uses and executory devises, collectively known as legal executory interests, thus took their place beside entails and remainders to make the common law of future interests the most elaborate folly ever built by logic.

A.W.B. Simpson, ***An Introduction to the History of the Land Law*** (Oxford University Press, 1961), pp. 189–192. [© A.W.B. Simpson 1961. Reprinted from *A History of the Land Law* by A.W.B. Simpson (1st ed. 1961) by permission of Oxford University Press.]

One other sort of use or trust was not executed by the Statute—the use upon a use. Until the eighteenth century no conveyancer ever deliberately conveyed land to A to the use of B to the use of C, but this might be the accidental effect of what he did. Since the Statute a bargain and sale passed a legal estate, and had the effect of a feoffment. Thus in *Jane Tyrrel's Case* in 1557 Jane Tyrrel bargained and sold lands to her son in fee simple to her own use for life, with remainders over. When analysed, the situation now was that Jane was seised to the use of her son to the use of herself, and so she, or her conveyancer, had limited a use on a use. The common law courts would not execute the second use, but said it was a mere contradiction of the first, and the Chancellor would not protect it in Equity; no doubt he realized that if he did so, such second users would before long be deliberately created. But this attitude on the part of Chancery was hard and unsympathetic, for everybody knew that the use on a use had only arisen through a mistake, and in *Sambach v. Dalston* (1634), where a simple slip was made, we find the first instance of Equity intervening. But this intervention did not take the form of a holding that whilst the first *cestui que use* had the legal title yet he must hold the legal estate in trust for the second *cestui que use*. The Chancellor simply ordered that the legal estate be conveyed to the second *cestui que use*. This amounts to saying that since the Statute of Uses fails to execute the second use, yet, since it was unconscionable not to execute it Equity would insist upon its execution by private conveyance. The decision in *Sambach v. Dalston* did not therefore open any doors to deliberate evasion of the Statute's design to end the separation of legal and equitable ownership.

After the Statute of Tenures the next step was taken. In *Ash v. Gallen* in 1668 there was another blunder. The parties to a conveyance had intended to convey by feoffment to uses, but the conveyance had been mismanaged and there had been a bargain and sale to uses; thus inadvertently but incompetently they had limited a use upon a use. It was suggested that the second use could be enforced as a trust, and in the context this seems to envisage the first *cestui que use* holding in trust for the second, rather than actually conveying the land. The case was compromised without a decision. About this time, however, it is clear from a number of sources of information that the second use would be so enforced in Chancery, probably by an order to convey. Equity dispensed with the need for the conveyance, which at first had been insisted upon, around 1700. In the late seventeenth century Equity was developing too a doctrine of implied trusts, where good conscience led to the conclusion that the wrong person had come into the legal title to lands. One situation of this sort rose where A had bargained and sold lands to B, but C had provided the purchase money. At law A held to the use of B, and the Statute of Uses passed the legal estate to B. Equity, however, held that B held in trust for C by implication. The trust in favour of C, even if it had been recognized at law, would be a use upon a use, but in Equity it was enforceable as a trust. Again the Chancellor could have ordered a conveyance to C, but instead he preferred to protect the *cestui que trust*, who obtained his interest under the doctrines of Equity, by purely equitable means. By the close of the century it was recognized that a use upon a use deliberately created would be enforced as a trust, as

> '...where lands are limited to the use of A in trust to permit B to receive the rents and profits'.

But uses upon uses deliberately created in this way were rarely met with in practice; the only passive trusts to be deliberately created at all commonly were trusts limited on a term of years, not trusts of freeholds.

With growing recognition of trusts some terminological confusion was cleared up. In 1535 the terms 'trust' and 'use' were interchangeable. It became the practice in the seventeenth century to employ the term 'use' solely for uses executed by the Statute. The term 'trust' became appropriated for interests protected by Equity only. Thus it became proper to speak of a conveyance of a term of years 'to A in trust for B', and of a conveyance 'to A to the use of B in trust for C'. This terminological usage must not be allowed to obscure the fact that the trust concept and the use concept were basically the same, nor that the trust is nothing else but the old use, slightly modified, in a new guise.

LEGAL FICTIONS

Illustration 9-10   The Walrus and the Carpenter, from Lewis Carroll, *Through the Looking Glass* (London, 1871). Contemporary Illustration by John Tenniel.

'It seems a shame, the Walrus said,
'To play them such a trick.
After we've brought them out so far,
And made them trot so quick!'
The Carpenter said nothing but
'The butter's spread too thick!'
'I weep for you,' the Walrus said:
'I deeply sympathize.'
With sobs and tears he sorted out
Those of largest size,
Holding his pocket-handkerchief
Before his streaming eyes.
'O Oysters,' said the Carpenter,
'You've had a pleasant run!

> Shall we be trotting home again?'
> But answer came there none—
> And this was scarcely odd, because
> They'd eaten every one."

For a full background, see *The Annotated Alice* (ed. Martin Gardner), New York, 1960, 233–237.

Henry Sumner Maine, *Ancient Law* (1st American, from 2nd English edition, New York, 1864), 23–32.

CHAPTER II

Legal Fictions

* * * * * * * * * *

I confine myself in what follows to the progressive societies. With respect to them it may be laid down that social necessities and social opinion are always more or less in advance of Law. We may come indefinitely near to the closing of the gap between them, but it has a perpetual tendency to re-open. Law is stable; the societies we are speaking of are progressive. The greater or less happiness of a people depends on the degree of promptitude with which the gulf is narrowed.

A general proposition of some value may be advanced with respect to the agencies by which Law is brought into harmony with society. These instrumentalities seem to me to be three in number, Legal Fictions, Equity, and Legislation. Their historical order is that in which I have placed them. Sometimes two of them will be seen operating together, and there are legal systems which have escaped the influence of one or other of them. But I know of no instance in which the order of their appearance has been changed or inverted. The early history of one of them, Equity, is universally obscure, and hence it may be thought by some that certain isolated statutes, reformatory of the civil law, are older than any equitable jurisdiction. My own belief is that remedial Equity is everywhere older than remedial Legislation; but, should this be not strictly true, it would only be necessary to limit the proposition respecting their order of sequence to the periods at which they exercise a sustained and substantial influence in transforming the original law.

I employ the word "fiction" in a sense considerably wider than that in which English lawyers are accustomed to it, and with a meaning much more extensive than that which belonged to the Roman "fictiones." Fictio, in old Roman law, is properly a term of pleading, and signifies a false averment on the part of the plaintiff which the defendant was not allowed to traverse; such, for example, as an averment that the plaintiff was a Roman citizen when in truth he was a foreigner. The object of these "Fictiones" was, of course, to give jurisdiction, and they therefore strongly resembled the allegations in the writs of the English Queen's Bench and Exchequer, by which those Courts contrived to usurp the jurisdiction of the Common Pleas:—the allegation that the defendant was in custody of the king's marshal, or that the plaintiff was the king's debtor, and could not pay his debt by reason of the defendant's default. But now I employ the expression "Legal Fiction" to signify any assumption which conceals, or affects to conceal, the fact that a rule of law has undergone alteration, its letter remaining unchanged, its operation being modified. The words, therefore, include the instances of fictions which I have cited from the English and Roman law, but they embrace much more, for I should speak both of the English Case-law and of the Roman Responsa Prudentum as resting on fictions. Both these examples will be examined presently. The *fact* is in both cases that the law has been wholly changed; the *fiction* is that it remains what it always was. It is not difficult to understand why fictions in all their forms are particularly congenial to the infancy of society. They satisfy the desire for improvement, which is not quite wanting, at the same time that they do not offend the superstitious disrelish for change which is always present. At a particular stage of social progress they are invaluable expedients for overcoming the rigidity of law and, indeed, without one of them, the Fiction of Adoption which permits the family tie to be artificially created, it is difficult to understand how society would ever have escaped from its swaddling clothes, and taken its first steps towards civilisation. We must, therefore, not suffer ourselves to be affected by the ridicule which Bentham pours on legal fictions wherever he meets them. To revile them as merely fraudulent is to betray ignorance of their peculiar office in the historical development of law. But at the same time it would be equally foolish to agree with those theorists who, discerning that fictions have had their uses, argue that they ought to be stereotyped in our system. There are several Fictions still exercising powerful influence on English jurisprudence which could not be discarded without a severe shock to the ideas, and considerable change in the language, of English practitioners; but there can be no doubt of the general truth that it is unworthy of us to effect an admittedly beneficial object by so rude a device as a legal fiction. I cannot admit any anomaly to be innocent, which makes the law either more difficult to understand or harder to arrange in harmonious order. Now, among other disadvantages, legal fictions are the greatest of obstacles to symmetrical classification. The rule of law remains sticking in the system, but it is a mere shell. It has been long ago undermined, and a new rule hides itself under its cover. Hence there is at once a difficulty in knowing whether the rule which is actually operative should be classed in its true or in its apparent place, and minds of different casts will differ as to the branch of the alternative which ought to be selected. If the English law is ever to assume an orderly distribution, it will be necessary to prune away the legal fictions which, in spite of some recent legislative improvements, are still abundant in it.

The next instrumentality by which the adaptation of law to social wants is carried on I call Equity, meaning by that word any body of rules existing by the side of the original civil law, founded on distinct principles and claiming incidentally to supercede the civil law in virtue of a superior sanctity inherent in those principles. The Equity whether of the Roman Praetors or of the English Chancellors, differs from the Fictions which in each case preceded it, in that the interference with law is open and avowed. On the other hand, it differs from Legislation, the agent of legal improvement which comes after it, in that its claim to authority is grounded, not on the prerogative of any external person or body, not even on that of the magistrate who enunciates it, but on the special nature of its principles, invested with a higher sacredness than those of the original law and demanding application independently of the consent of any external body, belongs to a much more advanced stage of thought than that to which legal fictions originally suggested themselves.

Legislation, the enactments of a legislature which, whether it take the form of an autocratic prince or of a parliamentary assembly, is the assumed organ of the entire society, is the last of the ameliorating instrumentalities. It differs from Legal Fictions just as Equity differs from them, and it is also distinguished from Equity, as deriving its authority from an external body or person. Its obligatory force is independent of its principles. The legislature, whatever be the actual restraints imposed on it by public opinion, is in theory empowered to impose what obligations it pleases on the members of the community. There is nothing to prevent its legislating in the wantoness of caprice. Legislation may be dictated by equity, if that last word be used to indicate some standard of right and wrong to which its enactments happen to be adjusted; but then these enactments are indebted for their binding force to the authority of the legislature, and not to that of the principles on which the legislature acted; and thus they differ from rules of Equity, in the technical sense of the word, which pretend to a paramount sacredness entitling them at once to the recognition of the courts even without the concurrence of prince or parliamentary assembly. It is the more necessary to note these differences because a student of Bentham would be apt to confound Fictions, Equity, and Statute law under the single head of legislation. They all, he would say, involve *law-making*; they differ only in respect of the machinery by which the new law is produced. That is perfectly true, and we must never forget it; but it furnishes no reason why we should deprive ourselves of so convenient a term as Legislation in the special sense. Legislation and Equity are disjoined in the popular mind and in the minds of most lawyers; and it will never do to neglect the distinction between them, however conventional, when important practical consequences follow from it.

It would be easy to select from almost any regularly developed body of rules examples of *legal fictions*, which at once betray their true character to the modern observer. In the two instances which I proceed to consider, the nature of the expedient employed is not so readily detected. The first authors of these fictions did not perhaps intend to innovate, certainly did not wish to be suspected of innovating. There are, moreover, and always have been, persons who refuse to see any fiction in the process, and conventional language bears out their refusal. No examples, therefore, can be better calculated to illustrate the wide diffusion of legal fictions, and the efficiency with which they perform their two-fold office of transforming a system of laws and of concealing the transformation.

We in England are well accustomed to the extension, modification, and improvement of law by a machinery which, in theory, is incapable of altering one jot or one line of existing jurisprudence. The process by which this virtual legislation is effected is not so much insensible as unacknowledged. With respect to that great portion of our legal system which is enshrined in cases and recorded in law reports, we habitually employ a double language, and entertain, as it would appear, a double and inconsistent set of ideas. When a group of facts come before an English Court for adjudication, the whole course of the discussion between the judge and the advocate assumes that no question is, or can be, raised which will call for the application of any principles but old ones, or of any distinctions but such as have long since been allowed. It is taken absolutely for granted that there is somewhere a rule of known law which will cover the facts of the dispute now litigated, and that, if such a rule be not discovered, it is only that the necessary patience, knowledge or acumen, is not forthcoming to detect it. Yet the moment the judgment has been rendered and reported, we slide unconsciously or unavowedly into a new language and a new train of thought. We now admit that the new decision *has* modified the law. The rules applicable have, to use the very inaccurate expression sometimes employed, become more elastic. In fact they have been changed. A clear addition has been made to the precedents, and the canon of law elicited by comparing the precedents is not the same with that which would have been obtained if the series of cases had been curtailed by a single example. The fact that the old rule has been repealed, and that a new one has replaced it, eludes us, because we are not in the habit of throwing into precise language the legal formulas which we derive from the precedents, so that a change in their tenor is not easily detected unless it is violent and glaring. I shall not now pause to consider at length the causes which have led English lawyers to acquiesce in these curious anomalies. Probably it will be found that originally it was the received doctrine that somewhere, *in nubibus* or *in gremio magistratuum*, there existed a complete, coherent, symmetrical body of English law, of an amplitude sufficient to furnish principles which would apply to any conceivable combination of circumstances. The theory was at first much more thoroughly believed in that it is now, and indeed it may have had a better foundation. The judges of the thirteenth century may have really had at their command a mine of law unrevealed to the bar and to the lay-public, for there is some reason for suspecting that in secret they borrowed freely, though not always wisely, from current compendia of the Roman and Canon laws. But that storehouse was closed as soon as the points decided at Westminster Hall became numerous enough to supply a basis for a substantive system of jurisprudence; and now for centuries English practitioners have so expressed themselves as to convey the paradoxical proposition that, except by Equity and Statute law, nothing has been added to the basis since it was first constituted. We do not admit that our tribunals legislate; we imply that they have never legislated; and yet we maintain that the rules of the English common law, with some assistance from the Court of Chancery and from Parliament, are coextensive with the complicated interests of modern society.

Jerome Frank, *Law and the Modern Mind* (Brentano's, Inc., 1930), 338–339.

Appendix VII
NOTES ON FICTIONS

In a book with a remarkable history, "The Philosophy of As If," Vaihinger has given the world a brilliant exposition of the function of fictions. Some of his salient points are as follows:

1. "In fictions thought makes deliberate errors." For a fiction is an error, a "more conscious, more practical and more fruitful error." One who employs a fiction makes a statement which deviates from or contradicts reality, but with full awareness of this deviation or contradiction. A fiction is a "conscious mistake" or a "conscious contradiction." A statement made with full consciousness, at the moment of utterance, that it does not correspond to the truth of the matter, is a fiction.

2. The chief characteristics of a fiction are:

    a. Its arbitrary deviation from reality.

    b. Its tentativeness: It is a point of transition for the mind, a mere temporary halting place for thought.

    c. "The express awareness that the fiction is just a fiction, in other words, the consciousness of its fictional nature and the absence of any claim to actuality." Fictions are "assumptions made with a full realization of the impossibility of the thing assumed."

    d. The requirement that it be useful. A fiction is a means to an end, it is an expedient. "When there is no expediency the fiction is unscientific." Every fiction must justify itself, must perform a service. The fiction is a "legitimatized error," i.e., "a fictional conceptual construct that has justified its existence by its success."

One must guard against the vice of assuming that, because a fiction is useful, it therefore has objective validity. "The gulf between reality and fiction must always be stressed"; one must avoid "the fundamental error of converting fictions into reality."

            *   *   *   *   *   *   *   *   *   *

"Fictions are falsehoods, and the judge who invents a fiction ought to be sent to jail," wrote Bentham. He seems to have considered fictions in law as the entire equivalent of lies and unmitigatedly evil. He apparently made no distinction between (1) legal lies (*i.e.*, misstatements designated to deceive others), (2) legitimate legal fictions (*i.e.*, inaccurate statements made for convenience, with full knowledge of their departure from reality and with the intention that the auditor or reader should be aware of their "untruth"), and (3) legal myths (*i.e.*, erroneous statements uttered without knowledge of their falsity and therefore based on self-delusion). Legal lies, legal fictions and legal myths—he lumped them all together under the name of "legal fictions" and denounced them all as falsehoods, as "the most pernicious form of lying."

That clearer understanding of the validity of legitimate legal fictions which has, since Bentham's day, been brought about by the writings of Vaihinger and Tourtoulon was not, it seems, a part of Bentham's equipment. C.K. Ogden, however, has recently published a previously unprinted manuscript of Bentham on which Ogden bases the contention that Bentham had in his day worked out a theory of fictions which not only anticipated Vaihinger's theory but, in some respects, cut deeper in its analysis.

Now it must be admitted that this recently discovered manuscript discloses surprising subtlety on Bentham's part with respect to fictions generally. Bentham, without doubt, had some discernment of the nature of a valid fiction as an object spoken of, for convenience, as existing, but with full awareness of the fact that it has no existence. Such "fictitious entities," says Bentham in effect, are indispensable and not harmful so long as persons observe their lack of correspondence with reality. He gives as examples the words, "motion, relation, faculty, power."

So far so good. If the Bentham essay, published by Ogden, had made no mention of legal fictions, one might have assumed that Bentham intended to carry over his fiction theory to the field of law and was revising his earlier and more naive notions of legal fictions. But, alas, Bentham, for all his sophisticated remarks on fictions in general, at the close of this very essay uses the following sentence:

"By the priest and the lawyer, in whatsoever shape fiction has been employed, it has had for its object or effect, or both, to deceive and, by deception, to govern, and by governing to promote the interest, real or supposed, of the party addressing, at the expense of the party addressed."

* * * * * * * * * *

Illustration 10-1 Sir Edward Coke (1552–1634). Chief Justice, Common Pleas (1606–1613), Chief Justice, King's Bench (1613–1616). From the frontispiece of his *First Institutes* (4th ed, 1639). [Author's Collection.]

X

LAW REPORTS, PASSION AND JUDGES
SIR FRANCIS BACON, SIR EDWARD COKE, AND THE INTELLECTUAL SEEDS OF CIVIL WAR

The "Tudor Compromise," so well illustrated by the Statute of Uses, became endangered by Elizabeth I's lack of an heir. Ever mindful of her legal loss of control if she married, Elizabeth—a passionate individual—never did. On her death, the closest heirs were the House of Stuart, the Kings of Scotland, and its head, James VI of Scotland, to become James I of England.[1]

James was perhaps the most intellectual of English sovereigns, and he wrote a number of learned treatises.[2] But he came to the monarchy with some inherent disadvantages. First, he was King of Scotland, and the "Aulde Alliance" between Scotland and Continental powers made some of his new English subjects suspicious. This suspicion was a primary barrier to one of James's most dearly held hopes, to achieve the legal unification of Scotland and England. The influence of civil law in Scotland was significant, and the common lawyers were on full alert to protect the nationalism of the common law. In the back corridors, some whispered even more damaging rumors, that James was secretly Catholic and partial to the "Spanish faction" at court. That James was almost openly gay, and appointed his male consorts to high positions, bothered the English much less.[3]

It was James's intellect that led to one of his biggest problems. Henry VIII and his daughter, Elizabeth, would willingly leave a matter of theory ambiguous as long as they held the practical power. James, on the other hand, loved to debate issues of theology and ideology. *The Political Works of James I* remains, by far, the most impressive intellectual achievement of any English monarch. There is a good example of his ability in the *Materials, infra*, James's "Charge to the Judiciary." This set out the elements of James' famous "Divine Right" theory, and his

---

1. James descended from Henry VII's daughter, Margaret, who married James IV of Scotland. Thus his nearest common ancestor with Elizabeth was a great, great grandfather.

2. True, one of his first books was a demonstration of the reality of witchcraft, *Daemonologie* (1597).

3. See J.P. Kenyon, *Stuart England* (2d ed., London, 1985), 57–82; Godfrey Davies, *The Early Stuarts 1603–1660* (Oxford, 1959), 1–33.

311

concept of the modern absolute monarchy as the cornerstone of the modern centralized state. It is easy today to characterize a powerful state anchored in a totalitarian king as regressive, but to many of James' compatriots the enlightened, centralized monarchy was the wave of the future. Indeed, it was still decades before the "Sun King" reigned in France, Peter and Catherine in Russia, or Frederick in Prussia. The Tudor "model" represented an old-fashioned, quite literally "feudal" arrangement, with reciprocal obligations between subject and sovereign based on ancient contracts and even older ritual. The new "rationalism" promised to do better through a powerful "new deal" of central government.[4]

A. THE DIALECTIC: FRANCIS BACON AND EDWARD COKE

James' court attracted great minds like his own. Probably the greatest was Francis Bacon (1561–1626). Youngest son of Elizabeth's Lord Keeper, Nicholas Bacon, Francis was disinherited, probably because his father never got around to making the legal arrangements necessary to provide for him. Bacon went to the bar to support himself, like many younger sons. Bacon knew Elizabeth personally from an early age. The Queen called him "my little Lord Keeper" and bounced him on her knee. But Bacon was never advanced by Elizabeth. She was a shrewd judge of character, and she was suspicious of him.[5] Instead, her favor fell on an older man, an experienced practitioner devoted to the common law of the yearbooks and the forms of action, Sir Edward Coke. She made Coke Attorney General, to Bacon's deep jealousy.

On Elizabeth's death, Bacon hurried to ingratiate himself with James. Bacon offered to assist James in reforming English law, and in combining the two legal systems of England and Scotland, a project dear to James' heart.[6] James recognized Bacon's great intelligence, and steady promotions followed, first to Solicitor General (1607), then Attorney General (1613) and finally Lord Keeper (1617) and Lord Chancellor (1618), thus fulfilling Bacon's dream of following in his father's footsteps.

Meanwhile, Edward Coke, with strong Parliamentary support, had been appointed Chief Justice of the Common Pleas (1606) and then Chief Justice of the Kings Bench (1613). As we have seen, the Lord Chancellor was always a symbol of royal discretion and prerogative, while the great common law courts, the Common Pleas and the King's Bench, were the bulwarks of the ancient common law, binding king and subject alike. The two contrasting personalities of Bacon and Coke came to further symbolize these differences, and not just in their rival judicial capacities as Lord Chancellor and Chief Justice. The two men were also philosophical opposites, with very different juristic and ideological beliefs.

---

4. See D.R. Coquillette, *The Civilian Writers, supra*, 39–41.

5. Bacon's friendship with the Earl of Essex, Elizabeth's tragic consort who threatened her and was executed, could not have helped. Bacon was forced by Elizabeth to aid the prosecution. See D.R. Coquillette, *Francis Bacon, supra*, 15–16, 312–314.

6. Political union was not to occur until 1707. See, for a full account, Brian P. Levack, *The Formation of the British State* (Oxford, 1987). Legal union has never occurred, and Scots law is decidedly different from English law.

Bacon, today, is most famous for his great philosophical treatises, the *Advancement of Learning* (1605), the *Novum Organum* (1620), and *De Augmentis* (1623), and for his pioneering work on the scientific method. He was also a great writer, and a man who knew Shakespeare, Raleigh, Spenser, Donne and Harvey. Bacon has been accused of writing Shakespeare, something he did not do, but he has never been given the proper credit for two things he did accomplish. First, the discovery of a new manuscript suggests that Bacon had a major influence on his favorite secretary, Thomas Hobbes, the great political theorist.[7] Second, Bacon's juristic writing, long overlooked, makes him the first analytical, critical jurist of the common law.[8]

These last two achievements grew from Bacon's powerfully held views concerning the function of law and government. Like Hobbes, Bacon believed that individual human nature was imperfect, and he was skeptical about democracy. Bacon's last work was the incomplete, prophetic *New Atlantis* (posthumous, 1626). There, he correctly foresaw that scientific technology was two-edged, with both the profound promise to rescue humanity from suffering and disease, and also the power to destroy. Bacon believed that only powerful, collectivist, and elitist states could control human nature and harness the promise of science safely. No wonder he influenced Marx and Darwin alike, and has been the subject of intense study from Russia to China.[9]

In such a state, law is tested logically by only one thing, its "instrumental" success. Bacon's *Novum Organum* (1620) ("New Tool") called for new philosophical tools to further the interests of humanity. Law was just another tool, an "instrument" whose success or failure could be measured by empirical methods. If the problem was crime, the criminal law was successful if crime was reduced. If crime increased, the law could not be the best.

"Rational" control of the law as a policy instrument meant long-range planning, a vision of social ends, and the ability to amend and reform the law prospectively. This, in Bacon's view, was the function of an enlightened Sovereign-Legislator, a modern Justinian. "Judge made law" was acceptable as a necessary "fine tuning," particularly through equity, but, as Bacon wrote in his masterful essay, "Of Judicature," "[j]udges ought to remember that their office is '*jus dicere*' and not '*jus dare*'; to interpret law, and not to make law, or give law...."[10] Characteristically, Bacon's great legal writing was in the form of treatises which collected and analyzed legal principles and suggested methodologies of law reform, works like his *Maximes of the Law* (1596–7); *Reading Upon the Statute of Uses* (1600); *A Proposition to His Majesty Touching the Compiling and Amendment of the Laws of England* (1616); and the jurisprudential sections of the *De Augmentis* (1623).

Coke's intellectual style and philosophy of law stood in marked contrast. Bacon was a common lawyer and trained in the Inns of Court, but he wrote like an analytical civilian.[11] Coke, on the other hand, was true to the old faith. For

---

7. See Mark S. Neustadt, *The Making of the Instauration* (Ph.D. thesis, 1987), 247–299. D.R. Coquillette, *Francis Bacon, supra*, 237–256.

8. *Id.*, 277–297.

9. See *Id.*, 18, n. 3.

10. *Materials, infra*, p. 336.

11. See D.R. Coquillette, *Civilian Writers, supra*, 257–259.

Coke, the common law embodied a wisdom that could not be safely assessed in purely instrumentalist terms. It was created by the folk spirit of the land, and by God. Its most reliable sources were not in the analytical books of the civilians. To Coke "these books have glorious and goodly titles...but there is *mors in olla*: They are like to Apothecaries boxes...whose titles promise remedies, but the boxes themselves contain poison."[12] Nor was legislation inherently superior to the common law, in either wisdom or legitimacy. In cases such as *Dr. Bonham's Case* (1610), *Materials, infra*, Coke edged toward modern notions of judicial review, only to retreat when James seized control of the judiciary, leaving the Parliament alone as a safeguard of property and the individual.

Coke saw the old treatises, particularly *Bracton* and *Littleton*, as authentic sources of the "pure" common law, but he particularly looked to the incremental decisions of the courts, as recorded in the Yearbooks. Coke's greatest professional writing, his four *Institutes*, painstakingly collected these precedents. But, as we have discussed, Yearbooks were an imperfect vehicle for theory—being in essence practitioner's guides. Perhaps Coke's greatest contribution was his full appreciation of the law report as a source of legal authority. We have already examined Coke's report of *Slade's Case* (1602) and *William Aldred's Case, Materials, supra*, Chap. IX. We will now carefully examine *Dr. Bonham's Case* (1610) and the politically inflammatory *Prohibition del Roy* (1608), published posthumously in 12 *Coke's Reports* (1655).

Coke's Reports were different from modern law reports. Much of the account was just Coke's own, and he was sometimes the advocate, and sometimes the judge. Indeed, modern study has shown that *Slade's Case* probably did not decide what Coke said it did, and Dr. *Bonham's Case* and the *Prohibition del Roy* were probably not accurate accounts either.[13] But Coke's format was a major breakthrough. It provided more than the pleadings of the yearbooks and the bare outcomes of the plea rolls, and included the theoretical justifications of the judges. While other reporters, such as Plowden or Dyer, predated Coke, their reports were hard to distinguish from later yearbooks. But *Coke's Reports* were distinctive. From their first appearance, in eleven installments from 1600 to 1615, with two posthumous parts in 1655 and 1658, they became known as simply "*the Reports*," as indeed that is how they are still cited today in English courts.

Coke's notion of fundamental inalienable justice, defended by judicial precedent, was to have wide political, as well as legal, consequences. And not just in England. Among the first law books ordered by the Puritan settlers of Massachusetts were *Coke's Reports*. *Coke's Reports* were cited in the American Revolution, and, today, Coke's statue looks down on the courtroom of the Supreme Court of the United States, perhaps his truest monument.[14]

In the following original accounts, we will follow the legal and political battles between these two giants, Bacon and Coke, battles that would eventually be resolved only by the English Civil War. But the legal record does not tell the depth of the conflict. As a young man, Bacon had proposed to a great heiress, Lady

---

12. Edward Coke, "Preface" to 7 *Coke's Reports* (London, 1608), 8th unpaginated page.

13. See sources cited at "For Further Reading," Section III, *infra*.

14. According to T. F. T. Plucknett, we owe to Coke "the bold experiment of making a written constitution which should have judges and a court for its guardians." T. F. T. Plucknett, *Studies in English Legal History* (London, 1983), XIV, 70.

Elizabeth Hatton. She chose Coke instead, and suffered a deeply unhappy marriage. At one point, she actually petitioned the Lord Chancellor, traditional protector of the helpless, to save her daughter from another forced marriage. (Coke was forcing his daughter to marry the brother of the King's favorite, the Duke of Buckingham.) The Lord Chancellor to whom Lady Hatton was forced to turn was no less than Francis Bacon. No soap opera could approach the real passion of these true events.[15]

It could be said that Bacon and Coke destroyed each other professionally. In the *Case of the Commendams, Materials, infra,* Bacon assisted the King in forcing Coke from office in 1616. Coke became powerful in Parliament, however, and even regained the Council in 1617, largely through the forced marriage of his daughter discussed above. In 1621, Coke and the Parliament struck back, impeaching Bacon for taking bribes—a true charge, but, as Bacon put it, "I was the justest judge that was in England these fifty years; but it was the justest censure in Parliament that was these two hundred years."[16]

Yet, it could also be said these two great men challenged each other to supreme efforts in their chosen areas of expertise, and that their rivalry brought out high achievement. Coke's name has become synonymous with fundamental human rights and judicial precedent. Bacon's *Essays* are still in print in almost every bookstore, and his great treatises established new social sciences and modern linguistics. Bacon also developed an entirely new approach in English law, critical jurisprudence.[17] The original materials contained in this Chapter, many of which were prepared by my great teacher, John P. Dawson, and generously given to me to use, tell much of the story.

B. THE "CASE" OF THE PROHIBITIONS DEL ROY (1608)

By 1608, Coke was Chief Justice of the Common Pleas. He had already begun his *Reports,* eight years before, but the report of the *Prohibitions Del Roy,* set out in *Materials, infra,* was never to be published in his lifetime. It was far too controversial. Instead, it was published after the Civil War, in 1655, from papers Coke left behind (carefully protected from the King's agents, who, reportedly, reached Coke's rooms immediately after his death).

It is also less a report of a law case, than an account of an ongoing dispute between the King and the common law judges, represented by Coke. The dispute began because the Archbishop of Canterbury greatly resented the writs of prohibition which were being issued by the common law courts to limit Church courts' jurisdiction. Ecclesiastical patronage was valuable to both the Archbishop and the King, and the King, in his role as the Head of the Anglican Church, took the Archbishop's side. The King finally lost his patience with the common law judges, and sought to intervene directly in what he saw as a dispute between two branches of his "own" court system.

---

15. For a highly readable account, see Elizabeth Drinker Bowen, *The Lion and the Throne* (Boston, 1956), 393–411. See also D.R. Coquillette, *Francis Bacon, supra,* 221.

16. See D.R. Coquillette, *Francis Bacon, supra,* 222.

17. See *Id.,* 277–292.

This was the King's argument:

> Concerning the high commission [an ecclesiastical court] or in any other case in which there is not express authority in law, the King himself may decide it in his Royal person; and that the Judges are but the delegates of the King, and that the King may take what causes he shall please to determine, from the determination of the Judges, and may determine them himself. And the Archbishop said, that this was clear in divinity, that such authority belongs to the King by the word of God in the Scripture. (*Materials, infra*).

Coke replied:

> To which it was answered by me, in the presence, and with the clear consent of all the judges of England, and Barons of the Exchequer, that the King in his own person cannot adjudge any case, either criminal, as treason, felony, & c. or betwixt party and party, concerning his inheritance, chattels, or goods, & c. but this ought to be determined and adjudged in some Court of Justice, according to the law and custom of England. (*Materials, infra*).

Typically, Coke then cited to dozens of old Yearbook authorities to back his position. The King was unimpressed. Coke's concluding argument, that the King lacked legal training and the "artificial reason" it represented, clearly infuriated James. James was a highly intelligent man, and considered himself a better philosopher than Coke.

> Then the King said, that he thought the law was founded upon reason, and that he and others had reason, as well as the Judges: to which it was answered by me, that true it was, that God had endowed His Majesty with excellent science, and great endowments of nature; but his Majesty was not learned in the laws of his realm of England, and causes which concern the life, or inheritance, or goods, or fortunes of his subjects, are not to be decided by natural reason but by the artificial reason and judgment of law, which law is an act which requires long study and experience, before that a man can attain to the cognizance of it: that the law was the golden met-wand and measure to try the causes of the subjects; and which protected His Majesty in safety and peace: with which the King was greatly offended, and said, that then he should be under the law, which was treason to affirm, as he said; to which I said, that Bracton saith, *quod Rex non debet esse sub homine, sed sub Deo et lege.* ["the king should not be under man but under God and the law."] (*Materials, infra*).

Thus, Coke's final appeal was, predictably, to the thirteenth century and to the great feudal treatise of *Bracton*.

As we shall see, this confrontation has become a symbol of the rule of law courageously defying totalitarianism, and was invoked by American revolutionaries and English parliamentarians alike. That the true occurrence may have been rather different, is of no real consequence. (Another first-hand report, set out at *Materials, infra*, has the King striking Coke in a most unroyal way, with Coke himself lying on the floor "on all fours," begging forgiveness). Indeed, as with

Coke's report of *Slade's Case*, the account became more important than the actuality. One of the great lessons of Coke's career was the importance of being the one who conveyed the report to posterity.

C. COKE'S INSTITUTES

Coke's twelfth and thirteenth *Reports* were published posthumously, in part because they contained controversial accounts like the *Prohibitions Del Roy*. Also published after his death were his *Second, Third* and *Fourth Institutes*,[18] all by special order of the House of Commons. The excerpts set out in the *Materials* give a hint why. The first comes from the *Third Institutes*, first published in 1641. It focused on criminal law. In this excerpt, Coke asserts that torture was contrary to the common law.

This may seem uncontroversial today, but torture was routinely used in Coke's time, particularly by the Star Chamber. Coke himself interrogated tortured prisoners for the Council.[19] So did Bacon, who probably saw justifiable aspects to torture, particularly in cases of great importance to the state and where evidence obtained by confession was used only when externally verifiable.[20] Coke, however, saw that the dignity of the individual, even a guilty individual, could be more important than ascertaining the truth. To Bacon, and to many civilian jurists, truth was the essence of justice. If torture led to truth, it could certainly be justifiable in sufficiently important cases. To Coke, the dignity of the individual, founded on personal freedom and private property, could outweigh any state interest in the truth. Coke's *Third Institutes* lay the foundation for the modern American constitutional doctrines of cruel and unusual punishment, of exclusion of evidence illegally obtained, and — indirectly — of the right of privacy.

Coke's *Fourth Institute* was also published in 1641. It focused on the jurisdiction of English courts, including local, conciliar, and Church courts. In the section on Parliament, included because of its function as an ultimate court, Coke articulated a doctrine of Parliamentary sovereignty.

> Of the power and jurisdiction of the parliament, for making of laws in proceeding by bill, it is so transcendent and absolute, as it cannot be confined either by causes or persons within any bounds. Of this court it is truly said: *Si antiquitatem spectes, est vetustissima, si dignitatem, est honoratissima, si jurisdictionem, est capacissima* ["If you look to antiq-

---

18. *The First Institute*, called "Coke on Littleton," was a vast commentary that was based on the structure and text of a tiny treatise on land law, *Littleton's Tenures* (1481). (Coke's elaborate comments literally surrounded the text of Littleton like the "glosses" on the early Roman law texts. See Illustration 1-4.) It focused on civil law of real property, although the comments covered almost everything. It was published in Coke's lifetime in 1628. The *Second Institute* (1642) focused on famous statutes, including the *Magna Carta*. The Third Institute (1644) focused on Criminal law and the *Fourth Institute* (1644), on court jurisdiction.

19. See John H. Langbein, *Torture and the Law of Proof* (Chicago, 1976), 115, 117, 119, 126.

20. *Id.*, 85, 117, 119, 121, 125, 129, 139. See D.R. Coquillette, *Francis Bacon, supra,* 279–280, 325.

uity it is the most ancient, to dignity it is the most honored, to jurisdiction it is the widest"]. *Huic ego nec metas rerum, nec tempora pono* ["Upon it I place no limits of matters or time."]. (*Materials, infra*).

As we will see, England later developed an "unwritten" constitution that put a high premium on parliamentary sovereignty, at least compared to the United States. Coke eventually was expelled from the courts, and had to fight the Crown from the Parliament. Whether the views of the *Fourth Institutes* reflected an older Coke, more restrained in his belief in court-made law, is hard to tell. Some of Coke's earlier writing suggested a different view, that Parliament, like the Monarch, was constrained by some of the traditional rules of common law. One of these was his famous report of *Dr. Bonham's Case* (1610).

D. DR. BONHAM'S CASE

Dr. Bonham's Case, unlike *Prohibition del Roy*, appeared during Coke's lifetime in 8 *Coke's Reports* 114 (1610). Physicians, like lawyers, were organized into guilds in London. The Royal College of Physicians, in particular, controlled the right to practice medicine in London, pursuant to royal letters patent of 1519. This charter gave the College the actual right to fine and imprison those who defied its authority. Of particular importance was the fact that this royal charter had been ratified in all respects by Parliament in 1523 and 1553.

Dr. Bonham had a doctorate in medicine from Cambridge University, Coke's *alma mater*. When he was examined by the College of Physicians, however, he was found to be "insufficiently trained." *Materials, infra*. But he continued to practice. He was first fined by the College, and then imprisoned for 7 days, pursuant to the charter. Dr. Bonham, presumably on his release, sued the four physicians who signed the warrant for the College, and the two "yeomen" who executed it. He brought an action for false imprisonment in the Common Pleas, where Coke was Chief Justice.[21]

After delivering himself of an ode in honor of his *alma mater*, Coke stated that a doctor from one of the ancient universities should be presumed "profound, sad, discreet, groundedly learned and profoundly studied" and that the College of Physician's statutory authority to fine and imprison must be read or limited to "delicts" in practice. Here, Dr. Bonham had been found merely "unlicensed, not inexpert," and the imprisonment was, therefore, illegal.[22] In this holding, Coke was joined by his colleagues, Justices Warburton and Daniel.

Coke, however, added another argument, which was apparently joined only by himself, and thus *dicta*: that no person should be "a judge of his own matter." Here, the College was both accuser and judge, in a case in which its own interests were deeply involved. In Coke's words:

---

21. False imprisonment was an action for damages related to trespass. It was appropriate where the prisoner was already free, and therefore, *habeas corpus* was not an effective remedy. See J.H. Baker, *Introduction, supra*, 168.

22. *Materials, infra*, p. 340.

The censors cannot be judges, ministers and parties; judges to give sentence or judgment; ministers to make summons; and parties to have the moiety of the forfeiture [because one should not be judge in his own cause, indeed it is unjust for one to be a judge of his own matter]; and one cannot be Judge and attorney for any of the parties, Dyer 3 E.6.65. 38 E.3.15. 8 H.6.19b.20a. 21 E.4.47a. & c. And it appears in our books, that in many cases, the common law will control Acts of Parliament, and sometimes adjudge them to be utterly void: for when an Act of Parliament is against common right and reason, or repugnant, or impossible to be performed, the common law will control it, and adjudge such an Act to be void; and therefore, in 8 E.3.30a.b.; Thomas Tregor's case on the statute of W.2.c.38. and Articuli super Chartas, c.9. Herle saith, some statutes are made against common law and right, which those who made them perceiving, would not put them in execution.... (*Materials, infra*).

Much has been written about *Dr. Bonham's Case,* and those fateful words "the common law will control Acts of Parliament, and sometimes adjudge them to be utterly void..." In particular, it can be forcefully argued that Coke was only referring to the old notion of "equity of the statute," i.e., a statute will be void if it is impossible to perform or unjust to enforce in particular situations.[23] But the facts of *Dr. Boham's Case* were not those of such an *ad hoc* case, but of a routine enforcement of a statutory power which, in its essence, violated a common law principle. Did the Coke who reported *Dr. Bonham's Case* change his mind before he wrote the sections on parliamentary sovereignty "so transcendent and absolute, as it cannot be confined...," in the *Fourth Institutes,* discussed above? Or has *Dr. Bonham's Case* been misread?

Two things are certain. First, Coke's words in *Dr. Bonham's Case* may have been *dicta,* and may have been read out of context, but they were to have a second life of glory on another continent. To this day they are widely believed to be the "birth" of judicial review and the doctrine of *Marbury vs. Madison,* 5 U.S. (1 Cranch.) 137 (1803). Second, whatever Coke's views were on parliamentary sovereignty in 1610, he would soon experience extraordinary pressures that would drive him out of the courts and into Parliament. Did these events ultimately convince Coke to look to the Parliament, rather than the common law courts, as the ultimate bulwark for the human freedom and private property rights that Coke held so dear? Fortunately, we can examine the historical record for ourselves, in following the compelling events known as the "*Case of the Commendams.*"

E. THE CASE OF THE COMMENDAMS (1616)

The "*Case of the Commendams*" was not a reported law case at all but, like *Prohibitions del Roy,* was really a series of confrontations between the King in Council and the common law judges. The record comes from the *Acts of the Privy Council,* and tells the tale from the Council's perspective. Also like the *Prohibitions del Roy,* this "case" involved a clash between Church authorities and

---

23. See T. F. T. Plucknett, "Bonham's Case and Judicial Review" in *Studies in English Legal History* (London, 1983), XIV, 30–70; J. H. Baker, *Introduction, supra,* 241–242.

the common law courts, with the Crown intervening, quite personally, for the Church.

A "commendam" was a temporary Church benefice, "commended" to the care of the holder pending a permanent appointment. See *Materials, infra*. Although temporary, it could be very lucrative, just like a feudal wardship where the holder enjoyed the profits of the land temporarily, i.e., until the ward reached his or her majority. In particular, the friends of the King, including his bishops, could hold multiple "commendams," doubtless assigning junior clergy to do the actual work at a fraction of the true income of the holding, while the holder kept the rest. To the extent the King controlled these appointments, they could be valuable perquisites for the Crown. In this case, the Crown had claimed power of appointment to such a commendam because a parsonage had allegedly been vacant for more than 18 months. The owners of the advowson, with the power of permanent appointment to the parsonage, disagreed, and brought suit in the Common Pleas in 1613 to defeat the King's appointment. Power to appoint a parson was like today's political "jobs." It was very valuable to those who controlled the patronage, and was seen as a kind of property. The King, in this case, purported to appoint the commendam to the wealthy Bishop of Coventry and Lichfield, a loyal supporter who doubtless held many more such positions.

When he heard of the Common Pleas action to defeat his appointment, James was furious. He summoned all twelve Common law judges before his Council.

> His Majestie, havinge this day given order for meetings of the Council, and that all the Judges (being twelve in number) should bee sent for to bee present; when the Lordes were sett, and the Judges readie attendinge, his Majestie came himself in person to Councell, and opened unto them the cause of that assembly; which was, that hee had called them togeather concerninge a question that had relacion to noe private person, but concerned God and the Kinge, the power of his Crowne, and the state of his Church, whereof hee was Protector; and that there was noe fitter place to handle it then at the head of his Councell Table; that there had ben a question pleaded and argued concerninge *commendams*, the proceedings wherein had either ben misreported, or mishandled; for his Majestie a yeare since had receaved advertizement concerninge that case in twoe extreames: by some, that it did trench farr into his Prerogative Royall, in the general power of grauntinge commendams; and by others, that the doubt rested only upon a speaciall nature of a commendam, such as in respect of the incongruitie and exorbitant forme therof might bee questioned, without impeachinge or weakeninge the generall power at all. (*Materials, infra.*)

By 1613, Coke had been transferred from the office of Chief Justice of the Common Pleas to that of Chief Justice of the King's Bench. This was actually done at the King's wish. His hope was that Coke would become more of a protector of the Crown in the King's Bench, particularly as Coke would now be appointed to the King's Council. This may even have been Bacon's suggestion, who by now was Attorney General and a close advisor of the King. In any event, the scheme failed. As Chief Justice of the King's Bench, Coke was even more a leader of the other judges, and even more stubborn.

The next step in the *Commendams* controversy was a letter from Bacon, as Attorney General, to Coke, as Chief Justice, declaring the King's "express pleasure" that the case be halted until the King was "consulted." Courageously, the judges refused.

> Wee holde it our duties to informe your Majestie that our oathe is in theis expresse wordes: That in case anie letters come unto us contrary to lawe, that wee doe nothings by such letters, but certefie your Majestie thereof, and goe forth to doe the lawe, notwithstaundinge the same letters. Wee have advisedly considered of the said letters of Mr. Attorney, and with one consent doe holde the same to bee contrary to lawe, and that wee could not yield to the same by our oath; assuredly persuadinge ourselves that your Majestie, beinge truly informed that it staundeth not with your royall and just pleasure to give way to them, and therefore knowinge your Majesty's zeale to justice, and to bee most renowned therefore, wee have, according to our oathes, and duties (at the day openly prefixed the last tearme) proceeded, and thereof certefyed your Majestie, and shall ever pray to the Almightie for your Majestie in all honor, health, and happiness longe to raigne over us." (*Materials, infra*).

The King was again furious and again summoned the judges to his Council. As to the judges' letter, he observed:

> As for the forme of the letter, his Majestie noated that it was a newe thinge, and very undecent, and unfitt for subjects to disobey the Kinges commaundement, but most of all to proceede in the meanetime, and to retorne unto him a bare certificate; whereas they ought to have concluded with the layinge downe and representinge of their reasons modestly unto his Majestie, why they should proceede, and soe to have submitted the same to his princely judgment, expectinge to knowe from him wheather they had given him satisfaccion. (*Materials, infra*).

The effect on the judges was predictable. To go on further risked loss of office, and worse. They capitulated.

> After this his Majesty's declaration, all the Judges fell downe upon their knees, and acknowledged their error, for matter of forme, humbly cravinge his Majesty's gracious favour and pardon for the same. (*Materials, infra*)

Only Coke continued to resist and argue. He was recalled by the King, this time alone, to hear charges of contempt against himself. See *Materials, infra*. He was then barred from the King's Council and prohibited from hearing cases on assize that summer. The most striking punishment, however was the last. Coke was ordered to censor his own *Reports*.

> Lastly: that durioge this vacacion, while hee hath time to live privately and dispose himself at home, hee take into his consideracion and review his bookes of Reportes, wherin (as his Majestie is informed) there bee manie exorbitaunt and extravagant opinions sett downe and published

for positive and good lawe; and if, in the review and reading thereof, hee finde anie things fitt to be altred or amended, the correctinge thereof is leaft to his discretion. Amongst other thinges, his Majestie was not well pleased with the tytle of those bookes, wherein hee styled himself Lord Chiefe Justice of Englaunde, whereas hee could challendge noe more then Chiefe Justice of the Kinges Bench. And havinge corrected what in his discretion hee found meete in those Reportes, his Majesty's pleasure was, that hee should bringe the same privately to himself, that hee might consider thereof, as in his princely judgement should bee found expedient. Hereunto the Secretary advised him to conforme himself in all dutie and obeydience, as hee ought, whereby hee might hope that his Majestie in time would receave him againe to his gracious and princely favour. (*Materials, infra*).

This was surely a striking acknowledgment of Coke's power as a reporter. Did Bacon draft this punishment? In all events, Coke came back in the fall with five minor typographical or factual errors, out of his 500 reported cases then published. This defiance meant the end of Coke's judicial career. On November 14, 1616, Coke was dismissed from office. Bacon himself drafted the King's letter of dismissal. As Lord Ellesmere observed to the new Chief Justice, "He [the King] putteth down one, and setteth up another; a lesson to be learned of all, and to be remembered and feared of all that sit in Judicial places." *Materials, infra.*

Almost immediately after the *Case of the Commendams*, the King appointed Bacon Lord Keeper (1617) and then Lord Chancellor (1618), with elevation to the peerage as Baron Verulam. On January 27, 1621 Bacon was further elevated to Viscount St. Albans. Meanwhile, Coke poured his energy into his new role in Parliament. On March 14, 1621, the first charges of bribery were brought against Bacon by the House of Commons. Popular resentment against the King's favorite, Buckingham, grew rapidly. Apparently to save Buckingham, the King elected to sacrifice Bacon. Bacon made no defense against the charges, probably at the King's direction. Bacon was impeached on May 1, 1621. He retired to the country, after nominal imprisonment, to write his greatest philosophy.

James doggedly hung on to power, calling Parliament as little as possible. On March 27, 1625, he died. He was succeeded by his son, Charles I. Bacon died soon after, on April 9, 1626.

F. THE FIVE KNIGHTS' CASE (1627) AND THE PETITION OF RIGHT (1628)

Charles I was not to die in bed, but to be executed by the Parliament after a bloody Civil War. While neither Bacon nor Coke would live to see the outbreak of hostilities, both must have sensed the deterioration of the English political fabric. To an astonishing extent, the English Civil War was defined by the very legal issues over which Coke and Bacon fought in court. The "beginning of the end," for peaceful government, was the "*Five Knights' Case.*"

In some ways, Charles was one of the most attractive of all English monarchs. Unlike more than one of his later namesakes, he was faithful to his beautiful wife, and he was hardworking and honest. But he had three, quite literally, fatal flaws. First, he was even more devoted than his father to theoretical divine rule. Second, he desperately needed money. Third, he was widely believed to be a secret Catholic, and in league with England's arch enemy, Spain. The Parliament was determined to use its financial power to bring Charles to heel. He was determined to resist. In the end, Charles was forced to dissolve Parliament and to try live without special subsidies. This was to be called the period of "Personal Rule."

The two critical elements of successful "Personal Rule" were exploiting all of the King's "personal" revenue, including feudal dues, to the utmost, and maintaining peace with England's neighbors. In pursuing the first goal, Charles was determined to use every means possible. His advisors hit on the idea of "loan-money," using the Lords Lieutenant of each county to assess "loans" from people of substance in their individual shires. Technically, this was not a tax. The money was just "a loan" to "help" the King. Of course, this was all a fiction, and those who refused to "loan" the requested sum were imprisoned, including five knights. They were Sir Thomas Daniel, Sir John Corbet, Sir Walter Earl, Sir John Heveninghan, and Sir Edmund Hampden. Their lawyers, who included the great legal historian, John Selden, and Sergeant John Bramston, brought a writ of *habeas corpus* in the King's Bench to test the legality of the imprisonment.

The *habeas* writ issued, and the jailor brought in the warrant for imprisonment. This warrant gave no reason for the imprisonment, except the words, "*per speciale mandatum domini regis*" ("by special order of the lord king..."). In one of the outstanding legal arguments of English history, John Selden appealed to *Magna Carta*.

> Now, my lord, I will speak a word or two to the matter of the return; and that is touching the imprisonment, '*per speciale mandatum domini regis*,' by the lords of the council, without any cause expressed: and admitting of any, or either, or both of these to be the return; I think that by the constant and settled laws of this kingdom, without which we have nothing, no man can be justly imprisoned by either of them, without a cause of the commitment expressed in the return. My lord, in both the last arguments the statutes have been mentioned and fully expressed: yet I will add a little to that which hath been said.

> The statute of Magna Charta, cap. 29, that statute if it were fully executed as it ought to be, every man would enjoy his liberty better than he doth. The law saith expressly, 'No freeman shall be imprisoned without due process of the law;' out of the very body of this act of parliament, besides the explanation of other statutes, it appears, '*Nullus liber homo capiatur vel imprisonatur nisi per legem terrae.*' My lord, I know these words '*legem terrae*,' do leave the question where it was, if the interpretation of the statute were not. But I think under your lordship's favour, there it must be intended by due course of law, to be either by presentment or indictment...

> *Materials, infra.*

The imprisonment was clearly illegal, but the circumstance had now occurred which Coke foresaw. The courts had lost their independence. In a pathetic opinion, Hyde C.J. refused to release the prisoners. Addressing the knights, he stated:

> Mr. Attorney hath told you that the King hath done it, and we trust him in great matters, and he is bound by law, and he bids us proceed by law, as we are sworn to do, and so is the king; and we make no doubt but the king, if you seek to him, he knowing the cause why you are imprisoned, he will have mercy; but we leave that. If in justice we ought to deliver you, we would do it; but upon these grounds, and these Records, and the Precedents and Resolutions, we cannot deliver you, but you must be remanded. Now if I have mistaken any thing, I desire to be righted by my brethren, I have endeavoured to give the Resolutions of us all.
>
> *Materials, infra.*

Now the scene shifted to Parliament. Desperate for money, Charles was forced to call a new Parliament in 1628. Charles knew they would do nothing with the five knights in jail. They were thus released by the King on January 29, 1628. When Parliament convened on March 22, 1628, the first order of business was the five knights. One of the authorities cited by the King's Solicitor to defend their imprisonment was a 1616 opinion by Coke. In a dramatic moment, the old judge, now a member of Parliament, rose from his seat:

> Then *Sir Edward Coke* stood up and said, The glass of Time runs out, and something cast upon us hath retarded us; when I spake against the Loans and this matter, I expected blows, and somewhat was spoken, though not to the matter. Concerning that (that hath been objected), I did when I was a Judge, I will say somewhat. Indeed, a motion was made, but no argument or debate, or resolution upon advice; I will never palliate with this house, there is no Judge that hath an upright heart to God, and a clear heart to the world, but he hath some warrant for every thing that he doth. I confess when I read Stamford then, and had it in my hands, I was of that opinion at the Council-Table; but when I perceived that some members of this house were taken away, even in the face of this house, and sent to prison, and when I was not far off from that place myself, I went to my book, and would not be quiet till I had satisfied myself. Stamford at the first was my guide, but my guide had deceived me, therefore I swerved from it: I have now better guides, Acts of Parliament and other precedents, these are now my guides. I desire to be free from the imputation that hath been laid upon me. . . .
>
> *Materials, infra.*

The Parliament then unanimously voted the famous *Petition of Right*, set out in the *Materials, infra*. The *Petition* encapsulated all of Coke's fundamental principles, but now in the form of a statutory enactment. (Although, like the *Magna Carta*, the *Petition of Right* can be read as a declaration of existing law, rather than new legislation.) The two basic points of the petition were 1) that *habeas corpus* must not be denied (i.e., no free person imprisoned without legal cause) and 2) "[t]hat it is antient and indubitable right of every Freeman, that he hath a full and absolute property in his goods and estate...and no tax...ought to be commanded...without common consent by act of parliament." *Materials, infra.* Personal freedom and private property were Coke's two great principles, his bulwarks against Bacon's ideal of a collectivist state. The issue was fairly joined, and war loomed.

The King appeared to assent to the *Petition of Right* on June 3, 1628, but on July 26th he dissolved Parliament and repealed his "assent." No further Parliament would be called for eleven years. The period of "Personal Rule" had begun in earnest. At first, it was surprising success, but an uprising of the Scots destroyed a fragile fiscal balance. More political blunders by Charles followed. The result was to be a bloody Civil War that wracked the heart of England and led to the execution of the King on January 30, 1649.

G. A FINAL NOTE

This is primarily a book about English legal history. But by the date of these events, tiny groups of immigrants were settling on the coast of another continent, vast and wild. By 1631, some had settled in rough houses across the street from Boston College Law School, where they traded with Native Americans whose camps were by the Charles River, named for Charles I. A dangerous ocean separated them from their homes, but they were literate and even legalistic. Word of the great struggles between King and Parliament reached them in fragments, and they were deeply concerned. Indeed, the trauma of the Civil War that followed was to influence the convictions of their children, and their children's children.[24] In many ways, the core values of American Constitutionalism were forged in reaction to these far away, but terrifying events. From now on, our study is not just the study of the law of England, but of America, too.

FOR FURTHER READING

I.   The Era of the Early Stuarts

For a concise introduction to the political events leading to the English Civil War, see, once again, *The Oxford History of Britain* (Kenneth O. Morgan, ed. Oxford, 1988), the relevant section is by John Morrill, "The Stuarts," *Id.* at 327–363. For a more detailed political history, see J.P. Kenyon, *Stuart England* (London, 2d. ed., 1985), 1–194, and Godfrey Davies, *The Early Stuarts 1603–1660* (Oxford, 2d ed., 1959). For an account full of dramatic writing with a true Tory perspective, see Winston S. Churchill, *A History of the English-Speaking Peoples* (London, 1956), vol. 2, 119–224. For an excellent general reference, see C.P. Hill, *Who's Who in Stuart Britain* (London, 1988).

---

24. See D.R. Coquillette, "Introduction: the Countenance of Authoritie," *Law in Colonial Massachusetts* (eds. Coquillette, Brink, Menand, Boston, 1984), xxi–lx.

II.   Bacon and Coke

For a book-length analysis of Francis Bacon's career as a lawyer, see Daniel R. Coquillette, *Francis Bacon* (Edinburgh and Stanford, 1992). For much racier accounts, see Daphne Du Maurier, *The Winding Stair* (New York, 1977) and *Golden Lads: A Study of Anthony Bacon, Francis and Their Friends* (London, 1975). For a most readable, and justly famous, account of the life and times of Sir Edward Coke, see Catherine Drinker Bowen, *The Lion and the Throne* (Boston, 1956). While there is no complete scholarly biography of Coke, see Stephen D. While, *Sir Edward Coke and "The Grievances of the Commonwealth 1621–1628"* (Chapel Hill, 1979) for the definitive study of Coke's final "parliamentary" stage.

III.   The Emergence of Law Reporting

For the historical context of *Coke's Reports*, see John P. Dawson, *The Oracles of the Law* (Ann Arbor, 1968), 65–99. There is also a description of Bacon's efforts to ensure accurate reports (unlike some of Coke's!) by providing for two professional reporters. *Id.* 73. See also D.R. Coquillette, *Francis Bacon, supra*, at 214–215, n.54. For a more detailed study see L.W. Abbott, *Law Reporting in England, 1485–1585* (London, 1973), particularly 240–256. See also the classic account in Percy H. Windfield, *The Chief Sources, of English Legal History* (Cambridge, 1925), 145–199. For an important scholarly study of the manuscript origins of *Coke's Reports*, see J.H. Baker, "Coke's Notebooks and the Sources of His Reports" in *The Legal Profession and the Common Law* (London, 1986), 177–204. See also "The Genesis of Coke's Reports" in T.F.T. Plucknett, *Studies in English Legal History* (London, 1985), XV, 190–213.

As for specific studies relating to the controversies surrounding *Dr. Bonham's Case*, see "Bonham's Case and Judicial Review" in T.F.T. Plucknett, *Studies, supra.*, XIV, 33–70. (Plucknett concludes that we owe to Coke "the bold experiment of making a written constitution which should have judges and a court for its guardians." *Id.*, 70.) J.H. Baker points out that the crucial *dicta* "was Coke's considered opinion at the time, for the passage has been found written out twice in his own autograph," J.H. Baker, *Introduction, supra*, 241, although Baker notes that there is "some doubt... whether it reflected the views of his brethren." See also S.E. Thorne, "Dr. Bonham's Case" in 54 *Law Quarterly Review*, 543–552 (1938); and C.M. Gray, "Bonham's case Revisited" (1972) *116 Proc. American Philosophical Society*, 35–58.

IV.   Constitutional Issues

For a concise summary of the constitutional issues leading to the English Civil War, see S.B. Chrimes, *English Constitutional History* (4th ed., Oxford, 1967), 87–120. For a more detailed account, with original documents, see J.P. Kenyon, *The Stuart Constitution* (Cambridge, 1966). As for issues relating to the unification of England and Scotland, see Brian P. Levack, *The Formation of the British State* (Oxford, 1987). Finally, on controversies relating to the relative values of human dignity and judicial truth-finding, as symbolized by debates on use of torture, see John H. Langbein, *Torture and the Law of Proof* (Chicago, 1976) and D.R. Coquillette, *Francis Bacon, supra*, 279–280, 325.

Illustration 10-2 One of the common law courts at Westminster, from *The Modern Assurancer, or the Clarks Directory* (London, 1658). This is probably the Court of Common Pleas, as the King's Bench had three judges at the time. (My gratitude to Professor J.H. Baker for this insight.) Note that this is after Charles I's execution, and the arms above the judicial bench are not royal. [Author's Collection.]

MATERIALS

Note: Throughout this book, I am deeply indebted to my late teacher, friend, and colleague, John P. Dawson, Fairchild Professor of Law, Harvard Law School. On his retirement, he gave me and a group of other students, accumulated notes, files and materials to "make what use you can." Today, many of these students are legal historians. The following materials are particularly indebted to him, a great teacher of legal history.

THE JURISPRUDENCE OF JAMES I AND BACON

James I (with possible assistance of Francis Bacon), *The Political Works of James I* (Cambridge, Mass., 1918), 326–27, 333–35. (As edited by J.P. Dawson)

Charge to the Judiciary

Give thy Judgments to the King, O God, and thy righteousness to the Kings son.

These be the first words of one of the Psalms of the Kingly Prophet David, whereof the literal sense runs upon him, and his son Salomon, and the mystical sense upon GOD and CHRIST his eternal Son: but they are both so woven together, as some parts are, and can only be properly applied unto GOD and CHRIST.... Now God cannot give to himself. In another part of the same Psalm, where it is said, that "Righteousness shall flourish, and abundance of Peace, as long as the Moon endureth," it signifieth eternity, and cannot be properly applied but to GOD and CHRIST: But both senses, as well literal as mystical, serve to Kings for imitation, and especially to Christian Kings: for Kings sit in the Throne of GOD, and they themselves are called Gods....

But Justice in a King avails not, unless it be with a clean heart: for except he be Righteous as well as Just he is no good King; and whatsoever justice he doeth; except he doeth it for Justice sake, and out of the pureness of his own heart, neither from private ends, vain-glory, or any other by-respects of his own, all such Justice is unrighteousness, and no true Justice. From this imitation of God and Christ, in whose Throne we sit, the government of all Common-wealths, and especially Monarchies, hath been from the beginning settled and established. Kings are properly Judges, and Judgment properly belongs to them from GOD: for Kings sit in the Throne of GOD, and thence all Judgment is derived.

In all well settled Monarchies, where Law is established formerly and orderly, there Judgment is deferred from the King to his subordinate Magistrates; not that the King takes it from himself, but gives it unto them....

As Kings borrow their power from God, so Judges from Kings: And as Kings are to account to God, so Judges unto God and Kings; and both Kings and Judges by imitation, have two qualities from God and his Christ, and two qualities from David and his Salomon: Judgment and Righteousness, from God and Christ: Godliness and Wisdom from David and Salomon. And as no King can discharge his account to God, unless he make conscience not to alter, but to declare and establish the will of God: So Judges cannot discharge their accounts to

Illustration 10-3 James I. From a painting by Paul Van Somer in the National Portrait Gallery. By courtesy of the National Portrait Gallery, London.

Kings, unless they take the like care, not to take upon them to make Law, but joined together after a deliberate consultation, to declare what the Law is; For as Kings are subject unto God's Law, so they to man's Law. It is the King's Office to protect and settle the true interpretation of the Law of God within his Dominions: And it is the Judge's office to interpret the Law of the King, whereto themselves are also subject....

Now my Lords the Judges for your parts, the Charge I have to give you, consists likewise in three parts.

First in general, that you do Justice uprightly, as you shall answer to GOD and me: For as I have only GOD to answer to, and to expect punishment at his hands, if I offend; So you are, to answer both to GOD and to me, and expect punishment at GOD's hands and mine, if you be found in fault.

Secondly, to do Justice indifferently between Subject and Subject, between King and Subject, without delay, partiality, fear or bribery, with stout and upright hearts, with clean and uncorrupt hands.

When I bid you do Justice boldly, yet I bid you do it fearfully; fearfully in this, to utter your own conceits, and not the true meaning of the Law: And remember you are no makers of Law, but Interpreters of Law, according to the true sense thereof; for your office is *Ius dicere*, and not *Ius dare*: And that you are so far from making Law, that even in the higher house of Parliament, you have no voice in making of a Law, but only to give your advice when you are required.

And though the Laws be in many places obscure, and not so well known to the multitude as to you; and that there are many parts that come not into ordinary practice, which are known to you, because you can find out the reason thereof by books and precedents; yet know this, that your interpretations must be always subject to common sense and reason....

For though the Common Law be a mystery and skill best known unto your selves, yet if your interpretation be such, as other men which have logic and common sense understand not the reason, I will never trust such an interpretation.

Remember also you are Judges and not a Judge, and divided into Benches, which showeth that what you do, that you should do with advice and deliberation, not hastily and rashly, before you well study the case, and confer together; debating it duly, not giving single opinions, *per emendicata suffragia*; and so to give your Judgment, as you will answer to God and me.

Now having spoken of your office in general, I am next to come to the limits wherein you are to bound your selves, which likewise are three. First, encroach not upon the Prerogative of the Crown: if there fall out a question that concerns my Prerogative or mystery of State, deal not with it, till you consult with the King or his Council, or both: for they are transcendent matters, and must not be sliberely carried with over-rash wilfulness; for so may you wound the King through the sides of a Private person: and this I commend unto your special care, as some of you of late have done very well, to blunt the sharp edge and vain popular humour of some lawyers at the bar, that think they are not eloquent and bold spirited enough, except they meddle with the King's Prerogative: But do not you suffer this; for certainly if this liberty be suffered, the King's Prerogative, the Crown, and I, shall be as much wounded by their pleading, as if you resolved what they disputed: That which concerns the mystery of the King's power, is not lawful to be disputed; for that is to wade into the weakness of Princes, and to take away the mystical reverence, that belongs unto them that sit in the Throne of God.

Secondly, That you keep your selves within your own Benches, not to invade other Jurisdictions, which is unfit, and an unlawful thing; In this I must enlarge my self. Besides the Courts of Common Law, there is the Court of Requests; the Admiralty Court; the Court of the President and Council of Wales, the President and Council of the North; High Commission Courts, every Bishop in his own Court.

These Courts ought to keep their own limits and bounds of their commission and instructions, according to the ancient precedents: And like as I declare that my pleasure is, that every of these shall keep their own limits and bounds; so the Courts of Common Law are not to encroach upon them, no more than it is my pleasure that they should encroach upon the Common Law. And this is a thing Regal, and proper to a King, to keep every Court within its own bounds....

Keep you therefore all in your own bounds, and for my part, I desire you to give me no more right in my private Prerogative, than you give to any subject; and therein I will be acquiescent: As for the absolute Prerogative of the Crown, that is no Subject for the tongue of a lawyer, nor is lawful to be disputed.

It is atheism and blasphemy to dispute what God can do: good Christians content themselves with his will revealed in his word, so, it is presumption and high contempt in a subject, to dispute what a King can do, or say that a King cannot do this, or that but rest in that which is the King's revealed will in his Law.

The King's-Bench is the principal Court for criminal causes, and in some respects it deals with Civil causes.

Then is there a Chancery Court; this is a Court of Equity, and hath power to deal likewise in Civil causes: It is called the dispenser of the King's Conscience, following always the intention of Law and Justice; not altering the Law, not making that black which other Courts made white, nor *e converso*; But in this it exceeds other Courts, mixing Mercy with Justice, where other Courts proceed only according to the strict rules of Law: And where the rigour of the Law in many cases will undo a subject, there the Chancery tempers the Law with equity and so mixeth Mercy with Justice, as it preserves men from destruction.

And thus (as before I told you) is the King's Throne established by Mercy and Justice.

The Chancery is independent of any other Court, and is only under the King: There it is written *Teste meipso*; from that Court there is no Appeal. And as I am bound in my Conscience to maintain every Court's Jurisdiction, so especially this, and not suffer it to sustain wrong yet so to maintain it, as to keep it within its own limits, and free from corruption....

It is the duty of Judges to punish those that seek to deprave the proceedings of any the King's Courts, and not to encourage them any way: And I must confess I thought it an odious and inept speech, and it grieved me very much that it should be said in *Westminster* Hall, that a *Premunire* lay against the Court of the Chancery and Officers there: How can the King grant a *Premunire* against himself?

It was a foolish, inept, and presumptuous attempt, and fitter for the time of some unworthy King: understand me aright; I mean not, the Chancery should exceed his limit; but on the other part, the King only is to correct it, and none else: And therefore I was greatly abused in that attempt: For if any was wronged there, the complaint should have come to me. None of you but will confess you have a King of reasonable understanding, and willing to reform; why then should you spare to complain to me, that being the high way, and not go the other way, and back way, in contempt of our Authority?

And therefore sitting here in a seat of Judgment, I declare and command, that no man hereafter presume to sue a *Premunire* against the Chancery; which I may the more easily do, because no *Premunire* can be sued but at my Suit: And I may justly bar myself at mine own pleasure.

As all inundations come with overflowing the banks, and never come without great inconvenience, and are thought prodigious by astrologers in things to come: So is this overflowing the banks of your Jurisdiction in itself inconvenient, and may prove prodigious to the State.

Remember therefore, that hereafter you keep within your limits and Jurisdictions. It is a special point of my Office to procure and command, that amongst Courts there be a concordance, and musical accord; and it is your parts to obey, and see this kept....

Illustration 10-4 Francis Bacon (1561–1626). Lord Keeper (1617), Lord Chancellor (1618–1621). From the frontispiece to Illustration 10-5, *infra*. The following 3 illustrations all come from this book, the 1674 edition of Bacon's *Advancement of Learning*. [Author's Collection.]

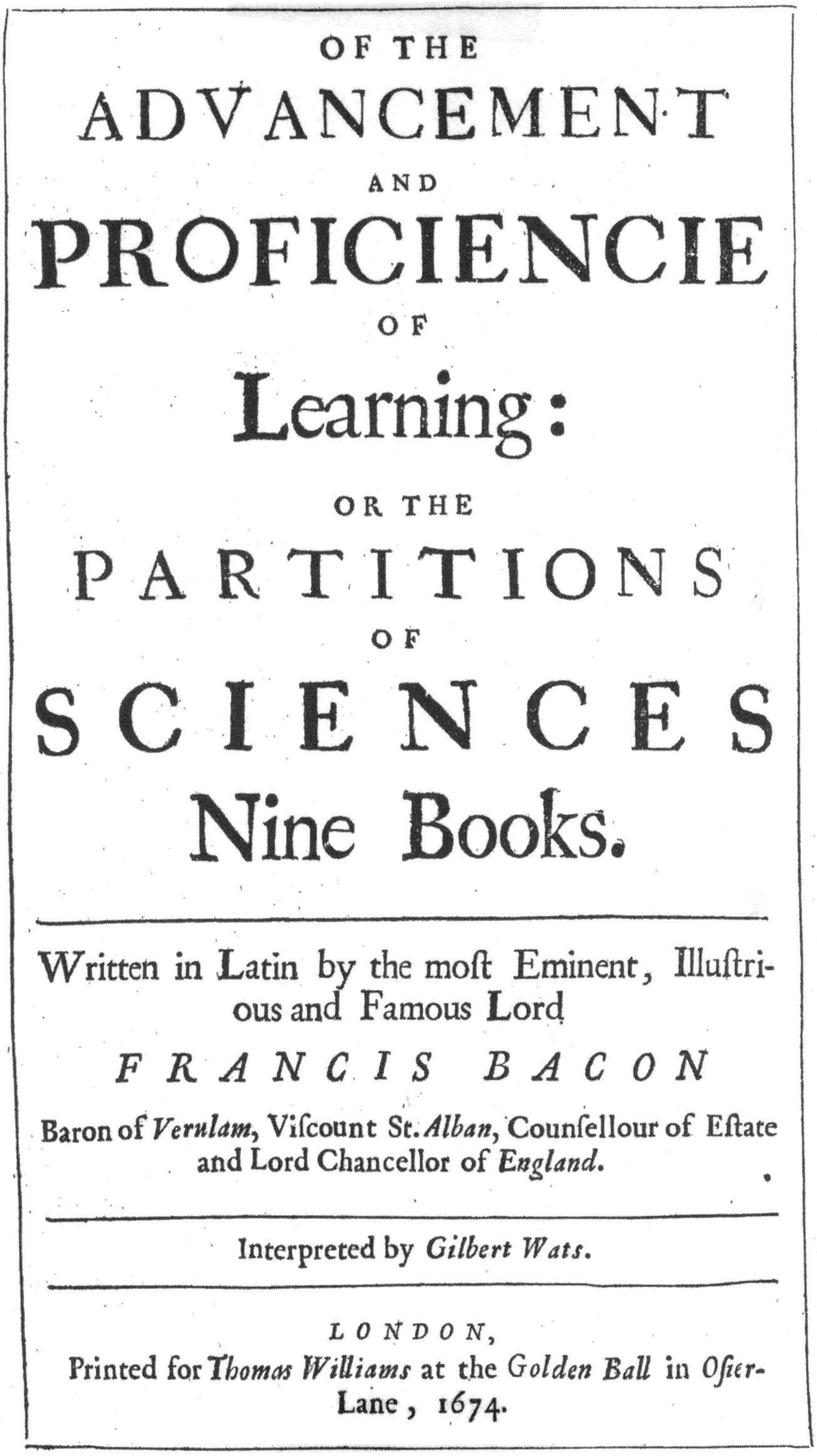

OF THE

ADVANCEMENT

AND

PROFICIENCIE

OF

Learning:

OR THE

PARTITIONS

OF

SCIENCES

Nine Books.

Written in Latin by the moſt Eminent, Illuſtri-
ous and Famous Lord

FRANCIS BACON

Baron of *Verulam*, Viſcount St. *Alban*, Counſellour of Eſtate
and Lord Chancellor of *England*.

Interpreted by *Gilbert Wats*.

LONDON,
Printed for *Thomas Williams* at the *Golden Ball* in *Oſier-*
Lane, 1674.

Illustration 10-5 Francis Bacon, *Advancement of Learning* (London, 1674), title page.
[Author's Collection.]

TITLE I.

Of the first Dignity of Laws, that they be Certain.

APHORISM VIII.

CErtainty is so Essential to a *Law*, as without it a *Law* cannot be *Just*; *Si enim incertam vocem det Tuba, quis se parabit ad Bellum?* So if the Law give an *uncertain sound*, who shall prepare himself to obey? A Law then ought to give warning before it strike : and it is a good Rule, *That is the best Law which gives least liberty to the Arbitrage of the Judge,* which is that, the *Certainty* thereof affecteth.

APHORISM. IX.

Incertainty *of Laws* is of two sorts; one where *no Law is prescribed*; the other, *when a Law is difficile and dark :* we must therefore first speak of *Causes omitted* in the *Law*; that in these likewise there may be found some Rule of *Certainty.*

Of Cases omitted in Law.

APHORISM X.

THe narrow compass of man's wisdom, cannot comprehend all cases which time hath found out; and therefore *Cases omitted, and new* do often present themselves. In these cases there is applied a threefold remedy, or supplement; either by a proceeding upon *like Cases,* or by the use of *Examples,* though they be not grown up into Law; or by *Jurisdictions,* which award according to the Arbitrement of some Good Man, and according to sound judgement; whether they be *Courts Pretorian,* or of *Equity,* or *Courts Censorian or of Penalty.*

Of Proceeding upon like Presidents; *and of the* Extensions of *LAWS.*

APHORISM XI

IN *Cases omitted,* the Rule of Law is to be deduced from *Cases of like nature*; but with Caution and Judgement. Touching which these Rules following are to be observed. *Let Reason be fruitful*; *Custom be barren, and not breed Cases.* Wherefore whatsoever is accepted against the *Sence and Reason* of a Law; or else where the *Reason* thereof is not apparent, the same must not be drawn into consequence.

APHO-

Illustration 10-6 Francis Bacon, *Advancement of Learning* (London, 1674), page 294.

APHORISM XII.

A singular Publick Good doth necessarily introduce *Cases pre-termitted*. Wherefore when a Law doth notably and extraordinarily respect, and procure the profit and advantage of a State, *Let the interpretation be ample and extensive.*

APHORISM XIII.

. *It is a hard Case to torture Laws, that they may torture Men.* We would not therefore *that Laws Penal, much less Capital, should be extended to new Offences :* yet if it be an old Crime, and known to the Laws, but the Prosecution thereof falls upon a new Case, not foreseen by the Laws ; we must by all means depart from the *Placits of Law,* rather than that offences pass unpunisht.

APHORISM XIV.

In those statutes, which the *Common Law* (specially concerning cases frequently incident, and are of long continuance) doth absolutely repeal; *We like not the proceeding by similitude, unto cases omitted :* for when a *State* hath for a long time wanted a *whole Law,* and that, in *Cases expreſſ* ; there is no great danger if the *cases omitted* expect a remedy by a *new statute.*

APHORISM XV.

Such constitutions as were manifestly, *the Laws of Time,* and sprung up from emergent Occasion , then prevailing in the *Common-wealth* ; the state of times once changed, they are reverenc'd enough, if they may conserve their authority within the limits of their own proper cases: and it were preposterous any way to extend and apply them to *Cases omitted.*

APHORISM XVI.

There can be no *Sequel of a Sequel,* but the extention must be arrested within the limits of *immediate Cases :* otherwise we fall by degrees upon *unresembling Cases* ; and the subtilty of wit will be of more force, than the Authority of Law.

APHORISM XVII.

In Laws and Statutes of a *compendious stile, extention* may be made more freely ; but in those *Laws* which are punctual in the *enumeration of Cases* Particular, more verily : for as *exception* strengthens the force of a *Law,* in *Cases not excepted* ; so *enumeration* weakens it, in Cases not *enumerated.*

APHO-

Illustration 10-7   Francis Bacon, *Advancement of Learning* (London, 1674), page 295.

Francis Bacon, "Of Judicature," from *The Essays*, vol. 1, *The Works of Francis Bacon* (Montagu ed., London, 1825), 179–184.

LVI. OF JUDICATURE.

Judges ought to remember that their office is "*jus dicere*," and not "*jus dare*;" to interpret law, and not to make law, or give law; else will it be like the authority claimed by the church of Rome, which under pretext of exposition of scripture, doth not stick to add and alter, and to pronounce that, which they do not find, and by shew of antiquity to introduce novelty. Judges ought to be more learned, than witty, more reverend, than plausible, and more advised than confident. Above all things, integrity is their portion and proper virtue. "Cursed (saith "the law) is he that removeth the landmark." The mislayer of a mere stone is to blame; but it is the unjust judge that is the capital remover of landmarks, when he defineth amiss of lands and property. One foul sentence doth more hurt than many foul examples; for these do but corrupt the stream, the other corrupteth the fountain: so saith Solomon, "*Fons turbatus, et vena corrupta est justus cadens in causa sua coram adversario.*" The office of judges may have reference unto the parties that sue, unto the advocates that plead, unto the clerks and ministers of justice underneath them, and to the sovereign or state above them.

First, for the causes or parties that sue. "There be (saith the Scripture) that turn judgment into "wormwood;" and surely there be, also, that turn it into vinegar; for injustice maketh it bitter, and delays make it sour. The principal duty of a judge is, to suppress force and fraud; whereof force is the more pernicious when it is open, and fraud when it is close and disguised. Add thereto contentious suits, which ought to be spewed out, as the surfeit of courts. A judge ought to prepare his way to a just sentence, as God useth to prepare his way, by raising valleys and taking down hills: so when there appeareth on either side an high hand, violent prosecution, cunning advantages taken, combination, power, great counsel, then is the virtue of a judge seen to make inequality equal; that he may plant his judgment as upon an even ground. "*Qui fortiter emungit, elicit sanguinem*;" and where the wine-press is hard wrought, it yields a harsh wine, that tastes of the grape-stone. Judges must beware of hard constructions, and strained inferences; for there is no worse torture than the torture of laws: especially in case of laws penal, they ought to have care that that which was meant for terror be not turned into rigour; and that they bring not upon the people that shower whereof the Scripture speaketh, "*Pluet super eos laqueos*;" for penal laws pressed, are a shower of snares upon the people: therefore let penal laws, if they have been sleepers of long, or if they be grown unfit for the present time, be by wise judges confined in the execution: "*Judicis officium est, ut res, ita tempora rerum*," &c. In causes of life and death judges ought, (as far as the law permitteth) in justice to remember mercy, and to cast a severe eye upon the example, but a merciful eye upon the person.

Secondly, for the advocates and counsel that plead. Patience and gravity of hearing is an essential part of justice; and an overspeaking judge is no well-tuned cymbal. It is no grace to a judge first to find that which he might have heard in due time from the bar; or to show quickness of conceit in cutting off evidence or counsel too short, or to prevent information by questions, though pertinent. The parts of a judge in hearing are four: to direct the evidence; to moderate length, repetition, or impertinency of speech; to recapitulate, select, and collate the material points of that which hath been said, and to give the rule, or sentence. Whatsoever is above these is too much, and proceedeth either of glory and willingness to speak, or of impatience to hear, or of shortness of memory, or of want of a staid and equal attention. It is a strange thing to see that the boldness of advocates should prevail with judges; whereas they should imitate God, in whose seat they sit, who represseth the presumptuous, and giveth grace to the modest: but it is more strange, that judges should have noted favourites, which cannot but cause multiplication of fees, and suspicion of by-ways. There is due from the judge to the advocate some commendation and gracing, where causes are well handled and fair pleaded, especially towards the side which obtaineth not; for that upholds in the client the reputation of his counsel, and beats down in him the conceit of his cause. There is likewise due to the public a civil reprehension of advocates, where there appeareth cunning counsel, gross neglect, slight information, indiscreet pressing, or an over-bold defence; and let not the counsel at the bar chop with the judge, nor wind himself into the handling of the cause anew after the judge hath declared his sentence; but, on the other side, let not the judge meet the cause half way, nor give occasion to the party to say, his counsel or proofs were not heard.

Thirdly, for that that concerns clerks and ministers. The place of justice is an hallowed place; and therefore not only the bench but the foot-pace and precincts, and purprise thereof ought to be preserved without scandal and corruption; for, certainly, "Grapes, (as the Scripture saith,) will not be "gathered of thorns or thistles;" neither can justice yield her fruit with sweetness amongst the briers and brambles of catching and polling clerks and ministers. The attendance of courts is subject to four bad instruments: first, certain persons that are sowers of suits, which make the court swell, and the country pine: the second sort is of those that engage courts in quarrels of jurisdiction, and are not truly "*amici curiae,*" but "*parasiti curiae,*" in puffing a court up beyond her bounds for their own scraps and advantage: the third sort is of those that may be accounted the left hands of courts: persons that are full of nimble and sinister tricks and shifts, whereby they pervert the plain and direct courses of courts, and bring justice into oblique lines and labyrinths: and the fourth is the poller and exacter of fees: which justifies the common resemblance of the courts of justice to the bush, whereunto, while the sheep flies for defence in weather, he is sure to lose part of his fleece. On the other side, an ancient clerk, skilful in precedents, wary in proceeding, and understanding in the business of the court, is an excellent finger of a court, and doth many times point the way to the judge himself.

Fourthly, for that which may concern the sovereign and estate. Judges ought, above all, to remember the conclusion of the Roman twelve tables, "*Salus populi suprema lex*;" and to know that laws, except they be in order to that end, are but things captious, and oracles not well inspired: therefore it is an happy thing in a state, when kings and states do often consult with judges; and again, when judges do often consult with the king and state; the one, when there is matter of law intervenient in business of state; the other, when there is some consideration of state intervenient in matter of law; for many times the things deduced to judgment may be "*meum*" and "*tuum*," when the reason and consequence thereof may trench to point of estate: I call matter of estate, not only the parts of sovereignty, but whatsoever introduceth any great alteration, or dangerous precedent; or concerneth manifestly any great portion of people: and let no man weakly conceive that just laws, and true policy, have any antipathy; for they are like the spirits and sinews, that one moves with the other. Let judges also remember, that Solomon's throne was supported by lions on both sides: let them be lions, but yet lions under the throne: being circumspect, that they do not check or oppose any points of sovereignty.

CASES OF SIR EDWARD COKE

The case of *"Prohibitions del Roy"* (1608). This case, dating from 1608, was included in Coke's famous *Reports*, but was only released in a part published in 1655, long after Coke's death in 1634.

Prohibitions del Roy, 12 Coke Rep. 63 (1608).

Note, upon Sunday the 10th of November in this same term, the King, upon complaint made to him by Bancroft, Archbishop of Canterbury, concerning prohibitions, the King was informed, that when the question was made of what matters the Ecclesiastical Judges have cognizance, either upon the exposition of the statutes concerning tithes, or any other thing ecclesiastical, or upon the statute 1 El. concerning the high commission or in any other case in which there is not express authority in law, the King himself may decide it in his Royal person; and that the Judges are but the delegates of the King, and that the King may take what causes he shall please to determine, from the determination of the Judges, and may determine them himself. And the Archbishop said, that this was clear in divinity, that such authority belongs to the King by the word of God in the Scripture. To which it was answered by me, in the presence, and with the clear consent of all the judges of England, and Barons of the Exchequer, that the King in his own person cannot adjudge any case, either criminal, as treason, felony, &c. or betwixt party and party, concerning his inheritance, chattels, or goods, &c. but this ought to be determined and adjudged in some Court of Justice, according to the law and custom of England and always judgments are given, *ideo consideratum est per Curiam*, so that the Court gives the judgment; and the King hath his Court, viz. in the Upper House of Parliament, in which he with his Lords is the supreme Judge over all other Judges; for if error be in the Common Pleas, that may be reversed in the King's Bench; and if the Court of King's Bench err, that may be reversed in the Upper House of Parliament, by the King, with the assent of the Lords Spiritual and Temporal, without the Commons: and in this respect the King is called the Chief Justice, 20 H. 7.7a. by Brudnell: and it appears in our books, that the King may sit in the Star-Chamber; but this was to consult with the justices, upon certain questions proposed to them, and not *in judicio*: so in the King's Bench he may sit, but the Court gives the judgment: and it is commonly said in our books, that the King is always present in Court in the judgment of law; and upon this he cannot be nonsuit: but the judgments are always given *per Curiam*; and the Judges are sworn to execute justice according to law and the custom of England. And it appears by the Act of Parliament of 2 Ed.3. cap.9. 2 Ed-3. cap.1. that neither by the Great Seal, nor by the Little Seal, justice shall be delayed; *ergo*, the King cannot take any cause out of any of his Courts, and give judgment upon it himself, but in his own cause he may stay it, as it doth appear 11 H.4.8. And the Judges informed the King, that no King after the Conquest assumed to himself to give any judgment in any cause whatsoever, which concerned the administration of justice within this realm, but these were solely determined in the Courts of Justice: and the King cannot arrest any man, as the book is in 1 H.7.4. for the party cannot have remedy against the King; so if the King give any judgment, what remedy can the party have. *Vide* 39 Ed.3.14. one who had a judgment reversed before the Council of State; it was held utterly void for that it was not a place where judgment may be reversed. *Vide* 1 H.7.4. Hussey Chief Justice, who was attorney to Ed. 4. reports that Sir John Markham, Chief Justice, said to King Ed. 4. that the King cannot arrest a man for suspicion of treason or felony, as others of his lieges may; for that if it be a wrong to the party grieved, he can have no remedy: and it was greatly marvelled that the archbishop durst inform the King, that such absolute power and authority, as is aforesaid, belong to the King by the word of God. *Vide* 4 H.4.cap.22. which being translated into Latin, the effect is, *judicia in Curia Regis reddita non annihilentur, sed stet judicium in suo robore quousque per judicium Curiae Regis tanquam erroneum, &c. vide* West.2.cap.5. *Vide le stat. de Marlbridge, cap.l. Provisum est, concordatum, et concessum, quod tam majores quam minores justitiam habeant et recipiant in Curia domini Regis, et vide le stat. de Magna Charta*, cap.29. 25 Ed.3.cap.5. [judgments in the king's court are not annulled but the judgment stays in force until by the decision of the king's court they are annulled as erroneous, etc. See Westm. 2, c.5 and the statute of Marlbridge, c.l. It is provided, agreed and granted that both the great and the lesser shall have and receive justice in the court of the lord king. And see the statute of Magna Carta, c.29. 25 Edw. III, c.5]. None may be taken by petition or suggestion made to our lord the King or his Council, unless by judgment: and 43 Edw.3.cap.3. no man shall be put to answer without presentment before the justices, matter of record, or by due process, or by writ original, according to the ancient law of the land: and if any thing be done against it, it shall be void in law and held for error. *Vide* 28 Edw.3. c.3. 37 Edw.3.cap.18. *Vide* 17 R.2. ex rotulis *Parliamenti in Turri*, art. 10. A controversy of land between parties was heard by the King, and sentence given, which was repealed for this, that it did belong to the common law: then the King said, that he thought the law was founded upon reason, and that he and others had reason, as well as the Judges: to which it was answered by me, that true it was, that God had endowed His Majesty with excellent science, and great endowments of nature; but his Majesty was not learned in the laws of his realm of England, and causes which concern the life, or inheritance, or goods, or fortunes of his subjects, are not to be decided by natural reason but by the artificial reason and judgment of, law, which law is an act which requires long study and experience, before that a man can attain to the cognizance of it: that the law was the golden met-wand and measure to try the causes of the subjects; and which protected His Majesty in safety and peace: with which the King was greatly offended, and said, that then he should be under the law, which was treason to affirm, as he said; to which I said, that Bracton saith, *quod Rex non debet esse sub homine, sed sub Deo et lege*. ["the king should not be under man but under God and the law."]

Sir Rafe Boswell to Dr. Milborne.

"Besides I must tell you the Archbishop of Canterburie resolued to try the validitie of our letters patentes: whereof Sir Christofer [Parkins] did faythfully assure me, and which I understand likewise from many others neerest my lo. grace. Whereunto I presume his Lp. might be the rather encouraged in regard of the late high Grace shewed to him on Sunday last at Whitehall before the King, where the Prohibitions were Debated by the Common lawyers. There the lo. Coke humbly prayed the king to haue respect to the Common Lawes of his land etc. he prayed his Majesty to consider that the Ecclesiasticall Iurisdiction was forren. After which his Majestie fell into that high indignation as the like was neuer knowne in him, looking and speaking fiercely with bended fist, offering to strike him etc., which the lo. Cooke perceiving fell flatt on all fower; humbly beseeching his Majestie to take compassion on him and to pardon him, if he thought zeale had gone beyond his dutie and allegiance. His Majesty not herewith contented, continued his indignation. Whereuppon the Lo. Treasurer, the lo. Cookes uncle by marriage, kneeled downe before his Majestle and prayed him to be favourable. To whome his Majestle replied saying, what hast thou to doe to intreate for him. He aunswered in regard he hath married my neerest kinswoman. etc....

From: R.G. Usher, "James I and Sir Edward Coke," *18 English Historical Review*, 664, 668–675. (Edited, J.P. Dawson)

Dr. Bonham's Case, 8 Coke Rep. 113b (1610). (Edited and summarized by J.P. Dawson.)

[On April 10, 1606 Thomas Bonham was summoned by the president and censors of the Royal College of Physicians to be examined by them concerning the sufficiency of his training for the practice of medicine. On April 14 Dr. Bonham appeared, was examined, and was found to be insufficiently trained. The president and censors imposed an amercement of 100 shillings and forbade him to practice in London under pain of imprisonment. Dr. Bonham continued to practice in London, was ordered to appear again on Oct. 22, 1606 but defaulted. The amercement was then raised to £10 and he was ordered imprisoned. On Nov. 7, 1606 Dr. Bonham appeared before an assembly of the president and censors, asserted that he had been granted a doctorate in medicine by the University of Cambridge, claimed that the Royal College had no authority over those who were doctors of the University, and refused to submit to the orders that had been issued against him. Dr. Bonham was then arrested and imprisoned for seven days under a warrant issued by the president and censors. The present action is for false imprisonment against the four physicians who had issued the warrant and two yeomen who had executed it.

The Royal College of Physicians had been incorporated by royal letters patent of 1519, with a governing board of a president and five censors. The charter conferred on the College regulatory powers over the practice of medicine in the City of London and for a seven-mile radius around it. Two clauses of the charter were mainly involved, the first dealing with *unlicensed* practice and the second with *inexpert practice*. The first clause provided that

"no one in the said city or for seven miles around it shall practice the said faculty of medicine unless he has been admitted to practice by the said president and college or their successors for the time being by letters under their common seal, under penalty of 100 shillings for each month in which, when not so admitted, he practices the said faculty, half of this sum to go to the king and his heirs and half to the said college."

The second clause authorized the Royal College "by fines, amercements and imprisonment of their bodies and by other reasonable and suitable means" to punish persons practicing in the designated area

"for their defaults in not properly executing, doing or using" [the faculty of medicine].

The charter of 1519 had been expressly confirmed and ratified in all respects by statutes of 1523 and 1553, the latter statute adding a general command to all jailers to hold in custody all persons that the president and censors had committed to prison for disobedience of their orders.

Coke's report first summarizes the arguments of counsel and then quotes himself, sitting as Chief Justice of the Common Pleas, in a tribute to the Universities of Oxford and Cambridge (he himself was a graduate of Cambridge). Admitting that the members of the Royal College of Physicians deserved the praise that had been heaped upon them for their professional skill, he quotes himself as saying that "the university is *alma mater*, from whose breasts those of that private college have sucked all their science and knowledge." This led him to the conclusion that every person with a doctorate from one of the universities should be presumed to be "profound, sad, discreet, groundedly learned and profoundly studied," and that the power of the Royal College to fine and imprison must be read as extending only to cases of malpractice — "for delicts in not properly executing, acting or using the faculty of medicine." Then Coke, C. J., and Justices Warburton and Daniel are reported to have given judgment that plaintiff's arrest was illegal, for five reasons of which the first three and the fifth can be summarized as follows:

(1) The two clauses were not only separate but the sanctions provided were different — 100 shillings fine, no more and no less, for each month of *unlicensed* practice but a wide discretion as to the nature and extent of the penalty (fines, amercements and imprisonments "and other reasonable and suitable means") for *inexpert* practice, this discretion being required by the fact that "the hurt that may come thereby may be little or great."

(2) The harm that may come from *inexpert* practice affects the body of the patient and therefore it was reasonable for the offender to be punished through imprisonment of his own body, but *unlicensed* practice "in a good manner" harms no one and therefore only a money fine, not imprisonment, was authorized in clause one.

(3) *Unlicensed* practice was required by the first clause to continue for a full month, but no time was fixed in the second clause, so that whenever *inexpert* practice occurred it could be punished.

(5) If the unlicensed physician could be fined 100 shillings for a month's London practice under the first clause and could also be punished under the second clause, he could be punished "not only twice but many times for one and the same offense... and the law saith no one should be punished for one wrong." Furthermore, it would be absurd, both to require a month's practice and to limit the fine to 100 shillings under the first clause, and then by the second clause to impose severe, unrestricted penalties for practicing the same offense on a single day.

[These arguments all drove toward the conclusion that the Royal College had no power under clause two to imprison Dr. Bonham, since he had been found merely to be unlicensed, not inexpert. But Coke also injected the following fourth argument, which was later to become famous.]

(4) The censors cannot be judges, ministers and parties; judges to give sentence or judgment; ministers to make summons; and parties to have the moiety of the forfeiture [because one should not be judge in his own cause, indeed it is unjust for one to be a judge of his own matter]; and one cannot be Judge and attorney for any of the parties, Dyer 3 E.6.65. 38 E.3.15. 8 H.6.19b.20a. 21 E.4.47a. &c. And it appears in our books, that in many cases, the common law will control Acts of Parliament, and sometimes adjudge them to be utterly void: for when an Act of Parliament is against common right and reason, or repugnant, or impossible to be performed, the common law will control it, and adjudge such Act to be void; and therefore, in 8 E.3.30a. b. *Thomas Tregor's case* on the statute of W.2.c.38. et Artic Super Chartas, c.9. Herle saith, some statutes are made against law and right, which those who made them perceiving, would not put them in execution....

And Coke, Chief Justice, in the conclusion of his argument, observed seven things for the better direction of the president and commonalty of the said college for the future. 1. That none can be punished for practising physic in London, but by forfeiture of £5 by the month, which is to be recovered by the law. 2. If any practise physic there for a less time than a month, that he shall forfeit nothing. 3. If any person prohibited by the statute offends in not properly executing, etc. they may punish him according to the statute within the month. 4. Those who they may commit to prison by the statute ought to be committed presently. 5. The fines which they set, according to the statute, belong to the King. 6. They cannot impose a fine, or imprisonment without a record of it. 7. The cause for which they impose fine and imprisonment ought to be certain, for it is traversable: for although they have letters patent and an Act of Parliament, yet because the party grieved has no other remedy, neither by writ of error or otherwise, and they are not made judges, nor a Court given them, but have an authority only to do it, the cause of their commitment is traversable in an action of false imprisonment brought against them.... For otherwise the party grieved may be perpetually, without just cause, imprisoned by them: but the record of a force made by a justice of peace is not traversable, because he doth it as Judge, by the statutes of 15 Rich. 2 and 8 Hen. 6 and so there is a difference when one makes a record as a Judge, and when he doth a thing by special authority, (as they did in the case at Bar) and not as a Judge. And afterwards for the said two last points judgment was given for the plaintiff, *nullo contradicente* [no one dissenting] as to them.

The "*Case of the Commendams*" (1616). This controversy led to the dismissal of Coke as Chief Justice in 1616. Is this really "a case"? This represented a shift from the judicial arena to politics and confrontation. The notes were originally prepared by J. P. Dawson, my late friend and teacher. Note the influence of Francis Bacon as Attorney General. Note also that this record is not from a case reporter, but from the *Acts of the Privy Council*, 1615–1616, 595.

At Whitehall, the 6 of June, 1616.

Present: The Kinges Majestie, Lord Archbishop of Canterburie, Lord Chancellor, Lord Treasurer, Lord Privie Seale, Lord Stewarde, Lord Chamberlein, Lord

Viscount Fenton, Lord Bishop of Winchester, Lord Zouch, Lord Knollis, Lord Wotton, Lord Stanhope, Mr. Vice-Chamberlein, Mr. Secretary Winwoode, Mr. Secretary Lake, Mr. Chancellor of the Exchequer, Master of the Roles.

His Majestie, havinge this day given order for meetinge of the Councell, and that all the Judges (being twelve in nomber) should bee sent for to bee present; when the Lordes were sett, and the Judges readie attendinge, his Majestie came himself in person to Councell, and openned unto them the cause of that assembly; which was, that hee had called them togeather concerninge a question that had relacion to noe private person, but concerned God and the Kinge, the power of his Crowne, and the state of his Church, whereof hee was Protector; and that there was noe fitter place to handle it then at the head of his Councell Table; that there had ben a question pleaded and argued concerninge *commendams*, the proceedinges wherein had either ben misreported, or mishandled; for his Majestie a yeare since had receaved advertizement concerninge that case in twoe extreames: by some, that it did trench farr into his Prerogative Royall, in the generall power of grauntinge commendams; and by others, that the doubt rested only upon a speciall nature of a commendam, such as in respect of the incongruitie and exorbitant forme therof might bee questioned, without impeachinge or weakeninge the generall power at all.

[A commendam was an ecclesiastical benefice "commended" to the care of a holder pending permanent appointment of an incumbent. It could be used to augment the income of higher churchmen; to permit, in effect, multiple holdings, with dispensatioin from requirements of residence. Earlier church legislation, starting with the Council of Constance in 1417, had attempted to restrict the practice. In 1610 the Bishop of Coventry and Lichfield had secured a general dispensation authorizing multiple holdings of benefices up to a ceiling of 200 marks income per year. In 1613 the Bishop had secured royal letters patent granting him in commendam the parsonage of Clifton Camvill. The reference by King James at the Privy Council meeting was to a case pending in the Common Pleas, *Colt and Glover v. Bishop of Coventry and Lichfield*, Hobart, 140 (1613). The plaintiffs claimed ownership of the advowson—power of appointment—to the parsonage; the crown claimed that this power of appointment had lapsed because the parsonage had been vacant for 18 months, so that the power accrued to the king, who exercised it by naming the Bishop of Coventry and Lichfield.]

Whereupon his Majestie, willinge to knowe the true state thereof, comaunded the Lord Bishop of Winchester and Mr. Secretarie Winwoode to bee present at the next argument, and to reporte the state of the question and proceedinges unto his Majestie; but Mr. Secretary Winwoode, beinge absent by occasion, the Lord [Bishop] of Winchester only was present, and gave informacion to his Majestie of the particulars thereof; which his Majestie commaunded him to reporte to the Boarde. Whereupon the Lord [Bishop] of Winchester stoode up and reported: That Sergeant Clibborne (who argued the case against the commendams) had maintayned divers assertions and positions very prejudiciall to his Majesty's Prerogative Royall:

As first, that the translacion of bishopps was against the cannon lawe, and, for authoritie, vouched the cannons of the Councell of Sardis.

That the Kinge had noe power to graunt commendams, but in case of necessitie.

That there could bee noe necessitie, because there was noe neede of augmentacion of livinges, for noe man was bounde to keepe hospitallitie above his meanes.

Besydes manie other partes of his argument tending to the overthrowe of his Majesty's prerogative in cases of commendam.

The Lord [Bishop] of Winchester havinge made this reporte, his Majestie resumed his former narrative, lettinge the lordes knowe that after the Lord [Bishop] of Winchester had made unto his Majestie a reporte of that which passed at the argument of the case, like in substaunce to that which hee had now made, his Majestie, apprehendinge the matter to bee so soe hiegh a nature, commaunded his Attorney Generall to signifie his Majesty's pleasure to the Lord Chiefe Justice; that in regarde of his Majesty's other most waighty occasions, and for that his Majestie helde it necessary (upon the Lord [Bishop] of Winchester's reporte), that his Majestie bee first consulted with, before the Judges proceeded to argument; therefore the day appointed for the Judges' arguments should bee putt of, till they might speake with his Majestie....

[The Privy Council Register then quotes a letter of April 25, 1616 from Francis Bacon, Attorney General, to Chief Justice Coke declaring that it was the King's "express pleasure" that there be no further proceedings in the pending case until the King had been first consulted. At Coke's request similar letters were then sent by Bacon to all the other judges of both Benches.]

Whereupon all the said Judges assembled, and by their letter under their haundes certefyed his Majestie that they helde those letters (importinge the significacion aforesaid) to bee contrary to lawe, and such as they could not yeild to the same by their oath; and that thereupon they had proceeded at the day, and did nowe certefie his Majesty thereof; which letter of the Judges his Majestie alsoe commaunded to bee openly read, the tenor whereof followeth, *in haec verba*: —

Most dread and most gracious Soveraigne.

It may please your most excellent Majestie to bee advertized that this letter inclosed was delivered to mee, your Chiefe Justice, on Thursday last in the afternoone, by a servaunt of your Majesty's Attorney Generall, and letters of like effect were, on the day followinge, sent from him by his servaunt to us, your Majesty's other Justices of every of your Courtes at Westminster. Wee are and ever wilbe readie with all faithfull and true hartes, accordinge to our bounden duties to serve and obey your Majestie, and thinke ourselves most happie to spende our lives and abillities to doe your Majestie faithfull and true service. In this present case, mencioned in this letter, what informacion hath ben made unto yow (whereupon Mr. Attorney doth ground his letter), from the report of the Bishop of Winchester, wee knowe not. This wee knowe, that the true substance of the case summarily is thus. It consisteth principally upon the construccion of twoe Acts of Parliament, the one of the 25 yeare of King Edward 3, and the other of the 25 yeare of King Henry 8; whereof your Majesty's Judges, upon their oathes, and accordinge to their best knowledge and learninge, are bounde to deliver the true understaundinge faithfully and uprightly. And the case is betweene subjects for private interrest and inheritaunce, earnestly called on for justice and expedition. Wee holde it our duties to informe your Majestie that our oathe is in theis expresse wordes: That in case anie letters come unto us contrary to lawe, that wee doe nothinge by such letters, but certefie your Majestie thereof, and goe forth to doe the lawe, notwithstaundinge the same letters. Wee have advisedly considered of the said letters of Mr. Attorney, and with one consent doe holde the same to bee contrary to lawe, and that wee could not yeild to the same by our oath; assuredly persuadinge ourselves that your Majestie, being truly informed that it staundeth not with your royall and just pleasure to give way to them, and therefore knowinge your Majesty's zeale to justice, and to bee most renowned therefore, wee have, accordinge to our oathes, and duties (at the day openly prefixed the last tearme) proceeded, and thereof certefyed your Majestie, and shall ever pray to the Almightie for your Majestie in all honor, health, and happiness longe to raigne over us."

Your Majesty's most humble and faithfull subjects and servaunts,

Edw. Coke, Henry Hobart, Laur. Tanfeilde, P. Warburton, Geo. Snigge, James Altham, Edw. Bromley, Jo. Croke, H. Winche, John Doddridge, Augustine Nicolls, Rob. Houghton.
Serjants' Inne, 27 April. . . .

[The King replied with the following letter.]

"Trustie and well-beloved Councellor, and trustie and wel-beloved; wee greete yow well. Wee perceave by your letter that you conceave the commaundement given yow by our Attorney Generall, in our name, to have proceeded upon wronge informacion. But if yee list to remember, what princely care wee have ever had, since our comeinge to this Crowne, to see justice duly administred to our subjects with all possible expedicion, and howe farr wee have ever benn from urginge the delay thereof in anie sorte, yee may easely persuade yourselves that it was noe smale reason which moved us to send yow that direccion. Yee might very well have spared your labor in informeinge us of the nature of your oath, for, although wee never studied the common lawe of Englaunde, yet are wee not ignoraunt of anie pointes which belonnge to a kinge to knowe. Wee are therefore to enforme yow hereby, that wee are farr from crossirge or delayinge anie thinge which may belonnge to the interest of anie private partie in this case. But wee cannot bee contented to suffer the prerogative royall of our Crowne to be wounded, through the sydes of a private person. Wee have noe care at all which of the parties shall wynn this processe in this case, soe right prevaile, and that justice bee duly administered. But upon the other parte, wee have reason to foresee, that nothinge be donn in this case which may wound our prerogative in generall; and, therefore, soe that wee may be sure that nothing shalbe debated amongst yow, which may concerne our generall power of givinge commendams, wee desire not the parties to have an hower's delay of justice. But, that our prerogative should not bee wounded in that regarde for all times hereafter, upon pretexte of a private partie's interrest wee sent yow that direccion; which wee accounte to be wounded aswell, if it bee publickly disnuted upon, as if anie sentence were given against it. We are therefore to admonish yow that, since the prerogative of our Crowne hath ben more boldly dealt withall in Westminster Hall duringe the time of our raigne then ever it was before in the raignes of divers princes ymediatly precedinge us, that wee will noe longer endure that popular and unlawfull libertie; and, therefore, were wee justly moved to sende yow that direccion to forbeare to meddle anie further in a case of soe tender a nature, till wee had further thought upon it. Wee have cause inded to rejoyce of your zeale for the speedie execution of justice; but wee would bee gladd that all our good subjects might soe finde the fruites thereof, as that noe pleas before yow were of older date then this is. But as to your argument which yow found upon your oath, yow give our predecessors, who first founded that oath, a very uncharitable meetinge, in pervertinge their intention and zeale to justice, to make a weapon of it to use against their successors. For, although your oath bee, that yow shall not delay justice betwixt anie private parties, yet was it not meant that the Kinge should thereby receave harme, before hee bee forewarned thereof. Neither can yee denye but that every tearme yee will, out of your owne discretions, for reasons knowne unto yow, put of either the hearinge or determininge of an ordinary cause amongst private persons, till the next tearme followings. Our pleasure therefore is, who are the heade and fountaine of justice under God, in our dominions, and wee, out of our absolute authoritie royall, doe commaunde yow, that yow forbeare to meedle anie further in this plea, till our comeinge to the towne, and that out of our owne mouth yow may heare our pleasure in this business; which wee doe only out of the care wee have that our prerogative may not receave an unwittinge and indirect blowe, and not to hinder justice to bee ministred to anie private parties; which noe importunitie shall persuade us to move yow in, like as only for avoydinge the unreasonable importunitie of suitors in their owne particular, that oath was by our predecessors ordayned to be ministered unto yow. Soe wee hartely wish yow well to fare.

Postscript.—Yow shall upon the receipt of this our letter call our Attorney Generall unto yow, who will informe yow of the particular pointes which wee are unwillinge should bee publickly disputed in this case."

This letter beinge read, his Majestie resorted to take into his consideracion the partes of the Judges' letter, and other their proceedinges in that cause, and the errors therein committed and contayned: which errors his Majestie did sett forth to bee both in matter and manner: in matter, as well by way of omission as commission; for omission, that it was a faulte in the Judges that when they hearde a Councellor at the bar presume to argue against his Majesty's prerogative (which in this case was in effect his supremacy), they did not interrupt him, and reproove sharply that loose and bold course of disaffirmeinge and impeachinge thinges of soe hiegh a nature, by discourse; especially since his Majestie had observed, that ever since his comeinge to this Crowne the popular sorte of lawiers have ben the men that most affrontedly in all Parlaments have troden upon his prerogative; which beinge most contrary to their vocation of anie men, since the lawe, nor lawyers can never bee respected if the Kinge bee not reverenced, it therefore best became the Judges of anie to checque and brydle such impudent lawyers, and in their severall Benches to disgrace them that beare soe litle respect to the King's authoritie and prerogative. That his Majestie had a doble prerogative, whereof the one was ordinary, and had relacion to his private interrest, which mought bee, and was, every day disputed in Westminster Hall. The other was of a hiegher nature, referringe to his supreme and imperiall power and soveragnitie, which ought not to bee disputed or handled in vulgar argument; but that of late the Courtes of the Common Lawe were growne soe vaste and transcendent, as they did both meddle with the King's prerogative, and had incroached upon all other Courtes of Justice, as the High Commission, the Councells established in Wales and Yorke, the Court of Requests. Concerninge that which might be tearmed Comission, his Majestie tooke exception to the Judges' letter, both in matter and forme. For matter, his Majestie did plainely demonstrate that, whereas it was contayned in the Judges' letter, that the significacion of his Majesty's pleasure as aforesaid was contrary to lawe and not agreeable to the oath of a Judge, that could not bee.

First, for that the puttinge of hearinge, or proceedinge upon, just and necessary cause is no denyinge or delay of justice, but a wisedome and maturitie of proceedinge, and that there cannot bee a more just and necessary cause of stay then the consultinge with the Kinge, when the cause concernes the Crowne, and that the Judges did dayly put of causes upon lighter occasions. And likewise his Majestie did desire to knowe of the Judges how his callinge them to consulte with him was contrary to lawe, which they never could aunsweare unto.

Secondly, that it was noe bare supposition or surmize that this case concerned the Kinges prerogative, for that it had ben directly and largly disputed at the barr, and the very disputinge thereof in a publicke audience is both daingerous and dishonorable to his Majestie.

Thirdly, that the manner of puttinge of which the Kinge required was not infinite, nor for lounge time, but grounded upon his Majesty's waighty occasions, which were notorious; by reason whereof hee could not speake with the Judges before the argument, and that there was a certaine expectation of his Majesty's speedie retorne at Whitsuntide, and likewise that the case had ben soe lately argued, and could not receave judgment till Easter tearme next, as the Judges themselves afterwardes confessed.

And lastlie, because there was another just cause of absence for the twoe Cheife Justices, for that they ought to have assisted the Lord Chancellor the same day in a great cause of the Kinges, followed by the Lord Hunsdon against the Lord William Howarde in Chancerie; which cause of the Kinges (specially beinge soe waightie) ought to have had precedence before anie cause betweene partie and partie.

Also, whereas it was contayned in the Judges' letter that the case of the commendams was but a case of private interrest betweene partie and partie, his Majestie shewed plainely the contrary, not only by the argument of Serjaunt Chibborne, which was before his commaundement, but by the argument of the Judges themselves (namely Justice Nicholls), which was after; but especially since one of the parties is a Bishopp, who pleads for the commendam, only by the virtue of his Majesty's prerogative.

Also, whereas it was contayned in the Judges' letter that the parties called upon them earnestly for justice, his Majestie conceaves it to bee but pretence, urgeing them to prove that there was anie sollicitation by the parties for expedicion, otherwise then in an ordinary course of attendaunce, which they could never prove.

As for the forme of the letter, his Majestie noated that it was a newe thinge, and very undecent, and unfitt for subjects to disobey the Kinges commaundment, but most of all to proceede in the meanetime, and to retorne unto him a bare certificate; whereas they ought to have concluded with the layinge downe and repesentinge of their reasons modestly unto his Majestie, why they should proceede, and soe to have submitted the same to his princely judgment, expectinge to knowe from him wheather they had given him satisfaccion.

After this his Majesty's declaration, all the Judges fell downe upon their knees, and acknowledged their error, for matter of forme, humbly cravinge his Majesty's gracious favour and pardon for the same.

But for the matter of the letter, the Lord Cheife Justice of the Kinges Bench entred into a defence thereof, the effect whereof was, that the stay required by his Majestie was a delay of justice, and, therefore, contrary to lawe and the Judges' oath; and that the Judges knewe well amongst themselves, that the case (as they meant to handle it) did not concerne his Majesty's prerogative of graunt of commendams, and that if the day had not helde by the not-comeinge of the Judges, the suite had ben discontinewed; which had ben a faylinge in justice, and that they could not adjourne it, because Mr. Attorney's letter mencioned noe day certaine, and that an adjornment must alwaies bee to a day certaine.

Unto which aunsweare of the Chiefe Justice, his Majestie did replye, that for the last conceipt, it was meere sophistrie, for that they might in their discretions have prefixed a convenient day, such as there might have ben time for them to consult with his Majestie before the same, and that his Majestie leafte that pointe of forme to themselves.

And for that other pointe, that they should take upon them peremptorily to discerne whether the case concerned the Kinges prerogative, without consultinge with his Majestie first, an informeinge his princely judgment, was a thing preposterous, for that they ought first to have made that appeare to his Majestie, and soe to have given him assurance thereof, upon consultacion with him.

And as for the mayne matter, that it should bee against the lawe, and against their oath, his Majestie sayde hee had sayed enough before; unto which the Lord Chiefe Justice in effect had made no aunsweare, but only insisted upon the former opinion; and therefore the Kinge required the Lord Chancellor to deliver his opinion upon that pointe, whether the stay that had ben required by his Majestie were contrary to lawe, or against the Judges' oath....

[The Chancellor first asked Bacon, Attorney General, to give his opinion, which was strongly to the effect that the oaths of the judges required them to consult with the King when called on to do so. Coke objected, saying that the Attorney General was supposed to "plead before the Judges, but not to dispute with them." The King replied that Bacon had acted in accordance with his duty, in whose performance the King would "mayntaine" him.]

After this the Lord Chancellor delivered his opinion, cleerely and plainely, that the stay which had beene by his Majestie required was not against lawe, nor any breach of a Judge's oath, and required that the oath itself might bee read out of the statute, which was donn by the Kinges Sollicitor, and all the wordes thereof waighed and considered.

Thereupon his Majestie and the Lordes thought good to aske the Judges severally their opinion; the question beinge put in this manner: Whether if at anie time in a case dependinge before the Judges, which his Majestie conceaved to concerne him, either in power or profitt, and thereupon required to consult with him, and that they should stay proceedinges in the meanetime, they ought not to stay accordingly. They all (the Lord Chiefe Justice only excepted) yeilded that they would, and acknowledged it to bee their dutie soe to doe; only the Lord Chiefe Justice of the King's Bench sayd for aunsweare that when that case should bee, hee would doe that should bee fitt for a Judge to doe, and the Lord Chiefe Justice of the Common Pleas, who had assented with the rest, added, that hee would ever trust the justnes of his Majesty's comaundement.

After this was put to a pointe, his Majestie thought fitt, in respect of the further day of argument appointed the Saturday followeinge for the commendams, to knowe from his Judges what hee might expect from them concerninge the same. Whereupon the Lord of Canterburie breakeinge the case into some questions, his Majestie did require his Judges to deale plainely with him, whether they meant in their argument to touch the generall power of grauntinge commendams, yea or noe. Whereupon all his said Judges did promisse and assure his Majestie that, in the argument of the said case of commendams, they would speake nothinge which should weaken, or drawe into doubte, his Majesty's prerogative for the grauntinge of them, but intended particularly to insist upon the pointe of the laps, and other individuall pointes of this case, which they conceaved to bee of a forme differringe from all other commendams which have ben practized.

The Judges alsoe went further, and did promise his Majestie that they would not only abstaine from speakeinge anie thinge to weaken his Majesty's prerogative of commendams, but would directly and in plaine tearmes affirme the same, and correct the erronious and bold speeches which had ben used at the barr in derogation thereof.

Alsoe, all the Judges did in generall acknowledge and professe, with greate forwardnes that it was their dutie, if anie councellor at the barr presumed at anie time to call in question his Majesty's hiegh prerogatives and regallities, that they ought to reprehende them and silence them; and all promised soe to doe hereafter.

Lastly, the twoe Judges, which were then next to argue, Mr. Justice Dodridge and Mr. Justice Winche, openned themselves unto his Majestie thus farr, that they would insist chiefely upon the laps, and some pointes of uncertaintie, repugnancy and absurditie, beinge peculiar to this commendam, and that they would shewe their dislike of that which had ben sayde at the barr for the weakeninge of the generall power; and Mr. Justice Doddridge sayde that he would conclude for the Kinge that the Church was voyde, and in his Majesty's guifte; and alsoe sayde that the King might give a commendam to a Bishop, either before or after his consecretion, and that hee might either give it him duringe his life, or for a certaine number of yeares.

The Judges havinge thus farr submitted and declared themselves, his Majestie admonished them to keepe the boundes and lymitts of their several Courtes, not to suffer his prerogative to bee wounded by rash and unadvised pleadinge before them, or by newe inventions of lawe. For as hee well knewe that the true and ancient common lawe is the most favourable for kinges of anie lawe in the worlde; soe hee advised them to apply themselves to the studie and practize of that ancient and best lawe, and not to extende the power of anie of their Courtes beyounde their due lymitts, followinge the president of the best ancient Judges, in the times of best Govermentes and that then they might assure themselves that hee for his parte in the proteccion of them and expediting of justice, would walke in the stepps of the ancient and best kinges. And thereupon gave them leave to proceede in their argument.

When the Judges were removed, his Majestie, that had forborne to aske the votes and opinions of his councell before the Judges, because hee would not prejudicate the freedome of the Judges' opinions concerninge the point; whether the stay of proceedinges that had ben by his Majestie required, could by anie construccion bee thought to bee within the compasse of the Judges' oath (which they had hearde reade unto them), did then put the question to his Councell, who all with one consent did give opinion that it was farr from anie colour or shadowe of such interpretacion, and that it was against common sence to thinke the contrary, especially since there is noe mention made in their oath of the delay of justice, but only that they shall not deny justice, nor bee moved by anie of the Kinges letters to doe any thinge contrary to lawe, or justice.

> G. Cant., T. Ellesmere, Canc., T. Suffolke,
> E. Worcester, Lenox, Nottingham, Pembroke,
> W. Knollis, John Digbye, Raphe Winwoode,
> Tho. Lake, Fulk Grevill, Jul. Caesar,
> Fr. Bacon.

Note (J.P. Dawson)

On June 26 and again on June 30, 1616 Coke was called before the Privy Council for further discussion. The following report to the King from the Privy Council of the conversations that ensued is recorded in the Privy Council Register.

Acts of the Privy Council, 1615–1616, 644–650.

June 26. It may please your most excellent Majestie.

The Lorde Chiefe Justice, presentinge himself on his knee at the Boarde, your Sollictor signifyed: That hee was by your commaundement to charge him for certaine acts and speeches, wherein your Majestie was much unsatisfyed; which were in nomber three.

1. First, an act donn.

2. Secoundly, speeches of hiegh contempt utterred in a seate of justice.

3. Thirdly, uncomely and undutifull carryage in the presence of your Majestie, your Privie Councell, and your Judges....

[The first charge against Coke was that in 1604, while Attorney-General, he had helped to draft two recognizances that were executed by his stepson and made payable to Coke himself, by which payment was deferred of a debt due the King from Sir Christopher Hatton, former Chancellor and deceased father of the obligor. As to this charge, Coke's main defenses were the absence of any harm to the King's interests or of any profit to himself.]

The secounde pointe was, wordes spoken in the Kinges Bench, the last day of Hillary tearme last, in a case of Glanvile and Allen, whereof your Sollicitor made a narrative relacion, and charged the Lord Chiefe Justice to have given too much harte and incoragement to that cause. That hee had too constauntly directed the jury, turned them thrice from the barr, threatenned to comitt them, examined them by the pole, and tolde them that they had ben tamperred withall. That hee had given warneinge to the councellors at the barr that, if they sett their haundes to a Bill after judgment, hee would foreclose them the Courte; and further in another case the same day sayde, that the Common Lawe of Englaunde would bee overthrowen, and that the light of the lawe would bee obscurred, and that all this was confirmed by good wittnes.

The thirde and last pointe was, his undecent behaviour before your Majestie, your Councell, and your Judges; and that consisted of twoe partes. First, the exception hee tooke at your learned councell in your presence for speakinge by your commaundement.

The second, that your Majestie havinge opennned yourself in the case of commendams, and satisfyed the Judges, that your Majestie sendinge unto them had noe intent to delay justice; and question beinge putt to the rest of the Judges, whether they did hold it for a delay of justice, that your Majestie had sent in that cause, or if yow shoulde send hereafter in a like case, wherein your Majesty's prerogative were interressed, the rest of the Judges submittinge themselves, hee alone dissented from all the rest.

This beinge the effect of your Solicitor's charge, the Lord Chiefe Justice made aunsweare: That hee would by their lordship's favours, beginn with the last, and sayde, that for the pointe of challendginge and takeinge exception at your Majesty's councell learned speakinge in the case of comendams by your Majesty's commaundement, hee acknowledged it for an error, and humbly submitted himself.

To the pointe, that upon the question asked the Judges touchinge stay of proceedinges, hee did deny, when all the rest of the Judges did yeild, his aunsweare was: that the question included a multitude of particulars, which suddenly occurringe to his minde, caused him to make that aunsweare, that when that time should bee, hee would doe that which should become an honest and just Judge....

For his speeches in the Kinges Bench, etc., hee sayeth first, that whatsoever was donn, was donn by common consent, and for those speeches, manie of them were spoken and hee knewe by whom they were spoken, but not by himself: and then offerred fower consideracions.

1. That the commission (unto which nevertheles hee did in noe wise except) was *ad informandum non ad convincendum*.

2. That there were but witnesses on one syde.

3. That the interrogatories might bee drawne too shorte.

4. That it was concerninge wordes spoken fower moneths agoe, which beinge spoken amongst manie might bee reported diversly, and thereupon produced a paper writen by himself, contayneinge (as hee sayeth) the true passages of that day; which paper wee present to your Majestie herewithall, beinge, as hee sayd, sette downe by himself the next after, *sedato animo*.

And touchinge the wordes: that the common lawe would bee overthrowen, and that the Judges would have but little to doe at Assizes, because the light of the lawe would bee obscured, hee confesseth the wordes, but sayth they were not spoken the same day, but another time in a cause of Sir Anthonie Mildmaies; and added, that hee will not maintaine the differrence betweene the twoe Courtes, nor bringe it into question; yet, if it were an error, hee may say *Erravimus cum patribus*; and thereupon alleadged three examples: first, the articles against Cardinall Wolsey, 21 Henry 8, wherein the same wordes are used that such proceedinges in Chancery tended to the subversion of the common lawe; secoundly, the booke called the *Doctor and Student*; and thirdly, an opinion of the Judges in Throgmorton's case in Queen Elizabeth's time: addinge further that for the time to come there was noe dainger; for that the Judges, havinge receaved your Majesty's commaundement, by your Attorney Generall, that noe Bills of that nature should hereafter bee receaved, hee and his bretheren have caused the same to bee entred as an order in the same Courte, which shalbe observed.

Which beinge the effect of his aunsweare, wee have thought good withall to add that before us, aswell in speech as in action, hee behaved himself very modestly and submissively.

This certificate was made the 26 day of this present June.

At the Court at Greenewich, Sonday morneineinge (*sic*), the 30th of June, 1616.

Present: Lord Archbishop of Canterburie, Lord Treasurer, Lord Privie Seale, Lord Zouch, Lord Knollis, Lord Wotton, Mr. Vice-Chamberlein, Mr. Secretary Winwoode, Mr. Secretary Lake, Mr. Chancellor of the Exchecquer, Master of the Roles, Mr. Attorney Generall.

Sir Edward Coke, knight, Chiefe Justice of the King's Bench, presentinge himself this day at thes Boarde, upon his knees, Mr. Secretary Winwoode signifyed unto him that their lordships had made reporte to his Majestie of that which passed on Wednesday last at Whithall, where hee was charged by his Majesty's Sollicitor with certaine thinges, wherein his Majesty was much unsatisfyed: which report contayned a true and just relacion, aswell of those thinges which were then objected against him, as of his aunsweares thereunto in particular, and that, rather to his advantage then otherwise; which beinge delivered in writinge, and in his princely judgment duly waighed and considered of, his Majestie was noe way satisfyed with his aunsweares to anie of those three pointes, wherewith he stood charged, vizt.: neither in that which hee made concerninge the bonde and defeasaunce upon the installment of a debte of Sir Christopher Hatton, late Lord Chancellor of Englaund; nor yet in that which hee maketh concerninge his speeches of hiegh contempt, utterred as he sate in the seate of justice, concerninge the overthrowe of the common law; nor lastly, in the aunsweare hee offereth to excuse his uncivill and indiscreete carryage before his Majestie, assisted with his Privie Councell and his Judges: but that the charge lyeth still upon him, notwithstandinge anie thinge contayned in his said aunsweares.

Nevertheles, such is his Majesty's clemencie and goodnes, as hee is pleased not to proceede heavely against him but rather to looke upon the meritt of his former services; and accordingly hath decreed.

First: that hee bee sequestred from the Councell Table, untill his Majesty's pleasure be further knowne.

Secoundly: that hee doe forbeare to ryde this sommer's circuit as Justice of Assize.

Lastly: that duringe this vacacion, while hee hath time to live privately and dispose himself at home, hee take into his consideracion and review his bookes of Reportes, wherein (as his Majestie is informed) there bee manie exorbitaunt and extravagant opinions sett downe and published for positive and good lawe; and if, in the review and reading thereof, hee finde anie thinge fitt to be altred or amended, the correctinge thereof is leaft to his discretion. Amongst other thinges, his Majestie was not well pleased with the tytle of those bookes, wherein hee styled himself Lord Chiefe Justice of Englaunde, whereas he could challendge noe more then Chiefe Justice of the Kinges Bench. And havinge corrected what in his discretion hee found meete in those Reportes, his Majesty's pleasure was, that hee should bringe the same privately to himself, that he might consider thereof, as in his princely judgement should bee found expedient. Hereunto the Secretary advised him to corforme himself in all dutie and obeydience, as hee ought, whereby hee might hope that his Majestie in time would receave him againe to his gracious and princely favour.

Hereunto the Lord Chiefe Justice made aunsweare; that hee did in all humillitie prostrate himself to his Majesty's good pleasure: that he acknowledged the decree to bee just, and proceeded rather from his Majesty's exceedinge mercie, then from his justice; gave humble thankes to their lordships for their favour and goodnes towards him, and hoped that his behaviour for the future should bee such as should deserve their lordship's favour.

My lordes havinge thus farr proceeded, the Lorde Treasurer told him that hee had one thinge more to lett him knowe, which belounged to the Erles Marshall's to take notice, of, and was, that his coachman used of late to ryde bareheaded before him, which was more than hee could anie way challendge or assume to himself, and required him to forbeare it for the future. To which the Lord Chiefe Justice aunsweared: that the coachman did it for his owne ease, and not by his commaundement. And soe, with the like submission and acknowledgment of favour, departed.

NOTE [J.P. Dawson]

As directed by the King, Coke spent the summer reviewing the eleven volumes of his Reports that had so far been published, containing more than 500 reported cases. He came back early in October with a list of five minor mistakes of fact or in translation. There followed a period of indecision on the part of James and his advisers, of whom the most prominent was Francis Bacon. Finally, on Nov. 14, 1616 the King's letter of dismissal from judicial office, drafted by Bacon, was handed to Coke.

Lord Chancellor Ellesmere, at the induction of Sir Henry Mountague as Coke's successor as Chief Justice of the King's Bench, opened his speech with a passage that probably expressed the views of many contemporaries.

Ellesmere's Speech to Sir Henry Mountague, Nov. 18, 1616 (Moore, 826).

Sir Henry Mountague,

The Kings Majesty in the governing of his Subjects, representeth the Divine Majesty of almighty God; for it is truly said of God, that *Infima per media ducit ad summa* [The lowest leads through the middle to the highest]. This I said lately in another place upon another occasion: this is my case, and this is your case, for after almost 14 years experience of your Wisdom, Learning, and Integrity, his Majesty is now graciously pleased to addresse unto you his Writ, under the Great Seal, calling you thereby to be his Chief Justice in this place, for Pleas to be holden before himself. A case rare, for you are called to a place vacant, not by death or cession, but by amotion and deposing of him that held the place before you, and that not as Sir William Thorpe in the time of the absence of King Ed. 3 when there was a Custos Regni; nor as Sir Robert Tresilian in the disordered and unruly time of King R.2. But in the peaceable and happy Reign of Great King James the great King of Great Brittain, wherein you see the Prophet Davids words true, He putteth down one, and setteth up another; a Lesson to be learned of all, and to be remembered and feared of all that sit in Judicial places.

THE FIVE KNIGHTS' CASE (1627)

Note: This case resulted in the great "Petition of Right." There is irony in Coke's role at this time. He has ceased to be a judge, and is now a leader in the Parliament, opposed to the King. John Selden (1584–1654), who argued this case, was one of the first genuinely analytical English legal historians, for whom the Selden Society is named. He was a man of courage!

THE FIVE KNIGHTS' CASE, 3 STATE TRIALS 1 (1627)

The king having deprived himself of the prospect of all parliamentary Aids, by dissolving the parliament, and yet resolving to prosecute the war; it was necessary to project all possible ways and means of raising money; to which end letters were sent to the Lords Lieutenants of the counties, to return the names of the persons of ability, and what sums they could spare; and the Comptroller of the king's Household issued forth letters in the king's name, under the privy seal, to several persons returned for the Loan-money; some were assessed £20, some £15, and others £10 and Commissioners were appointed with private instructions how to behave themselves in this affair, and divers lords of the council were appointed to repair into their counties to advance the Loan. Collectors were also appointed to pay into the exchequer the sums received, and to return the names of such as refused, or discovered a disposition to delay the payment of the sums imposed. This assessment of the general-Loan did not pass currently with the people, for divers persons refused to subscribe or lend at the rate proposed; the non-subscribers of high rank in all counties were bound over by recognizances to tender their appearance at the Council-board, and performed the same accordingly, and divers of them committed to prison: which caused great murmuring. But amongst those many gentlemen who were imprisoned throughout England, for refusing to lend upon the Commission of Loans, only five of them brought their Habeas Corpus, viz. sir Thomas Darnel, sir John Corbet, sir Walter Earl, sir John Heveningham, and Sir Edmund Hampden.

Mr. SELDEN'S Argument at the King's-bench bar the same day.

My Lords; I am of counsel with sir Edm. Hampden; his case is the same with the other two gentlemen: I cannot hope to say much, after that that hath been said; yet if it shall please your lordship, I shall remember you of so much as is befallen my lot. Sir Edmund Hampden is brought hither by a writ of Habeas Corpus, and the keeper of the Gatehouse hath returned upon the writ, that sir Edm. Hampden is detained in prison 'per speciale mandatum domini regis, mihi significatum per warrantum duorum privati concilii dicti domini regis.' [by special command of the lord king, to me signified by the warrant of two of the Privy Council of the said lord king]. And then he recited the warrant of the lords of the council, which is, that they do will and require him to detain this gentleman still in prison, letting him know that his first imprisonment, &c. May it please your lordship, I shall humbly move you that this gentleman may also be bailed; for under favour, my lord there is no cause to the return, why he should be any farther imprisoned and restrained of his liberty.

My lord, I shall say something to the form of the writ; and of the return; but very little to them both, because there is a very little left for me to say....

Now, my lord, I will speak a word or two to the matter of the return; and that is touching the imprisonment, 'per speciale mandatum domini regis,' by the lords of the council, without any cause expressed: and admitting of any, or either, or both of these to be the return; I think that by the constant and settled laws of this kingdom, without which we have nothing, no man can be justly imprisoned by either of them, without a cause of the commitment expressed in the return. My lord, in both the last arguments the statutes have been mentioned and fully expressed: yet I will add a little to that which hath been said.

The statute of Magna Charta, cap. 29, that statute if it were fully executed as it ought to be, every man would enjoy his liberty better than he doth. The law saith expressly, 'No freeman shall be imprisoned without due process of the law;' out of the very body of this act of parliament, besides the explanation of other statutes, it appears, '*Nullus liber homo capiatur vel imprisonatur nisi per legem terrae.*' My lord, I know these words '*legem terrae,*' do leave the question where it was, if the interpretation of the statute were not. But I think under your lordship's favour, there it must be intended by due course of law, to be either by presentment or by indictment....

The Judgement

On Thursday the 28th of November, Michaelis, 3 Caroli Regis, [1627] Chief-Justice Hyde, Justice Doderidge, Justice Jones, and Justice Whitlock on the bench: Sir John Corbet, sir Walter Earl, sir John Heveningham, and sir Edmund Hampden at the bar.

HYDE, C. J. I am sure you here expect the resolution of the whole Court, as accordingly yesterday we told you you should have. This is a case of very great weight and great expectation, and it had been fit we should have used more solemn arguments of it than now for the shortness of the time we can do; for you have been long in prison, and it is fit you should know whereunto you should trust: I am sure you expect justice from hence, and God forbid we should sit here but to do justice to all men according to our best skill and knowledge, for it is our oaths and duties so to do, and I am sure there is nothing else expected of us. We are sworn to maintain all Prerogatives of the king, that is one branch of our oath; and we are likewise sworn to administer justice equally to all people.

These three Statutes, as for example, the Statute of Magna Charta, 25 E. 3, and 36 E. 3, and the Statute of Westminster primo, and divers other statutes that have been alledged, and particularly disputed of, we all acknowledge and resolve, that they are good laws, and that they be in force: but the interpretation of them at this time belongs not to us, for we are driven to another point; and though the meaning of them belongs to the one way or the other, yet our judgment must be the same; for that which is now to be judged by us is this, Whether one that is committed by the king's authority, and no cause declared of his commitment, according as here it is upon this return, whether we ought to deliver him by bail, or to remand him back again? Wherein you must know this which your counsel will tell you, we can take notice only of this return; and when the case appears to come to us no otherwise than by the return, we are not bound to examine the truth of the return, but the sufficiency of it, for there is a great difference between the sufficiency and the truth.

We cannot judge upon rumours nor reports, but upon that which is before us on record....

Now the Precedents, you urged them to be so many, and so fully to the point, that we may thereby see that it is good to hear what can be said on both sides, and for to hear all, and view the Records themselves; and therefore we required you to bring the Records to us, and you did so, and you brought us more than you mentioned here; and we have perused them all.... But this I dare affirm, that no one of the Records that you have cited, doth inforce what you have concluded out of them, no not one; and therefore as you have cited Records and Precedents, Precedents shall judge this case....

Now here I shall trouble you with no more Precedents, and you see your own what conclusion they produce. And as to those strong precedents alledged on the other side, we are not wiser than they that went before us; and the common custom of the law is, the Common Law of the land, and that hath been the continual common custom of the law, to which we are to submit, for we come not to change the law, but to submit to it....

But the question now is, Whether we may deliver this gentleman or not? You see what hath been the practice in all the kings times heretofore, and your own Records; and this resolution of all the Judges teacheth us, and what can we do but walk in the steps of our forefathers? If you ask me which way you should be delivered, we shall tell you, we must not counsel you.

Mr. Attorney hath told you that the king hath done it, and we trust him in great matters, and he is bound by law, and he bids us proceed by law, as we are sworn to do, and so is the king; and we make no doubt but the king, if you seek to him, he knowing the cause why you are imprisoned, he will have mercy; but we leave that. If in justice we ought to deliver you, we would do it; but upon these grounds, and these Records, and the Precedents and Resolutions, we cannot deliver you, but you must be remanded. Now if I have mistaken any thing, I desire to be righted by my brethren, I have endeavoured to give the Resolutions of us all.

THE PARLIAMENTARY PROCEEDINGS

The Five Knights continued in custody until January 29, 1628, when they were released by the King. It was no coincidence that a new Parliament was to be called. One of its first items of business was to discuss the Five Knights, commencing on March 22, 1628.

[On March 25 the Commons resolved itself into a committee of the whole to discuss "the Subject's Liberty in his Person." On March 29 the King's Solicitor cited Coke's own decision in 1616, refusing to release a prisoner arrested on an order of the Privy Council.]

To this sir *Edward Coke* replied: This report moves not me at all; that report is not yet 21 years old, but under age, being in 13 Jac. In truth, when I read Stamford, I was of his opinion at the first, but since, looking into those Records before-mentioned, I was of another mind. He brings in an ill time 13 Jac. when there was clashing between the Court of King's-bench and Chancery, as also there were then many of the traitors that were of the Powder-Treason, committed 'per mandatum concilii.'

Upon Monday, April 1, the Debate being re-assumed, sir Robert Philips moved, That considering the house was now ready for the question, they might hear the resolution read of all the Judges in 34 Eliz. about this matter.
Then

Sir *Edward Coke* stood up and said, The glass of Time runs out, and something cast upon us hath retarded us; when I spake against the Loans and this matter, I expected blows, and somewhat was spoken, though not to the matter. Concerning that (that hath been objected), I did when I was a Judge, I will say somewhat. Indeed, a motion was made, but no argument or debate, or resolution upon advice;

I will never palliate with this house, there is no Judge that hath an upright heart to God, and a clear heart to the world, but he hath some warrant for every thing that he doth. I confess when I read Stamford [Staunford] then, and had it in my hands, I was of that opinion at the Council-Table; but when I perceived that some members of this house were taken away, even in the face of this house, and sent to prison, and when I was not far off from that place myself, I went to my book, and would not be quiet till I had satisfied myself. Stamford at the first was my guide, but my guide had deceived me, therefore I swerved from it: I have now better guides, Acts of Parliament and other precedents, these are now my guides. I desire to be free from the imputation that hath been laid upon me....

[The House of Commons then proceeded to vote unanimously for the following resolution:]

"I. That no Freeman ought to be detained or kept in prison, or otherwise re-strained by the command of the king or privy-council, or any other, unless some cause of the commitment, detainer or restraint be expressed, for which by law he ought to be committed, detained or restrained.

"II. That the Writ of Habeas Corpus may not be denied, but ought to be granted to every man that is committed or detained in prison, or otherwise re-strained, though it be by the command of the king, the privy-council, or any other, he praying the same.

"III. That if a Freeman be committed or detained in prison, or otherwise re-strained by the command of the king, the privy-council, or any other, no cause of such commitment, detainer, or restraint being expressed, for which by law he ought to be committed, detained, or restrained, and the same be returned upon an Habeas Corpus, granted for the said party; then he ought to be delivered or bailed.

"IV. That it is the antient and indubitable Right of every Freeman, that he hath a full and absolute property in his goods and estate; that no Tax, Taillage, Loan Benevolence, or other like charge ought to be commanded, or levied by the king, or any of his ministers, without common consent by act of parliament."

Note 1.

The above Items I-IV are the famous "Petition of Right." After much debate, the House of Lords also assented to the "Petition" and, after further delay, the King appeared to assent on June 3, 1628. On June 26, 1628, however the King dissolved the Parliament and retrenched on his assent to the "Petition." From 1629 to 1640, no Parliament was called, and by 1642 civil war had broken out. It still remains unclear as to what "assent" was actually given to the "Petition" and whether it has any status as law. There can be no doubt, however, of its fundamental symbolic importance. This was certainly noted, over time, in England's American colonies.

Note 2. (J.P. Dawson)

In later times the common law judges have been much criticized for their failure to give greater effect to the Petition of Right in the decade 1630–1640. Whether this criticism was just must depend in part on the legal effect that the Petition was intended to have. It seems clear that this experiment in constitution-making was not thought of by its sponsors as a statute. The most plausible view is that

"What they really seem to be doing is petitioning the King that a particular interpretation of certain laws in certain specific cases is to be regarded by the courts as the right one.... The great gain the Commons
had made, was that it had placed on record the King's acceptance of the
statement that according to these laws certain definite grievances were illegal. But it went no further than this: it laid down no wide constitutional principles that the judges could regard as binding."

(E.R. Adair, "The Petition of Right," 5 *History* n.s. 99).

Note 3.

Notice how Coke's role at this time is no longer that of a judge, but of a
politician. Was it reasonable to expect the judges, at this time of political confrontations, to enforce the Petition of Right? Or are some matters too fundamentally political for the courts? What if Nixon had refused the tapes subpoena? In
any event, such questions certainly indicate that a justice system has come to
great danger. In the case of England in 1628, a terrible civil war was just ahead.
It is interesting to note that the American Civil War was also preceded by important court cases and legal controversies, such as the infamous *Dred Scott v. Sandford* case, 60 U.S. (19 How.) 393 (1857), set out in Chapter XIII, *infra*.

As we will see in the next chapter (XI), the American colonists took careful
note of the Petition of Right and the events that led to the English Civil War.
When they eventually formed their own government, they attempted to avoid
prior mistakes, and to establish a strong, independent judiciary. Although the
issue of slavery defeated their initial goals, the long-run solutions embodied in the
American Constitution have proved strong over time. For this, in a sense, we can
thank the lessons of the cases set out above, so carefully learned by our founders.

COKE'S INSTITUTES

In addition to his famous *Reports*, Coke wrote four "Institutes," or treatises
about the English law. Of these, only the first was published during his lifetime.
That "Institute," the *First Institute* or *Coke on Litteton*, was published in 1628. It
was an elaborate commentary on a small earlier text on land law, Littleton's
Tenures, written before 1481. See Illustration 9-1, *supra*. The remaining three *Institutes* were inherently more controversial. The *Second Institutes*, published in 1642,
was a commentary on important statues, including the *Magna Carta*. The *Third Institutes*, published in 1644, focused on criminal law, and the *Fourth Institutes*, also
published in 1644, focused on the jurisdiction of the courts, including Parliament.

The first of the two following excerpts comes from the *Third Institutes* and deals
with torture. Here Coke asserted, for the first time, that torture is contrary to the
common law of England. What basis was there, in reality, for Coke's assertion? See
John H. Langbein, *Torture and the Law of Proof* (Chicago, 1976).

The second excerpt is from the *Fourth Institutes*. Is this assertion of the absolute
power of the Parliament consistent with *Dr. Bonham's Case, Materials, supra*? Did
Coke's experiences in the *Case of the Commendams* and other matters change his
views on legislative sovereignty? Regardless, Coke today is remembered for his
courageous defense of individual rights and judicial independence. His statue, in
fact, looks down on the courtroom of the Supreme Court of the United States.

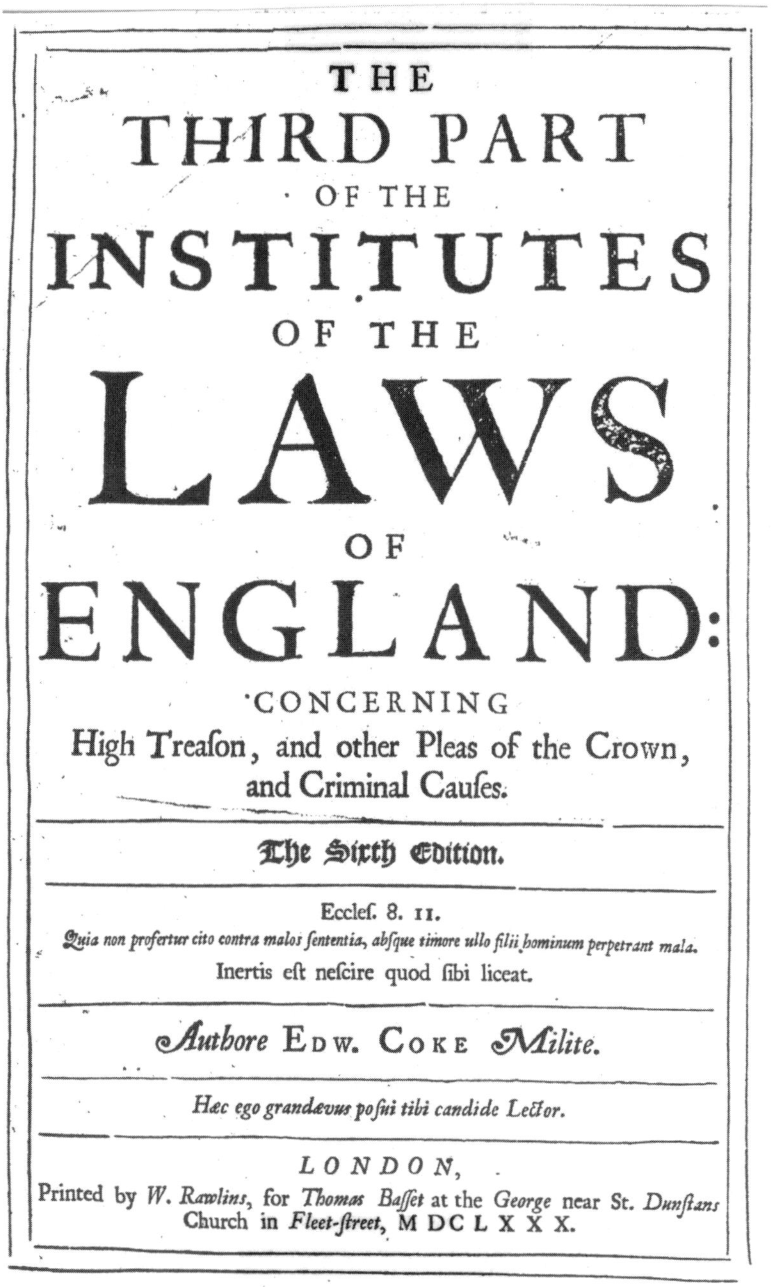

THE
THIRD PART
· OF THE
INSTITUTES
OF THE
LAWS
OF
ENGLAND:

·CONCERNING

High Treaſon, and other Pleas of the Crown,
and Criminal Cauſes.

𝕿𝖍𝖊 𝕾𝖎𝖝𝖙𝖍 𝕰𝖉𝖎𝖙𝖎𝖔𝖓.

Ecclef. 8. 11.

Quia non profertur cito contra malos ſententia, abſque timore ullo filii hominum perpetrant mala.

Inertis eſt neſcire quod ſibi liceat.

Authore EDW. COKE *Milite.*

Hæc ego grandævus poſui tibi candide Lector.

LONDON, .

Printed by *W. Rawlins,* for *Thomas Baſſet* at the *George* near St. *Dunſtans*
Church in *Fleet-ſtreet,* M DC L X X X.

Illustration 10-8.   Title page, 6th edition of Coke's *Third Institutes*. [Author's Collection.]

Coke's Institutes

[From: Sir Edward Coke, *The Third Part of the Institutes of the Laws of England* (London, 1644), p. 35. ("Concerning High Treason, and other Pleas of the Crown and Criminal Causes.")]

So as hereby it appeareth, that where the law requires that a prisoner should be kept in safe and close custody, yet that must be without pain or torment to the prisoner. Hereupon two questions do arise, when and by whom the rack or break in the Tower was brought in.

To the first, John Holland, Earl of Huntington, was by King Henry VI created Duke of Exeter and *anno* 26 Henry VI [1447–1448] the king granted to him the constableship of the Tower: he and William de la Pole, Duke of Suffolk, and others, intended to have brought in the civil laws. For a beginning whereof, the Duke of Exeter being constable of the Tower first brought into the Tower the rack or brake allowed in many cases by the civil law: and thereupon the rack is called the Duke of Exeter's daughter, because he first brought it thither.

To the second upon this occasion, Sir John Fortescue, Chief Justice of England wrote his book in commendation of the laws of England, and therein preferreth the same for the government of this country before the civil law; and particularly that all tortures and torments of parties accused were directly against the common laws of England, and showed the inconvenience thereof by fearful example, to whom I refer you being worthy your reading. So as there is no law to warrant tortures in this land, nor can they be justified by any prescription being so lately brought in.

And the poet [Virgil] in describing the iniquity of Radamanthus, that cruel judge of hell, saith: *Castigatque, auditque dolos, subigitque fateri*—First he punished before he heard, and when he had heard his denial, he compelled the party accused by torture to confess it. But far otherwise doth Almighty God proceed *postquam reus diffamatus est. 1. Vocat. 2. Interrogat. 3. Judicat* [after the accused is charged. 1. He summons. 2. He interrogates. 3. He judges—citing Luke 16.1,2 and John 7.51]. To conclude this point it is against Magna Carta, c . 29: "No free man..." And accordingly all the said ancient authors are against any pain or torment to be put or inflicted upon the prisoner before attainder [of treason] nor after attainder but according to the judgment. And there is no one opinion in our books or judicial record (that we have seen and remember) for the maintenance of tortures or torments.

* * * * *

[From: Sir Edward Coke, *The Fourth Part of the Institutes of the Laws of England* (London, 1644), p. 36–38.]

Of the power and jurisdiction of the parliament, for making of laws in proceeding by bill, it is so transcendent and absolute, as it cannot be confined either by causes or persons within any bounds. Of this court it is truly said: *Si antiquitatem spectes, est vetustissima, si dignitatem, est honoratissima, si jurisdictionem, est capacissima* ["If you look to antiquity it is the most ancient, to dignity it is the most honored, to jurisdiction it is the widest"].

Huic ego nec metas rerum, nec tempora pono

["Upon it I place no limits of matters or time."]

Yet some examples are desired. Daughters and heirs apparant of a man or woman, may by act of parliament inherit during the life of the ancestor.

It may adjudge an infant, or minor of full age.

To attaint a man of treason after his death.

To naturalize a mere alien, and make him a subject born.

It may bastard a childe that by law is legitimate, viz. begotten by an adulterer, the husband being within the foure seas.

To legitimate one that is illegitimate, and born before marriage absolutely....

Crofs   fecit

non
legunt

Illustration 11-1 Oliver Cromwell (1599–1658), Lord Protector of England (1653–1658). Contemp. Engraving. [Author's Collection.]

XI

LAWMAKING
AND REVOLUTION

It is impossible to discuss here the many political and military events of the English Civil War. All civil wars are traumatic, particularly when they are fought over issues of principle. The English Civil War was no exception. The Wars of the Roses may have lasted longer, but casualties were light and the "battles" were largely engagements between relatively small numbers of armed aristocrats and their supporters, fighting over what was basically a series of coups between leading families. In contrast, the English Civil War split the country along religious, regional and class lines, and was fought fiercely and with genuine armies. Like the American Civil War, fundamental political ideas were involved—in the English case the division of power between King and Parliament—and, like the American Civil War, the trauma of the fighting led to a political reaction.

The English Civil War lasted from 1642 until 1646. The victory of Parliament was assured by the control of London, with its wealth and population centers, and by the "New Model Army," a professional military force based on modern principles of central command and regular pay. The decision to execute Charles in 1649 was highly controversial. The formal execution of a reigning sovereign was something that went beyond contemporary European experience, and caused widespread horror at home and abroad, even among Charles' enemies. Despite his political blunders, Charles was a highly moral person in his private life, and he died a martyr's death with great dignity. In English churches to this day prayers are said for "Charles the Martyr" and on the walls of his places of imprisonment are carved "Lest We Forget."

His execution also left the victorious Parliament with a dilemma, how to rule? From 1649 to 1653 the Parliament tried to rule by itself. This was the so-called "Rump Parliament." Then the Army, which had refused to be disbanded following some brutal campaigns in Ireland and Scotland, simply took over, and placed its commander, Oliver Cromwell, in office as Lord Protector and Head of State.

Cromwell was a deeply religious man, who ruled the country by a system of military local governments. He called Parliament regularly, but packed the House with his supporters. He widely imprisoned subjects without trial. His supporters repeatedly offered him the Crown, partly because they believed it would serve "to limit his power, to bind him with precedents and with the rule of law."[1] Cromwell saw himself as ruled by God, and saw little point in the trappings of monarchy. In many ways, he was not unlike the modern military dictators we know so well today, particularly the more idealistic and personally honest ones.

Like these modern dictators, Cromwell left no permanent system of government behind him. His son was unable to take over at Cromwell's death in September, 1658, and within a year and a half Parliament and the Army agreed to restore Charles' son, Charles II, to the throne.

The restoration was unconditional. True, it was agreed that the King would not restore the Privy Council and its hated prerogative courts, such as the Star Chamber, but this was little more than what Charles I had agreed to before the war. As for the legal order of the Republic, it was to be wiped from memory. Every parliamentary act during the Interregnum was declared null and void. It was even impolite to talk about it. The King had just been, as he said, "on his travels."

A. RADICALISM

Even if it officially "did not happen," there were some powerful lessons to be learned from the War and the Republic. One lesson was that a failure to resolve conflicting legal values within a justice system can have truly catastrophic consequences. Both the American Civil War and the English Civil War were preceded by futile legal struggles and efforts at political resolution. The failure of the legal process in both cases would leave a permanent scar in the national confidence. A second lesson of both the English and the American Civil War was that the immediate results of battle rarely cure the core problems, and often bring on a counterproductive reaction.

To jurists, however, some of the most interesting aspects of the English Civil War and Republic were not tied up in these core lessons. Rather, they were the development of advanced political theories, by-products of the struggle. The importance of these theories would only become clear centuries later.

One example was early communism. Among small political fragments of the Parliamentary forces, particularly the most "left-wing" soldiers of Cromwell's New Model Army, there arose an extraordinary movement, the "Levellers and the Diggers." These proto-communists were a good example of an early "radical" movement.

What do we mean by "radical?" The word itself derives from the Latin *radix* or *radicis* (root). A radical movement seeks to change society fundamentally, "by its roots," to substitute an entirely new set of ruling principles. This is what the "Levellers and Diggers" wished.

Led by men like Hugh Peter (1598–1660), Chaplain of the New Model Army, and Jerrard Winstanley, the Levellers and the Diggers believed that all men and women were equal, (hence "Levellers") and that government should be based on complete suffrage. Thus, the Parliament should be elected in frequent and fair elections. Furthermore, wealth should be distributed more equally, and the labor of those who worked the land (the "Diggers") should be more valued than the

---

1. John Morrill, "The Stuarts," in *The Oxford History of Britain, supra*, 377.

passive control of wealth. Finally, religion should be up to each individual, and compulsory support of state religions should cease.

Important to Leveller and Digger philosophy was the Protestant precedent of "priesthood of believers." These Protestants believed that no person needs a priest to find God, only a Bible in English. The same was true with law and government. The jargon and complexity of statutes and the legal process were just "covers" for self-dealing and exploitation. If priests were not needed to know God, why should lawyers be needed to know the law?

The Levellers and Diggers were regarded as irritants by both sides of the English Civil War. After all, both the King and the Parliament were ancient institutions, and the leaders of both sides were people of conventional wealth and power. The country aristocracy had largely sided with the King, and the wealthy merchants ("princes of commerce") had largely sided with the Parliament. Neither side was pleased with genuine "left wing" radicals, and Hugh Peter was executed in 1660.

But it is important for students of legal history to listen closely to radical or dissident voices, even to those who never succeed. A good example of a "different voice" was Jerrard Winstanley's "The Law of Freedom in a Platform," published in 1652, and excerpted in the *Materials, infra*. Interestingly enough, its anger is directed primarily at Cromwell, who is both praised for defeating Charles and sternly reminded "that the Kingly Conqueror was not beaten by you only as you are a single man...but by the hand and assistance of Commoners." *Materials, infra.*

The Levellers had very strong ideas about the law, and accessibility to law by the people. They certainly did not like lawyers.

> If we go to the lawyer, we find him to sit in the Conquerors Chair, though the Kings be removed, maintaining the Kings Power to the height, for in many Courts and cases of Law, the Will of a Judge & Lawyer rules above the letter of the Law, and many Cases and Suits are lengthened to the great vexation of the Clients, and to the lodging of their Estates in the purse of the unbounded Lawyer: So that we see, though other men be under a sharp Law, yet many of the great Lawyers are not, but still do act their will, as the Conqueror did; as I have heard some belonging to the Law say, *What cannot we do?*
>
> Say they, If we look upon the Customs of the Law itself, it is the same it was in the Kings days, only the name is altered; as if the Commoners of *England* had paid their Taxes, Free-quarter, and shed their blood, not to reform, but to baptize the Law in to a new name, from *Kingly Law*, to *State Law*; by reason whereof, the spirit of discontent is strengthened, to increase more Suits of Law, then formerly was known to be: And so as the Sword pulls down Kingly Power with one hand, the Kings old Law builds up Monarchy again with the other.
>
> And indeed the main Work of Reformation lies in this, to reform the Clergy, Lawyers, and Law; for all the Complaints of the Land are wrapped up within them three, not in the person of a King.
>
> Shall men of other Nations say, That notwithstanding all those rare wits in the Parliament and Army of *England*, yet they could not reform the Clergy, Lawyer, and Law, but must needs establish all as the Kings left them?
>
> *Materials, infra.*

It is easy for us, as lawyers, to laugh at such arguments and, indeed, the Levellers and Diggers were quickly suppressed. But radical movements can play a valuable role in testing a legal establishment. There is a limit of patience in ordinary people for the complexities and the petty (and large) corruptions that come with a "mature" legal system. At least in a democracy, people have a right to be able to know the law that governs them. Few in America today can read a simple tax return. There is a warning here.

In addition, radicals can be prophets. The Levellers and Diggers sought things regarded as outrageous by mainstream English society, such as equality of men and women and complete suffrage. They were executed or had their ears chopped off, but we have now adopted some of their goals as our core values.

Even in their own time, some very simple goals were met. All law books were translated, by order of Parliament, from Latin and Law French into English. And, as we will see, Puritans and Quakers were already trying experiments in simplifying law and government in a new land, America.

B. THE "GLORIOUS REVOLUTION"

The King was "restored," but Charles II was very different from his father. A total pragmatist, he was determined not to "resume" his travels. He formally forgave all of his parliamentary enemies, except those who signed his father's death warrant.[2] The Act of Indemnity and Oblivion, designed to bring the period of unrest to a close, was so generous that one bitter royalist said it was an "act of indemnity to the King's enemies and of oblivion to his friends." Charles' family were all Catholic, except his sister Mary who married the Protestant Dutchman, William of Orange. Secretly, Charles was Catholic too, but he saw nothing wrong with hiding the fact until his death bed. It made it easier to get on with Parliament.

While Charles I was the most chaste of men, Charles II had a bevy of beautiful mistresses, and 17 illegitimate children. If you go to Goodwood House today, you can walk past wall after wall of portraits of Charles' beautiful "companions" and his "royal" children. But Charles was faithful to his wife, Catherine, in one important way. She was barren, and he would not divorce her just to have an heir. This had consequences of the greatest import, because it put Charles' brother, James, in line for the throne, and James was openly Catholic. Had another Stuart of Charles II's accommodating and cheerfully unprincipled nature succeeded to the throne, the English monarchs might still be Stuarts. But brother James was a very different matter.

Even before Charles II's death, an important group tried, unsuccessfully, to block James' succession by passing an Act of Exclusion. They were led by Lord Shaftsbury and tended to come from the "upper middle class," i.e., gentlemen farmers, lawyers, doctors, merchants, bankers and practical "low Church" clergy. They were devoted to the practical, the profitable and the conventional. They saw James as nothing but

---

2. Some of the "regicides" fled to America, and hid in caves above New Haven, where it was even hard to order a pizza. Thus, did far off battles touch Connecticut!

trouble. But they couldn't agree on a successor, and the nimble Charles II out maneuvered them politically. Although they lost their first confrontation, this group became the first modern political party, and were called "the Whigs." Maybe the name comes from the fact that they were all middle-aged, boring, bald men![3]

Charles II died in 1685. In three short years his brother wrecked all his political efforts. Some have called James II "a bigot," but many of his proposed measures—including equal acceptance of Catholic and other dissenters with Anglicans in civil worship and government positions—seem enlightened today. But James was a political disaster. The Whigs had always opposed him. The traditional royalists, now called "Tories," were particularly devoted to the idea of the King as Head of the Anglican Church. But James was openly Catholic. He desperately tried to create a third party of Catholics and Dissenters, and actually called in the charters of most towns to try to place Catholics and Dissenters in control. It was politically insane. There just weren't enough of either group.

James had a barren marriage of ten years, and Whigs and Tories alike began to look forward to his death without an heir. That would bring his sister, Mary, to the throne. She was sensible and Protestant, and married to that nice (i.e., anti-Spanish) Dutch leader, William. But, to their horror, James announced that he and his Catholic wife, Mary of Modena, had given birth to a son. His subjects were so suspicious that many in Parliament wanted to have a Commission to investigate the little baby's legitimacy. (The baby was allegedly smuggled into the room in a bed pan, the so-called "bed pan baby.") Whig and Tory leaders met at once. There was little disagreement. James' sister, Mary, was invited to take the throne with William. William landed with an army at Torbay on November 5, 1688. James, at the head of the royal troops, moved to meet him, but suffered "what can only be called a complete mental collapse."[4] His men deserted him. William was desperate to have him escape safely to France. James could not even do this right, and was captured by fishermen, who were doubtless surprised that their feat was so unwelcome. The second time James successfully escaped to the protection of his cousin, the mighty Louis XIV of France. His son, also called James, escaped with him. For centuries, bands of Jacobites remained loyal to the Stuart pretenders, holding their wine glasses during the "loyal toasts" over their water glasses—meaning that their true allegiance was to the "King over the water."

This collection of blunders was called the "Glorious Revolution." One reason for calling it "glorious" might be the non-existent casualty list. More to the point, however, was that William and Mary were now fully aware that they were guests at the sufferance of Parliament. The Age of Absolute Monarchy in England was absolutely over.

Legally, this was symbolized by a series of Parliamentary enactments, asserted by William and Mary, which were really the constitutional underpinnings of a limited monarchy. The most important was the Bill of Rights of 1689, set out in the *Materials, infra*. These enactments even made the future succession perfectly clear. In default of issue to William and Mary, Mary's safely Protestant sister,

---

3. The true origin of "Whig" probably derived from a derogatory term for the followers of Lord Shaftesbury, "Whiggamers," meaning to drive ("whig") a mare. See *The Concise Oxford Dictionary* (8th ed., 1990), 1397.

4. John Morrill, "The Stuarts (1603–1688)" in *The Oxford History of Britain*, 387.

Anne, was to be called to the Throne. (This, indeed, took place.) All "popish" princes were barred, and royalty were forbidden to "marry a papist." Additional enactments guaranteed free elections to Parliament, free speech in Parliament, jury trial, and independence of the judiciary. While the English monarch retained important executive powers, there was now no question as to where the ultimate power lay. Across the ocean, in Boston, New York, Philadelphia, New Haven, Charleston, Williamsburg, and many other cities, towns and villages, the Americans took notice.

C. AMERICA

I. A COLONIAL EXPERIMENT

Along the Atlantic seaboard there were now pockets of English settlers. In old settlements, such as Boston and Cambridge, there were schools, and in Cambridge, a printing press and a university. Most important, there were already second and third generation immigrants. The upheaval of the English Civil War had one clear effect on American settlements, they were left largely to fend for themselves. And they liked it that way.

Take Massachusetts as just one example. As with many other colonies, it was founded by religious refugees, in this case Puritans. The legal form of government was a corporate charter, issued by the Crown, giving the corporate proprietors power to exercise civil government and to pass any laws "not inconsistent" with English law. The Crown officers had named wealthy Puritan merchants, safely resident in England, among the proprietors. The Crown's intention had been to control the colony through these established proprietors, and by amending the Charter, which the Crown assumed would remain in London. The night before the expedition sailed, however, the resident proprietors resigned *en mass* and named replacements who were going with the fleet. When the ships left, the Charter was also on board. As the *Arbella* arrived off the coast of New England on June 12, 1630, there was nothing left in England to provide easy legal control. In any event, the royal government was completely distracted. Charles I had just decided to embark on the agony of "Personal Rule." Controversy was everywhere. By comparison, nobody cared about the Corporation of Massachusetts Bay. It was a perfect formula for being left alone.

Among the 1,005 settlers aboard the flotilla of 17 tiny ships were ten legally trained Puritans, products of the Inns of Court and English legal practice.[5] John Winthrop himself, the first Governor, was a member of Gray's Inn and Inner Temple. When the Puritans arrived, they met, to their total horror, another lawyer who was already here, the notorious Thomas Morton. Morton lived alone on a hill, now in Wollaston, Massachusetts, which he called "Merry Mount." He claimed to be a "gentleman of Cliffords Inn," an Inn of Chancery,

---

5. See Thomas G. Barnes, "Thomas Leckford and the Earliest Lawyering in Massachusetts, 1638–1641," and George L. Haskins, "Lay Judges: Magistrates and Justices in Early Massachusetts," *Law in Colonial Massachusetts 1630–1800* (eds. D.R. Coquillette, R.J. Brink, C.S. Menand, 1984), 3–38, 39–56.

but what he did in the New World was to trade guns and liquor to the Indians for furs and sex. He even had erected a Maypole on Merry Mount, and had huge, drunken parties. The famous historian, Samuel Eliot Morison, was descended himself from Puritans. Morison observed that, among modern lawyers, there were "more spiritual descendants of Thomas Morton than John Winthrop."[6] But no one has yet founded a Thomas Morton Law Club, at least at my law school. The Puritans sent Morton back to England.

Despite their legal training, the leaders of the Bay Colony were suspicious of the English legal establishment and of English law. They also had to face tension within the colony between the proprietorial "magistrate" class, consisting of the Governor, Deputy Governor, and the Eighteen "Assistants" who were given executive power by the Charter, and the "freemen," those entitled to assemble in the annual General Court. The "freemen" were all Puritans and men of substance, and they wanted more say in colonial governance. Ironically, within this tiny puritan enclave, the "Tory" and "Whig" perspectives seemed to automatically emerge. Both political groups were highly conservative, but one was more autocratic and elitist than the other.

This tension resulted in an extraordinary experiment, an effort to draft a codified law. As John Winthrop observed: "The deputies having conceived great danger to our state in regard that our magistrates, for want of positive laws, in many cases, might proceed according to their discretions, it was agreed that, some men should be appointed to frame a body of grounds of laws, in resemblance to a *Magna Charta*, which being allowed by some of the ministers and the general court, should be received for fundamental laws."[7] The result of these experiments was to be a law that all could read and understand, not unlike the later goals of the Levellers and Diggers in England. Indeed, the same religious conviction of a "priesthood of all believers" and free access to the scriptures, the "law of God," probably was the foundation in both cases. Again, if everyone should have free access to the law of God without the necessary intervention of priests, why should they not have free access to the civil law without an intervening priesthood of lawyers?

The *Materials* contain an analysis of the outcome of these experiments, the famous *Lawes and Libertyes...of Massachusetts* (Cambridge, 1648), the first law book printed in North America. It survives in only one copy, a treasure of the Huntington Library in California. See *Materials, infra.* Published separately as a broadside were the famous *Capitall Lawes of New-England.* These were distributed to towns which, in turn, gave a copy to each household to put up, as it were, on the refrigerator. Both derive from an early manuscript, *The Body of Liberties* of 1641, written by Nathaniel Ward, a brilliant Puritan minister with a legal background.

Reading these materials certainly brings home two lessons. First, the original settlers of this part of America took law very seriously, and wanted it to be accessible to all. Second, this did not mean they were prepared to import English law and the English legal profession wholesale. There is not a single citation to English law in the *Capitall Lawes*, which refers to biblical authority instead. There are very few English citations in the *Lawes and Libertyes*. There were certain "loyalist" malcontents, usually Anglican "high church" believers who felt isolated among the

---

6. See Samuel Eliot Morison, *Builders of the Bay Colony* (Boston, 1930), 16–17.

7. William H. Whitmore, "Introduction," *The Colonial Laws of Massachusetts* (Boston, 1889), 5.

"low church" Puritans. These "loyalists" occasionally tried to take legal matters on appeal to the Privy Council in London, but few succeeded. Until Charles II revoked the Charter in 1684, more than a generation later, these Americans were allowed to develop their own approach to a new legal order. The *Lawes and Libertyes* were republished in amended editions in 1660 and 1672, and then updated through 1686.

Read the *Lawes and Libertyes* excerpts in the *Materials* with care. Note the fundamental principles articulated in the Preamble, and the alphabetical structure of the excerpts that follow, covering all topics from "Appeal" to "Bakers." "A" to "Z," it was all the law you had to know.

In the attached analysis, "Radical Lawmakers in Colonial Massachusetts," I argue that the Puritans who drafted these documents were familiar with civil law tradition. (Indeed, they were all fluent in Latin, and Hebrew too, and *Justinian's Institutes* was in the Harvard College Library, probably before 1645.) But in 1647 they also ordered law books from England, including Coke's *Reports* and Coke's *First Institutes* ("Sir Edward Cooke upon Littleton") and *Second Institutes* ("Sir Edward Cooke upon *Magna Charta*").[8] Their problem was how to incorporate their English legal heritage with both the harsh reality of a frontier society, and also their dreams for a better future. It was a demanding challenge.

2. A CHALLENGE TO COMMON LAW INCORPORATION: RACISM AND SLAVERY

The additional American materials relate to this challenge of incorporation. Most of the American Colonies succeeded in evading the unwanted attention of the later Stuart monarchs by the convenient intervention of the "Glorious Revolution." William and Mary were sympathetic Protestants, and preoccupied with European wars. But a far more terrible evil had already arrived in the colonies: slavery. Even in the *Lawes and Libertyes*, the section on "Bond-slavery" is disturbingly ambiguous.

Bond-slavery

It is Ordered by this Court & Authority thereof; That there shall never be any bond slavery villenage or capitivity amongst us, unles it be Lawfull captives, taken in just warrs, as willingly sell themselves, or are told to us, and such shall have the liberties, & christian usuage, which the Law of God established in Israel, concerning such persons, doth morally require, provided this exempts none from servitude who shall be judged thereto by Authority. [1641]

Materials, 363

By 1700, slaves were to be found in all colonies, and the trade in human souls from Africa was growing rapidly.

English law, in theory, did not recognize race slavery at least within England. The earlier notions of "unfree" tenure came with major safeguards—you could

---

8. See D.R. Coquillette, "Radical Lawmakers in Colonial Massachusetts," 67 *New England Quarterly* (1994), 179–194.

not break up serf families, you could not separate serfs from their land, you could not hit or injure serfs except through legal process. Race discrimination was not a factor in unfree tenure, nor was it a factor in Roman slavery, where slaves often were captives in war — and came from all classes and racial backgrounds.

Thus the new race slavery presented an "incorporation" problem of the most ghastly type. Despite their English legal heritage, many Americans wanted this cruel "law of property." We will see in the next chapter that William Blackstone, the first true "law professor" of the common law, wrote a *Commentary on the Laws of England* (1765) that was to be a handbook to Americans and English alike. It was clearly written, and well organized. Hundreds of Americans, including future leaders of the new Republic like James Otis, John Adams, James Madison, Thomas Jefferson, and Alexander Hamilton, all ordered copies. Blackstone indicated, in the clearest terms, that English law prohibited slavery.[9]

The first American edition of Blackstone's *Commentaries*, published in 1771 in Philadelphia, was pirated. It was published, without copyright permission, by one Robert Bell. Its title page is reproduced in the *Materials, infra*, along with Bell's explanation for his piracy. It is fair to say that Blackstone became the "common law" of the colonies, to the extent such a thing existed at all. But not as to slavery.

In 1803, a distinguished Virginian jurist, St. George Tucker, published an edition of Blackstone's *Commentaries*. St. George Tucker added notes to Blackstone's text where the law of Virginia was different. The *Materials* set out some of Blackstone's key passages on civil liberty, along with St. George Tucker's notes relating to the Virginian law of slavery, and how it differed from the English law. Not only did Virginia have a law of chattel slavery, but St. George Tucker also discusses "our *free* negros and mulattos; whose civil incapacities are almost as numerous as the civil rights of our free citizens." *Materials, infra*. These civil incapacities were based on race alone, and there were elaborate tests as to who was a negro, who was a "mulatto" (one-fourth or more "negroe blood") and who was "white." St. George Tucker clearly disliked these systems, but he presented it as the law of Virginia.

The issues presented by slavery and racism were thus "part and parcel" of the question of what English law should be incorporated, and what rejected. Among that rejected in many colonies was the English safeguards of civil liberty for the

---

9. Blackstone equivocated only on the issue of indentured servitude, which did exist in England. To the extent that a master might still have some contractual rights to a former slave's services, the right to those services may still exist at English law. The former slave, however, would no longer be a slave, but a free person. As Blackstone put it:

The idea and practice of this political or civil liberty flourish...in their highest vigor in these kingdoms, where it falls little short of perfection, and can only be lost or destroyed by the folly or demerits of it's owner: the legislature, and of course the laws of England, being peculiarly adapted to the preservation of this inestimable blessing even in the meanest subject. Very different from the modern constitutions of other states, on the continent of Europe, and from the genius of the imperial law; which in general are calculated to vest an arbitrary and despotic power, of controlling the actions of the subject, in the prince, or in a few gradees. And this spirit is so deeply implanted in our constitution, and rooted even in our very soil, that a slave or a negro, the moment he lands in England, falls under the protection of the laws; and so far becomes a freeman; though the master's right to his service may *possibly* still continue. (*Materials, infra*).

most "unfree." The English legal culture was never perfect, but on this topic it far exceeded the colonial monstrosities. Here, English legal models would have saved us from the terror of our Civil War and the continuing cost of national racism.

3. SOURCES OF LAW AND LEGITIMACY

That we did benefit from the English Civil War experience in other ways is certain. In particular, the trauma of the English Civil War and the settlement represented by the "Glorious Revolution" inspired an outburst of English political writing. Two of the most famous theorists were Thomas Hobbes (1588–1679) and John Locke (1632–1704).

Hobbes and Locke both had a great effect on modern political philosophy, but they derived very different lessons from the English Civil War. Hobbes wrote his famous *Leviathan* (1651) while he was in exile. Although not a lawyer, Hobbes had been Bacon's secretary, and had a good understanding of legal theory. He had two major ideas, both of which were far too radical to be accepted by any contemporary political faction. The first was that religion must be subordinated to secular authority. This was a direct reaction to Hobbes' despair over the events in England, which were driven in part by religious hatreds. Second, was the idea that law is ultimately an issue of power, not of morals, and a strong government is the only alternative to anarchy. Government may be set up by the governed to avoid anarchy, but it was itself not part of any "covenant" with the people. Hobbes was traumatized by the disorder of the Long Parliament, the execution of the Monarch, and uncertainties of the Republic. He preferred absolute monarchy to such chaos. But his reaction to the English Civil War was even too cynical for the monarchists. In the twentieth century, however, Hobbes' *Leviathan* has become a philosophical basis for secular, totalitarian regimes. As Bertrand Russell observed: "Hobbes prefers monarchy, but all his abstract arguments are equally applicable to all forms of government in which there is one supreme authority not limited by the legal rights of other bodies."[10]

Locke took a different approach. He was an archetypal Whig, and was in exile in Holland from 1683–1689, the last years of the Stuart monarchy. He returned with William and Mary at the "Glorious Revolution," and was very much the chief theoretician for the new constitutional monarchy. He wrote his *Two Treatises on Civil Government* in 1690 as an effort to refute Hobbes. Like Hobbes, Locke also had two fundamental ideas. First, was that the consent of the governed is required for there to be a legitimate state. Where Hobbes saw a unilateral grant of power, Locke saw mutual contract, conditional on the sovereign's good conduct. Second, Locke believed that the powers of the government should be divided into "balancing" branches, so that no one branch could become a source of tyranny. In Locke's view, James II forfeited the Crown because he had abused his side of the contract (as, it could be argued, had his father, Charles I). But Parliament, too, must be subjected to

---

10. Bertrand Russell, *History of Western Philosophy* (London, 1961), 535.

checks and balances, to avoid tyranny of the majority. An independent executive and judiciary were important. Moderate and balanced, Locke was a perfect Whig, and his ideas appealed to middle class, conventional souls, who
wanted some genuine representational government. There were a lot of people
like that in the American colonies, and Locke was to become the chief theoretical architect of both the Declaration of Independence, and the Constitution of
the United States.[11]

While Locke's theories would help shape the tone and structure of American
Independence, he did not answer the question of where the new sovereign states
could, or should, obtain their law. One solution was simply to carry over the old
English law, statutes and all, and then modify it as necessary by new legislation
or case law. This was certainly a most practical approach in a land where, even
in Massachusetts, there was only one unpublished law report before Independence and where, despite the Puritan experiments of the prior century, there were
really no legal treatises.[12] Another approach would be to adopt the English common law, but only those statutes that were re-enacted after Independence—an
approach advocated in several states.

A third, a more radical, approach was proposed by Jesse Root (1763–1822).
He was a Connecticut lawyer who had been admitted to the bar in 1763. After
the Revolution, he became Chief Justice of the Connecticut Superior Court and
founded the second *Connecticut Law Reports* (1798), one of the earliest sets of
law reports in America. His "Preface" to the first volume, entitled "The Origin of
Government and Laws in Connecticut, 1798," is set out in the *Materials, infra.*

Put bluntly, Root felt that the common law of Connecticut was derived from
the law of nature, not from the common law of England.

> Our ancestors, who emigrated from England to America, were pos-
> sessed of the knowledge of the laws and jurisprudence of that country;
> but were free from any obligations of subjection to them. The laws of
> England had no authority over them, to bind their persons. Nor were
> they in any measure applicable to their condition and circumstances
> here. Nor was it possible they should be: for the principle of their gov-
> ernment, as it respected the prerogatives of the crown, the estates, rights
> and power of the lords, and the tenure of their lands, were derived from
> the feudal system. The privilege of sending members to parliament, from
> the towns, cities, and boroughs, to compose one branch of the legisla-
> ture, called the House of Commons, and an exemption from taxation,
> only by their consent, was extorted from the kings by the barons, and is
> confirmed by the great charter of liberties as of his gift and grant. Their
> laws were calculated for a great commercial nation. As to their criminal
> code, it was adapted to a people grown old in the habits of vice, where
> the grossest enormities and crimes were practiced. In every respect there-
> fore their laws were inapplicable to an infant country or state, where the
> government was in the peoples, and which had virtue for its principle,

---

11. Ultimately, the lesson Hobbes learned from the English Civil War was to fear breakdown of state power, whereas Locke feared concentrations of such power. Their conflicting
views are still evident in both American and English political debates.

12. See Morris L. Cohen, "Legal Literature In Colonial Massachusetts," in *Law In Colonial Massachusetts* (ed. D.R. Coquillette, R. Brink, K. Menand, Boston, 1984) 243–272.

and the public good for its object and end, where the tenure of their lands was free and absolute, the objects of trade few, and the commission of crimes rare.

Our ancestors, therefore, as a free, sovereign, and independent people, very early established a constitution of government by their own authority; which was adapted to their situation and circumstances, and enacted laws for the due and regular administration of justice, for the propagation of knowledge and virtue, for the preservation of the public peace, and for the security and defense of the state against their savage enemies.

Materials, infra.

But if the common law of Connecticut were not the common law of England, from whence should it be derived?

[It should be] derived from the law of nature and of revelation — those rules and maxims of immutable truth and justice, which arise from the eternal fitness of things, which need only to be understood, to be submitted to, as they are themselves the highest authority; together with certain customs and usages, which had been universally assented to and adopted in practice, as reasonable and beneficial...

Materials, infra.

These rights and liberties are our own, not holden by the gift of a despot. Our government and our rulers are from amongst ourselves; chosen by the free, uninfluenced suffrages of enlightened freemen; not to oppress and devour, but to protect, feed, and bless the people, with the benign and energetic influence of their power (as ministers of god for good to them). This shows the ignorance of those who are clamorous for a new constitution, and the mistake of those who suppose that the rules of the Common Law of England are the common law of Connecticut, until altered by a statute.

Materials, infra.

As attractive as Root's argument might be in the abstract, however, it presented severe problems in practice. Where there were Connecticut statutes in place, all agreed they should have precedence. But what about the jurisprudence surrounding the statute *Quia Emptores* (1290) or the *Statute of Uses* (1536)? This ancient law underlay the common law of real property or trusts in most states. Was it "repealed" by the Revolution? Should a state legislature go through the English statute books and "re-enact" the statutes they like? (Some, in essence, did.) What about the *Magna Carta* (1215) itself?

In Root's view there were only two legitimate sources of law: 1) the State legislature; and 2) "Connecticut" or "American" common law. The latter was derived from three sources: 1) "the perfection of reason, arising from the nature of God, of man and of things, and from their relations, dependencies, and connections;" 2) universal usages and customs, "universally assented to and adopted in practice by citizen at large, or by particular classes of men, as the farmers, the merchants etc." and 3) "the adjudications of the courts of justice and the rules of practice adopted in them." *Materials, infra.* The last source, court "adjudication," was conventional enough, but who was to determine the first two, "perfection of reason" and "universal usage?" Connecticut was still a fairly rural, sparsely inhabited state. There was one law school, a proprietary school unconnected with any university, and only one volume of reports.[13] There were no efforts at codification yet, and many holes in every statutory scheme. Root's arguments doubtless swelled the patriotic chests of the American bar with pride, but the shelves of their offices were filled with English reports, English treatises, and, most of all, a dog-eared *Blackstone's Commentaries*, filled with English law.

We will return to this problem of "incorporation" in Chapter XIII, "The Nineteenth Century." Indeed, the "Codification Movement" in New York and elsewhere was strongly motivated by a desire to establish a "Code American," a purely American legal system. But it was to be based on systematic legislation, not common law. See Chapter XIII, *infra*. And things changed slowly. In the 1850s, Abraham Lincoln practiced law in the new State of Illinois with just eight law books stuck in the saddle bags of his horse, as he followed the state judges "on circuit." (Still the English assize system!) Four of the eight books were purely English law, the four volumes of *Blackstone's Commentaries*. In the next chapter, we will return to England and eighteenth century developments there, and learn more about Blackstone's role in his own country.

FOR FURTHER READING

I.   General Background: The English Civil War and the "Glorious Revolution"

For a concise general background of the political and constitutional struggle, see John Morrill, "The Stuarts (1603–1688)," 363–398, and Paul Langford, "The Eighteenth Century (1688–1789)," 399–409, in *The Oxford History of Britain* (ed. Kenneth O. Morgan, Oxford, 1988); J.P. Kenyon, *Stuart England* (London, 2d. ed., 1985) 131–313; S.B. Chrimes, *English Constitutional History* (Oxford, 4th ed., 1967) 100–119. For fully detailed, political accounts see Godfrey Davies, *The Early Stuarts 1603–1660* (Oxford, 1959) 81–214, 237–260, and Sir George Clark, *The Later Stuarts 1660–1714* (Oxford, 2d. ed., 1956) 1–27, 144–248. The two volumes above also contain extensive literary, economic, religious and sociological accounts. The best collections of documents and commentary is J.P. Kenyon, *The Stuart Constitution 1603–1688, Documents and Commentary* (Cambridge, 1966).

For a passionate, eminently enjoyable account of these times, it is still hard to surpass Sir Winston Churchill's *A History of the English-Speaking Peoples* (London, 1956), vol. 2, 153–325. For the "Cast of Characters," see C.P. Hill, *Who's Who in Stuart Britain* (London, 1988). For how this all related to the world of law and lawyers see Alan Harding, *A Social History of English Law* (London,

---

13. The extraordinary, and now extinct, proprietary law school was at Litchfield, Connecticut. It was founded in 1784. It was the oldest law school in America when it closed in 1833. It included among its graduates "sixteen United States senators, fifty congressmen, forty justices of higher courts, including eight chief justices, two justices of the United States Supreme Court, ten governors, [and] five cabinet members." See Arthur E. Sutherland, *The Law at Harvard* (Cambridge, 1967), 28.

1966), 265–282. For an account which unites this chapter intellectually with the previous chapter and the struggles of Coke and Bacon, see Christopher Hill, *Intellectual Origin of the English Revolution* (Oxford, 1980).

II. The Birth of Anglo-American Radicalism

For an excellent, scholarly account, see Donald Veall, *The Popular Movement for Law Reform 1640–1660*, particularly pp. 74–126. See also Gerrard Winstanley, *The Law of Freedom in a Platform* (orig. ed. 1652, London) (ed. Robert W. Kenny, New York, 1941) i–40; George H. Sabine, *The Works of Gerrard Winstanley*, (New York, 1965); Stuart E. Prall, *The Agitation for Law Reform During the Puritan Revolution, 1640–1660* (Hague 1960); G.B. Nourse, "Law Reform under the Commonwealth and Protectorate, "75 *Law Quarterly Review* (1959) 512–529. For an excellent account of Oliver Cromwell's life and his philosophy of government, see Christopher Hill, *God's Englishman: Oliver Cromwell and the English Revolution* (London, 1970).

III.   The Early American Legal Experience

For a good concise account of law in the American colonies, see Lawrence M. Friedman, *A History of American Law* (New York, 2d. ed., 1985) 31–104. For an in-depth analysis of Massachusetts colonial law, including full bibliographies and lists of original sources, see *Law in Colonial Massachusetts: 1630–1800* (eds. D.R. Coquillette, R.J. Brink, K. Menand, Boston, 1984). The classic account remains George L. Haskins, *Law and Authority in Early Massachusetts* (Lanham, Md., 1985). See also David P. Koenig, *Law and Society in Colonial Massachusetts* (Chapel Hill, N.C. 1979) and the excellent collections of studies in *Essays in the History of Early American Law* (D.H. Flaherty ed., Chapel Hill, N.C. 1969) and *Law and Authority in Colonial America* (George A. Billias, ed., Barre, Mass. 1965).

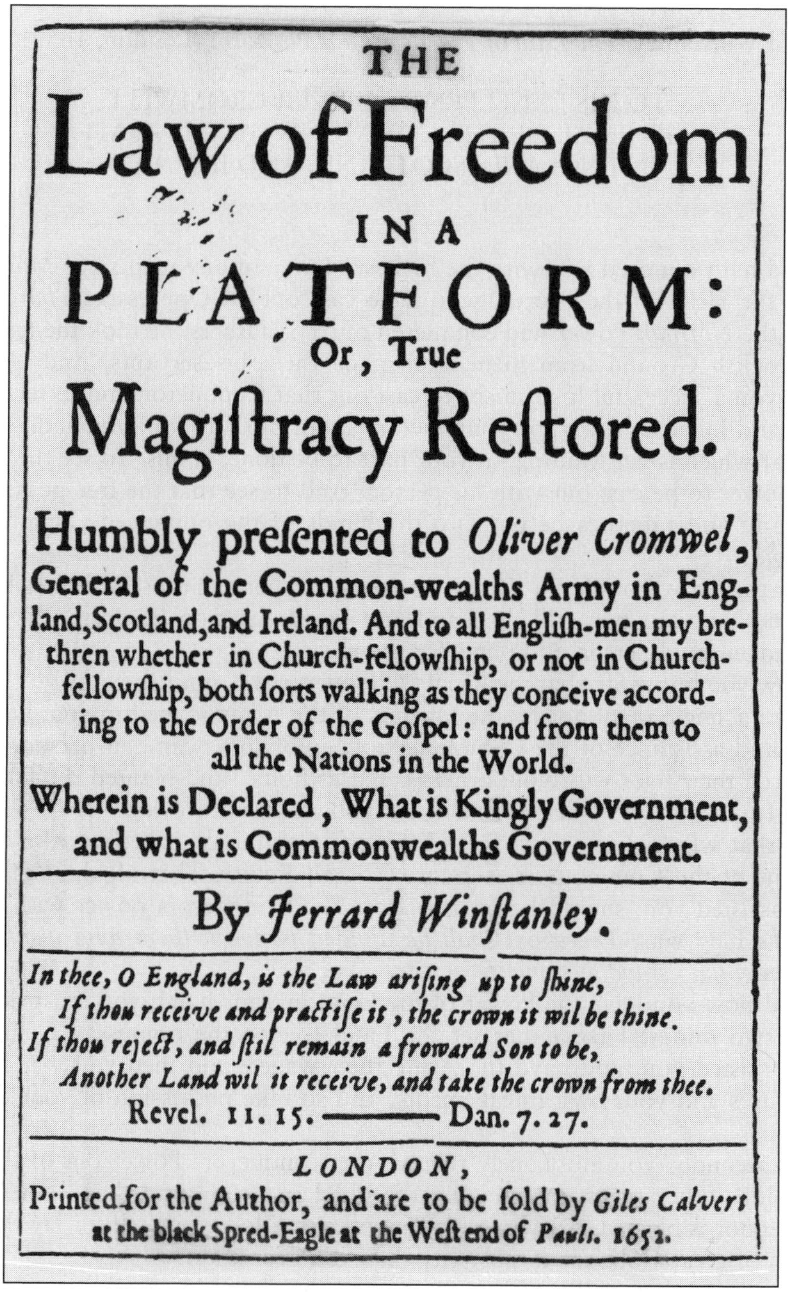

THE
Law of Freedom
IN A
PLATFORM:
Or, True
Magiſtracy Reſtored.

Humbly preſented to *Oliver Cromwel*, General of the Common-wealths Army in England, Scotland, and Ireland. And to all Engliſh-men my brethren whether in Church-fellowſhip, or not in Church-fellowſhip, both ſorts walking as they conceive according to the Order of the Goſpel: and from them to all the Nations in the World.

Wherein is Declared, What is Kingly Government, and what is Commonwealths Government.

By *Jerrard Winſtanley*.

In thee, O England, is the Law ariſing up to ſhine,
If thou receive and practiſe it, the crown it wil be thine.
If thou rejeɛt, and ſtil remain a froward Son to be,
Another Land wil it receive, and take the crown from thee.
Revel. 11. 15. ———— Dan. 7. 27.

LONDON,
Printed for the Author, and are to be ſold by *Giles Calvert* at the black Spred-Eagle at the Weſt end of *Pauls.* 1652.

Illustration 11-2 (Title page, Jerrard Winstanley, *The Law of Freedom in a Platform*, London, 1652).

MATERIALS

Jerrard Winstanley, *The Law of Freedom in a Platform* (London, 1652) 3–15.

TO HIS EXCELLENCY OLIVER CROMWELL,
GENERAL OF THE COMMONWEALTHS ARMY
IN ENGLAND, SCOTLAND, AND IRELAND

SIR,

God hath honored you with the highest Honor of any man since *Moses* time, to be the Head of the People, who have cast out an Oppressing *Pharoah*: For when the *Norman* Power had conquered our Forefathers, he took the free use of our English Ground from them, and made them his servants. And God hath made you a successful Instrument to cast out that Conqueror, and to recover our Land and Liberties again, by your Victories, out of that *Norman* hand.

That which is yet wanting on your part to be done, is this, To see the Oppressors power to be cast out with his person; And to see that the free possession of the Land and Liberties be put into the hands of the oppressed Commoners of *England*.

For the Crown of Honor cannot be yours, neither can those Victories be called Victories on your part, till the Land and Freedoms won be possessed by them who adventured person and purse for them.

Now you know Sir, that the Kingly Conqueror was not beaten by you onely as you are a single man, nor by the Officers of the Army joyned to you; but by the hand and assistance of the Commoners, whereof some came in person, and adventured their lives with you; others stayd at home, and planted the Earth, and payd Taxes and Freequarter to maintain you that went to war.

So that whatsoever is recovered from the Conqueror, is recovered by a joynt consent of the Commoners: therefore it is all Equity, That all the Commoners who assisted you, should be set free from the Conquerors power with you: As *David's* Law was, *The spoyl shall be divided between them who went to war, and them who stayd at home.*

And now you have the Power of the Land in your hand, you must do one of these two things: First, either set the Land free to the oppressed Commoners, who assisted you, and payd the Army their wages: and then you will fulfil the Scriptures and your own Engagements, and so take possession of your deserved Honor.

Or secondly, you must onely remove the Conquerors Power out of the Kings hand into other mens, maintaining the old Laws still: And then your Wisdom and Honor is blasted for ever; and you will either lose your self, or lay the Foundation of greater Slavery to posterity then you ever knew.

You know that while the King was in the height of his oppressing Power, the People onely whispered in private Chambers against him: But afterwards it was preached upon the house tops, That he was Tyrant and a Traytor to *Englands* peace; and he had his overturn.

The righteous Power in the Creation is the same still: If you, and those in power with you, should be found walking in the Kings steps, can you secure your selves or posterities from an overturn? Surely No.

The Spirit of the whole Creation (who is God) is about the Reformation of the World, and he will go forward in his work: For if he would not spare Kings, who have sat so long at his right hand, governing the World, neither will he regard you, unless your ways be found more righteous then the Kings.

You have the eyes of the People all the Land over, nay I think I may say all neighboring Nations over, waiting to see what you will do: And the eyes of your oppressed friends, who lie yet under kingly power, are waiting to have the possession given them of that Freedom in the Land, which was promised by you, if in case you prevailed. Lose not your Crown; take it up, and wear it. But know, that it is no Crown of Honor, till Promises and Engagements made by you be performed to your friends. *He that contnues to the end, shall receive the Crown.* Now you do not see the end of your work, unless the Kingly Law and Power be removed as well as his person.

Jonah's Gourd is a remembrancer to men in high places.

The worm in the Earth gnawed the root, and the Gourd dyed, and *Jonah* was offended.

Sir, I pray bear with me; my spirit is upon such a lock that I must speak plain to you, lest it tell me another day, If thou hadst spoke plain, things might have been amended.

The Earth wherein your Gourd grows is the Commoners of *England.*

The Gourd is that Power which covers you, which will be established to you by giving the People their true Freedoms, and not otherwise.

The root of your Gourd is the heart of the People, groaning under Kingly Bondage, and desiring a *Commonwealths* Freedom in their English Earth.

The worm in the Earth, now gnawing at the root of your Gourd, is Discontents, because Engagements and Promises made to them by such as have power, are not kept.

And this worm hath three heads: The first is a spirit waiting opportunities till a blasting wind arise to cause your Gourd to wither; and yet pretends fair to you, &c.

Another spirit shelters under your Gourd for a livelyhood, and will say as you say in all things; and these are called honest, yet no good friends to you nor the *Commonwealth,* but to their own bellies.

There is a third spirit, which is faithful indeed, and plain-dealing, and many times for speaking truth plainly he is cashiered, imprisoned, and crushed: And the Oppressions layd upon this spirit kindles the fire, which the two former waits to warm themselves at.

Would you have your Gourd stand for ever? Then cherish the root in the Earth; that is, the heart of your friends, the oppressed *Commoners of England,* by killing the Worm. And nothing will kill this worm, but performance of professions, words, and promises, that they may be made free men from Tyranny.

It may be you will say to me, *What shall I do?* I answer, You are in place and power to see all Burthens taken off from your friends, the *Commoners of England.* You will say, *What are those Burthens?*

I will instance in some, both which I know in my own experience, and which I hear the people dayly complaining of, and groaning under, looking upon you and waiting for Deliverance.

Most people cry, We have payd Taxes, given Freequarter, wasted our Estates, and lost our Friends in the Wars, and the Taskmasters multiply over us more then formerly. I have asked divers this question, *Why do you say so?*

Some have answered me, That Promises, Oaths, and Engagements have been made as a Motive to draw us to assist in the Wars; That Priviledges of Parliament and Liberties of Subjects should be preserved, and that all Popery, and Episcopacy, and Tyranny should be rooted out; and these promises are not performed: Now there is an opportunity to perform them.

For first, say they, The current of succeeding Parliaments is stopt, which is one of the greatest Priviledges (and peoples Liberties) for Safety and Peace; and if that continue stopt, we shall be more offended by an hereditary Parliament, then we were oppressed by an hereditary King.

And for the Commoners, who were called Subjects, while the Kingly Conqueror was in power, have not as yet their Liberties granted them; I will instance them in order, according as the common whisperings are among the people.

For say they, The burdens of the Clergy remains still upon us, in a three-fold nature.

First, If any man declare his Judgment in the things of God, contrary to the Clergies report, or the mind of some high Officers, they are cashiered, imprisoned, crushed, and undone, and made sinners for a word, as they were in the Popes and Bishops days; so that though their names be cast out, yet their High Commission Courts Power remains still, persecuting men for Conscience sake, when their actions are unblameable.

Secondly, In many Parishes there are old formal ignorant Episcopal Priests established; and some Ministers, who are bitter Enemies to Commonwealths Freedom, and Friends to Monarchy, are established Preachers, and are continually buzzing their subtle principles into the minds of the people, to undermine the Peace of our declared Commonwealth, causing a disaffection of spirit among neighbors, who otherwise would live in peace.

Thirdly, The burden of Tythes remains still upon our Estates, which was taken from us by the Kings, and given to the Clergy, to maintain them by our labours: so that though their preaching fill the minds of many with madness, contention, and unsatisfied doubting, because their imaginary and ungrounded Doctrines cannot be understood by them, yet we must pay them large Tythes for so doing; this is Oppression.

Fourthly, If we go to the Lawyer, we find him to sit in the Conquerors Chair, though the Kings be removed, maintaining the Kings Power to the height, for in many Courts and cases of Law, the Will of a Judge & Lawyer rules above the letter of the Law, and many Cases and Suits are lengthened to the great vexation of the Clients, and to the lodging of their Estates in the purse of the unbounded Lawyer: So that we see, though other men be under a sharp Law, yet many of the great Lawyers are not, but still do act their will, as the Conqueror did; as I have heard some belonging to the Law say, *What cannot we do?*

Fifthly, Say they, If we look upon the Customs of the Law it self, it is the same it was in the Kings days, only the name is altered; as if the Commoners of *England* had paid their Taxes, Free-quarter, and shed their blood, not to reform, but to baptize the Law into a new name, from *Kingly Law*, to *State Law*; by reason whereof, the spirit of discontent is strengthened, to increase more Suits of Law, then formerly was known to be: And so as the Sword pulls down Kingly Power with one hand, the Kings old Law builds up Monarchy again with the other.

And indeed the main Work of Reformation lies in this, to reform the Clergy, Lawyers, and Law; for all the Complaints of the Land are wrapped up within them three, not in the person of a King.

Shall men of other Nations say, That notwithstanding all those rare wits in the Parliament and Army of *England*, yet they could not reform the Clergy, Lawyer, and Law, but must needs establish all as the Kings left them?

Will not this blast all our Honor, and make all Monarchial Members laugh in their sleeves, to see the Government of our Commonwealth to be built upon the Kingly Laws and Principles?

I have asked divers Souldiers what they fought for; they answered, they could not tell; and it is very true, they cannot tell indeed, if the Monarchial Law be established without Reformation. But I wait to see what will be done; and I doubt not but to see our Commonwealths Government to be built upon his own Foundation.

Sixthly, If we look into Parishes, the burdens there are many.

First, For the Power of Lords of Manors remains still over their Brethren, requiring Fines and Heriots; beating them off the free use of the Common Land, unless their Brethren will pay them Rent; exacting obedience, as much as they did, and more, when the King was in Power.

Now saith the people, By what Power do these maintain their Title over us? Formerly they held Title from the King, as he was the Conquerors Successor: But have not the Commoners cast out the King, and broke the band of that Conquest? Therefore in equity they are free from the slavery of that Lordly Power.

Secondly, In Parishes where Commons lie, the rich *Norman* Freeholders, or the new (more covetous) Gentry, over-stock the Commons with Sheep and Cattle; so that inferior Tenants and poor Laborers can hardly keep a Cow, but half starve her; so that the poor are kept poor still, and the Common Freedom of the Earth is kept from them, and the poor have no more relief then they had when the King (or Conqueror) was in power.

Thirdly, In many Parishes two or three of the great ones bears all the sway, in making Assessments, over-awing Constables and other Officers; and when time was to quarter Souldiers, they would have a hand in that, to ease themselves, and over-burden the weaker sort; and many times make large sums of money over and above the Justices Warrant in Assessments, and would give no account why, neither durst the inferior people demand an account, for he that spake should be sure to be crushed the next opportunity; and if any have complained to Committees or Justices, they have been either wearied out by delays and waiting, or else the offence hath been by them smothered up; so that we see one great man favored another, and the poor oppressed have no relief.

Fourthly, There is another grievance which the people are much troubled at, and that is this; Country people cannot sell any Corn or other fruits of the Earth in a Market Town, but they must either pay Toll, or be turned out of Town: Now say they, This is a most shameful thing, that we must part with our estates in Taxes and Free-quarter to purchase the Freedom of the Land, and the Freedom of the Towns, and yet this Freedom must be still given from us, into the hands of a covetous *Norman* Toll-Taker, according to the Kings old burdensom Laws, and contrary to the Liberty of a free Commonwealth.

Now saith the whisperings of the people, The inferior Tenants and Laborers bears all the burdens, in laboring the Earth, in paying Taxes and Free-quarter beyond their strength, and in furnishing the Armies with Souldiers, who bear the greatest burden of the War; and yet the Gentry, who oppress them, and that live idle upon their labours, carry away all the comfortable livelyhood of the Earth.

For is not this a common speech among the people, We have parted with our Estates, we have lost our Friends in the Wars, which we willingly gave up, because Freedom was promised us; and now in the end we have new Task-masters, and our old burdens increased: and though all sorts of people have taken an Engagement to cast our Kingly Power, yet Kingly Power remains in power still in the hands of those who have no more right to the Earth then our selves.

For say the people, If the Lords of Manors and our Task-masters hold Title to the Earth over us from the old kingly power, behold that power is beaten and cast out.

And two Acts of Parliament are made. The one to cast out Kingly power, back'd by the Engagement against King and House of Lords. The other to make *England* a free Commonwealth.

And if Lords of Mannors lay claim to the earth over us, from the Armies Victories over the King; then we have as much right to the Land as they, because our labours, and blood, and death of friends, were the purchasers of the Earths freedome as well as theirs.

And is not this a slavery, say the People, That though there be Land enough in *England*, to maintain ten times as many people as are in it, yet some must beg of their brethren, or work in hard drudgery for day wages for them, or starve, or steal, and so be hanged out of the way, as men not fit to live in the earth, before they must be suffered to plant the waste land for their livelihood, unless they will pay Rent to their brethren for it? Wel, this is a burthen the Creation groans under; and the subjects (so called) have not their Birth-right Freedomes granted them from their brethren, who hold it from them by club law, but not by righteousness.

And who now must we be subject to, seeing the Conqueror is gone?

I Answer, we must either be subject to a Law, or to mens wils. If to a Law, then all men in *England* are subjects, or ought to be, thereunto: but what Law that is to which every one ought to be subject is not yet established in execution. If any say the old Kings Laws are the Rule, then it may be Answered, That those Laws are so full of confusion, that few knows when they obey and when not, because they were the Laws of a Conqueror to hold the people in subjection to the will of the Conqueror; therefore that cannot be the rule for every one: besides, we dayly see many actions done by State Officers, which they have no Law to justifie them in, but their Prerogative will.

And again if we must be subject to men, then what men must we be subject to, seeing one man hath as much right to the earth as another, for no man now stands as a Conqueror over his Brethren by the Law of righteousness?

You will say, We must be subject to the Ruler; it is true, but not to suffer the Rulers to call the Earth theirs and not ours, for by so doing they betray their trust, and run into the line of Tyranny, and we lose our freedome, and from thence Enmity and Wars arise.

A Ruler is worthy double honour when he rules well, that is, when he himself is subject to the Law, and requires all others to be subject thereunto and makes it his work to see the Laws obeyed, and not his own will, and such Rulers are faithfull, and they are to be subjected unto us therein, for all Commonwealths Rulers are servants to, not Lords and Kings over the people. But you will say, Is not the Land your brothers? And you cannot take away another mans Right by claiming a share therein with him.

I Answer, it is his either by creation right, or by right of Conquest: If by Creation right he call the earth his and not mine; then it is mine as well as his, for the Spirit of the whole Creation, who made us both, is no respecter of persons.

And if by Conquest he call the earth his and not mine, it must be either by the Conquest of the Kings over the Commoners, or by the Conquest of the Commoners over the Kings.

If he claim the earth to be his from the Kings Conquest, The Kings are beaten and cast out and that title is undone.

If he claim Title to the earth to be his from the Conquest of the Commoners over the Kings, then I have right to the Land as well as my brother, for my brother without me, nor I without my brother, did not cast out the Kings, but both together assisting with person and purse, we prevailed, so that I have by this Victory as equall a share in the earth which is now redeemed as my brother, by the Law of righteousnesse.

If my brother still say he will be Landlord (through his covetous ambition) and I must pay him Rent, or else I shall not live in the Land, then does he take my right from me, which I have purchased by my money in Taxes, free quarter and blood. And O thou Spirit of the whole Creation, who hath this Title to be called *King of Righteousness, and Prince of Peace*; judge thou between my brother and me, Whether this be righteous, &c.

And now, say the people, is not this a grievous thing that our brethren that will be Landlords right or wrong, will make Laws, and call for a law to be made to imprison, crush, nay put to death, any that denies God, Christ, and Scripture; and yet they will not practise that golden Rule, *Do to another as thou wouldst have another do to thee*, which God, Christ, and Scriptures, hath Enacted for a Law? Are not these men guilty of death by their own Law, which is the words of their own mouth? Is it not a flat denyall of God and Scripture?

O the confusion and thick darkness that hath over-spread our Brethren is very great, I have no power to remove it, but lament it in the secrets of my heart; when I see Prayers, Sermons, Fasts, Thanksgiving, directed to this God in words and shews, and when I come to look for actions of obedience to the Righteous Law, suitable to such a profession, I finde them men of another Nation, saying, and not doing; like an old Courtier saying *Your Servant*, when he was an Enemy. I wil say no more, but groan and waite for a restoration.

Thus Sir, I have reckoned up some of those burdens which the people groan under.

And I being sensible hereof was moved in my self, to present this Platform of Commonwealths Government unto you, wherein I have declared a full Commonwealths Freedome, according to the Rule of Righteousness, which is Gods Word. It was intended for your view above two years ago, but the disorder of the Times caused me to lay it aside, with a thought never to bring it to light, &c. Likewise I hearing that M. *Peters* and some others Propounded this request, That the Word of God might be consulted with to finde out a healing Government, which I liked well, and waited to see such a Rule come forth, for there are good rules in the Scripture if they were obeyed and practised: thereupon

I laid aside this in silence, and said, I would not make it publick; but this word was like fire in my bones ever and anon, *Thou shalt not bury thy talent in the earth*, therefore I was stirred up to give it a resurrection, and to pick together as many of my scattered papers as I could finde, and to compile them into this method, which I do here present to you, and do quiet my own spirit.

And now I have set the candle at your door, for you have power in your hand, in this other added opportunity, to Act for Common Freedome if you will; I have no power.

It may be here are some things inserted which you may not like, yet other things you may like, therefore I pray you read it, and be as the industrious Bee, suck out the honey and cast away the weeds.

Though this Platform be like a peece of Timber rough hewd, yet the discreet workmen may take it, and frame a handsome building out of it.

It is like a poor man that comes cloathed to your door in a torn country garment, who is unacquainted with the learned Citizens unsetled forms and fashions; take of the clownish language, for under that you may see beauty.

It may be you will say, If Tythes be taken from the Priests and Impropriators, and Copy-hold Services from Lords of Mannors, how shal they be provided for again; for is it not unrighteous to take their estates from them?

I Answer, when Tythes were first enacted, and Lordly power drawn over the backs of the oppressed, the Kings and Conquerors made not scruple of Conscience to take it, though the people lived in·sore bondage of poverty for want of it; and can there be scruple of conscience to make restitution of this which hath been so long stoln goods? It is not scruple arising from the Righteous Law, but from covetousness, who goes away sorrowfull to heare he must part with all to follow Righteousness and Peace.

But though you do take away Tythes, and the Power of Lords of Mannors, yet there will be no want to them, for they have the freedome of the Common stock, they may send to the Storehouses for what they want, and live more free then now they do, for now they are in care and vexation by servants, by casualties, by being cheated in buying and selling, and many other incumbrances, but then they will be free from all, for the common Storehouses is every mans riches, not any ones.

Is not buying and selling a righteous Law? No, It is the Law of the Conqueror, but not the righteous Law of Creation: how can that be righteous which is a cheat? for is not this a common practise, when he hath a bad Horse or Cow, or any bad commodity, he will send it to the Market, to cheat some simple plain-hearted man or other, and when he comes home, will laugh at his neighbours hurt, and much more &c.

When Mankinde began to buy and sell, then did he fall from his Innocency; for then they began to oppress and cozen one another of their Creation Birth-right: As for example; If the Land belong to three persons, and two of them buy and sell the Earth, and the third give no consent, his Right is taken from him, and his posterity is engaged in a War.

When the Earth was first bought and sold, many gave no consent: As when our Crown Lands, and Bishops Lands were sold, some foolish Soldiers yeelded, and covetous Officers were active in it, to advance themselves above their Brethren: but many, who payd Taxes and Free-quarter for the purchase of it, gave no consent, but declared against it, as an unrighteous thing, depriving posterity of their Birth-rights and Freedoms.

Therefore this buying and selling did bring in, and still doth bring in discontents and wars, which have plagued Mankinde sufficiently for so doing. And the Nations of the world will never learn to beat their swords into plowshares, and their spears into pruning hooks, and leave of warring, until this cheating device of buying and selling be cast out among the rubbish of Kingly power.

But shall not one man be richer then another?

There is no need of that; for Riches make men vain-glorious, proud, and to oppress their Brethren; and are the occasion of wars.

No man can be rich, but he must be rich, either by his own labors, or by the labors of other men helping him: If a man have no help from his neighbor, he shall never gather an Estate of hundreds and thousands a year: If other men help him to work, then are those Riches his Neighbors, as well as his; for they be the fruit of other mens labors as well as his own.

But all rich men live at ease, feeding and clothing themselves by the labors of other men, not by their own; which is their shame, and not their Nobility; for it is a more blessed thing to give then to receive: But rich men receive all they have from the laborers hand, and what they give, they give away other mens labors, not their own; Therefore they are not righteous Actors in the Earth.

But shall not one man have more Titles of Honor then another?

Yes: As a man goes through Offices, he rises to Titles of Honor, till he comes to the highest Nobility, to be a faithful Commonwealths man in a parliament house. Likewise he who findes out any secret in *Nature*, shall have a Title of Honor given him, though he be a young man. But no man shall have any Title of Honor till he win it by industry, or come to it by age, or Office-bearing. Every man that is above sixty years of age shall have respect as a man of honor by all others that are younger, as is shewed hereafter.

Shall every man count his Neighbors house as his own, and live together as one Family?

No: Though the Earth and Storehouses be common to every Family, yet every Family shall live apart as they do; and every mans house, wife, children, and furniture for ornament of his house, or any thing which he hath fetched in from the Storehouses, or provided for the necessary use of his Family, is all a propriety to that Family, for the peace thereof. And if any man offer to take away a mans wife, children, or furniture of his house, without his consent, or disturb the peace of his dwelling, he shall suffer punishment as an Enemy to the *Commonwealths* Government; as is mentioned in the Platform following.

Shall we have no Lawyers?

There is no need of them, for there is to be no buying and selling; neither any need to expound Laws; for the bare letter of the Law shall be both Judg and Lawyer, trying every mans actions: And seeing we shall have successive *Parliaments* every year, there will be Rules made for every action a man can do.

But there is to be Officers chosen yearly in every parish, to see the Laws executed according to the letter of the Laws; so that there will be no long work in trying of Offences, as it is under Kingly Government, to get the Lawyers mony, and to enslave the Commoners to the Conquerors prerogative Law, or Will. The sons of contention, *Simeon* and *Levi*, must not bear Rule in a free *Commonwealth*.

At the first view, you may say, this is a strange Government: but I pray judg nothing before tryal. Lay this Platform of Commonwealths Government in one scale, and lay Monarchy, or Kingly Government, in the other scale, and see which give true weight to righteous Freedom and Peace. There is no middle path between these two; for a man must either be a free and true Commonwealths man, or a Monarchial tyrannical Royalist.

If any say, This will bring poverty; surely they mistake: for there will be plenty of all Earthly Commodities, with less labor and trouble then now it is under Monarchy. There will be no want, for every man may keep as plentiful a house as he will, and never run into debt, for common stock pays for all.

If you say, Some will live idle; I answer, No: It will make idle persons to become workers, as is declared in the *Platform*; There shall be neither Beggar nor idle person.

If you say, This will make men quarrel and fight:

I answer, No: It will turn swords into plowshares, and settle such a peace in the Earth, as Nations shall learn War no more. Indeed the Government of Kings is a breeder of Wars, because men being put into the straits of poverty, are moved to fight for Liberty, and to take one anothers Estates from them, and to obtain Mastery. Look into all Armies, and see what they do more, but make some poor, some rich; put some into freedom, and others into bondage: And is not this a plague among Mankinde?

Well, I question not but what Objections can be raised against this *Commonwealths Government*; they shall finde an Answer in this *Platform* following. I have been something large, because I could not contract my self into a lesser volume, having so many things to speak of.

I do not say, nor desire, That every one shall be compelled to practice this *Commonwealths Government*; for the spirits of some will be Enemies at first, though afterwards will prove the most cordial and true friends thereunto.

Yet I desire, That the *Commonwealths* Land, which is the ancient Commons and waste Land, and the Lands newly got in, by the Armies Victories, out of the oppressors hands, as Parks, Forests, Chases, and the like, may be set free to all that have lent assistance, either of person or purse, to obtain it; and to all that are willing to come in to the practice of this Government, and be obedient to the Laws thereof: And for others, who are not willing, let them stay in the way of buying and selling, which is the Law of the Conqueror, till they be willing.

And so I leave this in your hand, humbly prostrating my self and it before you, and remain

A true Lover of Commonwealths Government, Peace, and Freedom,

Jerrard Winstanley, Novemb. 5, 1651

* * * * *

TO THE FRIENDLY AND UNBYASSED READER

READER,

It was the Apostles advice formerly, to try all things, and to hold fast that which is best. This Platform of Government which I offer, is the Original Righteousness and Peace in the Earth, though he hath been buried under the clods of kingly Covetousness, Pride and Oppression a long time.

Now he begins to have his Resurrection, despise it not while it is small; though thou understand it not at the first sight, yet open the door, and look into the house, for thou mayst see that which will satisfie thy heart in quiet rest.

To prevent thy hasty rashness, I have given thee a short Compendium of the whole.

First, Thou knowest that the Earth in all Nations is governed by buying and selling, for all the Laws of kings hath relation thereunto.

Now this Platform following declares to thee the Government of the Earth without buying and selling, and the Laws are the Laws of a free and peaceable Commonwealth, which casts out every thing that offends; for there is no pricking Briar in all this holy Mountain of the righteous Law or peaceable Ruler.

Every Family shall live apart, as now they do; every man shall enjoy his own wife, and every woman her own husband, as now they do; every Trade shall be improved to more excellency then now it is; all children shall be educated, and be trained up in subjection to parents and elder people more then now they are: The Earth shall be planted, and the fruits reaped, and carried into Store-houses by common assistance of every Family: The riches of the Store-houses shall be the Common stock to every Family: There shall be no idle person nor Beggar in the Land.

And because offences may arise from the spirit of unreasonable ignorance, therefore was the Law added.

The Bill of Rights, 1689 (I Will. & Mary, sess. 2, c.2)

An act for declaring the rights and liberties of the subject and settling the succession of the crown.

Whereas the lords spiritual and temporal, and commons, assembled at Westminster, lawfully, fully, and freely representing all the estates of the people of this realm, did upon the thirteenth day of February, in the year of our Lord one thousand six hundred eighty eight, present unto their Majesties, then called and known by the names and stile of William and Mary, prince and princess of Orange, being present in their proper persons, a certain declaration in writing, made by the said lords and commons, in the words following: viz.

Whereas the late King James The Second, by the assistance of divers evil counsellors, judges, and ministers employed by him, did endeavour to subvert and extirpate the protestant religion, and the laws and liberties of this kingdom.

1. By assuming and exercising a power of dispensing with and suspending of laws, and the execution of laws, without consent of parliament.
2. By committing and prosecuting divers worthy prelates, for humbly petitioning to be excused concurring to the said assumed power.
3. By issuing and causing to be executed a commission under the great seal for erecting a court called, The court of commissioners for ecclesiastical causes.
4. By levying money for and to the use of the crown, by pretence of prerogative, for other time, and in other manner, than the same was granted by parliament.
5. By raising and keeping a standing army within this kingdom in time of peace, without consent of parliament, and quartering soldiers contrary to law.

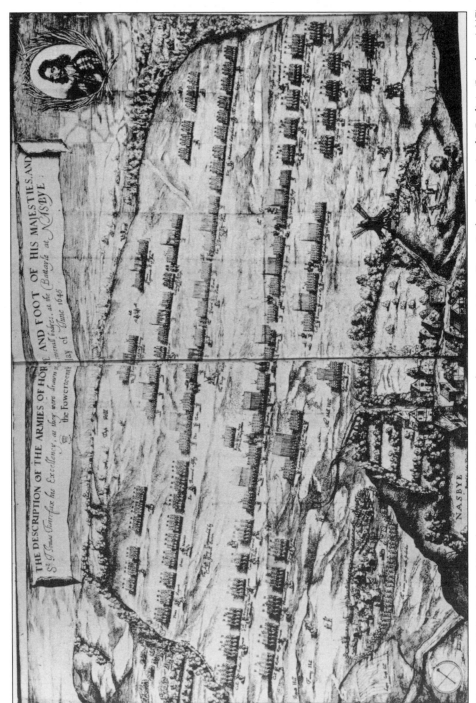

Illustration 11-3 Battle of Naseby (June 14, 1645). A great parliamentarian victory. From Joshua Sprigg, *Anglia Rediviva* (London, 1647).

6. By causing several good subjects, being protestants, to be disarmed, at the same time when papists were both armed and employed, contrary to law.
7. By violating the freedom of election of members to serve in parliament.
8. By prosecutions in the court of King's bench, for matters and causes cognizable only in parliament; and by divers other arbitrary and illegal courses.
9. And whereas of late years, partial, corrupt, and unqualified persons have been returned and served on juries in trials and particularly divers jurors in trials for high treason, which were not freeholders.
10. And excessive bail hath been required of persons committed in criminal cases, to elude the benefit of the laws made for the liberty of the subjects.
11. And excessive fines have been imposed; and illegal and cruel punishments inflicted.
12. And several grants and promises made of fines and forfeitures, before any conviction or judgment against the persons, upon whom the same were to be levied.

All which are utterly and directly contrary to the known laws and statutes, and freedom of this realm.

And whereas the said late King James the Second having abdicated the government, and the throne being thereby vacant, his highness the Prince of Orange (whom it hath pleased Almighty God to make the glorious instrument of delivering this kingdom from popery and arbitrary power) did (by the advice of the lords spiritual and temporal, and divers principal persons of the commons) cause letters to be written to the lords spiritual and temporal, being protestants; and other letters to the several counties, cities, universities, boroughs, and cinqueports, for the choosing of such persons to represent them, as were of right to be sent to parliament, to meet and sit at Westminster upon the two and twentieth day of January, in this year one thousand six hundred eighty eight, in order to such an establishment, as that their religion, laws, and liberties might not again be in danger of being subverted: upon which letters, elections have been accordingly made,

And thereupon the said lords spiritual and temporal, and commons, pursuant to their respective letters and elections, being now assembled in a full and free representative of this nation, taking into their most serious consideration the best means for attaining the ends aforesaid; do in the first place (as their ancestors in like case have usually done) for the vindicating and asserting their ancient rights and liberties, declare;

1. That the pretended power of suspending of laws, or the execution of laws, by regal authority, without consent of parliament, is illegal.
2. That the pretended power of dispensing with laws, or the execution of laws, by regal authority, as it hath been assumed and exercised of late, is illegal.
3. That the commission for erecting the late court of commissioners for ecclesiastical causes, and all other commissions and courts of like nature are illegal and pernicious.
4. That levying money for or to the use of the crown, by pretence of prerogative, without grant of parliament, for longer time, or in other manner than the same is or shall be granted, is illegal.

5. That it is the right of subjects to petition the King, and all committments and prosecutions for such petitioning are illegal.
6. That the raising or keeping a standing army within the kingdom in time of peace, unless it be with consent of parliament, is against law.
7. That the subjects which are protestants, may have arms for their defence suitable to their conditions, and as allowed by law.
8. That election of members of parliament ought to be free.
9. That the freedom of speech, and debates or proceedings in parliament, ought not to be impeached or questioned in any court or place out of parliament.
10. That excessive bail ought not to be required, nor excessive fines imposed; nor cruel and unusual punishments inflicted.
11. That jurors ought to be duly impanelled and returned, and jurors which pass upon men in trials for high treason ought to be freeholders.
12. That all grants and promises of fines and forfeitures of particular persons before conviction, are illegal and void.
13. And that for redress of all grievances, and for the amending, strengthening and preserving of the laws, parliaments ought to be held frequently.

And they do claim, demand, and insist upon all and singular the premisses, as their undoubted rights and liberties; and that no declarations, judgments, doings or proceedings, to the prejudice of the people in any of the said premisses, ought in any wise to be drawn hereafter into consequence or example.

To which demand of their rights they are particularly encouraged by the declaration of his highness the prince of Orange, as being the only means for obtaining a full redress and remedy therein.

Having therefore an entire confidence, That his said highness the Prince of orange will perfect the deliverance so far advanced by him, and will still preserve them from the violation of their rights, which they have here asserted, and from all other attempts upon their religion, rights, and liberties.

II. The said lords spiritual and temporal, and commons, assembled at Westminster, do resolve, That William and Mary prince and princess of Orange be, and be declared, King and Queen of England, France and Ireland, and the dominions thereunto belonging, to hold the crown and royal dignity of the said kingdoms and dominions to them and the said prince and princess during their lives, and the life of the survivor of them; and that the sole and full exercise of the regal power be only in, and executed by the said prince of Orange, in the names of the said prince and princess, during their joint lives; and after their deceases, the said crown and royal dignity of the said kingdoms and dominions to be to the heirs of the body of the said princess; and for default of such issue to the princess Anne of Denmark and the heirs of her body; and for default of such issue to the heirs of the body of the said prince of Orange. And the lords spiritual and temporal, and commons, do pray the said prince and princess to accept the same accordingly.

III. And that the oaths hereafter mentioned be taken by all persons of whom the oaths of allegiance and supremacy might be required by law, instead of them; and that the said oaths of allegiance and supremacy may be abrogated.

I A.B. do sincerely promise and swear, That I will be faithful, and bear true allegiance, to their Majesties King William and Queen Mary:

So help me God.

I A.B. do swear, That I do from my heart abhor, detest, and abjure as impious and heretical, that damnable doctrine and position, That princes excommunicated or deprived by the pope, or any authority of the see of Rome, may be deposed or murdered by their subjects, or any other whatsoever. And I do declare, That no foreign prince, person, prelate, state, or potentate hath, or ought to have any jurisdiction, power, superiority, pre-eminence, or authority, ecclesiastical or spiritual, within this realm:

So help me God.

IV. Upon which their said Majesties did accept the crown and royal dignity of the kingdoms of England, France, and Ireland, and the dominions thereunto belonging, according to the resolution and desire of the said lords and commons contained in the said declaration.

V. And thereupon their Majesties were pleased, That the said lords spiritual and temporal, and commons, being the two houses of parliament, should continue to sit, and with their Majesties royal concurrence make effectual provision for the settlement of religion, laws and liberties of this kingdom, so that the same for the future might not be in danger again of being subverted; to which the said lords spiritual and temporal, and commons, did agree and proceed to act accordingly.

VI. Now in pursuance of the premisses, the said lords spiritual and temporal, and commons, in parliament assembled, for the ratifying, confirming and establishing the said declaration, and the articles, clauses, matters, and things therein contained, by the force of a law made in due form by authority of parliament, do pray that it may be declared and enacted, That all and singular the rights and liberties asserted and claimed in the said declaration, are the true, ancient, and indubitable rights and liberties of the people of this kingdom, and so shall be esteemed, allowed, adjudged, deemed, and taken to be, and that all and every the particulars aforesaid shall be firmly and strictly holden and observed, as they are expressed in the said declaration; and all officers and ministers whatsoever shall serve their Majesties and their successors according to the same in all times to come.

VII. And the said lords spiritual and temporal, and commons, seriously considering how it hath pleased Almighty God, in his marvellous providence, and merciful goodness to this nation, to provide and preserve their said Majesties royal persons most happily to reign over us upon the throne of their ancestors, for which they render unto him from the bottom of their hearts their humblest thanks and praises, do truly, firmly, assuredly, and in the sincerity of their hearts think, and do hereby recognize, acknowledge and declare, That King *James* the Second having abdicated the government, and their Majesties having accepted the crown and royal dignity as aforesaid, their said majesties did become, were, are, and of right ought to be, by the laws of this realm, our sovereign liege and lady, King and Queen of *England, France*, and *Ireland*, and the dominions thereunto belonging, in and to whose princely persons the royal state, crown, and dignity of the said realms, with all honours, stiles, titles, regalities, prerogatives, powers, jurisdictions and authorities to the same belonging and appertaining, are most fully, rightfully, and intirely invested and incorporated, united and annexed.

VIII.   And for preventing all questions and divisions in this realm, by reason of any pretended titles to the crown, and for preserving a certainty in the succession thereof, in and upon which the unity, peace, tranquillity, and safety of this nation doth, under God, wholly consist and depend, The said lords spiritual and temporal, and commons, do beseech their Majesties that it may be enacted, established and declared, That the crown and regal government of the said kingdoms and dominions, with all and singular the premisses thereunto belonging and appertaining, shall be and continue to their said Majesties, and the survivor of them, during their lives, and the life of the survivor of them; And that the intire, perfect, and full exercise of the regal power and government be only in, and executed by his Majesty, in the names of both their Majesties during their joint lives; and after their deceases the said crown and premisses shall be and remain to the heirs of the body of her Majesty; and for default of such issue, to her royal highness the princess *Anne* of *Denmark*, and the heirs of her body; and for default of such issue, to the heirs of the body of his said Majesty; And thereunto the said lords spiritual and temporal, and commons do, in the name of all the people aforesaid, most humbly and faithfully submit themselves, their heirs and posterities for ever; and do faithfully promise, That they will stand to, maintain, and defend their said Majesties, and also the limitation and succession of the crown herein specified and contained, to the utmost of their powers, with their lives and estates against all persons whatsoever, that shall attempt any thing to the contrary.

IX. *And whereas it hath been found by experience, that it is inconsistent with the safety and welfare of this protestant kingdom, to be governed by a popish prince, or by any King or Queen marrying a papist*; the said lords spiritual and temporal, and commons, do further pray that it may be enacted, That all and every person and persons that is, are or shall be reconciled to, or shall hold communion with, the see or church of *Rome*, or shall profess the popish religion, or shall marry a papist, shall be excluded, and be for ever incapable to inherit, possess, or enjoy the crown and government of this realm, and *Ireland*, and the dominions thereunto belonging, or any part of the same, or to have, use, or exercise any regal power, authority, or jurisdiction within the same; and in all and every such case or cases the people of these realms shall be, and are hereby absolved of their allegiance; and the said crown and government shall from time to time descend to, and be enjoyed by such person or persons, being protestants, as should have inherited and enjoyed the same, in case the said person or persons so reconciled, holding communion, or professing, or marrying as aforesaid, were naturally dead.

X. And that every King and Queen of this realm, who at any time hereafter shall come to and succeed in the imperial crown of this kingdom, shall on the first day of the meeting of the first parliament, next after his or her coming to the crown, sitting in his or her throne in the house of peers, in the presence of the lords and commons therein assembled, or at his or her coronation, before such person or persons who shall administer the coronation oath to him or her, at the time of his or her taking the said oath (which shall first happen) make, subscribe, and audibly repeat the declaration mentioned in the statute made in the thirtieth year of the reign of King *Charles* the Second, intituled, *An act for the more effectual preserving the King's person and government, by disabling papists from sitting in either house of parliament.* But if it shall happen, that such King or Queen, upon his or her succession to the crown of this realm, shall be under the age of twelve years, then every such King or Queen shall make, subscribe, and audibly repeat the said declaration at his or her coronation, or the first day of the meeting of the first parliament as aforesaid, which shall first happen after such King or Queen shall have attained the said age of twelve years.

XI. All which their Majesties are contented and pleased shall be declared, enacted, and established by authority of this present parliament, and shall stand, remain, and be the law of this realm for ever; and the same are by their said Majesties, by and with the advice and consent of the lords spiritual and temporal, and commons, in parliament assembled, and by the authority of the same, declared, enacted, and established accordingly.

XII. And be it further declared and enacted by the authority aforesaid, That from and after this present session of parliament, no dispensation by *non obstante* of or to any statute, or any part thereof, shall be allowed, but that the same shall be held void and of no effect, except a dispensation be allowed of in such statute, and except in such cases as shall be specially provided for by one or more bill or bills to be passed during this present session of parliament.

XIII.   Provided that no charter, or grant, or pardon, granted before the three and twentieth day of *October* in the year of our Lord one thousand six hundred eighty nine shall be any ways impeached or invalidated by this act, but that the same shall be and remain of the same force and effect in law, and no other than as if this act had never been made.

THE WORKS OF JOHN LOCKE (1632–1704)

The Twelfth Edition
Volume The Fourth
(London, 1824.) Chapter XIX

The Treatises of Government

Of the Dissolution of Government (1689)

He that will with any clearness speak of the dissolution of government ought in the first place to distinguish between the dissolution of the society and the dissolution of the government. That which makes the community and brings men out of the loose state of nature into one politic society is the agreement which everybody has with the rest to incorporate and act as one body, and so be one distinct commonwealth. The usual and almost only way whereby this union is dissolved is the inroad of foreign force making a conquest upon them; for in that case, not being able to maintain and support themselves as one entire and independent body, the union belonging to that body which consisted therein must necessarily cease, and so every one return to the state he was in before, with a liberty to shift for himself and provide for his own safety, as he thinks fit, in some other society. Whenever the society is dissolved, it is certain the government of that society cannot remain. Thus conquerors' swords often cut up governments by the roots and mangle societies to pieces, separating the subdued or scattered multitude from the protection of and dependence on that society which ought to have preserved them from violence. The world is too well instructed in, and too forward to allow of, this way of dissolving of governments to need any more to be said of it; and there wants not much argument to prove that where the society is dissolved, the government cannot remain—that being as impossible as for the frame of a house to subsist when the materials of it are scattered and dissipated by a whirlwind, or jumbled into a confused heap by an earthquake.

Besides this overturning from without, governments are dissolved from within.

First, when the legislative is altered. Civil society being a state of peace amongst those who are of it, from whom the state of war is excluded by the umpirage which they have provided in their legislative for the ending all differences that may arise amongst any of them, it is in their legislative that the members of a commonwealth are united and combined together into one coherent living body. This is the soul that gives form, life, and unity to the commonwealth; from hence the several members have their mutual influence, sympathy, and connection; and, therefore, when the legislative is broken or dissolved, dissolution and death follows; for the essence and union of the society consisting in having one will, the legislative, when once established by the majority, has the declaring and, as it were, keeping of that will. The constitution of the legislative is the first and fundamental act of society, whereby provision is made for the continuation of their union under the direction of persons and bonds of laws made by persons authorized thereunto by the consent and appointment of the people, without which no one man or number of men amongst them can have authority of making laws that shall be binding to the rest. When any one or more shall take upon them to make laws, whom the people have not appointed so to do, they make laws without authority, which the people are not therefore bound to obey; by which means they come again to be out of subjection and may constitute to themselves a new legislative as they think best, being in full liberty to resist the force of those who without authority would impose anything upon them. Everyone is at the disposure of his own will when those who had by the delegation of the society the declaring of the public will are excluded from it, and others usurp the place who have no such authority or delegation.

This being usually brought about by such in the commonwealth who misuse the power they have, it is hard to consider it aright, and know at whose door to lay it, without knowing the form of government in which it happens. Let us suppose then the legislative placed in the concurrence of three distinct persons:

(1) A single hereditary person having the constant supreme executive power, and with it the power of convoking and dissolving the other two within certain periods of time.
(2) An assembly of hereditary nobility.
(3) An assembly of representatives chosen *pro tempore* by the people. Such a form of government supposed, it is evident,

First, that when such a single person or prince sets up his own arbitrary will in place of the laws which are the will of the society declared by the legislative, then the legislative is changed; for that being in effect the legislative whose rules and laws are put in execution and required to be obeyed. When other laws are set up, and other rules pretended and enforced than what the legislative constituted by the society have enacted, it is plain that the legislative is changed. Whoever introduces new laws, not being thereunto authorized by the fundamental appointment of the society, or subverts the old, disowns and overturns the power by which they were made, and so sets up a new legislative.

Secondly, when the prince hinders the legislative from assembling in its due time, or from acting freely pursuant to those ends for which it was constituted, the legislative is altered; for it is not a certain number of men, no, nor their meeting, unless they have also freedom of debating and leisure of perfecting what is for the good of the society, wherein the legislative consists. When these are taken away or altered so as to deprive the society of the due exercise of their power, the legislative is truly altered; for it is not names that constitute governments but the use and exercise of those powers that were intended to accompany them, so that he who takes away the freedom or hinders the acting of the legislative in its due seasons in effect takes away the legislative and puts an end to the government.

Thirdly, when, by the arbitrary power of the prince, the electors or ways of election are altered without the consent and contrary to the common interest of the people, there also the legislative is altered; for if others than those whom the society has authorized thereunto do choose, or in another way than what the society has prescribed, those chosen are not the legislative appointed by the people.

Fourthly, the delivery also of the people into the subjection of a foreign power, either by the prince or by the legislative, is certainly a change of the legislative, and so a dissolution of the government; for the end why people entered into society being to be preserved one entire, free, independent society, to be governed by its own laws, this is lost whenever they are given up into the power of another.

Why in such a constitution as this the dissolution of the government in these cases is to be imputed to the prince is evident. Because he, having the force, treasure, and offices of the state to employ, and often persuading himself, or being flattered by others, that as supreme magistrate he is incapable of control—he alone is in a condition to make great advances toward such changes, under pretense of lawful authority, and has it in his hands to terrify or suppress opposers as factious, seditious, and enemies to the government. Whereas no other part of the legislative or people is capable by themselves to attempt any alteration of the legislative, without open and visible rebellion apt enough to be taken notice of, which, when it prevails, produces effects very little different from foreign conquest. Besides, the prince in such a form of government having the power of dissolving the other parts of the legislative, and thereby rendering them private persons, they can never in opposition to him or without his concurrence alter the legislative by a law, his consent being necessary to give any of their decrees that sanction. But yet, so far as the other parts of the legislative in any way contribute to any attempt upon the government, and do either promote or not, what lies in them, hinder such designs, they are guilty and partake in this, which is certainly the greatest crime men can be guilty of one toward another.

There is one way more whereby such a government may be dissolved, and that is when he who has the supreme executive power neglects and abandons that charge, so that the laws already made can no longer be put in execution. This is demonstratively to reduce all to anarchy, and so effectually to dissolve the government; for laws not being made for themselves, but to be by their execution the bonds of the society, to keep every part of the body politic in its due place and function, when that totally ceases, the government visibly ceases, and the people become a confused multitude, without order or connection. Where there is no longer the administration of justice for the securing of men's rights, nor any remaining power within the community to direct the force to provide for the necessities of the public, there certainly is no government left. Where the laws cannot be executed, it is all one as if there were no laws; and a government without laws is, I suppose, a mystery in politics, inconceivable to human capacity and inconsistent with human society.

In these and the like cases, when the government is dissolved, the people are at liberty to provide for themselves by erecting a new legislative, differing from the other by the change of persons or form, or both, as they shall find it most for their safety and good; for the society can never by the fault of another lose the native and original right it has to preserve itself, which can only be done by a settled legislative, and a fair and impartial execution of the laws made by it. But the state of mankind is not so miserable that they are not capable of using this remedy till it be too late to look for any. To tell people they may provide for themselves by erecting a new legislative, when by oppression, artifice, or being delivered over to a foreign power, their old one is gone, is only to tell them they may expect relief when it is too late and the evil is past cure. This is in effect no more than to bid them first be slaves, and then to take care of their liberty; and when their chains are on, tell them they may act like freemen. This, if barely so, is rather mockery than relief; and men can never be secure from tyranny if there be no means to escape it till they are perfectly under it; and therefore it is that they have not only a right to get out of it, but to prevent it.

There is, therefore, secondly, another way whereby governments or the prince, either of them, act contrary to their trust.

First, the legislative acts against the trust reposed in them when they endeavor to invade the property of the subject, and to make themselves or any part of the community masters or arbitrary disposers of the lives, liberties, or fortunes of the people.

The reason why men enter into society is the preservation of their property; and the end why they choose and authorize a legislative is that there may be laws made and rules set as guards and fences to the properties of all the members of the society to limit the power and moderate the dominion of every part and member of society; for since it can never be supposed to be the will of the society that the legislative should have a power to destroy that which every one designs to secure by entering into society, and for which the people submitted themselves to legislators of their own making. Whenever the legislators endeavor to take away and destroy the property of the people, or to reduce them to slavery under arbitrary power, they put themselves into a state of war with the people who are thereupon absolved from any further obedience, and are left to the common refuge which God has provided for all men against force and violence. Whensoever, therefore, the legislative shall transgress this fundamental rule of society, and either by ambition, fear, folly, or corruption, endeavor to grasp themselves, or put into the hands of any other, an absolute power over the lives, liberties, and estates of the people, by this breach of trust they forfeit the power the people had put into their hands for quite contrary ends, and it devolves to the people, who have a right to resume their original liberty and, by the establishment of a new legislative, such as they shall think fit, provide for their own safety and security, which is the end for which they are in society. What I have said here concerning the legislative in general holds true concerning the supreme executor, who having a double trust put in him—both to have a part in the legislative and the supreme execution of the law—acts against both when he goes about to set up his own arbitrary will as the law of the society. He acts also contrary to his trust when he either employs the force, treasure, and offices of the society to corrupt the representatives and gain them to his purposes, or openly pre-engages the electors and prescribes to their choice such whom he has by solicitations, threats, promises, or otherwise won to his designs, and employs them to bring in such who have promised beforehand what to vote and what to enact. Thus to regulate candidates and electors, and new-model the ways of election, what is it but to cut up the government by the roots, and poison the very fountain of public security? For the people, having reserved to themselves the choice of their representatives, as the fence to their properties, could do it for no other end but that they might always be freely chosen, and, so chosen, freely act and advise as the necessity of the commonwealth and the public good should upon examination and mature debate be judged to require. This those who give their votes before they hear the debate and have weighed the reasons on all sides are not capable of doing. To prepare such an assembly as this, and endeavor to set up the declared abettors of his own will for the true representatives of the people and the lawmakers of the society, is certainly as great a breach of trust and as perfect a declaration of a design to subvert the government as is possible to be met with. To which if one shall add rewards and punishments visibly employed to the same end, and all the arts of perverted law made use of to take off and destroy all that stand in the way of such a design, and will not comply and consent to betray the liberties of their country, it will be past doubt what is doing. What power they ought to have in the society who thus employ it contrary to the trust that went along with it in its first institution is easy to determine; and one cannot but see that he who has once attempted any such thing as this cannot any longer be trusted.

To this perhaps it will be said that, the people being ignorant and always discontented, to lay the foundation of government in the unsteady opinion and uncertain humor of the people is to expose it to certain ruin; and no government will be able long to subsist if the people may set up a new legislative whenever they take offense at the old one. To this I answer: Quite the contrary. People are not so easily got out of their old forms as some are apt to suggest. They are hardly to be prevailed with to amend the acknowledged faults in the frame they have been accustomed to. And if there be any original defects, or adventitious ones introduced by time or corruption, it is not an easy thing to get them changed, even when all the world sees there is an opportunity for it. This slowness and aversion in the people to quit their old constitutions has in the many revolutions which have been seen in this kingdom, in this and former ages, still kept us to, or after some interval of fruitless attempts still brought us back again to, our old legislative of king, lords, and commons; and whatever provocations have made the crown be taken from some of our princes' heads, they never carried the people so far as to place it in another line.

But it will be said this hypothesis lays a ferment for frequent rebellion. To which I answer:

First, no more than any other hypothesis; for when the people are made miserable, and find themselves exposed to the ill-usage of arbitrary power, cry up their governors as much as you will for sons of Jupiter, let them be sacred or divine, descended or authorized from heaven, give them out for whom or what you please, the same will happen. The people generally ill-treated, and contrary to right, will be ready upon any occasion to ease themselves of a burden that sits heavy upon them. They will wish and seek for the opportunity, which in the change, weakness, and accidents of human affairs seldom delays long to offer itself. He must have lived but a little while in the world who has not seen examples of this in his time, and he must have read very little who cannot produce examples of it in all sorts of governments in the world.

Secondly, I answer, such revolutions happen not upon every little mismanagement in public affairs. Great mistakes in the ruling part, many wrong and inconvenient laws, and all the slips of human frailty will be born by the people without mutiny or murmur. But if a long train of abuses, prevarications, and artifices, all tending the same way, make the design visible to the people, and they cannot but feel what they lie under and see whither they are going, it is not to be wondered that they should then rouse themselves and endeavor to put the rule into such hands which may secure to them the ends for which government was at first erected, and without which ancient names and specious forms are so far from being better that they are much worse than the state of nature or pure anarchy—the inconveniences being all as great and as near, but the remedy farther off and more difficult.

Thirdly, I answer that this doctrine of a power in the people of providing for their safety anew by a new legislative, when their legislators have acted contrary to their trust by invading their property, is the best fence against rebellion, and the probablest means to hinder it; for rebellion being an opposition, not to persons, but authority which is founded only in the constitutions and laws of the government, those, whoever they be, who by force break through, and by force justify their violation of them, are truly and properly rebels; for when men, by entering into society and civil government, have excluded force and introduced laws for the preservation of property, peace, and unity amongst themselves, those who set up force again in opposition to the laws do *rebellare*—that is, bring back again the state of war—and are properly rebels; which they who are in power, by the pretense they have to authority, the temptation of force they have in their hands, and the flattery of those about them, being likeliest to do, the properest way to prevent the evil is to show them the danger and injustice of it who are under the greatest temptation to run into it.

In both the aforementioned cases, when either the legislative is changed or the legislators act contrary to the end for which they were constituted, those who are guilty are guilty of rebellion; for if any one by force takes away the established legislative of any society, and the laws of them made pursuant to their trust, he thereby takes away the umpirage which every one had consented to for a peaceable decision of all their controversies, and a bar to the state of war amongst them. They who remove or change the legislative take away this decisive power which nobody can have but by the appointment and consent of the people, and so destroying the authority which the people did, and nobody else can, set up, and introducing a power which the people has not authorized, they actually introduce a state of war which is that of force without authority; and thus by removing the legislative established by the society—in whose decisions the people acquiesced and unite as to that of their own will—they untie the knot and expose the people anew to the state of war.

*   *   *   *   *

Here, it is like, the common question will be made: Who shall be judge whether the prince or legislative act contrary to their trust? This, perhaps, ill-affected and factious men may spread amongst the people, when the prince only makes use of his due prerogative. To this I reply: The people shall be judge; for who shall be judge whether his trustee or deputy acts well and according to the trust reposed in him but he who deputes him and must, by having deputed him, have still a power to discard him when he fails in his trust? If this is reasonable in particular cases of private men, why should it be otherwise in that of the greatest moment where the welfare of millions is concerned, and also where the evil, if not prevented, is greater and the redress very difficult, dear, and dangerous?

But further, this question, Who shall be judge? cannot mean that there is no judge at all; for where there is no judicature on earth to decide controversies amongst men, God in heaven is Judge. He alone, it is true, is Judge of the right. But every man is judge for himself, as in all other cases, so in this, whether another has put himself into a state of war with him, and whether he should appeal to the Supreme Judge, as Jephthah did.

If a controversy arise betwixt a prince and some of the people in a matter where the law is silent or doubtful, and the thing be of great consequence, I should think the proper umpire in such a case should be the body of the people; for in cases where the prince has a trust reposed in him and is dispensed from the common ordinary rules of the law, there, if any men find themselves aggrieved and think the prince acts contrary to or beyond that trust, who so proper to judge as the body of the people (who, at first, lodged that trust in him) how far they meant it should extend? But if the prince, or whoever they be in the administration, decline that way of determination, the appeal then lies nowhere but to heaven; force between either persons who have no known superior on earth, or which permits no appeal to a judge on earth, being properly a state of war wherein the appeal lies only to heaven; and in that state the injured party must judge for himself when he will think fit to make use of that appeal and put himself upon it.

To conclude, the power that every individual gave the society when he entered into it can never revert to the individuals again as long as the society lasts, but will always remain in the community, because without this there can be no community, no commonwealth, which is contrary to the original agreement; so also when the society has placed the legislative in any assembly of men, to continue in them and their successors with direction and authority for providing such successors, the legislative can never revert to the people while that government lasts, because having provided a legislative with power to continue for ever, they have given up their political power to the legislative and cannot resume it. But if they have set limits to the duration of their legislative and made this supreme power in any person or assembly only temporary, or else when by the miscarriages of those in authority it is forfeited, upon the forfeiture, or at the determination of the time set, it reverts to the society, and the people have a right to act as supreme and continue the legislative in themselves, or erect a new form, or under the old form place it in new hands, as they think good.

AMERICA

Note: The following addresses the issue of the earliest legal developments in Massachusetts. Appropriately enough, it was a guest lecture at the celebration of the Columbus Quincentenary in Genoa.

Daniel R. Coquillette, "Radical Lawmakers in Colonial Massachusetts: The "Countenance of Authoritie" and *the Lawes and Libertyes*," 67 *The New England Quarterly* 179 (1994), 179–195, 204–206. Also published in Italian, (EDAM, Milan, 1994). Address Delivered at the Columbus Quincentenary "Il Diritto Dei Nuovi Mondi," Università di Genova 5 November 1992.

Genoa, the city and its university, celebrated the Columbus Quincentenary in grand style during the fall of 1992. Among the festivities were a number of distinguished international conferences and addresses, including the conference "Il diritto dei nuovi mondi" (the "law of new worlds"), which both looked back to the historical effects of Columbus's discoveries on modern law and forward to the "new worlds" of the future, including the new legal worlds of computer technology, satellites, and space exploration. The following paper was delivered at that conference through the kind invitation and support of the University of Genoa, Professor Giovanna Visintini, and Professor Vito Piergiovanni.

With the reader's kind forbearance, I would like to "set the scene." Those familiar with modern Italy will accept at once the paradox of Janus, the bifrons *Roman god of gates and doorways whose double face looks backward and forward simultaneously. The Columbus lectures, including those on space law and satellite communications, took place in the sixteenth-century Palace of the Jesuits. At intervals, meticulous waiters in white gloves served coffee from elegant silver pots. In the busy medieval streets below, shops whose crumbling façades date from the Crusades offered the latest in avant-garde Italian design, be it handbags, furniture, automobiles, or calculators.*

Genoa today is one of the largest and wealthiest ports in the world, the key southern outlet of the European Common Market. Vast ultra-modern sea and rail terminals serve dozens of ships concurrently, and the streets are crowded with sailors and silk-suited merchants from all corners of the globe. Here, unlike Venice, is no museum. In contrast to its archrival, Genoa lives and breathes. It is ancient and modern, tough and suave, all at once. The great palazzos are still occupied by families, banks, and institutions that can afford to shut their doors. The city's treasures are rarely seen, and private.

For the Quincentenary, however, the gates were opened to receive Genoa's guests. The receptions and dinners were simply stunning. My most vivid recollection is of arriving at a grand sixteenth-century palazzo in my rumpled suit, a victim of ten hours of flying, to watch the sleek, black Alfa Romeos pull down the medieval street and men and women of matchless Italian elegance, the family jewels glittering in the great gas torches, disembarking. Against the baroque fountains playing in the sunset., one could just see the detachment of Italian

Illustration 11-4 First Governor of Massachusetts, John Winthrop (1587/88–1649). Member of Gray's Inn and Inner Temple, Inns of Court. Admitted, Court of Wards and Liveries. Courtesy, Massachusetts Historical Society, from copy of a portrait painted in England before 1630.

carabinieri, machine guns at the ready, who were guarding the event. Inside, a magnificent mural depicted the arrival of an earlier group of guests, probably for some sixteenth-century "Cleopatra's feast," all in the fancy dress of the day but with the same diamonds sparkling and the same armed guards, here clutching their halberds, standing watch. What the radical lawmakers of the early Bay Colony would have thought of this scene, I would not dare to guess, but one thing is certain: Columbus himself would have felt right at home in his native city.

(I am particularly grateful to my research assistant, Mark A. Walsh, whose hard work and intelligence is evident on every page of this paper and in the excellent Annotated Bibliography, for which he is responsible.)

DISTINGUISHED COLLEAGUES:

On behalf of North America, and particularly on behalf of the hundreds of thousands of North Americans who proudly trace their ancestry to Italy and, indeed, to Genoa, I congratulate you on this great anniversary of your native son, Christopher Columbus.

The topic I would like to explore with you today concerns the ways in which the opening of the New World created radically different views about law in one of North America's oldest English colonies, Massachusetts, and how, in an extraordinary fashion, these new and creative approaches to law were indebted to Italy. For while the original settlers of Massachusetts were English Puritans, Protestant refugees who seem at superficial glance to have had little in common with the Latin world, in fact they were proud of their classical learning, and many of the books to be found in their libraries were in Latin, not English. [1] So if today I must address you in a barbaric tongue, many of the earliest leaders of the Massachusetts Bay Colony would have suffered no such embarrassment. Indeed, fluency in Latin, and Hebrew too, was crucial to their definition of an educated leader, as their 1636 founding of Harvard College, "first flower of their wilderness," so strongly attests.

The "Countenance of Authoritie"

It would be impossible to survey the legal history of colonial Massachusetts in the time allotted for my paper today. Spanning the eventful years between the landing of the ship *Arbella* in 1630, which carried to the New World not only the founders of Boston but the Massachusetts Bay Colony Charter, to the outbreak of violent revolution in the dawn hours of 19 April 1775, this period included nearly six generations of Americans and their laws.[2] Instead, I intend to

---

1. See Hugh Amory, *First Impressions: Printing in Cambridge, 1639–1989* (Cambridge: Harvard University Press, 1989), pp. 43, 46, 49. For example, Amory notes, Richard Bellingham, who became Governor in 1665, brought with him a Glanville *Tractatus de legibus & consuetudinibus regni Angliae* (1604) bound with a Latin version of St. Germain's *Doctor & Student, Dialogus de fundamentis legum Angliae et de conscientiae* (1604) (p. 49). As we shall see, there was a *Corpus Juris Civilis* in the Harvard College Library (ed. Jacques Cujas, 1625) at least by 1723, when the first library catalogue was completed. The library burned in 1764, so it is impossible to say how early the *Corpus Juris Civilis* was acquired, but there is no reason to believe that it was not purchased fairly soon after the foundation of the library in 1638. As Amory observes, "The Library catalogue of 1723 lists only twelve Anglo-American law books, mostly statutes; there were vastly more works of Roman and civil law" (Amory, *First Impressions*, pp. 43, 46). See Samuel E. Morison, *The Founding of Harvard College* (Cambridge: Harvard University Press, 1935), pp. 263–70; *Harvard College in the Seventeenth Century* (Cambridge: Harvard University Press, 1936), pp. 285–97.

2. For a full survey, see *Law in Colonial Massachusetts, 1630–1800*, ed. Daniel R. Coquillette, Robert J. Brink, Catharine S. Menand (Boston: Colonial Society of Massachusetts, 1984).

❖❖❖

The Capitall Lawes of *New-England*, as they ſtand now in force in the Common-Wealth.

BY THE COVRT,

In the Years 1641. 1642.

Capitall Lawes, Eſtabliſhed within the Iuriſdiction of *Maſſachuſets*.

1. IF any man after legall conviction, ſhall have or worſhip any o'her God, but the Lord God, he ſhall be put to death. *Deut.* 13. 6, &c. and 17. 2. &c. *Exodus* 22. 20.

2. IF any man or woman be a Witch, that is, hath or conſulteth with a familiar ſpirit, they ſhall be put to death. *Exod.* 22. 18. *Lev.* 20. 27. *Deut.* 18. 10, 11.

3. IF any perſon ſhall blaſpheme the Name of God the Father, Sonne, or Holy Ghoſt, with direct, expreſſe, preſumptuous, or high-handed blaſphemy, or ſhall curſe God in the like manner, he ſhall be put to death. *Lev.* 24. 15, 16.

4. IF any perſon ſhall commit any wilfull murther, which is manſlaughter, committed upon premeditate malice, hatred, or cruelty, not in a mans neceſſary and juſt defence, nor by meer caſualtie, againſt his will ; he ſhall be put to death. *Exod.* 21. 12, 13, 14. *Num.* 35. 30, 31.

5. IF any perſon ſlayeth another ſuddenly in his anger, or cruelty of paſſion, he ſhall be put to death. *Num.* 35. 20, 21. *Lev.* 24. 17.

6. IF any perſon ſhall ſlay another through guile, either by poyſonings, or other ſuch diviliſh practice ; he ſhall be put to death. *Exod.* 21. 14.

7. IF a man or woman ſhall lye with any beaſt, or bruit creature, by carnall copulation, they ſhall ſurely be put to death ; and the beaſt ſhall be ſlaine, and buried. *Lev.* 20. 15, 16.

8. IF a man lyeth with mankinde, as he lyeth with a woman, both of them have committed abomination, they both ſhall ſurely be put to death. *Lev.* 20. 13.

9. IF any perſon committeth adultery with a married, or eſpouſed wife, the Adulterer, and the Adultereſſe, ſhall ſurely be put to death. *Lev.* 20. 10. and 18. 20. *Deut.* 22. 23, 24.

10. IF any man ſhall unlawfully have carnall copulation with any woman-childe under ten yeares old, either with, or without her conſent, he ſhall be put to death.

11. IF any man ſhall forcibly, and without conſent, raviſh any maid or woman that is lawfully married or contracted, he ſhall be put to death. *Deut.* 22. 25. &c.

12. IF any man ſhall raviſh any maid or ſingle woman (committing carnall copulation with her by force, againſt her will) that is above the age of ten yeares ; he ſhall be either puniſhed with death, or with ſome other grievous puniſhment, according to circumſtances, at the diſcretion of the Judges : and this Law to continue till the Court take further order.

13. IF any man ſtealeth a man, or man-kinde, he ſhall ſurely be put to death. *Exod.* 21. 16.

14. IF any man riſe up by falſe witneſſe wittingly, and of purpoſe to take away any mans life, he ſhall be put to death. *Deut.* 19. 16. 18, 19.

15. IF any man ſhall conſpire, or attempt any invaſion, inſurrection, or publick rebellion againſt our Common-wealth, or ſhall indeavour to ſurprize any Towne or Townes, Fort or Forts therein ; or ſhall treacherouſly, or perfidiouſly attempt the alteration and ſubverſion of our frame of pollity, or government fundamentally, he ſhall be put to death. *Num.* 16. 2 *Sam.* 3. & 18. & 20.

Per exemplar Incre, Nowel, Secret.

Printed firſt in *New-England*, and re-printed in *London* for *Ben. Allen* in *Popes-head Allen.* 1643.

Illustration 11-5 *The Capitall Lawes of New England* (1641) published as a single page "broadside," exactly as above. Courtesy of Art and Visual Materials, Special Collections, Harvard Law School. (This copy was published in London, and is one of two known.) As discussed above, it was distributed to individual households.

concentrate on just one example of this rich and exciting heritage, the famous *Book of the General Lawes and Libertyes Concerning the Inhabitants of Massachusetts* (hereafter the *Lawes and Libertyes*). First printed in 1648, it was truly the "first flower" of American jurisprudence.

The *Lawes and Libertyes* were concerned with what the colonists called the "Countenance of Authoritie." By this they meant the process by which the coercive power of the Commonwealth was exercised. This "Countenance" could represent either justice or tyranny, depending on the nature of the process. To the Massachusetts colonists, who were escaping political and religious oppression, the difference between a good and evil "Countenance" lay in the rule of law, to which they were passionately devoted. The opening passage of the *Lawes and Libertyes* makes this abundantly clear.

> That no mans life shall be taken away; no mans honour or good name shall be stayned; no mans person shal be arrested, restrained, bannished, dismembered nor any wayes punished; no man shall be deprived of his wife or children; no mans goods or estate shall be taken away from him; nor any wayes indamaged under colour of law or Countenance of Authoritie unles it be by the vertue or equity of some express Law of the country warranting the same established by a General Court & sufficiently published; or in case of the defect of a law in any particular case by the word of God.[3]

These words issued from the first printing press in North America only eighteen years after their authors landed in what was almost unbroken wilderness. There can be no doubt that the *Lawes and Libertyes* was the first great printed affirmation of the American rule of law and of that particular "Countenance of Authoritie" for which it stands. Today, nearly three hundred and fifty years later, it remains among the most remarkable.

The Early Efforts: "Moses his Judicialls" (1636) and "The Body of Liberties" (1641)

Led by the *Arbella*, a battered flotilla of seventeen tiny ships arrived, one by one, off the rugged north shore of Massachusetts throughout the early summer of 1630. Aboard were one thousand and five immigrants, many ill and the majority anxious about the wilderness before them and the hostile English government of uncertain intent they had left behind. Yet fears were overmatched by enormous dreams, for smuggled on board at the last moment was the precious royal Charter of 1629, which granted the colony's leaders "full and absolute power and authority to correct, punish, pardon, govern and rule...according to the orders, laws, ordinances, instructions, and directions aforesaid, not being repugnant to the laws and statutes of our realm of England."[4] At the last minute as

---

3. *The Laws and Liberties of Massachusetts* (reprinted from the 1648 edition), ed. M. Farrand (Cambridge: Harvard University Press, 1929), p. 1. See also the photofacsimile edition, *The Book of the General Lawes and Libertyes Concerning the Inhabitants of Massachusetts*, ed. Thomas G. Barnes (San Marino, Calif.: Huntington Library, 1975), p. 1. Due to the clarity of the 1929 reprinting, reference will usually be made to that edition rather than the occasionally faint facsimile edition of 1975. The pagination of the text is identical in both modern editions.

4. *The Charters and General Laws of the Colony and Province of Massachusetts Bay*, Published by Order of the General Court (Boston, 1814), p. 15. In a great historical irony,

well, those proprietors not on the ship, wealthy Puritans in London whom the Crown had hoped to use as checks on the colony's independence, had resigned *en masse* in favor of leaders on the ship, thus freeing the colony entirely from direct control. Fervent religious refugees, with the hope of establishing a "City Upon a Hill" as a beacon to a sinful Europe, the colonial leaders were conscious of making history. As they drew close to that grey Massachusetts coast, they knew that the new order would have to be legal, as well as religious, in character.

The refugees on the ship were highly educated, and they included leaders with substantial legal training. John Winthrop, the first Governor, was a member of Gray's Inn and Inner Temple and an attorney to the Court of Wards and Liveries. His son, John Winthrop, Jr., was also a trained lawyer, as were Isaac Johnson, John Humfry, Roger Ludlow, Richard Bellingham, Simon Bradstreet, Herbert Pelham, Thomas Dudley, and Nathaniel Ward.[5] They were well acquainted with a fully developed legal system in their home country, complete with great legal guild halls, the Inns of Court, and an extensive professional literature with many hundreds of specialized treatises. They were also comfortable with a system of civil procedure based on writs and causes of action which was centuries old, a trained and professional judiciary sitting in ancient and established courts, and a rapidly emerging system of law reports, including *Plowden's Reports* (1571), *Dyer's Reports* (1585), *Croke's Reports* (1582–1641, published 1657, 1661), and the famous *Reports* of Edward Coke (1600–1615, 2 volumes posthumously published 1655, 1658).[6] Most important, the English legal profession was, by 1630, rigidly structured, with its own "universities" in the Inns of Court and its own, highly characteristic methods of legal training and jurisprudence, built almost exclusively around the common law courts.[7] With this system, the founders of Massachusetts were intimately familiar. To be sure, some were members of these powerful professional guilds or graduates of their training programs.

We should note here one important exception to the dominant common law tradition in England. Legal education in the English "ancient universities" had always focused on Roman-based civil and canon law and, after Henry VIII's "reforms," they taught Roman civil law exclusively. The actual law of the royal courts, the "common law," was not to be taught at Oxford or Cambridge until Blackstone's famous lectures in 1758. Further, certain specialized English courts, most notably the Court of Requests and the Admiralty Court, traditionally applied the civil, not the common, law.[8]

---

the first page of the priceless Charter of 1629 was stolen in 1984 and recovered in a drug raid.

5. See my "Introduction: The 'Countenance of Authoritie,'" in *Law in Colonial Massachusetts*, pp. xxvii–xxviii.

6. See John P. Dawson, *The Oracles of the Law* (Ann Arbor: University of Michigan Law School, 1968), pp. 65–80; J.H. Baker, *An Introduction to English Legal History* (London: Butterworths, 1990), pp. 204–14.

7. See Baker, *English Legal History*, pp. 177–99; Wilfrid R. Priest, *The Inns of Court Under Elizabeth I and the Early Stuarts, 1590–1640* (London and Totowa, N.J.: Rowan and Littlefield, 1972); J.H. Baker, *The Third University of England: The Inns of Court and the Common Law Tradition, Selden Society Lecture* (London, 1990).

8. See my *The Civilian Writers of Doctors' Commons, London* (Berlin: Duncker and Humblot, 1988), pp. 22–32.

The Puritans valued university education, and an extraordinarily high percentage of original settlers in the Massachusetts Bay Colony were university graduates, particularly of the nonconformist colleges at Cambridge, such as Emmanuel, the model for Harvard.[9] Indeed, it has been remarked that there were books on Boston's Beacon Hill while there were still "wolves on the slopes." It was true.

Given this high level of education, the strong professional tradition of the English common law by 1630, and the provisions of the Charter that the colonial laws not be "repugnant" to the English law, one might expect that the Puritans would have established a largely English legal system in Massachusetts. This was certainly the intent of the English government, but it was realized in only a very limited way. True, the language of the law was English, and certain important institutions, such as the jury and the justice of the peace, were adapted to New World conditions. But there were to be no law reports in Massachusetts until nearly two centuries later,[10] no formal organization of the bar for more than a century,[11] no formally trained judiciary for more than a century,[12] and only the seeds of a successful practicing bar for generations.[13] None of this could be explained by lack of educational institutions, illiteracy, lack of a printing press, or lack of an indigenous colonial legal literature. Not only was Harvard College in full operation, but the settlers had excellent primary schools, were highly literate, and had a printing press operating in Cambridge by 1638, the first in North America. Finally, there was indeed a flourishing colonial legal literature, but it was radically different in emphasis from its English counterpart.

Much of it could be explained, of course, by the very reasons for founding the colony, at least from the Puritans' perspective. They were religious refugees, who sought to establish a society where "God's will was done," or at least done more so than in England.[14] Further, they believed firmly in the "priesthood of all believers," all of whom should be able to apprehend God's will directly from the Holy Scriptures; thus Latin, Greek, and Hebrew languages were studied by the learned, and good, plain translations of the Scriptures in English were made

---

9. See Morison, *Founding of Harvard*, pp. 60–116, 148–209, and *Harvard in the Seventeenth Century*, pp. 3–25. For the familiarity later American lawyers demonstrated with Roman law precedents, see my "Justinian in Braintree: John Adams, Civilian Learning and Legal Elitism, 1758–1775," in *Law in Colonial Massachusetts*, pp. 359–418, and R. H. Helmholz, "Use of the Civil Law in Post-Revolutionary American Jurisprudence," *Tulane Law Review* 66 (June 1992): 1649.

10. John D. Cushing, "Sources for the Study of Law in Colonial Massachusetts at the Massachusetts Historical Society," in *Law in Colonial Massachusetts*, p. 584.

11. See my "Justinian in Braintree." p. 376.

12. George L. Haskins, "Lay Judges: Magistrates and Justices in Early Massachusetts," in *Law in Colonial Massachusetts*, pp. 39–55, and my "Justinian in Braintree," p. 376.

13. Thomas G. Barnes, "Thomas Lechford and the Earliest Lawyering in Massachusetts," in *Law in Colonial Massachusetts*, pp. 3–38. There was still a shortage of lawyers in 1689, when the Governor's secretary wrote to England:

> I have wrote you the want we have of two, or three, honest attorneys, (if any such thing in nature).
>
> Edward Randolph, Secretary to Governor Andros,
> Letter to England 1689.

See my introduction to *Law in Colonial Massachusetts*, pp. xxi.

14. See George L. Haskin's classic *Law and Authority in Early Massachusetts* (New York: Macmillan, 1960), pp. 1–93.

available for the less-educated settlers, as were Indian translations for the Native Americans the Puritans met and sought to convert.

But, if access to God's Law could, and should, be open to all believers, surely the same should be true of the secular law. And if there was no need for a "priesthood" to provide access to God's Law, surely a "priesthood" of lawyers was even more of an abomination. To the early Puritan leaders, religious learning was highly desirable, as was legal learning, but professional barriers to lay knowledge were shunned, both in a theological and a legal context. For this reason, colonial leaders expelled Massachusetts' first practicing lawyer, Thomas Lechford, in 1641 and initially ruled against representation in Court by paid counsel.[15] Again, the colony's early political leaders were trained lawyers themselves and considered legal learning, including Lechford's, useful. But, in complete contrast to the English models they had left behind, they were opposed to a professionalization of their system of justice. Lawyers such as Lechford were tolerated as long as they gave learned advice, but Lechford was accused of jury tampering and of questioning the religious orthodoxy of the colony. He had to go, and was not replaced for years, despite the highly litigious nature of the colonists.[16]

The early products of the Cambridge printing press were also evidence of these strongly held beliefs about the accessibility of law as well as religion. The first North American imprint, run on the press in 1638 or 1639, was a legal document, "The Oath of a Free Man."[17] Over its active life, from 1638 to 1692, legal publications were nearly as important to the business of the press as religious tracts and academic work for Harvard. Nearly forty legal imprints were published. Most strikingly, none were reprints of English law books. All were original to the colony.

Of all of these, the most important was the *Lawes and Libertyes* of 1648. This extraordinary book was the result of a deliberate and careful attempt to publish all "lawes of generall concernment" for the edification of all citizens. Even more important, it attempted to define the rights and duties of all inhabitants of the colony in a specific and positive way.[18] As such, it was quite unlike anything previously known to the preceding seven centuries of the English common law.

The book was a direct outcome of a political struggle within the colony between the magistrate class and the freemen. The magistrate class consisted of the Governor, the Deputy Governor, and the eighteen Assistants, who were given executive power by the Charter of 4 March 1629. The freemen of the colony were those who assembled in the annual General Court, first in person and then through elected deputies. Almost without exception, the freemen were also members of the established church and men of substance but not as prominent as the

---

15. Clause 26 of "The Body of Liberties" of 1641 stated that "every man that findeth himselfe unfit to plead his owne cause in any Court shall have Libertie to imploy any man against whom the Court doth not except, to helpe him, Provided he give him noe fee or reward for his paines," but this clause was one of the few in "The Body of Liberties" to be dropped by the *Lawes and Libertyes* in 1648. See Barnes, "Thomas Lechford," pp. 3–38.

16. Barnes, "Thomas Lechford," pp. 11–38.

17. See Amory, *First Impressions*; George Parker Winship, *A Preliminary Check List of Cambridge, Massachusetts, Imprints, 1638–1692* (Boston: Colonial Society of Massachusetts, 1939), p. 1.

18. See Barnes, introduction to *Lawes and Libertyes*, pp. 5–10

magistrates. At first, the magistrates resisted efforts to share power and even refused to show the Charter to the freemen and their deputies. By 1635, pressure from the freemen had resulted in the formation of a committee of magistrates and deputies to "make a draught of such lawes, as they shall judge useful for the well ordering of this plantation." As John Winthrop observed: "The deputies having conceived great danger to our state in regard that our magistrates, for want of positive laws, in many cases, might proceed according to their discretions, it was agreed, that some men should be appointed to frame a body of grounds of laws, in resemblance to a Magna Charta, which being allowed by some of the ministeries and the general courts, should be received for fundamental laws."[19]

Between 1635 and 1639 a number of experiments were undertaken, and at least two very different draft codes were created. One was by Boston's eminent divine, the Rev. John Cotton. A second was by another clergyman, but one with extensive prior legal training in England, the Rev. Nathaniel Ward.[20]

Cotton's draft was entitled "Moses his Judicialls." Although it was presented to the General Court as early as October 1636, it was never printed in America. It was, however, printed in London in 1641 under the title *An Abstract Or* [sic] *the Lawes of New England, As they are now established*. Reprinted in London in 1655, when it was first attributed to Cotton, the book probably resulted from a mistake by one of Cotton's London correspondents who, having received Cotton's draft manuscript, wrongly assumed it had been adopted into law by the colony.[21]

Indeed, Cotton's code was never to be adopted. Deriving the authority for all regulation of property rights, commerce, military affairs, and punishment from biblical authority, Cotton emphasized the colonial government's sources of power, not its limitations. Cotton closed his draft with stern, yet hopeful, lines from Isaiah 33.22: "The Lord is our Judge, the Lord is our Lawgiver, the Lord is our King, He will save us."[22] This was hardly the document the freemen sought. It set out few, if any, restraints on the magistrates' power. It was, however, remarkable in one respect. Not one word of "Moses his Judicialls," as embodied in the *Abstract*, referred to the authority of the English Crown, or even to English law. As such, its London printing was, in itself, significant. Appearing in the midst of tempestuous times there, the document is an example of how colonial legal thought was influencing England, rather than, as one might expect, England influencing the colonies. But again, and the point bears repeating, "Moses his Judicialls" never became law in Massachusetts.[23] As the dedicatory epistle to the

---

19. William H. Whitmore, introduction to *The Colonial Laws of Massachusetts. Reprinted from the edition of 1660, with the supplements to 1672* (Boston: Published by order of the City Council, 1889), pp. 2, 4, 5.

20. Whitmore, *Colonial Laws*, p. 9.

21. Cushing, "Sources for the Study of Law in Colonial Massachusetts at the Massachusetts Historical Society," p. 570.

22. *An Abstract of the Laws of New England* (London, 1641), *in Thomas Hutchinson's A Collection of Original Papers Relative to the History of the Colony of Massachusetts Bay* (Boston: Thomas and John Fleet, 1769), republished as *Hutchinson Papers* (Albany, N.Y.: J. Munsell, 1865; reprinted, New York: B. Franklin, 1967), pp. 183, 205.

23. Whitmore, Colonial Laws, pp. 12–13. "The next step is shown by the order passed by the General Court, November 5, 1639 (Records, i. 279), viz.: ___"

"It is ordered that the Governor [J. Winthrop], Deputy Governor [Thomas Dudley], Treasurer and Mr. Stoughton or any three of them, with two or more of the deputies of Boston, Charlestown or Roxbury, shall peruse all those models which have been or shall be

Lawes and Libertyes states, "[a]bout nine years since [1639] wee used the help of some of the Elders of our Churches to compare a modell of the Judiciall lawes of Moses...with intent to make use of them in composing our lawes, but not to have them published as the lawes of this Jurisdiction, nor were they voted in Court."[24]

Much more successful was the draft prepared by Nathaniel Ward, called "The Body of Liberties." This draft was certainly finished and circulated by 1639. The epistle to the *Lawes and Libertyes* of 1648 states that "The Body of Liberties" was "published about seven years since [1641]," but no printed copy has ever been found. We do know that it was circulated in manuscript form to every town and discussed so "that if any man should think fit, that any thing therein ought to be altered, he might acquaint the same for the deputies therewith against the next Court." Apparently, Cotton's draft was circulated with it. According to John Winthrop's notes of November 1639:

> The people had long desired a body of laws, and thought their condi-
> tion very unsafe, while so much power rested in the discretion of magis-
> trates. Divers attempts had been made at former courts, and the matter
> referred to some of the magistrates and some of the elders; but still it
> came to no effect; for, being committed to the care of many, whatsoever
> was done by some, was still disliked or neglected by others. At last it was
> referred to Mr. Cotton and Mr. Nathaniel Warde, &c., and each of them
> framed a model, which were presented to this General Court, and by
> them committed to the Governor and Deputy and some others, to con-
> sider of, and so prepare it for the Court in the third month next. Two
> great reasons there were, which caused most of the magistrates and some
> of the elders not to be very forward in this matter. One was, want of suf-
> ficient experience of the nature and disposition of the people, considered
> with the condition of the country and other circumstances, which made
> them conceive, that such laws would be fittest for us, which should arise
> *pro re nata* on occasions, &c., and so the laws of England and other
> states grew, and therefore the fundamental laws of England are called
> customs, *consuetudines*. 2. For that it would professedly transgress the
> limits of our charter, which provide, we shall make no laws repugnant to
> the laws of England, and that we were assured we must do. But to raise
> up laws by practice and custom had been no transgression; as in our
> church discipline, and in matters of marriage, to make a law that mar-
> riages shall not be solemnized by ministers, is repugnant to the laws of
> England; but to bring it to a custom by practice for the magistrates to
> perform it, is no law made repugnant, &c. At length (to satisfy the
> people) it proceeded, and the two models were digested with divers alter-
> ations and additions, and abbreviated and sent to every town, (12) to be
> considered of first by the magistrates and elders, and then to be pub-

---

further presented to this Court, or themselves, concerning a form of government and laws to be established, and shall draw up into one body, (altering, adding or omitting what they shall think fit,) and shall take order, that the same shall be copied out and sent to the several towns, that the elders of the churches and freemen may consider of them against the next General Court, and the charges to be defrayed by the Treasurer. [p. 7]"

24. Barnes, *Lawes and Libertyes*, p. A2.

lished by the constables to all the people, that if any man should think fit, that any thing therein ought to be altered, he might acquaint some of the deputies therewith against the next Court.[25]

Fortunately, a manuscript copy of "The Body of Liberties" has survived, and it was first printed in 1889.[26] Unlike Cotton's draft, it enumerates the fundamental rights of the colonial inhabitants rather than justifications for the government's authority. It was organized, like a classical Roman code, by theoretical categories. It first listed the rights and duties of all colonists and then described the rights and duties associated with more specific conditions: i.e., (II) "Rites, Rules and Liberties concerning Juditiall proceedings," (III) "Liberties more peculiarlie concerning the free men," (IV) "Liberties of Woemen," (V) "Liberties of Children," (VI) "Liberties of Servants," (VII) "Liberties of Forreiners and Strangers," (VIII) "Off the Bruite Creature," (IX) "Capitall Laws," and finally (X) "A Declaration of the Liberties the Lord Jesus hath given to the Churches." As stated in the preamble, "We hould it therefore our dutie and safetie whilst we are about the further establishing of this Government to collect and expresse all such freedomes as for the present we foresee may concerne us."[27]

---

25. Whitmore, *Colonial Laws*, pp. 7–9. See Morris L. Cohen, "Legal Literature in Colonial Massachusetts," in *Law in Colonial Massachusetts*, pp. 250–51. The records of the General Court of 7 October 1641 state that "The Governor [Bellingham] and Mr. Hawthorne were desired to speak to Mr. Ward for a copy of the Liberties and of the Capital laws to be transcribed and sent to the several towns" (Whitmore, p. 9). The records of 10 December 1641 also stated that "Mr. Deputy Endicot, Mr. Downing, and Mr. Hawthorne are authorized to get nineteen copies of the Laws, Liberties and the forms of oaths transcribed and subscribed by their several hands, and none to be authentic but such as they subscribe, and to be paid for by the Constable of each Town, ten shillings a piece for each copy, and to be prepared within six weeks" (Whitmore, p. 9). These records indicate that "The Body of Liberties" was transcribed, not printed.

According to Whitmore, some of the copies were made by Thomas Lechford, as appears by his "Note Book" (Boston, 1885, pp. 237–38). Lechford recorded that:

"I writt 5 copies more of the Lawes for the Country by the direction of our Governor. 11.8, 1639. Seven of them and the former had 3 lawes added. A Coppie of the Abstract of the Lawes of New England delivered to the Governor, 11.15.1639. And 12 coppies of the said Lawes first delivered, viz., in 10 last. For writing a Coppy of the breviat of the body of Lawes for the Country. 12.5.39. the 3 lawes added to the Copie of Lawes for Dorchester, delivered to the Constable, 12.6.1639. The 3 lawes added to 4 more of the said Coppies brought by the marshall. 12.11.39. Three Copyes of the said breviat delivered to the Governor besides the first, 12.12.1639....One copy of the said breviate delivered to Mr. Bellingham, with one coppy of the originall Institution and limitation of the Councell, 12.17.1639. Seven coppyes more of the said breviate. [Whitmore, p.8, n.6]"

Again, despite all these transcribed manuscript versions, no printed copy of "The Body of Liberties" is known. See Thorp L. Wolford, "The Laws and Liberties of 1648," in *Essays in the History of Early American Law*, ed. David H. Flaherty (Chapel Hill: University of North Carolina Press, 1969), pp. 147–85. In his *Preliminary Check List*, Winship reserved an entry for a possible printing (p. 1), and it has been assigned an "Evans Number," i.e. No. 6. It is not inconceivable that a printed copy might turn up.

26. Whitmore, *Colonial Laws*, pp. 29–61. The manuscript was preserved in a volume kept by Elisha Hutchinson, the grandfather of Thomas Hutchinson. It is now in the Boston Athenaeum, Ms.-L-350. The 1889 edition reproduces the manuscript in facsimile, each page faced by a printed text version. (Whitmore, pp. 10–11).

27. Whitmore, *Colonial Laws*, p. 33. According to Governor Winthrop, the "bodye of lawes, formerly sent forth among the "freemen" was actually "voted to stand in force" by

"The Body of Liberties" must have met with great approval, for almost all of its provisions were ultimately incorporated into the *Lawes and Libertyes*. Some of the provisions, particularly those related to extending dower rights of women and abolishing pure primogeniture (stated as a "Libertie of Children") were radically different from English law. Others, such as the strict rules against battering wives or servants, demonstrated advanced humanitarianism. The laws protecting "Bruite Creatures" were the first extensive animal protection laws to be proposed anywhere. And, like Cotton's draft, there was absolutely no reference to the Crown, the Charter, or to English authority. Nothing like this had been seen before. This was a totally new initiative in lawmaking.

There was one section of "The Body of Liberties," however, that was relatively primitive in its bluntness and that relied entirely on Old Testament authority: a listing of all crimes punishable by death, the so-called "*Capitall Lawes*." Whether this section was Ward's work or the product of an earlier hand, it was printed separately in 1642 as a broadside. It was also reprinted in England in 1643.[28]

The conclusion of "The Body of Liberties" established a three-year period for experimental consideration:

> Lastly because our dutie and desire is to do nothing suddainlie which fundamentally concerne us, we decree that these rites and liberties, shall be Audably read and deliberately weighed at every Generall Court that shall be held, within three yeares next insueing, And such of them as shall not be altered or repealed they shall stand so ratified, That no man shall infringe them without due punishment.
>
> And if any Generall Court within these next thre yeares shall faile or forget to reade and consider them as abovesaid. The Governor and Deputy Governor for the time being, and every Assistant present at such Courts shall forfeite 20sh. a man, and everie Deputie 10sh. a

---

the General Court in 1641. See vol. 1 of *Records of the Governor and Company of Massachusetts Bay*, ed. Nathaniel B. Shurtleff (Boston: William White, 1853), p. 346.

28. *The Capitall Lawes of New-England* (London: B. Allen, 1643). See Amory, *First Impressions*, p. 55. *The Capitall Lawes of 1642* was hardly a sophisticated document. It listed all crimes for which the death sentence was imposed, beginning with idolatry and witchcraft. The only "legal" authority cited was the Old Testament. Thus, the first two sections read, as follows:

Sect. 1

If any man after legal conviction shall have or worship any other God but the Lord God, he shall be put to death, Exod. 22.20. Deut. 13.6,10. Deut.17.2,6.

Sect. 2

If any man or woman be a witch, that is, hath or consulteth with a familiar spirit, they shall be put to death. Exod. 22.18. Levit. 20.27. Deut. 18.10, 11.

But the purpose of the document was salutary, to warn all in the colony, in clear, plain language, of the various causes for which they might be executed. As such the broadside was widely read in the colony, and specific measures were taken to ensure that it was taught to children and apprentices. Two thousand copies were printed, but they went out slowly, with Watertown voting as late as 1674 to require that "Each man heave in his house a coppy" to be paid for out of the rates. Today, only two copies survive, both London reprints. See Amory, *First Impressions*, p. 13, where he attributes the drafting of the *Capitall Lawes* to Nathaniel Ward.

man for each neglect, which shall be paid out of their proper estate, and not by the Country or the Townes which choose them, and whensover there shall arise any question in any Court amonge the Assistants and Associates thereof about the explanation of these Rites and liberties, the Generall Court onely shall have power to interpret them.[29]

At the end of this experimental period, political events in the colony forced more drastic measures. In 1646, the General Court was confronted by a *Remonstrance and Petition* issued by Robert Child and six other non-freemen. Their complaint was that the government of the colony was arbitrary and not consistent with the laws of England, as required by the Charter. They further attacked the Puritan theocracy by denying the government's right to require church attendance, to levy taxes to support Puritan ministers, and to restrict freemanship—and thus the ability to vote and hold office—to church members.[30] The remonstrants claimed that members of the Church of England were thus abused, and they threatened to appeal to England directly. They even cited the high mortality rate and a recent plague as evidence of divine disapproval of the colony.

The General Court responded in a long document, the *Declaration of 1646*, which attacked the text of the Remonstrance and asserted that the colonial government was indeed consistent with the Charter and the laws of England, although the *Declaration* added, parenthetically, that such laws had been supplemented by "words of eternal truth and righteousness."[31] Close examination of the *Declaration's* parallel citation of colonial and English law, however, has shown that its arguments are dangerously loose at best and at worst deliberately deceiving.[32] Most revealing, it was only with this document, and when they were under attack, that the Puritan leaders finally felt compelled to refer specifically to English law and the Charter.

The leaders may even have lacked English law books, at least initially. On 11 November 1647, doubtless in reaction to the *Remonstrance*, the General Court, "to the end we may have better light for making and proceeding about lawes," ordered four English law books in double copies: "[F]or the use of the Courte from time to time:—Two of Sir Edward Cooke upon Littleton; two of the Books of Entryes; two of Sir Edward Cooke upon Magna Charta; two of the new Tearmes of the Lawe; two Dalton's Justice of peace; two of Sir Edward Cooke reports." By November 1647, clearly before these English law books could have arrived, the General Court had already ordered that the colonial "lawes...be put in print" and that another committee be formed "for perfecting the lawes."[33] From this committee's proceedings would emerge the famous *Lawes and Libertyes* of 1648.

The "Lawes and Libertyes" of 1648

The Lawes and Libertyes was an extraordinary achievement. The first printed collection of laws in North America, it was published by the new press in Cam-

---

29. Whitmore, *Colonial Laws*, p. 61.
30. Whitmore, *Colonial Laws*, pp. 15–16.
31. Whitmore, *Colonial Laws*, pp. 15–16.
32. Richard B. Morris, "Massachusetts and the Common Law: The Declaration of 1646," in *Essays in the History of Early American Law*, pp. 135–46.
33. Farrand, introduction to *Lawes and Libertyes*, p. vii.

bridge in 1648, exactly ten years after the press's foundation and only eighteen after the landing of the *Arbella*.[34] There can be no doubt that the primary source was Ward's unprinted "Body of Liberties" (1641), for whole sections were extracted from it almost verbatim, including almost all of the new safeguards for oppressed women, servants, children, and animals. The three-year "discussion period" that followed the circulation of Ward's document also produced many amendments and new provisions. Indeed, while the *Lawes and Libertyes* incorporated many previously enacted laws, a full one third of the text was totally new. Another new, rather startling development was that unlike any previous English book, but very much like Justinian's *Institutes*, the *Lawes and Libertyes* was, upon publication, enacted into law.

*   *   *   *   *

The *Lawes and Libertyes* appeared in 1648, as the second phase of the English Civil War was raging. Doubtless the Massachusetts colonists knew that the King had lost all real power in 1646; they also knew that this was an auspicious moment for issuing a code that acknowledged no royal allegiance. Less than a year later, on 30 January 1649, Charles I was beheaded, a revolutionary act that stunned Europe. Of the 600 printed copies of the *Lawes and Libertyes*, the only one surviving, like the two known copies of the *Capitall Lawes* of 1641, was found in England, which raises an interesting question about transatlantic influence.

There is evidence that at least some participants in the English Civil War and some new theories of English government emerging from that struggle were affected by developments in the New World. Certainly English Puritans and the Levellers and Diggers who formed the ideological left wing of Cromwell's New Model Army knew of the exciting experiments in Massachusetts. Writers like Gerrard Winstanley, whose radical *The Law of Freedom* in a Platform appeared in 1652, must have been aware of the London edition of the *Abstract* of 1641, and the 1648 edition of the *Lawes and Libertyes* itself may have been distributed among Puritan radicals.[61] If cross-pollination of radical ideas did occur, some assuredly spread from the New World to Old. Thomas Barnes correctly argues that the *Lawes and Libertyes* was "an important model for the colonists' co-religionists in England who sought—albeit without success—the reform of English law during Cromwell's brief 'Godly commonwealth.'"[62]

Indeed, if an English jurisdiction had influenced the framers of the *Lawes and Libertyes* at all, it would have been the tiny neighboring colony of Plymouth,

---

34. Hailed at its discovery in 1906 by the American newspapers as "The Most Valuable American Printed Book," only one copy has survived of 600 originally printed. See Wolford, "The Laws and Liberties of 1648," p. 147.

61. See Gerrard Winstanley, *The Law of Freedom in a Platform* (London, 1652), ed. Robert W. Kenny (New York: Schocken Books, 1973), pp. 1–40; George H. Sabine, *The Works of Gerrard Winstanley* (New York: Russell and Russell, 1965); Stuart E. Prall, *The Agitation for Law Reform During the Puritan Revolution, 1640–1660* (The Hague: Martinus Nijhoff, 1966); Donald Veall, *The Popular Movement for Law Reform, 1640–1660* (Oxford: Clarendon Press, 1970); G.B. Nourse, "Law Reform Under the Commonwealth and Protectorate," *Law Quarterly Review* 75 (October 1959): 512–29.

62. Barnes, *Lawes and Libertyes*, p. 9. See also Haskins, *Law and Authority*, pp. 191–92.

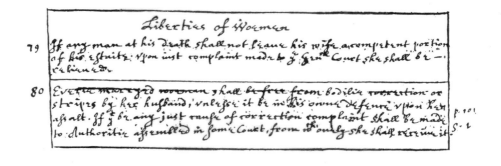

Liberties of Woemen.

79 | If any man at his death shall not leave his wife a competent portion of his estaite, upon just complaint made to the Generall Court she shall be relieved.

80 | Everie marryed woeman shall be free from bodilie correction or stripes by her husband, unlesse it be in his owne defence upon her assalt. If there be any just cause of correction complaint shall be made to Authoritie assembled in some Court, from which onely she shall receive it.

Illustration 11-6 The guarantees of married women's rights in the *Body of Liberties* (1641), facsimile from the Hutchinson Manuscript (Boston Athenaeum), W.H. Whitmore, *The Colonial Laws of Massachusetts* (Boston, 1889), 50, 51.

which had drafted a manuscript system of laws in 1636.[63] This effort, however, was quite primitive and heavily cited English authority. The first printed *General Laws of...New Plimouth* did not appear until 1672, from the Cambridge press, which issued the first edition of Connecticut's *The Book of the General Laws* the following year.[64] Both were clearly indebted to the Lawes and Libertyes, which went into its second edition in 1660 and its third in 1672.[65]

But that would not be all. A century later, Americans such as James Otis and John Adams would turn again to the great ideas of the *Lawes and Libertyes*, and, as their own Revolution drew near, they would seek in it models of radical legal reform. Even today, we look with wonder at the bold achievement of the *Lawes and Libertyes*, at its unquenchable optimism, at its faith in law as the guarantor

---

63. See George L. Haskins, "The Legal Heritage of Plymouth County," *in Essays in the History of Early American Law*, pp. 121, 123–25.

64. See the facsimile of *The Book of the General Laws of the Inhabitants of the Jurisdiction of New Plimouth* (Cambridge, 1672), printed in *The Compact with the Charter and Laws of The Colony of New Plymouth*, ed. William Brigham (Boston: Dutton and Wentworth, 1836; reprinted Buffalo: W.S. Hein Co., 1986), pp. 241 ff.; Winship, *Preliminary Check List*, p. 25.

65. Winship, *Preliminary Check List*, pp. 9, 24. These are reproduced in facsimile in Whitmore, *Colonial Laws of Massachusetts*, p. 119 ff., and in *The Colonial Laws of Massachusetts, Reprinted from the edition of 1672, with the supplements throughout 1686*, ed. William H. Whitmore (Boston: Rockwell and Churchill, 1890), p. 151 ff.

T H E
BOOK OF THE GENERAL
LAVVES AND LIBERTYES
CONCERNING THE INHABITANTS OF THE
MASSACHUSETS, COLLECTED OUT OF THE *RECORDS* OF
THE GENERAL COVRT, FOR THE SEVERAL YEARS
WHERIN THEY WERE MADE AND
ESTABLISHED.

And

Now Revifed by the fame Court, and difpofed into an
Alpbabetical order, and publifhed by the fame
Authority in the General Court holden
at *Bofton,* in *May* .
1 6 4 9.

VVbofoever therefore refifteth the Power, refifteth the Ordinance of God,
and they that refift , receive to themfelves damnation. Rom: **13.2.**

C A M B R I D G E,
Printed according to Order of the *GENERAL COVRT.*
1 6 6 0.

Illustration 11-7   A 1660 reprinting of the original *Lawes and Libertyes*, 1648, surviving in
a single copy at the Huntington Library, San Marino, California. Reproduced from W.H.
Whitmore, *The Colonial Laws of Massachusetts* (Boston, 1889), 19.

TO OUR BELOVED BRETHREN AND NEIGHBOURS
The Inhabitants of the Maſſachuſets, the Governour, Aſſiſtants and Deputies Aſſembled in the Generall Court of that Juriſdiction Wiſh Grace and Peace in our Lord Jeſus Chriſt.

THE Books of Lawes, of the firſt Impreſſion, not being to be had for the ſupply of the Country, put us upon thoughts of a ſecond; and conceiving the Charge would not be conſiderable, in reſpect of the benfit, if all our Lawes were (upon this occaſion) Reviſed, Compoſed and Reduced unto the firſt method, we have through the bleſſing of God upon our endeavours, effected the ſame.

The former Epiſtle tells you there would be need of alterations and additions, and experience doth witneſs the ſame, for while men either through ignorance or enmity, deny or oppoſe principles and actions of Righteouſneſs, the preſervation of humane Society will neceſſitate the enacting of new Lawes, or alteration of old, to fit the remedy to the diſeaſe; So it hath been in former ages, ex malis moribus bonæ legis, There is the leſs need of an Apologie for this work, not that we conceive it perfect, ſome few alterations are made, ſuch Lawes as have been repealed are left out, and ſuch Lawes of a general nature, as have bien made ſince the firſt Impreſſion, till this preſent, and are yet in force, are placed under the former heads, in an Alphabetical order, which method being at firſt taken up (though perhaps not the moſt exact) hath this conveniency and eaſe, that all Lawes referring to ſuch an head, are preſented to veiw at once whereby the Reader may with more facility comprehend the ſcope & meaning of the Law.

If any ſhall complain of incongruous expreſſions or obſcurity in ſome paſſages, let them be ſure it be ſo, before they affirm it; Conſidering the Supreme Court (which ought to be honoured) hath peruſed them, and hath judged meet to publiſh them as they ſtand: Neither would the time or their Honour permit them, as Criticks, to call every word to the Tryall before a Jury of Grammarians. Let it ſuffice that the meaning is intelligible, though the dreſs be not the moſt poliſhed; nor is it neceſſary, ſeeing mens Legis eſt Lex.

They, to whom theſe Laws are commended as Rules to which they ought to conform, may find better exerciſe for themſelves by endeavoring to make them live by executing of them, which will add a greater luſtre to them, then elegancy of expreſſion: When Laws may be read in mens lives, they appear more beautifull than in the faireſt Print, and promiſe a longer duration, than engraven in Marble. Weaker fences will ſecure againſt gentle Creatures, though walls of Braſs be inſufficient againſt forcible Obtruders. If breach of order doth argue violence of men, more than weakneſs of the Law, it will be every mans prudence to defend the Authority of the Laws, to avoid the cenſure of Impetuous, and to cover rather then make gaps, whereat the moſt innocent may enter, and deſtroy that proviſion which was made for their preſervation.

Laws are the peoples Birth-right, and Law makers the Parents of the Country: Undutifull unthrifts may deſpiſe the one and other, but many obligations command reverence to both. The light of Nature taught the Heathen to account them Sacroſancto, inviolable: Religion and civil Order ſhould make as deep Impreſſions in Chriſtians, eſpecially where Benefit and Damage are conſtant attendants. By this Hedge their All is ſecured againſt the Injuries of men, and whoſoever breaketh this hedge, a Serpent ſhall bite him: They that ruſh againſt it, will find the thornes will prick them; they that fly to it for ſhelter, may find the leaves to ſhade them: To ſuch as you, we need no other inducemens but the authority of the Apoſtle, 1 Pet.2. 13. & 17. Submit your ſelves to every Ordinance of man for the Lords ſake: Fear God; Honour the King.

By Order of the Generall Court,

Edward Rawſon Secret:

Illustration 11-8 The Preamble to the 1660 *Lawes and Libertyes, supra.*

T H E
GENERAL *L A U U E S* OF THE MASSACHUSETS COLONY, REVISED AND PUBLISHED BY *O R D E R O F T H E G E N E R A L C O U R T* in October 1 6 5 8.

 Orasmuch as the free fruition of such liberties, immunities, priviledges as humanity, civillity & Chrstianity, call for as due to every man in his place, & proportion, without impeachment and infringement, hath ever been, and ever will be, the tranquillity & stability of Churches, and Common-wealth, and the denyal or deprival thereof, the disturbance, if not ruine of both. It is therefore Ordered by this Court & the Authority thereof. That no mans life shall be taken away, no mans honour or good name shal be stained; no mans person shall be arrested, restrained, banished dismembred, nor any wayes punished no man shall be deprived of his wife, or children. no man's goods or estate shall be taken away from him, nor any wayes indamaged, under colour of Law, or countenance of Authority, unles it be by virtue or equity, of some expres Law of the Country warranting the same, established by a General Court, and sufficiently published; or in Case of the defect of a Law, in any particular Case, by the word of God. And in Capital Cases, or in cases concerning dismembring or banishment, according to that word, to be judged by the General Court. [1641]

Illustration 11-9 The famous first paragraph from 1660 *Lawes and Libertyes, supra,* tracking the 1648 1st edition.
Note: *Illustration 11-10,* following, is a typical following page, including everything from "Ballast Stones" to "Bond-Slavery," organized under "B" in alphabetical order. This page, of course, is included because of the highly important section on "Bond-Slavery." Is it consistent with the opening paragraph?

of human dignity. We talk in our twentieth-century classrooms, courts, and law offices about "demystifying" the law, about equal access to legal rights, and about a legal order that all people, rich and poor, empowered and weak, can understand and call their own. This was the dream of the *Lawes and Libertyes,* the dream of a New World. It was the dream of a rule of law. Is it not still our dream?[66]

Thank you.

---

66. As Thomas Barnes observed: "To borrow the Civil Law aphorism that the dedicatory epistle uses to justify the making of law, "Crescit in Orbe dolus": indeed evil does grow in the world, but known and established laws such as those set forth in the *Lawes and Libertyes* of 1648 provided a foundation not only for the punishment of malefactors but for the preservation of civil liberties. Those two sides of the same coin, the law, have been a fundamental element in the development of this country" (*Lawes and Libertyes,* p. 9).

| Ballaſt. | Barratrie. | Benevolence. | Bills. | Bondſlavery. | 5 |

and ſo proportionably, under the penaltie of forfeiting all ſuch bread, as ſhall not be of the ſeveral aſhizes aforementioned, to the uſe of the poor of the town, where the offence is committed, & otherwiſe as is hearafter expreſſed, & for the better execution of this preſent order; there ſhall be in every market town, & all other towns needful one or two able perſons annually choſen by each town, who ſhal be ſworn at the next County Court, or by the next Magiſtrate, unto the faithfull diſcharge of his or their office; who are hereby authorized, to enter into all houſes, either with a Conſtable or without, where they ſhall ſuſpect, or be informed of any bread baked for ſale and alſo to weigh the ſaid bread as oft as they ſee cauſe, & ſeize all ſuch as they find defective. As alſo to weigh all butter, made up for ſale, & bringing unto, or being in the town or market to be ſold by weight which if found light after notice once given, ſhall be forfeited in like manner. The like penaltie ſhall be for not marking all bread made for ſale. And the ſayd officer, ſhall have one third part of all forfeitures for his paines; the reſt to the poor as aforeſaid. [1646.]

Clarke of ṣ market.

Their pow-er.

Clarks fee.

A: 52: p: 8:

2 Whereas it appeares to this Court, that there is much deceit uſed by ſome Bakers, & others, who when the Clarke of the market cometh, to weigh their bread, pretend they have none, but for their owne uſe, & yet afterward putt their bread to ſale, which upon tryal hath been found too light; For prevention of ſuch abuſes for time to come. It is ordered That all perſons within this Juriſdiction, who ſhall uſually ſell bread within dores, or without, ſhall at all times hereafter, have all their bread, that they either putt to ſale or ſpend in their families, made of the due aſhizes, marked & yeilded to tryal of the ſaid Clarks as is directed in the order aforeſaid under the penaltie therein expreſt. [1652.]

To prevent deceit in Bakers

Ballaſt.

IT is Ordered by this Court & Authority thereof. That no Ballaſt ſhall be tak-en from any town ſhore, by any perſon whatſoever, without allowance under the hands of the ſelect men, upon the penaltie of ſix pence, for every ſhovel-full ſo taken, unleſs ſuch ſtones as they had lay there before? It is alſo Ordered; that no ſhip, nor other veſſel, ſhall caſt out any ballaſt in the channel, or other place inconvenient, in any harbour within this juriſdiction, upon the penalty of ten pounds. [1646.]

Ballaſt not to be taken without leav

nor caſt into ṣ channel.

Barratrie.

IT is Ordered, decreed & by this Court declared; that if any man be proved, and judged a common barrater, vexing others with unjuſt, frequent & endles ſuites. it ſhall be in the power of the Court, both to reject his cauſe, and to puniſh him for his Barratry. [1641]

Benevolence.

IT is Ordered, that this Court heer after will graunt no benevolence, except in forraine occaſions, and when there is mony in the treaſury ſufficient, and our debts firſt ſatisfied. [1641]

Bills.

IT is Ordered by the Authority of this Court; That any debt, or debts due upon bill or other ſpecialty aſſigned to another, ſhall be as good a debt & eſtate to the Aſſignee, as it was to the aſſigner, at the time of its aſſignation; And that it ſhall be Lawful for the ſayd Aſſignee, to ſue for, & recover the ſaid debt due upon bill, & ſo aſſigned, as fully as the original creditor might have done; provided the ſayd aſſignement be made upon the back-ſide of the bill or ſpecialtie. [1647]

Bils aſſigned good debt to the aſſigne,

Bona-ſlavery.

IT is Ordered by this Court & Authority thereof; That there ſhall never be any bond ſlavery villenage or captivity amongſt us, unles it be Lawfull captives, taken in juſt warrs, as willingly ſell themſelves, or are ſold to us. and ſuch ſhall have the liberties, & chriſtian uſuage, which the Law of God eſtabliſhed in Iſrael, concerning ſuch perſons, doth morally require, provided this exempts none from ſervitude who ſhall be judged thereto by Authority. [1641]

A 3

Bond

Illustration 11-10   The 1660 *Lawes and Libertyes, supra,* page 5. Note "Barratrie" and "Bond-slavery."

St. George Tucker's *Blackstone* (1st ed., 1803) (see Illustration 11-13), vol. 1, 62, 67, 124–127. Excerpts from Appendices, vol. 2, 73–74, vol. 5, 36–38. [The Notes and Appendices are St. George Tucker's effort to adapt Blackstone to Virginia.]

SECTION THE THIRD
OF THE LAWS OF ENGLAND.*

The municipal law of England, or the rule of civil conduct prescribed to the inhabitants of this kingdom, may with sufficient propriety be divided into two kinds; the *lex non scripta*, the unwritten or common law; and the *lex scripta*, the written or statute law.

The *lex non scripta*, or unwritten law, includes not only *general customs*, or the common law properly so called; but also the *particular customs* of certain parts of the kingdom; and likewise those *particular laws*, that are by custom observed only in certain courts and jurisdictions.[1]

*   *   *   *   *

I. As to general customs, or the common law, properly so called; this is that law, by which proceedings and determinations in the king's ordinary courts of justice are guided and directed. This, for the most part, settles the course in which lands descend by inheritance; the manner and form of acquiring and transferring property; the solemnities and obligation of contracts; the rules of expounding wills, deeds, and acts of parliament; the respective remedies of civil injuries; the several species of temporal offences, with the manner and degree of punishment; and an infinite number of minuter particulars, which diffuse themselves as extensively as the ordinary distribution of common justice requires. Thus, for example, that there shall be four superior courts of record; the chancery, the king's bench, the common pleas, and the exchequer....that the eldest son alone is heir to his ancestor....that property may be acquired and transferred by writing....that a deed is of no validity unless sealed and delivered....that wills shall be construed more favourably, and deeds more strictly....that money lent upon bond is recoverable by action of debt....that breaking the public peace is an offence, and punishable by fine and imprisonment....all these are doctrines that are not set down in any written statute or ordinance, but depend merely upon immemorial usage, that is, upon common law, for their support.

---

* Before we proceed with the Commentator to consider the subject of the ensuing Section, it will be proper to bestow some attention on those Acts of the PEOPLE OF THIS COMMONWEALTH, in particular, and the UNITED STATES, in general, to which nothing similar occurs in the Constitution and Government of England, or of Great Britain; being Laws, not only to the individual, and to the other departments of the Government, but to the Legislature, also. These are, the CONSTITUTION of the State of VIRGINIA, for which we must refer the Student to the Appendix to this part, Note C; and the CONSTITUTION of the UNITED STATES, which will be treated of in the Appendix, Note D.

1. From what circumstance the *general* customs, or *common law* of England, properly so called, obtains authority in these states will be the subject of future enquiry: but, with respect to particular customs, these, with the single exception of the Custom of Merchants, being merely local, could not be translated by our Ancestors to their new settlements in this Western World; and consequently have no authority, or existence here: as to the third branch of the *lex non scripta*, or particular Laws observed by custom in particular courts, a very small portion of them, indeed, will be found in the civil establishments of Virginia, even before the revolution.

IN CONGRESS, JULY 4, 1776.

A

DECLARATION

BY THE

REPRESENTATIVES

OF THE

UNITED STATES OF AMERICA,

IN CONGRESS ASSEMBLED.

WHEN in the courfe of human events,
it becomes neceffary for one people
to diffolve the political bands which have connected them with another, and to affume
among the powers of the earth, the feparate
and equal ftation to which the laws of nature
and of nature's God entitle them, a decent
refpect to the opinions of mankind requires
that they fhould declare the caufes which impel them to the feparation.

We hold thefe truths to be felf-evident, that
all men are created equal; that they are endowed by their Creator with certain unaliena-
ble rights; that among thefe are life, liberty,
and the purfuit of happinefs; that to fe-
cure thefe rights, governments are inftituted
among men, deriving their juft powers from
the confent of the governed; that whenever
any form of government becomes deftructive
of thefe ends, it is the right of the people to
alter or to abolifh it, and to inftitute new
government, laying its foundation on fuch
A 2   principles,

Illustration 11-11   Declaration of Independence (1797 ed.) [Author's Collection].

TO THE AMERICAN WORLD.

THE inhabitants of this continent have now an easy and advantageous opportunity of effectually establishing literary manufactures in the British colonies, at moderate prices calculated for this meridian, the establishment of which will absolutely and eventually produce mental improvement, and commercial expansion, with the additional recommendation of positively saving thousands of pounds to and among the inhabitants of the British empire in America.—Thus—The importation of one thousand sets of Blackstone's Commentaries, manufactured in Europe, at ten pounds per set, is sending very near ten thousand pounds across the great Atlantic ocean. Whereas—One thousand sets manufactured in America, and sold at the small price of three pounds per set, is an actual saving of seven thousand pounds to the purchasers, and the identical three thousand pounds which is laid out for our own manufactures is still retained in the country, being distributed among manufacturers and traders, whose residence upon the continent of course causeth the money to circulate from neighbour to neighbour, and by this circulation in America there is a great probability of its revolving to the very hands from which it originally migrated.—

American Gentlemen or Ladies who, at this juncture, retain any degrees of that antient and noble, but now almost extinguished, affection denominated patriotism, and are now pleased to exemplify it by extending with celerity and alacrity their auspicious patronage through the cheap mode of reposing their names and residences (*no money expected till the delivery of an equivalent*) with any Bookseller or Printer on the continent, as intentional purchasers of any of the literary works now in contemplation to be reprinted by subscription in America——will render an essential service to the community, by encouraging native manufactures——and therefore deserve to be had in grateful remembrance——by their country——by posterity——and by their much obliged, humble servant, the Publisher——

ROBERT BELL.

SUBSCRIPTIONS for Hume, Blackstone, and Ferguson, are received by said Bell, at the late Union Library, in Third-street, Philadelphia; and by the Booksellers and Printers in America.

Printed SPECIMENS, with Conditions annexed, for reprinting the above Books by Subscription, may be seen at all the great Towns in America.

Illustration 11-12 Robert Bell's subscription notice for the first (and uncopyrighted) American edition of Blackstone's *Commentaries* (Philadelphia, 1771). The subscription list contained the names of many American patriots. [Author's Collection].

*   *   *   *   *

CHAP. 1.

OF THE RIGHTS OF PERSONS.

*   *   *   *   *

The absolute rights of man, considered as a free-agent, endowed with discernment to know good from evil, and with power of choosing those measures which appear to him to be most desirable, are usually summed up in one general appellation, and denominated the natural liberty of mankind. This natural liberty consists properly in a power of acting as one thinks fit, without any restraint or control, unless by the law of nature; being a right inherent in us by birth, and one of the gifts of God to man at his creation when he endued him with the faculty of free-will. But every man, when he enters into society, gives up a part of his natural liberty, as the price of so valuable a purchase; and, in consideration of receiving the advantages of mutual commerce, obliges himself to conform to those laws, which the community has thought proper to establish. And this species of legal obedience and conformity is infinitely more desirable than that wild and savage liberty which is sacrificed to obtain it. For no man, that considers a moment, would wish to retain the absolute and uncontrolled power of doing whatever he pleases: the consequence of which is, that every other man would also have the same power; and then there would be no security to individuals in any of the enjoyments of life. Political, therefore, or civil liberty, which is that of a member of society, is no other than natural liberty so far restrained by human laws (and no farther) as is necessary and expedient for the general advantage of the public.[2] Hence we may collect that the law, which restrains a man from doing mischief to his fellow-citizens, though it diminishes the natural,[3] increases the

---

2. "Political liberty consists in the power of doing whatever does not injure another: the exercise of the natural rights of every man has no other limits than those which are necessary to secure to every other man the free exercise of the same rights; and these limits are determinable only by the law." Declaration of the rights of man, and of citizens, by the national assembly of France....1789.

3. Man in a state of nature has no more right to do mischief, than in a state of society: the restrictions of society, therefore, do not diminish any natural right, when they prohibit the doing mischief: they only restrain the exercise of a natural power to which no right was ever annexed. We must be careful, therefore, not to confound the term natural liberty, with natural right. Man, when he enters into society, may sacrifice a portion of his natural liberty in the sense here spoken of, without a particle of his natural rights. "It is a long received doctrine, that in a sate of society, or government, men give up a portion of their natural rights, in order to have the residue secured to them; by which it must be understood, that the rights possessed and enjoyed in a state of government, are necessarily fewer than those possessed, in what has been called, a state of nature. A man who adopts this opinion, is naturally enough inclined to look on government with a jealous eye; to esteem it, at best, but as the least of two evils; and to feel the restraints, or obligations imposed by it, as an abridgement of his natural liberty. This position conveys an idea altogether untrue, and highly derogatory to the noblest of all human institutions; an institution so fundamentally necessary, that without it, no other could take place, of any nature whatever. Without it, men must forever remain in a state of savage ignorance and wretchedness; in a condition more miserable, and more contemptible than that of the vilest brutes, or reptiles. If we could suppose men in that state, which is falsely called a state of nature, their rights would be extremely few, of very little value, and wholly destitute of protection and security. And unless

civil liberty of mankind; but that every wanton and causeless restraint of the will of the subject, whether practised by a monarch, a nobility, or a popular assembly, is a degree of tyranny: nay, that even laws themselves, whether made with or without our consent, if they regulate and constrain our conduct in matters of mere indifference, without any good end in view, are regulations destructive of liberty: whereas, if any public advantage can arise from observing such precepts, the control of our private inclinations, in one or two particular points, will conduce to preserve our general freedom in others of more importance; by supporting that state of society, which alone can secure our independence. Thus the statute of king Edward IV, which forbad the fine gentlemen of those times (under the degree of a lord) to wear pikes upon their shoes or boots of more than two inches in length, was a law that savoured of oppression; because, however ridiculous the fashion then in use might appear, the restraining it by pecuniary penalties could serve no purpose of common utility. But the state of king Charles II, which prescribes a thing seemingly as indifferent, (a dress for the dead, who are all ordered to be buried in woollen) is a law consistent with public liberty; for it encourages the staple trade, on which in great measure depends the universal good of the nation. So that laws, when prudently framed, are by no means subversive, but rather introductive of liberty; for (as Mr. Locke has well observed) where there is no law there is no freedom. But then, on the other hand, that constitution or frame of government, that system of laws is alone calculated to maintain civil liberty, which leaves the subject entire master of his own conduct, except in those points wherein the public good requires some direction or restraint.

The idea and practice of this political or civil liberty flourish in their highest vigour in these kingdoms, where it falls little short of perfection, and can only be lost or destroyed by the folly or demerits of it's owner: the legislature, and of course the laws of England, being peculiarly adapted to the preservation of this inestimable blessing even in the meanest subject. Very different from the modern constitutions of other states, on the continent of Europe, and from the genius of the imperial law; which in general are calculated to vest an arbitrary and despotic power, of controlling the actions of the subject, in the prince, or in a few grandees. And this spirit of liberty is so deeply implanted in our constitution, and

---

we include among the natural rights of man, his right of connecting himself with others in a state of civil society, his existence would be too wretched to be worth preserving. By legitimate government, his rights, so far from being diminished, are multiplied a thousand fold. To government he is indebted for every comfort, every convenience, and every enjoyment of life. He binds himself to certain duties, which are the conditions by which he becomes entitled to the benefits of government. But these duties, except on extraordinary occasions, are extremely light, whilst the benefits they procure are immense in value, and almost infinite in number. Were it possible in the jurisprudence of a democratic government, to deprive men of the benefits of government in exact proportion to their neglect of their obligations to it, it would be a code founded in severe justice; and every one would become sensible, how incomparably more numerous and valuable are the rights acquired by the stipulations of compact, than those which belong to a state of nature. All would then be induced to make a proper estimate of the blessings of a well ordered community, and to be in love with legitimate government, as the fountain of true liberty, and of every thing valuable in human life. No one should dare to talk of the rights of man who is unwilling to perform the duties of a citizen. Such a person would, in strict justice, have no rights, but those of a savage: for the essential rights of man are acquired by purchase, and the price must be paid to make the title good. This price is, obedience to the laws." Oration in commemoration of American independence, July 4, 1795, by T.T.T. of South-Carolina, Vol. 11.

rooted even in our very soil, that a slave or a negro, the moment he lands in England, falls under the protection of the laws; and so far becomes a freeman; though the master's right to his service may *possibly* still continue.[4]

The absolute rights of every Englishman, (which, taken in a political and extensive sense, are usually called their liberties) as they are founded on nature and reason, so they are coeval with our form of government; though subject at times to fluctuate and change; their establishment (excellent as it is) being still human. At some times we have seen them depressed by overbearing and tyrannical princes; at others so luxuriant as even to tend to anarchy, a worse state than tyranny itself, as any government is better than none at all. But the vigour of our free constitution has always delivered the nation from these embarrassments: and as soon as the convulsions consequent on the struggle have been over, the balance of our rights and liberties has settled to it's proper level; and their fundamental articles have been from time to time asserted in parliament, as often as they were thought to be in danger.

First, by the great charter of liberties, which was obtained, sword in hand, from king John, and afterwards, with some alterations, confirmed in parliament by king Henry the third, his son. Which charter contained very few new grants; but, as Sir Edward Coke observes, was for the most part declaratory of the principal grounds of the fundamental laws of England. Afterwards by the statute called *confirmatio cartarum*, whereby the great charter is directed to be allowed as the common law; all judgments contrary to it are declared void; copies of it are ordered to be sent to all cathedral churches, and read twice a year to the people; and sentence of excommunication is directed to to be as constantly denounced against all those that by word, deed, or counsel, act contrary thereto, or in any degree infringe it......Next, by a multitude of subsequent corroborating statutes (Sir Edward Coke, I think, reckons thirty-two), from the first Edward to Henry the fourth. Then, after a long interval, by the *petition of right*; which was a parliamentary declaration of the liberties of the people, assented to by king Charles the first in the beginning of his reign....

＊　＊　＊　＊　＊

Excerpts from St. George Tucker's Appendices

APPENDIX.
NOTE E.
SUMMARY VIEW OF THE LAWS CONCERNING SLAVES AS
PROPERTY IN VIRGINIA.
(Philadelphia, 1803)

[Appendix Vol. II, 73–74]

In considering the various acts which relate to slaves as property, it may be of use to premise some few observations on the nature, properties, qualities, and incident, appertaining to the objects of real and personal estates, respectively, and as distinguishing the one from the other.

---

4. The act for preventing the further importation of slaves, declared all slaves thereafter imported into Virginia by sea or land, contrary to the true intent of that act, to become free upon such importation. L.V.1778, c. 1, but a subsequent act unfortunately extended the period when they should become free to twelve months. L.V.1785, c. 77. Edi. 1794, c. 103.

BLACKSTONE'S COMMENTARIES:

WITH

NOTES OF REFERENCE,

TO

THE CONSTITUTION AND LAWS,

OF THE

FEDERAL GOVERNMENT OF THE UNITED STATES;

AND OF THE

COMMONWEALTH OF VIRGINIA.

IN FIVE VOLUMES.

WITH AN APPENDIX TO EACH VOLUME,

CONTAINING

SHORT TRACTS UPON SUCH SUBJECTS AS APPEARED NECESSARY
TO FORM A CONNECTED

VIEW OF THE LAWS OF VIRGINIA,

AS A MEMBER OF THE FEDERAL UNION.

BY ST. GEORGE TUCKER,

PROFESSOR OF LAW, IN THE UNIVERSITY OF WILLIAM AND MARY, AND
ONE OF THE JUDGES OF THE GENERAL COURT IN VIRGINIA.

PHILADELPHIA:

PUBLISHED BY WILLIAM YOUNG BIRCH, AND ABRAHAM SMALL,
NO. 17, SOUTH SECOND-STREET.

ROBERT CARR, PRINTER.

1803.

Illustration 11-13 St. George Tucker's *Blackstone* (1st ed., Philadelphia, 1803) with the "View of the Laws of Virginia" added. This was, in essence, the first American legal treatise. [Author's Collection].

The primary object of real property is land; whatever is permanently annexed to, or connected with it, or arises out of it, or issues from it, are considered as secondary objects of the same nature; because whilst they remain in such a state of connexion with it, they are regarded as a part of the land itself; but when severed from it, they cease to be considered as the objects of real property.

The primary, and almost universal objects of personal property are all things of a moveable and transitory nature; which may attend the person of the owner wherever he goes.

Hence there is in the nature of these primary objects, a permanent and irreconcileable difference, depending upon their several properties and qualities. This difference consists in the immoveable and permanent nature of land; and in the moveable and perishable properties and qualities, of such things as are neither annexed to, nor connected with it, or inseparable from it.

This difference being founded in the nature of the objects themselves, the one fixed, immoveable and perpetual, the other moveable and perishable, must ever remain unchanged, as the properties and qualities upon which the difference is founded. But the *incidents* to real and personal property, respectively, being merely creatures of the *juris positivi*, or civil institutions of different countries, there is no such irreconcileable difference between them, but that the same positive rules of law may be applied indifferently, to both, according to the will of the legislature, as good policy may require.

Thus an estate in lands, if limited for any number of years, even a thousand, is regarded as a chattel; whilst an estate in the precarious life of a villein might be an inheritance in fee simple, and as such, considered as a real estate. Co. Litt. 307. These instances demonstrate that the incidents to real and personal property, respectively, are merely creatures of the *juris positivi*, or ordinary rules of law concerning them; and may be altered and changed to suit the circumstances, convenience, interest and advantages of society.....Thus in England it might be for the benefit of commerce to consider a lease for a thousand years, in lands, as a mere chattel; and in Virginia it might have been equally for the advantage of agriculture to consider the slave who cultivated the land as real estate. And probably the rule of law might be applied with as little difficulty in the one case, as in the other.

This rule of positive law, whereby a slave whose breath is in his nostrils, or who may run away, and escape from his master forever, might be regarded as real estate, was not unknown to the antient common law of England. For a man might have an estate in fee, or in tail, or for life, or for years in a villein. Co. Litt. 307. And of an estate of inheritance in a villein, a woman might have been endowed, and a man tenant by the curtesy, Ibid. 307 and 124. And in this latter case the property in the villein should descend to the heir and not go to the executor. Ibid. 183. But if he had only an estate for years, and not an inheritance in the villein, the executor and not the heir should have him. Ibid. 117, 124. A villein also might have been annexed to lands, so as to descend and pass with them, by deed or devise, in which case he was called a villein regardant. Litt.§.181. Of these rules of the antient law the legislature cannot be presumed to have been uninformed.

Having premised these few observations, I shall now proceed to consider the several acts which relate to slaves, step by step; and thereby endeavor to discover their operation and effect from time to time.

* * * * *

[Appendix, Vol. I, pt. 2, 36–38]

II. Civil liberty, according to judge Blackstone, being no other than natural liberty so far restrained by human laws, and no farther, as is necessary and expedient for the general advantage of the public[1], whenever that liberty is, by the laws of the state, further restrained than is necessary and expedient for the general advantage, a state of *civil slavery* commences immediately: this may affect the whole society, and every description of persons in it, and yet the constitution of the state be perfectly free. And this happens whenever the laws of a state respect the form, or energy of the government, more than the happiness of the citizen; as in Venice, where the most oppressive species of civil slavery exists, extending to every individual in the state, from the poorest gondolier to the members of the senate, and the doge himself.

This species of slavery also exists whenever there is inequality of rights, or privileges, between the subjects or citizens of the same state, except such as necessarily results from the exercise of a public office; for the pre-eminence of one class of men must be founded erected upon the depression of another; and the measure of exaltation in the former, is that of the slavery of the latter. In all governments, however constituted, or by what description soever denominated, wherever the distinction of rank prevails, or is admitted by the constitution, this species of slavery exists. It existed in every nation, and in every government in Europe before the French revolution. It existed in the American colonies before they became independent states; and notwithstanding the maxims of equality which have been adopted in their several constitutions, it exists in most, if not all, of them, at this day, in the persons of our *free* negroes and mulattoes; whose civil incapacities are almost as numerous as the civil rights of our free citizens. A brief enumeration of them, may not be improper before we proceed to the third head.

Free negroes and mulattoes are by our constitution excluded from the right of suffrage*, and by consequence, I apprehend, from office too: they were formerly incapable of serving in the militia, except as drummers or pioneers, but of late years I presume they were enrolled in the lists of those that bear arms[2], though formerly punishable for presuming to appear at a musterfield[3]. During the revolutionary war many of them were enlisted as soldiers in the regular army. Even slaves were not rejected from military service at that period of their enlistment, were emancipated by an act passed after the conclusion of the war[4]. An act of justice to which they were entitled upon every principle. All but housekeepers, and persons residing upon the frontiers, are prohibited from keeping, or carrying

---

1. Blacks. Com. 125. I should rather incline to think this definition of *civil* liberty more applicable to *social* liberty, for reasons mentioned in a note, page 145, Vol. 1. of Blackstone's Commentaries.

* (The constitution of Virginia, Art. 7, declares, that the right of suffrage shall remain as then exercised: the act of 1723, c. 4, (Edi. 1733,) Sec. 23, declared, that no negroe, mulattoe, or Indian, shall have any vote at the election of burgesses, or any other election whatsoever. This act, it is presumed, was in force at the adoption of the constitution. The act of 1785, c. 55, (Edi. Of 1794, c. 17,) also expressly excludes them from the right of suffrage.

2. This was the case under the laws of the state; but the act of 2 Cong. C. 33, for establishing an uniform militia throughout the United States, seems to have excluded all but free white men from bearing arms in the militia.

3. 1723, c. 2.

4. Oct. 1783, c. 3.

any gun, powder, shot, club, or other weapon offensive or defensive[5]: Resistance to a white person, in any case, was, formerly, and now, in any case, except a wanton assault on the negroe or mulattoe, is punishable by whipping[6]. No negroe or mulattoe can be a witness in any prosecution, or civil suit in which a white person is a party[7]. Free negroes, together with slaves, were formerly denied the benefit of clergy in cases where it was allowed to white persons; but they are now upon an equal footing as to the allowance of clergy[8]. Emancipated negroes may be sold to pay the debts of their former master contracted before their emancipation; and they may be hired out to satisfy their taxes where no sufficient distress can be had. Their children are to be bound out apprentices by the overseers of the poor. Free negroes have all the advantages in capital cases, which white men are entitled to, except a trial by a jury of their own complexion: and a slave suing for his freedom shall have the same privilege. Free negroes residing, or employed to labour in any town, must be registered; the same thing is required of such as go at large in any county. The penalty in both cases is a fine upon the person employing, or harbouring them, and imprisonment of the negroe. [note omitted] The migration of free negroes or mulattoes to this state is also prohibited; and those who do migrate hither may be sent back to the place from whence they came. Any person, not being a negroe, having one-fourth or more negroe blood in him, is deemed a mulattoe. The law formerly made no other distinction between negroes and mulattoes, whether slaves or freemen. But now the act of 1796, c.2, which abolishes the punishment of death, except in case of murder, in all cases where any free person may be convicted, creates a most important distinction in their favour; slaves not being entitled to the same benefit.

Jesse Root, "Preface," *Connecticut Reports* (1798).

Jesse Root (1736–1822) was admitted to the Connecticut bar in 1763 and became Chief Justice of the Connecticut Superior Court. The following was the "Preface" to *Root's Reports* (1798), covering the period 1789–1798. There had been one prior Connecticut report, *Kirby's Reports* (1789), covering 1785–1788.

THE ORIGIN OF GOVERNMENT AND
LAWS IN CONNECTICUT, 1798

Our ancestors, who emigrated from England to America, were possessed of the knowledge of the laws and jurisprudence of that country; but were free from any obligations of subjection to them. The laws of England had no authority over them, to bind their persons. Nor were they in any measure applicable to their condition and circumstances here. Nor was it possible they should be: for the principle of their government, as it respected the prerogatives of the crown, the estates, rights and power of the lords, and the tenure of their lands, were derived from the feudal system. The privilege of sending members to parliament, from the towns, cities, and boroughs, to compose one branch of the legislature, called the House of Commons, and an exemption from taxation, only by their

---

5. 1748, c. 31. Ed. 1794.
6. Ibid. c. 103.
7. 1794, c. 141.
8. 1794, c. 103.

consent, was extorted from the kings by the barons, and is confirmed by the great charter of liberties as of his gift and grant. Their other laws were calculated for a great commercial nation. As to their criminal code, it was adapted to a people grown old in the habits of vice, where the grossest enormities and crimes were practised. In every respect therefore their laws were inapplicable to an infant country or state, where the government was in the peoples, and which had virtue for its principle, and the public good for its object and end, where the tenure of their lands was free and absolute, the objects of trade few, and the commission of crimes rare.

Our ancestors, therefore, as a free, sovereign, and independent people, very early established a constitution of government by their own authority; which was adapted to their situation and circumstances, and enacted laws for the due and regular administration of justice, for the propagation of knowledge and virtue, for the preservation of the public peace, and for the security and defense of the state against their savage enemies. New Haven did the same with little variation in point of form.

Their common law was derived from the law of nature and of revelation — whose rules and maxims of immutable truth and justice, which arise from the eternal fitness of things, which need only to be understood, to be submitted to, as they are themselves the highest authority; together with certain customs and usages, which had been universally assented to and adopted in practice, as reasonable and beneficial....

This constitution of our government, framed by the wisdom of our ancestors about 160 years ago, adapted to their condition and circumstances, was so constructed as to enable the legislature to accommodate laws to the exigencies of the state, through all the changes it hath undergone. And [it] is nearly coëval with our existence as a community, and analogous to the spirit of which all our laws have been made, from time to time, as cases occurred and the good of the public requires. And can it be said, with the least color of truth, that the laws of the state are not adequate to all the purposes of government and of justice?

We need only compare the laws of England with the laws of Connecticut, to be at once convinced of the difference which pervades their whole system. This is manifest in the spirit and principles of the laws, the objects, and in the rules themselves: with respect to the tenure of lands, descents, and who are heirs, and the settlement of insolvent estates, and of other estates testate and intestate, the probate of wills, registering of deeds, the arrangement and jurisdiction of our courts, the forms of civil processes, and the mode of trial, the appointing and returning jurors; and with respect to the settlement and support of the poor, the appointment and regulation of sheriffs, gaols and gaolers, the orderly celebration of marriages and granting of divorces; the means of propagating knowledge, and with respect to the punishments annexed to crimes; and in innumerable other instances, too tedious to mention, which every lawyer is acquainted with. May the citizens of Connecticut glory in this system of government and jurisprudence; which, at first, was the produce of wisdom, is perfected and matured by long experience; which has carried us safe through many a storm, withstood every attack, for more than a century and a half, is grown venerable by age and the wisdom of its regulations, and the rich profusion of blessings which it confers, as the nobles birthright of themselves and their children; and the highest interest and honor of the state as an independent member of a great nation, the rising empire of America!

These rights and liberties are our own, not holden by the gift of a despot. Our government and our rulers are from amongst ourselves; chosen by the free, uninfluenced suffrages of enlightened freemen; not to oppress and devour, but to protect, feed, and bless the people, with the benign and energetic influence of their power (as ministers of God for good to them). This shows the ignorance of those who are clamorous for a new constitution, and the mistake of those who suppose that the rules of the Common Law of England are the common law of Connecticut, until altered by a statute.

ON THE COMMON LAW OF CONNECTICUT

These questions are frequently asked, What is the Common law of America? Have we any common law in Connecticut? I know not how I can better resolve these questions than by answering another, (viz.) What is common law? And first, common law is the perfection of reason, arising from the nature of God, of man, and of things, and from their relations, dependencies, and connections: It is universal and extends to all men, and to all combinations of men, in every possible situation, and embraces all cases and questions that can possibly arise. It is in itself perfect, clear and certain; it is immutable, and cannot be changed or altered, without altering the nature and relation of things; it is superior to all other laws and regulations, by it they are corrected and controlled. All positive laws are to be construed by it, and wherein they are opposed to it, they are void. It is immemorial, no memory runneth to the contrary of it; it is co-existent with the nature of man, and commensurate with his being. It is most energetic and coercive, for every one who violates its maxims and precepts are sure of feeling the weight of its sanctions.

Nor may we say, who will ascend into heaven to bring it down, or descend into the depths to bring it up, or traverse the Atlantic to import it? It is near us, it is within us, written upon the table of our hearts, in lively and indelible characters; by it we are constantly admonished and reproved, and by it we shall finally be judged. It is visible in the volume of nature, in all the works and ways of God. Its sound is gone forth into all the earth, and there is no people or nation so barbarous, where its language is not understood.

The dignity of its original, the sublimity of its principles, the purity, excellency and perpetuity of its precepts, are most clearly made known and delineated in the book of divine revelations; heaven and earth may pass away and all the systems and works of man sink into oblivion, but not a jot or tittle of this law shall ever fall.

By this we are taught the dignity, the character, the rights and duties of man, his rank and station here and his relation to futurity, that he hath a property in himself, his powers and faculties, in whatever is produced by the application of them, that he is a free agent subject to the control of none, in his opinions and actions but to his God and the laws, to which he is amenable. This teaches us, so to use our own as not to injure the rights of others. This enables us, to explain the laws, construe contracts and agreements, to distinguish injuries, to determine their degree and the reparation in damages which justice requires. This designates crimes, discovers their aggravations and ill-tendency, and measures out the punishments proper and necessary for restraint and example. This defines the obligations and duties between husbands and wives, parents and children, brothers and sisters, between the rules and the people, and the people or citizens towards each other. This is the Magna Charta of all our natural and religious rights and liberties—and the only solid basis of our civil constitution and privileges—in short, it supports, pervades and enlightens all the ways of man, to the noblest ends by the happiest means, when and wherever its precepts and instructions are observed and followed—the usages and customs of men and the decisions of the courts of justice serve to declare and illustrate the principles of this law. But the law exists the same—nor is this a matter of speculative reasoning merely; but of knowledge and feeling. We know that we have a property in our persons, in our powers and faculties, and in the fruits and effects of our industry. We know that we have a right to think and believe as we choose, to plan and pursue our own affairs and concerns, whatever [we] judge to be for our advantage, our interest or happiness, provided we do not interfere with any principle of truth or of reason and justice. We know the value of a good name, and the interest we have in it. We know that every man's peace and happiness is his own. Nay, more when our persons are assaulted, our lives attacked, our liberties infringed, our reputation scandalized, or our property ravaged from us or spoiled, we feel the injury that is done to us, and by an irrepressible impulse of nature, resent the violation of our rights, and call upon the powerful arm of justice to administer redress. We also know that other men have the same rights, the same sensibility of injuries. When their rights are violated, this law is therefore evidenced both by the knowledge and the feelings of men. These ought to be the governing principles with all legislators in making of laws, with all judges in construing and executing the laws, and with all citizens in observing and obeying them.

Secondly, another branch of common law is derived from certain usages and customs, universally assented to and adopted in practice by the citizens at large, or by particular classes of men, as the farmers, the merchants, etc. as applicable to their particular business, and to all others of the same description, which are reasonable and beneficial.

These customs or regulations, when thus assented to and adopted in practice, have an influence upon the course of trade and business, and are necessary to be understood and applied in the construction of transactions had and contracts entered into with reference to them. To this end the courts of justice take notice of them as rules of right, and as having the force of laws formed and adopted under the authority of the people.

That these customs and usages must have existed immemorially, and have been compulsory, in order to their being recognized to be law, seems to involve some degree of absurdity—that is, they must have the compulsory force of laws, before they can be recognized to be laws, when they can have no compulsory force till the powers of government have communicated it to them by declaring them to be laws. That [is], so long as any one living can remember when they began to exist they can be of no force or validity whatever, however universally they may be assented to and adopted in practice; but as soon as this is forgotten and no one remembers their beginning, then and not until then they become a law.

This may be necessary in arbitrary governments, but in a free government like ours, I suppose, the better reason to be this:

That as statutes are positive laws enacted by the authority of the legislature, which consists of the representatives of the people, being duly promulgated, are binding upon all, as all are considered as consenting to them by their representatives: So these unwritten customs and regulations, which are reasonable and beneficial, and which have the sanction of universal consent and adoption in practice amongst the citizens at large or particular classes of them, have the force of laws under the authority of the people. And the courts of justice will recognize and declare them to be such, and to be obligatory upon the citizens as necessary rules of construction and of justice. The reasonableness and utility of their operation, and the universality of their adoption, are the better evidences of their existence and of their having the general consent and approbation, than the circumstance of its being forgotten when they began to exist.

Thirdly, another important source of common law is, the adjudications of the courts of justice and the rules of practice adopted in them. These have been learned by practice only, as we have no treatises upon the subject, and but one small volume of reports containing a period of about two years only, and a treatise lately wrote by Mr. Swift, containing a commentary on the government and laws of this state. We learn from history, the constitutions of government and the laws of foreign countries, the adjudications and rules of practice adopted in their courts of justice. But this will not give us the knowledge of our own, and although we may seem to have borrowed from them, yet ours is essentially different from all, in that it is highly improved and ameliorated in its principles and regulations, and simplified in its forms, is adapted to the state of our country, and to the genius of the people, and calculated in an eminent manner to improve the mind by the diffusion of knowledge, and to give effectual security and protection to the persons, rights, liberties and properties of the citizens, and is clothed with an energy, derived from a source, and rendered efficacious by a power, unknown in foreign governments, (viz.) the attachment of the citizens who rejoice in being ruled and governed by its laws, for the blessings it confers. Let us, Americans then, duly appreciate our own government, laws and manners, and be what we profess—an independent nation—and not plume ourselves upon being humble imitators of foreigners, at home and in our own country. But let our manners in all respects be characteristic of the spirit and principles of our independence.

I trust by this time the reader has anticipated in his own mind the answer to the questions, what is the common law of America? And have we any common law in the State of Connecticut? These principles, as applied to the situation and genius of the people, the spirit of our government and laws, the tenure of our lands, and the vast variety of objects, civil and military, ecclesiastical and commercial, in our own state have been exemplified in practice, defined, explained and established by the decisions of the courts in innumerable instances, although reports of but few of them have been published. To these I think we ought to resort, and not to foreign systems, to lay a foundation, to establish a character upon, and to rear a system of jurisprudence purely American, without any marks or servility to foreign power or states; at the same time leave ourselves open to derive instruction and improvement from the observations, discoveries, and experience of the literate, in all countries and nations, respecting jurisprudence and other useful arts and sciences. And indeed, a great part of our legal ideas were originally derived from the laws of England and the civil law, which being duly arranged, have been incorporated into our own system, and adapted to our own situation and circumstances.

*　　*　　*　　*　　*

Note: Do you think Root's "purely American" law makes sense? Or is he just a romantic? What do you think actually took place in Connecticut? Why would Root's view make some of his contemporaries nervous?

Illustration 12-1   Sir William Blackstone (1723–80) [Contemporary print, Author's Collection].

XII

"LAW AND ORDER" IN EIGHTEENTH-CENTURY ENGLAND

BLACKSTONE, "SOCIOLOGICAL HISTORY," AND THE "INCORPORATION" OF THE LAW MERCHANT

The "Glorious Revolution" instituted a long period of outward stability in English national life. Between England's new constitutional settlement in 1688 and England's ultimate victory over Napoleon in the treaties of the Congress of Vienna in 1815, 127 years passed. William and Mary failed to produce any heir, and the Crown passed to Anne, Mary's sister, in 1702. She also failed to produce an heir, and at her death in 1714, the Crown passed to the heirs of James I's sister Elizabeth, who had married a Protestant, Frederick, the Elector of Palatine, in Germany. This family, the so called Hanoverian Dynasty, are the direct ancestors of the contemporary English royal family, who exchanged the Germanic family name of "Saxe Coburg-Gotha" for the more patriotic "Windsor." (The German connection has been, at times, an embarrassment. The Kaiser was a relative. Edward VIII, who left his throne to marry a divorcee in 1936, can be seen in awkward photographs chatting amicably with Adolf Hitler.)

The Hanoverians were, by all accounts, very dull. George I and George II barely spoke English. They certainly spoke in German at court, and surrounded themselves with German favorites. They were not very articulate or intelligent. But this had a good side. The Hanoverians had to leave the business of government to able English politicians. While the monarchs still had great power by modern standards, the "Georges" certainly had no personal charisma or personal following of the kind that would permit them to challenge Parliament. The Whigs, in particular, flourished in this period, and their solid, commercial, bourgeoisie values became the national values. Despite great gaps between rich and poor, and the cruel dislocations inherent in growing industrialization, England remained internally at peace.

This long period of domestic stability, remarkable in the history of any nation, was particularly striking because of revolution elsewhere. This period saw the American Revolution: the Declaration of Independence was promulgated in 1775, and war followed soon afterwards. While these events made a profound impression on the English political leadership, even this trauma paled before the French Revolution of 1789, a bloody upheaval that was to change the feudal world of Europe forever.

Why stability in England and revolution elsewhere? It could be explained by domestic contentment, yet recent studies by the "Warwick" school of social history present a different picture, one full of smoldering class and regional antagonism and outright exploitation of the poor by the powerful. E.P. Thompson's great study, *Whigs and Hunters: The Origin of the Black Act* (London, 1975), is particularly recommended for those wishing a graphic picture of the daily realities of country life in Georgian England. Yet, with the exception of the ubiquitous highway man and the occasional London riot, these resentments and injustices would remain under the surface until the great statutory reforms of the nineteenth century. How could this have been achieved in a country which had no regular police, little internal security forces, and practically no real prisons?

America today is also enjoying a sustained period of relative domestic stability. But we are paying a high price for inequalities and hardships in our society. Our imprisonment rate is among the highest ever seen in recorded history, and certainly the highest in any free society without political prisoners. It is currently the highest in the world, three or four times the rate in European nations and ten times the rate found in China or Japan. In the United States as of January, 1998, an astonishing 1,725,842 people are in prison, at the annual cost of over $30,000 each, and, according to the Department of Justice, the number is growing by about 96,000 a year. The national figure could reach two million by 2000 A.D. In some neighborhoods, one out of two young men has a police record. Recent federal legislation will add to a domestic army of regular, armed police.

How could a society like that of Georgian England, where poverty and vast class exploitation were common, exist without a high rate of imprisonment or a regular police force? Indeed, it not only existed, it flourished without apparent fundamental reform for more than four generations. Part of the answer, of course, was in the administration of the criminal law, and part in the popular perception of the idea of law itself.

This is all the more curious given the dramatic economic change in eighteenth-century England. England entered the eighteenth century a colonial power, but with the balance of economic and political power still firmly in the hands of a landed aristocracy whose basic income remained, as always, the output of their great farms and herds, particularly sheep. Yet change was afoot. The Bank of England had been founded in 1694. Its initial deposits in 1696 were an amazing 2 million pounds. By 1796, that figure stood at 13,457 million pounds, the largest source of capital the world had ever seen.[1] In addition, the scattered colonies that had been a source of high risk adventure during the sixteenth and seventeenth centuries had become, with the conquest of India and the opening of China, a vast worldwide empire, with British colonies and surrogate governments standing guard on every major trade route, be it in the Caribbean, Africa, America, India, China, or in those great empty lands, Canada, Australia and New Zealand.

With the expansion of English trade and industry came demands on the common law system undreamt of a century before. Complex commercial transactions replaced land settlements at the heart of the production and protection of wealth, and these transactions frequently had an international scope. How did the English common law, based on feudal rights in land and ancient causes of action, adapt? The question becomes particularly compelling when two additional historical

---

1. See Daniel R. Coquillette, "The Mystery of the New Fashioned Goldsmiths: From Usury to the Bank of England (1622–1694)" in 12 *Comparative Studies in Continental and Anglo-American Legal History* (V. Piergiovanni ed., Berlin, 1993), 91–117.

facts are fully appreciated. First, the eighteenth century did not see the great statutory changes in the law that marked the reform of the feudal system, or were to come later in the nineteenth century. Most of the major changes were achieved by judge-made common law. Second, not only did the common law adapt to these profound economic and social changes, but it became established throughout this vast and growing empire, as perhaps England's most permanently enduring export. Even where, as in America, English rule itself was ousted, the English law remained. Today, there is little enthusiasm for the English colonial period among the young educated elites of Kenya, Nigeria, Ghana, India, Pakistan, Jamaica, or even in Hong Kong or Australia, but the young lawyers of these countries still come today to study at the Inns of Court and still stand proudly, in fiercely independent national courts, wearing the wig of the English barrister, while arguing principles of English common law to English style juries. Indeed, except for the wigs, this is still largely true throughout America.

A. BLACKSTONE

A single figure has come to symbolize the concept of the common law so dominant in the Georgian Age, and also its spread throughout the English colonies. This was Sir William Blackstone (1723–1780). While Blackstone became a judge of the King's Bench and the Common Pleas, his fame was not as a judge. Nor, despite his extensive legal writing, was he considered a jurist of the first rank. He never led major law reform projects, and he certainly did not achieve the political power of a Bacon or a Coke.

Blackstone was, first and foremost, a teacher and a popularizer of the common law. Strictly speaking, he was actually the first "law professor," in the sense of a university professor who taught common law. Of course, university professors had been teaching Roman and Canon law in English Universities since Vacarius in 1149 A.D., but common law training was restricted to the Inns of Court. Blackstone began lecturing privately on English law at Oxford in about 1753, where he was a Fellow of All Souls College, a graduate foundation. In that year, a man named Charles Viner completed the last volume of one of the most extensive and authoritative abridgments of English case law ever created, *A General Abridgment of Law and Equity* (23 volumes, 1742–53), otherwise known as "*Viner's Abridgment*." On Viner's death, in 1756, he left a major bequest to Oxford University. This established the Vinerian Professorship of English Law, the first position in any university for teaching the common law. Blackstone was appointed to the chair, and began to give regular university lectures in common law in 1758. These annual lectures, in turn, became the basis of a four volume summary of the entire common law, *Commentaries on the Laws of England* (Oxford 1765–1770), or "*Blackstone's Commentaries*."[2]

Blackstone's Commentaries became, in only a few years, the most popular legal treatise in common law history, comparable only to that "all time best seller" and civil law masterpiece, *The Institutes of Justinian*. Between 1765 and 1876, there were 23 editions of the *Commentaries* and more than 60 printings.

---

2. See *Materials*, Chapter I, *supra*.

As discussed in Chapter XI, *supra*, the *Commentaries* were published in a "pirated" edition in America in 1771, and by 1897 there were 13 American printings, and thousands of English copies were imported, as well. The most important feature of *Blackstone's Commentaries* was that it could be read and understood by intelligent laymen. Among his many books on military strategy and agriculture, George Washington had a set, so did John Adams, Jefferson, Hamilton and Madison.[3] And so did the colonial settlers of India, Hong Kong, Jamaica, Canada, and Australia, to name only a few colonies.

One colonist greatly impressed by Blackstone was a resident of Medford, Massachusetts named Isaac Royall. Royall had made a fortune in sugar plantations on Antigua, and had retired to New England, like many planters, to rest from the unhealthy climate of the Caribbean. (Certainly a switch on today's perspectives!) Royall was a loyalist at the outset of the Revolution, and went into exile in England. There he executed a will, and died in 1781. Royall's will, like Viner's, endowed a "Professor of Law," but this time at Harvard University in America.[4]

From the bequests of Viner and Royall evolved the great modern legal faculties of Oxford and Harvard. This process certainly took time. At Oxford, a respectable "school" of common law studies really only began with the 1850 commissions and reached its maturity only after another generation.[5] The oldest continuous university law school in America, Harvard was founded as "a school for the instruction of students at law, at Cambridge, under the patronage of the University" in 1817.[6] It, too, took a generation to come of age. But both of these great law schools, and dozens more, were inspired by the idea of the Vinerian Professorship and by the teaching of Blackstone. As Sutherland observed:

> Blackstone's lectures and books seized the imagination of thousands of men in America. The new study of law "as a science" in England and the new study in America had antecedents in common. The law at Harvard probably has some collateral as well as some direct kinship with the law at Blackstone's Oxford.[7]

Thus Blackstone's two great contributions were to prepare a clear restatement of the common law—a restatement whose lucidity was doubtless developed by hours in the classroom—and to unite the study of common law with the great Western university curriculum. This was to be a formidable combination, entrenching common law doctrine and methodologies in the minds of hundreds of thousands of lawyers. Even today, when one enters the luxurious office of a

---

3. In 1760, Adams wrote in his *Diary* that what he needed was "Mr. Blackstone's Analysis." James Iredell, future justice of the Supreme Court of the United States, wrote to his father in London in 1771 asking him to "be so obliging as to procure Dr. Blackstone's Commentaries...and send them by the first opportunity...They are books admirably calculated for a young student, and indeed may interest the most learned." In 1775, Edmund Burke told the House of Commons that almost as many copies of *Blackstone's Commentaries* had been sold in America as England. See Arthur E. Sutherland, *The Law at Harvard* (Cambridge, MA 1967) 24–25. By this, Burke meant to warn his colleagues that the Americans knew their rights under law.

4. See *Id.*, 32–42. Today, the Dean of Harvard Law School, Robert C. Clark, holds the Isaac Royall Professorship.

5. See F. H. Lawson, *The Oxford Law School 1850–1965* (Oxford, 1968) 1–33.

6. See Arthur E. Sutherland, *The Law at Harvard* (Cambridge, MA 1967) 32–91.

7. *Id.*, 31.

Texas oil law specialist, it may be that the lawyer's true pride and joy will be a set of the first edition of *Blackstone's Commentaries*, gleaming on the bookshelf.

Blackstone was not without his critics, both now and then. We will study in the next chapter the fierce attacks on Blackstone by reformers and codifiers, such as Jeremy Bentham.[8] In Bentham's eyes, Blackstone's vice was his uncritical acceptance and restatement of common law doctrine and process, regardless of utility and reason. Others have criticized Blackstone for overlooking important areas of contract and mercantile law, and failing to understand the importance of equity.[9] Duncan Kennedy, a leader of the Critical Legal Studies School, analyzed Blackstone as late as 1979 from a "structuralist or phenomenological, or neo-Marxist" perspective.[10] He concluded, "the enterprise [Blackstone's influence] goes on to this day, sustained in bankruptcy like the rail system or a defense conglomerate, by the combination of naiveté, self-interest and fear of the alternatives."[11]

The critics can say what they like. American law today is not a monument to Benthamite codification or to neo-Marxist deconstruction. Its fundamental principles are a reliance on the slow evaluation of common law principles, largely through judicial opinions, taught and analyzed in university law schools. Good or bad, this is the legacy of William Blackstone. We will now turn to a specific examination of one small section of the *Commentaries*, Book IV, Chapter 32 "Of Execution."[12] Our task will be to compare the law of Blackstone to the reality of the eighteenth century.

B. ALBION'S FATAL TREE

Thomas Green, in his "Introduction" to vol. 4 of a modern edition of *Blackstone's Commentaries* by the University of Chicago Press (1979, Chicago), refers to Blackstone's concluding essay in the *Commentaries* as "a whig panegyric."[13] "Sweeping in scope, majestic in style, this final paean to the elegance, wisdom, and humanity of English laws displays both Blackstone the optimistic and complacent eighteenth-century gentleman and Blackstone the proponent of measured reform."[14] Panegyrics are important, but so is the actual operation of the law in practice.

Take capital punishment as an example. Blackstone duly listed those crimes punishable by death, and the mechanics of carrying out the terrible sentence.[15] There was interest expressed as to the form of the warrant (a marginal note next to the prisoner's name of "suspendus per collum, or "sus. per coll."), as to whether the King could substitute another form of death (such as the "noble" ex-

---

8. See *Materials*, Chapter XIII, *infra*.

9. See, for example, David M. Walker, *The Oxford Companion to Law* (Oxford, 1980), 136. "His [Blackstone's] account of the law of contract is underdeveloped and he treats equity very lightly." *Id.*, 136.

10. Duncan Kennedy, "The Structure of Blackstone's Commentaries," 28 *Buffalo Law Review* (1979) 205, 209.

11. *Id.*, 382. See excerpts set out in *Materials*, Chapter XIV, *infra*.

12. *Materials, infra*, p. 456.

13. Thomas A. Green, "Introduction," William Blackstone, *Commentaries on the Laws of England* vol. 4 (Chicago, 1979), xi.

14. *Id.*, xi–xii.

15. *Materials, infra*, pp. 456–459.

ecutions of beheading) for hanging, and to exactly when the sentence must be carried out ("on the next day but one after sentence passed"). There is only one comment on the policy behind the sentence.

> It has been well observed, that it is of great importance, that the punishment should follow the crime as early as possible; that the prospect of gratification or advantage, which tempts a man to commit the crime, should instantly awake the attendant idea of punishment. Delay of execution serves only to separate these ideas; and the execution itself affects the minds of the spectators rather as a terrible sight, than as the necessary consequence of transgression.[16]

Based on reading *Blackstone's Commentaries* alone, a legal historian would envisage a society in which public order was maintained by rapid and severe punishment for even tiny acts of wrongdoing. Theft of a loaf of a bread was a capital offense, as was forging a check or setting a trap for a rabbit in any of the vast royal forests. Most threats to private property were capital offenses, and one could be excused for thinking that the state of the law was good evidence for Locke's assertion that "Government has no other end but the preservation of property."[17]

But the law in the books told only part of the true story. One recent development in legal history has been at the Centre for the Study of Social History at the University of Warwick. Scholars associated with that Centre have been conducting research into the eighteenth-century punishment of crime using modern statistical analysis, demographic data, and all available popular records, including newspapers, diaries, and broadsides, to supplement the formal legal records. This modern approach to legal history, set in its full social and political context, has been called the "Warwick School." It counts among its members distinguished scholars such as Douglas Hay, E.P. Thompson, Peter Linebaugh, John C. Ryle and Cal Winslow.[18]

Some of their conclusions have changed our views of the past. For example, despite the proliferation of crimes punishable by death, executions were, in fact, surprisingly rare.[19] Despite the severity of the law in *Blackstone*, there were, in practice, many ways to avoid an actual hanging, even after conviction. Two of the most common of these "escapes" were benefit of clergy and pardons.

Benefit of clergy originated in the middle ages as a privilege of ordained clergy accused of felonies. The theory was that such clergy had a right to be tried by ecclesiastical courts, but as a practical matter, this rarely happened. By 1350 anyone who could read the "neck verse" (Psalm 51:1) was presumed to be clergy for this purpose. By 1705 even the necessity of this reading was abolished, and the privilege became available for all.

From almost the beginning, certain heinous offenses were excluded from the benefit, and from the reign of Henry VII those claiming benefit of clergy were, on

---

16. *Materials, infra*, p. 457.
17. *Materials, supra*, p. 393 ff.
18. Particularly recommended are E.P. Thompson's great study of the anti-poaching laws, *Whigs and Hunters: The Origin of the Black Act* (New York, 1975) and *Albion's Fatal Tree* (eds. D. Hay, P. Linebaugh, J. Rule, E.P. Thompson, C. Winslow, New York, 1975).
19. See *Materials, infra*, p. 462 ff.

conviction, branded, and could not claim it again, unless they were actually in orders. In 1717, "it was enacted that persons not in orders convicted for a clergyable offense were to be transported (to the colonies) for seven years."[20] So most first offenders were not executed, but were branded or transported. These were both efficient punishments that involved little cost and either removed criminals from society altogether or provided warning to those who encountered them. Large sections of Australia and America, particularly Georgia, were settled this way.

If a criminal was convicted again for a capital offense, there was still a chance for pardon. This was usually done in a way that emphasized the guilt and remorse of the criminal and the mercy and compassion of the state. Modern American criminal process discourages confessions and encourages a steadfast denial of guilt. Many convicted defendants, even those guilty as charged, come out of the modern process convinced they have been wronged by society. This is natural, as their defense lawyers will have been arguing procedural or other errors throughout the trial and appeal. The eighteenth-century pardon, on the other hand, rewarded acknowledgment of guilt and open remorse. Both the confession and the pardon were done in public. The criminal became an "object lesson" for others, while the state appeared to be both powerful and compassionate.

The "Warwick School" research also discovered that, when executions actually did occur, they were orchestrated for maximum public impact. Thanks to benefit of clergy and the pardon, the convicted felon was usually a repeat offender and the case symbolically appropriate. The offender, and family, would often make money by printing broadsides for sale at the execution site, and these were usually pious recantations. Stands for spectators would be erected. If the focus was London, the execution took place at Tyburn, where there were often extensive stands and hundreds, if not thousands, of spectators. It was a "media" event, featured in the newspaper and in broadsides throughout the city. Today's equivalent would be full coverage by CNN and "Larry King Live."

A particular fuss was made where the offender provided some special object lesson. The execution of an aristocrat, such as Lord Ferrers in 1760, was celebrated in dozens of books and pamphlets as evidence of equality of all before the law.[21] The modern equivalent would be the execution of a well-known broker for securities fraud on prime time T.V., complete with an exhortation by the offender about avoiding the evils of insider securities trading. It would make an impression.

The effectiveness of a few severe punishments, of a highly dramatic and symbolic sort, was important to maintaining order in Georgian England without prisons or police. The other secret was the ever present Justice of the Peace. Minor crimes and misdemeanors were not tried in the royal courts before juries, but were tried before lay magistrates, usually leading land owners or citizens in the town. These "amateurs" had the power to inflict minor penalties, such as whippings, stocks, or small fines. They used such punishment to enforce the public order, and also to be sure public duties were fulfilled, including keeping public ways in repair and providing child support. Justices of the Peace, as "amateurs,"

---

20. David M. Walker, *supra*, 124.
21. See Douglas Hay, "Property, Authority and the Criminal Law," *Albion's Fatal Tree*, *supra*, 34.

frequently resorted to handy manuals, such as Michael Dalton's *Justice of the Peace*, or, of course, *Blackstone's Commentaries*, which could be found on thousands of study shelves. Real lawyers were rarely involved, and the hearing room was often the front parlor in the Justice's home. (Some Old English houses still have a "Justice's room.") See Illustration 12-11, *infra*.

Local justices were usually knowledgeable about all aspects of the crime and the criminal. Most punishments were public and symbolic, and also highly personal. If the misdemeanors were by a juvenile, the justice would probably know the parents, and also the village parson and the schoolmates. This form of local, lay justice was imported widely into America, and still persists in England today.[22]

Jurists refer to punishments that are designed to be highly educational and symbolic as "didactic" punishments. A "didactic" punishment tries to address two groups, the convicted criminals and the rest of the public, simultaneously. The goal with the convicted criminal is to get the criminal to recognize the evil of the conduct and the justness of the punishment. The goal with regard to the rest of the public is to teach the difference between right and wrong, and also the ultimate supremacy of the state over the individual.

Modern criminal punishments tend to focus on either "reform" of the criminal or "deterrence." Both of these theories focus primarily on the individual criminals, and not the public. "Reform" theory tries to change the criminal so that the desire to commit antisocial acts disappears. While this initially would seem to be a "humane" approach, "reforming" the human personality can approximate the "brainwashing" in *A Clockwork Orange*, particularly when the techniques used include isolation and long imprisonment. "Deterrence" theory on the other hand, does not attempt to change the criminal's antisocial urges, but simply exacts a cost so high that the illegal act, no matter how desirable to the criminal, is not worth the penalty. This theory requires that most crimes be solved quickly and accurately, but does respect the dignity of the human personality—including the dignity of the guilty—more than "reform" theory. It does, after all, give the criminal a "free will" choice.[23]

Didactic punishments, on the other hand, can be purely retributive, i.e., designed for revenge. Take, for example, a man who poisons a spouse who is suffering from an incurable disease. That person will never commit another crime, and no "reform" or "deterrence" will have any effect for good or bad. A public execution, however, will teach about that state's view on the sanctity of human life and on the evil of murder. Indeed, it could be argued, the more compelling the passion to murder, the greater the lesson. Perhaps even more "instructive" would be a contrite expression of remorse by convicted offenders, followed by a dramatic pardon by the "compassionate" state. Such were the symbols used by the eighteenth-century English state to educate and awe the populace.

Before we dismiss too lightly the story of "Albion's Fatal Tree" and the lessons of the Warwick School, it is important to contemplate the effectiveness of our

---

22. See the masterful study by John P. Dawson, *A History of Lay Judges* (Cambridge, Mass., 1960) 136–145, 178–286.

23. Another theory, "expiation," argues that punishment can be good for a criminal, and that true confession and penitence promote healing. This view is promoted by Judeo-Christian religious doctrine.

own system of modern criminal punishment. Is it a system that educates the convicted defendant and treats that defendant humanely? Does it also educate the public about right and wrong? What are the ultimate financial and social costs of our system? No one, certainly not this writer, seeks a return to the "Fatal Tree" and the eighteenth-century public hanging—nor necessarily any capital punishment. But our current system could benefit from study of the symbolic role of didactic punishment in social order, whether in the punishment of severe crimes, or in the approach to minor, local crimes. In both cases, there is much to be learned from the Warwick School and the eighteenth century.

C. LORD MANSFIELD AND THE "INCORPORATION" OF THE LAW MERCHANT

Earlier, we discussed the "incorporation" controversies which surround the "reception" of Roman or civil law principles into the common law of England.[24] Civilian doctrines certainly were important in the specialist "conciliar" courts, such as the Admiralty, and in ecclesiastical jurisdictions, but these courts were isolated from the common law jurisdictions in very much the same way as the Roman Law curriculum of the universities had little relation with the Inns of Court. "Incorporation" of the law merchant was a different proposition, although willingness to consider the usefulness of "foreign" doctrines to common law jurisdictions was a common factor in both cases, and great "incorporation" judges, such as Lord Mansfield, were knowledgeable of both commercial practices and civilian legal doctrines.[25]

In an odd way, the "law merchant" was hardly a "law" at all. Some have regarded it as solely a kind of expedited procedure.[26] Its origins were in the local fair court of the "pied-poudre" and the local courts of port and market towns, where speed was of the essence, as merchants were constantly on the move. But some aspects of this "law" were also substantive. In particular, merchants were always looking for ways to avoid carrying large amounts of currency—a highly dangerous practice then as now. The result was a body of commercial practices that was accepted in the customary dealing of merchants both in England and abroad, arguably before it received full protection of common law. This included bills of exchange and negotiable commercial paper generally. In addition, proof of contractual obligations relied somewhat less on formality and writing, a natural result where much depended on oral bargains and mutual trust.

During the seventeenth and eighteenth centuries, mercantile transactions and practices were certainly becoming more important in England. The opening up of

---

24. See *Materials*, Chapter VII, *supra*. See also D.R. Coquillette, "Legal Ideology and Incorporation I: The English Civilian Writers, 1523–1607," 61 *Boston Univ. L. Rev.* 1, 3–35 (1981).

25. See D.R. Coquillette, "Legal Ideology and Incorporation IV: The Nature of Civilian Influence on Modern Anglo-American Commercial Law," 67 *Boston Univ. Law Review* (1987) 877, 934–970.

26. See D.R. Coquillette, "Legal Ideology and Incorporation II: Sir Thomas Ridley, Charles Malloy, and the Literary Battle for the Law Merchant, 1607–1676," 61 *Boston Univ. L. Rev.* 315, 346–351.

important trade routes to India, China, and the Americas, the founding of the Bank of England, and the spread of the Empire resulted in new class of the very rich whose fortunes were based almost exclusively on trade.[27] These "nabobs," as they were called, quickly acquired country estates and the trappings of the old landed aristocracy, but their economic center of gravity was in shipping contracts and joint-ventures, not feudal estates. The source of wealth was shifting from the land to industry and trade, and the focus of the legal system rarely lagged far behind the money.

No judge was more concerned with such commercial issues than the great William Murray, Lord Mansfield (1705–1793). Mansfield followed other great common law judges, including Mathew Hale (1609–1676) and Sir John Holt (1642–1710), but he brought the development of common law doctrine by "incorporation" of mercantile practices to a new height. Indeed, Mansfield was one of the greatest judges that ever lived, and perhaps the most important Anglo-American jurist to date to convey his or her ideas primarily through decided cases.

Mansfield was a Scot. Scotland had, then as now, a separate legal system that included more civilian elements. As a young man Mansfield went to Christ Church College, Oxford, where he attended lectures on Justinian's *Digest*, translated Cicero's orations from Latin and won a major prize with a Latin poem.[28] His interest in Roman law and fluency in Latin were to continue, but on graduation he set his back on both Rome and Scotland and was admitted to Lincoln's Inn of the Inns of Court. From there on, his career was as a common lawyer, and he rose to the top of the common law system when he became Chief Justice of the King's Bench in 1756, a position he was to hold for thirty-two years.

One of the reasons for Mansfield's great reputation as a judge was the development of reliable law reports. While some important seventeenth-century judges, including Coke himself, published their own reports, the quality of law reports in the seventeenth century was generally uneven. Despite the efforts of Francis Bacon to appoint official law reporters as early as 1614, no genuinely "official reports" were published until the incorporated Council of Law Reporting for England and Wales was established in 1865.[29] But, by Mansfield's day, there were some "quasi-authorized" reporters who had highly professional standards. One of the best was Sir James Burrow. His *Burrow's Reports* covered 1756–1772, the heart of Mansfield's career. When it is recalled that English decisions were usually delivered orally from the bench, the importance of the reporter becomes obvious. Burrow was so good that his reports have been termed "works of art."[30] Such praise might be a bit extreme, but Mansfield's close reasoning and wide ranging intellect certainly was preserved in Burrow's pages. This was most important as, like some other great judges, Mansfield left little in the way of other formal jurisprudence. (Recently, Mansfield's important trial note-

---

27. See D.R. Coquillette, "The Mysteries of the New Fashioned Goldsmiths: From Usury to the Bank of England (1622–1694)," *supra*, 91–117.

28. See C.H.S. Fifoot, *Lord Mansfield* (Oxford, 1936), 27–51. Mansfield's interest in Roman and International Law followed him all his life, as his proposed course of study for the Duke of Portland demonstrated. This was published in 1757 as *A Treatise on the Study of the Law*, containing Directions to Students. *Id.*, 29.

29. Daniel R. Coquillette, *Francis Bacon* (Stanford, 1992), 102.

30. See James W. Wallace, *The Reporters* (Boston, 1882), 449.

books have been discovered by James C. Oldham and published as *The Mansfield Manuscripts and the Growth of the English Law in the Eighteenth Century* (Chapel Hill, 1992).)

Some of the most famous Mansfield cases reported by Burrow involved contract law and commercial transactions. Contract law was not regarded as a major subject in the old common law, and there is little in *Blackstone's Commentaries* about this subject, compared to the law of inheritance or land law. The triumph of the individual "will," as expressed in the power to contract, over "status," which was vested at birth, was an important result of the new industry and commerce of the eighteenth century. Indeed, Sir Henry Maine regarded the development "from status to contract" as an intrinsic part of legal "progress." See *Materials, infra.* Today, some of the greatest forms of wealth are stored in contracts, be they sports contracts, movie rights, commodities or stock options, or even insurance contracts or annuities, rather than in goods or land. Most people would regard their employment contract at least as valuable as their house. In Mansfield's day, these changes were certainly in the air.

The *Materials* contain two famous Mansfield contract cases, *Pillans v. Van Miérop*, 3 Burrow 1663 (1765 K.B.) and *Rann v. Hughes*, as reversed by the House of Lords in 1778, 4 *Brown*, P.C. 27: 7 T.R.350, n. The first was an excellent example of "incorporation" of commercial law practices into the common law.

At an early time, perhaps as early as the middle of the fourteenth century, English merchants imported a continental idea called the "bill of exchanges." Originally these bills were a method of transporting value without bullion and for facilitating mercantile credit.[31] The idea was simple. Suppose an English merchant "A" wished to buy cloth in Flanders. He did not wish to carry gold, because of highway men and pirates. He could visit a partner "B" of a Flemish firm in London, and pay him £100 of English money. The partner "B" would then draft a note to his partner "C" in Flanders as follows: "To C... 'Greetings' pay to D 100 guilders on 30 days sight. Yours, "B." "D" could be "A's" agent, or "A" himself if he wished to travel to Flanders. When the slip of paper was presented to "C," he would wait 30 days, and then pay "D" 100 guilders cash. (The "30 days sight," or delay, guarded against forgery and fraud.)

Illustration 12-2   A "Bill of Exchange"

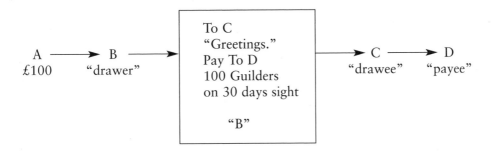

---

31. See D.R. Coquillette, "Legal Ideology and Incorporation IV: The Nature of Civilian Influence on Modern Anglo-American Commercial Law," 67 *Boston Univ. Law Rev.* (1987) 877, 881–914.

How did "C" have 100 guilders cash to pay to "D"? Probably because a Flemish merchant wished to buy wool in England. He would give "C" 100 guilders and get a bill of exchange to "B" in London to pay him 100 pounds. "B," of course, would have "A's" 100 pounds on hand. In real practice, of course, both "B" and "C" would take a "cut," usually by exchanging the currency at rates advantageous to them, as modern banks still do.

From a very early time, this "exchange" also concealed interest for loans, something usually prohibited in the open by usury laws.[32] Suppose "A" didn't have £100. "B" might write him a bill of exchange anyway, at an exchange rate highly favorable to "B" and "C's" partnership. "A" would be required to pay the £100 later by a covenant, and the actual interest would be concealed in the exchange rate.

Such bills of exchange were enforced by English courts, particularly the Admiralty, as part of the custom of merchants. This probably began as early as 1437.[33] In addition, English courts later recognized bills of exchange which read "Pay to "D" *or to his order.*" Such bills could be endorsed on the back by "D" and assigned to another, say "E." Such "negotiable" bills were just as good as money and, in some ways, better, because they were risky for a thief to cash or negotiate.

But if such bills of exchange between merchants in foreign trade were so useful, why could not they be used in domestic commerce? Indeed, the seventeenth century saw the use of "inland notes," instruments identical to bills of exchange except that they were issued between domestic merchants. There were, however, two major doctrinal problems with recognizing these "inland" notes as enforceable at law. First, if the note was actually concealing a loan from "B" to "A," there was no exchange rate between currencies in which to hide the interest. Second, while there was privity of contract and consideration between "A" and "B," there was no privity between "C" and "D" on the other end, and no consideration.

The first problem was resolved by a more enlightened view in the seventeenth century, which permitted taking reasonable commercial interest.[34] The second problem, however, rankled. In *Buller v. Crips*, 6 Mod. 29 (QB, 1704), Mansfield's distinguished predecessor, Chief Justice Holt, heard extensive argument as to the practice of merchants in London. The facts were simple.

> A note was in this form: "I promise to pay John Smith, or order, the sum of one hundred pounds, on account of wine had from him." John Smith endorses this note to another; the indorsee brings an action against him that drew this note, and declares upon the custom of merchants as upon a bill of exchange.[35]

According to Holt,

---

32. Daniel R. Coquillette, "The Mystery of the New Fashioned Goldsmiths: From Usury to the Bank of England (1622–1694)," *supra*, 92–99.

33. Daniel R. Coquillette, "Legal Ideology and Incorporation IV," *supra*, 895.

34. See D.R. Coquillette, "The Mystery of the New Fashioned Goldsmiths: From Usury to the Bank of England (1622–1694)," 96–99.

35. *Materials, infra*, pp. 477–478.

Holt, C.J.: I remember when actions upon inland bills of exchange did first begin; and there they laid a particular custom between London and Bristol, and it was an action against the acceptor. The defendant's counsel would put them to prove the custom; at which Hale, C.J., who tried it, laughed and said they had a hopeful case of it. And in my Lord North's time it was said that the custom in that case was part of the common law of England; and these actions since became frequent, as the trade of the nation did increase; and all the difference between foreign bills and inland bills is, that foreign bills must be protested before a public notary before the drawer can be charged, but inland bills need no protest, and the notes in question are only an invention of the goldsmiths in Lombard street, who had a mind to make a law to bind all those that did deal with them; and sure to allow such a note to carry any lien with it were to turn a piece of paper, which is in law but evidence of a parol contract, into a specialty. And, besides it would empower one to assign that to another which he could not have himself; for since he to whom this note was made could not have this action, how can his assignee have it? And these notes are not in the nature bills of exchange; for the reason of the custom of bills of exchange is for the expedition of trade and its safety; and likewise it hinders the exportation of money out of the realm.[36]

Holt also got information directly from the merchants themselves.

At another day, Holt, C.J. declared that he had desired to speak with two of the most famous merchants in London, to be informed of the mightily ill consequences that it was pretended would ensue by obstructing this course: and that they had told him it was very frequent with them to make such notes, and that they look upon them as bills of exchange, and that they had been used for a matter of thirty years, and that not only notes, but bonds for money were transferred frequently, and indorsed as bills of exchange. Indeed, I agree, a bill of exchange may be made between two persons without a third; and, if there be such a necessity of dealing that way, why do not dealers use that way which is legal? and may be this; as, A. has money to lodge in B.'s hands, and would have a negotiable note for it, it is only saying thus, "Mr. B., pay me, or order, so much money value to yourself," and signing this, and B. accepting it; or he may take the common note and say thus, "For value to yourself, pay me (or indorsee) so much," and good.[37]

In the end, however, Holt refused to recognize inland bills as legally enforceable. His reporters were not as good or as complete as Burrows, so it was never fully recorded why. Perhaps Holt believed such a radical change should be achieved by statute. If so, he soon got his wish in the famous Act of 1704 which made inland bills enforceable and extended the negotiable features of bills of exchange to promissory notes.[38] Holt was actually ordered before the House of

---

36. *Id.*
37. *Id.*
38. 3 & 4 Anne, ch. 9 (1704).

Lords to assist with the preparation of the bill.[39] The result was something very close to the ordinary negotiable bank check of today.

Illustration 12-3 An "inland bill"

"To Bank of New England

"Greetings" pay David Price, or to His order,

$10

Dan Coquillette"

If Holt looked to legislation to "incorporate" mercantile practice, Mansfield rarely felt so constrained. The famous case of *Pillans v. Van Miérop*, 3 Burrow 1663 (1765) like *Buller v. Crips*, involved a commercial obligation which was a "nude pact" i.e., without regular contractual consideration. But Mansfield looked to customary commercial practice and enforced the obligation.

The facts were these. An Irish merchant named White asked the plaintiffs, who were Dutch merchants named Pillans, to pay £800 in Rotterdam to a merchant named Clifford. White offered to repay Pillans by a credit "upon a good house in London," i.e., a reputable banking or merchant firm. The Dutch merchants, quite prudently, wished a "confirmed" credit upon such a London firm in White's name before paying the money. White gave them the name of Van Miérop and Hopkins, the defendants. Pillans then paid out the £800.

Illustration 12-4

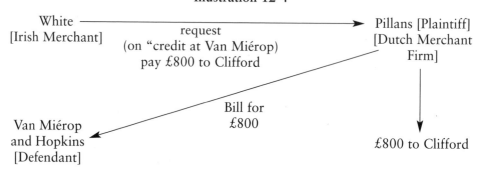

After paying the money, Pillans contacted Van Miérop and Hopkins and asked if they would honor a bill for £800 on White's credit. The defendants said "yes," and Pillans then proceeded to draw a bill for £800 payable by Van Miérop and Hopkins. Before the bill came to Van Miérop and Hopkins to be paid, White failed. Van Miérop and Hopkins then refused to pay the £800, and Pillans sued them.

The legal issue was simple. If Pillans had obtained assurances from Van Miérop *before* paying out the £800, or had done so at Van Miérop's request, or had paid consideration for Van Miérop's guarantee, the defendants would have

---

39. See D.R. Coquillette, "Legal Ideology and Incorporation IV: The Nature of Civilian Influence on Modern Anglo-American Commercial Law," *supra*, 934–948.

had a weaker case. But Pillans obtained Van Miérop's guarantee *after* paying the money, and no consideration had been received by Van Miérop for the guarantee. As Van Miérop's lawyers said, this was "a promise to pay a past debt...void at common law for want of consideration" and "[a] naked promise [*nudum pactum*] is a void promise: the consideration must be executory, not past or executed."[40] The fact that the guarantee was in writing should make no difference.

Yet Mansfield disagreed. He began:

> "This is a matter of great consequence to trade and commerce in every light.
>
> If there was any kind of fraud in this transaction, the collusion and *mala fides* would have vacated the contract. But....it seems to me clear that there was none....
>
> If there be no fraud, it a mere question of law. The Law of Merchants and the Law of the Land is the same. A witness cannot be admitted to prove the Law of Merchants: we must consider it as a point of law. A *nudum pactum* does not exist in the usage and law of merchants.
>
> I take it that the ancient notion about the want of consideration was for the sake of evidence only: for when it is reduced into writing, as in covenants, specialties, bonds, etc., there was no objection to the want of consideration. And the Statute of Frauds proceeded upon the same principle.
>
> In commercial cases among merchants the want of consideration is not an objection.
>
> This is just the same thing as if White had drawn on Van Miérop and Hopkins, payable to the plaintiffs. It had been nothing to the plaintiffs whether Van Miérop and Co. had effects of White's in their hands or not, if they had accepted his bill. And this amounts to the same thing: 'I will give the bill due honor' is, in effect, accepting it....This is an engagement to accept the bill, if there was a necessity to accept it, and pay it when due; and they could not afterwards retract. It would be very destructive to trade and to trust in commercial dealing, if they could. There was nothing of *nudum pactum* mentioned to the Jury; nor was it, I dare say, at all in their idea or contemplation.
>
> I think the point of law is with the plaintiffs.[41]

This holding rejected the need for consideration in commercial cases if a promise was in writing. It was radical. But Mansfield's colleagues on the King's Bench followed his brave lead. One, Justice Wilmot, supported the decision by reference to Roman law principles and the international law of the *ius gentium*.

> Mr. Justice Wilmot: The question is whether this action can be supported upon the breach of this agreement.
>
> I can find none of those cases, that go upon its being *nudum pactum* that are in writing: they are all upon parol.

---

40. *Materials, infra*, p. 480.
41. *Materials, infra*, p. 482.

I have traced this matter of the *nudum pactum*, and it is very curious....[It is] echoed from the Civil Law—*ex nudo pacto non oritur actio*. Vinnius gives the reason in *Lib. 3. Tit. De Obligationibus, 4to Edition*, 596. If by stipulation (and a *fortiori* if by writing) it was good without consideration. There was no radical defect in the contract for want of consideration. But it was made requisite in order to put people upon attention and reflection and to prevent obscurity and uncertainty; and, in that view, either writing or certain formalities were required. *Idem*, on *Justinian, 4to Edition*, 614. Therefore it was intended as a guard against rash inconsiderate declarations. But if an undertaking was entered into upon deliberation and reflection it had activity, and such promises were binding. Both Grotius and Puffendorff hold them obligatory of the Law of Nations. *Grot. Lib 2.c. 11: De Promissis. Puffend. Lib 3.c.5*. They are morally good and only require ascertainment. Therefore there is no reason to extend the principle or carry it further.

There would have been no doubt upon the present case according to the Roman Law, because here is both stipulation (in the express Roman form) and writing.

Bracton (who wrote *temp. Hen. 3*) is the first of our lawyers who mentions this. His writings interweave a great many things out of the Roman law. In his third Book, *Cap. 1. De Actionibus*, he distinguishes between naked and clothed contracts. He says that *Obligatio est mater actionis*, and that it may arise *ex contractu multis modis, sicut ex conventione, etc., sicut sunt pacta conventa quae nuda sunt aliquando, aliquando vestita, etc.*

Our own lawyers have adopted exactly the same idea as the Roman Law. *Plowden*, 308*b* in the case of *Sheryngton v. Strotton* mentions it; and not one contradicted it. He lays down the distinction between contracts or agreements in words (which are more base) and contracts or agreements in writing (which are more high); and puts the distinction upon the want of deliberation in the former case and the full exercise of it in the latter. His words are the marrow of what the Roman lawyers had said. 'Words pass from men lightly': but where the agreement is made by Deed, there is more stay....'The delivery of the Deed is a ceremony in law, signifying fully his good will that the thing in the Deed should pass from him who made the Deed to the other. And therefore a Deed, which must necessarily be made upon great thought and deliberation, shall bind, without regard to consideration.'[42]

Wilmot closed with an important appeal to the *ius gentium*.

All nations ought to have their laws conformable to each other in such cases. *Fides Servanda est: simplicitas Juris Gentium praevaleat. Hodierni mores* are such that the old notion about the *nudum pactum* is not strictly observed as a rule. On a question of this nature—whether by the Law of Nations such an engagement as this shall bind—the Law is to judge.[43]

---

42. *Materials, infra*, p. 482.
43. *Materials, infra*, pp. 483–484.

Pillans v. Van Miérop was a great departure from the English doctrine of contractual consideration, and it was justified through "incorporating" principles of the Roman Law and the law merchant. Mansfield, however, was even bolder than that. In a leading decision that had nothing to do with mercantile customs and practices, he also rejected the doctrine of consideration if there was a moral reason to enforce an agreement.

The case, *Rann v. Hughes*, 4 Brown, P.C. 27 (1778) was as follows. A dispute arose between a John Hughes and a Mary Hughes. It was submitted to arbitration, and the arbitrator awarded Mary Hughes £983. Before the sum was paid, both parties died. The administratrix to John Hughes' estate was Isabella Hughes. She made a promise, assumed by the appellate court to be in writing, to pay the £983 to the executors of Mary Hughes' estate, Joseph and Arthur Rann. Then apparently she got some legal advice, and was correctly told that personal actions, at common law, terminate with the death of the parties. She therefore had no legal obligation to pay. At least, there was no legal obligation *except* for her subsequent promise to pay, which was without consideration. So Mary Hughes refused to pay and was sued by Joseph and Arthur Rann on her "nude" promise.

Illustration 12-5   "Moral" Consideration?

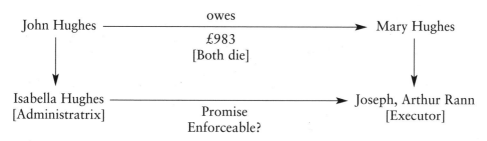

Rann v. Hughes [Mansfield]

In a dramatic judgment, Mansfield, sitting as a trial judge in Westminster Hall, refused to set aside a jury verdict for the plaintiffs Rann, which included £483 damages, plus costs. Mansfield believed that "moral consideration" supported the promise by Isabella. The defendant Hughes brought a writ of error in the Exchequer Chamber.[44] After *two* full arguments, Mansfield's decision was set aside. The plaintiff then brought a writ of error in the highest court in the kingdom, the House of Lords.

The House of Lords upheld the Exchequer Chamber and not only reversed Lord Mansfield in *Rann v. Hughes*, but disapproved of *Pillans v. Van Miérop* as well. The final decision approved the language of Lord Chief Baron Skynner in the Exchequer Chamber, as follows:

> It is undoubtedly true that everyman is by the law of nature bound to
> fulfil his engagements. It is equally true that the law of this country sup-

---

44. To review the common law appellate process, see *Materials, supra,* Chapter VIII.

plies no means nor affords any remedy to compel the performance of an agreement made without sufficient consideration. Such agreement is *nudum pactum ex quo non oritur actio*; and whatsoever may be the sense of this maxim in the civil law, it is in the last-mentioned sense only that it is to be understood in our law. The declaration states that the defendant, being indebted as administratrix, promised to pay when requested, and the judgment is against the defendant generally. The being indebted is of itself a sufficient consideration to ground a promise, but the promise must be co-extensive with the consideration unless some particular consideration of fact can be found here to warrant the extension of it against the defendant in her own capacity. If a person, indebted in one right, in consideration of forbearance for a particular time promise to pay in another right, this convenience will be a sufficient consideration to warrant an action against him or her in the latter right. But here no sufficient consideration occurs to support this demand against her in her personal capacity; for she derives no advantage or convenience from the promise here made. For if I promise generally to pay upon request what I was liable to pay upon request in another right, I derive no advantage or convenience from this promise, and therefore there is not sufficient consideration for it.

But it is said that, if this promise is in writing, that takes away the necessity of a consideration and obviates the objection of *nudum pactum*, for that cannot be where the promise is put into writing, and that, if it were necessary to support the promise that it should be in writing, it will after verdict be presumed that it was in writing; and this last is certainly true. But, that there cannot be *nudum pactum* in writing, whatever may be the rule of the civil law, there is certainly none such in the law of England. His Lordship observed upon the doctrine of *nudum pactum* delivered by Mr. Justice WILMOT in the case of *Pillans v. Van Miérop*, that he contradicted himself and was also contradicted by Vinnius in his Comment on Justinian.[45]

Every Anglo-American law student who struggles through the illogicalities of the doctrine of consideration should reflect on Mansfield. Stripping the doctrine to its utilitarian and moral essentials, he would have reformed the common law for all time. But in 1776, he had gone too far for his contemporaries. Later, in the nineteenth-century and twentieth-century codification projects, many of his holdings would be established by legislation. But, as a common law judge, Mansfield had explored the outer limits of "judge-made law."[46]

Toward the end of Mansfield's great career, students would come to sit at the back of the court just to see him in action. One of them was the great Edmund

---

45. *Materials, infra*, pp. 485–486.
46. Mansfield's other great claim to lasting fame and respect was his unwavering opposition to religious bigotry. This resulted in the destruction of his town house by anti-Catholic mobs in the Gordon Riots. He was less forceful on issues of slavery, but did order a slave freed in the famous *Somersett's Case*. See C.H.S. Fifoot, *Lord Mansfield* (Oxford, 1936) 41–42. See William M. Wiecek, "*Somersett*: Lord Mansfield and the Legitimacy of Slavery in the Anglo-American World," 47 *Univ. Chicago L. Rev.* 86 (1974).

Burke (1729–1797), politician and political theorist.[47] Another was perhaps even greater still, Jeremy Bentham (1748–1832), the eccentric but brilliant author of utilitarian theory and the codification movement. As Bentham wrote:

> From the first morning on which I took my seat on one of the hired boards, that slid from under the officers' seats in the area of the King's Bench...at the head of the gods of my idolatry, had sitten the Lord Chief Justice...Days and weeks together have I made my morning pilgrimage to the chief seat of the living idol.[48]

Ultimately, Bentham would turn from his "living idol" and from judge-made law itself. He would adopt instead a new formula of statutory reform and advancement. As the nineteenth century dawned, the vast industrial slums of England multiplied. A society of unforeseen urban complexity brought new challenges and new solutions. But the ideals of the "judge-made law," even as they faded in England, were emerging with a new strength and purpose in another land. In 1803, *Marbury v. Madison* was decided. Most appropriately, Mansfield's statue stands today in the Supreme Court of the United States.[49]

FOR FURTHER READING

I.   General Background: Eighteenth Century

Highly recommended is the concise account by Paul Langford, "The Eighteenth Century (1688–1789)" in *The Oxford History of Britain* (ed. K.O. Morgan, Oxford, 1988) 399–469. See also John B. Owen, *The Eighteenth Century (1714–1815)* (New York, 1974). For a vivid social and economic account, see J.H. Plumb, *England in the Eighteenth Century* (1963, Harmondsworth), and for the usual elegant writing of Churchill, see Winston S. Churchill, *A History of English-Speaking Peoples*, vol. III, 87–190 (London, 1957). The best collection of original documents is E.N. Williams, *The Eighteenth Century Constitution:*

---

47. Burke wrote of Mansfield:
    His ideas go to the growing melioration of the law, by making its liberality keep pace with the demands of justice, and the actual concerns of the world; not restricting the infinitely diversified occasions of men, and the rules of natural justice, within artificial circumscriptions, but conforming our jurisprudence to the growth of our commerce and of our empire.
    See William Holdsworth, *Some Makers of English Law* (Cambridge, 1938), 169.
48. *Id.,* 169.
49. For those who are Mansfield enthusiasts, his magnificent "country" house, Kenwood, still stands in Hampstead Park, London, open to the public. There one can still see his great library, and have tea in the stables. Also up the road still stands the Spaniards' Inn. There London rioters, out to destroy Mansfield and his house for his tolerance of Catholics, were delayed by free drinks until troopers could come to the rescue. Not so lucky was Mansfield's "town" house. In the anti-Catholic Gordon Riots, it was burnt to the ground, with all of his personal books. Mansfield, although not a Catholic himself, was a great defender of civil rights.

Documents and Commentary (Cambridge, 1960). For a detailed political account, see Basil Williams, *The Whig Supremacy* 1714–1760 (2d ed. rev. C.H. Stuart, Oxford, 1965) and Steven Watson, *The Reign of George III 1760–1815* (Oxford, 1960).

II. Blackstone

There is an excellent new edition of Blackstone, *William Blackstone's Commentaries of the Laws of England* (Chicago, 1979). It is a facsimile of the first edition of 1765–1769 with fine scholarly introductions to each volume by Stanley N. Katz (vol. 1), A.W. Brian Simpson (vol. 2), John H. Langbein (vol. 3), and Thomas A. Green (vol. 4). For a concise introduction, see S.F.C. Milson, *The Nature of Blackstone's Achievement* (London, 1981). This was the Selden Society Lecture of 1980 commemorating Blackstone's bicentenary. See also William Holdsworth, *Some Makers of English Law* (Cambridge, 1966) 240–247. For an example of modern criticism, "structuralist or phenomenological, or neo-Marxist, or all three together," see Duncan Kennedy, "The Structure of Blackstone's Commentaries," 28 *Buffalo Law Review* 205 (1979).

III. "Law and Order in the Eighteenth Century"

For a good introduction to the substantive law of crime, see Thomas A. Green, "Introduction" to *Blackstone's Commentaries*, vol. IV (Chicago, 1979), iii-xiii. The "Warwick School," with its focus on the social context of legal history, is particularly well represented by E.P. Thompson, *Whigs and Hunters: The Origin of the Black Acts* (New York, 1975) and Douglas Hay, Peter Linebaugh, John C. Rule, E.P. Thompson, Cal Winslow, *Albion's Fatal Tree: Crime and Society in Eighteenth Century England* (New York, 1975).

IV. Mansfield

For an introduction to the commercial and economic context of Mansfield's achievement, see Alan Harding, *A Social History of English Law* (London, 1966) 265–329. For biographies of Mansfield's life see C.H.S. Fifoot, *Lord Mansfield* (Oxford, 1936) and Edmund Heward, *Lord Mansfield* (London, 1979). For a fine account of Mansfield's influence on the development of contract law, see C.H.S. Fifoot, *History and Sources of the Common Law* (London, 1949) 406–443. For specialized accounts of Mansfield's famous *Somersett Case*, see Edward Fiddes, "Lord Mansfield and the Somersett Case," 50 *L.Q. Rev.* 495 (1934) 499–511, James Oldham, "New Light on Mansfield and Slavery," 27 *Journal of British Studies* 45 (1988) and William M. Wiecek, "Somersett: Lord Mansfield and the Legitimacy of Slavery in the Anglo-American World," 47 *Chicago Law Rev.* 86, (1974). Mansfield's *A Treatise on the Study of Law* has been reprinted in *Classics in Legal History* (R.M. Mersky, J. Myron Jacobstein, eds., 1974) vol. 26. James C. Oldham has completed a major new study based on the discovery of Mansfield's trial notebooks entitled, *The Mansfield Manuscripts and the Growth of the English Law in the Eighteenth Century* (Chapel Hill, 1992). Finally, the best account of the evolution of commercial law is that of my distinguished colleague James S. Rogers, *The Early History of the Law of Bills and Notes* (Cambridge, 1995).

COMMENTARIES

Thomas Shelton ON THE *Robert Taylor's*

LAWS

OF *J. R. Stewart*

ENGLAND.

IN FOUR BOOKS.

BY

SIR WILLIAM BLACKSTONE, KNT.

ONE OF HIS MAJESTY's JUDGES OF THE COURT OF COMMON PLEAS.

RE-PRINTED FROM THE BRITISH COPY,
PAGE FOR PAGE WITH THE LAST EDITION.

AMERICA:

PRINTED FOR THE SUBSCRIBERS,

By ROBERT BELL, at the late UNION LIBRARY, in *Third-street*,

PHILADELPHIA. MDCCLXXI.

Illustration 12-6   The 1st American edition of Blackstone's *Commentaries*. [Author's Collection.]

CHAPTER THE THIRTY-SECOND.

OF EXECUTION.

THERE now remains nothing to speak of, but *execution*; the completion of human punishment. And this, in all cafes, as well capital as otherwife, must be performed by the legal officer, the sheriff or his deputy; whose warrant for so doing was antiently by precept under the hand and seal of the judge, as it is still practised in the court of the lord high steward, upon the execution of a peer[a] : though, in the court of the peers in parliament, it is done by writ from the king[b]. Afterwards it was established[c], that, in case of life, the judge may command execution to be done without any writ. And now the usage is, for the judge to sign the calendar, or list of all the prisoners' names, with their separate judgments in the margin, which is left with the sheriff. As, for a capital felony, it is written opposite to the prisoner's name " let him be hanged by the neck;" formerly, in the days of Latin and abbreviation[d], " *suf. per coll.*" for " *suspendatur per collum.*" And this is the only warrant that the sheriff has, for so material an act as taking away the life of another[e]. It may certainly afford matter of speculation, that in civil causes there should be such a variety of writs of execution to recover a trifling debt, issued in the king's name, and under the seal of the court, without which the sheriff

a 2 Hal. P. C. 409.   d Staundf. P. C. 182.
b See append. §. 5.   e 5 Mod. 22.
c Finch. L. 478.

cannot

Illustration 12-7   Book IV, Blackstone's *Commentaries* (9th ed., London, 1783, with last corrections of Blackstone). [Author's Collection.]

cannot legally ftir one ftep; and yet that the execution of a man, the moft important and terrible tafk of any, fhould depend upon a marginal note.

THE fheriff, upon receipt of his warrant, is to do execution within a convenient time; which in the country is alfo left at large. In London indeed a more folemn and becoming exactnefs is ufed, both as to the warrant of execution, and the time of executing thereof: for the recorder, after reporting to the king in perfon the cafe of the feveral prifoners, and receiving his royal pleafure, that the law muft take it's courfe, iflues his warrant to the fheriffs; directing them to do execution on the day and at the place affigned [f]. And, in the court of king's bench, if the prifoner be tried at the bar, or brought there by *habeas corpus*, a rule is made for his execution; either fpecifying the time and place [g], or leaving it to the difcretion of the fheriff [h]. And, throughout the kingdom, by ftatute 25 Geo. II. c. 37. it is enacted that, in cafe of murder, the judge fhall in his fentence direct execution to be performed on the next day but one after fentence paffed [i]. But, otherwife, the time and place of execution are by law no part of the judgment [k]. It has been well obferved [l], that it is of great importance, that the punifhment fhould follow the crime as early as poffible; that the profpect of gratification or advantage, which tempts a man to commit the crime, fhould inftantly awake the attendant idea of punifhment. Delay of execution ferves only to feparate thefe ideas: and then the execution itfelf affects the minds of the fpectators rather as a terrible fight, than as the neceffary confequence of tranfgreffion.

THE fheriff cannot alter the manner of the execution by fubftituting one death for another, without being guilty of felony himfelf, as has been formerly faid [m]. It is held alfo

[f] See appendix. §. 4.
[g] St Trials. VI. 332. Foft. 43.
[h] See appendix. §. 3.
[i] See pag. 202.

[k] So held by the twelve judges, Mich. 10 Geo. III.
[l] Beccar. ch. 19.
[m] See pag. 179.

by

Illustration 12-8   Book IV, Blackstone's *Commentaries* (9th ed., London, 1783, with last corrections of Blackstone). [Author's Collection.]

Ch. 32.   W R O N G S.   405

by fir Edward Coke [n] and fir Matthew Hale [o], that even the king cannot change the punifhment of the law, by altering the hanging or burning into beheading; though, when beheading is part of the fentence, the king may remit the reft. And, notwithftanding fome examples to the contrary, fir Edward Coke ftoutly maintains, that "*judicandum eft legi-*" *bus, non exemplis.*" But others have thought [p], and more juftly, that this prerogative, being founded in mercy and immemorially exercifed by the crown, is part of the common law. For hitherto, in every inftance, all thefe exchanges have been for more merciful kinds of death; and how far this may alfo fall within the king's power of granting conditional pardons, *(viz.* by remitting a fevere kind of death, on condition that the criminal fubmits to a milder) is a matter that may bear confideration. It is obfervable, that when lord Stafford was executed for the popifh plot in the reign of king Charles the fecond, the then fheriffs of London, having received the king's writ for beheading him, petitioned the houfe of lords, for a command or order from their lordfhips, how the faid judgment fhould be executed: for, he being profecuted by impeachment, they entertained a notion (which is faid to have been countenanced by lord Ruffel) that the king could not pardon any part of the fentence [q]. The lords refolved [r], that the fcruples of the fheriffs were unneceffary, and declared, that the king's writ ought to be obeyed. Difappointed of raifing a flame in that affembly, they immediately fignified [s] to the houfe of commons by one of the members, that they were not fatisfied as to the power of the faid writ. That houfe took two days to confider of it; and then [t] fullenly refolved, that the houfe was *content* that the fheriff do execute lord Stafford by fevering his head from his body. It is farther related, that when afterwards the fame lord Ruffel was condemned for high treafon upon indictment, the king while he remitted the ignominious part of

[n] 3 Inft. 52.
[o] 2 Hal. P. C. 412.
[p] Foft. 270. F. N. B. 244. h.
[19] Rym. *Foed.* 284.

[q] 2 Hume Hift. of G. B. 328.
[r] Lords Journ. 21 Dec. 1680.
[s] Com. Journ. 21 Dec. 1680.
[t] *Ibid.* 23 Dec. 1680.

the

Illustration 12-9   Book IV, Blackstone's *Commentaries* (9th ed., London, 1783, with last corrections of Blackstone). [Author's Collection.]

406   P U B L I C   BOOK **IV.**

the fentence, obferved, " that his lordfhip would now find " he was poffeffed of that prerogative, which in the cafe of " lord Stafford he had denied him ᵘ." One can hardly determine (at this diftance from thofe turbulent times) which moft to difapprove of, the indecent and fanguinary zeal of the fubject, or the cool and cruel farcafm of the fovereign.

To conclude: it is clear, that if, upon judgment to be hanged by the neck till he is dead, the criminal be not thoroughly killed, but revives, the fheriff muft hang him again ʷ. For the former hanging was no execution of the fentence; and, if a falfe tendernefs were to be indulged in fuch cafes, a multitude of collufions might enfue. Nay, even while abjurations were in force ˣ, fuch a criminal, fo reviving, was not allowed to take fanctuary and abjure the realm; but his fleeing to fanctuary was held an efcape in the officer ʸ.

AND, having thus arrived at the *laft* ftage of criminal proceedings, or execution, the end and completion of human *punifhment*, which was the fixth and laft head to be confidered under the divifion of *public wrongs*, the fourth and laft object of the laws of England; it may now feem high time to put a period to thefe commentaries, which, the author is very fenfible, have already fwelled to too great a length. But he cannot difmifs the ftudent, for whofe ufe alone thefe rudiments were originally compiled, without endeavouring to recall to his memory fome principal outlines of the legal conftitution of this country; by a fhort hiftorical review of the moft confiderable revolutions, that have happened in the laws of England, from the earlieft to the prefent times. And this tafk he will attempt to difcharge, however imperfectly, in the next or concluding chapter.

ᵘ 2 Hume. 360.
ʷ 2 Hal. P. C. 412. 2 Hawk. P. C. 463.

ˣ See pag. 326.
ʸ Fitzh. *Abr. t. corone.* 335. Finch. L. 467.

Illustration 12-10   Book IV, Blackstone's *Commentaries* (9th ed., London, 1783, with last corrections of Blackstone). [Author's Collection.]

Illustration 12-11   A poacher is brought before the country squire, typical of the "justice of the peace" class that kept order in 18th century England. Note the poacher's family begging for mercy. From Thomas Rowlandson, *The Dance of Life* (London, 1817). See E.P. Thompson, *Whigs and Hunters: The Origin of the Black Acts* (New York, 1975).

MATERIALS

CRIME

Albion's Fatal Tree (eds. D. Hay, P. Linebaugh, J.G. Ryle, E.P. Thompson, C. Winslow, New York, 1975), 13–15, 17–26, 33–39. [Notes omitted.] [Courtesy Douglas Hay.]

PREFACE

All the contributors to this book have been associated at one time in the Centre for the Study of Social History at the University of Warwick. We were all concerned with the social history of eighteenth-century England. And we were all centrally concerned with the law, both as ideology and as actuality and with that century's definition of crime. We were equally concerned with criminality itself, the offences, the offenders and the popular myths of offenders (such as highwaymen and smugglers) as part-hero, part dreadful moral exemplars.

These questions, we became convinced, were central to unlocking the meanings of eighteenth-century social history. From one aspect it appears as if 'crime' multiplied in this century. The statistics are still not fully established, and they present difficulties in interpretation. Contributors to this volume (notably Douglas Hay and Peter Linebaugh) are still engaged in their own investigation of these figures; and we have all benefited from the findings and advice of Professor J.M. Beattie of Toronto who has carried this investigation farthest. From another aspect it appears as if it is not just a matter of 'crime' enlarging but equally of a property-conscious oligarchy redefining, through its legislative power, activities, use-rights in common or woods, perquisites in industry, as thefts or offences. For as offences appear to multiply so also do statutes—often imposing the sanction of death—which define hitherto innocent or venial activities (such as some forms of poaching, wood-theft, anonymous letter-writing) as crimes. And the ideology of the ruling oligarchy, which places a supreme value upon property, finds its visible and material embodiment above all in the ideology and practice of the law. Tyburn Tree, as William Blake well understood, stood at the heart of this ideology; and its ceremonies were at the heart of the popular culture also.

This book begins to unlock these meanings; but we do not propose it as offering more than a partial disclosure. In one particular the book has not come out as we had planned it. It is rather easy, when taking a superficial view of eighteenth-century evidence, to propose two distinct kinds of offence and offenders. There are 'good' criminals, who are premature revolutionaries or reformers, forerunners of popular movements—all kinds of rioters, smugglers, poachers, primitive rebels in industry. This appears as 'social crime.' And there then are those who commit crime without qualification: thieves, robbers, highwaymen, forgers, arsonists and murderers. (Around the thieves of all degrees, with their necessary concomitant organization of receivers, informers, the drink and sex trades, it is deceptively easy to borrow contemporary criminological terms of 'deviance' and 'sub-culture.')

As it turns out, this book appears to draw heavily upon evidence from the first kind of offender. But this is in part accidental. Two or three contributors fell out, and we hope will publish their work subsequently in other places. Existing contributors found some of their materials (of the second sort) unmanageable within the confines of an essay and will be publishing their findings independently. Thus Peter Linebaugh is engaged upon exhaustive research into London criminality in the first half of the eighteenth century; Douglas Hay into Midlands evidence; while Edward Thompson's first submission to this book, on the origins of the Black Act of 1723 and the subsequent history of the act, grew to book-length and is being published as *Whigs and Hunters*.

As a result this book became more weighted towards 'social crime' than we had intended. But we should say that in our researches into legal archives and into the actual offences and offenders it became less possible to sustain any tidy notion of a distinction between these two kinds of crime. There is a real difference in emphasis at each pole: certainly the community (and its culture) was more likely to give shelter to some 'social' offenders (smugglers or rioters in popular causes) than to thieves or sheep-stealers. Yet in many cases we found little evidence of a morally endorsed popular culture here and a deviant sub-culture there. Several of the contributors have raised this question in the context of their own studies, and their conclusions differ in emphasis. In London it appears that the same kind of men and women, with the same kinds of life history, found their way to the gallows for both kinds of offence. In rural parishes, perhaps the more constricted horizon of village life sharpened the definitions about what was, and was not, crime, while certain communities were dependent upon certain products for their livelihood (for example, sheep or cloth) and united against offenders. On the other hand, the same kind of community, in west Yorkshire, appears to have tolerated or sheltered coiners. These distinctions (and our ignorance of popular attitudes in this area is only slowly shifting) were not, however, based on in-

hibitions upon violence. Poachers and smugglers punished informers and threatened life and property as readily as the Tyburn rioter. And in all spheres of popular culture informers and law-enforcers often lived in a symbiotic relationship
upon the structures of taking and receiving by which the poor redistributed some
small part of the wealth of England.

*   *   *   *   *

Douglas Hay, *Property, Authority and the Criminal Law*

I

The rulers of eighteenth-century England cherished the death sentence. The ora-
tory we remember now is the parliamentary speech, the Roman periods of Fox
or Burke, that stirred the gentry and the merchants. But outside Parliament were
the labouring poor, and twice a year, in most counties in England, the scarlet-
robed judge of assize put the black cap of death on top of his full-bottomed wig
to expound the law of the propertied, and to execute their will. 'Methinks I see
him,' wrote Martin Madan in 1785,

> with a countenance of solemn sorrow, adjusting the cap of judgement on
> his head...His Lordship then, deeply affected by the melancholy part of
> his office, which he is now about to fulfill, embraces this golden opportu-
> nity to do most exemplary good—He addresses, in the most pathetic
> terms, the consciences of the trembling criminals...shows them how just
> and necessary it is, that there should be laws to remove out of society
> those, who instead of contributing their honest industry to the public
> good and welfare, have exerted every art, that the blackest villainy can
> suggest, to destroy both...He then vindicates the *mercy*, as well as the
> *severity* of the law, in making such examples, as shall not only protect
> the innocent from outrage and violence, but also deter others from bring-
> ing themselves to the same fatal and ignominious end...He acquaints
> them with the certainty of speedy death, and consequently with the ne-
> cessity of speedy repentance—and on this theme he may so deliver him-
> self, as not only to melt the wretches at the bar into contrition, but the
> whole auditory into the deepest concern—Tears express their feelings—
> and many of the most thoughtless among them may, for the rest of their
> lives, be preserved from thinking lightly of the first steps to vice, which
> they now see will lead them to destruction. The dreadful sentence is now
> pronounced—every heart shakes with terror—the almost fainting crimi-
> nals are taken from the bar—the crowd retires—each to his several
> home, and carries the mournful story to his friends and neighbours;—
> the day of execution arrives—the wretches are led forth to suffer, and
> exhibit a spectacle to the beholders, too awful and solemn for descrip-
> tion.

This was the climactic moment in a system of criminal law based on *terror*: 'if
we diminish the terror of house-breakers,' wrote justice Christian of Ely in 1819,
'the terror of the innocent inhabitants must be increased, and the comforts of domestic life must be greatly destroyed.' He himself had dogs, firearms, lights and
bells at his own country home, and took a brace of double-barreled pistols to

bed with him every night. But his peace of mind mostly rested on the knowledge that the death sentence hung over anyone who broke in to steal his silver plate. A regular police force did not exist, and the gentry would not tolerate even the idea of one. They remembered the pretensions of the Stuarts and the days of the Commonwealth, and they saw close at hand how the French monarchy controlled its subjects with spies and informers. In place of police, however, propertied Englishmen had a fat and swelling sheaf of laws which threatened thieves with death. The most recent account suggests that the number of capital statutes grew from about 50 to over 200 between the years 1688 and 1820. Almost all of them concerned offences against property.

This flood of legislation is one of the great facts of the eighteenth century, and it occurred in the period when peers and gentry held power with least hindrance from Crown or people. The Glorious Revolution of 1688 established the freedom not of men, but of men of property. Its apologist, John Locke, distorted the oldest arguments of natural law to justify the liberation of wealth from all political or moral controls; he concluded that the unfettered accumulation of money, goods and land was sanctioned by Nature and, implicitly, by God. Henceforth among triumphant Whigs, and indeed all men on the right side of the great gulf between rich and poor, there was little pretence that civil society was concerned primarily with peace or justice or charity. Even interests of state and the Divine Will had disappeared. Property had swallowed them all: 'Government', declared Locke, 'has no other end but the preservation of property.' Most later writers accepted the claim uncritically. William Blackstone, the most famous eighteenth-century writer on the law and constitution, declared it self-evident that 'there is nothing which so generally strikes the imagination, and engages the affections of mankind, as the right of property; or that sole and despotic dominion which one man claims and exercises over the external things of the world, in total exclusion of the right of any other individual in the universe.' The common and statute law, it seems, extended throughout not only England but the cosmos. When Christian edited the twelfth edition of Blackstone's *Commentaries on the Laws of England* in 1793, he reduced the claim only a little, to 'that law of property, which nature herself has written upon the hearts of all mankind.'

Once property had been officially deified, it became the measure of all things. Even human life was weighed in the scales of wealth and status: 'the execution of a needy decrepit assassin,' wrote Blackstone, 'is a poor satisfaction for the murder of a nobleman in the bloom of his youth, and full enjoyment of his friends, his honours, and his fortune.' Again and again the voices of money and power declared the sacredness of property in terms hitherto reserved for human life. Banks were credited with souls, and the circulation of gold likened to that of blood. Forgers, for example, were almost invariably hanged, and gentlemen knew why: 'Forgery is a stab to commerce, and only to be tolerated in a commercial nation when the foul crime of murder is pardoned.' In a mood of unrivalled assurance and complacency, Parliament over the century created one of the bloodiest criminal codes in Europe. Few of the new penalties were the product hysteria, or ferocious reaction; they were part of the conventional wisdom of England's governors. Locke himself defined political power as the right to create the penalty of death, and hence all lesser ones. And Shaftesbury, the enlightened rationalist who attacked both Hobbes and the Church for making fear the cement of the social order, at the same time accepted that the 'mere Vulgar of

Mankind' might perhaps 'often stand in need of such a rectifying Object as *the Gallows* before their Eyes.'

Eighteenth-century lawyers were well aware that never before had the legislature passed such a mass of new capital statutes so quickly. They floundered, however, when seeking for explanations. Many men, including learned ones, blamed the ever-increasing depravity of the people. In the 1730s Lord Chancellor Hardwicke blamed 'the degeneracy of human nature'; almost a century later, Justice Christian indicted 'the wicked inventions, and the licentious practices of modern times.' He drew a picture of a besieged government gradually making harsh new penalties as outrages demonstrated the uselessness of the old. But other observers were aware that the larger changes of trade, commerce and manufacturing might have something to do with the increasing weight of the statute book. Justice Daines Barrington cited 'the increase of trade': the great circulation of new and valuable commodities made any comparison of England's laws with those of other states unsound, for 'till a country can be found, which contains equal property and riches, the conclusion cannot be a just one.' In similar vein, the editor of the sixth edition of Hawkins's *Pleas of the Crown* wrote in 1788 that 'the increase of commerce, opulence, and luxury' since the first edition of 1715 'has introduced a variety of temptations to fraud and rapine, which the legislature has been forced to repel, by a multiplicity of occasional statutes, creating new offences and afflicting additional punishments.'

Undoubtedly this is a more persuasive explanation than 'degeneracy.' The constant extension of inland and foreign trade from the late seventeenth century, the exploitation of new mines, the wealth of London and the spas and the growth of population all increased the opportunities for theft. The relationship of each of these factors to the level of crime is still uncertain; indeed, whether there was any increase in the amount of theft *per capita* is the subject of current research. What is certain is that Parliament did not often enact the new capital statutes as a matter of conscious public policy. Usually there was no debate, and most of the changes were related to specific, limited property interests, hitherto unprotected for one reason or another. Often they were the personal interest of a few members, and the Lords and Commons enacted them for the mere asking.

Three bills from mid-century illustrate the process. An act of 1753 prescribing hanging for stealing shipwrecked goods was brought in on behalf of the 'Merchants, Traders and Insurers of the City of London' whose profits were being diminished by the activities of wreckers; the existing laws were declared to be too gentle. In 1764 Parliament decreed that the death penalty would apply to those who broke into buildings to steal or destroy linen, or the tools to make it, or to cut it in bleaching-grounds. But the penalties were contained in an incidental clause in an act passed to incorporate the English Linen Company, whose proprietors included lord Verney and the Right Honourable Charles Townshend; the death penalty was routinely added to protect their investments. Finally, a law of 1769 suggests how the class that controlled Parliament was using the criminal sanction to enforce two of the radical redefinitions of property which gentlemen were making in their own interests during the eighteenth century. The food riot was an organized and often highly disciplined popular protest against the growing national and international market in foodstuffs, a market which alarmed the poor by moving grain from their parishes when it could compel a higher price elsewhere, and which depended on a growing corps of middlemen whom the rioters knew were breaking Tudor and Stuart legislation by wholesale trading in food. Country gentlemen often tolerated such a 'riot,' or at least handled it sensibly, but Parliament was not prepared to let property suffer. Some mills had been torn down in the nation-wide riots of 1766 and 1767, and the 1769 act plugged a gap in the law by making such destruction a capital offence. If death for food rioters was an excellent idea, so was transportation for enclosure rioters. Within three days the bill was enlarged so that gentlemen busy on the expropriation of common lands by Act of Parliament were as well protected as the millers. By the time the bill became law two weeks later, it had also become a transportable offence to meddle with the bridges and steam-engines used in the mines which were bringing ever-increasing revenues to the gentry and aristocracy. As the decades passed, the maturing trade, commerce and industry of England spawned more laws to protect particular kinds of property. Perhaps the most dramatic change in the organizational structure of British capital was the growth of promissory notes on banks as a medium of exchange, and the increase in negotiable paper of all kinds. This new creation was exposed to fraud in many ways never foreseen by the ancient criminal law. The result was a rash of capital statutes against forgeries and frauds of all kinds, laws which multiplied towards the end of the century.

These, then, were the legal instruments which enforced the division of property by terror. They were not the largest parts of the law—much more dealt with land, 'with its long and voluminous train of descents and conveyances, settlements, entails, and incumbrances,' and commerce, for which the eighteenth-century judges at last created a coherent framework. The financial details of the marriage settlement, so often the sacrament by which land allied itself with trade, provided the best lawyers with a good part of their fees. But if most of the law and the lawyers were concerned with the civil dealings which propertied men had with one another, most men, the unpropertied labouring poor, met the law as criminal sanction: the threat or the reality of whipping, transportation and hanging. Death had long been a punishment for theft in England, and several of the most important statutes were passed in Tudor times. But the gentry and merchants and peers who sat in Parliament in the eighteenth century set new standards of legislative industry, as they passed act after act to keep the capital sanction up to date, to protect every conceivable kind of property from theft or malicious damage.

Yet two great questions hang over this remarkable code. The first concerns the actual number of executions. The available evidence suggests that, compared to some earlier periods, the eighteenth-century criminal law claimed few lives. At the beginning of the seventeenth century, for example, it appears that London and Middlesex saw four times as many executions as 150 years later. Equally interesting is the fact that in spite of the growth in trade and population, the increasing number of convictions for theft, and the continual creation of new capital statutes throughout the eighteenth-century, the number of executions for offences against property remained relatively stable, especially after 1750. The numbers of executions did not increase to match the number of convictions because of the increasing use of the royal pardon, by which transportation could be substituted for hanging, on the recommendation of the judges. Sir Leon Radzinowicz, in the most complete study of the subject, has shown that in London and Middlesex the proportion of death sentences commuted increased as the century progressed. He has argued that Parliament intended their legislation to be strictly enforced, and that the judges increasingly vitiated that intention by extending pardons freely. But this is an unsatisfactory conclusion. A conflict of such magnitude between Parliament and the judiciary would have disrupted eighteenth-century politics, and nothing of the sort happened. With few exceptions, gentlemen congratulated themselves on living in a century when the bench was wise and incorruptible, one of the glories of the constitution. Secondly, we shall see that the men who controlled Parliament were precisely those who usually brought their influence to bear in requesting pardons for condemned convicts from the judges and the king. We have yet to explain the coexistence of bloodier laws and increased convictions with a declining proportion of death sentences that were actually carried out.

This first problem is related to a second one. Most historians and many contemporaries argued that the policy of terror was not working. More of those sentenced to death were pardoned than were hanged; thieves often escaped punishment through the absence of a police force, the leniency of prosecutors and juries, and the technicalities of the law; transported convicts were so little afraid that they often returned to England to pick pockets on hanging days; riot was endemic. The critics of the law argued that the gibbets and corpses paradoxically weakened the enforcement of the law: rather than terrifying criminals, the death penalty terrified prosecutors and juries, who feared committing judicial murder on the capital statutes. Sir Samuel Romilly and other reformers led a long and intelligent campaign for the repeal of some laws, arguing from statistics that convictions would become more numerous once that fear was removed. The reformers also used the arguments of Beccaria, who suggested in 1764 that gross and capricious terror should be replaced by a fixed and graduated scale of more lenient but more certain punishments. His ideas were widely canvassed in England, as well as on the continent. Even Blackstone, the high priest of the English legal system, looked forward to changes on these lines. Yet Parliament resisted all reform. Not one capital statute was repealed until 1808, and real progress had to wait until the 1820s and 1830s.

Why the contradiction? If property was so important, and reform of the criminal law would help to protect it, why did gentlemen not embrace reform? Given the apparently fierce intentions of the legislature, why was the law not changed to make enforcement more certain? Historians searching for the roots of the modern criminal law and the modern police usually devote most of their attention to the triumph of reform in the nineteenth century. But the victors in the eighteenth century were the conservatives, the hangers and gibbeters, and they resolutely ignored over fifty years of cogent criticism. Two immediate explanations are commonly given. The gentry undoubtedly refused to create a regular police force, a necessary part of the Beccarian plan. Moreover, the lack of secondary punishments, and the unsatisfactory nature of those in use, such as transportation, made it seem desirable to keep the death penalty for the incorrigible rogue. Neither fact, however, explains why there was such unbending opposition to the repeal of even those capital statutes that were seldom used. This determination of Parliament to retain all the capital statutes, even when obsolete, and to continue to create new ones, even when they were stillborn, suggests that the explanation for the failure of reform lies deeper in the mental and social structure of eighteenth-century England. A few historians have attempted explanations, but they are usually vague or tautological: that the industrial revolution, as a time of social change, induced conservatism; that the French Revolution did the same; that legal reform in England is always, and inevitably, slow. These explanations ignore the underlying assumptions of the governors of England, and do not show how the old criminal law matched that mental world. For it is difficult to believe that Parliament would have been so complacently conservative about the unreformed law unless they were convinced that it was serving their interests. And here the testimony of conservatives is more helpful than the claims of reformers.

Timothy Nourse antedated Beccaria and Romilly by a good half-century, but he expressed an enduring belief of the gentry when he declared that many of the common people were 'very rough and savage in their Dispositions, being of levelling Principles, and refractory to Government, insolent and tumultuous.' Civility only made them saucy.

> The best way therefore will be to bridle them, and to make them feel the spur too, when they begin to play their Tricks, and kick. The Saying of an *English* gentleman was much to the purpose, That three things ought always to be kept under, our Mastiff-Dog, a Stone-Horse, and a Clown: And really I think a snarling, cross-grained Clown to be the most unlucky Beast of the three. Such Men then are to be look'd upon as trashy Weeds or Nettles, growing usually upon Dunghills, which if touch'd gently will sting, but being squeez'd hard will never hurt us.

The instruments to deal with such 'stubborn, cross-grain'd rogues' were at hand: '*Beadles, Catchpoles, Gaolers, Hangmen,*...such like Engines of Humanity are the fittest Tools in the World for a Magistrate to work with in the Reformation of an obdurate Rogue, all which, I say, may be so used and managed by him as not to endanger his own fingers, or discompose his thoughts.' This is language far removed from Romilly's cool calculation of rates of conviction, or even Justice Christian's hysterical talk of alarms, watch-dogs and double-barreled pistols. Nourse knew instinctively that the criminal law is as much concerned with authority as it is with property. For wealth does not exist outside a social context, theft is given definition only within a set of social relations, and the connections between property, power and authority are close and crucial. The criminal law was critically important in maintaining bonds of obedience and deference, in legitimizing the status quo, in constantly recreating the structure of authority which arose from property and in turn protected its interests.

But terror alone could never have accomplished those ends. It was the raw material of authority, but class interest and the structure of the law itself shaped it into a much more effective instrument of power. Almost a century after Nourse, another defender of the unreformed system described the other side of authority: 'Could we view our own species from a distance, or regard mankind with the same sort of observation with which we read the natural history, or remark the *manners*, of any other animal,' he wrote in 1785,

> there is nothing in the human character which would more surprise us, than the almost universal subjugation of strength to weakness—than to see many millions of robust men, in the complete use and exercise of their faculties, and without any defect of courage, waiting upon the will

of a child, a woman, a driveller, or a lunatic. And although...we suppose perhaps an extreme case; yet in all cases, even in the most popular forms of civil government, *the physical strength lies in the governed*. In what manner opinion thus prevails over strength, or how power, which naturally belongs to superior force, is maintained in opposition to it; in other words, by what motives the many are induced to submit to the few, becomes an inquiry which lies at the root of almost every political speculation...Let civil governors learn hence to respect their subjects; let them be admonished, that the physical strength resides in the governed; that this strength wants only to be felt and roused, to lay prostrate the most ancient and confirmed dominion; that civil authority is founded in opinion; that general opinion therefore ought always to be treated with deference, and managed with delicacy and circumspection.

These are the words of Archdeacon Paley, and they were published a few years after the Gordon Riots. Paley is not usually quoted as an exponent of 'delicacy and circumspection,' but as the most eloquent defender of the old criminal law as a system of selective terror. He was cited by almost every subsequent opponent of reform, and has often been considered by later writers as little more than an ingenious apologist or uncritical conservative. But he was in fact an acute observer of the bases of power in eighteenth-century England, and although he did not make the connection explicit, the criminal law was extremely important in ensuring, in his words, that 'opinion' prevailed over 'physical strength.' The opinion was that of the ruling class; the law was one of their chief ideological instruments. It combined the terror worshipped by Nourse with the discretion stressed by Paley, and used both to mould the consciousness by which the many submitted to the few. Moreover, its effectiveness in doing so depended in large part on the very weaknesses and inconsistencies condemned by reformers and liberal historians. In considering the criminal law as an ideological system, we must look at how it combined imagery and force, ideals and practice, and try to see how it manifested itself to the mass of unpropertied Englishmen. We can distinguish three aspects of the law as ideology: majesty, justice and mercy. Understanding them will help us to explain the divergence between bloody legislation and declining executions, and the resistance to reform of any kind.

*   *   *   *   *

'Equality before the law' also implied that no man was exempt from it. It was part of the lore of politics that in England social class did not preserve a man even from the extreme sanction of death. This was not, of course, true. But the impression made by the execution of a man of property or position was very deep. As executions for forgery became increasingly common throughout the century, more such respectable villains went to the gallows. The crime was punished with unremitting severity even though it was often committed by impecunious lawyers of good family. This rigour was distressing to many middling men: the agitation led by Johnson against the execution of the Reverend Dr. Dodd, a former Royal Chaplain and lord Chesterfield's old tutor, was enormous. Dodd died at Tyburn in 1777 but he lived in popular culture for a long time, his case persuasive evidence that the law treated rich and poor alike. The occasional sentence of transportation or death passed on gentlemen with unusual sexual tastes or guilty of homicide, cases widely reported in the *Newgate Calendar* and other versions, similarly served to justify the law. Undoubtedly the most useful victim in this respect was Lawrence Shirley, Lord Ferrers, who killed his steward, was captured by his tenantry, tried in the House of Lords, sentenced to death, executed at Tyburn, and dissected 'like a common criminal' as the publicists never tired of repeating. He was hanged in his silver brocade wedding-suit, on a scaffold equipped with black silk cushions for the mourners. But hanging is hanging, the defenders of the law repeated enthusiastically. An enormous literature surrounded his execution in 1760, much of it devoted to celebrating the law. Later in the century the event was often recalled as an irrefutable proof of the justice of English society. An anti-Jacobin in the 1790s advised his 'brother artificers':

> We have long enjoyed that Liberty and Equality which the French have been struggling for: in England, ALL MEN ARE EQUAL; all who commit the same offences are liable to the same punishment. If the *very poorest and meanest man* commits murder, he is hanged with a hempen halter, and his body dissected. If the *Richest nobleman* commits a murder, *he* is hanged with a hempen halter, and his body dissected – *all are equal here.*

Hannah More used the same argument in her anti-Jacobin pamphlets for the poor; Ferrers became one of the best-known villains of the century. In some counties the story of the wicked aristocrat who met a just end on the scaffold was told at popular festivities until well into the 1800s.

In the parlour of the Justice of the Peace, *stare decisis* and due process were not always so much in evidence as in the high courts. Many justices convicted on flimsy evidence, particularly when they were subservient to a local magnate, and when they were enforcing the game laws. It was perfectly possible to combine arbitrary powers with an obeisance to the rules, however, and it appears that most JPs made an effort to appear, at least, to be acting legally. Moreover, even at the level of the justice the rules of law could be used effectively on behalf of a labouring man. It was not unknown for labourers caught deer-stealing to make an ingenious use of the contradictory statutes protecting informers to escape punishment. The occasional success of such ruses, and the attempts to use them, probably helped sustain the belief that the integrity of the law was a reality and not merely the rhetoric of judges the gentlemen. Perhaps even more important in this respect were the frequent prosecutions brought by common informers, where the poor could go before a JP and use the law in their own interests. Prosecutions under the excise, game and turnpike acts — often against farmers and tradesmen who on most other occasions were those who used the courts — occasionally allowed the powerless to make the law their servant, whether for personal revenge or the sake of the reward. Moreover, Justices of the Peace sometimes intervened in the administration of the poor laws, prosecuting callous overseers who forced paupers to marry to remove them from the rates, or who dumped them over parish boundaries to die at the expense of their neighbours. Every county saw trials for such cruelties every few years, and the gentlemen who brought them clothed the issue in the language of constitutionalism. An extremely pervasive rhetorical tradition, with deep historical roots, was invoked and strengthened on all such occasions. The law was held to be the guardian of Englishmen, of all Englishmen. Gentlemen held this as an unquestionable belief: that belief, too, gave the ideology of justice an integrity which no self-conscious manipulation could alone sustain. The real guarantees of the law were, moreover, confirmed in several celebrated political trials: Lord Mansfield's finding against general warrants in 1765, the Middlesex jury's acquittals of the leaders of the London Corresponding Society in 1794. In the latter case the striking contrast with the Scottish trials under Braxfield the year before was treated as an object lesson in the superiority of the English courts and bench.

Yet the idea of justice was always dangerous, straining the narrow definitions of the lawyers and judges. It was easy to claim equal justice for murderers of all classes, where a universal moral sanction was more likely to be found, or in political cases, the necessary price of a constitution ruled by law. The trick was to extend that communal sanction to a criminal law that was nine-tenths concerned with upholding a radical division of property. Though Justice seemed impartial in crimes against the person, wrote Mandeville,

> Yet, it was thought, the sword she bore
> Check'd but the Desp'rate and the Poor;
> That, urged by mere Necessity,
> Were tied up to the wretched Tree
> For Crimes, which not deserv'd that Fate
> But to secure the Rich, and Great.

In times of dearth, when the rulers of England were faced with food riots by men desperate with hunger and convinced of the rights of their case, the contradiction could become acute. At such times two conceptions of justice stood in sharp opposition: an older, Christian version of natural rights, which guaranteed even the poorest man at least life; and the justice of the law of property, sanctioned by the settlements of the seventeenth century. Keith Thomas has suggested that the erosion of the moral sanctions surrounding charity, and the ambiguity accompanying the birth of a more rationalized and less indulgent attitude to poverty, produced strong conflicts of guilt and blame, with seventeenth-century witch trials as their partial expression. A century later, the ambiguities had still not been altogether resolved in the law, which in its ideological role had to reconcile popular ideas of justice with the absolute claims of property. From time to time writers in jurisprudence took up with distaste the ancient civil doctrine that a starving man had the right to steal enough food to keep himself for a week. Hale had written in the seventeenth century that the rule had long been disused in England. Blackstone argue that in this, as in all things, English law was founded on the highest reason, 'for men's properties would be under a strange insecurity, if liable to be invaded according to the wants of others; of which wants no man can possibly be an adequate judge, but the party himself who pleads them.' The judges agreed, for it was impossible to admit poverty as a legal defence without wholly eroding the property statute. Rather then acknowledge an archaic, alien and dangerous legal doctrine, the bench stressed their deep concern for the little personal property that the ordinary Englishman did have. From time to time they passed harsh sentences for certain crimes, such as the theft of clothes, which they proclaimed in court to be particular misfortunes of the poor. A great many words were lavished also on particular statutes for the same reason. An act of 1713 punished with death any housebreaker who stole goods worth forty shillings or more. Opposing repeal in a major debate in 1811, Lord Eldon declared 'that the property of the industrious cottager should be protected, who is often obliged to leave his cottage, and his little hoard of perhaps not more than 40s deposited in a tin-box in a corner of a room.'

It is difficult to assess the weight such arguments had with the mass of Englishmen. Eldon's was jejune: few cottagers had savings of £2, the wages of a month or more, in the harsh year 1811. Equally few cottagers could afford to go to law to recover stolen goods. Ideologies do not rest on realities, however, but on appearances, and there were enough prosecutions on behalf of poor men to give colour to the Lord Chancellor's claims. Usually such cases were begun or paid for by employers, landlords or local associates for the prosecution of felons. The motives for men of property to assist the poor to prosecute were a rangle of self-interest and paternalism. Some gentlemen simply believed that the law was the birthright of every Englishman, and most were anxious to convict a thief who might prey on them as well. The consequence was that more poor men were able to use the law than the system of legal fees would otherwise have allowed. The poor suffer from theft as well as the rich, and in eighteenth-century England probably far more poor men lost goods to thieves, if only because the rich were few and their property more secure. In recognizing that fact, and extending its protection, however imperfectly, to ordinary men, the criminal law did much to justify itself and the gentlemen who administered it. Defending the constitution in the 1790s, Hannah More's ploughman sings,

> British laws for my guard,
> My cottage is barr'd,
> 'Tis safe in the light or the dark, Sir;
> If the Squire should oppress,
> I get instant redress:
> My orchard's as safe as his park, Sir.

The justice of English law was thus a powerful ideological weapon in the arsenal of conservatives during the French Revolution. Wicked Lord Ferrers, juries and *habeas corpus* were leading themes in anti-Jacobin popular literature. They were usually contrasted with tyrannical French aristocrats, the inquisitorial system of law and *lettres de cachet*. In countering the influence of Tom Paine, the conservatives repeatedly emphasized the central place of law in the English constitution. Gillray caught the spirit of the argument perfectly in a print of 1801. He drew two trees. One, the blasted and rotten stump of Opposition, was surmounted by a French cap of Liberty, and on its few remaining branches hung the withered fruits of Blasphemy, Sedition, Anarchy, Democracy. The other tree, flourishing and green, he gave roots of Kings, Lords and Commons, sweet apples of Peace, Happiness and Prosperity, and he labelled its massive trunk JUSTICE. It is important, however, to distinguish the argument against Paine from the wider ideological use of justice throughout the century. The author of *The Rights of Man* was in a peculiar position with respect to the law. As one of 'the middling sort' he was a man of moderate property, and he thought like one. He was not a critic of the institutions of the law. Indeed, Paine claimed that Quarter Sessions and assizes, as bodies of local administration, were two of the few organs of proper self-government. Nor did he criticize the law's tenderness for property. The only effective answer to the Tory position would have been a thoroughly egalitarian critique and this Paine was unwilling to begin. An egalitarian on the subject of hereditary monarchy and corrupt aristocracy and landed wealth, he was no leveller of all property distinctions. Hence he had to suffer the conservatives' encomiums of justice in silence.

Although Paine never lent his pen to the task, the institutions of the law were in fact exceedingly open to radical criticism. The conservatives based their defence on comparisons with French tyranny, the occasional punishment of a great man, the limited protection the law gave to the poor. They did not dare to attempt a reasoned examination of the whole legal system for the edification of the mob. All men of property knew that judges, justices and juries had to be chosen from their own ranks. The jury, the supposed guarantee that an Englishman would be tried by his equals had a sharp property qualification. The reason, simply put, was that the common Englishman could not be trusted to share in the operation of the law. A panel of the poor would not convict a labourer who stole wood from a lord's park, a sheep from a farmer's fold, or corn from a merchant's yard. As Gisborne pointed out, even as witnesses 'many of the common people...are found to make use of a very blameable latitude in their interpretation of the ninth commandment; and think that they are guilty of no breach of it in deviating, though upon oath, from strict truth, *in favour* of the party accused.' The cottager who appeared in court charged with theft had no illusions about being tried by 'his equals and neighbours,' whatever the writers of law books claimed. The twelve men sitting opposite him were employers, overseers of the poor, propertied men. In most cases they were the equals and neighbours of the prosecutor, not the accused, and this was especially true in cases of theft. The point is not that such juries convicted against the evidence, but rather that a more democratic jury might not have convicted at all. In the constitutional struggles of the seventeenth century, 'middling men' of moderate property had wanted the widest possible extension of trial by jury; the Crown had tried to restrict it because juries shielded sedition. There was another small group, however, who had also wanted to control juries. Winstanley and the Diggers repudiated them as protectors of property against the rights of the poor. There were no Diggers in the eighteenth century, but cottagers and labourers were undoubtedly aware that English justice was still the creature of judges and juries.

Eighteenth-century 'justice' was not, however, a nonsense. It remained a powerful and evocative word, even if it bore a much more limited meaning than a twentieth-century (or seventeenth- century) egalitarian would give it. In a society radically divided between rich and poor, the powerful and powerless, the occasional victory of a cottager in the courts or the rare spectacle of a titled villain on the gallows made a sharp impression. Moreover, it would be wrong to suggest that the law had to be wholly consistent to persuade men of its legitimacy. 'Justice,' in the sense of rational, bureaucratic decisions made in the common interest, is a peculiarly modern conception. It was gaining ground in the eighteenth century. Most reformers worked to bring about such law, and of all such schemes Jeremy Bentham's was the logical conclusion. Yet his plan for a criminal code that was precise, consistent and wholly enforced was alien to the thought of most eighteenth-century Englishmen. They tended to think of justice in personal terms, and were more struck by understanding of individual cases than by the delights of abstract schemes. Where authority is embodied in direct personal relationships, men will often accept power, even enormous, despotic

A. Doctor Vsher, Lord Pri
te of Ireland.
B the Sheriffes of London.
C, the Earle of Strafford.
D, his Kindred and friend

Illustration 12-12 Execution of the Earl of Strafford, May 12, 1641. See discussion in Blackstone's *Commentaries*, vol. 4, 405, at *Materials, supra,* p. 458. Contemporary print.

power, when it comes from the 'good King,' the father of his people, who tempers justice with mercy. A form of this powerful psychic configuration was one of the most distinctive aspects of the unreformed criminal law. Bentham could not understand it, but it was the law's greatest strength as an ideological system, especially among the poor, and in the countryside.

*   *   *   *   *

COMMERCIAL LAW

Sir Henry Maine, *Ancient Law* (1st American from 2d English ed., New York, 1864), 295–303.

CHAPTER IX.
THE EARLY HISTORY OF CONTRACT

There are few general propositions concerning the age to which we belong which seem at first sight likely to be received with readier concurrence than the assertion that the society of our day is mainly distinguished from that of preceding generations by the largeness of the sphere which is occupied in it by Contract. Some of the phenomena on which this proposition rests are among those most frequently singled out for notice, for comment, and for eulogy. Not many of us are so unobservant as not to perceive that in innumerable cases where old law fixed a man's social position irreversibly at his birth, modern law allows him

Illustration 12-13 "Britannia." Frontispiece to Charles Molloy's *De Jure Maritimo et Navali: or a Treatise of Affairs Maritime and of Commerce* (6th ed., London, 1707). [Author's Collection.]

to create it for himself by convention; and indeed several of the few exceptions which remain to this rule are constantly denounced with passionate indignation. The point, for instance, which is really debated in the vigorous controversy still carried on upon the subject of negro servitude, is whether the status of the slave does not belong to by-gone institutions, and whether the only relation between employer and labourer which commends itself to modern morality be not a relation determined exclusively by contract. The recognition of this difference between past ages and the present enters into the very essence of the most famous contemporary speculations. It is certain that the science of Political Economy, the only department of moral inquiry which has made any considerable progress in our day, would fail to correspond with the facts of life if it were not true that Imperative Law had abandoned the largest part of the field which it once occupied, and had left men to settle rules of conduct for themselves with a liberty never allowed to them till recently. The bias indeed of most persons trained in political economy is to consider the general truth on which their science reposes as entitled to become universal, and, when they apply it as an art, their efforts are ordinarily directed to enlarging the province of Contract and to curtailing that of Imperative Law, except so far as law is necessary to enforce the performance of Contracts. The impulse given by thinkers who are under the influence of these ideas is beginning to be very strongly felt in the Western world. Legislation has nearly confessed its inability to keep pace with the activity of man in discovery, in invention, and in the manipulation of accumulated wealth; and the law even of the least advanced communities tends more and more to become a mere surface-stratum, having under it an ever-changing assemblage of contractual rules with which it rarely interferes except to compel compliance with a few fundamental principles, or unless it be called in to punish the violation of good faith.

Social inquiries, so far as they depend on the consideration of legal phenomena, are in so backward a condition that we need not be surprised at not finding these truths recognised in the commonplaces which pass current concerning the progress of society. These commonplaces answer much more to our prejudices than to our convictions. The strong disinclination of most men to regard morality as advancing seems to be especially powerful when the virtues on which Contract depends are in question, and many of us have an almost instinctive reluctance to admitting that good faith and trust in our fellows are more widely diffused than of old, or that there is anything in contemporary manners which parallels the loyalty of the antique world. From time to time, these prepossessions are greatly strengthened by the spectacle of frauds, unheard of before the period at which they were observed, and astonishing from their complications as well shocking from criminality. But the very character of these frauds shows clearly that, before they became possible, the moral obligations of which they are the breach must have been more than proportionately developed. It is the confidence reposed and deserved by the many which affords facilities for the bad faith of the few, so that, if colossal examples of dishonesty occur, there is no surer conclusion than that scrupulous honesty is displayed in the average of the transaction which, in the particular case, have supplied the delinquent with his opportunity. If we insist on reading the history of morality as reflected in jurisprudence, by turning our eyes not on the law of Contract but on the law of Crime, we must be careful that we read it aright. The only form of dishonesty treated of in the most ancient Roman law is Theft. At the moment at which I write, the newest chapter in the English criminal law is one which attempts to prescribe punishment for the frauds of Trustees. The proper inference from this contrast is not that the primitive Romans practised a higher morality than ourselves. We should rather say that, in the interval between their day and ours, morality had advanced from a very rude to a highly refined conception—from viewing the rights of property as exclusively sacred, to looking upon the rights growing out of the mere unilateral reposal of confidence as entitled to the protection of the penal law.

The definite theories of jurists are scarcely nearer the truth in this point than the opinions of the multitude. To begin with the views of the Roman lawyers, we find them inconsistent with the true history of moral and legal progress. One class of contracts, in which the plighted faith of the contracting parties was the only material ingredient, they specifically denominated Contracts *juris gentium*, and though these contracts were undoubtedly the latest born into the Roman system, the expression employed implies, if a definite meaning be extracted from it, that they were more ancient than certain other forms of engagement treated of in Roman law, in which the neglect of a mere technical formality was as fatal to the obligation as misunderstanding or deceit. But then the antiquity to which they were referred was vague, shadowy, and only capable of being understood through the Present; nor was it until the language of the Roman lawyers became the language of an age which had lost the key to their mode of thought that a "Contract of the Law of Nations" came to be distinctly looked upon as a Contract known to man in a state of Nature. Rousseau adopted both the judicial and the popular error. In the Dissertation on the effects of Art and Science upon Morals, the first of his works which attracted attention and the one in which he states most unreservedly the opinions which made him the founder of a sect, the veracity and good faith attributed to the ancient Persians are repeatedly pointed out as traits of primitive innocence which have been gradually obliterated by civilisation; and at a later period he found a basis for all his speculations in the doctrine of an original Social Contract. The Social Contract or Compact is the most systematic form which has ever been assumed by the error we are discussing. It is a theory which, though nursed into importance by political passions, derived all its sap from the speculations of lawyers. True it certainly is that the famous Englishmen, for whom it had first had attraction, valued it chiefly for its political serviceableness, but, as I shall presently attempt to explain, they would never have arrived at it, if politicians had not long conducted their controversies in legal phraseology. Nor were the English authors of the theory blind to that speculative amplitude which recommended it so strongly to the Frenchmen who inherited it from them. Their writings show they perceived that it could be made to account for all social, quite as well as for all political phenomena. They had observed the fact, already striking in their day, that of the positive rules obeyed by men, the greater part were created by Contract, the lesser by imperative Law. But they were ignorant or careless of the historical relation of these two constituents of jurisprudence. It was for the purpose, therefore, of gratifying their speculative tastes by attributing all jurisprudence to a uniform source, as much as with the view of eluding the doctrines which claimed a divine parentage for Imperative Law, that they devised the theory that all Law had its origin in Contract. In another stage of thought, they would have been satisfied to leave their theory in the condition of an ingenious hypothesis or a convenient verbal formula. But that age was under the dominion of legal superstitions. The State of Nature had been talked about till it had ceased to be regarded as paradoxical, and hence it seemed easy to give a fallacious reality and definiteness to the contractual origin of Law by insisting on the Social Compact as a historical fact.

Our own generation has got rid of these erroneous juridical theories, partly by outgrowing the intellectual state to which they belong, and partly by almost ceasing to theorise on such subjects altogether. The favorite occupation of active minds at the present moment, and the one which answers to the speculations of our forefathers on the origin of the social state, is the analysis of society as it exists and moves before our eyes; but, through omitting to call in the assistance of history, this analysis too often degenerates into an idle exercise of curiosity, and is especially apt to incapacitate the inquirer for comprehending states of society which differ considerably from that to which he is accustomed. The mistake of judging the men of other periods by the morality of our own day has its parallel in the mistake of supposing that every wheel or bolt in the modern social machine had its counterpart in more rudimentary societies. Such impressions ramify very widely, and masque themselves very subtly, in historical works written in the modern fashion; but I find the trace of their presence in the domain of jurisprudence in the praise which is frequently bestowed on the little apologue of Montesquieu concerning the Troglodytes, inserted in the *Lettres Persanes*. The Troglodytes were a people who systematically violated their Contracts, and so perished utterly. If the story bears the moral which its author intended, and is employed to expose an anti-social heresy by which this century and the last have been threatened, it is most unexceptionable; but if the inference be obtained from it that society could not possibly hold together without attaching a sacredness to promises and agreements which should be on something like a par with the respect that is paid to them by a mature civilisation, it involves an error so grave as to be fatal to all sound understanding of legal history. The fact is that the Troglodytes have flourished and founded powerful states with very small attention to the obligations of Contract. The point which before all others has to be apprehended in the constitution of primitive societies is that the individual creates for himself few or no rights, and few or no duties. The rules which he obeys are derived first from the station into which he is born, and next from the imperative commands addressed to him by the chief of the household of which he forms a part. Such a system leaves the very smallest room for Contract. The members of the same family (for so we may interpret the evidence) are wholly incapable of contracting with each other, and the family is entitled to disregard the engagements by which any one of its subordinate members has attempted to bind it. Family, it is true, may contract with family, and chieftain with chieftain, but the transaction is one of the same nature, and encumbered by as many formalities, as the alienation of property, and the disregard of one iota of the performance is fatal to the obligation. The positive duty resulting from one man's reliance on the word of another is among the slowest conquests of advancing civilization.

Term. S. Mich. 2 Annae, in B.R., Buller *versus* Crips, (1704)
(6 Mod. 29)

A note was in this form: "I promise to pay John Smith, or order, the sum of one hundred pounds, on account of wine had from him." John Smith endorses this note to another; the indorsee brings an action against him that drew this note, and declares upon the custom of merchants as upon a bill of exchange.

A motion was made in arrest of judgment upon the authority of the case of *Martin v. Clarke*.

But *Brotherick* would distinguish this case from that: for there the party to whom the note was originally made brought the action, but here it is by the indorsee; and he that gave this note did, by the tenor thereof, make it assignable or negotiable by the words "or order," which amount to a promise or undertaking to pay it to any whom he should appoint, and the indorsement is an appointment to the plaintiff.

Holt, C.J.: I remember when actions upon inland bills of exchange did first begin; and there they laid a particular custom between London and Bristol, and it was an action against the acceptor. The defendant's counsel would put them to prove the custom; at which Hale, C.J., who tried it, laughed, and said they had a hopeful case of it. And in my Lord North's time it was said that the custom in that case was part of the common law of England; and these actions since became frequent, as the trade of the nation did increase; and all the difference between foreign bills and inland bills is, that foreign bills must be protested before a public notary before the drawer can be charged, but inland bills need no protest, and the notes in

Oafte *verfus* Taylor.

ASfumpfit, by David Oafte, Merchant-ftranger, againft William Taylor Merchant: For that whereas by the cuftom of London, between Merchants trafficking from London into the parts beyond Seas: If any Merchant, commorant in London, and trafficking beyond Seas, direct his Bill of Exchange, bona fide, and without Covin, to another Merchant, commorant beyond Seas, and trafficking betwixt London and the parts beyond Seas; Upon fuch a Merchants accepting a Bill, and fubfcribing it according to the ufe of Merchants, It hath the force of a promife, to compel him to pay it at the day appointed by the Bill; And alledgeth in facto, That William Kenton, being a Merchant, trafficking betwixt London and Middleburgh beyond Seas, and commorant in London, directed his Bill of Exchange to the Defendant, commorant in Middleburgh, and trafficking between London and Middleburgh, requiring him to pay 355 l. Flemifh, at the ufance of four months to the Plaintiff, being a Merchant: And that the Defendant accepted thereof, fecundum ufum Mercatorum, and fubfcribed it, and had not payed it: Whereupon, &c. After Verdict, upon Non affumpfit pleaded, and found for the Plaintiff, It was moved in arreft of Judgment, becaufe the Defendant is not averred to be a Merchant at the time of the Bill accepted.

Illustration 12-14 *Oaste v. Taylor (1612)*, *Croke's Reports*, 2nd part ("Cro. Jac."), 1683 ed., 306–307. [Author's Collection.]

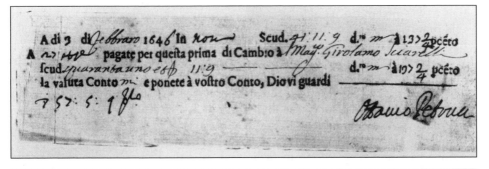

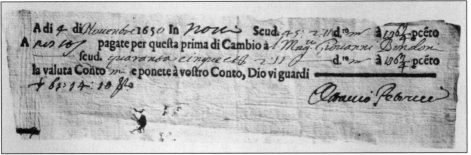

Illustration 12-15 Bills of exchange. Italian bills from 1646 and 1650. Siena-Monte Paschi Archives (no. 167, 176). With thanks to my brother-in-law, Patrick Rogers. Courtesy Siena-Monte Paschi Archives.

question are only an invention of the goldsmiths in Lombard street, who had a mind to make a law to bind all those that did deal with them; and sure to allow such a note to carry any lien with it were to turn a piece of paper, which is in law but evidence of a parol contract, into a specialty. And, besides, it would impower one to assign that to another which he could not have himself; for since he to whom this note was made could not have this action, how can his assignee have it? And these notes are not in the nature of bills of exchange; for the reason of the custom of bills of exchange is for the expedition of trade and its safety; and likewise it hinders the exportation of money out of the realm. He said, if the indorsee had brought this action against the indorser, it might peradventure lie; for the indorsement may be said to be tantamount to the drawing of a new bill for so much as the note is for, upon the person that gave the note; or he may sue the first drawer in the name of the indorser, and convert the money, when recovered, to his own use; for the indorsement amounts at least to an agreement that the indorsee should sue for money in the name of the indorser, and receive it to his own use; and, besides, it is a good authority to the original drawer to pay the money to the indorsee.

And Powell, J., cited one case, where a plaintiff had judgment upon a declaration of this kind in the Common Pleas; and that my Lord Treby was very earnest for it, as a mighty convenience for trade; but that, when they had considered well the reasons why it was doubted here, they began to doubt, too.

The whole court seemed clear for staying judgment.

At another day, Holt, C.J., declared that he had desired to speak with two of the most famous merchants in London, to be informed of the mighty ill consequences that it was pretended would ensue by obstructing this course; and that they had told him it was very frequent with them to make such notes, and that they looked upon them as bills of exchange, and that they had been used for a matter of thirty years, and that not only notes, but bonds for money, were transferred frequently, and indorsed as bills of exchange. Indeed, I agree, a bill of exchange may be made between two persons without a third; and, if there be such a necessity of dealing that way, why do not dealers use that way which is legal? and may be this; as, if A. has money to lodge in B.'s hands, and would have a negotiable note for it, it is only saying thus, "Mr. B., pay me, or order, so much money value to yourself," and signing this, and B. accepting it; or he may take the common note and say thus, "For value to yourself, pay me (or indorsee) so much," and good.

And the court at last took the vacation to consider of it.

Pillans and Ross v. Van Miérop and Hopkins (April 30, 1763)*
3 Burrow 1663

On Friday 25th of January last Mr. Attorney-General *Norton* on behalf of the plaintiffs moved for a new trial. He moved it as upon a verdict against evidence; the substance of which evidence was a follows.

One White, a merchant in Ireland, desired to draw upon the plaintiffs, who were merchants at Rotterdam in Holland, for £800, payable to one Clifford, and proposed to give them credit upon a good house in London for their reimbursement, or any other method of reimbursement.

The plaintiffs, in answer, desired a confirmed credit upon a house of rank in London as the condition of their accepting the bill. White names the house of the defendants as this house of rank, and offers credit upon them. Whereupon the plaintiffs honoured the draught and paid the money, and then wrote to the defendants, Van Miérop and Hopkins, merchants in London (to whom White also wrote about the same time), desiring to know whether they would accept such bills as they, the plaintiffs, should in about a month's time draw upon the said Van Miérop's and Hopkins' house here in London for £800 upon the credit of White. And they, having received their assent, accordingly drew upon the defendants. In the interim White failed, before their draught came to hand or was even drawn; and the defendants gave notice of it to the plaintiffs and forbad their drawing upon them. Which they nevertheless did; and therefore the defendants refused to pay their bills.

On the trial a verdict was found for the defendants.

*   *   *   *   *

Serjt. Davy (for the defendants): . . . A promise to pay a past debt of another person is void at Common Law for want of consideration, unless there be at least an implied promise from the debtee to forbear suing the original debtor. But here was a debt clearly contracted by White with the plaintiffs on the credit of White, and there is no promise from the plaintiffs to forbear suing White. A naked promise is a void promise: the consideration must be executory, not past or executed.

LORD MANSFIELD asked if any case could be found where the undertaking holden to be a *nudum pactum* was in writing.

---

* Some editing by C.H.S. Fifoot, *History and Sources of the Common Law* (London, 1945), 427–430.

REPORTS

OF

CASES

ADJUDGED IN THE

Court of King's Bench

Since the Time of LORD MANSFIELD's
Coming to preside in it.

By SIR JAMES BURROW

With TABLES,
Of the NAMES of the CASES,
AND
Of the MATTER contained in them.

VOLUME the SECOND:

Beginning with *Michaelmas* Term 32 *Geo.* 2. 1758.

AND

Ending with *Trinity* Term 1 *G.* 3. 1761, (inclusive.)

THE THIRD EDITION.

LONDON:

Printed by His Majesty's Law-Printers;

For EDWARD BROOKE (Successor to Messrs. WORRALL and
TOVEY) at the *Dove* in *Bell-Yard*, near *Temple-Bar*.
MDCCLXXVII.

Illustration 12-16   The 3d edition of the famous *Burrow's Reports*. [Author's Collection.]

Serjeant Davy—It was antiently doubted whether a written acceptance of a Bill of Exchange was binding for want of a consideration. It is so said somewhere in *Lutwyche*.

LORD MANSFIELD: This is a matter of great consequence to trade and commerce in every light.

If there was any kind of fraud in this transaction, the collusion and *mala fides* would have vacated the contract. But...it seems to me clear that there was none...

If there be no fraud, it is a mere question of law. The Law of Merchants and the Law of the Land is the same. A witness cannot be admitted to prove the Law of Merchants: we must consider it as a point of law. A *nudum pactum* does not exist in the usage and law of merchants.

I take it that the ancient notion about the want of consideration was for the sake of evidence only; for when it is reduced into writing, as in covenants, specialties, bonds, etc., there was no objection to the want of consideration. And the Statute of Frauds proceeded upon the same principle.

In commercial cases among merchants the want of consideration is not an objection.

This is just the same thing as if White had drawn on Van Miérop and Hopkins, payable to the plaintiffs. It had been nothing to the plaintiffs whether Van Miérop and Co. had effects of White's in their hands or not, if they had accepted his bill. And this amounts to the same thing: 'I will give the bill due honour' is, in effect, accepting it....This is an engagement to accept the bill, if there was a necessity to accept it, and to pay it when due; and they could not afterwards retract. It would be very destructive to trade and to trust in commercial dealing, if they could. There was nothing of *nudum pactum* mentioned to the Jury; nor was it, I dare say, at all in their idea or contemplation.

I think the point of law is with the plaintiffs.

Mr. Justice WILMOT: The question is whether this action can be supported upon the breach of this agreement.

I can find none of those cases, that go upon its being *nudum pactum*, that are in writing: they are all upon parol.

I have traced this matter of the *nudum pactum*, and it is very curious....[It is] echoed from the Civil Law—*ex nudo pacto non oritur actio*. Vinnius gives the reason in *Lib. 3. Tit. De Obligationibus*, 4to Edition, 596. If by stipulation (and *a fortiori* if by writing) it was good without consideration. There was no radical defect in the contract for want of consideration. But it was made requisite in order to put people upon attention and reflection and to prevent obscurity and uncertainty; and, in that view, either writing or certain formalities were required. *Idem*, on *Justinian*, 4to Edition, 614. Therefore it was intended as a guard against rash inconsiderate declarations. But if an undertaking was entered into upon deliberation and reflection it had activity, and such promises were binding. Both Grotius and Puffendorff hold them obligatory by the Law of Nations. *Grot. Lib. 2. c. 11: De Promissis. Puffend. Lib. 3. c. 5.* They are morally good and only require ascertainment. Therefore there is no reason to extend the principle or carry it further.

There would have been no doubt upon the present case according to the Roman Law, because here is both stipulation (in the express Roman form) and writing.

Bracton (who wrote *temp. Hen.* 3) is the first of our lawyers who mentions this. His writings interweave a great many things out of the Roman Law. In his third Book, *Cap.* 1. *De Actionibus*, he distinguishes between naked and clothed contracts. He says that *Obligatio est mater actionis*, and that it may arise *ex contractu multis modis, sicut ex conventione, etc., sicut sunt pacta conventa quae nuda sunt aliquando, aliquando vestita, etc.*

Our own lawyers have adopted exactly the same idea as the Roman Law. *Plowden*, 308*b*. in the case of *Sheryngton v. Strotton* mentions it; and no one contradicted it. He lays down the distinction between contracts or agreements in words (which are more base) and contracts or agreements in writing (which are more high); and puts the distinction upon the want of deliberation in the former case and the full exercise of it in the latter. His words are the marrow of what the Roman lawyers had said. 'Words pass from men lightly': but where the agreement is made by Deed, there is more stay.... 'The delivery of the Deed is a ceremony in law, signifying fully his good will that the thing in the Deed should pass from him who made the Deed to the other. And therefore a Deed, which must necessarily be made upon great thought and deliberation, shall bind, without regard to the consideration.'

The voidness of the consideration is the same in reality in both cases, and the reason of adopting the rule was the same in both cases; though there is a difference in the ceremonies required by each law. But no inefficacy arises merely from the naked promise. Therefore, if it stood only upon the naked promise, its being in this case reduced into writing is a sufficient guard against surprise; and therefore the rule of *nudum pactum* does not apply in the present case. I cannot find that a *nudum pactum* evidenced by writing has been ever holden bad, and I should think it good; though where it is merely verbal it is bad. Yet I give no opinion upon its being good *always*, when in writing.

Many of the old cases are strange and absurd. So also are some of the modern ones, particularly that of *Hayes v. Warren*. It is now settled that, where the act is done at the request of the person promising, it will be a sufficient foundation to graft the promise upon. In another instance the strictness has been relaxed; as, for instance, burying a son, or curing a son; the considerations were both past, and yet holden good. It has been melting down into common sense of late times.

However, I do here see a consideration. If it be a departure from any right, it will be sufficient to graft a verbal promise upon. Now here White, living in Ireland, writes to the plaintiffs 'to honour his draught for £800, payable ten weeks after.' The plaintiffs agree to it on condition that they be made safe at all events. White offers good credit on a House in London, and draws; and the plaintiffs accept his draught. Then White writes to them 'to draw on Van Miérop and Hopkins'; to whom the plaintiffs write to inquire if they will honour their draught. They engage that they will. This transaction has prevented, stopped and disabled the plaintiffs from calling upon White for the performance of his engagement 'to give them credit on a good House in London for reimbursement.' So that here is a good consideration. The Law does not weigh the *quantum* of the consideration. The suspension of the plaintiffs' right to call upon White for a compliance with his engagement is sufficient to support an action, even if it be a suspension of the right for a day only or for ever so little a time.

But to consider this as a commercial case. All nations ought to have their laws conformable to each other in such cases. *Fides servanda est: simplicitas Juris Gen-*

tium prævaleat. Hodierni mores are such that the old notion about the *nudum pactum* is not strictly observed as a rule. On a question of this nature—whether by the Law of Nations such an engagement as this shall bind—the Law is to judge....

[YATES, J. and ASTON, J. concurred].

Rann v. Hughes, (1778)
4 Brown, P.C. 27: 7 T.R. 350, n.

[The plaintiffs, as executors of Mary Hughes, declared that 'divers disputes' had arisen between Mary Hughes and one John Hughes, which had been referred to arbitration; that the arbitrator had awarded that John Hughes should pay to Mary Hughes £983 0s. 2 1/2d.; that John Hughes died intestate, possessed of effects sufficient to discharge the award; that the defendant, Isabella Hughes, was the administratrix; that the defendant, 'as administratrix aforesaid, became liable' to pay the said sum to the plaintiffs, as executors of Mary Hughes; 'and being so liable, the said Isabella, in consideration thereof, afterwards, to wit, on the same day and year last aforesaid at Westminster aforesaid undertook and to the said Joseph and Arthur then and there faithfully promised to pay them the said sum of money in the said award mentioned.']*

...The cause was tried before LORD MANSFIELD at the sittings in Westminster Hall after Trinity Term, 1774, when the jury found a verdict for the plaintiffs on the first count of the declaration, that the defendant did make the promise therein alledged, and gave the plaintiffs £483 damages and 40s. costs. The jury also found that the defendant Isabella had fully administered the effects of John Hughes.

In Michaelmas Term, 1774, a motion was made by the defendant in the Court of King's Bench to set aside the verdict and for a new trial. But the Court were unanimously of opinion that the verdict was well founded, both on the facts and the law of the case; whereupon in Easter Term, 1775, judgment was entered up against the defendant generally for £547 damages and costs.

Soon afterwards the defendant brought a writ of error in the Exchequer Chamber, where the case was twice argued; and in Michaelmas Term, 1776, the judgment of the Court of King's Bench was reversed.

But to reverse this judgment of reversal, the plaintiffs brought a writ of error in Parliament.

[*Buller* and *Dunning*, for the plaintiffs in error, set themselves, *inter alia*, to meet the objection that, 'supposing this to be a promise to pay the debt out of the effects of the administratrix, yet that promise was void in law'].

...The second objection, that the promise was void, was supported on two grounds; 1st, that it did not appear by the declaration that the promise was in writing; 2dly, that there was no consideration for the promise. As to the first ground, it is an adjudged point that the Statute of Frauds, which requires such promise to be in writing, makes no alteration in the mode of pleading, and, therefore, though the promise be not expressly alledged in the declaration to have been made in writing, yet it must necessarily be presumed to have been so; for, if it had not been so proved at the trial, which in fact it was, the plaintiffs

---

* Note, C.H.S. Fifoot, *History and Sources of the Common Law* (London, 1949), 430. Minor editing by C.H.S. Fifoot.

could not have obtained a verdict, and, after a verdict, everything is presumed which was necessary to be proved on the trial.

And as to the second ground, it was submitted that, in the case of a promise in writing, which this must be taken to be, it is not necessary to alledge any consideration in the declaration; but, if it were necessary, there was a sufficient consideration for the promise appearing upon this declaration. In reason, there is little or no difference between a contract which is deliberately reduced into writing and signed by the parties without seal, and a contract under the same circumstances, to which a party at the time of signing it puts a seal or his finger on cold wax. In the case of a deed, i.e., an instrument under seal, it must be admitted that no consideration is necessary; and in the year 1765 it was solemnly adjudged in the Court of King's Bench that no consideration was necessary when the promise was reduced into writing. That opinion has since been recognized in the same Court and several judgments founded upon it; all which judgments must be subverted and what was there conceived to be settled law totally overturned, if the plaintiffs in this cause were not entitled to recover. But, further, if a consideration were necessary, a sufficient one for the promise appeared upon the declaration in this case. The defendant was the administratrix of John Hughes, she had effects of his in her hands, she was liable to be called upon by the plaintiffs in an action to shew to what amount she had assets and how she had applied them; and under these circumstances she promised to pay the demand which the plaintiffs had against her....

After argument the following question was proposed to the Judges by the Lord Chancellor: 'Whether sufficient matter appeared upon the declaration to warrant after verdict the judgment against the defendant in error in her personal capacity'; upon which the Lord Chief Baron SKYNNER delivered the opinion of the Judges to this effect.—

It is undoubtedly true that every man is by the law of nature bound to fulfil his engagements. It is equally true that the law of this country supplies no means nor affords any remedy to compel the performance of an agreement made without sufficient consideration. Such agreement is *nudum pactum ex quo non oritur actio*; and whatsoever may be the sense of this maxim in the civil law, it is in the last-mentioned sense only that it is to be understood in our law. The declaration states that the defendant, being indebted as administratrix, promised to pay when requested, and the judgment is against the defendant generally. The being indebted is of itself a sufficient consideration to ground a promise, but the promise must be co-extensive with the consideration unless some particular consideration of fact can be found here to warrant the extension of it against the defendant in her own capacity. If a person, indebted in one right, in consideration of forbearance for a particular time promise to pay in another right, this convenience will be a sufficient consideration to warrant an action against him or her in the latter right. But here no sufficient consideration occurs to support this demand against her in her personal capacity; for she derives no advantage or convenience from the promise here made. For if I promise generally to pay upon request what I was liable to pay upon request in another right, I derive no advantage or convenience from this promise, and therefore there is not sufficient consideration for it.

But it is said that, if this promise is in writing, that takes away the necessity of a consideration and obviates the objection of *nudum pactum*, for that cannot be where the promise is put into writing, and that, if it were necessary to support the promise that it should be in writing, it will after verdict be presumed that it was in writing; and this last is certainly true. But, that there cannot be *nudum pactum* in writing, whatever may be the rule of the civil law, there is certainly none such in the law of England. His Lordship observed upon the doctrine of *nudum pactum* delivered by Mr. Justice WILMOT in the case of *Pillans v. Van Miérop,* that he contradicted himself and was also contradicted by Vinnius in his Comment on Justinian.

All contracts are by the laws of England distinguished into agreements by specialty and agreements by parol; nor is there any such third class as some of the counsel have endeavored to maintain as contracts in writing. If they be merely written and not specialties they are parol, and a consideration must be proved. But it is said that the Statute of Frauds has taken away the necessity of any consideration in this case. The Statute of Frauds was made for the relief of personal representatives and others, and did not intend to charge them further than by common law they were chargeable. His Lordship here read those sections of that Statute which relate to the present subject. He observed that the words were merely negative and that executors and administrators should not be liable out of their own estates, unless the agreement upon which the action was brought or some memorandum thereof was in writing and signed by the party. But this does not prove that the agreement was still not liable to be tried and judged of as all other agreements merely in writing are by the common law, and does not prove the converse of the proposition, that when in writing the party must be at all events liable.

He here observed upon the case of *Pillans v. Van Miérop* and the case *of Losh v. Williamson,* Mich. 16 Geo. 3 in B.R.; and, so far as these cases went on the doctrine of *nudum pactum,* he seemed to intimate that they were erroneous. He said that all his brothers concurred with him that in this case there was not a sufficient consideration to support this demand as a personal demand against the defendant, and that its being now supposed to have been in writing makes no difference. The consequence of which is that the question put to us must be answered in the negative.

And the judgment in the Exchequer Chamber was affirmed.

D.R. Coquillette, "Legal Ideology and Incorporation IV: The Nature of Civilian Influence on Modern Anglo-American Commercial Law," 67 *Boston Univ. Law Review* (1987) 877, 948–962. [Notes omitted.] © 1987 by Daniel R. Coquillette.

2. William Murray, Lord Mansfield

William Murray, Lord Mansfield (1705–1793), was Chief Justice of the King's Bench from 1756 until 1788. Holt was Chief Justice from 1689 to 1710. Their combined tenures represent over half a century in the most influential legal position in England. They both esteemed that office over any other available, and to keep it both declined invitations to become Lord Chancellor, as well as other powerful positions. They shared a faith in judge-made law, using the reported judicial case as a vehicle for reform, and, despite some evidence of corruption on Mansfield's part, their dedication to the rule of law was such that both faced either impeachment or angry mobs in its name. Even their jurisprudential achievements were similar; both made major contributions to the laws of personal freedom, the law of business and

Illustration 12-17   William Murray, Lord Mansfield (1705–1793). This early engraving shows Mansfield as a young lawyer of 28, just called to the bar two years before, and is after an even earlier portrait, possibly painted for his girlfriend. See Edmund Heward, *Lord Mansfield* (London, 1979), 14. By Courtesy of the National Portrait Gallery, London.

trade, and to the critical legal status of English law in the colonies. Mansfield's reported cases show, as one would expect, an intimate knowledge of Holt's decisions.

In spite of their similarities, their juristic styles were in sharp contrast. Holt was a focused problem solver, and Mansfield, a bold, free-ranging theorist. On the issue of incorporation of mercantile practice and foreign legal ideas, this difference in style became one of substance.

First, Mansfield was a Scot with a classical English education. While some have doubted Holt's familiarity with Roman law and foreign legal systems, Mansfield's knowledge is indisputable. A younger son of a poor, Jacobite Scottish peer, Mansfield studied, through the charity of friends, at Christ Church, Oxford. There he attended lectures on Justinian's *Digest* and translated Cicero into English and back into Latin. Surviving scraps of his student exercises show that Mansfield was, even as a young man, a genuine classicist. This is all quite apart from his portentous defeat of the young William Pitt for the Latin poetry prize on the death of George I, which earned him a lifelong enemy. Years later, the influence of this curriculum emerged in Mansfield's famous outlines of recommended study, prepared for the heir to the Duke of Portland. These displayed a profound and rich understanding of both classical and humanist legal studies. Mansfield's interests, however, were not limited to Roman law. His outlines and personal studies included many modern civilians, such as Grotius, Pufendorf, Vinius [sic], and Burlamaqui, and he was familiar with France's attempt to rationalize commercial custom by the *Ordonnance de la Marine* in 1681.

Mansfield's Scottish connections, and the patronage of Talbot and Yorke, secured him a Scottish appeals practice before the House of Lords. This further developed his learning. His early Scottish appellate cases "enabled him to display his culture and gratify the court by judicious selections from the law of nations, of Scotland and of Moses." His Scottish origins may have been a major social and professional handicap in some respects, but those origins led him to the unusual opportunities of this early law practice. Scottish appeals practice included explaining issues of Scottish law, with all of its civilian underpinnings, to English jurists. It practically forced Mansfield to be a comparativist, and led to professional success. Later, this success would attract bitter political attacks, including accusations that Mansfield was a secret Jacobite, a Catholic, and an absolutist. He was also charged "with the black offense of corrupting the ancient simplicity of the common law with principles drawn from the corpus juris." Ironically, these vicious attacks were identical to the libels suffered by the earlier English civilians.

Did Mansfield's civilian learning affect his jurisprudence? Again, we turn to our chosen "litmus test," commercial law and particularly bills of exchange. Shientag attempted to summarize all of Mansfield's contribution to the law of negotiable instruments in just one rather remarkable sentence!

> In Negotiable Instruments, he [Mansfield] harmonized the rules relating to the foreign bill of exchange, the inland bill of exchange, and the promissory note; he insisted on the rights of the innocent holder for value; he reiterated the principle that negotiable instruments were currency; he laid down the rule that the holder of a bearer note could maintain an independent action; he upheld the negotiability of bearer notes by delivery; he ruled that an acceptor who accepted a forged bill and paid it to a *bona fide* holder, could not recover the payment from such holder; he emphasized the necessity for certainty in determining what was a reasonable time for presenting a bill or giving notice of dishonor and the advisability of having the court determine that question, where possible, and he invoked the doctrine of equitable estoppel, where one placed in the hands of a broker a bill of lading so endorsed that the broker could deceive an innocent third party into believing that the broker owned the goods.

For the most part, Shientag accurately describes Mansfield's achievements, but he also claims too little and too much in terms of Mansfield's contributions to the law merchant. And he hides a major controversy. Let us start with the controversy.

Much of our view of Mansfield derives from Mr. Justice Buller's great tribute in *Lickbarrow v. Mason*, one year before Mansfield's retirement:

> Thus the matter stood till within these thirty years; since that time the commercial law of this country has taken a very different turn from what it did before....Before that period we find that in Courts of Law all the evidence in mercantile cases was thrown together; they were left generally to a jury, and they produced no established principle. From that time we all know that great study has been made to find some certain general principles, which shall be [made] known to all mankind, not only to rule the particular case then under consideration, but to serve as a guide for the future. Most of us have heard these principles stated, reasoned upon, enlarged, and explained, till we have been lost in admiration at the strength and stretch of the human understanding. And I should be very sorry to find myself under a necessity of differing from any case on this subject which has been decided by Lord Mansfield, who may be truly said to be the founder of the commercial law of this country.

Buller's opinion has been reinforced by Fifoot, Mansfield's most extensive legal biographer, who considered Mansfield "the founder of commercial law," and by Beutel, who described Mansfield as "the founder of modern English Commercial law."

Our examination of Holt has demonstrated that these accolades of Mansfield claim too much. Buller was simply wrong that Holt left everything to juries and produced "no established principles." While the notice of mercantile custom was limited, it was not always put to juries as a question of fact, as with a local custom. Holt, in fact, settled a great deal of law.

Not surprisingly, therefore, a rival group has emerged, consisting of such diverse bedfellows as Baker and Lord Campbell, who have challenged some of the claims made for Mansfield as a creative genius. Campbell insisted that Mansfield "cannot be considered a man of original genius. With great good sense, he adapted, he improved—but he never invented." Holden, a moderate member of this faction, correctly observed that Holt "commenced to take judicial notice of some of the more important mercantile customs," but that "Mansfield's work was certainly not confined to the re-definition of existing principles."

Both of these warring groups focus too much on doctrine and not enough on the judicial process. Mansfield certainly did not invent the modern law of negotiable instruments. As we have seen, it was largely in place at Holt's death. Yet Mansfield was the father of the modern judicial attitude toward commercial law, and in this he owed a great deal to civilian jurisprudence—a debt he candidly acknowledged.

Because Mansfield was not a treatise writer, law teacher, or publisher of legal tracts, we must, as we did with Holt, accept the fragmented, ad hoc evidence of reported cases. But we have an advantage here: the quality and modern format of Sir James Burrow's *Reports*, in which many of Mansfield's opinions appear. Burrow's *Reports* have a high reputation and have even been described, rather floridly, as "works of art." Their careful division of the case into facts stated, argument of counsel, and judical opinion, gave Mansfield one more advantage over Holt: we know what he really meant to decide. Rather ungenerously, Mansfield was quoted as saying that "Sir James Burrow's Reports were not always accurate."

But even Burrow's *Reports* cannot remedy the problem of deciding principles ad hoc, in isolated cases. Thus, to understand the evolution of Mansfield's judicial philosophy, we will have to look at two lines of case development. Not only will we look at cases relating to a specific topic in chronological order, focusing again on bills of exchange and negotiable instruments, but we will examine some doctrinally unrelated cases that nevertheless illustrate relevant points about Mansfield's use of the judicial process. The latter will not enlighten us much about commercial law doctrine, but will illustrate how civilian methodology became a part of Mansfield's judicial style. This had a great impact on his commercial cases, and on many of his decisions unrelated to commercial law.

For example, Mansfield demonstrated his remarkable knowledge of Roman law in *Windham v. Chetwynd*, just one year after his appointment to the bench. The case had nothing to do with law merchant, but it did demonstrate the determination of the new judge to appeal to universal and comparative standards in defending a decision, as well as to practical principles of utility and fairness. A will was being disputed. A creditor had been one of the three witnesses to the will. At issue was the meaning of the requirement, under the Statute of Frauds, of "three credible witnesses." Mansfield traced the Roman law of testament from the *Twelve Tables* to Justinian's *Digest*, demonstrating a genuine familiarity with Roman law and an extraordinary willingness to apply Roman standards to interpret an English statute. Finding no historical bases for disqualifying a creditor from being a subscribing witness, Mansfield concluded that to presume witnesses were not credible because they had an "interest at the time of subscription" due to a charge "to pay debts" would be "against Justice and Truth." He then turned to a practical consideration, observing that "[t]he Persons attendant upon a dying Testator...are generally in *some* Degree *Creditors*...Servants, Parson, Attorney, Apothecary, etc; And the disallowing such Persons to be Witnesses can not answer *Ends of public Utility*." Roman law and appeal to public utility; the message was plain: Mansfield intended to give opinions that not only established rules, but persuaded with their dual appeal to universal reason and practical fairness.

Mansfield decided his first important negotiable instrument case one year later, in *Miller v. Race*. There, he reasserted the rights of the innocent holder for value. A mail coach had been robbed. The thief had taken a bank note, which ended up in the hands of the plaintiff "for a full and valuable consideration, and in the usual course...of his business." Of course, the owner of the note had stopped payment. The bearer, citing Holt, argued that the owner of a bank bill would have trover against a stranger who found it, except when the finder transferred it for a valuable consideration, which "by reason of the *Course of Trade* creates a Property in the...Bearer." The owner, however, argued that the note "remains in the Man's Hands, and is not come into the Course of Trade," because the theft could not be regarded as wilfully introducing the note into the "Course of Trade." Rejecting this argument, Mansfield observed that "Ld., Ch. J. *Holt* could never say That an Action [in trover] would lie against the Person who, *for a valuable Consideration*, had received a *Bank-Note* which had been stolen or lost, and *bona fide paid to him*." He noted that Holt had decided otherwise just two years before the case cited by the bearer. Bank notes, concluded Mansfield, "are not like Lottery-Tickets, but *Money*...paid and received as Cash: And it is necessary, for the Purpose of Commerce, that their *Currency* should be *established* and *secured*." Mansfield didn't invent the notion of negotiable bank notes, but Mansfield restated the principle of negotiability in modern terms that could not be misinterpreted.

That same year, in *Heylyn v. Adamson*, Mansfield did more than merely restate Holt. In that case, Mansfield reexamined the legal differences between the three major classes of mercantile instruments: foreign bills of exchange, inland bills of exchange, and promissory notes. In so doing, he reaffirmed the different treatment of foreign bills of exchange and promissory notes, but held that foreign and inland bills should be treated identically, characterizing as erroneous a number of decisions allegedly to the contrary "quoted" to "My Ld. Ch. J. *Holt.*" According to Mansfield, the difference between foreign bills and promissory notes was required by practical considerations. Whereas the holder of a promissory note was required to make a demand on the original drawer before suing an endorser, the same requirement would be impracticable under a foreign bill of exchange, since the drawer often lived abroad, "perhaps in the Indies." Applying these same practical considerations, Mansfield saw no reason to distinguish between foreign and inland bills of exchange, observing that "except as to Degree of Inconvenience; All the Arguments from Law and the Nature of a Transaction, are exactly the same in both cases." Although Mansfield drew heavily from an earlier foreign bill case of 1713, it was the exposition in *Heylyn* that settled the law.

In the next three years, Mansfield gave three of his most important opinions: *Luke v. Lyde*, *Moses v. Macferlan*, and *Edie v. East India Company*. *Luke* and *Edie* were important commercial cases. *Moses*, while a case on quasi-contract and not a commercial case, clearly illustrates Mansfield's mode of juristic analysis. Taken together, they illustrate Mansfield's still young judicial philosophy.

Luke v. Lyde, the now famous story of privateering, salvage, and freight, is a study in Mansfield's attention to the *ius gentium*. After hearing extensive argument citing Malynes and Molloy, the great popularizers of the law merchant, Mansfield canvassed the *Rhodian Laws*, the *Consolato de mare*, the *Laws of Oleron*, the *Laws of Wisby*, and the "Ordinance of Lewis the fourteenth"—all to determine ratable freight on a cargo of Newfoundland fish. Mansfield explained his comprehensive survey in one sentence: "the Maritime Law is not the Law of a particular Country, but the general Law of Nations: *'Non erit alia Lex Romae, alia Athenis; alia nunc, alia posthac; sed et apud omnes gentes et omni tempore, una eademque Lex obtinebit.'*" Such universal standards were needed "[n]ot only for the greater Satisfaction of the Parties in the particular Cause, but to prevent other Disputes, by making the rules of the Law and the Ground upon which they are established *certain* and *notorious.*" It could have been Zouche, Gentilis, or Ridley speaking, but it was Mansfield.

If *Luke v. Lyde* established Mansfield's attention to the *ius gentium*, *Moses v. Macferlan* established his interest in moral obligation, unjust enrichment, and actions "*ex aequo et bono.*" The issue was whether the plaintiff could recover for unjust enrichment directly through an action upon the case for money had and received, instead of having to bring "a special action upon the contract." Holding that the special action was not required, Mansfield stated:

> One great benefit, which arises to suitors from the nature of *this* action, is, that the *Plaintiff needs not state the Special Circumstances* from which he concludes "that, *ex aequo & bono*, the Money received by the Defendant, ought to be deemed as belonging to him:" he may *declare*

generally, "that the Money was received to his Use;" and make out his Case, at the Trial.....

If one Man takes another's Money to do a Thing, and refuses to do it; it is a Fraud: And it is at the *Election* of the party injured, either to affirm the Agreement, by bringing an Action for the Non-performance of it; or to disaffirm the Agreement *ab initio*, by reason of the Fraud, and bring an Action for Money had and received to his Use.

The Damages recovered in that Case, shew the *Liberality* with which this kind of Action is considered: for though the Defendant received From the Plaintiff £262 10s. yet the *Difference Money Only*, £175 *was retained by him against* Conscience: And *therefore* the plaintiff, *ex aequo et bono*, ought to recover *no more*; agreeable to the rule of the Roman law—"*Quod condictio indebiti non datur ultra, quam locupletior factus est, qui accepit.*"

....

This kind of equitable Action, to recover back Money which ought not in justice to be kept, is *very beneficial*, and therefore *much encouraged*. It lies only for Money which, ex aequo et bono, the Defendant *ought* to refund.

In one Word, The Gist of this kind of Action is, that the Defendant, upon the Circumstances of the Case, is *obliged by the Ties of natural Justice and Equity to refund* the Money.

If *Luke v. Lyde* reads as if it were decided by Godolphin in the Admiralty, *Moses v. Macferlan* sounds like a case in the Chancery decided by an extraordinary chancellor. Indeed, it sounds as if it were decided by Francis Bacon.

One year after deciding *Moses v. Macferlan*, Mansfield encountered directly the theoretical problems of incorporation in *Edie v. East India Company*. The issue was whether a bill of exchange endorsed by a payee to "pay A," but which did not include an "or order" clause, could be transferred by A. Mansfield allowed evidence of mercantile usage to be put to the jury, who found that the form of the endorsement precluded transfer. On motion for a new trial, Mansfield learned of two prior cases to the contrary. In setting aside the verdict, Mansfield explained: "Since the trial I have looked into the cases....I ought not to have admitted any evidence of the particular usage of merchants in such a case. Of this, I say I am now satisfied; for the law is already settled."

This, of course, represented the conceptual "end of the line" for growth in the commercial law through evidence of mercantile usage. Mansfield's desire to do practical justice in accordance with commercial utility conflicted, not with any slavish adherence to legal precedent, but with another demand of commercial utility—certainty, which Mansfield later recognized to be the "great object" in "all mercantile transactions." It was an inherently irreconcilable conflict: the practical cost of incorporation of mercantile practice into rigid law as opposed to leaving it as a factual issue. As Mansfield would later say in *Buller v. Harrison*: "I desire nothing so much as that all questions of mercantile law be fully settled and ascertained; and it is of much more consequence that they should be so, than which way the decision is." Later in *Hankey v. Jones*, Mansfield confirmed his preferences:

I desired a case to be made for the opinion of the Court, for the sake of that, which perhaps is more important than doing right: to bring all questions upon mercantile transactions to a certainty. General verdicts do not answer the purpose: but when a case is made, the profession know the result, the merchants know the result....

In *Grant v. Vaughan*, decided three years after *Edie v. East India Company*, Mansfield again undertook to clarify the law of Holt. The case involved an inland bill of exchange payable to the "Ship Fortune or Bearer." It had been lost by the defendant and passed by an unknown finder to a bona fide plaintiff for good consideration (five pounds worth of tea). The defendant had stopped payment. The issue was whether a bearer could possess by delivery without endorsement. The defendant argued that Holt's opinion in *Nicholson v. Sedgwick* controlled, but Mansfield was not impressed, believing that case to be *"upon general Principles...not agreeable to Law and Justice."* Mansfield had originally put to the jury the question whether "such Draughts as this...were, in the course of Trade, Dealing and Business, *actually* Paid away and negotiated, or *In Fact* and *Practice* negotiable." The jury, a "special jury of merchants," came in for the defendant. Mansfield put this verdict aside, explaining that "I *ought not* to have left the *latter* Point to them: For it is a Question of *Law*, 'whether a Bill of Note be *negotiable*, or not.'" The bill, he observed, came *"bona fide* and in the *Course of Trade*, into the Hands of the present Plaintiff, who paid a *full and fair Consideration for it."* Mansfield concluded that both parties were innocent and "by Law" the loss falls on the defendant, rather than on a bona fide purchaser for good consideration.

The holding in *Grant v. Vaughan*, which remains good law in many jurisdictions, was later reinforced in *Peacock v. Rhodes*. There, an inland bill with a blank endorsement had been stolen and later negotiated. The innocent endorsee recovered against the drawer. Striving to develop a uniform holding with respect to the negotiability of bearer bills, Mansfield permitted only the issue of the endorsee's innocence to go to the jury:

> I see no difference between a note indorsed blank, and one payable to bearer. They both go by delivery, and possession proves property in both cases. The question of mala fides was for the consideration of the jury. The circumstances, that the buyer and also the drawers were strangers to the plaintiff, and that he took the bill for goods on which he had a profit, were grounds for suspicion, very fit for their consideration. But they have considered them, and have found it was received in the course of trade, and, therefore, the case is clear, and within the principle of all those Mr. Wood has cited, from that of *Miller v. Race*, downwards, to that determined by me at Nisi Prius.

The decision in *Grant v. Vaughan* reveals that Mansfield was undeterred by either adverse prior judicial precedent or adverse factual determination by a special jury of merchants. His desire to achieve uniformity in like cases was equally obvious in *Peacock v. Rhodes*. Both cases reflect deliberate, conscious judicial lawmaking, as systematic and principled as the case law format permitted.

The stage was now set for Mansfield's ultimate mercantile case, *Pillans v. Van Miérop*. The facts are familiar to generations of law students. Plaintiffs, Dutch merchants, sought a confirmed credit on a London banking "house of rank" as a condition for accepting a bill of exchange drawn on them by one White. White named the defendants, London merchants, and the plaintiffs honored the bill. At this point there had been no contract between the plaintiffs and defendants, but later the defendants agreed in writing to accept a bill for the same amount to be drawn on them in "a month's time" by plaintiffs on White's credit. White failed, and the defendants gave notice to the plaintiffs not to draw upon them. The defendants obtained a verdict at the trial, and on a motion for new trial, defendant's counsel argued that his client's undertaking was either a "naked promise" unsupported by any consideration, or that all the consideration was past, and this would not support an assumpsit.

Here was the opportunity to sweep the involved and complex doctrine of consideration away from commercial transactions. Mansfield seized it:

> This is a Matter of great Consequence to Trade and Commerce in every Light.
>
> If there was any kind of Fraud in this Transaction, the Collusion and *mala Fides* would have *vacated* the Contract. But from these Letters, it seems to Me clear that there was *none*.
>
> . . . .
>
> If there be *no* Fraud, it is a mere Question of Law. The Law of *Merchants* and the Law of the *Land* is the *same*: A Witness cannot be admitted, to prove the Law of Merchants. We must consider it as a Point of *Law*. A *nudum Pactum* does not exist, in the Usage and Law of Merchants.
>
> I take it that the ancient Notion about the Want of Consideration was for the Sake of *Evidence* only: For when it is reduced into *Writing*, as in Covenants, Specialties, Bonds, etc., there was no Objection to the Want of Consideration. And the Statute of Frauds proceded upon the same Principle.
>
> In *Commercial* Cases among Merchants, the Want of consideration is *not* an Objection.
>
> . . . .
>
> This is an Engagement 'to accept the Bill, ['] if there was a Necessity to 'accept it; and to pay it, when due:' And they [defendants] *could not afterwards retract*. It would be very destructive to Trade and to Trust in Commercial Dealing, if They could. There was Nothing of *nudum Pactum* mentioned to the Jury; nor was it, I dare say, at all in *their* Idea or Contemplation.

Only after wading through hundreds of earlier mercantile cases can one really appreciate the boldness of this decision. The radical step was not the statement that "The law of Merchants and the law of the Land is the same." Holt had recognized that, as did many before him. Nor was it the unqualified statement that "a witness cannot be admitted to prove the Law of Merchants." There were roots of that as well in the earlier notion of general mercantile usage. The truly courageous step was Mansfield's flat abolition of the doctrine of consideration in mercantile dealings, in the face of an adverse jury verdict and much precedent to the contrary, all in the name of "trade and . . . trust in commercial dealing." It was a bold, utilitarian principle.

Experts have argued endlessly about the *ratio decidendi* of Pillans *v.* Van Miérop. There were four judges. While all four unanimously set aside the verdict and ordered a new trial, the reasons given by the other three were far less clear. It has been said that the holding establishes the principle that the bill of exchange was a "specialty." As Judge Yates explained in his opinion, "bills of exchange are considered, and are declared upon as special contracts; though legally, they are only simple contracts: the declaration sets forth the bill and acceptance specifically: and that thereby the defendants, by the custom of merchants, become liable to pay it."

But there was no such accepted bill, drawn without consideration, in the case, but just "a gratuitous promise to accept" a future bill. In any event, *Rann v. Hughes* and the House of Lords would put an end to such a heresy in thirteen years. Mansfield's opinion there contained the seeds of another proposition, simpler and equally heretical. Unless the practicalities of evidence required otherwise, moral obligation should be equated with consideration. As Mansfield stated approximately fifteen years later in *Hawkes v. Saunders*:

> Where a man is under a legal or equitable obligation to pay, the law implies a promise, though none was ever actually made. *A Fortiori*, a legal or equitable duty is a sufficient consideration for an actual promise. Where a man is under a moral obligation, which no court of law or equity can enforce, and promises, the honesty and rectitude of the thing is a consideration."

This thesis would be continued in the context of bankruptcy.

Mansfield's determination to establish a certain and principled law of negotiable instruments eventually brought him into a series of conflicts with Guildhall juries. For example, in *Medcalf v. Hall*, the issue was whether the plaintiff had presented a bill for payment within a "reasonable time" when, having received a draft at one o'clock in the afternoon, he had failed to get it accepted at the appropriate address one-half mile distant by five o'clock that evening. The jury held that the plaintiff had acted reasonably, but Mansfield ordered a new trial. A second and third jury held for the plaintiff, and each time Mansfield brushed the verdict aside, recoiling at "the great inconvenience which it would occasion in the circulation of paper." Finally, the plaintiff gave up.

In *Appleton v. Sweetapple*, which involved the similar question of what constituted reasonable notice of dishonor before suing an endorser, Mansfield again ordered a new trial, prompting Justice Buller to observe:

> In a question of law, however unpleasant it may be to us, we must not yield to the decision of a jury. I do not doubt if a special jury in London will, if desired, find a special verdict. The usage is to be considered, but such usage must be reasonable, and it is for the Court to say whether it is good or bad.

Later, in *Tindal v. Brown*, Mansfield came just short of holding that "reasonable notice" was a question of law; although he ultimately retreated to the safer yet equally bold proposition that it was "partly a question of fact and partly a question of law." Was this Mansfield's last effort at establishing commercial certainty while retaining some input for usage as a matter of fact? If so, he was clearly attempting to keep the question of usage within the control of the court. Eventually, frustrated with the commercial jury and wanting "bright line" uniformity in commercial dealings, Mansfield moved closer in his last years on the bench to the ultimate modern solution: a codified commercial law containing carefully restricted "elastic" clauses for the trier of fact.

It would be too much to say that Mansfield "invented" English commercial law, but Joseph Story was correct in saying that Mansfield "was one of those great men raised up by Providence, at a fortunate moment he became what he intended, the jurist of the Commercial world." As Shientag observed, Mansfield "created a body of systematic legal principles, in conformity with the realities of business needs.... His decisions in this field amounted to judicial legislation of the first order."

Mansfield was a jurist in the finest sense. While he may not have invented the law of negotiable instruments or other commercial doctrines, his decisions gave English commercial law a far more systematic and rational structure. Mansfield also sought to make these principles persuasive and self-evident by demonstrating their utility, and he strove for consistency, certainty, and universality. Here Mansfield drew deeply on the comparativist and rationalist tradition of the English and continental civilian jurists. His decisions contain hundreds of citations to their treatises and sources. Like Bacon, Selden, and Hale, the character of Mansfield's juristic thought testified to this influence. Yet, unlike Bacon, Selden, and Hale, Mansfield's sole juristic vehicle was the reported decision—the case law tool of today's judiciary.

As young men, both Edmund Burke and Jeremy Bentham sat at the back of Mansfield's courtroom. It was, in Bentham's words, like visiting "the chief seat of the living idol." Both the inventor of conservative modern constitutional theory and the pioneer of the modern codification movement learned from Mansfield what modern adjudication could mean. Those that influenced Mansfield, influenced the entire future of the Anglo-American law.

XIII

THE NINETEENTH CENTURY
LEGAL INSTRUMENTALISM,
CODIFICATION AND UTILITARIANISM

As James Willard Hurst observed, the "nineteenth century" in the United States stretched from the "constitution-making years" (1776–1800) right up until Theodore Roosevelt's departure from the White House in 1908.[1] It was a period of profound economic, social and political change, pivoting around a brutal Civil War whose effects are still being felt today. The industrial revolution changed the life of the average person profoundly.

> "Capital put into manufacturing doubled every decade up to 1900 and thereafter increased more slowly. Net national product grew about three times from 1870 to 1900, while population less than doubled, so that national income per capita increased. The percentage of the labor force engaged in nonagricultural work rose from 28 per cent in 1820 to 36 per cent in 1850, to 47 per cent in 1870, to 62 per cent in 1900. Factories became larger, but in the last quarter of the century the larger firms grew at the faster rate. By 1904 manufacturing companies producing over $1 million of value added in manufacturing were less than one per cent of all such concerns, but accounted for about 30 per cent of the total value added by manufacturing. From 1890 to 1904 some 237 corporate consolidations occurred, each involving business of regional or national extent, each capitalized for more than $1 million, representing almost every important field of manufacture. Finance likewise changed character. From 1870 to 1900 around 6 to 7 per cent of a steadily rising national income went into new investment apart from replacement of old facilities. In the second quarter of the century railroad securities dislodged government and bank stocks from their market predominance. In 1867 only 15 industrial shares were traded on the New York Stock Exchange, but by 1896 that Exchange handled a total of 57 million shares, and by 1901, 266 million."[2]

Equally important, the American population simply exploded. While this was due partly to immigration, the leading cause was the high birthrate.

> The most spectacular rate of increase was before the Civil War; population increased eleven-fold (from 2,781,000 to 31,443,321) from 1780

---

1. James Willard Hurst, *Law and the Conditions of Freedom in Nineteenth Century United States* (Madison, 1956), 71.
2. *Id.*, 71–72.

Illustration 13-1   Dred Scott (1797–1858). The plaintiff in *Dred Scott v. Sandford*, 60 U.S. (19 Howard) 393 (1857). This picture, from the collection of the New York Historical Society, is by an unknown artist. It is based on a daguerreotype made in St. Louis in 1857 (negative 37000). [Collection of the New-York Historical Society.]

to 1869 and then grew less than two and a half times (to 75,994,575) from 1860 to 1900. But throughout the century both relative and absolute increases were such as to reshape the social environment. The main cause of our population increase was a high native birth rate. Immigration was a lesser factor; in 1900 the foreign-born were only about one-seventh of our people. However, the migration of 20 millions of people—12 million of them from 1870 to 1900 alone—could not but bring novel issues of social order. More and more people lived in urban areas; but what created the most unusual problems was the rapid growth of metropolitan areas. In 1880 we had 19 cities of 100,000 people or more; in 1900 we had 36; from 1880 to 1900 New York grew from about two to three and a half million, and Chicago from 500,000 to a million and a half; a junior metropolis might develop like Milwaukee, from 71,000 in 1870 to 285,000 in 1900.[3]

Coupled with all of this was a 600 percent growth in railroads, from 1865 to 1900, a massive switch from water power to steam engines, and the dramatic increase in the use of electricity.[4] For everyone—not just the rich and powerful, but for everyone—the world had changed.

Similar changes were certainly occurring in England. The first official population census was in 1801, and it registered 8.3 million. By 1831 the population had increased to 13.1 million, and by 1851 to 16.92 million, with equally dramatic upward changes in Scotland and Wales. Only Ireland saw fluctuation, swinging from 5.22 million in 1801, to 7.77 million in 1831, and, due to the terrible potato blight of 1845, 1846 and 1848, down again to 6.51 million in 1851.[5] The effect of industrialization was, if anything, more profound, with enormous increases in manufacturing, iron and coal output, and steam technology.[6] The result, as in America, was a vast shift of the population from traditional agrarian villages to the great industrial centers: Birmingham, Liverpool, Manchester, Nottingham, Derby, and London. Also, as in America, the development of canals and, then, the steam railway linked the population as never before.

The French Revolution had already terrorized the rural Whig squirearchy of England with the political consequences of social change. The long Whig epoch of the eighteenth century was not built on complacency, and the end of the postwar boom from the Napoleonic victories brought signs of severe danger from the new industrial towns, where widespread unemployment and a steep drop in wages brought new threats to the social order.[7] On August 16, 1819, soldiers, in an over-reaction to a large peaceful demonstration of workers at St. Peter's Fields in Manchester, killed eleven people. After this disaster, the so-called "Peterloo" massacre, the Parliament was ready to consider new initiatives for enlarged franchise and reform legislation.[8] When the Whig Reform Bill of 1830 was vetoed by the House of Lords, riots broke out in Nottingham, Bristol, and Wales. In 1832, the House of Lords backed off, reversing its decision by nine votes.[9] It was in London, in 1848, that Marx and Engels surveyed the new social order and wrote the *Communist Manifesto*, but long before the English establishment was alert to the need for change. The theoretical leader of the English reform movement was

---

3. *Id.*, 72.
4. *Id.*, 72.
5. Christopher Harvie, "Revolution and the Rule of Law (1789–1851)," *The Oxford History of Britain* (K.O. Morgan, ed., 1988), 477. Over two million emigrated from Ireland between 1845 and 1855. *Id.*, 506. The British Army was 42% Irish in 1830. *Id.*, 512.
6. *Id.*, 470–481.
7. *Id.*, 492–493.
8. *Id.*, 493.
9. *Id.*, 495.

to be a most unlikely figure—a strange, iconoclastic and eccentric individual who, nevertheless, struck exactly the right balance between the need for radical change and the fear of revolution. The catch words of the reform, "codification" and "utilitarianism," were all his invention. His name was Jeremy Bentham.

A. "LEGAL INSTRUMENTALISM"

In both England and America, the need for legal change to accommodate new economic and political realities led to a new view of the "common law." *Blackstone's Commentaries* (1765–70) still adhered to the spirit of Edward Coke. For Blackstone the common law was still the manifestation of the timeless folk wisdom of the land. While all knew it had to be restated and refined by judicial oracles, it was certainly not a tool of social engineering—and certainly not susceptible to a "testing" of its social utility.

But Jeremy Bentham had seen another face of the common law, Lord Mansfield. Along with other notables, including Edmund Burke, Bentham frequently sat at the back of Mansfield's courtroom. He even started a poem to Mansfield:

> Hail noble Mansfield! Chief among the just, The bad man's terror, and the good man's trust.[10]

In the end, however, Mansfield's judicial activism taught Bentham an unexpected lesson, that judge-made law was inherently founded on a myth of consent and interpretation. The reality was that judges like Mansfield made the law afresh, and, in Bentham's view, that was the true function of a legislative sovereign, not a judge. Not only was the legislative process more open to genuine political review and social consensus, it was also more likely to use scientifically valid criteria to test the usefulness of legal change.[11] The prospective nature of legislation was also inherently more fair and effective.

While Mansfield was Bentham's "idol," Bentham had a very different view of Blackstone. In 1776 Bentham published, anonymously, *A Fragment on Government, Being An Examination of…the introduction to Sir William Blackstone's Commentaries, with a Preface in which is given a Critique on the Work at Large.*[12] In Bentham's view, Mansfield at least changed the law with an open mind and a bold spirit directed to the specific usefulness of the law in its economic and social application. But Blackstone implied that this was both improper and contrary to the spirit of the common law. Blackstone's assertion that the common law contained a core of natural law—immutable and self evident—

---

10. W.S. Holdsworth, *Some Makers of English Law* (Cambridge, 1966), 169.

11. For useful basic introductions to Bentham's utilitarian philosophy, see *id.*, 246–256; and Bertrand Russell, *History of Western Philosophy* (London, 1946) 740–743. For more subtle analysis, see David Lyons, *In the Interest of the Governed* (Oxford, 1973), 82–137; Gerald J. Postema, *Bentham and the Common Law Tradition* (Oxford, 1986); and Jeremy Bentham, *Of Laws in General* (ed. H.L.A. Hart, London, 1970). Bentham's close friend, John Austin (1790–1859), established the positivist school of English jurisprudence in his posthumous masterpiece, *Jurisprudence* (London, 1861). See W.S. Holdsworth, *Some Makers of English Law, supra,* 256–264.

12. See *Materials, infra,* p. 523.

particularly infuriated Bentham. In *A Fragment*, Bentham attacked Blackstone relentlessly:

> Tis in a passage antecedent to the digression we are examining, but in the same section, that, speaking of the pretended law of Nature, and of the law of revelation, 'no human laws,' he [Blackstone] says, 'should be *suffered* to contradict these *Commentaries*. The expression is remarkable. It is not that no human laws should contradict them: but that no human laws should be *suffered* to contradict them. He then proceeds to give us an example. This example, one might think, would be such as should have the effect of softening the dangerous tendency of the rule: —on the contrary, it is such as cannot but enhance it; and, in the application of it to the rule, the substance of the latter is again repeated in still more explicit and energetic terms. 'Nay,' says he, speaking of the act he instances, 'if any human law should allow or enjoin us to commit it, we are *bound* to *transgress* that human law, or else we must offend both the natural and the divine.'
>
> The propriety of this dangerous maxim, so far as the Divine Law is concerned, is what I must refer to a future occasion for more particular consideration. As to the LAW *of Nature,* if (as I trust it will appear) it be nothing but a phrase; if there be no other medium for proving any act to be an offence against it, than the mischievous tendency of such act; if there be no other medium for proving a law of the *state* to be contrary to it, than the *inexpediency* of such law, unless the bare unfounded disapprobation of any one who thinks of it be called a proof; if a test for distinguishing such laws as would be *contrary* to the LAW *of Nature* from such as, *without* being contrary to it, are simply *inexpedient,* be that which neither our Author, nor any man else, so much as pretended ever to give; if, in a word, there be scarce any law whatever but what those who have not liked it have found, on some account or another, to be repugnant to some text of scripture; I see no remedy but that the natural tendency of such doctrine is to impel a man, by the force of conscience, to rise up in arms against any law whatever that he happens not to like. What sort of government it is that can consist with such a disposition, I must leave to our Author to inform us.[13]

To Bentham, there was only one test of the validity of any law:

> It is the principle of *utility,* accurately apprehended and steadily applied, that affords the only clue to guide a man through these straits. It is for that, if any, and for that alone to furnish a decision which neither party shall dare in *theory* to disavow. It is something to reconcile men even in theory. They are at least, *something* nearer to an effectual union, than when at variance as well in respect of theory as of practice.[14]

Bentham was far too radical for Americans—his offer to codify the laws of Pennsylvania was politely declined. Indeed, as Perry Miller observed, Bentham

---

13. *Materials, infra*, pp. 526–527.
14. *Id*, p. 529.

was condemned "sight unseen," but the very controversy engendered by his attack on the patron saint of American common law, Blackstone, gave Bentham's ideas wide American exposure. "Abusing Bentham was...a game at which ministers and jurists played with gusto...."[15] Nevertheless, Bentham's writings were consistent with a growing willingness by American judges and legislators alike to see law as a conscious tool for change, rather than as an unchanging standard. This sense of the law as a means to an end, as an "instrument" to reach certain political or economic results, was to have a profound effect, whatever was said of Bentham and his "utilitarianism" in public.

As we will see, one vehicle of "utilitarianism" was to be an effort, in both England and America, to achieve law reform by coordinated statutory change, the so-called "codification" movement. But, as Morton Horwitz has argued, the American judiciary also adopted an "instrumental conception" of law.[16] While leaders such as Jefferson took a dim view of the judicial activism of Mansfield—whom Jefferson accused of rendering the law "more uncertain under pretense of rendering it more reasonable"—they also failed to replace judicial reform with legislative codes.[17]

Judicial instrumentalism can be found in many leading American courts during this period. A particularly excellent example is the famous case of *Commonwealth v. Hunt*,[18] decided in 1842 by the Supreme Judicial Court of Massachusetts. The opinion was written by a true peer of Mansfield, the great Chief Justice of Massachusetts, Lemuel Shaw (1781–1861). Like Mansfield, Shaw was Chief Justice for more than thirty years (1830–1860), and changed the legal landscape of Massachusetts by common law adjudication.[19]

Commonwealth v. Hunt was a pioneer "union" case. The facts were these. One Jeremiah Horne, a boot-maker, was discharged by his employer because Horne was not willing to pay a penalty to the Boston Journeymen Bootmakers' Society, a union. Horne had been fined by the union for doing extra work without pay, a violation of union rules. His employer wished to enjoy good relations with the union and to avoid strikes. An indictment was then brought by the state against John Hunt and six other union leaders for conspiracy on three counts: (1) forming an "unlawful...combination" to "extort great sums of money" by imposing a rule that members would not work for an employer who hired non-members—today called a "closed shop" rule; (2) that Horne's employer was forced to discharge him for this reason; and (3) that the defendant thus "wicked and unjustly intending unlawfully, and by indirect means, to impoverish one Jeremiah Horne...and hinder him from following his trade..."[20]

In theory, this case was of the greatest interest. Freedom of contract was widely regarded as a fundamental right of the individual protected by the common law, closely analogous to the right to private property. Unlawful interference with the

---

15. Perry Miller, *The Life of the Mind in America* (1965), 243.

16. Morton Horwitz, *The Transformation of American Law 1780–1860* (Cambridge, Mass., 1977), 17–30.

17. Jefferson led an unsuccessful effort to codify the law of Virginia. *Id.*, 18; Perry Miller, *The Life of the Mind in America, supra*, 241.

18. See *Materials, infra.*

19. See Leonard Levy, *The Law of the Commonwealth and Chief Justice Shaw* (Cambridge, Mass., 1957), 183–206.

20. *Materials, infra*, pp. 529 ff.

right of a person to make contracts or to follow a legal trade had long been seen by Anglo-American common law as a "criminal conspiracy," similar to extortion.[21] Further, as James Willard Hurst pointed out, "contract and free private association" were seen as the cornerstones of the "release-of-energy" principle: i.e. that the elimination of archaic, status-oriented legal doctrines would free trade to reach its most beneficial and profitable potential, to the ultimate benefit of all.[22] According to this theory, the activities of the union not only violated Horne's common law rights as an individual, but also impeded the general public good.

But the case was even more important politically. Workers in the industrial states were discovering that any "equality" in bargaining their services with big employers was a myth. As Hurst observed:

> Economic growth tied the lives of an increasing proportion of people to the market and the division of labor; they were either wage or salary earners, or small producers or traders in specialized ranges of goods or services. Theoretically buyers consent to the practical compulsions of the market in which they buy; if they do not consent, they stay out. But men who find their whole livelihood in the market are too vulnerable to stay out. An outstanding recognition of this simple but slowly learned truth was the legislation which limited or abolished the employer's defense of assumption of risk in industrial accident cases.[23]

Contract law, uninformed by social policy, could be a "pretty blunt instrument." Again, Hurst stated the problem clearly:

> We had to learn a second major lesson about our release-of-energy principle. During the first half of the [nineteenth] century we expressed that principle chiefly through contract. But sound doctrine for so fundamental a community concern as the organization of power requires built-in points of view and procedures to take account of all important values in the situation. Contract was inherently too limited an institution to serve this need.[24]

How would Chief Justice Shaw deal with this dilemma?

First, Shaw affirmed that, in the absence of a relevant statute, the case should be decided by "the general rules of the common law."

> We have no doubt, that by the operation of the constitution of this Commonwealth, the general rules of the common law, making conspiracy an indictable offence, are in force here, and that this is included in the description of laws which had, before the adoption of the constitution, been used and approved in the Province, Colony, or State of Massachusetts Bay, and usually practised in the courts of law.[25]

---

21. See Leonard W. Levy. *The Law of the Commonwealth and Chief Justice Shaw*, *supra*, 183–185. See also, for example, *Rex v. Journeymen Tailors of Cambridge 8 Modern Reports* 10 (K.B., 1721).

22. James W. Hurst, *Law and the Conditions of Freedom in Nineteenth Century United States*, *supra* note 1, 74–75.

23. *Id.* 75.

24. *Id.*, 75–76.

25. *Materials, infra*, pp. 531–540.

But not all common law precedents are absolutely binding on Massachusetts courts. "[A]lthough the common law in regard to conspiracy in this Commonwealth is in force, yet it will not necessarily follow that every indictment at common law is a precedent for a similar indictment in the State."[26] For example,

> All those laws of the parent country, whether rules of the common law, or early English statutes, which were made for the purpose of regulating the wages of laborers, the settlement of paupers, and making it penal for any one to use a trade or handicraft to which he had not served a full apprenticeship—not being adapted to the circumstances of our colonial condition—were not adopted, used or approved, and therefore do not come within the description of the laws adopted and confirmed by the provision of the constitution already cited.[27]

But if the common law is not to be blindly followed where inappropriate to Massachusetts, and there is no legislative authority directly on point, how are cases involving major legal and political issues to be resolved? In the end, for Shaw, it was an issue of judicial authority. For over 20 pages, a huge opinion for the day, Shaw reviewed every statutory analogy and every relevant common law doctrine. His final conclusion was that the purpose of the union was "to induce all those engaged in the same occupation to become members of it" and that "[s]uch a purpose is not unlawful."[28] Nor were the means employed, withholding of labor, criminal.[29] Therefore the damage to Horne was simply that of a legal competition, allowable in everyday economic life. As Shaw observed:

> Suppose a baker in a small village had the exclusive custom of his neighborhood, and was making large profits by the sale of his bread. Supposing a number of those neighbors, believing the price of his bread too high, should propose to him to reduce his prices, or if he did not, that they would introduce another baker; and on his refusal, such other baker should, under their encouragement, set up a rival establishment, and sell his bread at lower prices; the effect would be to diminish the profit of the former baker, and to the same extent to impoverish him. And it might be said and proved, that the purpose of the associates was to diminish his profits, and thus impoverish him, though the ultimate and laudable object of the combination was to reduce the cost of bread to themselves and their neighbors. The same thing may be said of all competition in every branch of trade and industry; and yet it is through that competition, that the best interests of trade and industry are promoted. It is scarcely necessary to allude to the familiar instances of opposition lines of conveyance, rival hotels, and the thousand other instances, where each strives to gain custom to himself, by ingenious improvements, by increased industry, and by all the means by which he may lessen the price of commodities, and thereby diminish the profits of others.[30]

---

26. *Id.*, p. 531.
27. *Id.*, p. 532.
28. *Id.*, pp. 537–538.
29. *Id.*, p. 539.
30. *Id.*, p. 539.

Thus, as the indictment did not charge a "criminal conspiracy punishable by law," the judgment below was arrested. The union movement gained a landmark victory.[31]

The fundamental argument of scholars such as Morton Horwitz and others is that Shaw could have decided this case "either way," and that it is hard to assume that he was oblivious to the great social and political issues hinging on the outcome.[32] The need to "adapt" a non-statutory common law tradition to new settings gave powerful judges law-making opportunities equivalent to those of the legislatures themselves. The classical common law theory of law as immemorial custom was a shallow fiction.[33] Judges such as Shaw, boldly used judicial opinions to create a law for a new America. This was the point of "instrumentalism."

Of course, legal instrumentalism was not limited to evolving areas of contract, commercial, labor, and criminal law. The ancient common law domain of real property was involved as well, particularly in setting a balance between industrial exploitation of resources—with its concomitant externalization of costs through environmental waste and pollution—and other public and private rights in property. Leading cases in both England and America, including the famous House of Lords case of *St. Helen's Smelting Co. v. Tipping*, 11 Eng. Rep. 1483 (H.L. 1865), moved subtly away from absolute enforcement of nuisance doctrine, with its protection of private property owners from off-site interference from noise and pollution. See the discussion of *William Aldred's Case*, 9 *Coke's Reports* 57(b), at *Materials*, Chapter VIII, *supra*, and the *St. Helen's Smelting* case itself, set out in this chapter. Instead, there was the new "balancing of utilities" doctrine. This provided more discretion for industrial development, and included the now infamous notion of the "ruined" neighborhood whose inhabitants lose effective nuisance rights because they live in a very polluted city.[34]

Other cases saw judges revive ancient doctrines to restrict exploitation of public resources. In *Illinois Central Railroad v. Illinois*, 146 U.S. 387 (1892), the Supreme Court of the United States set aside a transfer by the Illinois state legislature of a grant in fee to the Illinois Central Railroad of a large section of land submerged beneath Lake Michigan in the Chicago harbor. The ruling was based on the ancient doctrine of *res communes*, i.e., that certain property is incapable of

---

31. See Leonard W. Levy, *The Law of the Commonwealth and Chief Justice Shaw, supra*, 166–196.

32. See Morton J. Horwitz, *The Transformation of American Law: 1780–1860, supra*, 40–41, 52–53, 89–90, 97, 209–210. Indeed, it has been argued that Shaw's opinion in *Commonwealth v. Hunt* was "Shaw's answer to the movement for the codification of the common law." See Leonard W. Levy, *The Law of the Commonwealth and Chief Justice Shaw, supra*, 196. Others have questioned whether Shaw was so calculating. *Id.*, 195–201. In event, an attempt to codify the Massachusetts criminal law failed two years later. *Id.*, 201. Levy observed that "In the last analysis, men like Joseph Story, Charles Jackson, Willard Phillips, and Luther Cushing, who composed the Massachusetts commissions on codification, posed no threat to Shaw's mistress, the common law." *Id.*, 201.

33. For an excellent discussion of "classical common law theory," see Gerald J. Postema, *Bentham and the Common Law Tradition, supra*, 3–38

34. See Daniel R. Coquillette, "Mosses from an Old Manse: Another Look at Some Historic Property Cases About the Environment," 64 *Cornell Law Review* 761, 784–790 (1979). Ironically, the famous *St. Helen Smelting* case itself introduced the "balancing test" as pure *dictum* by Lord Westbury. *Id.*, 789–791.

private ownership, but is held by the government in trust for the commonalty—a theory close to old English law of commons.[35] The Supreme Court's decision was despite the clear legislative action of Illinois and the obvious economic interests of the railroad. It set an important precedent for protecting public lands in other uniquely important areas.[36] No one could honestly argue that such a result was "dictated" by past precedents. In truth, the Supreme Court had been informed by past doctrines, but had made bold choices to protect certain perceived social ends, and to overlook others. Again, "instrumentalism" at work. As Morton Horwitz observed:

> By 1820 the legal landscape in America bore only the faintest resemblance to what existed forty years earlier. While the words were often the same, the structure of thought had dramatically changed and with it the theory of law. Law was no longer conceived of as an eternal set of principles expressed in custom and derived from natural law. Nor was it regarded primarily as a body of rules designed to achieve justice only in the individual case. Instead, judges came to think of the common law as equally responsible with legislation for governing society and promoting socially desirable conduct. The emphasis on law as an instrument of policy encouraged innovation and allowed judges to formulate legal doctrine with the self-conscious goal of bringing about social change. And from this changed perspective, American law stood on the verge of what Daniel Boorstin has correctly called one of the great "creative outbursts of modern legal history."[37]

B. CODIFICATION

It is easy to see how judicial instrumentalism would spawn a codification movement. As we have seen, Bentham, who actually invented the word "codification," was inspired by the instrumentalism of Mansfield.[38] But if the "unwritten" law is to be used as an explicit social tool, would not a written, prospective law be better? Once the myth of the "immemorial" common law as a static, unchanging monolith is exploded, how can one argue that a sovereign legislature should ever defer to judges? Most important, if law is seen solely as the enforced commands of a sovereign, as Bentham's friend Austin argued, is not a carefully organized, accessible, written scheme of law, prospectively applied, simply more useful, efficient and fair? As Bentham observed:

> Grant even the proposition in general: —What are we the nearer? Grant that there *are* certain bounds to the *authority* of the legislature: — Of what use is it to say so, when these bounds are what no body has ever attempted to mark out to any useful purpose; that is, in any such

---

35. *Id.*, 799–814.
36. *Id.*, 810–821, and cases cited.
37. Morton Horwitz, *The Transformation of American Law 1780–1860* (Cambridge, Mass., 1977), 30.
38. See note 11, *supra*.

manner whereby it might be known beforehand what description a law must be of to fall *within*, and what to fall *beyond* them? Grant that there *are* things which the legislature *can*not do;—grant that there *are* laws which exceed the *power* of the legislature to establish. What rules does this sort of discourse furnish us for determining whether any one that is in question is, or is not of the number? As far as I can discover, none. Either the discourse goes on in the confusion it began; either all rests in vague assertions, and no intelligible argument at all is offered; or if any, such arguments as are drawn from the principle of *utility*: arguments which, in whatever variety of words expressed, come at last to neither more nor less than this: that the tendency of the law is, to a greater or a less degree, pernicious. If this then be the result of the argument, why not come home to it at once? Why turn aside into a wilderness of sophistry, when the path of plain reason is straight before us?[39]

Codification movements occurred in both England and America. Given the colonial experiments, such as the remarkable *Lawes and Libertyes* of 1648,[40] and the revolutionary denunciation of the English common law by lawyers such as Jesse Root in his "The Origins of Government and Laws in Connecticut, 1798,"[41] it would be easy to imagine a great sweep of codification across America. This would seem even more likely when one considers the legal *tabula rasa* facing most former colonies, the lack of local law reports, legal treatises, and even law schools.[42] The spectacle of states such as Pennsylvania, where a statute of 1807 empowered the judges of the Supreme Court to decide which English statutes were in force, would be regarded by Benthamites as a great opportunity lost, and, indeed, powerful American advocates, such as Robert Rantoul and David Dudley Field, were soon calling for codes.[43] In 1836, Rantoul asked, "Why, is an *ex post facto* law, passed by the legislature, unjust, unconstitutional, and void, while judge-made law, which, from its nature, must always be *ex post facto*, is not only to be obeyed, but applauded?"[44] In 1855, Field addressed the graduating class of the Albany Law School. Field attacked the inherited common law, observing that "it is derived from the Common Law of England, but so mixed the blended with other rules and usages that it can hardly be called a system at all."[45] He called for "the greatest reform of all, *the establishment of 'a written and systematic code of the whole body of the law of this State.'* "[46] Is such a code a practical possibility? Field waxed eloquent:

> How, then, stands the question of practicability? Is a civil code practicable? The best answer to this question should seem to be the fact that civil codes have been established in nearly all the countries of the world,

39. *Materials, infra*, p. 529.

40. See *Materials* Chapter XI, *supra*.

41. See *Materials*, Chapter XI, *supra*.

42. See Lawrence M. Friedman, *A History of American Law* (2d ed., New York, 1985), 403–411.

43. Morton J. Horwitz, *The Transformation of American Law: 1780–1860; supra*, note 33, 23–24.

44. *Id.*, 18.

45. *Materials, infra*, p. 547.

46. *Id.*

from the time of the Lower Empire to the present day. Are we not as capable of performing a great act of legislation as Romans or Germans, as
Frenchmen or Italians? The very doubt supposes either that our abilities
are inferior or our law more difficult. The suggestion of inferior abilities
would be resented as a national insult; and who that knows anything of
it believes that Roman, French, or Italian law is easier to express or explain than our own? And he who does believe it should, in very consistency, straightway set about the amendment of our own, to render it as
easy to learn and as facile to express as these foreign laws."[47]

Would not a code remove "flexibility" from the system? But a "flexible" common law presents far worse problems.

> A law is a rule of action; to say that the rule is not fixed, that is, flexi-
> ble, is to say that it is no rule at all. When a decision is made upon the
> Common Law, it is announced as an authoritative declaration of an ex-
> isting rule; if it be not really that, then the Judges, instead of interpreting,
> are making law. If it be an exposition of existing law, then it is not alter-
> able by the Judges, and, of course, is no more flexible in their hands than
> a statute would be. A flexible Common Law, means, therefore, judicial
> legislation. Is that desirable? If there be any reason for the policy of sep-
> arating the different departments of government, the Judges should no
> more be permitted to make laws than the Legislature to administer them.
> All experience has shown that confusion in functions leads to confusion
> in government.[48]

What could be a more noble monument for a new transcontinental power, a
nation of "manifest destiny," than a code which, like its new railroads and
canals, stretched across the land. This vision Field called the "Code American."
Calling on the great names of both Bacon and Mansfield "and our own Marshall, Kent and Story," as well as the classical heritage of "Demosthenes,
Aeschines, Ulpian and Cicero" and the civilian Daguesseau, Field urged the graduates toward an entirely new threshold of law.

> Shall this imperial State be outstripped in the noble race by either of
> her sisters, or by that queenly island, mother of nations, which, having
> been our parent, now our rival? In material public works, in commerce
> with all the world, in the accumulation of wealth, in the possession
> and display of power, and in all the arts, we are contending with her
> preëminence; it is now to be determined which shall be the lawgiver of
> the race. Whether this crown shall be upon the head of the mother, or
> the youngest of the nations, is the problem which the men of this gen-
> eration shall solve. May it be so resolved as that we shall win the well-
> deserved prize; that we shall have a book of our own laws, a CODE

---

47. *Id*, p. 459.
48. *Id*, p. 550.

AMERICAN, not insular but continental, as simple as so vast a work can be made, free in it spirit, catholic in its principle![49]

How could such a vision, at such a time, but succeed?

But it did not succeed. With the exception of Field's own Code of Civil Procedure; adopted by New York in 1848 and by many Western states, there was no great "Code American." Field did not publish a full Civil Code until 1865, and then even New York would not adopt it. Eventually, only Field's Penal Code was adopted in New York, as late as 1881, and the Civil Code was rejected.[50] Men like James C. Carter organized the bar in opposition. According to Carter, the question was whether "growth, development and improvement of the law" should "remain under the guidance of men selected by the people on account of their special qualifications for the work" or "be transferred to a numerous legislative body, disqualified by the nature of their duties for the discharge of this supreme function?"[51] If Americans distrusted lawyers, they trusted politicians even less. With the notable exceptions of the Field Penal Code, the Negotiable Instruments Law (based on the English Bills-of-Exchange Act of 1882), its offspring the Uniform Commercial Code, and special situations in states like Louisiana and Georgia, there was to be no great Codification. As Lawrence Friedman observed: "As of 1900, American legal system was, as it had been, a system of astonishing complexity." Diversities as old as the seventeenth century still survived."[52] The "Code American" remained a dream.

If codification failed in the great new vista of America, how could it succeed in the ancient homeland of the common law, where the powerful Inns of Court held sway? Yet, here too the historical record surprises. To a much greater extent than America, England moved toward legislative reform, eventually embracing almost the entire legal system in new legislation. Even the courts themselves were completely reorganized by a series of statutes, culminating in the Judicature Act of 1875. That act establishing a new High Court of Justice which encompassed all of the traditional common law courts, plus a new Chancery Division and a new Admiralty Probate, Divorce Division, reflecting the old civilian specialties.[53]

What is equally astonishing is that these reforms were partly inspired, not by empirical studies or surveys, but by works of fiction. Charles Dickens (1812–1870) was the son of a clerk in the navy pay office. His father was imprisoned for debt, and he worked, at age 12, in a warehouse. He then became an office boy, and later a newspaper reporter. As a reporter, he frequently covered court cases, particularly the interesting domestic disputes in Doctors' Commons and the Chancery. From these experiences came unforgettable pictures of a corrupt and hopelessly unjust legal system filling the pages of novels such as *David Copperfield* (1849–1850)[54] and *Bleak House* (1852–1853).[55]

---

49. *Id.*, p. 551.

50. See Laurence M. Friedman, *A History of American Law, supra*, 403–411.

51. *Id.*, 403. See James C. Carter, *The Proposal Codification of Our Common Law* (New York, 1884).

52. Laurence M. Friedman, *A History of American Law, supra*, 411.

53. See *Materials, supra*.

54. See Chapter VIII, *supra*.

55. See the excerpt later in this chapter, *Materials, infra*, pp. 518–522.

This, of course, was only one aspect of Dickens' literary war on the grinding poverty and alienation that the industrial revolution had created among the urban poor. There was a sense of despair unknown in the traditional country-side, even among the most exploited farm labor. By 1848, it was becoming apparent that "capitalist industrialization" had "failed to improve the conditions of the working class."[56] If Marx became the ideologue of this failure, Dickens was its artistic soul. The opening paragraphs of *Bleak House* were the equivalent to several royal commissions on civil justice reform:

> On such an afternoon, if ever, the Lord High Chancellor ought to be sitting here — as here he is — with a foggy glory round his head, softly fenced in with crimson cloth and curtains, addressed by a large advocate with great whiskers, a little voice, and an interminable brief, and outwardly directing his contemplation to the lantern in the roof, where he can see nothing but fog. On such an afternoon, some score of members of the High Court of Chancery bar ought to be — as here they are — mistily engaged in one of the ten thousand stages of an endless cause, tripping one another up on slippery precedents, groping knee-deep in technicalities, running their goat-hair and horse-hair warded heads against walls of words, and making a pretence of equity with serious faces, as players might. On such an afternoon, the various solicitors in the cause, some two or three of whom have inherited it from their fathers, who made a fortune by it, ought to be — as are they not? — ranged in a line, in a long matted well (but you might look in vain for Truth at the bottom of it), between the registrar's red table and the silk gowns, with bills, cross bills, answers, rejoinders, injunctions, affidavits, issues, references to masters, masters' reports, mountains of costly nonsense, piled before them. Well may the court be dim, with wasting candles here and there; well may the fog hang heavy in it, as if it would never get out; well may the stained glass windows lose their color, and admit no light of day into the place; well may the uninitiated from the streets, who peep in through the glass panes in the door, be deterred from entrance by its owlish aspect, and by the drawl languidly echoing to the roof from the padded dais where the Lord High Chancellor looks into the lantern that has no light in it, and where the attendant wigs are all stuck in a fog-bank! This is the Court of Chancery; which has its decaying houses and its blighted lands in every shire; which has its worn-out lunatic in every madhouse, and its dead in every churchyard; which has its ruined suitor, with his slipshod heels and threadbare dress, borrowing and begging through the round of every man's acquaintance; which gives to monied might the means abundantly of wearing out the right; which so exhausts finances, patience, courage, hope; so overthrows the brain and breaks the heart; that there is not an honorable man among its practitioners who would not give — who does not often give — the warning, "Suffer any wrong that can be done you, rather than come here![57]

---

56. See Christopher Harvie, "Revolution of the Rule of Law (1789–1851)," *The Oxford History of Britain* (K.O. Morgan, ed., 1988), 470–517.

57. *Materials, infra,* p. 519.

Even before Dickens, it had become clear to the English establishment that reform was necessary. The turning point was the Reform Act of 1832. This greatly improved actual democratic representation, although much was left to be desired. This was followed closely by the Poor Law Amendment Act of 1834, which attempted to provide a basic reform of English local government.[58] Slow consolidation of the statute law had begun in 1825, with the repeal of 12 archaic acts and the replacement of 442 others.[59] The great reformer, Henry Brougham, founded a Royal Commission on statutory reform by 1833, and by 1854 a Statute Law Commission was appointed by the Lord Chancellor. Its original goal was to draft a "Code Victoria," perhaps drawing on the large-scale codification of the common law prepared between 1830 and 1860 for use in India.[60] An important part of the criminal law has consolidated and codified by 1861. From 1868 on, a series of Statute Law Revision Acts followed. The goal was better, clearer drafting of new statutes.[61] By 1869 the position of parliamentary draftsman was created, and professional drafting was assured. By 1860 the Report of the Commissioners on the Supreme Court of Law led to the more radical First Report of the Judicature Commission (1868) which in turn led to the radical reforms of the Judicature Act of 1875, which finally abolished the old common law courts, and replaced them with a new High Court of Justice and a Court of Appeals. Only the old names lived on. There was still a "Chancery Division" and a "Queen's Bench Division" (including the old Common Pleas and Exchequer after 1880), and a Probate, Divorce and Admiralty Division. But now all royal judges were "Justice of the Supreme Court" who could be assigned to any division if needed.[62] Just over twenty years after the first publication of *Bleak House*, the entire legal order that Dickens portrayed was changed.

Of course, as John Baker points out, this was far short of a "Code Victoria." True, Lord Westbury had raised the issue of a code in Parliament in 1863 "to enquire into the expediency of a Digest of Law."[63] In 1879, another Commission produced a draft of Criminal Code, which was defeated. The Bills of Exchange Act of 1882, the Partnership Act of 1890 and the Sale of Goods Act of 1893 were more successful. As Baker observed:

> "These digests were more in the tradition of Justinian, Staunford and Bacon than of Bentham. Their object was to restate in clear language the case-law of the time, all the texts being supportable by reference to cases on which they are based."[64]

---

58. See Christopher Harvie, "Revolution and the Rule of Law (1789–1851), *The Oxford History of Britain* (K.O. Morgan, ed., 1988) 495–496).

59. See Alan Harding, *A Social History of English Law* (London, 1966) 338–339. Bentham was actually greatly disappointed by the first reform statutes, which were passed just before his death in 1832. He thought them to be "woefully unsystematic." *Id.*, 335.

60. See *id.* 338 and J.H. Baker, *An Introduction to English Legal History* (3d ed., London, 1990), 251–252. See also A.H. Manchester, *A Modern Legal History of England and Wales 1750–1930* (London, 1980) 13–49.

61. *Alan Harding, A* Social History of English Law, supra, 338; J.H. Baker, *An Introduction to English Legal History, supra*, 250–251.

62. Alan Harding, *A Social History of English Law, supra*, 340–342.

63. J.H. Baker, *An Introduction to English Legal History, supra*, 251–252.

64. *Id.*, 251.

In the end, the codification movement in England resulted in such pragmatic, but highly useful statutes and restatements. As Pollock observed:

> "Codes are not meant to dispense lawyers from being learned, but for the ease of the lay person and the greater usefulness of the law. The right kind of consolidating legislation is that which makes the law more accessible without altering its principle or methods."[65]

It may not have been the "Code Victoria," but the English nineteenth century saw a growing body of reform legislation, increasingly professional in its conception and drafting.[66]

C. THE DRED SCOTT CASE (1857)

The optimism and innovation apparent in both legal instrumentalism and the codification movement cannot conceal one colossal failure of the nineteenth-century American legal system. The issue of race slavery threatened the very core of the law, and an increasingly desperate resort to the courts failed to prevent the resulting bloody Civil War. Even Chief Justice Shaw saw little choice but to enforce the savage Fugitive Slave Law, and return African Americans to slavery in the South.[67] The analogies with the English Civil War are striking. The prelude to both wars, to a surprising degree, saw key issues expressed as legal questions and presented to courts of law. In England, the "Five Knights Case" (1627) came to symbolize the ultimate conflict between the rule of law and parliament and the prerogatives of the crown.[68] The failure of the courts to protect individual rights and uphold the parliament's taxation power made war inevitable. In America, the equivalent last chance for the courts was the *Dred Scott Case*, 60 U.S. (19 How.) 393 (1857).

Dred Scott, an African American, had been held in slavery in Missouri. His master, an army surgeon, took him into a free territory, the upper Louisiana Territory. There slavery had been prohibited by the Missouri Compromise, an act of Congress of 1820. Scott returned with the surgeon to Missouri, where Scott later sued for freedom. His argument was simple. As slavery was prohibited by Congress in the upper Louisiana Territory, his residency there made him free. In an infamous opinion that was to ruin his reputation, Chief Justice Roger Brooke Taney not only held that Scott was still a slave under the laws of his present residence, Missouri, but that no African American was a citizen of the United States within the meaning of the constitution, and that Scott, therefore, could not sue

---

65. As cited by J.H. Baker. *Id.*, 232.

66. As J.H. Baker observes, the Law Commission (est. 1965), still has "a standing charge to review the law with a view to its development, reform and possible codification." *Id.*, 252. See the Law Commissions Act of 1965 (c. 22).

67. See Leonard Levy, *The Law of the Commonwealth and Chief Justice Shaw*, 72–91, 106–108 (Cambridge, Mass. 1957). See the discussion in D.R. Coquillette, *Lawyers and Fundamental Moral Responsibility* (Cincinnati, 1995), 191–202.

68. See *Materials, supra*, Chapter X.

for freedom in a federal court. Even worse, the court held that Congress exceeded its constitutional powers in adopting the Missouri Compromise, on the grounds that the prohibition of slavery deprived citizens of property contrary to the due process clause of the Fifth Amendment.[69]

In a brilliant dissent, Justice Benjamin Curtis attacked slavery as "contrary to natural right" and defended the power of the congress to prohibit slavery in the free territories.[70] Curtis' argument both symbolized the ability of the courts to attack deep political and moral issues by bold instrumentalist holdings, and the necessary power of the legislature to likewise attack such problems, Curtis' dissent was true to the spirit of instrumentalism and the legislative sovereignty inherent in codification, while Taney's invocation of common law "property" rights to stifle reform represented all that Bentham feared and hated about the judicial process.

As with the "Five Knights Case," *supra*, the failure of the judicial system to provide a viable solution to a major political problem led to war. Whether this was, in any way, the fault of the judges depends on your judicial philosophy. Some would argue that, short of a constitutional convention and the enactment of the Fourteenth Amendment, Chief Justice Taney had little choice. Others have had little hesitancy in attacking Taney for failing to recognize the right policy and pursuing that policy by the full use of judicial power, in the spirit of Lord Mansfield or Chief Justice Earl Warren.[71] In all events, no assessment of the nineteenth-century American judiciary can omit the terrible lessons of *Dred Scott*.

D. CONCLUSION

The nineteen century in both America and England saw enormous change in population, economic structure, and integration of the nations by new forms of transport. In both countries, industrialization led to a basic shift of labor and population from agrarian towns and villages into urban centers. The resulting work force was displaced and alienated, and initially had little to show for the "Industrial Revolution." Meanwhile, the nature and needs of commerce changed beyond recognition.

The legal "instrumentalism" of great judges, such as Lord Mansfield, provided a vehicle for bringing the common law in line with the times. In America, this legal instrumentalism was established by giants such as Lemuel Shaw, Marshall, Kent and Story. But the candid recognition of judicial power inherent in such "instrumentalism" provoked a backlash, and focused efforts to establish the law through well drafted codes and statutes on particular topics, such as commercial transactions. This "codification" movement and its patron saint, Jeremy Bentham, were not an unmitigated success in either nation, but they brought a bold notion that law was no more than what its social usefulness warrants. This no-

---

69. See *Scott v. Sandford, supra*, 60 U.S. at 450–452. See Laurence H. Tribe, *American Constitutional Law* (New York, 1978) 278, n. 12.

70. See *Materials, infra*.

71. For example, David M. Walker observes in his *Oxford Companion to Law* (Oxford, 1980) that Taney had been "an eminently competent chief justice," but that he "latterly became out of touch and the *Dred Scott* decision ruined his reputation." *Id.*, 1207.

tion in turn brought a new period of reflection and experimentation. If there was to be no "Code American" or "Code Victoria," at least there would be a Field Penal Code (Laws N.Y., 1881, ch. 676), a Sale of Goods Act of 1893 (56 & 57 Vict., c. 71) and, eventually, a Uniform Commercial Code (first adopted, Penn., 1953).

Of course, one is always left with the ancient folk dilemma of whether the cup was half empty or half filled. Bentham and codification left a permanent mark on Anglo-American law. But perhaps more remarkable and important was the stubborn persistence of the common law, now made more potent by legal instrumentalism. Indeed, despite the sad record on slavery, the persistence of traditional "judge made law" was even more conspicuous in the American "brave new World" than in England itself. Such are the ironies of legal history.

FOR FURTHER READING

I.   General Background: The Nineteenth Century

A.   *England*

For an excellent general introduction, see Christopher Harvie "Revolution and the Rule of Law (1789–1851)" and H.C.G. Mathew "The Liberal Age (1851–1914)" both in *The Oxford History of Britain* (ed. K.O. Morgan, Oxford, 1988) 470–517, 518–581, respectively. For an economic and social analysis, see David Thomson, *England in the Nineteenth Century* (London, 1978 rev. ed.), which has particularly good sections on constitutional, political, economic and social reforms at 56–98. See also Derek Beales, *From Castlereagh to Gladstone 1815–1885* (London, 1969), particularly pages 106–152. For an exhaustive political history of events and an extensive scholarly bibliography, see Sir Llewellyn Woodward, F.B.A., *The Age of Reform* 1815–1870 (Oxford, 2d ed. 1962). For a good brief overview of constitutional history and the reform of parliament, see S.B. Chrimes, *English Constitutional History* (Oxford, 4th ed., 1967). Unmatched for a combination of analysis of constitutional reform and a selection of original documents is H.J. Hanham, *The Nineteenth Century Constitution: Documents and Commentary* (Cambridge, 1969).

No general introductions to nineteenth-century English law and politics should be without some reading in Dickens. Particularly recommended by lawyers is the great *Bleak House* (London, 1853, first consolidated edition). See, for further suggestions and guidance, William S. Holdsworth, *Charles Dickens as a Legal Historian* (New Haven, 1928).

B.   *America*

The great classical accounts remain James Willard Hurst's *Law and the Conditions of Freedom in the Nineteenth Century United States* (Madison, 1956) and, for the latter part of the century, Richard Hofstadter, *The Age of Reform* (New York, 1955). For the intellectual history of the period, see Perry Miller's two classics: *The Legal Mind in America, from Independence to the Civil War*

(Garden City, NY, 1962) and *The Life of the Mind in America: From the Revolution to the Civil War* (New York, 1965). For an excellent social and economic history, see David J. Rothman's *The Discovery of the Asylum, Social Order and Disorder in the New Republic* (Boston, 1971), and Oscar Handlin and Mary Frug Handlin, *Commonwealth* (Cambridge, Mass., 1969).

II. Legal Instrumentalism and Legal History

A. *England*

The best brief introductory account is once again J.H. Baker, *An Introduction to English Legal History* (3d ed., London, 1990) particularly pages 246–252. More extensive, and very useful for this period, is Alan Harding, *A Social History of English Law* (London, 1966) 330–388. For a conventional, extensive and detailed account, see W. S. Holdsworth, *A History of English Law*, vols. XIV, XV, and XVI (A.L. Goodhart, H.G. Hanbury eds., London, 1965) ("From the Reform Act, 1832, to the Judicative Acts (1873–1875)"). Also highly useful are sections of A.H. Manchester's *A Modern Legal History of England and Wales 1750–1950* (London, 1980) particularly 1–110, and C.H.S. Fifoot, *Judge and Jurist in the Reign of Queen Victoria* (London, 1959) and the classic A.V. Dicey, *Law and Public Opinion in England During the 19th Century* (London, 1905).

B. *America*

The best general introduction to all phases of American legal history is Lawrence M. Friedman, *A History of American Law* (2d edition, New York, 1985). For the nineteenth century, see particularly pages 335–654. The leading scholarly account on legal instrumentalism in the early American nineteenth century is Morton J. Horwitz, *The Transformation of American Law, 1780–1860* (Cambridge, Mass., 1977). Unmatched for a sweeping view of the principal agencies of law in the United States from 1790–1940 is James Willard Hurst's *The Growth of America: The Law Markers* (Boston, 1950). Again for an excellent, compact anthology see Perry Miller, *The Legal Mind in America, From Independence to the Civil War* (Garden City, N.Y., 1962). There are also two excellent legal biographies of great instrumentalist judges: John P. Reid's *Chief Justice, the Judicial World of Charles Doe* (1967) and Leonard Levy's *The Law of the Commonwealth and Chief Justice Shaw* (Cambridge, Mass., 1957). The latter contains a good account of *Commonwealth v. Hunt. Id.*, 183–206. See also, Elijah Adlow, *The Genius of Lemuel Shaw* (Boston, 1962), for a more adulatory view.

III. Bentham and Codification

For a very concise introduction to Bentham and his circle, particularly John Austin, see W.S. Holdsworth, *Some Makers of English Law* (Cambridge, 1966) 248–264. For a sophisticated analysis of Bentham and detailed bibliographies, see David Lyons, *In the Interest of the Governed: A Study in Bentham's Philosophy of Utility and Law* (Oxford 1973) and Gerald J. Postema, *Bentham and the Common Law Tradition* (Oxford, 1986). See also H. Beynon, "Mighty Bentham" in *Journal of Legal History* (1981), 62–76. For a good account of the codification movement's early experiments, see B. Rudden, "A Code Too Soon:

The 1826 Property Code of James Humphrys" in *Essays in Memory of F.H. Lawson* (eds. Peter Wallington, Robert M. Merkin, London, 1986), 101–116. There is also a good introduction to Bentham's *A Fragment on Government* by Wilfrid Harrison, which contains excellent summaries of Bentham's analysis. See Wilfrid Harrison, "Introduction" to Jeremy Bentham, *A Fragment on Government and an Introduction to the Principles of Morals and Legislation*, (Oxford, 1967), vii–ixiv.

Bentham is not easy to read in the original. The most rewarding works are his *A Fragment on Government*, (see the Harrison edition, *supra*) and his *Of Laws in General* (ed. H.L.A. Hant, London, 1970).

Illustration 13-2   Chief Justice Lemuel Shaw (1781–1861). Chief Justice of Massachusetts for 30 years (1830–1860). Author of *Commonwealth v. Hunt*, 4 Metcalf 111 (1842), *infra*. Portrait from *Supreme Judicial Court of Massachusetts: 1602–1942* (Mass. Bar Association, 1942), sec. 2, 22.

MATERIALS

Charles Dickens, *Bleak House* (1st ed. London, 1853), 1–5

BLEAK HOUSE.
CHAPTER I.
IN CHANCERY.

LONDON. Michaelmas Term lately over, and the Lord Chancellor sitting in Lincoln's Inn Hall. Implacable November weather. As much mud in the streets, as if the waters had but newly retired from the face of the earth, and it would not be wonderful to meet a Megalosaurus, forty feet long or so, waddling like an elephantine lizard up Holborn-hill. Smoke lowering down from chimney-pots, making a soft black drizzle, with flakes of soot in it as big as full-grown snowflakes—gone into mourning, one might imagine, for the death of the sun. Dogs, undistinguishable in mire. Horses, scarcely better; splashed to their very blinkers. Foot passengers, jostling one another's umbrellas, in a general infection of ill-temper, and losing their foot-hold at street-corners, where tens of thousands of other foot passengers have been slipping and sliding since the day broke (if the day ever broke), adding new deposits to the crust upon crust of mud, sticking at those points tenaciously to the pavement, and accumulating at compound interest.

Fog everywhere. Fog up the river, where it flows among green aits and meadows; fog down the river, where it rolls defiled among the tiers of shipping, and the waterside pollutions of a great (and dirty) city. Fog on the Essex marshes, fog on the Kentish heights. Fog creeping into the cabooses of collier-brigs; fog lying out on the yards, and hovering in the rigging of great ships; fog drooping on the gunwales of barges and small boats. Fog in the eyes and throats of ancient Greenwich pensioners, wheezing by the firesides of their wards; fog in the stem and bowl of the afternoon pipe of the wrathful skipper, down in his close cabin; fog cruelly pinching the toes and fingers of his shivering little 'prentice boy on deck. Chance people on the bridges peeping over the parapets into a nether sky of fog, with fog all round them, as if they were up in a balloon, and hanging in the misty clouds.

Gas looming through the fog in divers places in the streets, much as the sun may, from the spongey fields, be seen to loom by husbandman and ploughboy. Most of the shops lighted two hours before their time—as the gas seems to know, for it has a haggard and unwilling look.

The raw afternoon is rawest, and the dense fog is densest, and the muddy streets are muddiest, near that leaden-headed old obstruction, appropriate ornament for the threshold of a leaden-headed old corporation: Temple Bar. And hard by Temple Bar, in Lincoln's Inn Hall, at the very heart of the fog, sits the Lord High Chancellor in his High Court of Chancery.

Never can there come fog too thick, never can there come mud and mire too deep, to assort with the groping and floundering conditions which this High Court of Chancery, most pestilent of hoary sinners, holds, this day, in the sight of heaven and earth.

On such an afternoon, if ever, the Lord High Chancellor ought to be sitting here—as here he is—with a foggy glory round his head, softly fenced in with crimson cloth and curtains, addressed by a large advocate with great whiskers, a little voice, and an interminable brief, and outwardly directing his contemplation to the lantern in the roof, where he can see nothing but fog. On such an afternoon, some score of members of the High Court of Chancery bar ought to be — as here they are — mistily engaged in one of the ten thousand stages of an endless cause, tripping one another up on slippery precedents, groping knee-deep in technicalities, running their goat-hair and horse-hair warded heads against walls of words, and making a pretence of equity with serious faces, as players might. On such an afternoon, the various solicitors in the cause, some two or three of whom have inherited it from their fathers, who made a fortune by it, ought to be — as are they not? —ranged in a line, in a long matted well (but you might look in vain for Truth at the bottom of it), between the registrar's red table and the silk gowns, with bills, crossbills, answers, rejoinders, injunctions, affidavits, issues, references to masters,, masters' reports, mountains of costly nonsense, piled before them. Well may the court be dim, with wasting candles here and there; well may the fog hang heavy in it, as if it would never get out; well may the stained glass windows lose their color, and admit no light of day into the place; well may the uninitiated from the streets, who peep in through the glass panes in the door, be deterred from entrance by its owlish aspect, and by the drawl languidly echoing to the roof from the padded dais where the Lord High Chancellor looks into the lantern that has no light in it, and where the attendant wigs are all stuck in a fog-bank! This is the Court of Chancery; which has its decaying houses and its blighted lands in every shire; which has its worn-out lunatic in every madhouse, and its dead in every churchyard; which has its ruined suitor, with his slipshod heels and threadbare dress, borrowing and begging through the round of every man's acquaintance; which gives to monied might the means abundantly of wearying out the right; which so exhausts finances, patience, courage, hope; so overthrows the brain and breaks the heart; that there is not an honorable man among its practitioners who would not give — who does not often give — the warning, "Suffer any wrong that can be done you, rather than come here!"

Who happen to be in the Lord Chancellor's court this murky afternoon besides the Lord Chancellor, the counsel in the cause, two or three counsel who are never in any cause, and the well of solicitors before mentioned? There is the registrar below the Judge, in wig and gown; and there are two or three maces, or petty-bags, or privy-purses, or whatever they may be, in legal court suits. These are all yawning; for no crumb of amusement ever falls from JARNDYCE and JARNDYCE (the cause in hand), which was squeezed dry years upon years ago. The short-hand writers, the reporters of the court, and the reporters of the newspapers, invariably decamp with the rest of the regulars when Jarndyce and Jarndyce comes on. Their places are a blank. Standing on a seat at the side of the hall, the better to peer into the curtained sanctuary, is a little mad old woman in a squeezed bonnet, who is always in court, from its sitting to its rising, and always expecting some incomprehensible judgment to be given in her favor. Some say she really is, or was, a party to a suit; but no one knows for certain, because no one cares. She carries some small litter in a reticule which she calls her documents; principally consisting of paper matches and dry lavender. A sallow prisoner has come up, in custody, for the half-dozenth time, to make a personal application "to purge himself of his contempt;" which, being a solitary surviving executor who has fallen into a state of conglomeration about accounts of which it is not pretended that he had ever any knowledge, he is not at all likely ever to do. In the meantime his prospects in life are ended. Another ruined suitor, who periodically appears from Shropshire, and breaks out into efforts to address the Chancellor at the close of the day's business, and who can by no means be made to understand that the Chancellor is legally ignorant of his existence after making it desolate for a quarter of a century, plants himself in a good place and keeps an eye on the Judge, ready to call out "My lord!" in a voice of sonorous complaint, on the instant of his rising. A few lawyers' clerks and others who know this suitor by sight, linger, on the chance of his furnishing some fun, and enlivening the dismal weather a little.

Jarndyce and Jarndyce drones on. This scarecrow of a suit has, in course of time, become so complicated, that no man alive knows what it means. The parties to it understand it least; but it has been observed that no two Chancery lawyers can talk about it for five minutes, without coming to a total disagreement as to all the premises. Innumerable children have been born into the cause; innumerable young people have married into it; innumerable old people have died out of it. Scores of persons have deliriously found themselves made parties in Jarndyce and Jarndyce, without knowing how or why; whole families have inherited legendary hatreds with the suit. The little plaintiff or defendant, who was promised a new rocking-horse when Jarndyce and Jarndyce should be settled, has grown up, possessed himself of a real horse, and trotted away into the other world. Fair wards of court have faded into mothers and grandmothers; a long procession of Chancellors has come in and gone out; the legion of bills in the suit have been transformed into mere bills of mortality; there are not three Jarndyces left upon the earth perhaps, since old Tom Jarndyce in despair blew his brains out at a coffee-house in Chancery-lane; but Jarndyce and Jarndyce still drags its dreary length before the Court, perennially hopeless.

Jarndyce and Jarndyce has passed into a joke. That is the only good that has ever come of it. It has been death to many, but it is a joke in the profession. Every master in Chancery has had a reference out of it. Every Chancellor was "in it," for somebody or other, when he was counsel at the bar. Good things have been said about it by blue-nosed, bulbous-shoed old benchers, in select port-wine committee after dinner in hall. Articled clerks have been in the habit of fleshing their legal wit upon it. The last Lord Chancellor handled it neatly, when, correcting Mr. Blowers the eminent silk gown who said that such a thing might happen when the sky rained potatoes, he observed, "or when we get through Jarndyce and Jarndyce, Mr. Blowers;"—a pleasantry that particularly tickled the maces, bags, and purses.

How many people out of the suit, Jarndyce and Jarndyce has stretched forth its unwholesome hand to spoil and corrupt, would be a very wide question. From the master, upon whose impaling files reams of dusty warrants in Jarndyce and Jarndyce have grimly writhed into many shapes; down to the copying clerk in the Six Clerks' Office, who has copied his tens of thousands of Chancery-folio-pages under that eternal heading; no man's nature has been made the better by it. In trickery, evasion, procrastination, spoliation, botheration, under false pretences of all sorts, there are influences that can never come to good. The very solicitors' boys who have kept the wretched suitors at bay, by protesting time out of mind that Mr. Chizzle, Mizzle, or otherwise, was particularly engaged and had appointments until dinner, may have got an extra moral twist and shuffle into themselves out of Jarndyce and Jarndyce. The receiver in the cause has acquired a goodly sum of money by it, but has acquired too a distrust of his own mother, and a contempt for his own kind. Chizzle, Mizzle, and otherwise, have lapsed into a habit of vaguely promising themselves that they will look into that outstanding little matter, and see what can be done for Drizzle—who was not well used—when Jarndyce and Jarndyce shall be got out of the office. Shirking and sharking, in all their many varieties, have been sown broadcast by the ill-fated cause; and even those who have contemplated its history from the outermost circle of such evil, have been insensibly tempted into a loose way of letting bad things alone to take their own bad course, and a loose belief that if the world go wrong, it was, in some off-hand manner, never meant to go right.

Thus, in the midst of the mud and at the heart of the fog, sits the Lord High Chancellor in his High Court of Chancery.

"Mr. Tangle," says the Lord High Chancellor, latterly something restless under the eloquence of that learned gentleman.

"Mlud," says Mr. Tangle. Mr. Tangle knows more of Jarndyce and Jarndyce than anybody. He is famous for it—supposed never to have read anything else since he left school.

"Have you nearly concluded your argument?"

"Mlud, no—variety of points—feel it my duty tsubmit—ludship," is the reply that slides out of Mr. Tangle.

"Several members of the bar are still to be heard, I believe?" says the Chancellor, with a slight smile.

Eighteen of Mr. Tangle's learned friends, each armed with a little summary of eighteen hundred sheets, bob up like eighteen hammers in a piano-forte, make eighteen bows, and drop into their eighteen places of obscurity.

"We will proceed with the hearing on Wednesday fortnight," says the Chancellor. For, the question at issue is only a question of costs, a mere bud on the forest tree of the parent suit, and really will come to a settlement one of these days.

The Chancellor rises; the bar rises; the prisoner is brought forward in a hurry; the man from Shropshire cries, "My lord!" Maces, bags, and purses, indignantly proclaim silence, and frown at the man from Shropshire.

"In reference," proceeds the Chancellor, still on Jarndyce and Jarndyce, "to the young girl—"

"Begludship's pardon—boy," says Mr. Tangle, prematurely.

"In reference," proceeds the Chancellor, with extra distinctness, "to the young girl and boy, the two young people,"

(Mr. Tangle crushed.)

"Whom I directed to be in attendance to-day, and who are now in my private room, I will see them and satisfy myself as to the expediency of making the order for their residing with their uncle."

Mr. Tangle on his legs again.

"Begludship's pardon—dead."

"With their," Chancellor looking through his double eye-glass at the papers on his desk, "grandfather."

"Begludship's pardon—victim of rash action—brains."

Suddenly a very little counsel, with a terrific bass voice, arises, fully inflated, in the back settlements of the fog, and says, "Will your lordship allow me? I appear

Illustration 13-3 Illustration by H.K. Browne from Charles Dickens' *Bleak House* (1st ed., London, 1853), facing 388. [Author's Collection.] There are also dramatic illustrations in the book of "denaturalized" neighborhoods, like the London slum "Tom-all-Alone's," facing 442.

for him. He is a cousin, several times removed. I am not at the moment prepared to inform the Court in what exact remove he is a cousin; but he *is* a cousin."

Leaving this address (delivered like a sepulchral message) ringing in the rafters of the roof, the very little counsel drops, and the fog knows him no more. Everybody looks for him. Nobody can see him.

"I will speak with the both the young people," says the Chancellor anew, "and satisfy myself on the subject of their residing with their cousin. I will mention the matter to-morrow morning when I take my seat."

The Chancellor is about to bow to the bar, when the prisoner is presented. Nothing can possibly come of the prisoner's conglomeration, but his being sent back to prison; which is soon done. The man from Shropshire ventures another remonstrative "My lord!" but the Chancellor, being aware of him, has dexterously vanished. Everybody else quickly vanishes too. A battery of blue bags is loaded with heavy charges of papers and carried off by clerks; the little mad old woman marches off with her documents; the empty court is locked up. If all the injustice it has committed, and all the misery it has caused, could only be locked up with it, and the whole burnt away in a great funeral pyre, —why, so much the better for other parties than the parties in Jarndyce and Jarndyce!

UTILITARIANISM

Jeremy Bentham, *A Fragment on Government* (Published anonymously in 1776)
[Selected notes omitted]

A FRAGMENT ON GOVERNMENT
BEING AN EXAMINATION OF WHAT IS DELIVERED, ON
THE SUBJECT OF GOVERNMENT IN GENERAL,
IN THE INTRODUCTION TO
SIR WILLIAM BLACKSTONE'S COMMENTARIES
WITH A PREFACE
IN WHICH IS GIVEN
A CRITIQUE ON THE WORK AT LARGE

Rien ne recule plus le progès des connoissances, qu'un mauvais ouvrage d'un
Auteur célèbre: parce qu'avant d'instruire, il faut commencer par détromper.
MONTESQUIEU, Esprit des Loix, L. XXX, Ch. XV

A FRAGMENT ON GOVERNMENT
Introduction

1. The subject of this examination is a passage contained in that part of Sir W.
BLACKSTONE'S COMMENTARIES on the LAWS of ENGLAND, which the Author has
styled the INTRODUCTION. This Introduction of his stands divided into four Sections. The *first* contains his discourse '*On the* STUDY *of the* LAW.' The *second*, entitled "*Of the* NATURE *of* LAWS *in general*,' contains his speculations concerning the
various objects, real or imaginary, that are in use to be mentioned under the common name of LAW. The *third*, entitled '*Of the* LAWS *of* ENGLAND,' contains such
general observations, relative to these last mentioned Laws, as seemed proper to be
premised before he entered into the details of any parts of them in particular. In the
fourth, entitled, '*Of the* COUNTRIES *subject to the* LAWS *of* ENGLAND,' is given a
statement of the different territorial extents of different branches of those Laws.

2. 'Tis in the *second* of these sections, that we shall find the passage proposed
for examination. It occupies in the edition I happen to have before me, which is
the *first* (and all the editions, I believe, are paged alike) the space of *seven* pages;
from the 47th to the 53d, inclusive.

*   *   *   *

36. As to the Original Contract, by turns embraced and ridiculed by our Author, a few pages, perhaps, may not be ill bestowed in endeavouring to come to a
precise notion about its reality and use. The stress laid on it formerly, and still,
perhaps, by some, is such as renders it an object not undeserving of attention. I
was in hopes, however, till I observed the notice taken of it by our author, that
this chimera had been effectually demolished by Mr. HUME. I think we hear not
so much of it now as formerly. The indestructible prerogatives of mankind have
no need to be supported upon the sandy foundation of a fiction.

37. With respect to this, and other fictions, there was once a time, perhaps,
when they had their use. With instruments of this temper, I will not deny but that
some political work may have been done, and that useful work, which, under the
then circumstances of things, could hardly have been done with any other. But

the season of *Fiction* is now over: insomuch, that what formerly might have been tolerated and countenanced under that name, would, if now attempted to be set on foot, be censured and stigmatized under the harsher appellations of *incroachment* or *imposture*. To attempt to introduce any *new* one, would be *now* a crime: for which reason there is much danger, without any use, in vaunting and propagating such as have been introduced already. In point of political discernment, the universal spread of learning has raised mankind in a manner to a level with each other, in comparison of what they have been in any former time: nor is any man now so far elevated above his fellows, as that he should be indulged in the dangerous licence of cheating them for their good.

38. As to the fiction now before us, in the character of an *argumentum ad hominem* coming when it did, and managed as it was, it succeeded to admiration.

That compacts, by whomsoever entered into, *ought* to be kept; — that men are *bound* by compacts, are propositions which men, without knowing or enquiring why, were disposed universally to accede to. The observance of promises they had been accustomed to see pretty constantly enforced. They had been accustomed to see Kings, as well as others, behave themselves as if bound by them. This proposition, then, 'that men are bound by *compacts*,' and this other, 'that, if one party performs not his part, the other is released from his,' being propositions which no man disputed, were propositions which no man had any call to prove. In theory they were assumed for axioms: and in practice they were observed as rules.[1] If, on any occasion, it was thought proper to make a show of proving them, it was rather for form's sake than for any thing else: and that, rather in the way of memento or instruction to acquiescing auditors, than in the way of proof against opponents. On such an occasion the common place retinue of phrases was at hand; *Justice, Right Reason* required it, the *Law of Nature* commanded it, and so forth; all which are but so many ways of intimating that a man is firmly persuaded of the truth of this or that moral proposition, though he either thinks he *need not*, or finds he *can't* tell *why*. Men were too obviously and too generally interested in the observance of these rules to entertain doubts concerning the force of any arguments they saw employed in their support. — It is an old observation how Interest smooths the road to Faith.

39. A compact, then, it was said, was made by the King and people: the terms of it were to this effect. The people, on their part, promised to the King a *general obedience*. The King, on his part, promised to *govern* the people in such a *particular* manner always, as should be *subservient* to their happiness. I insist not on the words: I undertake only for the sense; as far as an imaginary engagement, so loosely and so variously worded by those who have imagined it, is capable of any decided signification. Assuming then, as a general rule, that promises, when made, ought to be observed; and, as a point of fact, that a promise to this effect in particular had been made by the party in question, men were more ready to deem themselves qualified to judge when it was such a promise was *broken*, than to decide directly and avowedly on the delicate question, when it was that a King acted so far in *opposition* to the happiness of his people, that it were better no longer to obey him.

---

1. 1 Comm., p. 47.

40. It is manifest, on a very little consideration, that nothing was gained by this manoeuvre after all: no difficulty removed by it. It was still necessary, and that as much as ever, that the question men studied to avoid should be determined, in order to determine the question they thought to substitute in its room. It was still necessary to determine, whether the King in question had, or had not acted so far in *opposition* to the happiness of his people, that it were better no longer to obey him; in order to determine, whether the promise he was supposed to have made, had, or had not been broken. For what was the supposed purport of this promise? It was no other than what had just been mentioned.

*   *   *   *

13. This is not all. The most emphatical passage is yet behind. It is a passage in that short paragraph[2] which we found to contain such a variety of matter. He is there speaking of the several forms of government now in being. 'However they began,' says he, 'or by what right soever they subsist, there *is* and *must be* in all of them a *supreme, irresistible, absolute, uncontrolled* authority, in which the *jura summi imperii*, or the rights of sovereignty, reside.'

14. The vehemence... of this passage is remarkable. He ransacks the language: he piles up, one upon another, four of the most tremendous epithets he can find; he heaps Ossa upon Pelion: and, as if the English tongue did not furnish expressions strong or imposing enough, he tops the whole with a piece of formidable Latinity. From all this agitation, it is plain, I think, there is a something which he has very much at heart; which he wishes, but fears, perhaps, to bring out undisguised; which in several places, notwithstanding, bursts out involuntarily, as it were, before he is well ready for it; and which, a certain discretion, getting at last the upper hand of propensity, forces, as we have seen, to dribble away in a string of obscure sophisms. Thus oddly enough it happens, that that passage of them all, which, if I mistake not, is the only one that was meant to be dedicated expressly to the subject, is the least explicit on it.[3]

15. A courage much stauncher than our Author's might have wavered here. A task of no less intricacy was here to be travelled through, than that of adjusting the claims of those two jealous antagonists, Liberty and Government. A more invidious ground is scarcely to be found any where within the field of politics. Enemies encompass the traveller on every side. He can scarce stir but he must expect to be assaulted with the war-whoop of political heresy from one quarter or another. Difficult enough is the situation of him, who, in these defiles, feels himself impelled one way by fear, and another by affection.

16. To return to the paragraph which it was the more immediate business of this chapter to examine:—Were the path of obscurity less familiar to our Author, one should be tempted to imagine he had struck into it on the particular occasion before us, in the view of extricating himself from this dilemma. A discourse thus prudently indeterminate might express enough to keep fair with the rulers of the earth, without setting itself in direct array against the prejudices of the people. Viewed by different persons, it might present different aspects: to men in power

---

2. 1 Comm., p. 48, supra, ch. 11, par. 11.

3. Another passage or two there is which might seem to glance the same way: but these I pass over as less material, after those which we have seen.

it might recommend itself, and that from the first, under the character of a practical lesson of obedience for the use of the people; while among the people themselves it might pass muster, for a time at least, in quality of a string of abstract scientific propositions of jurisprudence. It is not till some occasion for making application of it should occur, that its true use and efficacy would be brought to light. The people, no matter on what occasion, begin to murmur, and concert measures of resistance. Now then is the time for the latent virtues of this passage to be called forth. The book is to be opened to them, and in this passage they are to be shewn, what of themselves, perhaps they would never have observed, a set of arguments curiously strung together and wrapped up, in proof of the universal expedience, or rather *necessity*, of submission: a necessity which is to arise, not out of the reflection that *the probable mischiefs of resistance are greater than the probable mischiefs of obedience*; not out of any such debatable consideration; but out of a something that is to be much more cogent and effectual: to wit, a certain *metaphysico-legal* impotence, which is to beget in them the sentiment, and answer all the purposes of a natural one. Armed, and full of indignation, our malcontents are making their way to the royal palace. In vain. A certain *estoppel* being made to bolt out upon them, in the manner we have seen, by the force of our Author's legal engineering, their arms are to fall, as it were by enchantment, from their hands. To disagree, to clamour, to oppose, to take back, in short, their wills again, is now, they are told, too late: it is what *can*not be done: their wills have been put in *hotchpot* along with the rest: they *have* 'united,'—they *have* 'consented,'—they *have* 'submitted.'—Our Author having thus *put his hook into their nose*, they are to go back as they came, and all is peace. An ingenious contrivance this enough: but popular passion is not to be fooled, I doubt, so easily. Now and then, it is true, one error may be driven out, for a time, by an opposite error: one piece of nonsense by another piece of nonsense: but for barring the door effectually and for ever against all error and all nonsense, there is nothing like the simple truth.

17. After all these pains taken to inculcate unreserved submission, would any one have expected to see our Author himself among the most eager to excite men to disobedience? and that, perhaps, upon the most frivolous pretences? in short, upon any pretence whatsoever? Such, however, upon looking back a little, we shall find him. I say, among the most eager; for other men, at least the most enlightened advocates for liberty, are content with leaving it to subjects to resist, for their own sakes, on the footing of *permission*: this will not content our Author, but he must be forcing it upon them as a point of *duty*.

18. 'Tis in a passage antecedent to the digression we are examining, but in the same section, that, speaking of the pretended law of Nature, and of the law of revelation, 'no human laws,' he says, 'should be *suffered* to contradict these.'[4] The expression is remarkable. It is not that no human laws should contradict them: but that no human laws should be SUFFERED to contradict them. He then proceeds to give us an example. This example, one might think, would be such as should have the effect of softening the dangerous tendency of the rule: —on the contrary, it is such as cannot but enhance it; and, in the application of it to the

---

4. 1 Comm., p. 42.

rule, the substance of the latter is again repeated in still more explicit and ener-getic terms. 'Nay,' says he, speaking of the act he instances, 'if any human law should allow or enjoin us to commit it, we are BOUND TO TRANSGRESS that human law, or else we must offend both the natural and the divine.'

19. The propriety of this dangerous maxim, so far as the Divine Law is con-cerned, is what I must refer to a future occasion for more particular considera-tion. As to the LAW *of Nature*, if (as I trust it will appear) it be nothing but a phrase; if there be no other medium for proving any act to be an offence against it, than the mischievous tendency of such act; if there be no other medium for proving a law of the *state* to be contrary to it, than the *inexpediency* of such law, unless the bare unfounded disapprobation of any one who thinks of it be called a proof; if a test for distinguishing such laws as would be *contrary* to the LAW *of Nature* from such as, *without* being contrary to it, are simply *inexpedient*, be that which neither our Author, nor any man else, so much as pretended ever to give; if, in a word, there be scarce any law whatever but what those who have not liked it have found, on some account or another, to be repugnant to some text of scripture; I see no remedy but that the natural tendency of such doctrine is to impel a man, by the force of conscience, to rise up in arms against any law whatever that he happens not to like. What sort of government it is that can con-sist with such a disposition, I must leave to our Author to inform us.

20. It is the principle of *utility*, accurately apprehended and steadily applied, that affords the only clue to guide a man through these straits. It is for that, if any, and for that alone to furnish a decision which neither party shall dare in *the-ory* to disavow. It is something to reconcile men even in theory. They are at least, *something* nearer to an effectual union, than when at variance as well in respect of theory as of practice.

21. In speaking of the supposed contract between King and people,[5] I have al-ready had occasion to give the description, and, as it appears to me, the only *gen-eral* description that *can* be given, of that juncture at which, and not before, re-sistance to government becomes *commendable*; or, in other words, reconcilable to just notions, whether of *legal* or not, at least of *moral*, and, if there be any dif-ference, *religious* duty.[6] What was there said was spoken, at the time, with refer-ence to that particular branch of government which was then in question; the branch that in this country is administered by the King. But if it was just, as ap-plied to *that* branch of government, and in *this* country, it could only be for the same reason that it is so when applied to the *whole* of government, and that in *any* country whatsoever. It is *then*, we may say, and not till then, allowable to, if not incumbent on, every man as well on the score of *duty* as of *interest*, to enter into measures of resistance; when, according to the best calculation he is able to make, *the probable mischiefs of resistance* (speaking with respect to the commu-nity in general) *appear less to him than the probable mischiefs of submission.* This then is to him, that is to each man in particular, the *juncture for resistance.*

22. A natural question here is — by what *sign* shall this juncture be known? By what *common* signal alike conspicuous and perceptible to all? A question which is readily enough started, but to which, I hope, it will be almost as readily per-

---

5. Ch. I.
6. See Ch. V. par. 7.

ceived that it is impossible to find an answer. *Common* sign for such a purpose, I, for my part, know of none: he must be more than a prophet, I think, that can shew us one. For that which shall serve a particular person, I have already given one—his own internal persuasion of a balance of *utility* on the side of resistance.

23. Unless such a sign then, which I think impossible, can be shewn, the *field*, if one may say so, of the supreme governor's authority, though not *infinite*, must unavoidably, I think, *unless where limited by express convention,*[7] be allowed to be *indefinite*. Nor can I see any narrower, or other bounds to it, under this constitution, or under any other yet *freer* constitution, if there be one, than under the most *despotic. Before* the juncture I have been describing were arrived, resistance, even in a country like this, would come too soon: were the juncture arrived *already*, the time for resistance would be come already under such a government even as any one should call *despotic*.

24. In regard to a government that is *free*, and one that is *despotic*, wherein is it then that the difference consists? Is it that those persons in whose hands that power is lodged which is acknowledged to be supreme, have less power in the one than in the other, when it is from custom that they derive it? By no means. It is not that the power of one any more than of the other has any certain bounds to it. The distinction turns upon circumstances of a very different complexion:—on the manner in which that whole mass of power, which, taken together, is supreme, is, in a free state, *distributed* among the several ranks of persons that are sharers in it: —on the *source* from whence their titles to it are successively derived: —on the frequent and easy *changes* of condition between govern*ors* and govern*ed*; whereby the interests of the one class are more or less indistinguishably blended with those of the other: —on the *responsibility* of the governors; or the right which a subject has of having the reasons publicly assigned and canvassed of every act of power that is exerted over him:—on the *liberty of the press*; or the security with which every man, be he of the one class or the other, may make known his complaints and remonstrances to the whole community:—on *the liberty of public association*; or the security with which malcontents may communicate their sentiments, concert their plans, and practise every mode of opposition short of actual revolt, before the executive power can be legally justified in disturbing them.

25. True then, it may be, that, owing to this last circumstance in particular, in a state thus circumstanced, the road to a revolution, if a revolution be necessary, is to appearance shorter; certainly more smooth and easy. More likelihood, certainly there is of its being such a revolution as shall be the work of a number; and in which, therefore, the interests of a number are likely to be consulted. Grant then, that by reason of these facilitating circumstances, the juncture itself may arrive sooner, and upon less provocation, under what it called a *free* government, than under what is called an *absolute* one: grant this; —yet till it *be* arrived, resistance is as much too soon under one of them as under the other.

26. Let us avow then, in short, steadily but calmly, what our Author hazards with anxiety and agitation, that the authority of the supreme body cannot, *unless where limited by express convention*, be said to have any assignable, any certain

---

7. This respects the case where one state, has, upon *terms*, submitted itself to the government of another: or where the governing bodies of a number of states agree to take directions in certain specified cases, from some *body* or other that is distinct from all of them: consisting of members, for instance, appointed out of each.

bounds. — That to say there is any act they *cannot* do, — to speak of any thing of theirs as being *illegal*, — as being *void*; — to speak of their exceeding their *authority* (whatever be the phrase) — their *power*, their *right*, — is, however common, an abuse of language.

27. The legislature *cannot* do it? The legislature *cannot* make a law to this effect? Why cannot? What is there that should hinder them? Why not this, as well as so many other laws murmured at, perhaps, as inexpedient, yet submitted to without any question of the *right*? With men of the same party, with men whose affections are already lifted against the law in question, any thing will go down: any rubbish is good that will add fuel to the flame. But with regard to an impartial bystander, it is plain that it is not denying the right of the legislature, their *authority*, their *power*, or whatever be the word — it is not denying that they *can* do what is in question — it is not that, I say, or any discourse verging that way that can tend to give *him* the smallest satisfaction.

28. Grant even the proposition in general: — What are we the nearer? Grant that there *are* certain bounds to the *authority* of the legislature: — Of what use is it to say so, when these bounds are what no body has ever attempted to mark out to any useful purpose; that is, in any such manner whereby it might be known beforehand what description a law must be of to fall *within*, and what to fall *beyond* them? Grant that there *are* things which the legislature *cannot* do; — grant that there *are* laws which exceed the *power* of the legislature to establish. What rule does this sort of discourse furnish us for determining whether any one that is in question is, or is not of the number? As far as I can discover, none. Either the discourse goes on in the confusion it began; either all rests in vague assertions, and no intelligible argument at all is offered; or if any, such arguments as are drawn from the principle of *utility*: arguments which, in whatever variety of words expressed, come at last to neither more nor less than this: that the tendency of the law is, to a greater or a less degree, pernicious. If this then be the result of the argument, why not come home to it at once? Why turn aside into a wilderness of sophistry, when the path of plain reason is straight before us?

INSTRUMENTALISM

Commonwealth vs. John Hunt & Others.
4 Metc. 111 (1842), 112–136.

This was an indictment against the defendants, (seven in number,) for a conspiracy. The first count alleged that the defendants, together with divers other persons unknown to the grand jurors, "on the first Monday of September 1840, at Boston, being workmen and journeymen in the art and manual occupation of boot-makers, unlawfully, perniciously and deceitfully designing and intending to continue, keep up, form, and unite themselves into an unlawful club, society and combination, and make unlawful by-laws, rules and orders among themselves, and thereby govern themselves and other workmen in said art, and unlawfully and unjustly to extort great sums of money by means thereof, did unlawfully assemble and meet together, and, being so assembled, did then and there unjustly and corruptly combine, confederate and agree together, that none of them should thereafter, and that none of them would, work for any master or person whatsoever, in the said art, mystery or occupation, who should employ any workman or journeyman, or

Illustration 13-4 A rally on April 10, 1848 on Kennington Common. These are "chartists," dedicated to universal manhood suffrage, equal electoral districts, and abolition of property qualification for MPs. Early union cases like *Commonwealth v. Hunt*, 4 Metc. 111 (1842), *infra*, whether in America or England, have to be seen against this political backdrop. W.E. Kilburn. Courtesy The Royal Archives, Windsor Castle. © Her Majesty Elizabeth II.

other person, in the said art, who was not a member of said club, society or combination, after notice given him to discharge such workman from the employ of such
master; to the great damage and oppression, not only of their said masters employing them in said art and occupation, but also of divers other workmen and journeymen in the said art, mystery and occupation; to the evil example of all others in
like case offending, and against the peace and dignity of the Commonwealth."

The second count charged that the defendants, and others unknown, at the
time and place mentioned in the first count, "did unlawfully assemble, meet, conspire, confederate and agree together, not to work for any master or person who
should employ any workman not being a member of a club, society or combination, called the Boston Journeymen Bootmakers' Society in Boston, in Massachusetts, or who should break any of their by-laws, unless such workman should
pay to said club and society such sum as should be agreed upon as a penalty for
the breach of such unlawful rules, orders and by-laws; and by means of said conspiracy, they did compel one Isaac B. Wait, a master cordwainer in said Boston,
to turn out of his employ one Jeremiah Horne, a journeyman boot-maker, because said Horne would not pay a sum of money to said society for an alleged
penalty of some of said unjust rules, orders and by-laws."

The third count averred that the defendants and others unknown, "wickedly
and unjustly intending unlawfully, and by indirect means, to impoverish one Jeremiah Horne, a journeyman boot-maker, and hinder him from following his
trade, did" (at the time and place mentioned in the former counts) "unlawfully
conspire, combine, confederate and agree together, by wrongful and indirect
means to impoverish said Horne, and to deprive and hinder him from following
his said art and trade of a journeyman boot-maker, and from getting his livelihood and support thereby;"

*   *   *   *

SHAW, C.J. Considerable time has elapsed since the argument of this case. It
has been retained long under advisement, partly because we were desirous of examining, with some attention, the great number of cases cited at the argument,
and others which have presented themselves in course, and partly because we
considered it a question of great importance to the Commonwealth, and one
which had been much examined and considered by the learned judge of the municipal court.

We have no doubt, that by the operation of the constitution of this Commonwealth, the general rules of the common law, making conspiracy an indictable offence, are in force here, and that this is included in the description of laws which
had, before the adoption of the constitution, been used and approved in the
Province, Colony, or State of Massachusetts Bay, and usually practised in the
courts of law. Const. Of Mass. c, VI. §6. It was so held in *Commonwealth v.
Boynton,* and *Commonwealth v. Pierpont,* cases decided before reports of cases
were regularly published, and in many cases since. *Commonwealth v. Ward,* 1
Mass. 473. *Commonwealth v. Judd,* and *Commonwealth v. Tibbetts,* 2 Mass.
329, 536. *Commonwealth v. Warren,* 6 Mass. 74. Still, it is proper in this connexion to remark, that although the common law in regard to conspiracy in this
Commonwealth is in force, yet it will not necessarily follow that every indictment at common law for this offence is a precedent for a similar indictment in
this State. The general rule of the common law is, that it is a criminal and in-

dictable offence, for two or more to confederate and combine together, by concerted means, to do that which is unlawful or criminal, to the injury of the public, or portions or classes of the community, or even to the rights of an individual. This rule of law may be equally in force as a rule of the common law, in
England and in this Commonwealth; and yet it must depend upon the local laws
of each country to determine, whether the purpose to be accomplished by the
combination, or the concerted means of accomplishing it, be unlawful or criminal in the respective countries. All those laws of the parent country, whether rules
of the common law, or early English statutes, which were made for the purpose
of regulating the wages of laborers, the settlement of paupers, and making it
penal for any one to use a trade or handicraft to which he had not served a full
apprenticeship — not being adapted to the circumstances of our colonial condition — were not adopted, used or approved, and therefore do not come within
the description of the laws adopted and confirmed by the provision of the constitution already cited. This consideration will do something towards reconciling
the English and American cases, and may indicate how far the principles of the
English cases will apply in this Commonwealth, and show why a conviction in
England, in many cases, would not be a precedent for a like conviction here. *The
King v. Journeymen Tailors of Cambridge*, 8 Mod. 10, for instance, is commonly
cited as an authority for an indictment at common law, and a conviction of journeymen mechanics of a conspiracy to raise their wages. It was there held, that the
indictment need not conclude *contra formam statuti*, because the gist of the offence was the conspiracy, which was an offence at common law. At the same
time it was conceded, that the unlawful object to be accomplished was the raising of wages above the rate fixed by a general act of parliament. It was therefore
a conspiracy to violate a general statute law, made for the regulation of a large
branch of trade, affecting the comfort and interest of the public; and thus the object to be accomplished by the conspiracy was unlawful, if not criminal.

But the rule of law, that an illegal conspiracy, whatever may be the facts which
constitute it, is an offence punishable by the laws of this Commonwealth, is established as well by legislative as by judicial authority. Like many other cases, that of
murder, for instance, it leaves the definition or description of the offence to the
common law, and provides modes for its prosecution and punishment. The Revised Statutes, *c.* 82, §28, and *c.* 86, §10, allowed an appeal from the court of
common pleas and the municipal court, respectively, in cases of a conviction for
conspiracy, and thereby recognized it as one of the class of offences, so difficult of
investigation, or so aggravated in their nature and punishment, as to render it fit
that the party accused should have the benefit of a trial before the highest court of
the Commonwealth. And though this right of appeal is since taken away, by *St.* of
1839, *c.* 161, this does not diminish the force of the evidence tending to show that
the offence is known and recognized by the legislature as a high indictable offence.

But the great difficulty is, in framing any definition or description, to be drawn
from the decided cases, which shall specifically identify this offence — a description broad enough to include all cases punishable under this description, without
including acts which are not punishable. Without attempting to review and reconcile all the cases, we are of opinion, that as a general description, though perhaps not a precise and accurate definition, a conspiracy must be a combination
of two or more persons, by some concerted action, to accomplish some criminal
or unlawful purpose, or to accomplish some purpose, not in itself criminal or un-

lawful, by criminal or unlawful means. We use the terms criminal or unlawful, because it is manifest that many acts are unlawful, which are not punishable by indictment or other public prosecution; and yet there is no doubt, we think, that a combination by numbers to do them would be an unlawful conspiracy, and punishable by indictment. Of this character was a conspiracy to cheat by false pretences, without false tokens, when a cheat by false pretences only, by a single person, was not a punishable offence. *Commonwealth v. Boynton*, before referred to. So a combination to destroy the reputation of an individual, by verbal calumny which is not indictable. So a conspiracy to induce and persuade a young female, by false representations, to leave the protection of her parent's house, with a view to facilitate her prostitution. *Rex v. Lord Grey*, 3 Hargrave's State Trials, 519.

But yet it is clear, that it is not every combination to do unlawful acts, to the prejudice of another by a concerted action, which is punishable as conspiracy. Such was the case of *The King v. Turner*, 13 East, 228, which was a combination to commit a trespass on the land of another, though alleged to be with force, and by striking terror by carrying offensive weapons in the night. The conclusion to which Mr. Chitty comes, in his elaborate work on *Criminal Law*, Vol. III. p. 1140, after an enumeration of the leading authorities, is, that "we can rest, therefore, only on the individual cases decided, which depend, in general, on particular circumstances, and which are not to be extended."

The American cases are not much more satisfactory. The leading one is that of *Lambert v. People of New York*, 9 Cow. 578. On the principal point, the court of errors were equally divided, and the case was decided in favor of the plaintiff in error, who had been convicted before the supreme court, by the casting vote of the president. The principal question was, whether an indictment, charging that several persons, intending unlawfully, by indirect means, to cheat and defraud an incorporated company, and divers others unknown, of their effects, did fraudulently and unlawfully conspire together, injuriously and unjustly, by wrongful and indirect means, to cheat and defraud the company and others of divers effects, and that, in execution thereof, they did, by certain undue, indirect and unlawful means, cheat and defraud the company, &c. was a good and valid indictment. As two distinguished senators, and members of the court of errors, took different sides of this question, the subject was fully and elaborately discussed; the authorities were all reviewed; and the case may be referred to, as a full and able exposition of the learning on the subject.

Let us, then, first consider how the subject of criminal conspiracy is treated by elementary writers. The position cited by Chitty from Hawkins, by way of summing up the result of the cases, is this: "In a word, all confederacies wrongfully to prejudice another are misdemeanors at common law, whether the intention is to injure his property, his person, or his character." And Chitty adds, that "the object of conspiracy is not confined to an immediate wrong to individuals; it may be to injure public trade, to affect public health, to violate public police, to insult public justice, or to do any act in itself illegal." 3 Chit. Crim. Law, 1139.

Several rules upon the subject seem to be well established, to wit, that the unlawful agreement constitutes the gist of the offence, and therefore that it is not necessary to charge the execution of the unlawful agreement. *Commonwealth v. Judd*, 2 Mass. 337. And when such execution is charged, it is to be regarded as proof of the intent, or as an aggravation of the criminality of the unlawful combination.

Another rule is a necessary consequence of the former, which is, that the crime is consummate and complete by the fact of unlawful combination, and, therefore, that if the execution of the unlawful purpose is averred, it is by way of aggravation, and proof of it is not necessary to conviction; and therefore the jury may find the conspiracy, and negative the execution, and it will be a good conviction.

And it follows, as another necessary legal consequence, from the same principle, that the indictment must — by averring the unlawful purpose of the conspiracy, or the unlawful means by which it is contemplated and agreed to accomplish a lawful purpose, or a purpose not of itself criminally punishable — set out an offence complete in itself, without the aid of any averment of illegal acts done in pursuance of such an agreement; and that an illegal combination, imperfectly and insufficiently set out in the indictment, will not be aided by averments of acts done in pursuance of it.

From this view of the law respecting conspiracy, we think it an offence which especially demands the application of that wise and humane rule of the common law, that an indictment shall state, with as much certainty as the nature of the case will admit, the facts which constitute the crime intended to be charged. This is required, to enable the defendant to meet the charge and prepare for his defence, and, in case of acquittal or conviction, to show by the record the identity of the charge, so that he may not be indicted a second time for the same offence. It is also necessary in order that a person, charged by the grand jury for one offence, may not substantially be convicted, on his trial, of another. This fundamental rule is confirmed by the Declaration of Rights, which declares that no subject shall be held to answer for any crime or offence, until the same is fully and plainly, substantially and formally described to him.

From these views of the rules of criminal pleading, it appears to us to follow, as a necessary legal conclusion, that when the criminality of a conspiracy consists in an unlawful agreement of two or more persons to compass or promote some criminal or illegal purpose, that purpose must be fully and clearly stated in the indictment; and if the criminality of the offence, which is intended to be charged, consists in the agreement to compass or promote some purpose, not of itself criminal or unlawful, by the use of fraud, force, falsehood, or other criminal or unlawful means, such intended use of fraud, force, falsehood, or other criminal or unlawful means, must be set out in the indictment. Such, we think, is, on the whole, the result of the English authorities, although they are not quite uniform. 1 *East P.C.* 461. 1 *Stark. Crim. Pl.* (2d ed.) 156. *Opinion of Spencer, Senator*, 9 *Cow.* 586, & *seq.*

In the case of a conspiracy to induce a person to marry a pauper, in order to change the burden of her support from one parish to another, it was held by Buller, J. that, as the marriage itself was not unlawful, some violence, fraud or falsehood, or some artful or sinister contrivance must be averred, as the means intended to be employed to effect the marriage, in order to make the agreement indictable as a conspiracy. *Rex v. Fowler*, 2 *Russell on Crimes*, (1st ed.) 1812 S.C. 1 *East P.C.* 461.

Perhaps the cases of *The King v. Eccles*, 3 Doug. 337, and *The King v. Gill*, 2 Barn. & Ald. 204, cited and relied on as having a contrary tendency, may be reconciled with the current of cases, and the principle on which they are founded, by the fact, that the court did consider that the indictment set forth a criminal, or at least an unlawful purpose, and so rendered it unnecessary to set forth the means; because a confederacy to accomplish such purpose, by any means, must be considered an indictable conspiracy, and so the averment of any intended means was not necessary.

With these general views of the law, it becomes necessary to consider the circumstances of the present case, as they appear from the indictment itself, and from the bill of exceptions filed and allowed.

One of the exceptions, though not the first in the order of time, yet by far the most important, was this:

The counsel for the defendants contended, and requested the court to instruct the jury, that the indictment did not set forth any agreement to do a criminal act, or to do any lawful act by any specified criminal means, and that the agreements therein set forth did not constitute a conspiracy indictable by any law of this Commonwealth. But the judge refused so to do, and instructed the jury, that the indictment did, in his opinion, describe a confederacy among the defendants to do an unlawful act, and to effect the same by unlawful means; that the society, organized and associated for the purposes described in the indictment, was an unlawful conspiracy, against the laws of this Commonwealth; and that if the jury believed, from the evidence in the case, that the defendants, or any of them, had engaged in such a confederacy, they were bound to find such of them guilty.

We are here carefully to distinguish between the confederacy set forth in the indictment, and the confederacy or association contained in the constitution of the Boston Journeymen Bootmakers' Society, as stated in the little printed book, which was admitted as evidence on the trial. Because, though, it was thus admitted as evidence, it would not warrant a conviction for any thing not stated in the indictment. It was proof, as far as it went to support the averments in the indictments. If it contained any criminal matter not set forth in the indictment, it is of no avail. The question then presents itself in the same form as on motion in arrest of judgment.

The first count set forth, that the defendants, with divers others unknown, on the day and at the place named, being workmen, and journeymen, in the art and occupation of bootmakers, unlawfully, perniciously and deceitfully designing and intending to continue, keep up, form, and unite themselves, into an unlawful club, society and combination, and make unlawful by-laws, rules and orders among themselves, and thereby govern themselves and other workmen, in the said art, and unlawfully and unjustly to extort great sums of money by means thereof, did unlawfully assemble and meet together, and being so assembled, did unjustly and corruptly conspire, combine, confederate and agree together, that none of them should thereafter, and that none of them would, work for any master or person whatsoever, in the said art, mystery and occupation, who should employ any workman or journeyman, or other person, in the said art, who was not a member of said club, society or combination, after notice given him to discharge such workman, from the employ of such master; to the great damage and oppression, &c.

Now it is to be considered, that the preamble and introductory matter in the indictment—such as unlawfully and deceitfully designing and intending unjustly to extort great sums, &c.—is mere recital, and not traversable, and therefore cannot aid an imperfect averment of the facts constituting the description of the offence. The same may be said of the concluding matter, which follows the averment, as to the great damage and oppression not only of their said masters, employing them in said art and occupation, but also of divers other workmen in the same art, mystery and occupation, to the evil example, &c. If the facts averred constitute the crime, these are properly stated as the legal inferences to be drawn from them. If they do not constitute the charge of such an offence, they cannot be aided by these alleged consequences.

Stripped then of these introductory recitals and alleged injurious consequences, and of the qualifying epithets attached to the facts, the averment is this; that the defendants and others formed themselves into a society, and agreed not to work for any person, who should employ any journeyman or other person, not a member of such society, after notice given him to discharge such workman.

The manifest intent of the association is, to induce all those engaged in the same occupation to become members of it. Such a purpose is not unlawful. It would give them a power which might be exerted for useful and honorable purposes, or for dangerous and pernicious ones. If the latter were the real and actual object, and susceptible of proof, it should have been specially charged. Such an association might be used to afford each other assistance in times of poverty, sickness and distress; or to raise their intellectual, moral and social condition; or to make improvement in their art; or for other proper purposes. Or the association might be designed for purposes of oppression and injustice. But in order to charge all those, who become members of an association, with the guilt of a criminal conspiracy, it must be averred and proved that the actual, if not the avowed object of the association, was criminal. An association may be formed, the declared objects of which are innocent and laudable, and yet they may have secret articles, or an agreement communicated only to the members, by which they are banded together for purposes injurious to the peace of society or the rights of its members. Such would undoubtedly be a criminal conspiracy, on proof of the fact, however meritorious and praiseworthy and declared objects might be. The law is not to be hoodwinked by colorable pretences. It looks at truth and reality, through whatever disguise it may assume. But to make such an association, ostensibly innocent, the subject of prosecution as a criminal conspiracy, the secret agreement, which makes it so, is to be averred and proved as the gist of the offence. But when an association is formed for purposes actually innocent, and afterwards its powers are abused, by those who have the control and management of it, to purposes of oppression and injustice, it will be criminal in those who thus misuse it, or give consent thereto, but not in the other members of the association. In this case, no such secret agreement, varying the objects of the association from those avowed, is set forth in this count of the indictment.

Nor can we perceive that the objects of this association, whatever they may have been, were to be attained by criminal means. The means which they proposed to employ, as averred in this count, and which, as we are now to presume, were established by the proof, were, that they would not work for a person, who, after due notice, should employ a journeyman not a member of their society. Supposing the object of the association to be laudable and lawful, or at least not unlawful, are these means criminal? The case supposes that these persons are not bound by contract, but free to work for whom they please, or not to work, if they so prefer. In this state of things, we cannot perceive, that it is criminal for men to agree together to exercise their own acknowledged rights, in such a manner as best to subserve their own interests. One way to test this is, to consider the effect of such an agreement, where the object of the association is acknowledged on all hands to be a laudable one. Suppose a class of workmen, impressed with the manifold evils of intemperance, should agree with each other not to work in a shop in which ardent spirit was furnished, or not to work in a shop with any one who used it, or not to work for an employer, who should, after notice, employ a journeyman who habitually used it. The consequences might be the same. A workman, who should still persist in the use of ardent spirit, would find it more difficult to get employment; a master employing such an one might, at times, experience inconvenience in his work, in losing the services of a skilful but intemperate workman. Still it seems to us, that as the object would be lawful, and the means not unlawful, such an agreement could not be pronounced a criminal conspiracy.

From this count in the indictment, we do not understand that the agreement was, that the defendants would refuse to work for an employer, to whom they were bound by contract for a certain time, in violation of that contract; nor that they would insist that an employer should discharge a workman engaged by contract for a certain time, in violation of such contract. It is perfectly consistent with every thing stated in this count, that the effect of the agreement was, that when they were free to act, they would not engage with an employer, or continue in his employment, if such employer, when free to act, should engage with a workman, or continue a workman in his employment, not a member of the association. If a large number of men, engaged for a certain time, should combine together to violate their contract, and quit their employment together, it would present a very different question. Suppose a farmer, employing a large number of men, engaged for the year, at fair monthly wages, and suppose that just at the moment that his crops were ready to harvest, they should all combine to quit his service, unless he would advance their wages, at a time when other laborers could not be obtained. It would surely be a conspiracy to do an unlawful act, though of such a character, that if done by an individual, it would lay the foundation of a civil action only, and not of a criminal prosecution. It would be a case very different from that stated in this count.

The second count, omitting the recital of unlawful intent and evil disposition, and omitting the direct averment of an unlawful club or society, alleges that the defendants, with others unknown, did assemble, conspire, confederate and agree together, not to work for any master or person who should employ any workman not being a member of a certain club, society or combination, called the Boston Journeymen Bootmaker's Society, or who should break any of their by-laws, unless such workmen should pay to said club, such sum as should be agreed upon as a penalty for the breach of such unlawful rules, &c.; and that by means of said conspiracy they did compel one Isaac B. Wait, a master cordwainer, to turn out of his employ one Jeremiah Horne, a journeyman boot-maker, &c. in evil example, &c. So far as the averment of a conspiracy is concerned, all the remarks made in reference to the first count are equally applicable to this. It is simply an averment of an agreement amongst themselves not to work for a person, who should employ any person not a member of a certain association. It sets forth no illegal or criminal purpose to be accomplished, nor any illegal or criminal means to be adopted for the accomplishment of any purpose. It was an agreement, as to the manner in which they would exercise an acknowledged right to contract with others for their labor. It does not aver a conspiracy or even an intention to raise their wages; and it appears by the bill of exceptions, that the case was not put upon the footing of a conspiracy to raise their wages. Such an agreement, as set forth in this count, would be perfectly justifiable under the recent English statute, by which this subject is regulated. *St.* 6 Geo. IV. *c.* 129. See *Roscoe Crim. Ev.* (2d Amer. Ed.) 368, 369.

As to the latter part of this count, which avers that by means of said conspiracy, the defendants did compel one Wait to turn out of his employ one Jeremiah Horne, we remark, in the first place, that as the acts done in pursuance of a conspiracy, as we have before seen, are stated by way of aggravation, and not as a substantive charge; if no criminal or unlawful conspiracy is stated, it cannot be aided and made good by mere matter of aggravation. If the principal charge falls, the aggravation falls with it. *State v. Rickey,* 4 Halst. 293.

But further; if this is to be considered as a substantive charge, it would depend altogether upon the force of the word "compel," which may be used in the sense of coercion, or duress, by force or fraud. It would therefore depend upon the context and the connexion with other words, to determine the sense in which it was used in the indictment. If, for instance, the indictment had averred a conspiracy, by the defendants, to compel Wait to turn Horne out of his employment, and to accomplish that object by the use of force or fraud, it would have been a very different case; especially if it might be fairly construed, as perhaps in that case it might have been, that Wait was under obligation, by contract, for an unexpired term of time, to employ and pay Horne. As before remarked, it would have been a conspiracy to do an unlawful, though not a criminal act, to induce Wait to violate his engagement, to the actual injury of Horne. To mark the difference between the case of a journeyman or a servant and master, mutually bound by contract, and the same parties when free to engage anew, I should have before cited the case of the *Boston Glass Co. v. Binney,* 4 Pick. 425. In that case, it was held actionable to entice another person's hired servant to quit his employment, during the time for which he was engaged; but not actionable to treat with such hired servant, whilst actually hired and employed by another, to leave his service, and engage in the employment of the person making the proposal, when the term for which he is engaged shall expire. It acknowledges the established principle, that every free man, whether skilled laborer, mechanic, farmer or domestic servant, may work or not work, or work or refuse to work with any company or individual, at his own option, except so far as he is bound by contract. But whatever might be the force of the word "compel," unexplained by its connexion, it is disarmed and rendered harmless by the precise statement of the means, by which such compulsion was to be effected. It was the agreement not to work for him, by which they compelled Wait to decline employing Horne longer. On both of these grounds, we are of opinion that the statement made in this second count, that the unlawful agreement was carried into execution, makes no essential difference between this and the first count.

The third count, reciting a wicked and unlawful intent to impoverish one Jeremiah Horne, and hinder him from following his trade as a boot-maker, charges the defendants, with others unknown, with an unlawful conspiracy, by wrongful and indirect means, to impoverish said Horne and to deprive and hinder him, from his said art and trade and getting his support thereby, and that, in pursuance of said unlawful combination, they did unlawfully and indirectly hinder and prevent, &c. and greatly impoverish him.

If the fact of depriving Jeremiah Horne of the profits of his business, by whatever means it might be done, would be unlawful and criminal, a combination to compass that object would be an unlawful conspiracy, and it would be unnecessary to state the means. Such seems to have been the view of the court in *The King v. Eccles*, 3 Doug. 337, though the case is so briefly reported, that the reasons, on which it rests, are not very obvious. The case seems to have gone on the ground, that the means were matter of evidence, and not of averment; and that after verdict, it was to be presumed, that the means contemplated and used were such as to render the combination unlawful and constitute conspiracy.

Suppose a baker in a small village had the exclusive custom of his neighborhood, and was making large profits by the sale of his bread. Supposing a number of those neighbors, believing the price of his bread too high, should propose to him to reduce his prices, or if he did not, that they would introduce another baker; and on his refusal, such other baker should, under their encouragement, set up a rival establishment, and sell his bread at lower prices; the effect would be to diminish the profit of the former baker, and to the same extent to impoverish him. And it might be said and proved, that the purpose of the associates was to diminish his profits and thus impoverish him, though the ultimate and laudable object of the combination was to reduce the cost of bread to themselves and their neighbors. The same thing may be said of all competition in every branch of trade and industry; and yet it is through that competition, that the best interests of trade and industry are promoted. It is scarcely necessary to allude to the familiar instances of opposition lines of conveyance, rival hotels, and the thousand other instances, where each strives to gain custom to himself, by ingenious improvements, by increased industry, and by all the means by which he may lessen the price of commodities, and thereby diminish the profits of others.

We think, therefore, that associations may be entered into, the object of which is to adopt measures that may have a tendency to impoverish another, that is, to diminish his gains and profits, and yet so far from being criminal or unlawful, the object may be highly meritorious and public spirited. The legality of such an association will therefore depend upon the means to be used for its accomplishment. If it is to be carried into effect by fair or honorable and lawful means, it is, to say the least, innocent; if by falsehood or force, it may be stamped with the character of conspiracy. It follows as a necessary consequence, that if criminal and indictable, it is so by reason of the criminal means intended to be employed for its accomplishment; and as a further legal consequence, that as the criminality will depend on the means, those means must be stated in the indictment. If the same rule were to prevail in criminal, which holds in civil proceedings—that a case defectively stated may be aided by a verdict—then a court might presume, after verdict, that the indictment was supported by proof of criminal or unlawful means to effect the object. But it is an established rule in criminal cases, that the indictment must state a complete indictable offence, and cannot be aided by the proof offered at the trial.

The fourth count avers a conspiracy to impoverish Jeremiah Horne, without stating any means; and the fifth alleges a conspiracy to impoverish employers, by preventing and hindering them from employing persons, not members of the Bootmakers' Society; and these require no remarks, which have not been already made in reference to the other counts.

One case was cited, which was supposed to be much in point, and which is certainly deserving of great respect. *The People v. Fisher*, 14 Wend. 1. But it is obvious, that this decision was founded on the construction of the revised statutes of New York, by which this matter of conspiracy is now regulated. It was a conspiracy by journeymen to raise their wages, and it was decided to be a violation of the statutes, making it criminal to commit any act injurious to trade or commerce. It has, therefore, an indirect application only to the present case.

A caution on this subject, suggested by the commissioners for revising the statutes of New York, is entitled to great consideration. They are alluding to the question, whether the law of conspiracy should be so extended, as to embrace every case where two or more unite in some fraudulent measure to injure an individual, by means not in themselves criminal. "The great difficulty," say they, "in enlarging the definition of this offence, consists in the inevitable result of depriving the courts of equity of the most effectual means of detecting fraud, by compelling a discovery on oath. It is a sound principle of our institutions, that no man shall be compelled to accuse himself of any crime; which ought not to be violated in any case. Yet such must be the result, or the ordinary jurisdiction of courts of equity must be destroyed, by declaring any private fraud, when committed by two, or any concert to commit it, criminal." 9 Cow. 625. In New Jersey, in a case which was much considered, it was held that an indictment will not lie for a conspiracy to commit a civil injury. *State v. Rickey*, 4 Halst. 293. And such seemed to be the opinion of Lord Ellenborough, in *The King v. Turner*, 13 East, 231, in which he considered that the case of *The King v. Eccles*, 3 Doug. 337, though in form an indictment for a conspiracy to prevent an individual from carrying on his trade, yet in substance was an indictment for a conspiracy in restraint of trade, affecting the public.

It appears by the bill of exceptions, that it was contended on the part of the defendants, that this indictment did not set forth any agreement to do a criminal act, or to do any lawful act by criminal means, and that the agreement therein set forth did not constitute a conspiracy indictable by the law of this State, and that the court was requested so to instruct the jury. This the court declined doing, but instructed the jury that the indictment did describe a confederacy among the defendants to do an unlawful act, and to effect the same by unlawful means—that the society, organized and associated for the purposes described in the indictment, was an unlawful conspiracy against the laws of this State, and that if the jury believed, from the evidence, that the defendants or any of them had engaged in such confederacy, they were bound to find such of them guilty.

In this opinion of the learned judge, this court, for the reasons stated, cannot concur. Whatever illegal purpose can be found in the constitution of the Bootmakers' Society, it not being clearly set forth in the indictment, cannot be relied upon to support this conviction. So if any facts were disclosed at the trial, which, if properly averred, would have given a different character to the indictment, they do not appear in the bill of exceptions, nor could they, after verdict, aid the indictment. But looking solely at the indictment, disregarding the qualifying epithets, recitals and immaterial allegations, and confining ourselves to facts so averred as to be capable of being traversed and put in issue, we cannot perceive that it charges a criminal conspiracy punishable by law. The exceptions must, therefore, be sustained, and the judgment arrested.

Illustration 13-5   A typical nineteenth-century scene. The central mill buildings date from 1862. The setting is comparable to the setting of *St. Helen's Smelting Co. v. Tipping* (1865), *infra*. (Courtesy AeroFilms.)

Note: As indicated in the "introduction" to this chapter, the case below was included to illustrate judicial instrumentalism and the development, or erosion, of environmental protection. But the case is also an excellent example of nineteenth-century English appellate procedure. Compare it with the cases discussed in Chapter VIII, *supra*. What are the differences between the case below and *Slade's Case, supra*?

St. Helen's Smelting Company vs. William Tipping
[June 30, July 5, 1865]
11 English Reports 1483 (H.L. 1865),
XI H.L.C. 642. 1483–1488.

This was an action brought by the Plaintiff to recover from the Defendants damages for injuries done to his trees and crops, by their works. The Defendants are the directors and shareholders of the St. Helen's Copper Smelting Company (Limited). The Plaintiff, in 1860, purchased a large portion of the Bold Hall estate, consisting of the manor house and about 1300 acres of land, within a short distance of which stood the works of the Defendants. The declaration alleged that, "the Defendants erected, used, and continued to use, certain smelting works upon land near to the said dwelling house and lands of the Plaintiff, and caused large quantities of noxious gases, vapours, and other noxious matter, to issue from the said works, and diffuse themselves over the land and premises of the Plaintiff, whereby the hedges, trees, shrubs, fruit, and herbage, were greatly injured; the cattle were rendered unhealthy, and the Plaintiff was prevented from having so beneficial a use of the said land and premises as he would otherwise have enjoyed, and also the reversionary lands and premises were depreciated in value." The Defendants pleaded, Not guilty.

The cause was tried before Mr. Justice Mellor at Liverpool in August 1863, when the Plaintiff was examined and spoke distinctly to the damage done to his plantations, and to the very unpleasant nature of the vapour, which, when the wind was in a particular direction, affected persons as well as plants in his grounds. On cross examination, he said he had seen the Defendants' chimney before he purchased the estate, but he was not aware whether the works were then in operation. On the part of the Defendants, evidence was called to show that the whole neighborhood was studded with manufactories and tall chimneys, that there were some alkali works close by the Defendants' works, that the smoke from one was quite as injurious as the smoke from the other, that the smoke of both sometimes united, and that it was impossible to say to which of the two any particular injury was attributable. The fact that the Defendants' works existed before the Plaintiff bought the property was also relied on.

The learned Judge told the jury that an actionable injury was one producing sensible discomfort; that every man, unless enjoying rights obtained by prescription or agreement, was bound to use his own property in such a manner as not to injure the property of his neighbours; that there was no prescriptive right in this case; that the law did not regard trifling inconveniences; that everything must be looked at from a reasonable point of view; and therefore, in an action for nuisance to property, arising from noxious vapours, the injury to be actionable must be such as visibly to diminish the value of the property and the comfort and enjoyment of it. That when the jurors came to consider the facts, all the circumstances, including those of time and locality, ought to be taken into consideration; and that with respect to the latter it was clear that in counties where great works had been erected and carried on, persons must not stand on their extreme rights and bring actions in respect of every matter of annoyance, for if so, the business of the whole country would be seriously interfered with.

The Defendants' counsel submitted that the three questions which ought to be left to the jury were, "whether it was a necessary trade, whether the place was a suitable place for such a trade, and whether it was carried on in a reasonable manner." The learned judge did not put the questions in this form, but did ask the jury whether the enjoyment of the Plaintiff's property was sensibly diminished, and the answer was in the affirmative. Whether the business there carried on was an ordinary business for smelting copper, and the answer was, "We consider it an ordinary business, and conducted in a proper manner, in as good a manner as possible." But to the question whether the jurors thought that it was carried on in a proper place, the answer was, "We do not." The verdict was therefore entered for the Plaintiff, and the damages were assessed at £361 18s. 4d. A motion was made for a new trial, on the ground of misdirection, but the rule was refused (4 Best and Sm. 608). Leave was however given to appeal, and the case was carried to the Exchequer Chamber, where the judgment was affirmed, Lord Chief Baron Pollock there observing, "My opinion has not always been that which it is now. Acting upon what has been decided *in this Court*, my brother Mellor's direction is not open to a bill of exception" (4 Best and Sm. 616). This appeal was then brought.

The judges were summoned, and Mr. Baron Martin, Mr. Justice Willes, Mr Justice Blackburn, Mr. Justice Keating, Mr. Baron Pigott, and Mr. Justice Shee, attended.

The Attorney-General (Sir R. Palmer), and Mr. Webster for the Appellants (Defendants in the Court below).—The law on this subject is doubtful, and requires to be settled by the authority of this House. A dictum of Lord Chief Baron Comyns (*Com. Dig. Action on the Case for Nuisance. C.*), declared that an action on the case will not lie "for a reasonable use of my right, though it be to the annoyance of another; as if a butcher, brewer, etc. use his trade in a convenient place, though it be to the annoyance of his neighbor." That dictum, for which it is admitted no authority is cited, nevertheless lays down the true principle. That principle was adopted in *Hole v. Barlow* (4 Com. Ben., N.S., 334). It was not distinctly dissented from in *Stockport Waterworks Company v. Potter* (7 Hurl. And N. 160). It was adopted in *Bamford v. Turnley* in the Court of Queen's Bench (3 Best and Sm. 62), but when that case was heard in the Exchequer Chamber (*id.* 66). *Hole v. Barlow* was expressly dissented from by several of the judges. Their dissent is not warranted by principle or authority. Our material question is the convenience or fitness of the place where the business is carried on.

In *Bamford v. Turnley* (3 Best and Sm. 74), it is said by Mr. Justice Williams, "It was therefore treated as a doctrine of law that if the spot should be proved by the jury to be proper or convenient, and the burning of the bricks a reasonable use of the land, these circumstances would constitute a bar to the action," and he then proceeds to argue that they would not do so if the work was carried elsewhere, or if it actually created a nuisance to a neighbour. But a part of the fallacy of the argument lies in this mode of stating the case. An act may be an annoyance without being a nuisance. If only an annoyance, then being performed in a convenient place, for the proper phrase is *convenient* and not *suitable*, and performed, as here it was expressly found to be, in a careful way, in "the best manner," it is no nuisance.

And in that case itself Mr. Baron Bramwell really has adopted these principles, for he says (3 Best and Sm. 82), "It is to be borne in mind however, that, in *fact*, the act of the Defendant is a nuisance." Now, that shows that even in his opinion the doctrine of nuisance would not be applicable except under a certain condition of fact; and it is clear from the verdict in this case that that condition of *fact* did not exist. In *Cavey v. Leadbitter* (13 Com Ben., N.S., 470), Lord Chief Justice [647] Erle distinctly states that he did not differ from the judgment of Mr. Justice Willes in *Hole v. Barlow*. Now in that case Mr. Justice Willes said (4 Com. Ben., N.S., 334), "The right of the owner of a house to have the air unpolluted is subject to this qualification, that necessities may arise for an interference with that right *pro bono publico*, to this extent, that such interference be in respect of a matter essential to the business of life, and be conducted in a reasonable and proper manner, and in a reasonable and proper place." The nature of the thing, the place where it is used, and the fair and proper use of it, are all circumstances to be considered before a thing can be pronounced a nuisance. When, therefore, by the use of certain manufactures, a neighbourhood is, as it may be said, denaturalised, a person who comes into that neighbourhood cannot complain that what was done before he came there is continued. Under such circumstances the ordinary use of property is really that of its use in the special manner, and such use cannot give rise to a right of action by a person who happens to suffer some annoyance from it; what is done around him assumes then the character of the ordinary and proper use of the property. In the *Wanstead Local Board of Health v. Hill* (13 Com. Ben., N.S., 479), it was decided that under the words of a particular statute, (11 and 12 Vict. C. 63), brickmaking was not a "noxious or offensive business," but that case is chiefly remarkable for the declaration of Mr. Justice Willes as to the unsettled state of the law on this matter. That learned Judge says, "It is still an open question to be determined by the highest tribunal, whether one who carries on a business under reasonable circumstances of place, time, and otherwise, can be said to be guilty of an actionable nuisance."

The old authorities show that ordinary trade reasonably carried on is not a nuisance. In *Jones v. Powell* (Palm. 536), the mere facts of the erection of a brewhouse, and of an ordinary use of sea coal, were not held to constitute a nuisance, but the erection of a *latrina* from which "unhealthy vapours arose," was, after verdict, held to warrant the action. In *Baines v. Baker* (Ambl. 158), Lord Hardwicke refused to grant an injunction to prevent the building of a small-pox hospital near Cold Bath Fields, laying down the principle that in all cases the Court must consider not merely the effect on the neighbouring property, but also the reasonableness of doing the thing in the particular place. The statement to the jury here that the business was actionable if it interfered with the comfort of the plaintiff was therefore a misdirection. That alone would not render it actionable; nor would the fact that it produced injury to the Plaintiff's trees and shrubs have that effect. It cannot be asserted as an abstract proposition of law that any act by which a man sends over his neighbour's land that which is noxious and hurtful is actionable, but the jury must be told to take into account the condition of the other property in the neighborhood, the nature of the locality, and the other circumstances which show the reasonable employment of the property, and even the employment of it in a particular manner in that particular locality. To ask the jury merely whether there has been a sensible injury to the Plaintiff's property, or to his enjoyment of it, is not sufficient.

Mr. Brett, Mr. Mellish, and Mr. Milward were for the Respondents, but were not called upon to address the House.

The Lord Chancellor (Lord Westbury).—My Lords, as your Lordships, as well as myself, have listened carefully to the able argument on the part of the Appellants, and are perfectly satisfied with the decision of the Court below, and are of opinion that, subject to what we may hear from the learned judges, the direction to the jury was right, I would submit that two questions should be put to the learned judges; but at the same time the learned judges will be good enough to understand that if they desire farther argument of the case the Respondent's counsel must be heard. Otherwise the following are the questions which I propose to be put to them: Whether directions given by the learned judge at *nisi prius* to the jury were correct? or, Whether a new trial ought to be granted in this case? The learned judges will intimate to your Lordships whether they desire to hear farther argument on the part of the Respondent's counsel, or whether they are prepared to answer the questions put to them by your Lordships.

Mr. Baron Martin said that the judges did not require the case to be farther argued, but they requested to have a few moments' consideration to give their answer to the questions put to them.

Adjourned for a short time, and resumed.

Mr. Baron Martin. — My Lords, in answer to the questions proposed by your Lordships to the judges, I have to state their unanimous opinion that the directions given by the learned judge to the jury were correct, and that a new trial ought not to be granted. As far as the experience of all of us goes, the directions are such as we have given in these cases for the last twenty years.

The Lord Chancellor (5 July). — My Lords, I think your Lordships will be satisfied with the answer we have received from the learned judges to the questions put by this House.

My Lords, in matters of this description it appears to me that it is a very desirable thing to mark the difference between an action brought for a nuisance upon the ground that the alleged nuisance produces material injury to the property, and an action brought for a nuisance on the ground that the thing alleged to be a nuisance is productive of sensible personal discomfort. With regard to the latter, namely, the personal inconvenience and interference with one's enjoyment, one's quiet, one's personal freedom, anything that discomposes or injuriously affects the senses or the nerves, whether that may or may not be denominated a nuisance, must undoubtedly depend greatly on the circumstances of the place where the thing complained of actually occurs. If a man lives in a town, it is necessary that he should subject himself to the consequences of those operations of trade which may be carried on in his immediate locality, which are actually necessary for trade and commerce, and also for the enjoyment of property, and for the benefit of the inhabitants of the town and of the public at large. If a man lives in a street where there are numerous shops, and a shop is opened next door to him, which is carried on in a fair and reasonable way, he has no ground for complaint, because to himself individually there may arise much discomfort from the trade carried on in that shop. But when an occupation is carried on by one person in the neighbourhood of another, and the result of that trade, or occupation, or business, is a material injury to property, then there unquestionably arises a very different consideration. I think, my Lords, that in a case of that description, the submission which is required from persons living in society to that amount of discomfort which may be necessary for the legitimate and fee exercise of the trade of their neighbours, would not apply to circumstances the immediate result of which is sensible injury to the value of the property.

Now, in the present case, it appears that the Plaintiff purchased a very valuable estate, which lies within a mile and a half from certain large smelting works. What the occupation of these copper smelting premises was anterior to the year 1860 does not clearly appear. The Plaintiff became the proprietor of an estate of great value in the month of June 1860. In the month of September 1860 very extensive smelting operations began on the property of the present Appellants, in their works at St. Helen's. Of the effect of the vapours exhaling from those works upon the plaintiff's property, and the injury done to his trees and shrubs, there is abundance of evidence in the case.

My Lords, the action has been brought upon that, and the jurors have found the existence of the injury; and the only ground upon which your Lordships are asked to set aside that verdict, and to direct a new trial, is this, that the whole neighbourhood where these copper smelting works were carried on, is a neighbourhood more or less devoted to manufacturing purposes of a similar kind, and therefore it is said, that inasmuch as this copper smelting is carried on in what the Appellant contends is a fit place, it may be carried on with impunity, although the result may be the utter destruction, or the very considerable diminution, of the value of the Plaintiff's property. My Lords, I apprehend that that is not the meaning of the word "suitable," or the meaning of the word "convenient," which has been used as applicable to the subject. The word "suitable" unquestionably cannot carry with it this consequence, that a trade may be carried on in a particular locality, the consequence of which trade may be injury and destruction to the neighbouring property. Of course, my Lords, I except cases where any prescriptive right has been required by a lengthened user of the place.

On these grounds, therefore, shortly, without dilating farther upon them (and they are sufficiently unfolded by the judgment of the learned judges in the Court below), I advise your Lordships to affirm the decision of the Court below, and to refuse the new trial, and to dismiss the appeal with costs.

Lord Cranworth.—My Lords, I entirely concur in opinion with my noble and learned friend on the Woolsack, and also in the opinion expressed by the learned judges, that this has been considered to be the proper mode of directing a jury, as Mr. Baron Martin said, for at least twenty years; I believe I should have carried it back rather farther. In stating what I always understood the proper question to be, I cannot do better than adopt the language of Mr. Justice Mellor. He says, "It must be plain, that persons using a limekiln, or other works which emit noxious vapours, may not do an actionable injury to another, and that any place where such an operation is carried on so that it does occasion an actionable injury to another, is not, in the meaning of the law, a convenient place." I always understood that to be so; but in truth, as was observed in one of the cases by the learned judges, it is extremely difficult to lay down any actual definition of what constitutes an injury, because it is always a question of compound facts, which must be looked to see whether or not the mode of carrying on a business did or did not occasion so serious an injury as to interfere with the comfort of life and enjoyment of property.

I perfectly well remember, when I had the honour of being one of the Barons of the Court of Exchequer, trying a case in the county of Durham, where there was an action for injury arising from smoke, in the town of Shields. It was proved incontestably that smoke did come and in some degree interfere with a certain person; but I said, "You must look at it not with a view to the question whether, abstractedly, that quantity of smoke was a nuisance, but whether it was a nuisance to a person living in the town of Shields;" because, if it only added in an infinitesimal degree to the quantity of smoke, I held that the state of the town rendered it altogether impossible to call that an actionable nuisance.

There is nothing of that sort, however, in the present case. It seems to me that the distinction, in matters of fact, was most correctly pointed out by Mr. Justice Mellor, and I do not think he could possibly have stated the law, either abstractedly or with reference to the facts, better than he has done in this case.

Lord Wensleydale.—My Lords, I entirely agree in opinion with both my noble and learned friends in this case. In these few sentences I think everything is included: The Defendants say, "If you do not mind you will stop the progress of works of this description." I agree that it is so, because, no doubt, in the county of Lancaster above all other counties, where great works have been created and carried on, and are the means of developing the national wealth, you must not stand on extreme rights and allow a person to say, "I will bring an action against you for this and that, and so on." Business could not go on if that were so. Everything must be looked at from a reasonable point of view; therefore the law does not regard trifling and small inconveniences, but only regards sensible inconveniences, injuries which sensibly diminish the comfort, enjoyment or value of the property which is affected."

My Lords, I do not think the question could have been more correctly laid down by any one to the jury, and I entirely concur in the propriety of dismissing this appeal.

Judgment of the Exchequer Chamber affirming the judgment of the Court of Queen's Bench affirmed; and appeal dismissed with costs. *Lords' Journals*, 5th July, 1865.

CODIFICATION

David Dudley Field (1805–94), *Reform in the Legal Profession and the Laws.* Address to the graduating class of the Albany Law School, March 23, 1855*

The present condition of our law is anomalous. For the main part, it is derived from the Common Law of England, but so mixed and blended with other rules and usages that it can hardly be called a system at all. The Constitution of the State declares that "such parts of the Common Law, and of the acts of the Legislature of the Colony of New York, as together did form the law of the said colony, on the 19th day of April, 1775," and the resolutions of the Congress of the said colony and of the Convention of the State of New York, in force on the 20th day of April, 1777, which have not since expired or been repealed or altered, and such acts of the Legislature of this State as are now in force, "shall be and continue the law of this State, subject to such alterations as the Legislature shall make concerning the same." The Constitution thereupon requires the Legislature, at its first session after the adoption of the Constitution, to "appoint three commissioners, whose duty it shall be to reduce into a written and systematic code the whole body of the law of this State, or so much and such parts thereof as to the said commissioners shall seem practicable and expedient." The wisdom of the latter provision will be apparent by-and-by.

What was this Common Law to which the Constitution referred, and which are those parts of it that formed the law of the colony in 1775? The Common Law, properly so called, is the customary law of England, as it existed before the coronation of Richard I, which was in 1189. But, as this would throw us back, nearly seven hundred years, upon a mass of usages which would not be thought tolerable for any existing civilization, the Courts have been obliged to hold that such acts of the English Parliament, in amendment of the Common Law, as were passed before the emigration of our ancestors, and are applicable to our situation, are to be considered as part and parcel of the Common Law. What an explanation is this to give to the citizen of the laws according to which he is to live!

---

* See commentary in *The Legal Mind in America* (ed. Perry Miller, New York, 1962) 284–287.

If he be certain that he knows what were the customs of England in the reign of Richard, how is he to know to what period of emigration the Constitution refers (for be it remembered that from the first emigration to the Revolution there passed a hundred and fifty years), and by what means can he guess which English statutes the Courts will consider applicable to our situation?...

To this unwritten or Common Law are to be added, according to the construction put by our Courts upon the constitutional declaration, the statutes of England applicable to our situation. Thus it is seen that the English portion of law which our English progenitors brought with them was not a homogeneous system, but an irregular mass of usage and statute, derived partly from the traditions of various and discordant tribes and races, partly from the enactments of tyrannical kings and struggling Parliaments, and partly, it may be added, from interpolations by judges and chancellors from the civil or canon law.

But, before the arrival of the English, there had settled in the land, and ruled for nearly half a century, a dissimilar people, whose laws, founded chiefly on the Roman codes, were yet modified by the local customs of the different provinces of the Netherlands. These laws, "the precious customs of Fatherland," as the Dutch settlers delighted to call them, and particularly the customs of Friesland, were the first laws of the colony, and, though long since, in most respects, supplanted by the English, traces of them still exist, and affect property in the oldest of the Dutch settlements.

Upon this English and Dutch stock was ingrafted colonial legislation, which consisted mainly of efforts to adapt the law of aristocratic and kingly England to the circumstances and wants of settlers in the forest on a different side of the ocean. No attempt was made to frame a new system, conformable to the new country, and to the new people that were to be born in it; but the old laws of old nations, strangely compounded of Saxon, Norman, and Dutch customs, of the laws of the Heptarchy, of Alfred, and the Conquest, of the statutes of Merton of Marleberge, Winchester, and Gloucester, were transferred from one continent to the other. Thus it happened that those feudal laws of real property were impressed upon the virgin wilderness, with which the Gothic invaders had afflicted the fair lands where the mild and rational system of the Roman law had prevailed before that fierce onslaught from the North:

> ...when her barbarous sons
> Came like a deluge on the South, and spread
> Beneath Gibraltar to the Libyan sands.

And thus also it happened that a most artificial system of procedure, conceived in the midnight of the dark ages, established in those scholastic times when chancellors were ecclesiastics, and logic was taught by monks, and perfected in a later and more venal period, with a view to the multiplication of offices and the increase of fees, was imposed upon the banks of the Hudson and the quiet valley of the Mohawk....

Let us return now from the consideration of these minor reforms to that greatest reform of all, *the establishment of "a written and systematic code of the whole body of the law of this State."* And first let me explain how the matter stands at present.

At the same time that the commission enjoined by the Constitution was created for the purpose of framing a general code, or code of rights and crimes, another commission, also enjoined by the Constitution, was created for the framing of a code of remedies. The former commission was dissolved without reporting a code. The latter framed, and reported to the Legislature, codes of civil and criminal procedure....

The prejudices that prevail on this subject among the members of the profession, both on the bench and at the bar, are well known, and I would not disguise the impediment which these prejudices create. But I have seen greater prejudices than these pass away: and, believing in the power of reason and the spread of truth, I feel confident that the day is near when we shall all smile at the fallacies which are now so dominant. It may well be true that not one lawyer in five believes in the practicability or expediency of a civil code; but not one in a hundred, ten years ago, believed in the possibility of administering legal and equitable relief in the same action, and by a uniform mode of proceeding; but who in this State doubts it now, or would go back to the separate processes if he could? And I may add that not one in twenty, here or in England, ten years ago, believed in the advantage or safety of making witnesses of parties, though the most conservative bar in Christendom now, as one man, pronounces in its favor, and the old rule of exclusion is thrown contemptuously aside for jest and derision.

How the establishment of a code should have been so long a problem with us is a curious subject of speculation, for certainly all the instincts of republicanism are in its favor. One of the distinctions of our scheme of government is the written Constitution. A written law rests upon the same principle. In monarchical or aristocratic governments it would not be so much to be wondered at that a class should arrogate to itself the knowledge and interpretation of laws; but that this should happen in a republic, where all the citizens both legislate and obey, is one of those anomalies which, however susceptible of explanation, seem at first sight incredible.

Is a civil code practicable, and, if practicable, expedient? These questions present the whole case, and should be answered in connection; for it is the habit of objectors to retreat in a circle from one to the other. If you answer the objection that the code is impracticable, you are then told that, though it might be practicable, it would not be expedient; and if you follow by proving the expediency, not unlikely you will hear again that, though expedient, it is not practicable. Show first that the work is practicable, and, that being done, let not your adversary escape from the position that the whole question has been narrowed to the one point of expediency, and that the decision of this closes the question.

How, then, stands the question of practicability? Is a civil code practicable? The best answer to this question should seem to be the fact that civil codes have been established in nearly all the countries of the world, from the time of the Lower Empire to the present day. Are we not as capable of performing a great act of legislation as Romans or Germans, as Frenchmen or Italians? The very doubt supposes either that our abilities are inferior or our law more difficult. The suggestion of inferior abilities would be resented as a national insult; and who that knows anything of it believes that Roman, French, or Italian law is easier to express or explain than our own? And he who does believe it should, in very consistency, straightway set about the amendment of our own, to render it as easy to learn and as facile to express as these foreign laws.

If it were assumed as essential to a code that it should contain a rule for every transaction that in the compass of time can possibly arise, the objection might have some force; but no sane person holds any such idea. We know that new relations will hereafter arise which no human eye has foreseen, and for which new laws must be made. The plan of a code does not include a provision for every future case, in all future times; it contemplates the collecting and digesting of existing rules and the framing of new ones, for all that man's wisdom can discern of what is to come hereafter. Every existing rule of law is written in some book; the books are infinite in number and abound in contradictions and anomalies. To have a code is to have these rules collected, arranged, and classified; the contradictions reconciled; the doubts settled; the bad laws eliminated, and the result written in one book, for the instruction and guidance of citizen and magistrate, lawyer and client.

This brings us to the remaining question of expediency. Is it better to have written or unwritten law; law collected in one book or scattered through a thousand; one system, congruous with itself, where the parts can be seen in their relation to the whole, or disjointed pieces of law, collected from different languages and nations?

There are two objections, which are the only ones that seem to me to be put forth with any appearance of confidence. The first asserts that an unwritten or customary law has this advantage over a written code, that the former is more pliable, and can be extended and molded to correspond with a changing and expanding social state. This is a favorite argument, but I conceive it to be altogether fallacious. It assumes two things, neither of which is true: first, that law is more flexible because unwritten; and, second, that flexibility in law is excellence. A law is a rule of action; to say that the rule is not fixed, that is, flexible, is to say that it is no rule at all. When a decision is made upon the Common Law, it is announced as an authoritative declaration of an existing rule; if it be not really that, then the Judges, instead of interpreting, are making law. If it be an exposition of existing law, then it is not alterable by the Judges, and, of course, is no more flexible in their hands than a statute would be. A flexible Common Law, means, therefore, judicial legislation. Is that desirable? If there be any reason for the policy of separating the different departments of government, the Judges should no more be permitted to make laws than the Legislature to administer them. All experience has shown that confusion in functions leads to confusion in government. Judges are not the wisest legislators, any more than legislators are the wisest Judges. And if it were otherwise, there is this difference between the two modes of legislation, that legislation by a Legislature is made known before it is executed, while legislation by a court occurs after the fact, and necessarily supposes a party to be the victim of a rule unknown until after the transaction which calls it forth.

The judiciary have no rightful concern with the policy of laws. If they need to be changed, the Legislature is the proper judge of the time and the manner of change. And before all other nations, ours is the one by which this rule should be inflexibly enforced; for, more than others, we hold to the entire separation and independence of the different departments of government, so that neither shall encroach upon the other, and the judiciary shall be independent of the executive, the executive of the judiciary, and the Legislature of both.

Then it is said that, if a code were once enacted, it should soon be overloaded with glosses and comments upon the texts, as numerous and contradictory as the cases upon the common law, which now fill the books. This, if it were true, would only prove that the process of codification must be repeated at certain intervals — an objection of no great force, especially as it assumes that, until the accumulation of glosses and comments, the code would have an advantage. But the fact is overstated. There would be glosses and comments, of course; but with a common tribunal to settle questions of doubtful construction, it should seem impossible that there should arise half the questions which now occur upon the common law, since the latter regards not merely the meaning but the existence of a rule, the extent of its design, its applicability to our situation, and also its policy.

This objection, moreover, is inconsistent with the first objection which I answered; for, if there are to be so many commentaries and different interpretations, the text and the comments will soon come to have that flexible character which is thought by some to be so beneficial an element of the common law.

Considering, then, these two objections to the expediency of a code to be satisfactorily answered, and turning to the other side, how great are the advantages which we can see in its accomplishment! The numerous collections of law-books upon the shelves of our libraries superseded by a single work; the whole law brought together, so that it can be seen at one view; the text spread before the eyes of all our citizens; old abuses removed, excrescences cut away, new life infused — these will be the beneficent effects of this vast work....

No undertaking which you could engage in would prove half so grand or beneficent. Your canals, your railways, your incalculable wealth, your ships cutting the foam of every sea, the enterprise of your merchants, the skill of your artisans, the fame of your ancestors — all would not exceed in glory the establishment of a code of laws, containing the wisest rules of past ages, and the most matured reflections of our own, which, instinct with the free spirit of our institutions, should become the guide and example for all the nations bearing the tie of our common language.

Shall this imperial State be outstripped in the noble race by either of her sisters, or by that queenly island, mother of nations, which, having been our parent, is now our rival? In material public works, in commerce with all the world, in the accumulation of wealth, in the possession and display of power, and in all the arts, we are contending with her for preëminence; it is now to be determined which shall be the lawgiver of the race. Whether this crown shall be upon the head of the mother, or the youngest of the nations, is the problem which the men of this generation shall solve. May it be so resolved as that we shall win the well-deserved prize; that we shall have a book of our own laws, a CODE AMERICAN, not insular but continental, as simple as so vast a work can be made, free in its spirit, catholic in its principles! And that work will go with our ships, our travelers, and our armies; it will march with the language, it will move with every emigration, and make itself a home in the farthest portion of our own continent, in the vast Australian lands, and in the islands of the southern and western seas.

Let us not fear that anything valuable will be lost from the accumulations of past generations. Whatever is beneficial as well as venerable, whatever is most wise, whatever is approved by time and or consecrated by habit, will be preserved and reënacted. Only that which is hurtful, unsuitable, or obsolete, will be laid aside, as it ought, no matter how long it may have lasted, or how strong become.

To the young men of this generation, more than any other that have ever lived, to you who are now going forth from study into professional life, the great task is committed of reforming and establishing the law. You are now enrolled in that profession upon which, more than any other, rest the functions of government and the preservation of social order. You stand in that great congregation, where also stand the most illustrious men of the past and present ages. Demosthenes, Aeschines, Ulpian, Cicero, Daguessau, Bacon, Mansfield, and our own Marshall, Kent, and Story, are your professional brethren. To be worthy to stand in such presence, to be influenced by such examples, to catch a portion of their spirit, are distinctions in themselves.

You stand, moreover, in the very portals of a new time. The world is soon to take its impulses from this side of the ocean. The language we speak, the institutions in which we participate, are to spread with our dominion —

From the world's girdle to the frozen pole — and beyond our dominion to remote islands and continents. Whence shall come the lawgiver of the new time? From our own soil, I would fain hope and believe. The materials are at hand, and the time is propitious. A new people, grown suddenly to the strength and civilization of the oldest and mightiest, with laws for the most part borrowed, finds that they need to be reëxamined, simplified, and reconstructed. The task is great, the object is greater, and the reward is ample. Let us, then, be up and doing, that we may have the merit and the satisfaction of having accomplished something toward it, before we rest from our labors.

DRED SCOTT

Dred Scott, Plaintiff in Error v. John F. A. Sandford
60 U.S. (19 Howard) 393 (1857), 403–404, 624–628.
[Notes omitted]

Opinion of the Court, Chief Justice Taney

* * * * *

The question is simply this: Can a negro, whose ancestors were imported into this country, and sold as slaves, become a member of the political community formed and brought into existence by the Constitution of the United States, and as such become entitled to all the rights, and privileges, and immunities, guarantied by that instrument to the citizen? One of which rights is the privilege of suing in a court of the United States in the cases specified in the Constitution.

It will be observed, that the plea applies to that class of persons only whose ancestors were negroes of the African race, and imported into this country, and sold and held as slaves. The only matter in issue before the court, therefore, is, whether the descendants of such slaves, when they shall be emancipated, or who are born of parents who had become free before their birth, are citizens of a State, in the sense in which the word citizen is used in the Constitution of the United States. And this being the only matter in dispute on the pleadings, the court must be understood as speaking in this opinion of that class only, that is, of those persons who are the descendants of Africans who were imported into this country, and sold as slaves.

The situation of this population was altogether unlike that of the Indian race. The latter, it is true, formed no part of the colonial communities, and never amalgamated with them in social connections or in government. But although they were uncivilized, they were yet a free and independent people, associated together in nations or tribes, and governed by their own laws.

*   *   *   *   *

The words "people of the United States" and "citizens" are synonymous terms, and mean the same thing. They both describe the political body who, according to our republican institutions, form the sovereignty, and who hold the power and conduct the Government through their representatives. They are what we familiarly call the "sovereign people," and every citizen is one of this people, and a constituent member of this sovereignty. The question before us is, whether the class of persons described in the plea in abatement compose a portion of this people, and are constituent members of this sovereignty? We think they are not, and that they are not included, and were not intended to be included, under the word "citizens" in the Constitution, and can therefore claim none of the rights and privileges which that instrument provides for and secures to citizens of the United States. On the contrary, they were at that time considered as a subordinate and inferior class of beings, who had been subjugated by the dominant race, and, whether emancipated or not, yet remained subject to their authority, and had no rights or privileges but such as those who held the power and the Government might choose to grant them.

It is not the province of the court to decide upon the justice or injustice, the policy or impolicy, of these laws. The decision of that question belonged to the political or law-making power; to those who formed the sovereignty and framed the Constitution. The duty of the court is, to interpret the instrument they have framed, with the best lights we can obtain on the subject, and to administer it as we find it, according to its true intent and meaning when it was adopted.

*   *   *   *   *

Mr. Justice Curtis (Dissent)

*   *   *   *   *

Slavery, being contrary to natural right, is created only by municipal law. This is not only plain in itself, and agreed by all writers on the subject, but is inferable from the Constitution, and has been explicitly declared by this court. The Constitution refers to slaves as "persons held to service in one State, under the laws thereof." Nothing can more clearly describe a *status* created by municipal law. In *Prigg v. Pennsylvania*, (10 Pet., 611,) this court said: "The state of slavery is deemed to be a mere municipal regulation, founded on and limited to the range of territorial laws." In *Rankin v. Lydia*, (2 Marsh., 12, 470,) the Supreme Court of Appeals of Kentucky said: "Slavery is sanctioned by the laws of this State, and the right to hold them under our municipal regulations is unquestionable. But we view this as a right existing by positive law of a municipal character, without foundation in the law of nature or the unwritten common law." I am not acquainted with any case or writer questioning the correctness of this doctrine. (See also 1 Burge, Col. And For. Laws, 738–741, where the authorities are collected.)

The *status* of slavery is not necessarily always attended with the same powers on the part of the master. The master is subject to the supreme power of the State, whose will controls his action towards his slave, and this control must be defined and regulated by the municipal law. In one State, as at one period of the Roman law, it may put the life of the slave into the hand of the master; others, as those of the United States, which tolerate slavery, may treat the slave as a person, when the master takes his life; while in others, the law may recognise a right of the slave to be protected from cruel treatment. In other words, the *status* of slavery embraces every condition, from that in which the slave is known to the law simply as a chattel, with no civil rights, to that in which he is recognised as a person for all purposes, save the compulsory power of directing and receiving the fruits of his labor. Which of these conditions shall attend the *status* of slavery, must depend on the municipal law which creates and upholds it.

And not only must the *status* of slavery be created and measured by municipal law, but the rights, powers, and obligations, which grow out of that *status*, must be defined, protected, and enforced, by such laws. The liability of the master for the torts and crimes of his slave, and of third persons for assaulting or injuring or harboring or kidnapping him, the forms and modes of emancipation and sale, their subjection to the debts of the master, succession by death of the master, suits for freedom, the capacity of the slave to be party to a suit, or to be a witness, with such police regulations as have existed in all civilized States where slavery has been tolerated, are among the subjects upon which municipal legislation becomes necessary when slavery is introduced.

Is it conceivable that the Constitution has conferred the right on every citizen to become a resident on the territory of the United States with his slaves, and there to hold them as such, but has neither made nor provided for any municipal regulations which are essential to the existence of slavery?

Is it not more rational to conclude that they who framed and adopted the Constitution were aware that persons held to service under the laws of a State are property only to the extent and under the conditions fixed by those laws; that they must cease to be available as property, when their owners voluntarily place them permanently within another jurisdiction, where no municipal laws on the subject of slavery exist; and that, being aware of these principles, and having said nothing to interfere with or displace them, or to compel Congress to legislate in any particular manner on the subject, and having empowered Congress to make all needful rules and regulations respecting the territory of the United States, it was their intention to leave to the discretion of Congress what regulations, if any, should be made concerning slavery therein? Moreover, if the right exists, what are its limits, and what are its conditions? If citizens of the United States have the right to take their slaves to a Territory, and hold them there as slaves, without regard to the laws of the Territory, I suppose this right is not to be restricted to the citizens of slaveholding States. A citizen of a State which does not tolerate slavery can hardly be denied the power of doing the same thing. And what law of slavery does either take with him to the Territory? If it be said to be those laws respecting slavery which existed in the particular State from which each slave last came, what an anomaly is this? Where else can we find, under the law of any civilized country, the power to introduce and permanently continue diverse systems of foreign municipal law, for holding persons in slavery? I say, not merely to introduce, but permanently to continue, these anomalies. For the offspring of the female must be governed by the foreign municipal laws to which the mother was subject; and when any slave is sold or passes by succession on the death of the owner, there must pass with him, by a species of subrogation, and as a kind of unknown *jus in re*, the foreign municipal laws which constituted, regulated, and preserved, the *status* of the slave before his exportation. Whatever theoretical importance may be now supposed to belong to the maintenance of such a right, I feel a perfect conviction that it would, if ever tried, prove to be as impracticable in fact, as it is, in my judgment, monstrous in theory.

* * * * *

Nor, in my judgment, will the position, that a prohibition to bring slaves into a Territory deprives any one of his property without due process of law, bear examination.

It must be remembered that this restriction on the legislative power is not peculiar to the Constitution of the United States; it was borrowed from *Magna Charta*; was brought to America by our ancestors, as part of their inherited liberties, and has existed in all the States, usually in the very words of the great charter. It existed in every political community in America in 1787, when the ordinance prohibiting slavery north and west of the Ohio was passed.

* * * * *

I am not aware that such laws, though they exist in many States, were ever supposed to be in conflict with the principle of *Magna Charta* incorporated into the State Constitutions. It was certainly understood by the Convention which framed the Constitution, and has been so understood ever since, that, under the power to regulate commerce, Congress could prohibit the importation of slaves; and the exercise of the power was restrained till 1808. A citizen of the United States owns slaves in Cuba, and brings them to the United States, where they are set free by the legislation of Congress. Does this legislation deprive him of his property without due process of law? If so, what becomes of the laws prohibiting the slave trade? If not, how can a similar regulation respecting a Territory violate the fifth amendment of the Constitution?

Some reliance was placed by the defendant's counsel upon the fact that the prohibition of slavery in this territory was in the words, "that slavery, &c., shall be and is hereby *forever* prohibited." But the insertion of the word *forever* can have no legal effect. Every enactment not expressly limited in its duration continues in force until repealed or abrogated by some competent power, and the use of the word "forever" can give to the law no more durable operation. The argument is, that Congress cannot so legislate as to bind the future States formed out of the territory, and that in this instance it has attempted to do so. Of the political reasons which may have induced the Congress to use these words, and which caused them to expect that subsequent Legislatures would conform their action to the then general opinion of the country that it ought to be permanent, this court can take no cognizance.

Illustration 14–1 Duncan Kennedy, Carter Professor of General Jurisprudence, Harvard Law School. Courtesy Harvard Law School Alumni Magazine and Professor Kennedy.

XIV

THE TWENTIETH CENTURY
THE "NEW JURISPRUDENCE,"
"CRITICAL LEGAL STUDIES,"
AND THE "POST-LIBERAL SOCIETY"

All self-respecting legal history is supposed to end by the twentieth century. As we approach our own lives, experience and training—and those events that we have actually witnessed—we allegedly lose that "objectivity" which makes the "science" of history itself possible. Certainly, there is no point in burdening the reader with the "original" materials, including cases and statutes, that make up the bulk of any legal education. But there are good reasons to reflect on our own legal century from an "historical perspective."

First, we can already discern certain forests through the trees that surround us. The early years of this century saw the development of a powerful new school of "sociological jurisprudence," or the "new jurisprudence," growing from the writing and judicial opinions of jurists such as Oliver Wendell Holmes Jr., Louis Brandeis, and Roscoe Pound. This new approach to judicial law making set the juristic underpinnings for Franklin Roosevelt's "New Deal" and the activist Supreme Court of the post war era. Optimistic and expansive in spirit, the "new jurisprudence" combined the utilitarian philosophy of Benthamism with an aggressive new judicial instrumentalism.

On a very different note has been the analysis of modern legal movements developed in Germany by Georg Hegel and Max Weber and applied, at least in part, in this country by theorists such as Duncan Kennedy, Morton Horwitz, and Roberto Unger. Both Weber and Unger have identified tendencies in modern legal systems that are cutting away at belief in a neutral rule of law and are threatening the legitimacy of the legal profession and the courts alike. In many ways, the observations of these writers challenge future generations of common lawyers to either reform their heritage or revert to political and economic tribalism.

A. THE "NEW JURISPRUDENCE"

The life of Oliver Wendell Holmes Jr. (1841–1935) spans much of American history. He was born into the aristocratic world of old Massachusetts, and was related to four great families, the Olivers, the Wendells, the Holmeses and the Jacksons. He met men such as John Quincy Adams, who had, in turn, intimately known the founders of the Republic. Holmes himself fought and was wounded

557

in the most terrible American experience of all time, the Civil War. Yet, his term as a Supreme Court Justice, from 1902 to 1932, saw the emergence of a new social, economic, and juristic era, whose "modern" influence we still feel strongly. Alger Hess, his law clerk, was prosecuted as a traitor by Richard Nixon. Louis Brandeis was Holmes' protégé. Many are still alive who remember clearly meeting and discussing law with the great old man, and I was once in a room with five of them. Holmes' life links us directly with the birth of the Republic.

But Holmes was always, as Commager said, "a generation ahead of his time."[1] And nothing symbolizes that better than his lectures and writings in the 1880s, particularly three: 1) the incomparable *The Spirit of the Common Law* (Boston, 1881), based on his Lowell Institute Lectures of 1880; 2) "The Path of the Law," an address at the dedication of a new hall at Boston University Law School in 1897, published in 10 *Harvard Law Review* 451 (1897); and 3) "Natural Law" published in 32 *Harvard Law Review* (1918). Such writing founded the "new jurisprudence," and led to the great departure from formalism that would mold American constitutional jurisprudence for the next century. The *Materials* for this chapter include excerpts from *The Common Law* (1881) and "Natural Law" (1918), written nearly forty years apart. The next chapter, XV, contains excerpts from "The Path of the Law" (1897).[2]

In November, 1880, Holmes addressed a hushed audience containing James Barr Ames, James Bradley Thayer, John Chipman Gray, and Christopher Columbus Langdell at the Lowell Institute Lectures. This was literally a "who's who" of the traditional natural law and common law schools of jurisprudence, jurists who emphasized the "gospel of Savigny" that the common law was fixed and immutable, almost like the laws of natural science itself. Holmes issued a direct challenge to them.

> "The life of the law has not been logic; it has been experience. The felt necessities of the time, the prevalent moral and political theories, intuitions of public policy, avowed or unconscious, even the prejudices which judges share with their fellow-men, have had a good deal more to do than the syllogism in determining the rules by which men should be governed."[3]

This challenge was repeated a year later by *The Common Law* (1881).

> "What has been said will explain the failure of all theories which consider the law only from its formal side, whether they attempt to deduce the *corpus* from *a priori* postulates, or fall into the humbler error of supposing the science of the law to reside in the *elegantia juris*, or logical cohesion of part with part. The truth is, that the law is always approaching, and never reaching, consistency. It is forever adopting new principles from life at one end, and it always retains old ones from history at the other, which have not yet been absorbed or sloughed off. It will become entirely consistent only when it ceases to grow."[4]

---

1. Henry Steele Commager, *The American Mind* (New Haven, 1950), 376.
2. *Materials, infra,* p. 610.
3. *Materials, infra,* p. 572.
4. O.W. Holmes, Jr., *The Common Law* (ed. Mark D. Howe, London, 1988), 32.

This was the essence of what Roscoe Pound would call "sociological jurisprudence." As Commager put it, it was, "[A] new way of thinking about law and applying it. It was a shift from absolutes to relatives, from doctrines to practices, from passive—and therefore pessimistic-determinism to creative—and therefore optimistic-freedom."[5]

But this was far from rationalist, codified utilitarianism. Holmes believed firmly in the history and tradition of the Common law as an essential part of a growing, living body of doctrine. As he put it in *The Common Law*:

> "However much we may codify the law into a series of seemingly self-sufficient propositions, these propositions will be but a phase in a continuous growth. To understand their scope fully, to know how they will be dealt with by judges trained in the past which the law embodies, we must ourselves know something of that past. The history of what the law has been is necessary to the knowledge of what the law is."[6]

Here was more of Mansfield than Bentham, and more of the secret innovative soul of Coke—who changed the law by judicial reports—than the self-declared legal science of Bacon.

But the glory of the "new jurisprudence" was its willingness to incorporate the lessons of social science and utilitarian with the goals of judicial instrumentalism. At the Lowell Lectures, along with the John Chipman Grays and the Langdells, also sat the young Louis Dembitz Brandeis (1856–1941). Although his great sociological brief in *Muller v. Oregon* (1908), the first "Brandeis Brief," was still twenty-eight years in the future, Brandeis was to become a great exponent of Holmes' principles—both in his distinguished Boston law practice and during twenty-three vitally significant years on the United States Supreme Court (1916–1939). Together with Harlan Stone, Benjamin Cardozo, and Felix Frankfurter, Brandeis was responsible for making sociological jurisprudence, after Roosevelt's 1937 "court packing" crisis, "the all but official doctrine of the Court."[7]

Holmes' doctrines also had a great impact on legal education. Christopher Columbus Langdell, who had established the "case method" at Harvard Law School, said in 1886 that "[L]aw is a science" and that law books were "to us all what laboratories of the university are to the chemists and physicists...."[8] Langdell resigned in 1895, after twenty-five years. Twenty years later, in 1916, Roscoe Pound took the deanship. During the next twenty years, he established "sociological jurisprudence" as a corner stone of a new approach to legal education.

"Sociological jurisprudence," Pound's own term, was very different from Langdell's "science." In Pound's words, it was

> "a process, an activity, not merely a body of knowledge or a fixed order of construction. It is a doing of things, not a serving as passive instruments through which mathematical formulas and mechanical laws real-

---

5. See Henry Steele Commager, *The American Mind* (New Haven, 1950) 374–381.
6. O.W. Holmes, Jr., *The Common Law, supra*, 33.
7. Henry Steele Commager, *supra*, 380–381.
8. Arthur E. Sutherland, *The Law at Harvard* (Cambridge, 1967), 175.

ize themselves in the eternally appointed way. The engineer is judged by what he does. His work is judged by its adequacy to the purposes for which it is done, not by its conformity to some ideal form of a traditional plan. We are beginning...to think of jurist and judge and lawmaker in the same way. We are coming to study the legal order instead of debating as to nature of law. We are thinking of interests, claims, demands, not of rights; of what we have to secure or satisfy, not exclusively of the institutions by which we have sought to secure or satisfy them, as if those institutions were ultimate things existing for themselves. (*Interpretations of Legal History*, p. 152)"[9]

At its core, the new jurisprudence was, in Pound's words, "a movement for pragmatism as a philosophy of law; for the adjustment of principles and doctrines to the human condition they are to govern rather than to assure first principles; for putting the human factor in the central place and relegating logic to its true position as an instrument."[10] Inherent in this new approach to law was both a new attitude as to the proper source of judicial principles and a new test of what made a law good or bad.

In the last century we studied law from within. The jurists of today are studying it from without. The past century sought to develop completely and harmoniously the fundamental principles which jurists discovered by metaphysics or by history. The jurists of today seek to enable and to compel lawmaking and also the interpretation and application of legal rules, to take more account and more intelligent account, of the social facts upon which law must proceed and to which it is to be applied. Where the last century studied law in the abstract, they insist upon study of the actual social effects of legal institutions and legal doctrines. Where the last century prepared for legislation by study of other legislation analytically, they insist upon sociological study in connection with legal study in preparation for legislation. Where the last century held comparative law the best foundation for wise lawmaking, they hold it not enough to compare the laws themselves, but that even more their social operation must be studied and the effects which they produce, if any, when put in action. Where the last century studied only the making of law, they hold it necessary to study as well the means of making legal rules effective. (*The Spirit of the Common Law*, pp. 212–213).[11]

The impact of this new approach on legal study and legal policy, particularly in the area of criminal law, was "immediate and far reaching."[12] But, in Commager's words, "[I]ts most dramatic, and perhaps its most consequential results were to be found...in the area of constitutional law."[13] Formulated in lectures and legal writings of a man who had met John Quincy Adams and fought in the Civil War, the "new jurisprudence" was to become the ideological backbone of

---

9. Henry Steele Commager, *The American Mind, supra,* 378.
10. *Id.,* 378.
11. *Id.,* 379.
12. *Id.,* 380.
13. *Id.,* 380.

the "Warren Court," and the monumental cases of *Gideon, Miranda, Brown v. Board, Roe v. Wade*, and *Griswold v. Connecticut* are its lasting heritage.[14]

B. THE QUALITIES OF MODERN LAW AND THE "POSTLIBERAL SOCIETY"

Just as the "new jurisprudence" grew from the instrumental optimism of nineteenth-century America, but reached its full fruition decades later, so the "critical realism" movement of the last twenty years grew from the hard lesson of the economic "Great Depression" in Europe and America and the World Wars. The first to articulate the elements of modern law in ways that reflected these lessons was Max Weber (1864–1920), the great German economist and scholar.

In his *Law in Economy and Society*, Weber identified three "qualities of modern law" that clearly challenged the existence of "law" as a concept independent of raw political and economic power. The first was "specialization." In Weber's words, "the legal ignorance of the layman will increase" as legal rules became more complex and technical.[15] Equally important was the "anti-formalistic tendencies of modern legal development," i.e., the tendency of courts to depart from rigid, objective rules to resolve cases, and to rely more on subjective "economical utilitarian meaning."[16] Finally, there was the "lay justice and corporate tendencies in the modern legal profession," i.e. the increasing reliance on subjective lay decision making—whether by jury, arbitration or mediator—and the erosion of significant distinction between "private" and "public" legal decision making.[17]

Weber warns that there is a price to be paid for these developments. As law becomes increasingly obscure, technical, subjective and private, the source of its moral force is eroded. In Weber's words:

> "Whatever form law and legal practice may come to assume under the impact of these various influences, it will be inevitable that, as a result of technical and economic developments, the legal ignorance of the layman will increase. The use of jurors and similar lay judges will not suffice to stop the continuous growth of the technical element in the law and hence of its character as a specialists' domain. Inevitably, the notion must expand that the law is a rational technical apparatus, which is continually transformable in the light of experiential considerations and devoid of all sacredness of content."[18]

A law "devoid of all sacredness of content" would, in the eyes of Blackstone or Coke, lead quickly to tyranny, yet Weber saw this as an inevitable result of the new "sociological jurisprudence"—the "dark side," as it were, of the promise of legal instrumentalism. Again in Weber's words:

---

14. See Archibald Cox, *The Warren Court* (Cambridge, 1968).
15. *Materials, infra*, p. 582.
16. *Id.*, p. 577.
17. *Id.*, p. 580.
18. *Id.*, p. 582.

This fate may be obscured by the tendency of acquiescence in the existing law, which is growing in many ways for several reasons, but it cannot really be stayed. All of the modern sociological and philosophical analyses, many of which are of a high scholarly value, can only contribute to strengthen this impression, regardless of the content of their theories concerning the nature of law and the judicial process.[19]

Certainly the "deconstruction" of "sacred texts" of the law, including Blackstone's *Commentaries*, has been one product of modern critical legal scholarship. A particularly good example is Duncan Kennedy's controversial "The Structure of Blackstone's Commentaries," 28 *Buffalo Law Review* 209 (1979), excerpted in the *Materials, supra*. Kennedy, a leader of the "critical studies movement" and now Carter Professor of General Jurisprudence at Harvard, acknowledges the influence of E.P. Thompson, discussed above in Chapter XII, and Hegel. His purpose in analyzing Blackstone is to strip away the pretense of Blackstone's "desire to legitimate the legal *status quo*" and to establish a method of "discovering hidden political intentions beneath the surface of legal exposition."[20]

Weber's message has been further developed in the work of Roberto Mangabeira Unger, another law professor at Harvard. In his view, the rule of law has been "the soul of the modern state."[21] In particular, belief in a neutral, all pervading rule of law and a careful division between state and private ordering is at the heart of our notion of a liberal, constitutional state. But, argues Unger, the rule of law is currently in "disintegration," and our belief in the United States as a "liberal" state is actually belief in a myth. Rather, we are now entering a "post-liberal" society which is marked by a gradual abandonment of formal, neutral, public rulemaking.[22]

Two forces are leading us to this end. The first is "the overt intervention of government in areas previously regarded as beyond the proper reach of state action," a tendency that Unger labels the "welfare state" function.[23] The second is "the reverse side of the events just enumerated: the gradual approximation of state and society, of the public and the private sphere." This Unger calls the "corporatist" tendency, borrowing a term from Weber.[24] The latter tendency is well illustrated by nominally "private" entities, such as utilities, hospitals, private universities, and large industrial enterprises, that actually have acquired bodies of rules, powers and responsibilities that are very like public governments. According to Unger:

> Corporatism's most obvious influence on the law is its contribution to the growth of a body of rules that break down the traditional distinction between public and private law. Thus, administrative, corporate, and

---

19. *Id.*, pp. 582–583.
20. *Id.*, p. 583 ff.
21. *Id.*, p. 586.
22. *Id.*, p. 586 ff.
23. *Id.*, p. 586.
24. *Id.*, p. 590.

labor law merge into a body of social law that is more applicable to the structure of private-public organizations than to official conduct or private transactions. But though this development undermines the conventional contrast of public and private law, it does not necessarily destroy the broader difference between the law of the state and the internal, privately determined regulations of private associations. Insofar as private law is laid down by the state, it too is, in this more comprehensive sense, public.

The deepest and least understood impact of corporatism is the one it has on the very distinction between the law of the state and the spontaneously produced normative order of nonstate institutions. As private organizations become bureaucratized in response to the same search for impersonal power that attracts government to the rule of law principle, they begin to acquire the features, and to suffer the problems, of the state. At the same time, the increasing recognition of the power these organizations exercise, in a quasi-public manner, over the lives of their members makes it even harder to maintain the distinction between state action and private conduct. Finally, the social law of institutions is a law compounded of state-authored rules and of privately sponsored regulations or practices; its two elements are less and less capable of being separated. All these movements, which tend to destroy the public character of law, carry forward a process that begins in the failure of liberal society to keep its promise of concentrating all significant power in government.

The tendency of large corporate organizations to become bureaucratized and to produce a body of rules with many of the characteristics of state law should not be confused with an increasing regulation of the corporation by the state. In fact, quite the opposite may be true: the bureaucratization of corporate institutions may be associated with their ability to become relatively independent power centers with decisive influence over government agencies.[25]

The growth of the welfare state and the power of corporatism eat at the neutral rule of law in at least three ways. First, the welfare state encourages "open-ended standards and general clauses in legislation" that take away the certainty and objectivity of legal rules. Second, law in the welfare state turns "from formalistic to purposive or policy-oriented styles of legal reasoning and from concerns with formal justice to an interest in procedural and substantive justice."[26] Finally, the

---

25. *Id.*, pp. 590–591.

26. *Id.,* 580. Unger defines "formal," "substantive" and "procedural" justice as follows: "An ideal of justice is formal when it makes the uniform application of general rules the keystone of justice or when it establishes principles whose validity is supposedly independent of choices among conflicting values. It is procedural when it imposes conditions on the legitimacy of the processes by which social advantages are exchanged or distributed. It is substantive when it governs the actual outcome of distributive decisions or of bargains. Thus, in contract law, the doctrine that bargains are enforceable given certain externally visible manifestations of intent exemplifies formal justice; the demand that there be equality of bargaining power among contracting parties illustrates procedural justice; and the prohibition of ex-

erosion of the ideals of formal justice eventually leads to a breakdown in the difference between public and private and between law and pure economic and political power.

> The decline in the distinctiveness of legal reasoning is connected with the need administrators and judges have of reaching out to the substantive ideals of different groups, of drawing upon a conventional morality or a dominant tradition. These changes in the substance and method of law also help undercut the identity of legal institutions and of the legal profession. Courts begin to resemble openly first administrative, then other political institutions. Thus, the difference between lawyers and other bureaucrats or technicians starts to disappear.[27]

In these predictions, Unger follows and develops the early observations of Weber.[28]

Suddenly, however, Unger advances two extraordinarily original—and alternative—hypotheses about legal history itself. In his words:

> The first hypothesis might be summarized by the metaphor of the closed circle. It would present the entire history of law as one of movement toward a certain point, followed by a return to the origin. We have seen how, in Western legal history, bureaucratic law, with its public and positive rules, builds upon customary practices, and how this bureaucratic law is in turn partly superseded by the rule of law, with its commitment to the generality and the autonomy of legal norms. The welfare trend in postliberal society moves the rule of law ideal back in the direction of bureaucratic law by undermining the social and ideological bases of that deal. The corporatist tendency and the communitarian aspirations that follow it begin to subvert bureaucratic law itself. Thus, they prepare the way for the return to the custom of each group as the fundamental and almost exclusive instrument of social order.[29]

In short, Unger proposes as hypothesis that legal history could be purely cyclical, rather than progressive. This is a rather pessimistic view. Is it right?

The "stages" of Unger's cycle are worth examining closely, and they also provide a convenient way to re-examine and review the materials in this book. Here is a rough diagram of Unger's cycle.

---

changes of two performances of unequal value, however value may be assessed, represents substantive justice." *Id.*, p. 587.

27. *Id.*, pp. 589–590.

28. Unger's observations also reflect the historical theories of scholars such as Morton Horwitz, whose *The Transformation of American Law* (1780–1860) (Cambridge, 1977) traced what he found to be an "emergence of an instrumental conception of law" which led to a breakdown in true distinctions between law and politics and economics. See *id.*, xi–xvii, 1–30.

29. *Materials, infra*, p. 594.

Chart 14-1

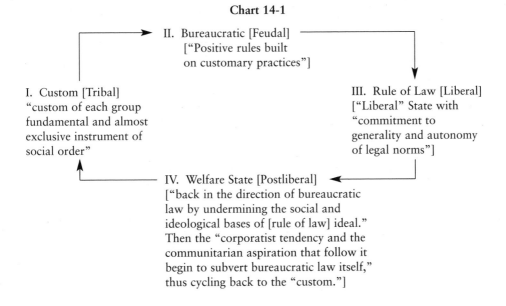

I have taken one liberty with Unger's terminology and inserted the words "tribal," "feudal," "liberal" and "postliberal." In particular, I like to use "feudal" with "bureaucratic" to describe Unger's "Stage II." That is because a society with "positive rules built on customary practices" which also has a strong notion of "corporatist" and "welfare" elements—i.e., where the public and private spheres are commingled and where there is a paternalistic responsibility for collective welfare—closely resembles the "feudal" model that we discussed at length in Chapter IV.

How does this chart reflect this course and the "progression" or, if Unger's cycle is correct, the "flow" of Anglo-American legal history? Obviously, Stage I, "Custom," would correspond with our Chapter II, the "Anglo-Saxon Period," particularly the period before 900 AD. Stage II, "Bureaucratic," closely resembles the evolution of a positive law based on custom during the "feudal" period of England as pointed out above. This period is covered in our Chapters III, IV, and V. The development of royal courts, the treatise *Bracton*, the invention of formulary pleading, and the great medieval statutes, such as *Quia Emptores* (1290) and *De Donis* (1285) could all be seen as part of this stage. Stage III, "Rule of Law," with a "commitment to the generality and the autonomy of legal norms," could be seen as the essence of the struggles led by Coke and other great common lawyers during the sixteenth, seventeenth and eighteenth centuries, leading to the great confrontation of the *Prohibitions del Roy*, 12 *Coke Reports*, 63 (1608),[30] The *Five Knights Case*, 3 *State Trials* 1 (1627),[31] the "Petition of Right" (1628),[32] the *Bill of Rights* (1689),[33]

---

30. *Materials, supra*, p. 338.
31. *Id.*, p. 353.
32. *Id.*, p. 357.
33. *Id.*, p. 387.

and in a very real sense, our own *Constitution*. These developments are described in Chapters IX, X, XI, and XII of this book.

These three "stages" are frequently described as a progressive evolution from pure tribalism to our contemporary, modern "rule of law," as extolled in countless law school graduation and bar admissions ceremonies. But here is where Unger becomes controversial. He, like Weber, sees forces at work in our modern legal system and state that are undermining the rule of law and making it a fiction or a myth. He advances, therefore, at least one hypothesis that sees us returning to a feudal or bureaucratic ["welfare"] state, where public and private norms again commingle, and eventually, to where the "corporatist tendency and the communitarian aspirations that follow it begin to subvert bureaucratic law itself" leading to "the return to the custom of each group as the fundamental and almost exclusive instrument of social order."[34] Some see today a return in America to feudal corporate entities and to vast, faceless paternal bureaucracies, each with their own rules, and then to fragmented economic, ethnic, racial, and sociopolitical "special interest" or "tribal" groups. Such a "balkanization" of American political life, away from consensus politics to the politics of "special interest groups," and to "fractionalized politics" would make Unger's cycle seem credible.

But Unger had a second hypothesis. This theory is a bit more optimistic. Instead of an eternal cycle, legal history may "spiral" upward, like this:

Illustration 14-2

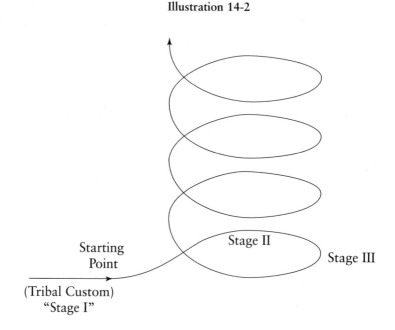

In Unger's own words:

> An alternative approach to the prospects of modern society and to their legal implications might be represented by the metaphor of a spiral

---

34. *Materials, infra,* p. 594.

that reverses direction without returning to its starting point. This would mean that individual freedom could be rescued from the demise of the rule of law and brought into harmony with the reassertion of communitarian concerns. It would also signify that the capacity to see and to treat each form of social life as a creation rather than as a fate could survive the disintegration of public and positive law reconciled with the sense of an immanent order in society.[35]

What would be required to ensure an upward spiral rather than a continuous cycle without progress? Unger believes that legal systems must refine "ancient methods for the dispersal of power" while also distinguishing between "legitimate and illegitimate uses of power" and between "permissible and prohibited inequalities."[36] He also believes that the law must retain what Weber termed "sacredness of content," i.e., not just be an arbitrary exercise of power promoting arbitrary ends.[37] Again, in Unger's words:

> The problem of power carries us to the other aspect of the spiral like process I envisage. Unless people regain the sense that the practices of society represent some sort of natural order instead of a set of arbitrary choices, they cannot hope to escape from the dilemma of unjustified power. But how can this perception of immanent order be achieved in the circumstances of modern society?[38]

The chronicles contained in this book offer every lawyer a chance to answer these fundamental questions for themselves. It is worth recalling Chapter I. This book does not begin with Unger's first stage with a tribal, customary system. Rather, Chapter I is about a highly sophisticated legal system, the Roman system, which was certainly a "Stage 2," if not also a "Stage 3" and "Stage 4" system. The Roman system governed the entire civilized world for centuries, but disappeared without a trace in England. There was a complete return to warring tribes. Elegantly written commercial codes which governed shipments of English tin to Syria, and Egyptian rings to the fingers of wealthy English farmers, were replaced with crude "price lists" to govern blood feud negotiations, i.e., "If an ear is cut off, 30 shillings shall be paid…"[39] The bricks that formed the walls for central heating systems within the walls of spacious villas were literally quarried out to make walls to surround primitive huts. Could it happen again? Photographs in 1994 of abandoned schools and factories in the former Yugoslavia, covered with weeds as ethnic tribes fight from village to village, remind us that social order, upon which civilization and prosperity rest, can be fragile indeed.

But the Roman law chapter was not included in this book at the beginning to make some philosophical or moral point. It is there because Roman law, in fact, came before the Anglo-Saxon period. Does this confirm Unger's grimmer hypothesis? In one way, probably so. At least Western legal science as manifested in English history cannot be regarded as purely "progressive." But the Roman law

---

35. *Id.*, p. 594.
36. *Id.*, pp. 595–596.
37. *Id.*, pp. 595–596.
38. *Id.*, p. 595.
39. *Materials, supra*, Chapter II.

chapter, Chapter I, does not just conclude with Roman times. Rather, it extends to writings by Francis Bacon, during the English Renaissance, and by John Adams, during the dawn of American constitutionalism. Both relied heavily on Roman learning.[40] Indeed, throughout the history of English law we return to the influence of Roman legal science, in Bracton's *De Legibus* of 1265 A.D.,[41] in the development of the notion of equity by St. German in his classic *Doctor and Student* (1523),[42] in the specialized "civilian" courts of Doctors' Commons which flourished from 1511 to 1858, over three centuries,[43] and in the commercial law jurisprudence of Holt and Mansfield,[44] to name but a few examples. Seen from this perspective, Roman legal science was not "lost," but recycled, and recycled in a form both more humane and arguably more sophisticated. The commercial law of Mansfield rivaled that of Ulpian and Gaius, but it did not have to be illustrated by the sale of slaves—at least in England.

Much depends on whether our legal science is progressive. "Progress" in technology can be a two-edged sword unless it is accompanied by a stable and humane social order, as the Cold War reminds us. Search for this social order unites us, as lawyers, with a long line of lawyers, extending into the distant past, who worked for the same goal. As Unger concludes:

> The search for this latent and living law—not the law of prescriptive rules or of bureaucratic policies, but the elementary code of human interaction—has been the staple of the lawyer's art whenever this art was practiced with most depth and skill. What united the great Islamic 'ulama,' the Roman jurisconsults, and the English common lawyers was the sense they shared that the law, rather than being made chiefly by judges and princes, was already present in society itself. Throughout history there has been a bond between the legal profession and the search for an order inherent in social life. The existence of this bond suggests that the lawyer's insight, which preceded the advent of the legal order, can survive its decline.
>
> The same processes that promise to reconcile freedom and transcendence with community and immanent order also threaten to sacrifice the former to the latter. In a brief passage of his *Republic*, Plato evokes a society in which men, reduced to animal contentment, have lost the capacity of self-criticism together with the sense of incompleteness. He calls this society the City of Pigs. The significance of the historical tendencies discussed in this chapter lies in this: with a single gesture they frighten us with the image of the City of Pigs and entice us with the prospect of the Heavenly City. By offering us the extremes of good and evil, they speak at once to what is bestial and to what is sublime in our humanity.[45]

---

40. *Id.*, Chapter I.
41. *Id.*, Chapter III.
42. *Id.*, Chapter VI.
43. *Id.*, Chapter VII.
44. *Id.*, Chapter XII. See Daniel R. Coquillette, *The Civilan Writers of Doctors' Commons, London* (Berlin, 1988), 271–296, for a full account of Roman law influence on Holt and Mansfield.
45. *Materials, infra*, p. 596.

This much is certainly true. The history of Anglo-American law leaves us with no easy answers. At the Saxon "Law Rock," or on the meadow at Runnymede, or in the Privy Council Chamber as Edward Coke alone stood fast before the enraged King, or in a small room in Braintree as John Adams begins to draft the Constitution, or on the picket lines, or on the battlefields of world wars or Selma, progress in legal institutions has been won only through struggle and has been retained only through constant vigilance and effort.

FOR FURTHER READING

I. The "New Jurisprudence"

See the classic articulation of the "New Jurisprudence" in Henry Steele Commager, *The American Mind: An Interpretation of American Thought and Character Since the 1880s* (New Haven, 1950), 374–390. There is also a good summary of the historical context in an "Epilogue: American Law in the 20th Century" in Lawrence M. Friedman, *A History of America's Law* (New York, 2d. ed., 1985), 655–695.

Friedman has called Oliver Wendell Holmes Jr.'s *The Common Law* (Boston, 1881) "the most important 19th century [law] book." *Id.*, 545. But, as Commager pointed out, Holmes' "thought was a generation ahead of his time," and Holmes only *began* his thirty years on the Supreme Court in 1902. See Henry Steele Commager, *The American Mind, supra*, 376. Thus, Holmes was a genuine figure of the twentieth century. *The Common Law* remains in print. See the excellent edition by Mark DeWolfe Howe, O.W. Holmes, *The Common Law* (ed. M. DeWolfe Howe, London, 1968). Also powerfully impressive are Holmes' less well known legal addresses, including several on legal scholarship and the legal profession in O.W. Holmes, *Speeches* (Boston, 1891). See also O.W. Holmes, *Collected Legal Papers* (Harold J. Laski ed., New York, 1920). Holmes' brilliance is also preserved in his great correspondence with Sir Frederick Pollock and with Harold Laski. See *Holmes - Pollock Letters* (ed. Mark DeWolfe Howe, Cambridge, 1961); *Holmes - Laski Letters 1916–1935* (ed. Mark DeWolfe Howe, Cambridge, 1923). See also "The Early Critical and Philosophical Writings of Justice Holmes" (ed. with introduction by Michael H. Hoffheimer, 30 *Boston College Law Review* (1989) 1221. For a modern analysis, see the incomparable Holmes Lectures of 1981 of Benjamin Kaplan, Patrick Atiyah, and Jay Vetter printed in *Holmes and The Common Law: A Century Later* (Cambridge, 1983). There is also David J. Seipp's brilliant essay on the 125th anniversary of "The Path of the Law." See David J. Seipp, "Holmes's Path," 77 *Boston Univ. L. Rev.* 515 (1997), and the fine work of my valued colleague, Catherine Wells. See Catherine P. Wells, "Old-Fashioned Postmodernism and the Legal Theories of Oliver Wendell Holmes, Jr.," 63 *Brooklyn Law Rev.* 63 (1997). Finally, there is Catherine Drinker Bowen's wonderful *Yankee from Olympus* (Boston, 1944), a biography as insightful as it is accessible.

There are many surviving books and articles of Roscoe Pound (1870–1964), including his monumental five volume *Jurisprudence* (Cambridge, 1959). By far the most important, however, is the little treatise containing a series of his lectures called *The Spirit of the Common Law* (Cambridge, 1921). See also Pound's

Interpretations of Legal History (Cambridge, 1923), his famous Trinity College, Cambridge, lecture of 1922. The scholarly biography is Paul L. Sayre, *Life of Roscoe Pound* (Iowa City, 1948). For a guide to the great canon of Supreme Court decisions and articles by Louis Dembitz Brandeis, see Alpheus T. Mason, *Brandeis, A Free Man's Life* (New York, 1946).

II. "Post-Liberal Society"

The patron saint of modern legal analysis remains Max Weber (1869–1920). See particularly his *Law in Economy and Society* (trans. from *Wirtschaft und Gesellschaft* by Shils) (Rheinstein, ed., Cambridge, Mass. 1954). See also Max Weber, *General Economic History* (trans. Knight, New York, 1961), 249–258. The leading contemporary commentator on the legal characteristics of "post liberal society" is Roberto Mangaberia Unger who, with other scholars such as Duncan Kennedy and Morton Horwitz, formed the "critical legal studies" group at Harvard in the late 1970s. See Roberto M. Unger's *Law in Modern Society* (New York, 1976) and *Knowledge and Politics* (New York, 1975), Morton Horwitz's *The Transformation of American Law: 1780–1860* (Cambridge, Mass., 1977), and Duncan Kennedy's *Legal Education and the Reproduction of Hierarchy* (Cambridge, Mass., 1983).

For those wishing to complete their overview of English developments up through the aftermath of World War II see R.M. Jackson's classic *The Machinery of Justice in England* (Cambridge, 1940), Sir Carleton Kemp Allen's equally distinguished *Law and Orders* (3d ed., London, 1965) and Robert Stevens' fascinating *Law and Politics: The House of Lords as a Judicial Body, 1800–1976* (Chapel Hill, 1978).

Illustration 14-3   Oliver Wendell Holmes, Jr. (1841–1935). Associate Justice (1882–1899), Chief Justice (1899–1902), Massachusetts Supreme Judicial Court; Associate Justice (1902–1932), Supreme Court of the United States. Photograph by "E.G.M." in 1899. Courtesy of Art & Visual Materials, Special Collections, Harvard Law School.

MATERIALS

O.W. Holmes, Jr., *The Common Law* (Boston, 1881), 1–5.

LECTURE I
EARLY FORMS OF LIABILITY

The object of this book is to present a general view of the Common Law. To accomplish the task, other tools are needed besides logic. It is something to show that the consistency of a system requires a particular result, but it is not all. The life of the law has not been logic: it has been experience. The felt necessities of the time, the prevalent moral and political theories, intuitions of public policy, avowed or unconscious, even the prejudices which judges share with their fellow-men, have had a good deal more to do than the syllogism in determining the rules by which men should be governed. The law embodies the story of a nation's development through many centuries, and it cannot be dealt with as if it contained only the axioms and corollaries of a book of mathematics. In order to know what it is, we must know what it has been, and what it tends to become. We must alternately consult history and existing theories of legislation. But the most difficult labor will be to understand the combination of the two into new products at every stage. The substance of the law at any given time pretty nearly corresponds, so far as it goes, with what is then understood to be convenient; but its form and machinery, and the degree to which it is able to work out desired results, depend very much upon its past.

In Massachusetts to-day, while, on the one hand, there are a great many rules which are quite sufficiently accounted for by their manifest good sense, on the other, there are some which can only be understood by reference to the infancy of procedure among the German tribes, or to the social condition of Rome under the Decemvirs.

I shall use the history of our law so far as it is necessary to explain a conception or to interpret a rule, but no further. In doing so there are two errors equally to be avoided both by writer and reader. One is that of supposing, because an idea seems very familiar and natural to us, that it has always been so. Many things which we take for granted have had to be laboriously fought out or thought out in past times. The other mistake is the opposite one of asking too much of history. We start with man full grown. It may be assumed that the earliest barbarian whose practices are to be considered, had a good many of the same feelings and passions as ourselves.

The first subject to be discussed is the general theory of liability civil and criminal. The Common Law has changed a good deal since the beginning of our series of reports, and the search after a theory which may now be said to prevail is very much a study of tendencies. I believe that it will be instructive to go back to the early forms of liability, and to start from them.

It is commonly known that the early forms of legal procedure were grounded in vengeance. Modern writers have thought that the Roman law started from the blood feud, and the authorities agree that the German law began in that way. The feud led to the composition, at first optional, then compulsory, by which the feud was bought off. The gradual encroachment of the composition may be traced in the Anglo-Saxon laws, and the feud was pretty well broken up, though not extinguished, by the time of William the Conqueror. The killings and house-burnings of an earlier day became the appeals of mayhem and arson. The appeals *de pace et plagis* and of mayhem became, or rather were in substance, the action of trespass which is still familiar to lawyers. But as the compensation recovered in the appeal was the alternative of vengeance, we might expect to find its scope limited to the scope of vengeance. Vengeance imports a feeling of blame, and an opinion, however distorted by passion, that a wrong has been done. It can hardly go very far beyond the case of a harm intentionally inflicted: even a dog distinguishes between being stumbled over and being kicked.

Whether for this cause or another, the early English appeals for personal violence seem to have been confined to intentional wrongs. Glanvill mentions mêlées, blows, and wounds,—all forms of intentional violence. In the fuller description of such appeals given by Bracton it is made quite clear that they were based on intentional assaults. The appeal *de pace et plagis* laid an intentional assault, described the nature of the arms used, and the length and depth of the wound. The appellor also had to show that he immediately raised the hue and cry. So when Bracton speaks of the lesser offences, which were not sued by way of appeal, he instances only intentional wrongs, such as blows with the fist, flogging, wounding, insults, and so forth. The cause of action in the cases of trespass reported in the earlier Year Books and in the *Abbreviatio Placitorum* is always an intentional wrong. It was only at a later day, and after argument, that trespass was extended so as to embrace harms which were foreseen, but which were not the intended consequence of the defendant's act. Thence again it extended to unforeseen injuries.

It will be seen that this order of development is not quite consistent with an opinion which has been held, that it was a characteristic of early law not to penetrate beyond the external visible fact, the *damnum corpore corpori datum*. It has been thought that an inquiry into the internal condition of the defendant, his culpability or innocence, implies a refinement of juridical conception equally foreign to Rome before the *Lex Aquilia*, and to England when trespass took its shape. I do not know any very satisfactory evidence that a man was generally held liable either in Rome or England for the accidental consequences even of his own act. But whatever may have been the early law, the foregoing account shows the starting-point of the system with which we have to deal. Our system of private liability for the consequences of a man's own acts, that is, for his trespasses, started from the notion of actual intent and actual personal culpability.

The original principles of liability for harm inflicted by another person or thing have been less carefully considered hitherto than those which governed trespass, and I shall therefore devote the rest of this Lecture to discussing them. I shall try to show that this liability also had its root in the passion of revenge, and to point out the changes by which it reached its present form. But I shall not confine myself strictly to what is needful for that purpose, because it is not only most interesting to trace the transformation throughout its whole extent, but the story will also afford an instructive example of the mode in which the law has grown, without a break, from barbarism to civilization. Furthermore, it will throw much light upon some important and peculiar doctrines which cannot be returned to later.

A very common phenomenon, and one very familiar to the student of history, is this. The customs, beliefs, or needs of a primitive time establish a rule or a formula. In the course of centuries the custom, belief, or necessity disappears, but the rule remains. The reason which gave rise to the rule has been forgotten, and ingenious minds set themselves to inquire how it is to be accounted for. Some ground of policy is thought of, which seems to explain it and to reconcile it with the present state of things; and then the rule adapts itself to the new reasons which have been found for it, and enters on a new career. The old form receives a new content, and in time even the form modifies itself to fit the meaning which it has received. The subject under consideration illustrates this course of events very clearly.

*   *   *   *   *

Oliver Wendell Holmes, Jr., "Natural Law," 32 Harvard Law Review 40 (1918) [Notes omitted].

NATURAL LAW

It is not enough for the knight of romance that you agree that his lady is a very nice girl—if you do not admit that she is the best that God ever made or will make, you must fight. There is in all men a demand for the superlative, so much so that the poor devil who has no other way of reaching it attains it by getting drunk. It seems to me that this demand is at the bottom of the philosopher's effort to prove that truth is absolute and of the jurist's search for criteria of universal validity which he collects under the head of natural law.

I used to say, when I was young, that truth was the majority vote of that nation that could lick all others. Certainly we may expect that the received opinion about the present war will depend a good deal upon which side wins (I hope with all my soul it will be mine), and I think that the statement was correct in so far as it implied that our test of truth is a reference to either a present or an imagined future majority in favor of our view. If, as I have suggested elsewhere, the truth may be defined as the system of my (intellectual) limitations, what gives it objectivity is the fact that I find my fellow man to a greater or less extent (never wholly) subject to the same *Can't Helps*. If I think that I am sitting at a table I find that the other persons present agree with me; so if I say that the sum of the angles of a triangle is equal to two right angles. If I am in a minority of one they send for a doctor or lock me up; and I am so far able to transcend the to me convincing testimony of my senses or my reason as to recognize that if I am alone probably something is wrong with my works.

Certitude is not the test of certainty. We have been cock-sure of many things that were not so. If I may quote myself again, property, friendship, and truth have a common root in time. One can not be wrenched from the rocky crevices into which one has grown for many years without feeling that one is attacked in one's life. What we most love and revere generally is determined by early associations. I love granite rocks and barberry bushes, no doubt because with them were my earliest joys that reach back through the past eternity of my life. But while one's experience thus makes certain preferences dogmatic for oneself, recognition of how they came to be so leaves one able to see that others, poor souls, may be equally dogmatic about something else. And this again means scepticism. Not that one's belief or love does not remain. Not that we would not fight and die for it if important—we all, whether we know it or not, are fighting to make the kind of a world that we should like—but that we have learned to recognize that others will fight and die to make a different world, with equal sincerity or belief. Deep-seated preferences can not be argued about—you can not argue a man into liking a glass of beer—and therefore, when differences are sufficiently far reaching, we try to kill the other man rather than let him have his way. But that is perfectly consistent with admitting that, so far as appears, his grounds are just as good as ours.

The jurists who believe in natural law seem to me to be in that naïve state of mind that accepts what has been familiar and accepted by them and their neighbors as something that must be accepted by all men everywhere. No doubt it is true that, so far as we can see ahead, some arrangements and the rudiments of familiar institutions seem to be necessary elements in any society that may spring from our own and that would seem to us to be civilized—some form of permanent association between the sexes—some residue of property individually owned—some mode of binding oneself to specified future conduct—at the bottom of all, some protection for the person. But without speculating whether a group is imaginable in which all but the last of these might disappear and the last be subject to qualifications that most of us would abhor, the question remains as to the *Ought* of natural law.

It is true that beliefs and wishes have a transcendental basis in the sense that their foundation is arbitrary. You can not help entertaining and feeling them, and there is an end of it. As an arbitrary fact people wish to live, and we say with various degrees of certainty that they can do so only on certain conditions. To do it they must eat and drink. That necessity is absolute. It is a necessity of less degree but practically general that they should live in society. If they live in society, so far as we can see, there are further conditions. Reason working on experience does tell us, no doubt, that if our wish to live continues, we can do it only on those terms. But that seems to me the whole of the matter. I see no *a priori* duty to live with others and in that way, but simply a statement of what I must do if I wish to remain alive. If I do live with others they tell me that I must do and abstain from doing various things or they will put the screws on to me. I believe that they will, and being of the same mind as to their conduct I not only accept the rules but come in time to accept them with sympathy and emotional affirmation and begin to talk about duties and rights. But for legal purposes a right is only the hypostasis of a prophecy—the imagination of a substance supporting the fact that the public force will be brought to bear upon those who do things said to contravene it—just as we talk of the force of gravitation accounting for the conduct of bodies in space. One phrase adds no more than the other to what we know without it. No doubt behind these legal rights is the fighting will of the subject to maintain them, and the spread of his emotions to the general rules by which they are maintained; but that does not seem to me the same thing as the supposed *a priori* discernment of a duty or the assertion of a preexisting right. A dog will fight for his bone.

The most fundamental of the supposed pre-existing rights—the right to life—is sacrificed without a scruple not only in war, but whenever the interest of society, that is, or the predominant power in the community, is thought to demand it. Whether that interest is the interest of mankind in the long run no one can tell, and as, in any event, to those who do not think with Kant and Hegel it is only an interest, the sanctity disappears. I remember a very tenderhearted judge being of opinion that closing a hatch to stop a fire and the destruction of a cargo was justified even if it was known that doing so would stifle a man below. It is idle to illustrate further, because to those who agree with me I am uttering commonplaces and to those who disagree I am ignoring the necessary foundations of thought. The *a priori* men generally call the dissentients superficial. But I do agree with them in believing that one's attitude on these matters is closely connected with one's general attitude toward the universe. Proximately, as has been suggested, it is determined largely by early associations and temperament, coupled with the desire to have an absolute guide. Men to a great extent believe what they want to—although I see in that no basis for a philosophy that tells us what we should want to want.

Now when we come to our attitude toward the universe I do not see any rational ground for demanding the superlative—for being dissatisfied unless we are assured that our truth is cosmic truth, if there is such a thing—that the ultimates of a little creature on this little earth are the last word of the unimaginable whole. If a man sees no reason for believing that significance, consciousness and ideals are more than marks of the finite, that does not justify what has been familiar in French sceptics; getting upon a pedestal and professing to look with haughty scorn upon a world in ruins. The real conclusion is that the part can not swallow the whole—that our categories are not, or may not be, adequate to formulate what we cannot know. If we believe that we come out of the universe, not it out of us, we must admit that we do not know what we are talking about when we speak of brute matter. We do know that a certain complex of energies can wag its tail and another can make syllogisms. These are among the powers of the unknown, and if, as may be, it has still greater powers that we can not understand, as Fabre in his studies of instinct would have us believe, studies that gave Bergson one of the strongest strands for his philosophy and enabled Maeterlinck to make us fancy for a moment that we heard a clang from behind phenomena—if this be true, why should we not be content? Why should we employ the energy that is furnished to us by the cosmos to defy it and shake our fist at the sky? It seems to me silly.

That the universe has in it more than we understand, that the private soldiers have not been told the plan of campaign, or even that there is one, rather than some vaster unthinkable to which every predicate is an impertinence, has no bearing upon our conduct. We still shall fight—all of us because we want to live, some, at least, because we want to realize our spontaneity and prove our powers, for the joy of it, and we may leave to the unknown the supposed final valuation of that which in any event has value to us. It is enough for us that the universe has produced us and has within it, as less than it, all that we believe and love. If we think of our existence not as that of a little god outside, but as that of a ganglion within, we have the infinite behind us. It gives us our only but our adequate significance. A grain of sand has the same, but what competent person supposes that he understands a grain of sand? That is as much beyond our grasp as man. If our imagination is strong enough to accept the vision of ourselves as parts inseverable from the rest, and to extend our final interest beyond the boundary of our skins, it justifies the sacrifice even of our lives for ends outside of ourselves. The motive, to be sure, is the common wants and ideals that we find in man. Philosophy does not furnish motives, but it shows men that they are not fools for doing what they already want to do. It opens to the forlorn hopes on which we throw ourselves away, the vista of the farthest stretch of human thought, the chords of a harmony that breathes from the unknown.

Max Weber, *Law in Economy and Society* (trans. from *Wirtschaft und Gesellschaft* by Edward Shils.) (Rheinstein ed. Harvard Univ. Press, 1954), 301, 302–304, 315–321. [Courtesy Harvard University Press.]

CHAPTER XI
THE FORMAL QUALITIES OF MODERN LAW

I. Specialization in Modern Law. As we have seen, the specifically modern occidental type of administration of justice has arisen on the basis of rational and systematic legislation. However, its basic formal qualities are by no means unambiguously definable. Indeed, this ambiguity is a direct result of more recent developments.

The ancient principles which were decisive for the interlocking of "right" and law have disappeared, especially the idea that one's right has a "valid" quality only by virtue of one's membership in a group of persons by whom this quality is monopolized. To the past now also belongs the tribal or status-group quality of the sum total of a person's rights and, with it, their "particularity" as it once existed on the basis of free association or of usurped or legalized privilege. Equally gone are the estatist and other special courts and procedures. Yet neither all special and personal law nor all special jurisdictions have disappeared completely. On the contrary, very recent legal developments have brought an increasing specialization within the legal system.

*   *   *   *   *

2. The Anti-Formalistic Tendencies of Modern Legal Development. From a theoretical point of view, the general development of law and procedure may be viewed as passing through the following stages: first, charismatic legal revelation through "law prophets"; second, empirical creation and finding of law by legal honoratiores, i.e., law creation through cautelary jurisprudence and adherence to precedent; third, imposition of law by secular or theocratic powers; fourth and finally, systematic elaboration of law and professionalized administration of justice by persons who have received their legal training in a learned and formally logical manner. From this perspective, the formal qualities of the law emerge as follows: arising in primitive legal procedure from a combination of magically conditioned formalism and irrationality conditioned by revelation, they proceed to increasingly specialized juridical and logical rationality and systematization, passing through a stage of theocratically or patrimonially conditioned substantive and informal expediency. Finally, they assume, at least from an external viewpoint, an increasingly logical sublimation and deductive rigor and develop an increasingly rational technique in procedure.

Since we are here only concerned with the most general lines of development, we shall ignore the fact that in historical reality the theoretically constructed stages of rationalization have not everywhere followed in the sequence which we have just outlined, even if we ignore the world outside the Occident. We shall not be troubled either by the multiplicity of causes of the particular type and degree of rationalization that a given law has actually assumed. As our brief sketch has already shown, we shall only recall that the great differences in the line of development have been essentially influenced, first, by the diversity of political power relationships, which, for reasons to be discussed later, have resulted in very different degrees of power of the imperium vis-à-vis the powers of the kinship groups, the folk community, and the estates; second, by the relations between the theocratic and the secular powers; and, third, by the differences in the structure of those legal honoratiores who were significant for the development of a given law and which, too, were largely dependent upon political factors.

*   *   *   *   *

3. *Contemporary Anglo-American Law.* The differences between continental and common law methods of legal thought have been produced mostly by factors which are respectively connected with the internal structure and the modes of existence of the legal profession as well as by factors related to differences in political development. The economic elements, however, have been determinative only in connection with these elements. What we are concerned with here is the fact that, once everything is said and done about these differences in historical developments, modern capitalism prospers equally and manifests essentially identical economic traits under legal systems containing rules and institutions which considerably differ from each other at least from the juridical point of view. Even what is on the face of it so fundamental a concept of continental law as *dominium* still does not exist in Anglo-American law. Indeed, we may say that the legal systems under which modern capitalism has been prospering differ profoundly from each other even in their ultimate principles of formal structure.

Even today, and in spite of all influences by the ever more rigorous demands for academic training, English legal thought is essentially an empirical art. Precedent still fully retains its old significance, except that it is regarded as unfair to invoke a case from too remote a past, which means older than about a century. One can also still observe the charismatic character of lawfinding, especially, although not exclusively, in the new countries, and quite particularly the United States. In practice, varying significance is given to a decided case not only, as happens everywhere, in accordance with the hierarchical position of the court by which it was decided but also in accordance with the very personal authority of an individual judge. This it true for the entire common-law sphere, as illustrated, for instance, by the prestige of Lord Mansfield. But in the American view, the judgment is the very personal creation of the concrete individual judge, to whom one is accustomed to refer by name, in contrast to the impersonal "District Court" of Continental-European officialese. The English judge, too, lays claim to such a position. All these circumstances are tied up with the fact that the degree of legal rationality is essentially lower than, and of a type different from, that of continental Europe. Up to the recent past, and at any rate up to the time of Austin, there was practically no English legal science which would have merited the name of "learning" in the continental sense. This fact alone would have sufficed to render any such codification as was desired by Bentham practically impossible. But it is also this feature which has been responsible for the "practical" adaptability of English law and its "practical" character from the standpoint of the public.

The legal thinking of the layman is, on the one hand, literalistic. He tends to be a definition-monger when he believes he is arguing "legally." Closely connected with this trait is the tendency to draw conclusions from individual case to individual case; the abstractionism of the "professional" lawyer is far from the layman's mind. In both respects, however, the art of empirical jurisprudence is cognate to him, although he may not like it. No country, indeed, has produced more bitter complaints and satires about the legal profession than England. The formularies of the conveyancers, too, may be quite unintelligible to the layman, as again is the case in England. Yet, he can understand the basic character of the English way of legal thinking, he can identify himself with it and, above all, he can make his peace with it by retaining once and for all a solicitor as his legal father confessor for all contingencies of life, as is indeed done by practically every English businessman. He simply neither demands nor expects of the law anything which could be frustrated by "logical" legal construction.

Safety valves are also provided against legal formalism. As a matter of fact, in the sphere of private law, both common law and equity are "formalistic" to a considerable extent in their practical treatment. It would hardly be otherwise under a system of stare decisis and the traditionalist spirit of the legal profession. But the institution of the civil jury imposes on rationality limits which are not merely accepted as inevitable but are actually prized because of the binding force of precedent and the fear that a precedent might thus create "bad law" in a sphere which one wishes to keep open for a concrete balancing of interests. We must forego the analysis of the way in which this division of the two spheres of *stare decisis* and concrete balancing of interests is actually functioning in practice. It does in any case represent a softening of rationality in the administration of justice. Alongside all this we find the still quite patriarchal, summary and highly irrational jurisdiction of the justices of the peace. They deal with the petty causes of everyday life and, as can be readily seen in Mendelssohn's description, they represent a kind of Khadi justice which is quite unknown in Germany. All in all, the Common Law thus presents a picture of an administration of justice which in the most fundamental formal features of both substantive law and procedure differs from the structure of continental law as much as is possible within a secular system of justice, that is, a system that is free from theocratic and patrimonial powers. Quite definitely, English law-finding is not, like that of the Continent, "application" of "legal propositions" logically derived from statutory texts.

These differences have had some tangible consequences both economically and socially; but these consequences have all been isolated single phenomena rather than differences touching upon the total structure of the economic system. For the development of capitalism two features have been relevant and both have helped to support the capitalistic system. Legal training has primarily been in the hands of the lawyers from among whom also the judges are recruited, i.e., in the hands of a group which is active in the service of propertied, and particularly capitalistic, private interests and which has to gain its livelihood from them. Furthermore and in close connection with this, the concentration of the administration of justice at the central courts in London and its extreme costliness have amounted almost to a denial of access to the courts for those with inadequate means. At any rate, the essential similarity of the capitalistic development on the Continent and in England has not been able to eliminate the sharp contrasts between the two types of legal systems. Nor is there any visible tendency towards a transformation of the English legal system in the direction of the continental under the impetus of the capitalist economy. On the contrary, wherever the two kinds of administration of justice and of legal training have had the opportunity

to compete with one another, as for instance in Canada, the Common Law way
has come out on top and has overcome the continental alternative rather
quickly. We may thus conclude that capitalism has not been a decisive factor in
the promotion of that form of rationalization of the law which has been peculiar to the continental West ever since the rise of Romanist studies in the medieval universities.

4. *Lay Justice and Corporative Tendencies in the Modern Legal Profession.*
Modern social development, aside from the already mentioned political and
internal professional motives, has given rise to certain other factors by which
formal legal rationalism is being weakened. Irrational Khadi justice is exercised today in criminal cases clearly and extensively in the "popular" justice
of the jury. It appeals to the sentiments of the layman, who feels annoyed
whenever he meets with formalism in a concrete case, and it satisfies the emotional demands of those underprivileged classes which clamor for substantive
justice.

Against this "popular justice" element of the jury system, attacks have been
directed from two quarters. The jury has been attacked because of the strong
interest orientation of the jurors as against the technical matter-of-factness of
the specialist. Just as in ancient Rome the jurors' list was the object of class
conflict, so today the selection of jurors is attacked, especially by the working
class, as favoring class justice, upon the ground that the jurors, even though
they may be "plebeians," are picked predominantly from among those who
can afford the loss of time. Although such a test of selection can hardly be
avoided entirely, it also depends, in part at least, on political considerations.
Where, on the other hand, the jurors' bench is occupied by working-class
people, it is attacked by the propertied class. Moreover, not only "classes" as
such are the interested parties. In Germany, for instance, male jurors can practically never be moved to find a fellow male guilty of rape, especially where
they are not absolutely convinced of the girl's chaste character. But in this connection we must consider that in Germany female virtue is not held in great respect anyway.

From the standpoint of professional legal training lay justice has been criticized on the ground that the laymen's verdict is delivered as an irrational oracle
without any statement of reasons and without the possibility of any substantive
criticism. Thus one has come to demand that the lay judges be subjected to the
control of the legal experts. In answer to this demand there was created the system of the mixed bench, which, however, experience has shown to be a system in
which the laymen's influence is inferior to that of the experts. Thus their presence
has practically no more significance than that of giving some compulsory publicity to the deliberation of professional judges in a way similar to that of Switzer-
land, where the judges must hold their deliberation in full view of the public. The
professional judges, in turn, are threatened, in the sphere of criminal law, by the
overshadowing power of the professional psychiatrist, onto whom more and
more responsibility is passed, especially in the most serious cases, and on whom
rationalism is thus imposing a task which can by no means be solved by means
of pure science.

Obviously all of these conflicts are caused by the course of technical and economic development only indirectly, namely in so far as it has favored intellectu-
alism. Primarily they are rather consequences of the insoluble conflict between

the formal and the substantive principles of justice, which may clash with one another even where their respective protagonists belong to one and the same social class. Moreover, it is by no means certain that those classes which are underprivileged today, especially the working class, may safely expect from an informal administration of justice those results which are claimed for it by the ideology of the jurists. A bureaucratized judiciary, which is being planfully recruited in the higher ranks from among the personnel of the career service of the prosecutor's office and which is completely dependent on the politically ruling powers for advancement, cannot be set alongside the Swiss or English judiciary, and even less the (federal) judges in the United States. If one takes away from such judges their belief in the sacredness of the purely objective legal formalism and directs them simply to balance interests, the result will be very different from those legal systems to which we have just referred. However, the problem does not belong to this discussion. There remains only the task of correcting a few historical errors.

Prophets are the only ones who have taken a really consciously "creative" attitude toward existing law; only through them has new law been consciously created. For the rest, as must be stressed again and again, even those jurists who, from the objective point of view, have been the most creative ones, have always and not only in modern times, regarded themselves to be but the mouthpiece of norms already existing, though, perhaps, only latently, and to be their interpreters or appliers rather than their creators. This subjective belief is held by even the most eminent jurists. It is due to the disillusionment of the intellectuals that today this belief is being confronted with objectively different facts and that one is trying to elevate this state of facts to the status of a norm for subjective judicial behavior. As the bureaucratization of formal legislation progresses, the traditional position of the English judge is also likely to be transformed permanently and profoundly. On the other hand, it may be doubted whether, in a code country, the bestowal of the "creator's" crown upon bureaucratic judges will really turn them into law prophets. In any case, the juristic precision of judicial opinions will be seriously impaired if sociological, economic, or ethical argument were to take the place of legal concepts.

All in all the movement is one of those characteristic onslaughts against the dominance of "specialization" and rationalism, which latter has in the last analysis been its very parent. Thus the development of the formal qualities of the law appears to have produced peculiar antinomies. Rigorously formalistic and dependent on what is tangibly perceivable as far as it is required for security to do business, the law has at the same time become informal for the sake of business loyalty, in so far as required by the logical interpretation of the intention of the parties or by the "good usage" of business intercourse, which is understood to be tending toward some "ethical minimum."

The law is drawn into antiformal directions, moreover, by all those powers which demand that it be more than a mere means of pacifying conflicts of interests. These forces include the demand for substantive justice by certain social class interests and ideologies; they also include the tendencies inherent in certain forms of political authority of either authoritarian or democratic character concerning the ends of law which are respectively appropriate to them; and also the demand of the "laity" for a system of justice which would be in-

Illustration 14-4   Louis Dembitz Brandeis (1856–1941), Associate Justice (1916–1939), Supreme Court of the United States. Photographer and date unknown. Courtesy Art & Visual Materials, Special Collections, Harvard Law School.

telligible to them; finally, as we have seen, anti-formal tendencies are being promoted by the ideologically rooted power aspirations of the legal profession itself.

Whatever form law and legal practice may come to assume under the impact of these various influences, it will be inevitable that, as a result of technical and economic developments, the legal ignorance of the layman will increase. The use of jurors and similar lay judges will not suffice to stop the continuous growth of the technical element in the law and hence of its character as a specialists' domain. Inevitably the notion must expand that the law is a rational technical apparatus, which is continually transformable in the light of expediential considerations and devoid of all sacredness of content. This fate may be obscured by the tendency of acquiescence in the existing law, which is growing in many ways for several reasons, but it cannot really be stayed. All of the modern sociological and philosophical analyses, many of which are of a high scholarly value, can only contribute to strengthen this impression, regardless of the content of their theories concerning the nature of law and the judicial process.

Duncan Kennedy, "The Structure of Blackstone's Commentaries," Vol. 28 *Buffalo Law Review* 209 (1979) 209–211, 381-382. [Notes omitted.] [Courtesy *Buffalo Law Review* and Duncan Kennedy.]

"[T]he material relations of production of the capitalist epoch only are what they are in combination with the forms in which they are reflected in the pre-scientific and bourgeois-scientific consciousness of the period; and they could not subsist in reality without these forms of consciousness." [K. Korsch, *Marxism and Philosophy* 88–89 (F. Halliday trans. 1970).]

INTRODUCTION

This article is a version of the first chapter of a book on the history of American legal thought. It has two purposes. The first is to provide an introduction to Blackstone's *Commentaries on the Laws of England*, an important 18th century legal treatise that all legal scholars have heard of but practically no one knows anything about. The second is to introduce the reader to a method for understanding the political significance of legal thinking, a method that might be called structuralist or phenomenological, or neo-Marxist, or all three together.

I don't intend to provide any background information on Blackstone, except to say that he published his treatise in England between 1765 and 1769, and that aside from Chancellor Kent's *Commentaries on the Laws of the United States*, published between 1820 and 1825, Blackstone's work is the only systematic attempt that has been made to present a theory of the whole common law system. It is the single most important source on English legal thinking in the 18th century, and it has had as much (or more) influence on American legal thought as it has had on British.

The method this study exemplifies is, like the *Commentaries*, familiar in name but altogether unfamiliar in practice to most American legal scholars. For this reason, I begin with a methodological excursion. As for the origins of the method, let me say only that I am trying to apply to legal thought techniques developed over two centuries in what is sometimes called the "continental" tradition of philosophy, social theory, history, psychology and anthropology. My approach owes a great deal to the work of Peter Gabel and Roberto Unger, and to that of Al Katz, whose essay in this issue of the *Buffalo Law Review* has greatly influenced my thinking.

Everything that I will have to say flows from (but is in no sense logically entailed by) a premise about legal thinking. This premise is that the activity of categorizing, analyzing, and explaining legal rules has a double motive. On the one hand, it is an effort to discover the conditions of social justice. On the other, it is an attempt to deny the truth of our painfully contradictory feelings about the actual state of relations between persons in our social world. In its first aspect, it is a utopian enterprise constituting, in E.P. Thompson's phrase, a "cultural achievement of universal significance." In its second aspect, it has been (as a matter of historical fact rather than of logical necessity) an instrument of apology—an attempt to mystify both dominators and dominated by convincing them of the "naturalness," the "freedom" and the "rationality" of a condition of bondage. I will be concerned in this paper with the second aspect—of denial and apology—but I don't want to be understood to deny the first, utopian aspect.

From this perspective, Blackstone is important on three distinct grounds. First, he was a pivotal figure in the development of what I will call the liberal mode of American legal thought. His work set out together, for the first time in English, all the themes that right to the present day characterize attempts to legitimate the status quo through doctrinal exegesis. Second, he presented these familiar arguments and categories as parts of a larger structure that is quite unfamiliar to the modern reader. By analyzing that structure, we can get a sense of the contingency of our accustomed modes of thought in approaching what seem the most elementary legal issues.

Third, Blackstone is supremely unconvincing. Although he made many contributions to the utopian enterprise of legality, his *Commentaries* as a whole quite patently attempt to "naturalize" purely social phenomena. They restate as "freedom" what we see as servitude. And they cast as rational order what we see as something like chaos. At least since Bentham's *Fragment on Government*, critics have linked these traits of the *Commentaries* to Blackstone's desire to legitimate the legal status quo of the England of his day. Thus Blackstone serves both as a convenient starting point for the substantive history of American legal thought *and* as a relatively easy object for the method of discovering hidden political intentions beneath the surface of legal exposition.

*   *   *   *   *

Blackstone developed his structural opposition between natural liberty and the general welfare achieved through regulation as an aspect of his strategy for legitimating the "artificial" institutions (feudal and capitalist) of the legal system of his time. He devised a sort of compromise in which both hierarchical formal inequality and substantive inequality through property rights could seem to flow from the postulated equality of the state of nature. But the devices he employed transformed and greatly strengthened the theory on which they were parasitic. Rights were, and are, much more plausible if we can base their definition simultaneously on a libertarian logic of "nature" and on the "only apparently" contradictory needs of the community.

To my mind, Blackstone's enduring success in America is better explained in these terms than in the more prosaic and therefore more plausible ones that come readily to mind. It is true that the *Commentaries* were the only convenient way for several generations of American lawyers to learn law. His very irrelevance to 19th century America made him an invaluable asset in the professional game of rendering professional knowledge inaccessible to the layman. And there were his fragmentary but important contributions to particular aspects of liberal theory, like the separation of powers or executive subordination to the rule of law. His histories of land law and of the gradual constriction of royal prerogative through the rise of the commons gave 19th century American law both a sense of where it came from and a sense of where it was going.

But Blackstone stood for more than any of these. The pre-legal natural liberty of antagonistic individuals became, in conflicts mediated by the ideas of convenience and implied consent, the fully legal absolute and relative rights of persons. That same natural liberty, clashing with sovereignty, began its transmutation into the legal but limited constitutional rights against the state of American citizens. Sovereignty—unrestrained and unrestrainable state power—went through its own transformation. In the same conflict that limited and legalized natural liberty, the mediation of convenience and implied consent turned sovereignty into something like our legislative police power. The relations of men in the state of nature, and the relation of natural right to sovereignty, were conundrums of political theory. But the relations of legal rights to one another and to the police power were *legal* problems.

A final picture may help here:

Illustration 14-5

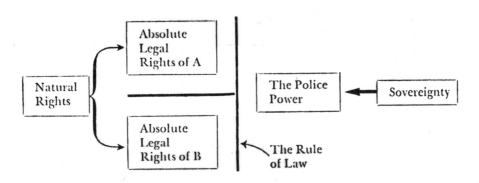

The body of the *Commentaries*, seen in this light, was a vast explication of the single notion that the conflict of right with right was illusory, and that the same was therefore true of the conflict of right with power. Where Hobbes and Locke were opposite sides of a coin, Blackstone argued that law was *the coin itself*. He invited generations of liberal legal thinkers to find legal answers to the problem of conflict, because he presented the problem at the same time as the linchpin of liberal theory, and as a surmountable challenge to theoretical ingenuity. The enterprise goes on to this day, sustained in bankruptcy, like the rail system or a defense conglomerate, by the combination of naivete, self-interest and fear of the alternatives. But even thus reduced, it still plays the role Rousseau identified: "The strong is never strong enough to be always the strongest, unless he transforms strength into right, and obedience into duty."

Roberto M. Unger, *Law in Modern Society* (The Free Press, 1976) pp. 192–202, 205–208, 209–210, 213–214, 238–242. [Courtesy the Free Press, an imprint of Simon & Schuster.]

THE DISINTEGRATION OF THE RULE OF LAW
IN POSTLIBERAL SOCIETY

Postliberal society

An understanding of liberal society illuminates, and is illuminated by, an awareness of that society's legal order and legal ideals. For the rule of law has been truly said to be the soul of the modern state. The study of the legal system takes us straight to the central problems faced by the society itself.

If this hypothesis, which underlies my argument, is correct, then any revision of the nature and uses of law will reveal changes in the basic arrangements of society and in men's conceptions of themselves. At the same time, whatever we can learn about these social changes will help us reinterpret the transformation of the legal order. In this spirit, I discuss on the following pages some aspects of the way certain countries, the Western capitalist social democracies, have become postliberal societies.

The characteristics of these societies undermine the rule of law and they strengthen tendencies in belief and organization that ultimately discourage reliance on public and positive rules as bases of social order. These startling trends will force us to reexamine our view of the situation and the prospects of postliberal societies. For immediate purposes, it is enough to emphasize two commonly observed sets of features of this novel form of social life.

The first group of features refers to the overt intervention of government in areas previously regarded as beyond the proper reach of state action. The response to the problems of unjustified hierarchy, a response the rule of law failed to provide, is now sought from the government. The rank order itself increasingly moves to the center of political debate and political action. As the state becomes involved in the tasks of overt redistribution, regulation, and planning, it changes into a welfare state.

The other notable set of attributes of postliberal society is but the reverse side of the events just enumerated: the gradual approximation of state and society, of the public and the private sphere. For one thing, the state's pretense to being a neutral guardian of the social order is abandoned. For another thing, private organizations are increasingly recognized and treated as entities with the kind of power that traditional doctrine viewed as the prerogative of government. People may become more conscious of what was always partly true, though perhaps less so in earlier periods: society consists of a constellation of governments, rather than an association of individuals held together by a single government. The state that has lost both the reality and the consciousness of its separation from society is a corporate state.

Now let us see how these welfare and corporatist tendencies affect the society's normative order.

The welfare state and the decline of the rule of law

Welfare state developments influence the legal order of postliberal society in a variety of ways. But two kinds of immediate influence seem particularly significant.

The first type of effect is the rapid expansion of the use of open-ended standards and general clauses in legislation, administration, and adjudication. For example, the courts may be charged to police unconscionable contracts, to void unjust enrichment, to control economic concentration so as to maintain competitive markets, or to determine whether a government agency has acted in the public interest. Such indeterminate prescriptions have always existed in the law, but they grow rapidly in prominence because of the transformations to which I refer.

The second major impact of the welfare state on law is the turn from formalistic to purposive or policy-oriented styles of legal reasoning and from concerns with formal justice to an interest in procedural and substantive justice. Before further discussion, these terms should be defined.

Legal reasoning is formalistic when the mere invocation of rules and the deduction of conclusions from them is believed sufficient for every authoritative legal choice. It is purposive when the decision about how to apply a rule depends on a judgment of how most effectively to achieve the purposes ascribed to the rule. The difference between these two types of legal reasoning is one between the criteria thought appropriate to the overt justification or criticism of official decisions; it does not pretend to describe the actual causes and motives of decision.

An ideal of justice is formal when it makes the uniform application of general rules the keystone of justice or when it establishes principles whose validity is supposedly independent of choices among conflicting values. It is procedural when it imposes conditions on the legitimacy of the processes by which social advantages are exchanged or distributed. It is substantive when it governs the actual outcome of distributive decisions or of bargains. Thus, in contract law, the doctrine that bargains are enforceable given certain externally visible manifestations of intent exemplifies formal justice; the demand that there be equality of bargaining power among contracting parties illustrates procedural justice; and the prohibition of exchanges of two performances of unequal value, however value may be assessed, represents substantive justice.

A formal view of justice requires, to be coherent, a belief in the possibility of formalistic legal reasoning. And it is likely to be most persuasive in the realm of exchanges among individuals rather than in that of governmental distribution, which inevitably involves choices among conflicting interests. Thus, it tends to distinguish sharply between an impersonal justice of reciprocity that dispenses with distributive premises and an arbitrary justice of distribution whose pronouncements are never impartial and general enough to have anything more than the appearance of law.

Procedural or substantive notions of justice become important as purposive forms of legal reasoning are adopted, and they in turn give impetus to those varieties of argument. For policy-oriented legal discourse forces one to make explicit choices among values, and the pursuit of procedural or substantive justice requires that rules be interpreted in terms of ideals that define the conception of justice. Hence, every decision about the principles that govern exchange is seen to rest upon procedural or distributive premises and to have procedural or distributive consequences.

Postliberal society witnesses an escalating use of open-ended standards and a swing toward purposive legal reasoning and procedural or substantive approaches to justice. This is a change of emphasis rather than a sequence of clearly differentiated stages. In few societies have these shifts followed a line of uninterrupted progression. Periods of greater stress on formalistic legal reasoning and formal justice have followed eras of a more policy-oriented mode of legal discourse, as in nineteenth-century American. Even during the hegemony of formalism, there has often been a widespread awareness of the fact that the legal order was redistributing resources among groups and classes. Nevertheless, I shall argue later that present-day tendencies differ from their earlier counterparts not merely because of the more pronounced, persistent and universal character of the contemporary developments, but, above all, because of the emergence in the welfare-corporate state of a unique relationship among problems of formality, equity, community, and equality in law.

The immediate causes of the postliberal moves toward purposive legal reasoning and procedural or substantive justice are directly connected with the inner dynamic of the welfare state. These moves appear as ways to deal with concentrated power in the private order or to correct the effects of a system of formal rules. As government assumes managerial responsibilities, it must work in areas in which the complexity and variability of relevant factors of decision seem too great to allow for general rules, whence the recourse to vague standards. These standards need to be made concrete and individualized by persons charged with their administrative or judicial execution.

The reasons for the greater emphasis on purposive legal reasoning and on procedural or substantive justice are more obscure and less amenable to a comprehensive interpretation. Changes in the theoretical understanding of language, in the character of common beliefs about the basis and scope of legitimate state action, and in the structure of the rank order all seem to play a part. Language is no longer credited with the fixity of categories and the transparent representation of the world that would make formalism plausible in legal reasoning or in ideas about justice. In the absence of belief in the naturalness of existing hierarchies of power or distribution, the legitimacy of governmental, including judicial, activity comes to depend increasingly on the welfare consequences of that activity. Finally, the vicissitudes of class struggle strip the state of every pretense to impartiality and transform it into an acknowledged tool of factional interest in a social situation in which the dictates of justice are still believed to be unknowable.

Whatever the causes of the trends I have described and however much they may vary from one country to another, their chief effects on the law seem clear. They repeatedly undermine the relative generality and the autonomy that distinguish the legal order from other kinds of law, and in the course of so doing they help discredit the political ideals represented by the rule of law.

Open-ended clauses and general standards force courts and administrative agencies to engage in ad hoc balancings of interest that resist reduction to general rules. One of the corollaries of generality in law is a severe limitation of the range of facts considered relevant to the making of official choices. If the number of pertinent factors of decision is too large, and each of them is constantly shifting, then categories of classification or criteria of analogy will be hard to draw and even harder to maintain. But the kinds of problems to which comprehensive standards characteristically apply tend to defy such limitations. They involve the conflict of numerous and inchoate interests against the background of a refusal to sacrifice any one of these interests completely to the others.

When attempts are made to codify standards, to reduce them to rules, their character is distorted. Either a large area of uncontrolled discretion and individualization subsists under the trappings of general norms, or the flexibility needed to make managerial decisions or to produce equitable results is lost. The same dialectic of illusion and petrification can be observed in the analogous processes by which Roman praetorian law was overtaken by imperial legislation, English equity lost out to common law, and the customary or sacred laws of non-Western societies were codified by colonial administrators.

Purposive legal reasoning and nonformal justice also cause trouble for the ideal of generality. The policy-oriented lawyer insists that part of interpreting a rule is to choose the most efficient means to the attainment of the ends one assigns to it. But the circumstances to which decisions are addressed change and as the decisionmaker's understanding of the means available to him varies, so must the way he interprets rules. This instability of result will also increase with the fluctuations of accepted policy and with the variability of the particular problems to be resolved. Hence, the very notion of stable areas of individual entitlement and obligation, a notion inseparable from the rule of law ideal, will be eroded.

The quest for substantive justice corrupts legal generality to an even greater degree. When the range of impermissible inequalities among social situations expands, the need for individualized treatment grows correspondingly. No matter how substantive justice is defined, it can be achieved only by treating different situations differently. Thus, for example, it may become necessary to compensate for an existing inequality with a reverse preference afforded by the legal order to the disadvantaged group. Priorities among groups in turn shade imperceptibility into preferences among individuals and individual situations.

The history of the law of obligations and of liability rules in many Western social democracies illustrates another way in which the insistence on substantive justice enters into conflict with established notions of generality. Classic theories of contractual and delictual liability drew a sharp line between the allegedly impersonal justice of reciprocity, with which they were concerned, and distributive justice, which, if it existed at all, was the province of politics and the marketplace. At the same time, they confined liability to areas of conduct that seemed amenable to general rules and they asserted its absolute character within those confines.

In the era of the welfare state and of policy-oriented legal discourse, there is a firmer recognition that exchange rules do have a distributive significance. Nonetheless, the attempt to take distributive criteria into account in an adjudicative setting unavoidably forces the courts into fields in which the complexity of relevant factors and the lack of widely shared standards of justice make generalization hard to come by and to stick with. The situation is aggravated by the impulse to extend liability, in response to equitable considerations, to areas where the same sorts of problems arise. And the difficulty is compounded still further by the willingness, in criminal as well as in private law, to admit a growing list of exculpatory conditions within this enlarged sphere of liability. For the granting of an excuse turns on judgments about particular persons and individualized situations, judgments that resist statement as rules.

The same events that subvert the generality also tend to destroy the relative autonomy of the legal order in its substantive, methodological, institutional, and occupational dimensions.

Overarching standards invite their appliers to make use of the technician's conception of efficiency or the layman's view of justice. If, for example, one seeks to give content to the conception of good faith in contract law, one must go outside the narrow confines of lawyers' learning to consult the practices and enter into the thought patterns of a certain social group.

As purposive legal reasoning and concerns with substantive justice begin to prevail, the style of legal discourse approaches that of commonplace political or economic argument. All are characterized by the predominance of instrumental rationality over other modes of thought. Indeed, policy-oriented legal argument represents an unstable accommodation between the assertion and the abandonment of the autonomy of legal reasoning, just as procedural justice mediates between formal and substantive justice.

The decline in the distinctiveness of legal reasoning is connected with the need administrators and judges have of reaching out to the substantive ideals of different groups, of drawing upon a conventional morality or a dominant tradition.

These changes in the substance and method of law also help undercut the identity of legal institutions and of the legal profession. Courts begin to resemble openly first administrative, then other political institutions. Thus, the difference between lawyers and other bureaucrats or technicians starts to disappear.

The cumulative impact of the movements discussed in the preceding pages is to encourage the dissolution of the rule of law, at least insofar as that form of legality is defined by its commitment to the generality and autonomy of law. To be sure, autonomy and generality could never be meant as completely actualized descriptions of the legal order in liberal society; they are no more than ideals which the liberal form of social life makes necessary to entertain and impossible to achieve fully. What distinguishes the law of the postliberal period is primarily the turning away from these ideals, a change of course that, despite its apparent insignificance, indicates important shifts in human belief and social order.

The corporate state and the attack on public and positive law

The corporatist tendencies of postliberal society have potentially an even more dramatic effect on the law than the welfare state trends. If the latter contribute to the disintegration of the rule of law, the former ultimately challenge the more universal and elementary phenomenon of bureaucratic law, law that is public and positive.

The spearhead of corporatism is the effacement both in organization and in consciousness of the boundary between state and society, and therefore between the public and the private realm. As the state reaches into society, society itself generates institutions that rival the state in their power and take on many attributes formerly associated with public bodies. It is doubtless true that much of the earlier separation of government and society may have been more a matter of vision than of reality. But here one must tread carefully. The images people hold of their social situation are an integral part of those situations; indeed, they establish their specifically social meaning. Thus, a modest change of emphasis in forms of organization may be important if it is accompanied by a transformation of belief. The corporatist developments, like the welfare state ones mentioned earlier, seem to exemplify this principle.

Corporatism's most obvious influence on the law is its contribution to the growth of a body of rules that break down the traditional distinction between public and private law. Thus, administrative, corporate, and labor law merge into a body of social law that is more applicable to the structure of private-public organizations than to official conduct or private transactions. But though this development undermines the conventional contrast of public and private law, it does not necessarily destroy the broader difference between the law of the state and the internal, privately determined regulations of private associations. Insofar as private law is laid down by the state, it too is, in this more comprehensive sense, public.

The deepest and least understood impact of corporatism is the one it has on the very distinction between the law of the state and the spontaneously produced normative order of nonstate institutions. As private organizations become bureaucratized in response to the same search for impersonal power that attracts government to the rule of law principle, they begin to acquire the features, and to suffer the problems, of the state. At the same time, the increasing recognition of the power these organizations exercise, in a quasi-public manner, over the lives of their members makes it even harder to maintain the distinction between state action and private conduct. Finally, the social law of institutions is a law compounded of state-authored rules and of privately sponsored regulations or practices; its two elements are less and less capable of being separated. All these movements, which tend to destroy the public character of law, carry forward a process that begins in the failure of liberal society to keep its promise of concentrating all significant power in government.

The tendency of large corporate organizations to become bureaucratized and to produce a body of rules with many of the characteristics of state law should not be confused with an increasing regulation of the corporation by the state. In fact, quite the opposite may be true: the bureaucratization of corporate institutions may be associated with their ability to become relatively independent power centers with decisive influence over government agencies.

*   *   *   *   *

Formality and equity. The polar opposite to justification by rules is equity, the intuitive sense of justice in the particular case. The formalist views equity as amorphous because it cannot be codified as a system of rules and as tyrannical because all moral judgments are subjective even if they are widely shared. Hence, the most that may be granted to equity is the role of tempering the consequences of formalism that seem intolerably harsh in the light of prevailing moral ideas.

The more equity is sacrificed to the logic of rules, the greater the distance between official law and the lay sentiment of right. As a result, the law loses its intelligibility as well as its legitimacy in the eyes of the layman; he knows it either as a chest of magical tools to be used by the well-placed or as a series of lightning bolts falling randomly on the righteous and the wicked.

To understand why the conflict between formality and equity is unavoidable, we must consider the cognate of equity, which is solidarity.

Formality and solidarity. Legality, which operates through rules established before disputes arise, differs from procedures of justification that resist yielding clear-cut rules. Such might be procedures that were concerned primarily with reconciling the parties or with vindicating, harmonizing, and developing, in the context of dispute settlement, moral ideals cherished by the broader communities to which the judge and the litigants belonged. For this moral sense of the community seems to transcend any system of rules or principles in which one tries to express or to encase it.

What accounts for our seeming inability to devise a set of prescriptions that adequately reflects the subtlety and richness of our moral ideas? Surely the complexity of our ethical commitments is not in and of itself a sufficient explanation; all rules are outcomes of a multitude of conflicting aspirations and interests. The true reason lies in the central role which the idea of solidarity plays in the moral life and in the impossibility of solving the problem of solidarity by any system of rights based upon equality of respect or variations of desert.

The kernel of solidarity is our feeling of responsibility for those whose lives touch in some way upon our own and our greater or lesser willingness to share their fate. Solidarity is the social face of love; it is concern with another as a person rather than just respect for him as a bearer of formally equal rights and duties or admiration for his gifts and achievements.

Respect is owed to men for what they have in common by virtue of their equal dignity; it sets aside each individual's distinctiveness. Admiration recognizes another's skills or accomplishments. Love differs from respect because it prizes the loved one's humanity in the unique form of his individual personality. It differs from admiration because it addresses the total personality rather than some facet of it and because it surpasses the limits of praise and blame. Love is neither an act nor an emotion, but a gift of self, an opening up to another person, which may, for external reasons, fail to eventuate in acts and may also exist in the presence of hostile emotions the lover is unable to overcome. Solidarity does not differ in kind from love; it is merely love struggling to move beyond the circle of intimacy. When we fail to achieve the fuller communion and knowledge required by love, we may nevertheless be able to acknowledge another's unique value as a person to the extent of sharing in some predicament he faces.

There is a simple reason why no set of rules and principles can do justice to the sentiment of solidarity. A legal order confers entitlements and obligations; the more formal it becomes, the more does it treat each entitlement as a power to be exercised in the discretion of the powerholder. An individual's rights and duties, whether assumed by contract or imposed directly by law, become part of his objective situation. They resemble the forces of nature in the way they set limits to his striving.

But solidarity means that one takes no entitlements for granted. A powerholder who acts out of a sense of solidarity will always have to ask himself whether the exercise of his power in a particular situation would be consistent with the aim of sharing the burden of the people with whom he is dealing. To this question, there can never be a general answer, laid down in advance. Everything will depend on issues like the degree to which the other person has acted wrongly in the particular relationship and his ability to bear the loss that would result from the exercise of the power. These are not factors that can be made the basis of rules; instead, they are elements of decision that bear on how one uses the rights allocated by existing rules.

Take, for instance, the issue of liability on a contract in the event of changed and unforeseen circumstances. At what point does a shift in the market value of the commodities to be sold by an executory contract become so great that the enforcement of the bargain would violate the duties of solidarity owed by the parties to each other and by the judge to the parties? A contracting party or a judge who acts in the spirit of solidarity will not be satisfied with references to party intent as to the allocation of risks, even if intent seems unequivocal. He will also want to know whether one party is more blameworthy than another for the occurrence of the event that overtook the contractual relation and how any given allocation of losses would affect each party. He will deny that the administration of the rules governing exchange is independent from either conceptions of moral fault or goals of distributive justice.

*   *   *   *   *

Purposes and standards. The legal order as a system of formality encounters two great problems, which dominate modern legal thought. The first is the struggle to escape from the dilemma of blind formalism and arbitrary, tyrannical equity; the second is the effort to make a peace between legality and morality by rejecting the extremes of individualism and collectivism and providing a larger place within the law for the values of solidarity. The various trends described earlier by which the rule of law is eroded in contemporary society must be understood in the context of these aspirations. But now we can make our understanding of such trends more comprehensive.

The characteristic response of modern lawyers to the problem of formality and equity is purposive legal reasoning. One treats the law as a system of intelligible rules whose meaning is controlled by beneficial purposes which the law applier must attribute to the rules, for the intent of the lawmaker is likely to be or ought to be inconclusive. By this means, one hopes to moderate the tension between formality and equity and to avoid unpalatable outcomes in the great majority of cases.

The result, however, is, as I suggested before, a style of legal discourse that eats away at generality and autonomy without necessarily increasing one's assurance that he is doing justice. The attempted compromise between formalism and equity is inherently dissatisfying and unstable; it does not resolve the problem of subjective value that lies at the root of the dilemma of formality and equity, nor need it contribute to transform the circumstances of domination that deprive people of confidence in their own moral judgments. Consequently, the policies by which the modern lawyer wants to justify his elaborations of the law tend either to become abstract to the point of meaninglessness or to appear as expressions of an effort to manipulate all rules so as to further the arbitrary preferences of particular interest groups.

*   *   *   *   *

Cycle or progression? We now have the means with which to answer my question as to whether a heightened interest in equity and solidarity is simply the most recent turn in a cyclical process or whether, on the contrary, it is a stage in a progressive, though halting and sinuous, evolution. If there is something that distinguishes contemporary experiments in solidarity and equity from earlier movements in legal history, it would have to be the intimate association between this modern tendency and the attack on structures of domination in the name of substantive justice. Only to the extent that this attack occurs and succeeds dare one hope that equity and solidarity will become major sources of normative order rather than just residual limitations on formality.

The subversion of personal dependency relationships saves equitable and communitarian ideas from serving as apologies for established power. It also creates the conditions within which people can arrive at judgments about the dictates of equity and solidarity without feeling that these judgments are rendered suspect by the circumstances in which they were made.

Hence, the question as to whether the movement toward equity and solidarity in contemporary law is simply a cyclical reversion or a genuinely novel breakthrough is more a political question for the future than a historical one about the past. Whether the antinomian tendencies within modern law will or should prevail depends on the degree to which they are connected with the development of doctrines of substantive justice and with the actual disruption of the social mechanisms of personal dependence.

We can now also understand more clearly the sense in which the public and the positive character of law as well as its autonomy and generality are at stake in these developments. The greater the commitment to equity and solidarity as sources and ideals of law, the less it is possible to distinguish state law from ideas of moral obligation or propriety that are entertained in the different social settings within which disputes may arise. And the less importance do positive rules have in the law.

* * * * *

LAW BEYOND MODERN SOCIETY: TWO POSSIBILITIES

There are two main ways in which one can interpret the significance for law of the tendencies at work in modern, and particularly in postliberal, society. Neither interpretation can be proved true or false at the present time, for both represent possibilities intrinsic to modernism.

The first hypothesis might be summarized by the metaphor of the closed circle. It would present the entire history of law as one movement toward a certain point, followed by a return to the origin. We have seen how, in Western legal history, bureaucratic law, with its public and positive rules, builds upon customary practices, and how this bureaucratic law is in turn partly superseded by the rule of law, with its commitment to the generality and the autonomy of legal norms. The welfare trend in postliberal society moves the rule of law ideal back in the direction of bureaucratic law by undermining the social and ideological bases of that ideal. The corporatist tendency and the communitarian aspirations that follow it begin to subvert bureaucratic law itself. Thus, they prepare the way for the return to the custom of each group as the fundamental and almost exclusive instrument of social order.

This hypothetical development would have a profound impact on morals and politics. The rule of law is intimately associated with individual freedom, even though it fails to resolve the problem of illegitimate personal dependency in social life. Bureaucratic law is premised on the conception that social arrangements can be grasped by the mind and transformed by the will; it refuses to treat them as an unchanging part of nature.

Thus, the decline of the rule of law might endanger, or even destroy, individual freedom. The abandonment of bureaucratic law could mean a relapse into the logic of tribalism, which sanctifies the existing order of the group as an irrevocable decree of nature. If these were to be the outcomes of the transformation of modern society, the negative utopias of our day would have been vindicated. We would have lost the treasures of freedom and of transcendence and would have condemned ourselves to a society of unreflective adaptation, in which the power of criticism and the spirit of revolt would have been smothered.

An alternative approach to the prospects of modern society and to their legal implications might be represented by the metaphor of a spiral that reverses direction without returning to its starting point. This would mean that individual freedom could be rescued from the demise of the rule of law and brought into harmony with the reassertion of communitarian concerns. It would also signify that the capacity to see and to treat each form of social life as a creation rather than as a fate could survive the disintegration of public and positive law and be reconciled with the sense of an immanent order in society. Let us examine briefly each of these possibilities.

The rule of law is the liberal state's most emphatic response to the problems of power and freedom. But we have seen that whatever its efficacy in preventing immediate government oppression of the individual, the strategy of legalism fails to deal with these issues in the basic relationships of work and everyday life. Whether "public" persecution can still be prevented and "private" domination at last be tamed once the rule of law is given up depends in part on the possibility of refining ancient methods for the dispersal of power. The chief of these methods is the plurality of groups itself: the liberty of the individual to pass from one to another and to participate in the decisions that shape life in each of the associations to which he belongs.

But this by itself is not enough. One also needs criteria by which to choose among different ways of ranking, among legitimate and illegitimate uses of power, among permissible and prohibited inequalities. In the absence of such principles, the predicament of liberal society will simply be repeated: men will be condemned to search for a justice they cannot find, and all social arrangements will be rendered suspect by their lack of a moral foundation.

The problem of power carries us to the other aspect of the spirallike process I envisage. Unless people regain the sense that the practices of society represent some sort of natural order instead of a set of arbitrary choices, they cannot hope to escape from the dilemma of unjustified power. But how can this perception of immanent order be achieved in the circumstances of modern society?

The mere existence of moral agreement within a particular association would not bring about this end. First, it would be necessary for the subversion of inequality to proceed to such a point that people would be entitled to place greater confidence in collective choices as expressions of a shared human nature or of the intrinsic demands of social order rather than as a product of the interests of dominant groups. Second, it would be indispensable that this experience of increasing equality also make possible an ever more universal consensus about the immanent order of social life and thus help refine further the understanding of what equality means. The first condition without the second is empty. The second without the first is dangerous because it threatens to consecrate the outlook of the most powerful and articulate elements in the society.

Even if one assumes that the vision of an indwelling pattern of right be created and justified, one may still wonder whether this vision could be kept from stifling criticism and change. To preserve the possibility of transcending the present, it is important to remain aware of the inherent imperfection of any one system of community practices as a source of insight into the requirements of social life. For if one takes seriously the notion that men make themselves in history, these requirements develop over time rather than remain static. Openness toward the future means that one must value the conflictual process by which communities are created over time and satisfactory relations are established among them as much as the internal cohesion of any communal group.

Such a reconciliation of immanent order and transcendent criticism would imply a greater replacement than we could now comprehend of bureaucratic law or the rule of law by what in a sense could be called custom. This customary law would have many of the marks we associate with custom: its lack of a positive and a public character and its largely emergent and implicit quality. Yet it would differ from custom in making room for a distinction between what is and what ought to be. It would become less the stable normative order of a particular group than the developing moral language of mankind.

Whether one accepts the hypothesis of the circle or that of the spiral, it is important to remember that the three kinds of law present themselves historically as overlapping and interpenetrating realms, rather than as neatly separated worlds. The legal profession and legal education in postliberal society show the juxtaposition of concerns with all these forms of law and legal thought. This universe has an outer sphere of blackletter law: the area wherein the rule of law ideal and the specialized methods of legal analysis flourish. Then there is an inner sphere of bureaucratic law and bureaucratic rhetoric. At this level, law is approached instrumentally; one talks of costs and benefits, and one searches for a science of policy that can help the administrative and the professional elite exercise its power in the name of impersonal technique and social welfare. But, beyond legalistic formality and bureaucratic instrumentalism, lie the inchoate senses of equity and solidarity.

I have argued that these ideas of solidarity and equity can be seen in two different lights, which correspond respectively to the two senses of custom. On the one hand, they can be devices with which to defend the established beliefs and values of a particular community, as articulated by those who have governed it in the past or control it in the present. But, in conjunction with a program of substantive justice, they may also serve as the primitive form taken by the struggle to discover a universal given order in social life.

The search for this latent and living law—not the law of prescriptive rules or of bureaucratic policies, but the elementary code of human interaction—has been the staple of the lawyer's art wherever this art was practiced with most depth and skill. What united the great Islamic '*ulama*,' the Roman jurisconsults, and the English common lawyers was the sense they shared that the law, rather than being made chiefly by judges and princes, was already present in society itself. Throughout history there has been a bond between the legal profession and the search for an order inherent in social life. The existence of this bond suggests that the lawyer's insight, which preceded the advent of the legal order, can survive its decline.

The same processes that promise to reconcile freedom and transcendence with community and immanent order also threaten to sacrifice the former to the latter. In a brief passage of his *Republic*, Plato evokes a society in which men, reduced to animal contentment, have lost the capacity of self-criticism together with the sense of incompleteness. He calls this society the City of Pigs. The significance of the historical tendencies discussed in this chapter lies in this: with a single gesture they frighten us with the image of the City of Pigs and entice us with the prospect of the Heavenly City. By offering us the extremes of good and evil, they speak at once to what is bestial and to what is sublime in our humanity.

XV

CONCLUSION
LAW AND HISTORY

A. THE GREAT DEBATES

What is the fundamental significance of history in our law and legal system? One answer is that we are, of course, part of an historical process ourselves, a process of extraordinary continuity over centuries. As Frederick William Maitland put it, "Such is the unity of all history that any one who endeavours to tell a piece of it must feel that his first sentence tears a seamless web."[1]

But what is the significance, in practical terms, of being "part of history?" This is where the true debates begin and where, in the end, legal historians and reflective lawyers makes their own individual judgments. This concluding section features reflections by some of the most famous of all modern jurists: Oliver Wendell Holmes, Jr. (1841–1935); Benjamin Nathan Cardozo (1870–1938); and Roscoe Pound (1870–1964). Also included is a section by one of my professors, Harold Berman, former Ames Professor of Law at Harvard, and now Woodruff Professor at Emory, and a section by Laura Kalman, Professor of History at the University of California, another great legal historian. Such a galaxy of stars would seem to inhibit anyone making up their own mind about the role of legal history, except for one thing: these distinguished scholars largely disagree with each other.

First, I would like to return to an important hypothesis set out earlier in the *Materials*, in Chapter IX. This is Maine's theory of legal change. Sir Henry Sumner Maine (1822–1888), Corpus Professor of Jurisprudence at Oxford, was famous for his great book *Ancient Law* (1861).[2] He was a leading proponent of "historical jurisprudence" and of evolutionary views of law. Today he is largely known for some of his great sweeping "principles" of legal history, such as "[W]e may say that the movement of progressive societies has hitherto been a movement from *Status to Contract*."[3] As we have seen, feudal law was domi-

---

1. Sir Frederick Pollock, Frederick William Maitland, *The History of English Law Before the Time of Edward I* (2d ed., ed. S.F.C. Milsom, Cambridge, 1968), vol. 1, 1.

2. Maine did, of course, write many more books, including *Village Communities* (1871), *Early History of Institutions* (1875), *Dissertations on Early Law and Custom* (1883) and *International Law* (1888).

3. "The word Status may be usefully employed to construct a formula expressing the law of progress thus indicated, which, whatever be its value, seems to me to be sufficiently ascertained. All the forms of Status taken notice of in the Law of Persons were derived from, and

Illustration 15–1 Litta Belle Campbell (1886–1980) (center) with her sisters in 1910. Campbell graduated at the top of her class at the USC College of Law in 1911 and became the first female deputy district attorney in the United States. The first woman to obtain a law degree was Ada H. Kepley, who graduated from the Union College of Law in Chicago in 1870. (Photo courtesy Law School of the University of Southern California and Jean Campbell De Blasis and Family.)

nated by "status" relationships. Land could not even be left by will. Your identity, or "status," or birth was all important.[4] Later developments, such as eighteen-century English commercial law, saw an emergence of "will" based legal doctrines, such as consensual contracts.[5] These doctrines put a premium on an individual's act of will, what an individual *did*, rather than *who* the person was. But does this make the law "progressive?" And what about the modern developments observed by Weber and Unger that are stripping away genuine individual autonomy, such as vast bureaucracies and a "corporate" state?[6] Can anyone make the kind of assertion about legal history that Maine did and be correct?

One of Maine's other well known assertions is as follows:

---

to some extent are still coloured by, the powers and privileges anciently residing in the Family. If then we employ Status, agreeably with the usage of the best writers, to signify these personal conditions only, and avoid applying the term to such conditions as are the immediate or remote result of agreement, we may say that the movement of the progressive societies has hitherto been a movement *from Status to Contract*." Henry Sumner Maine, *Ancient Law* (10th ed., 1884, London), 164–165.

4. See *Materials, supra*, Chapter XII.

5. *Id.*, Chapter XII.

6. *Id.*, Chapter XIV.

"A general proposition of some value may be advanced with respect to the agencies by which Law is brought into harmony with society. These instrumentalities seem to me to be three in number, Legal Fictions, Equity and Legislation. Their historical order is that in which I have placed them."[7]

Throughout this course we have been discussing all three of these "instrumentalities." Is Maine correct? Is he even right about their "historical order?" The famous hypothesis is set out in full in the *Materials* in Chapter IX . The judgment is yours.

Next is set out Roscoe Pound's famous queries about legal history. Pound was a leader of the "New Jurisprudence" of the twentieth century, the so-called "Sociological School," that was discussed at length in Chapter XIV, above. In this excerpt he summarizes the legal history school of the past, and advances his own "overview." He boldly rejects the "evolutionary" nineteenth-century analysis.

"We may well believe, then, that an epoch in Juristic thought has come to an end, and that the time is ripe to appraise its work, to ask what of permanent value it has achieved, to inquire what are the present demands which it is unable to satisfy, and to consider wherein its way of unifying stability and change, with which men were content for a century, is no longer of service."[8]

In its place he proposes a new perspective on the history of law, a "complex picture" informed by "psychology and sociology." "We must think not in terms of an organism, growing because of and by means of some inherent property, but once more, as in the eighteenth century, in terms of a building, built...to satisfy human desires and continually repaired, restored, rebuilt and added to...."[9] What do you think of Pound's argument?

Two great American jurists, Holmes and Cardozo, recognized clearly the power that history exercises through the law. They also perceived both the promise and the danger that this represents to judges, lawyers, and historians alike. Included here are excerpts from their two best known essays on the relationship between law and history: Holmes' essay "The Path of the Law," first given as an address at Boston University School of Law in 1897, and Cardozo's famous *The Nature of the Judicial Process* (1921). Note Holmes' controversial distinction between law and morals. Does this view influence his attitude toward legal history? Holmes' view comes from the great nineteenth-century legal philosopher, Austin. Austin's work, and that of his close friend Bentham, greatly shaped the social and political attitudes of nineteenth-century lawyers.

Following the atrocities of the twentieth century, including mass genocide, and the resulting Nuremberg trials, the view that law and morals are and should be separate has come under attack. As you read these materials, keep in mind the question of law and morals. Think of how the lawyers of each generation approached this question and the institutional "vehicles" they used to solve moral

---

7. See *Id.*, Chapter IX.
8. Roscoe Pound, *Interpretation of Legal History* (Cambridge, 1923), 12.
9. *Id.*, 21.

problems.[10] Ask yourself if this controversy is merely a question of definitions and semantics, or does it say something fundamental about the role of law and lawyers during different historical periods?

Note also the view of the great legal historian, Maitland, that lawyers are fundamentally "anti-historical." "The lawyer must be orthodox," wrote Maitland, "otherwise he is not lawyer; and orthodox history seems to me a contradiction in terms."[11] Even Holmes seems "anti-historical" in this sense. According to Holmes, "I look forward to a time when the part played by history in the explanation of dogma shall be very small, and instead of ingenious research we shall spend our energy on a study of the ends sought to be attained and the reasons for desiring them."[12] Ask yourself whether Maitland is right about a fundamental contradiction between the intellectual function of practicing lawyers and the legal historians. If so, what is the point of taking this course? Remember, according to Holmes, antiquarianism for its own sake is a "pitfall."[13]

Benjamin Cardozo's great *Nature of the Judicial Process* may come to your rescue, at least in terms of providing answers to these questions. His discussion of the source of law in "the creative energy of custom" is particularly valuable.

But beware! Cardozo, a judge, characterizes scientific, rational jurisprudence as "the demon of formalism."[14] This "demon" is restrained by social policy and philosophical justice, applied, of course, by judges. These judges, in turn, rely on Cardozo's four "forces": history, philosophy, custom, and sociology, to legitimize their "flexibility," i.e., their discretionary power. Doesn't this view deny lawmakers the power to rationally plan into the future to achieve predetermined ends, free from the judicial arbitrariness and the legal fictions, which, in Holmes' view, have made the study of legal history a necessary evil? Or does this fundamentally misstate Cardozo's views? What, in the end, would Holmes say about Cardozo's arguments?

Throughout these materials, we have encountered a tension between the forces of "scientific jurisprudence," which take as their banner the power of human reason and the need for over-riding central legislation to make future planning possible, and the forces of individualism, whose *leitmotifs* are scepticism of human foresight and fear of centralized forces. Legal history not only tells the tale of this eternal struggle, but becomes a valuable weapon, used and abused by both sides. You will notice that the particular philosophic position of a judge or lawyer in this struggle may determine his or her view of the "proper role" of legal history. This will be true, even in your case. Your ultimate view of legal history will probably predict a great deal about the kind of lawyer you will become, both professionally and politically, and your study of legal history may even influence this future.

Concluding these materials are excerpts from Harold J. Berman's "Introduction" to his book *Law and Revolution* (Cambridge, Mass. 1983) and from Laura

---

10. See Daniel R. Coquillette, *Lawyers and Fundamental Moral Responsibility* (Cincinnati, 1995), 55–124.

11. See S.F.C. Milsom, "Introduction," F. Pollock, F.W. Maitland, *The History of English Law* (2d ed., Cambridge, 1968), vol. 1, XXIV–XXV.

12. *Materials, infra*, p. 614.

13. *Id.*, p. 614.

14. *Id.*, p. 616.

Kalman's *The Strange Career of Legal Liberalism* (New Haven, 1996). According to Berman, the "history of Western law is at a turning point as sharp and as crucial as that which was marked by the French Revolution of 1789 [and] the English Revolution of 1640..."[15] Berman sees part of the reason for this crisis as "cynicism about the law, and lawlessness, [which] will not be overcome by adhering to a so-called realism which denies the autonomy, the integrity, and the ongoingness of our legal tradition."[16] How would Berman view the "sociological" and "realist" approaches of Pound and Cardozo? What would he think of Holmes' "Path of the Law?" Does Berman represent a return to the world of Henry Sumner Maine, or something quite different?

Laura Kalman leads a new, brilliant generation of legal historians, many of whom hold both law degrees and graduate degrees in other disciplines and, perhaps most significantly, many of whom are women. Some other examples are my own valued colleagues, Mary S. Bilder and Catherine Wells, and Harvard's Christine A. Desan, Mary Ann Glendon, and Martha L. Minow. This generation seeks to use interdisciplinary insights to look beyond the history of legal doctrine and use history "with an eye to its relevance for the present."[17] Kalman repeats Bruce Ackerman's famous challenge that the task "is to locate ourselves in a conversation between generations."[18] Ackerman continues, "I propose...the beginning of a dialogue between past and present which will serve as our central technique for constitutional discovery."[19] What do you think about Laura Kalman's description of the "new historicism?" What does she mean when she says that "it would be unfortunate if law professors desert the barricades just as academics in other fields, such as historians, begin to show signs of appreciating what legal scholars are doing, and wanting to help?"[20]

B. ONE TEACHER'S VIEW

It is a favorite trick of law professors to avoid answering hard questions themselves by just asking more questions. With this in mind I have added a short excerpt from some of my own writing, the "Introduction" to *Law in Colonial Massachusetts* (Boston, Mass., 1984).[21] It addresses some of the same issues as Maine, Pound, Holmes, Cardozo, Berman, and Kalman did, but not so eloquently.

My view of legal history has been profoundly influenced by Felix Gilbert, a great history scholar and teacher. Gilbert poses this dilemma:

> "But what is our situation, for we believe neither in history as a means of teaching ethical values nor in the possibility of discovering laws to determine the process of world history?"[22]

---

15. *Id.*, p. 618.
16. *Id.*, p. 621.
17. *Id.*, p. 625.
18. *Id.*, p. 625.
19. *Id.*, p. 625.
20. *Id.*, p. 627.
21. *Id.*, p. 627.
22. Felix Gilbert, *History: Choice and Commitment* (Cambridge, 1977), 452.

He answers his own question as follows:

> Although we may not share the views of nineteenth-century historians on the purposes of historical study and what historical scholarship might achieve, we are still their heirs insofar as we are professors of history, and, as such, accept the framework established more than one hundred years ago—that is, recognition of the relationship between research and teaching, of the necessity for employing critical methods, and of the importance of maintaining professional standards. As remote as we seem to be from the assumptions and expectations of nineteenth-century historical scholarship, certain aspects of the history of the professor of history may still be relevant.
>
> One is the view that history is indivisible and that everything that happened in the past belonged to the domain of the professor of history. History became an independent and autonomous field of study because it was recognized that special methods and procedures were necessary to study the past, but also because these methods and procedures were regarded as applicable to any aspect and period of the past. Before the nineteenth century history was chiefly an auxiliary science, and as an auxiliary to other fields of knowledge, historical study and research will always remain alive—now, perhaps, as an aid to political science, sociology, and area studies, rather than, as in the past, to moral philosophy, theology, or law. But if historians want their discipline to be more than an auxiliary science and to remain an autonomous and independent field of study, we should keep in mind that isolating our subjects is only one part of our work; the other is to seek for relationships, comparisons, and analogies.
>
> A second aspect of the history of the professor of history is that history was expected to provide not only special and factual knowledge, but also general insights about the nature of man. We might not feel that we can set our sights as high as that any longer. But, after all reservations have been made, we ought to remain aware that the man who acted and was acted upon in the past is the same man who acts in the present, and that the past is one way—and not the worst way—of acquiring the right and the criteria to judge the present. Our willingness to see the past as a whole, our willingness to take a stand, constitute our card of identity.[23]

I very much agree with Gilbert about his "card of identity," but I am less sure that "the past is one way—and not the worst way—of acquiring the right and criteria to judge the present." What do you think?

C. "KINGLESS COMMONWEALTHS"

At the conclusion of his great *History of English Law*, Maitland made the following observation:

---

23. *Id.*, 452.

But of this there can be no doubt, that it was for the good of the whole world that one race stood apart from its neighbours, turned away its eyes at an early time from the fascinating pages of the *Corpus Iuris*, and, more Roman than the Romanists, made the grand experiment of a new formulary system. Nor can we part with this age without thinking once more of the permanence of its work. Those few men who were gathered at Westminster round Pateshull and Raleigh and Bracton were penning writs that would run in the name of kingless commonwealths on the other shore of the Atlantic Ocean; they were making right and wrong for us and for our children.[24]

We now represent the generations of which Maitland spoke, and we are the lawyers of those "kingless commonwealths on the other shore of the Atlantic." We can debate as long as we wish the significance of the history of our law, but we cannot escape it. It invades the sentences and the paragraphs of our cases, rules and statutes. It is, indeed, imbedded in the very words we use to describe all we do. But most of all, this history invades our legal culture, the very way we are taught to think. There is a power in this culture. Must it control us, or can we control it? Only by our understanding of our past can Cardozo's "demon of formalism" and Pound's "political" and "juristic" gods be brought to heel.[25]

Understanding of our legal heritage is particularly urgent today, in this "kingless commonwealth." On March 23, 1885, David Dudley Field addressed the graduating class of Albany Law School on the topic "Reform in the Legal Profession and the Laws." His concluding words to the graduates spoke of the "portals of a new time," and he asks "whence shall come the lawgiver of the new time?"

> You stand, moreover, in the very portals of a new time. The world is soon to take its impulses from this side of the ocean. The language we speak, the institutions in which we participate, are to spread with our dominion —
>
> From the World's girdle to the frozen pole — and beyond our dominion to remote islands and continents. Whence shall come the lawgiver of the new time? From our own soil, I would fain hope and believe. The materials are at hand, and the time is propitious. A new people, grown suddenly to the strength and civilization of the oldest and mightiest, with laws for the most part borrowed, finds that they need to be reexamined, simplified, and reconstructed. The task is great, the object is greater, and the reward is ample. Let us, then, be up and doing, that we may have the merit and the satisfaction of having accomplished something toward it, before we rest from our labors.[26]

There is a touch of imperialism in these sentences, but, like Field's graduates, we surely do stand on the "portals of a new time," a time whose rate of change, opportunities and dangers far exceed even the propitious and perilous years that

---

24. Sir Frederick Pollock, Frederick William Maitland, *The History of English Law Before the Time of Edward I* (2d ed., S.F.C. Milsom ed., Cambridge, 1968) vol. II, 674.

25. Roscoe Pound, *Interpretation of Legal History, supra,* 4, 6.

26. *Materials, infra,* Chapter XIII.

followed Field's 1855 address. And there can be no doubt from "whence shall come the lawgivers of the new time," for they are you.

FOR FURTHER READING

A concise bibliography covering most of the recent controversies about legal history, from Grant Gilmore's "The Age of Antiquarius: On Legal History in the Time of Troubles" to Robert W. Gordon's "Historicism in Legal Scholarship" can be found in the notes to the excerpt from my "Introduction" to *Law in Colonial Massachusetts* set out below in the *Materials*. Laura Kalman's *The Strange Career of Legal Liberalism* (Yale, 1996), published since my "Introduction," is worth reading from cover to cover. There is also a great new scholarly biography of Cardozo by Andrew Kaufman. See Andrew L. Kaufman, *Cardozo* (Cambridge, Mass., 1998).

Illustration 15-2 Roscoe Pound (1870–1964) was Dean of Harvard Law School from 1916–1936. Note his famous "green eyeshade." Photograph by Jim Hughes, *Christian Science Monitor*. Courtesy of Art & Visual Materials, Special Collections, Harvard Law School and the *Christian Science Monitor*.

MATERIALS

Roscoe Pound, *Interpretations of Legal History* (Cambridge, 1923), 1-2, 8–21.
[Notes omitted.]

I

LAW AND HISTORY

Law must be stable and yet it cannot stand still. Hence all thinking about law
has struggled to reconcile the conflicting demands of the need of stability and of
the need of change. The social interest in the general security has led men to seek
some fixed basis for an absolute ordering of human action whereby a firm and
stable social order might be assured. But continual changes in the circumstances
of social life demand continual new adjustments to the pressure of other social interests as well as to new modes of endangering security. Thus the legal order must
be flexible as well as stable. It must be overhauled continually and refitted continually to the changes in the actual life which it is to govern. If we seek principles,
we must seek principles of change no less than principles of stability. Accordingly
the chief problem to which legal thinkers have addressed themselves has been
how to reconcile the idea of a fixed body of law, affording no scope for individual wilfulness, with the idea of change and growth and making of new law; how
to unify the theory of law with the theory of making law and to unify the system
of legal justice with the facts of administration of justice by magistrates.

For, put more concretely, the problem of compromise between the need of stability and the need of change becomes in one aspect a problem of adjustment between
rule and discretion, between administering justice according to settled rule, or at
most by rigid deduction from narrowly fixed premises, and administration of justice
according to the more or less trained intuition of experienced magistrates. In one
way or another almost all of the vexed questions of the science of law prove to be
phases of this same problem. In the last century the great battles of the analytical
and the historical jurists were waged over the question of the nature of law—
whether the traditional or the imperative element of legal systems was to be taken as
the type of law—and over the related questions as to the nature of law-making—
whether law is found by judges and jurists or is made to order by conscious lawgivers—and as to the basis of the law's authority—whether it lies in reason and science or in command and sovereign will. But the whole significance of these questions lies in their bearing upon the problem of adjustment between or reconciliation
of rule and discretion, or, as it is ultimately, the problem of stability and change—of
the general security and the individual human life. And so it is with the philosophical problems of jurisprudence and with the most debated practical problems of law.
When we discuss the relation of law and morals or the distinction between law and
equity, or the respective provinces of court and jury, or the advisability of fixed rules
or of wide judicial power in procedure, or the much-debated question as to judicial
sentence or administrative individualization in the treatment of criminals, at bottom
we have to do with forms of the same fundamental problem.

*   *   *   *   *

English legal history-writing prior to the nineteenth century is more closely related to the legal history of that century in that it is nationalist, and has an im-

mediate practical purpose of setting up a historical authority as a basis for the legal order. Fortescue writes a historical sketch to show that England had always been governed by the same customs from pre-Roman Britain. He could not claim the authority of Justinian nor of any other sovereign law-giver for the unwritten common law of England. But the "written law" laid down that immemorial custom had authority as well as, and in the absence of, written laws, and the common law of England was shown by history to be the body of rules by which Englishmen had always been wont to adjudge controversies and to guide their conduct. Coke's *Second Institute* is a history of public law in which he seeks to make out the case of the common-law courts against the Stuart kings by setting forth the immemorial common-law rights of Englishmen, possessed by their forefathers from the beginning and declared by *Magna Carta*, by a long succession of statutes, and by a long and continuous succession of judicial decisions. The premises are the same as Fortescue's and the method is that of the advocate. The purpose is not to find a basis for authority but to identify authority. In Hale, also, with his proposition that the origins of English law are as undiscoverable as the sources of the Nile, we have the same idea of a historical identification of authority, although there is a suggestion of a combination of philosophy and history in a period of philosophical hegemony which reminds us of Gaius. Finally Blackstone, at the height of the reign of philosophy, reconciles stability and change by adopting the historical theory of continuity of an immemorial custom, as expounded by Fortescue, Coke, and Hale, and adding a doctrine of change by authority of Parliament, in terms of Coke and of the Revolution of 1688; unifying the two ideas by the philosophical theory of a law of nature of which each was declaratory and conformity whereto gave to each its ultimate validity.

Nineteenth-century legal history-writing had a radically different purpose. It did not think of a law which had always been the same but of a law which had grown. It sought stability through establishment of principles of growth, finding the lines along which growth had proceeded and would continue to proceed, and it sought to unify stability and change by a combination of historical authority and philosophical history. Utilizing the idea of authority, it sought to put a historical foundation under the seventeenth- and eighteenth-century theory of law as only declaratory of something having a higher authority than the pronouncement of legislator or judge as such. Law was not declaratory of morals or of the nature of man as a moral entity or reasoning creature. It was declaratory of principles of progress discovered by human experience of administering justice and of human experience of intercourse in civilized society; and these principles were not principles of natural law revealed by reason, they were realizings of an idea, unfolding in human experience and in the development of institutions—an idea to be demonstrated metaphysically and verified by history. All of this body of doctrine did not develop at once. But such was the creed of the school which was dominant in the science of law throughout the century and in one form or another this creed may be identified in all the varieties of juristic thinking during the century, even in schools which professed a different method.

After flourishing for a hundred years and ruling almost uncontested during the latter half of that period, the historical school came into marked disfavour at the end of the nineteenth century and broke down as completely at the beginning of the present century as the law-of-nature school had broken down at the end of the eighteenth century. As early as 1888 Stammler made a formidable philosophical attack upon it in his *Methode der geschichtlichen Rechtswissenschaft*, followed up in his well-known books of 1896 and 1902. In the latter year a leading exponent of the historical school in France accused it of "abdicating" and of leading to legal immobility and gave what proved a decisive impetus to the so-called revival of natural law in that country. In 1897 Mr. Justice Holmes, who had done notable work in the historical interpretation of Anglo-American law in the hey-day of the school, criticized its habitual failure to take conscious account of the considerations of social advantage on which rules of law must be justified, its negative attitude with respect to improvement of the law, and its rooted tendency to hold a rule wholly established as a suitable or even necessary rule of action today if it could but be shown that it obtained in embryo or in historical principle in the Year Books. Some of the historical school went over to positivism. Others turned to the economic interpretation of legal history, or to historical materialism. Others asserted that a distinction must be made "between history and the historical school," gave up historical jurisprudence, and confined themselves to a purely descriptive legal history and a purely descriptive teaching of law. Finally Kohler, who had done great things in historical jurisprudence, turned to philosophy and in his neo-Hegelian philosophical jurisprudence insisted upon the element of creative activity, upon the adapting of the legal materials of the past, shaped by and adapted to the civilizations of the past, to the exigencies of civilization in the present and the requirements of a continually changing and moving civilization. Indeed, this break-up of the historical school coincides with a general abandonment of the nineteenth-century historicophilosophical thinking in every field and the revival of faith in the efficacy of human effort with an accompanying call for philosophies of action and of creation in place of the political fatalism and juristic pessimism of the immediate past. All this was observable before the war, but the war gave it added impetus. For it demonstrated the role which human initiative, half blind, erroneous, misdirected as it may be, does play in the building of institutions and the shaping of human events; it visibly overturned the social and psychological foundations of nineteenth-century thought, already undermined but still standing. All the nineteenth-century schools were agreed upon the futility of conscious action, although for different reasons. They conceived of a slow and ordered succession of events and of institutions whereby things perfected themselves by evolving to the limit of their idea. Just as clearly all the recent philosophies of every type are philosophies of action.

Pragmatism sees validity in actions, not in that they realize the idea, but to the extent that they are effective for their purpose and in purposes to the extent that they satisfy a maximum of human demands. Bergson's intuitionism shows us how we act better than we know and achieve results by trial and error to meet human desires which we explain to ourselves by ideas. The implication is that we need not fear to act. Historical scepticism, in contrast with ancient scepticism, which taught men not to act, teaches action by attacking the dogma of historical fatalism and the doctrine that what does not exist in historical idea is an idle hope. Activist idealism reaches a result directly opposite to the conclusion of the idealism of the past, which regarded the man who acted as a vain disturber of the rational and foreordained order. The relativisms that are springing up on every hand are, on their practical side, philosophies of action with respect to something desired. Croce's identification of philosophy and history rejects the nineteenth-century philosophy of history and is a philosophy of life with all its variety and action and change and compromise and adaptation. When men are thinking thus a functional attitude in jurisprudence is inevitable. Nor is this way of thinking merely the natural and temporary attitude of those who have been actors in or spectators of the far-reaching changes of the past decade. It grows out of the need for action to meet the pressure of new demands consequent upon changes in the social order and of new desires both behind and involved in those changes. As the theory of the law of nature came in as one of growth and of creation, to take better account of the element of change in the reconciliation of stability and change, and ended in assuming that the key to reason had been found for all time and that social and legal and political charts had been drawn up by which men and law-makers and peoples might be guided forever, so, it may be, the historical theory, which sought a new reconciliation in an idea of growth and progress, had come to deny growth and progress in any effective sense through its belief that it had discovered finally the immutable lines of growth or had calculated once for all the fixed orbit of progress outside of which no movement could possibly take place.

We may well believe, then, that an epoch in juristic thought has come to an end, and that the time is ripe to appraise its work, to ask what of permanent value it has achieved, to inquire what are the present demands which it is unable to satisfy, and to consider wherein its way of unifying stability and change, with which men were content for a century, is no longer of service.

*   *   *   *   *

For the simple picture of the legal order painted by the historical school, with its one idea to which it attributed and by which it solved everything, must give way before the results of psychology and psychological sociology. We must give up the quest for the one solving idea. The actual legal order is not a simple rational thing. It is a complex, more or less irrational thing into which we struggle to put reason and in which, as fast as we have put some part of it in the order of reason, new irrationalities arise in the process of meeting new needs by trial and error.

On the one hand we must take account of the social or cultural needs of the time and place in all their possibilities of overlapping and of conflict and in all their phases, economic, political, religious and moral. On the other hand we must take account of suggestion, imitation, traditional faiths or beliefs, and particularly of the belief in logical necessity or authority expressing the social want or demand for general security. We must think not in terms of an organism, growing because of and by means of some inherent property, but once more, as in the eighteenth century, in terms of a building, built by men to satisfy human desires and continually repaired, restored, rebuilt and added to in order to meet expanding or changing desires or even changing fashions. We must think of a body of materials in actual use handed down from the past on which we work consciously and subconsciously to achieve the desires and satisfy the wants of the present; eking them out through suggestion and imitation, creating new ones now cautiously and now boldly when the old fail us, and moulding all to the form which those desires and wants have given to traditional faiths and beliefs; but held back by those traditional faiths and beliefs and especially in law by the rules and modes of thought of the art in which lawyers have been trained, become an instinct to follow logical compulsion and authority. Some such complex picture as this is given us by psychology and sociology in place of the simple pictures of the past. And yet in that complex picture there is something of each of those simple pictures to justify our looking at each of them in detail.

Oliver Wendell Holmes, *Collected Legal Papers* (New York, 1920), 167–168, 169–173, 179–182, 186–187, 188–189, 192, 194–195, 200–202.

THE PATH OF THE LAW

When we study law we are not studying a mystery but a well-known profession. We are studying what we shall want in order to appear before judges, or to advise people in such a way as to keep them out of court. The reason why it is a profession, why people will pay lawyers to argue for them or to advise them, is that in societies like ours the command of the public force is intrusted to the judges in certain cases, and the whole power of the state will be put forth, if necessary, to carry out their judgments and decrees. People want to know under what circumstances and how far they will run the risk of coming against what is so much stronger than themselves, and hence it becomes a business to find out when this danger is to be feared. The object of our study, then, is prediction, the prediction of the incidence of the public force through the instrumentality of the courts.

The means of the study are a body of reports, of treatises, and of statutes, in this country and in England, extending back for six hundred years, and now increasing annually by hundreds. In these sibylline leaves are gathered the scattered prophecies of the past upon the cases in which the axe will fall. These are what properly have been called the oracles of the law. Far the most important and pretty nearly the whole meaning of every new effort of legal thought is to make these prophesies more precise, and to generalize them into a thoroughly connected system.

* * * * *

I wish, if I can, to lay down some first principles for the study of this body of dogma or systematized prediction which we call the law, for men who want to use it as the instrument of their business to enable them to prophesy in their turn, and, as bearing upon the study, I wish to point out an ideal which as yet our law has not attained.

The first thing for a business-like understanding of the matter is to understand its limits, and therefore I think it desirable at once to point out and dispel a confusion between morality and law, which sometimes rises to the height of conscious theory, and more often and indeed constantly is making trouble in detail without reaching the point of consciousness. You can see very plainly that a bad man has as much reason as a good one for wishing to avoid an encounter with the public force, and therefore you can see the practical importance of the distinction between morality and law. A man who cares nothing for an ethical rule which is believed and practised by his neighbors is likely nevertheless to care a good deal to avoid being made to pay money, and will want to keep out of jail if he can.

I take it for granted that no hearer of mine will misinterpret what I have to say as the language of cynicism. The law is the witness and external deposit of our moral life. Its history is the history of the moral development of the race. The practice of it, in spite of popular jests, tends to make good citizens and good men. When I emphasize the difference between law and morals I do so with reference to a single end, that of learning and understanding of the law. For that purpose you must definitely master its specific marks, and it is for that I ask you for the moment to imagine yourselves indifferent to other and greater things.

I do not say that there is not a wider point of view from which the distinction between law and morals becomes of secondary or no importance, as all mathematical distinctions vanish in presence of the infinite. But I do say that that distinction is of the first importance for the object which we are here to consider — a right study and mastery of the law as a business with well understood limits, a body of dogma enclosed within definite lines. I have just shown the practical reason for saying so. If you want to know the law and nothing else, you must look at it as a bad man, who cares only for the material consequences which such knowledge enables him to predict, not as a good one, who finds his reasons for conduct, whether inside the law or outside of it, in the vaguer sanctions of conscience. The theoretical importance of the distinction is no less, if you would reason on your subject aright. The law is full of phraseology drawn from morals, and by the mere force of language continually invites us to pass from one domain to the other without perceiving it, as we are sure to do unless we have the boundary constantly before our minds. The law talks about rights, and duties, and malice, and intent, and negligence, and so forth, and nothing is easier, or, I may say, more common in legal reasoning, than to take these words in their moral sense, at some stage of the argument, and so to drop into fallacy. For instance, when we speak of the rights of man in a moral sense, we mean to mark the limits of interference with individual freedom which we think are prescribed by conscience, or by our ideal, however reached. Yet it is certain that many laws have been enforced in the past, and it is likely that some are enforced now, which are condemned by the most enlightened opinion of the time, or which at all events pass the limit of interference as many consciences would draw it. Manifestly, therefore, nothing but confusion of thought can result from assuming that the rights of man in a moral sense are equally rights in the sense of the Constitution and the law. No doubt simple and extreme cases can be put of imaginable laws which the statute-making power would not dare to enact, even in the absence of written constitutional prohibitions, because the community would rise in rebellion and fight; and this gives some plausibility to the proposition that the law, if not a part of morality, is limited by it. But this limit of power is not coextensive with any system of morals. For the most part it falls far within the lines of any such system, and in some cases may extend beyond them, for reasons drawn from the habits of a particular people at a particular time. I once heard the late Professor Agassiz say that a German population would rise if you added two cents to the price of a glass of beer. A statute in such a case would be empty words, not because it was wrong, but because it could not be enforced. No one will deny that wrong statutes can be and are enforced, and we should not all agree as to which were the wrong ones.

The confusion with which I am dealing besets confessedly legal conceptions. Take the fundamental question, What constitutes the law? You will find some text writers telling you that it is something different from what is decided by the courts of Massachusetts or England, that it is a system of reason, that it is a deduction from principles of ethics or admitted axioms or what not, which may or may not coincide with the decisions. But if we take the view of our friend the bad man we shall find that he does not care two straws for the axioms or deductions, but that he does want to know what the Massachusetts or English courts are likely to do in fact. I am much of his mind. The prophesies of what the courts will do in fact, and nothing more pretentious, are what I mean by the law.

*   *   *   *   *

So much for the limits of the law. The next thing which I wish to consider is what are the forces which determine its content and its growth. You may assume, with Hobbes and Bentham and Austin, that all law emanates from the sovereign, even when the first human beings to enunciate it are the judges, or you may think that law is the voice of the Zeitgeist, or what you like. It is all one to my present purpose. Even if every decision required the sanction of an emperor with despotic power and a whimsical turn of mind, we should be interested none the less, still with a view to prediction, in discovering some order, some rational explanation, and some principle of growth for the rules which he laid down. In every system there are such explanations and principles to be found. It is with regard to them that a second fallacy comes in, which I think it important to expose.

The fallacy to which I refer is the notion that the only force at work in the development of the law is logic. In the broadest sense, indeed, that notion would be true. The postulate on which we think about the universe is that there is a fixed quantitative relation between every phenomenon and its antecedents and consequents. If there is such a thing as a phenomenon without these fixed quantitative relations, it is a miracle. It is outside the law of cause and effect, and as such transcends our power of thought, or at least is something to or from which we cannot reason. The condition of our thinking about the universe is that it is capable of being thought about rationally, or, in other words, that every part of it is effect and cause in the same sense in which those parts are with which we are most familiar. So in the broadest sense it is true that the law is a logical development, like everything else. The danger of which I speak is not the admission that the principles governing other phenomena also govern the law, but the notion that a given system, ours, for instance, can be worked out like mathematics from some general axioms of conduct. This is the natural error of the schools, but it is not confined to them. I once heard a very eminent judge say that he never let a decision go until he was absolutely sure that it was right. So judicial dissent often is blamed, as if it meant simply that one side or the other were not doing their sums right, and, if they would take more trouble, agreement inevitably would come.

This mode of thinking is entirely natural. The training of lawyers is a training in logic. The processes of analogy, discrimination, and deduction are those in which they are most at home. The language of judicial decision is mainly the language of logic. And the logical method and form flatter that longing for certainty and for repose which is in every human mind. But certainty generally is illusion, and repose is not the destiny of man. Behind the logical form lies a judgment as to the relative worth and importance of competing legislative grounds, often an inarticulate and unconscious judgment, it is true, and yet the very root and nerve of the whole proceeding. You can give any conclusion a logical form. You always can imply a condition in a contract. But why do you imply it? It is because of some belief as to the practice of the community or of a class, or because of some opinion as to policy, or, in short, because of some attitude of yours upon a matter not capable of exact quantitative measurement, and therefore not capable of founding exact logical conclusions. Such matters really are battle grounds where the means do not exist for determinations that shall be good for all time, and where the decision can do no more than embody the preference of a given body in a given time and place. We do not realize how large a part of our law is open to reconsideration upon a slight change in the habit of the public mind. No concrete proposition is self evident, no mater how ready we may be to accept it, not even Mr. Herbert Spencer's "Every man has a right to do what he wills, provided he interferes not with a like right on the part of his neighbors."

*   *   *   *   *

The rational study of law is still to a large extent the study of history. History must be a part of the study, because without it we cannot know the precise scope of rules which it is our business to know. It is a part of the rational study, because it is the first step toward an enlightened scepticism, that is, towards a deliberate reconsideration of the worth of those rules. When you get the dragon out of his cave on to the plain and in the daylight, you can count his teeth and claws, and see just what is his strength. But to get him out is only the first step. The next is either to kill him, or to tame him and make him a useful animal. For the rational study of the law the black-letter man may be the man of the present, but the man of the future is the man of statistics and the master of economics.

*   *   *   *   *

Far more fundamental questions still await a better answer than that we do as our fathers have done. What have we better than a blind guess to show that the criminal law in its present form does more good than harm? I do not stop to refer to the effect which it has had in degrading prisoners and in plunging them further into crime, or to the question whether fine and imprisonment do not fall more heavily on a criminal's wife and children than on himself. I have in mind more far-reaching questions. Does punishment deter? Do we deal with criminals on proper principles?

...[I]f we consider the law of contract, we find it full of history. The distinctions between debt, covenant, and assumpsit are merely historical. The classification of certain obligations to pay money, imposed by the law irrespective of any bargain as quasi contracts, is merely historical. The doctrine of consideration is merely historical. The effect given to a seal is to be explained by history alone. Consideration is a mere form. Is it a useful form? If so, why should it not be required in all contracts? A seal is a mere form, and is vanishing in the scroll and in enactments that a consideration must be given, seal or no seal. Why should any merely historical distinction be allowed to affect the rights and obligations of business men?

*   *   *   *   *

I trust that no one will understand me to be speaking with disrespect of the law, because I criticise it so freely I venerate the law, and especially our system of law, as one of the vastest products of the human mind. No one knows better than I do the countless number of great intellects that have spent themselves in making some addition or improvement, the greatest of which is trifling when compared with the mighty whole. It has the final title to respect that it exists, that it is not a Hegelian dream, but a part of the lives of men. But one may criticise even what one reveres. Law is the business to which my life is devoted, and I should show less than devotion if I did not do what in me lies to improve it, and, when I perceive what seems to me the ideal of its future, if I hesitated to point it out and to press toward it with all my heart.

Perhaps I have said enough to show the part which the study of history necessarily plays in the intelligent study of the law as it is to-day.

* * * * *

We must beware of the pitfall of antiquarianism, and must remember that for our purposes our only interest in the past is for the light it throws upon the present. I look forward to a time when the part played by history in the explanation of dogma shall be very small, and instead of ingenious research we shall spend our energy on a study of the ends sought to be attained and the reasons for desiring them. As a step toward that ideal it seems to me that every lawyer ought to seek an understanding of economics. The present divorce between the schools of political economy and law seems to me an evidence of how much progress in philosophical study still remains to be made. In the present state of political economy, indeed, we come again upon history on a larger scale, but there we are called on to consider and weigh the ends of legislation, the means of attaining them, and the cost. We learn that for everything we have we give up something else, and we are taught to set the advantage we gain against the other advantage we lose, and to know what we are doing when we elect.

There is another study which sometimes is undervalued by the practical minded, for which I wish to say a good word, although I think a good deal of pretty poor stuff goes under that name. I mean the study of what is called jurisprudence. Jurisprudence, as I look at it, is simply law in its most generalized part. Every effort to reduce a case to a rule is an effort of jurisprudence, although the name as used in English is confined to the broadest rules and most fundamental conceptions. One mark of a great lawyer is that he sees the application of the broadest rules. There is a story of a Vermont justice of the peace before whom a suit was brought by one farmer against another for breaking a churn. The justice took time to consider, and then said that he had looked through the statutes and could find nothing about churns, and gave judgment for the defendant. The same state of mind is shown in all our common digests and text-books.

* * * * *

I have been speaking about the study of the law, and I have said next to nothing of what commonly is talked about in that connection—text-books and the case system, and all the machinery with which a student comes most immediately in contact. Nor shall I say anything about them. Theory is my subject, not practical details. The modes of teaching have been improved since my time, no doubt, but ability and industry will master the raw material with any mode. Theory is the most important part of the dogma of the law, as the architect is the most important man who takes part in the building of a house. The most important improvements of the last twenty-five years are improvements in theory. It is not to be feared as unpractical, for, to the competent, it simply means going to the bottom of the subject. For the incompetent, it sometimes is true, as has been said, that an interest in general ideas means an absence of particular knowledge. I remember in army days reading of a youth who, being examined for the lowest grade and being asked a question about squadron drill, answered that he never had considered the evolutions of less than ten thousand men. But the weak and foolish must be left to their folly. The danger is that the able and practical minded should look with indifference or distrust upon ideas the connection of which with their business is remote. I heard a story, the other day, of a man who had a valet to whom he paid high wages, subject to deduction for faults. One of his deductions was, "For lack of imagination, five dollars." The lack is not confined to valets. The object of ambition, power, generally presents itself nowadays in the form of money alone. Money is the most immediate form, and is a proper object of desire. "The fortune," said Rachel, "is the measure of the intelligence." That is a good text to waken people out of a fool's paradise. But, as Hegel says, "It is in the end not the appetite, but the opinion, which has to be satisfied." To an imagination of any scope the most far-reaching form of power is not money, it is the command of ideas. If you want great examples, read Mr. Leslie Stephen's *History of English Thought in the Eighteenth Century,* and see how a hundred years after his death the abstract speculations of Descartes had become a practical force controlling the conduct of men. Read works of the great German jurists, and see how much more the world is governed to-day by Kant than by Bonaparte. We cannot all be Descartes or Kant, but we all want happiness. And happiness, I am sure from having known many successful men, cannot be won simply by being counsel for great corporations and having an income of fifty thousand dollars. An intellect great enough to win the prize needs other food besides success. The remoter and more general aspects of the law are those which give it universal interest. It is through them that you not only become a great master in your calling, but connect your subject with the universe and catch an echo of the infinite, a glimpse of its unfathomable process, a hint of the universal law.

Benjamin Nathan Cardozo, *The Nature of the Judicial Process* (Yale University Press, New Haven, 1921), 64–66.

*   *   *   *   *

Three of the directive forces of our law, philosophy, history and custom, have now been seen at work We have gone far enough to appreciate the complexity of the problem. We see that to determine to be loyal to precedents and to the principles back of precedents, does not carry us far upon the road. Principles are complex bundles. It is well enough to say that we shall be consistent, but consistent with what? Shall it be consistency with the origins of the rule, the course and tendency of development? Shall it be consistency with logic or philosophy or the fundamental conceptions of jurisprudence as disclosed by analysis of our own and foreign systems? All these loyalties are possible. All have sometimes prevailed. How are we to choose between them? Putting that question aside, how do we choose between them? Some concepts of the law have been in a peculiar sense historical growths. In such departments, history will tend to give direction to development. In other departments, certain large and fundamental concepts, which comparative jurisprudence shows to be common to other highly developed systems, loom up above all others. In these we shall give a larger scope to logic and symmetry. A broad field there also is in which rules may, with approximately the same convenience, be settled one way or the other. Here custom tends to assert itself as the controlling force in guiding the choice of paths. Finally, when the social needs demand one settlement rather than another, there are times when we must bend symmetry, ignore history and sacrifice custom in the pursuit of other and larger ends.

From history and philosophy and custom, we pass, therefore, to the force which in our day and generation is becoming the greatest of them all, the power of social justice which finds its outlet and expression in the method of sociology.

The final cause of law is the welfare of society. The rule that misses its aim cannot permanently justify its existence. "Ethical consideration can no more be excluded from the administration of justice which is the end and purpose of all civil laws than one can exclude the vital air from his room and live." Logic and history and custom have their place. We will shape the law to conform to them when we may; but only within bounds. The end which the law serves will dominate them all. There is an old legend that on one occasion God prayed, and his prayer was "Be it my will that my justice be ruled by my mercy." That is a prayer which we all need to utter at times when the demon of formalism tempts the intellect with the lure of scientific order. I do not mean, of course, that judges are commissioned to set aside existing rules at pleasure in favor of any other set of rules which they may hold to be expedient or wise. I mean that when they are called upon to say how far existing rules are to be extended or restricted, they must let the welfare of society fix the path, its direction and its distance. We are not to forget, said Sir George Jessel, in an often quoted judgment, that there is this paramount public policy, that we are not lightly to interfere with freedom of contract. So in this field, there may be a paramount public policy, one that will prevail over temporary inconvenience or occasional hardship, not lightly to sacrifice certainty and uniformity and order and coherence. All these elements must be considered. They are to be given such weight as sound judgment dictates. They are constituents of that social welfare which it is our business to discover. In a given instance we may find that they are constituents of preponderating value. In others, we may find that their value is subordinate. We must appraise them as best we can.

Harold J. Berman, *Law and Revolution* (Harvard Univ. Press, Cambridge, Mass., 1983), 11-13, 36–41. [Notes omitted.] [Courtesy Harvard University Press.]

Introduction

Law and History

To follow the story of the Western legal tradition, and to accept it, is to confront implicit theories both of law and of history that are no longer widely accepted, at least in the universities. The theories that do prevail pose serious obstacles to an appreciation of the story.

The conventional concept of law as a body of rules derived from statutes and court decisions—reflecting a theory of the ultimate source of law in the will of the lawmaker ("the state")—is wholly inadequate to support a study of a transnational legal culture. To speak of the Western legal tradition is to postulate a concept of law, not as a body of rules, but as a process, an enterprise, in which rules have meaning only in the context of institutions and procedures, values, and ways of thought. From this broader perspective the sources of law include not only the will of the lawmaker but also the reason and conscience of the community and its customs and usages. This is not the prevailing view of law. But it is by no means unorthodox: it used to be said, and not long ago, that there are four sources of law: legislation, precedent, equity, and custom. In the formative era of the Western legal tradition there was not nearly so much legislation or so much precedent as there came to be in later centuries. The bulk of law was derived from custom, which was viewed in the light of equity (defined as reason and conscience). It is necessary to recognize that custom and equity are as much law as statutes and decisions, if the story of the Western legal tradition is to be followed and accepted.

Beyond that, it is necessary to recognize that law in the West is formed into integrated legal systems, in each of which the various constituent elements take their meaning partly from the system as a whole. Further, each system is conceived to be a developing one; therefore, the meaning of each constituent element is derived not only from what the system has been in the past but also from what it is coming to be in the future. These, too, are not conventional truths of the prevailing "analytical jurisprudence," which postulates a sovereign who issues commands in the form of rules and imposes sanctions for failure to apply them as "he willed" them to be applied—what Max Weber called the "formal rationality" or "logical formalism" of Western law. And this is widely believed to be an accurate description, both by those who are against formalism and by those who are for it. Weber thought it explained the utility of law for the development of capitalism. Such a concept of law is a formidable obstacle to an understanding of the story of the Western legal tradition, which originated in what is usually thought to be the era of feudalism, and which stemmed from the separation of the church from the secular order. The fact that the new system of canon law, created in the late eleventh and twelfth centuries, constituted the first modern Western legal system has been generally overlooked, perhaps just because it does not fit in with the prevailing theories of the nature of law.

If analytical jurisprudence, or, as it is now more often called, legal positivism, is an inadequate theoretical basis for grasping the narrative of the development of Western legal institutions, what theory or theories would provide a better basis? The chief alternatives presented by Western legal philosophy itself are "natural-law theory" and "historical jurisprudence." In addition, in recent times a new school called "sociological jurisprudence" has come to the fore. All of these schools have, of course, many variants. Yet each theory, taken by itself, focuses on only one aspect of the truth. None of them, standing alone, offers a basis for understanding the history of law in the West. The story of the Western legal tradition is itself, in part, a story of the emergence and clash of these various schools of legal philosophy. They do not explain history; it is history that explains them—why they emerged, and why different schools have prevailed in different places at different times.

In the formative era of the Western legal tradition, natural-law theory predominated. It was generally believed that human law derived ultimately from, and was to be tested ultimately by, reason and conscience. According not only to the legal philosophy of the time but also to positive law itself, any positive law, whether enacted or customary, had to conform to natural law, or else it would lack validity as law and could be disregarded. This theory had a basis in Christian theology as well as in Aristotelian philosophy. But it also had a basis in the history of the struggle between ecclesiastical and secular authorities, and in the politics of pluralism. One may compare it with the theory that accompanies the law of the United States, under which any positive law must conform to the constitutional requirements of "due process," equal protection," "freedom," "privacy," and the like, or lose its validity. "Due process of law" is, in fact, a fourteenth-century English phrase meaning natural law. Thus natural-law theory is written into the positive law of the United States. This does not, however, prevent one from giving a political ("positivist") explanation of it. It is easy enough to show that the state, or the powers that be, or the ruling class, benefits from the due process clause and "wills" it to be.

Similarly, historical jurisprudence—the theory that law derives its meaning and authority from the past history of the people whose law it is, from their customs, from the genius of their institutions, from their historic values, from precedents—has been built into the English legal *system* since the English Revolution of the seventeenth century; yet English legal *philosophy* has swung between positivism and natural-law theory, and historical jurisprudence has had relatively few adherents, at least in the twentieth century. It is Germany—which in contrast to England created its national law, especially in the nineteenth century, not so much out of its own historic legal institutions as out of a received "alien" Roman law—that has been the homeland of historical jurisprudence, in whose name the greatest German jurists have sung praises to German law as a reflection of the spirit of the German people.

Thus Western legal history has been the breeding ground of a variety of schools of legal philosophy, some of which have been dominant in some times and places and others in others, often for paradoxical reasons—as if in ideological reaction against the existing legal realities. Students of Western legal history must therefore guard against the limitations of each of the individual schools. It would be more appropriate, and more "Western," to use all of them as screens to be placed successively over historical experience rather than to attempt to use history as a buttress for any one of them.

*   *   *   *   *

The history of Western law is at a turning point as sharp and as crucial as that which was marked by the French Revolution of 1789, the English Revolution of 1640, and the German Revolution of 1517. The two generations since the outbreak of the Russian Revolution have witnessed—not only in the Soviet Union but throughout the West—a substantial break with the individualism of the traditional law, a break with its emphasis on private property and freedom of contract, its limitations on liability for harm caused by entrepreneurial activity, its strong moral attitude toward crime, and many of its other basic postulates. Conversely, they have witnessed a turn toward collectivism in the law, toward emphasis on state and social property, regulation of contractual freedom in the interest of society, expansion of liability for harm caused by entrepreneurial activity, a utilitarian rather than a moral attitude toward crime, and many other new basic postulates.

These radical changes constitute a severe challenge to traditional Western legal institutions, procedures, values, concepts, rules, and ways of thought. They threaten the objectivity of law, since they make the state an invisible party to most legal proceedings between individuals or corporate entities—the same state that enacted the applicable law and appointed the court. This invisible pressure is increased in Communist countries by virtue of strong central controls not only over economic life, but also over political, cultural, and ideological life; and in non-Communist countries, too, such central controls in the noneconomic sphere have increased, although they have usually been more in the hands of large bureaucratic organizations than of the state as such.

To the extent that the present crisis is comparable to revolutionary crises that have struck the Western legal tradition in the past, the resources of that whole tradition may be summoned to overcome it, as those resources have been summoned to overcome previous revolutionary crises. However, the present crisis goes deeper. It is a crisis not only of individualism as it has developed since the eighteenth century, or of liberalism as it has developed since the seventeenth century, or of secularism as it has developed since the sixteenth century; it is a crisis also of the whole tradition as it has existed since the late eleventh century.

Only four—the first four—of the ten basic characteristics of the Western legal tradition remain as basic characteristics of law in the West.*

1. Law is still relatively autonomous, in the sense that it remains differentiated from politics and religion as well as from other types of social institutions and other scholarly disciplines.

2. It is still entrusted to the cultivation of professional legal specialists, legislators, judges, lawyers, and legal scholars.

3. Legal training centers still flourish where legal institutions are conceptualized and to a certain extent systematized.

4. Such legal learning still constitutes a meta-law by which the legal institutions and rules are evaluated and explained.

It is important to stress the survival of these four characteristics of law, since in Russia during the first years of the revolution and again in the early 1930s strong attacks were made—as had been the case in the previous great revolutions—upon the autonomy of law, its professional character, and its character as a learned discipline and a science. In other countries of the West, as well, it was proposed from time to time in the 1920s and 1930s, partly under Marxist—Leninist influence, that law and lawyers should be eliminated, or at least greatly restricted in importance, as unnecessary and harmful to society. In the 1960s and early 1970s the Chinese Revolution took up this cry with great seriousness: all the law schools were closed and almost all lawyers disappeared. Only since the late 1930s in the Soviet Union and the late 1970s in the Chinese People's Republic has "legal nihilism" been denounced.

---

* According to Berman, the other six characteristics are: 5. that the law is conceived to be an integrated "coherent whole;" 6. the concept that the law "depends for its vitality on the belief in the ongoing character of law," its "capacity for growth;" 7. that this growth "is thought to have an internal logic;" 8. that "the historicity of law is linked with the concept of its supremacy over the political authorities;" 9. "the coexistence and competitions within the same community of diverse jurisdictions and diverse legal systems;" and 10. "a tension between the ideals and reality" between "the transcendence and the immanence of the Western legal tradition." See Harold J. Berman, *Law and Revolution* (Cambridge, Mass. 1983), 9–10.

All of the other six characteristics attributed to the Western legal tradition have been severely weakened in the latter part of the twentieth century, especially in the United States.

5. Law in the twentieth century, both in theory and in practice, has been treated less and less as a coherent whole, a body, a *corpus juris*, and more and more as a hodgepodge, a fragmented mass of ad hoc decisions and conflicting rules, united only by common "techniques." The old meta-law has broken down and been replaced by a kind of cynicism. Nineteenth-century categorizations by fields of law are increasingly viewed as obsolete. Still older structural elements of the law—such as, in England and America, the forms of action by which the common law was once integrated and which Maitland in 1906 said still "rule us from the grave"—are almost wholly forgotten. The sixteenth-century division of all law into public law and private law has had to yield to what Roscoe Pound in the mid-1930s called "the new feudalism." Yet it is a feudalism lacking the essential concept of a hierarchy of the sources of law by which a plurality of jurisdictions may be accommodated and conflicting legal rules may be harmonized. In the absence of new theories that would give order and consistency to the legal structure, a primitive pragmatism is invoked to justify individual rules and decisions.

6. The belief in the growth of law, its ongoing character over generations and centuries, has also been substantially weakened. The notion is widely held that the apparent development of law—its apparent growth through reinterpretation of the past, whether the past is represented by precedent or by codification—is only ideological. The law is presented as having no history of its own, and the history which it proclaims to present is treated as, at best, chronology, and at worst, mere illusion.

7. The changes which have taken place in law in the past, as well as the changes which are taking place in the present, are viewed not as responses to the internal logic of legal growth, and not as resolutions of the tensions between legal science and legal practice, but rather as responses to the pressure of outside forces.

8. The view that law transcends politics—the view that at any given moment, or at least in its historical development, law is distinct from the state—seems to have yielded increasingly to the view that law is at all times basically an instrument of the state, that is, a means of effectuating the will of those who exercise political authority.

9. The source of the supremacy of law in the plurality of legal jurisdictions and legal systems within the same legal order is threatened in the twentieth century by the tendency within each country to swallow up all the diverse jurisdictions and systems in a single central program of legislation and administrative regulation. The churches have long since ceased to constitute an effective legal counterweight to the secular authorities. The custom of mercantile and other autonomous communities or trades within the economic and social order has been overridden by legislative and administrative controls. International law has enlarged its theoretical claim to override national law, but in practice national law has either expressly incorporated international law or else has rendered it ineffectual as a recourse for individual citizens. In federal systems such as that of the United States, the opportunity to escape from one set of courts to another has radically diminished. Blackstone's concept of two centuries ago that we live

under a considerable number of different legal systems has hardly any counterpart in contemporary legal thought.

10. The belief that the Western legal tradition transcends revolution, that it precedes and survives the great total upheavals that have periodically engulfed the nations of the West, is challenged by the opposing belief that the law is wholly subordinate to revolution. The overthrow of one set of political institutions and its replacement by another leads to a wholly new law. Even if the old forms are kept, they are filled, it is said, with new content, they serve new purposes, and they are not to be identified with the past.

The crisis of the Western legal tradition is not merely a crisis in legal philosophy but also a crisis in law itself. Legal philosophers have always debated, and presumably always will debate, whether law is founded in reason and morality or whether it is only the will of the political ruler. It is not necessary to resolve that debate in order to conclude that as a matter of historical fact the legal systems of all the nations that are heirs to the Western legal tradition have been rooted in certain beliefs or postulates: that is, the legal systems themselves have presupposed the validity of those beliefs. Today those beliefs or postulates—such as the structural integrity of law, its ongoingness, its religious roots, its transcendent qualities—are rapidly disappearing, not only from the minds of philosophers, not only from the minds of lawmakers, judges, lawyers, law teachers, and other members of the legal profession, but from the consciousness of the vast majority of citizens, the people as a whole; and more than that, they are disappearing from the law itself. The law is becoming more fragmented, more subjective, geared more to expediency and less to morality, concerned more with immediate consequences and less with consistency or continuity. Thus the historical soil of the Western legal tradition is being washed away in the twentieth century, and the tradition itself is threatened with collapse.

The breakdown of the Western legal tradition springs only in part from the socialist revolutions that were inaugurated in Russia in October 1917 and that have gradually spread throughout the West (and throughout other parts of the world as well), albeit often in relatively mild forms. It springs only in part from massive state intervention in the economy of the nation (the welfare state), and only in part from the massive bureaucratization of social and economic life through huge centralized corporate entities (the corporate state). It springs much more from the crisis of Western civilization itself, commencing in 1914 with the outbreak of World War I. This was more than an economic and technological revolution, more even than a political revolution. If it had not been, Western society would be able to adapt its legal institutions to meet the new demands placed upon them, as it has done in revolutionary situations in the past. Western society would be able to accommodate socialism—of whatever variety—within its legal tradition. But the disintegration of the very foundations of that tradition cannot be accommodated; and the greatest challenge to those foundations is the massive loss of confidence in the West itself, as a civilization, a community, and in the legal tradition which for nine centuries has helped to sustain it.

Almost all the nations of the West are threatened today by a cynicism about law, leading to a contempt for law, on the part of all classes of the population. The cities have become increasingly unsafe. The welfare system has almost broken down under unenforceable regulations. There is wholesale violation of the tax laws by the rich and the poor and those in between. There is hardly a profession that is not caught up in evasion of one or another form of governmental regulation. And the government itself, from bottom to top, is caught up in illegalities. But that is not the main point. The main point is that the only ones who seem to be conscience-stricken over this matter are those few whose crimes have been exposed.

Contempt for law and cynicism about law have been stimulated by the contemporary revolt against what is sometimes called legal formalism, which emphasizes the uniform application of general rules as the central element in legal reasoning and in the idea of justice. According to Roberto M. Unger, with the development of the welfare state, on the one hand, and of the corporate state, on the other, formalism is yielding to an emphasis on public policy both in legal reasoning and in the idea of justice. Policy-oriented legal reasoning, Unger writes, is characterized by emphasis upon broad standards of fairness and of social responsibility. He connects this shift in "post-liberal" Western legal thought with a change in beliefs concerning language. "Language is no longer credited with the fixity of categories and the transparent representation of the world that would make formalism plausible in legal reasoning or in ideas about justice," he writes. Thus described, the revolt against legal formalism seems both inevitable and benign. Yet what is to prevent discretionary justice from being an instrument of repression and even a pretext for barbarism and brutality, as it became in Nazi Germany? Unger argues that this is to be prevented by the development of a strong sense of community within the various groups that comprise a society. Unfortunately, however, the development of such group pluralism is itself frustrated by some of the same considerations that underlie the attack on legal formalism. Most communities of more than face-to-face size can hardly survive for long, much less interact with one another, without elaborate systems of rules, whether customary or enacted. To say this is not to deny that in the late nineteenth and early twentieth centuries, in many countries of the West, there was an excessive concern with logical consistency in the law, which still exists in some quarters; the reaction against it, however, loses its justification when it becomes an attack on rules per se, and on the Western tradition of legality which strikes a balance among rule, precedent, policy, and equity—all four.

The attack on any one of these four factors tends to diminish the others. In the name of antiformalism, "public policy" has come dangerously close to meaning the will of those who are currently in control: "social justice" and "substantive rationality" have become identified with pragmatism; "fairness" has lost its historical and philosophical roots and is blown about by every wind of fashionable doctrine. The language of law is viewed not only as necessarily complex, ambiguous, and rhetorical (which it is) but also wholly contingent, contemporary, and arbitrary (which it is not). These are harbingers not only of a "post-liberal" age but also of a "post-Western" age.

Cynicism about the law, and lawlessness, will not be overcome by adhering to a so-called realism which denies the autonomy, the integrity, and the ongoingness of our legal tradition. In the words of Edmund Burke, those who do not look backward to their ancestry will not look forward to their posterity.

This certainly does not mean that the study of the past will save society. Society moves inevitably into the future. But it does so by walking backwards, so to speak, with its eyes on the past. Oliver Cromwell said, "Man never reaches so high an estate as when he knows not whither he is going." He understood the revolutionary significance of respect for tradition in a time of crisis.

*   *   *   *   *

Laura Kalman, *The Strange Career of Legal Liberalism* (Yale, New Haven, 1996), 139–143, 244–246. [Notes omitted.] [Courtesy Yale University Press.]

Note: Laura Kalman is a distinguished historian of liberalism. Here she is discussing "originalism," or constitutional doctrines based on an historical "original intent." Many of her observations, however, are relevant to all aspects of today's legal history. See also Laura Kalman, *Legal Realism at Yale 1927–1960* (Chapel Hill, 1986).

THE TURN TO HISTORY

Some legal liberals determined to appropriate originalism for themselves. They would meet the proponents of original intent on the battleground of history. They would advance alternative interpretations of the Founding to justify legal liberalism.

They had other reasons to turn to history. In 1969, C. Vann Woodward had used his presidential address to the American Historical Association to warn that history's popularity was waning. During the 1970s, philosophy, anthropology, and literary theory had sometimes seemed proudly ahistorical. "We're not concerned with the historical question here," Dworkin had said of himself and Rawls. "We're not concerned about how principles are in fact chosen. We're concerned about which principles are just." Some literary theory also made history irrelevant. When Derrida said "*il n'y a pas d'hors texte*" in *Of Grammatology*, he denied the possibility of access to external historical reality. Derrida spurned the "vulgar and mundane concept of temporality" and predicted "the end of linear writing."

In the 1980s, Americans nevertheless embarked on one of their periodic love affairs with the past. Even so, at the bicentennial, NEH director Lynne Cheney was cautioning that erosion of "historical consciousness" could destroy the nation. "Knowledge of the ideas that have molded us and the ideals that mattered to us functions as a kind of civic glue," she testified.

Allan Bloom's *Closing of the American Mind* appeared in time for the Bork battle and provided fodder for academics feeling besieged by liberals and the left. According to one law professor, "Bloom's work enraptured the book-buying public not because it was convinced by his plea for a return to Platonic dialogue and absolute values, but because it is enthralled by his marvelous depiction of the left-wing cowardice that has caused American universities to discard the values and principles that made them great." The culture wars were about to mushroom beyond the academy into a new phase, a battle between the university and its attackers.

Although the new "political correctness" phase remained for the moment a gleam in the right's eye, some disciplines displayed renewed interest in history. Given Gadamer's emphasis on the "the historicity of all understanding," the interpretive turn led naturally to a "historic turn." Anthropologists were about to promise that "rehistoricization" would allow their field to recapture some of the authority it had recently lost. Historical sociology was experiencing a "revival."

Literary theorists were also touting the new historicism, "a reciprocal concern with the historicity of texts and the textuality of histories," as "a response to that acceleration in the forgetting of history which seems to characterize an increasingly technocratic and commodified American academy and society." To some scholars who had come of age during the 1960s and had survived the revelations about Paul de Man's wartime activities as a collaborator, the new historicism apparently seemed more compatible than deconstruction with radical political critique. Whatever the reason for its emergence, the new historicism challenged deconstruction's domination of literary theory. Gayatri Spivak even charged that the new historicism was "a sort of academic media hype mounted against deconstruction." In his 1986 presidential address to the Modern Language Association, J. Hillis Miller complained about the "the so-called new historicism." Bemoaning the "shift from language to history," he decried literature's "sudden, almost universal turn away from theory in the sense of an orientation toward language as such and . . . [its] corresponding turn toward history, culture, society, politics, institutions, class and gender conditions, the social context, the material base."

That was unfair: the new historicists knew their Derrida, as well as their Foucault, Geertz, and Marx. Their work transformed their teaching. Wesleyan now required potential English majors to enroll in a year of coursework organized around "two platitudes":

> [E]very student should know how to read a text with careful and subtle attention to its language, and every student should be able to read a text with some appreciation of its historicity.
>
> From this plain credo we developed two semesters of study with a chasm between them. In English 201 the students read mainly lyric poems in the way that became traditional after World War II. One poem per fifty minutes; no intentional fallacy, no context, little intertextuality; key in on voice, register, metaphor, syntax, dramatic situation, prosody, and so on. In English 202, suddenly the texts are fat novels surrounded by journals, memoirs, documents, historical arguments, criticism, and so on, all somehow to be grasped as participating in the historical process. It is as if the English Department were kidnapped and taken en masse to a reeducation camp over winter break.

Most law professors had shied away from historicism, new or old. In fact, at the 1981 Yale conference on legal scholarship, critical legal scholar Robert Gordon argued that "historicism, the recognition of the historical and cultural contingency of law, is a perpetual threat to the aims of our legal scholarship as conventionally practiced; that to defend against the threat (or to protect themselves from becoming aware of it) legal scholars have regularly and recurrently resorted to certain strategies of response and evasion; and finally that these strategies have so influenced the practice of legal scholarship as severely to limit its intellectual options and imaginative range." Few law professors seemed eager to confront Gordon's challenge.

Neither English professors nor historians would point legal scholars to historicism. Those law professors who turned to literary theory in the early 1980s seemed unaware of the new historicism. They bypassed it for either Fish's or Derrida's forms of poststructuralism. And though adherents might credit the new historicism with making both context and text matter, it was too theoretical and acontextual for historians.

Ironically, the turn to history in the social sciences and humanities came when history itself was in poor shape. Though politics had not polarized them, historians were anxious about the future of their discipline. Bernard Bailyn's 1981 presidential address to the American Historical Association deplored "the absence of effective organizing principles" in contemporary historical work. "[L]arge areas of history, including some of the most intensively cultivated, have become shapeless, and scholarship is heavily concentrated on unconnected technical problems. Narratives that once gave meanings to the details have been undermined and discredited with the advance of technical scholarship, and no new narrative structures have been constructed to replace the old." Bailyn's plea "to bring order into large areas of history and thus to reintroduce history in a sophisticated form to a wider reading public, through synthetic works, narrative in structure, on major themes, works that explain some significant part of the story of how the present world came to be the way it is" inaugurated an argument about the fragmentation of history and the wisdom of reviving synthesis.

In many ways, this debate was a stand-in for one about the value of the social history that had proliferated in the 1960s and 1970s. It left historians with little time for law professors. Thus for legal scholars, the impulse to study history with an eye to its relevance for the present, along with an acknowledgment of the historicity of history, came from someone other than historians.

In addition to Gadamer, the impetus for the turn to history may have come from Geertz and Rorty. Because of his emphasis on historians' beloved context, Geertz was becoming the patron saint of cultural historians. Rorty's neopragmatism may have also led law professors to context. In the mid-1980s, Rorty promised the law professors Gordon had spooked the possibility of having it both ways. "There seems to be a dilemma: either we anachronistically impose enough of our problems and vocabulary on the dead to make them conversational partners, or we confine our interpretive activity to making their falsehoods look less silly by placing them in the context of the benighted times in which they were written," Rorty said. "These alternatives, however, do not constitute a dilemma. We should do both of these things." Rorty turned attention from the general human condition to the human condition in the twentieth century. Legal scholars could focus on history's message for twentieth-century law, a project that would have seemed especially appealing at a time when law apparently lacked a future as an autonomous discipline.

That enterprise meant law professors could conduct colloquies with the Founders *and* say something authoritative about the past. For example, Gregory Alexander explicitly accepted Rorty's challenge to make the dead "conversational partners." Bruce Ackerman reminded readers that the task "is to locate ourselves in a conversation between generations." Ackerman held out the hope history could be studied two ways. "My first aim is to place...[the] Founding...in historical context," he informed his readers. "My second aim is different, though not (I hope) inconsistent. I propose to use the Founding as the beginning of a dialogue between past and present which will serve as our central technique for constitutional discovery."

* * * * *

At a time when both the Prince of Wales and Pope John Paul II have discovered postmodern rhetoric, we might expect law professors to embrace disciplines

which do so too. There is something deeper to academic lawyers' frenzied interdisciplinary work, however, than their desire for trendiness. As one of them says,
"legal scholars are desperately groping for an external, non-legal source of legitimacy or authority."

Some law professors would say they are not finding it and that law remains an
autonomous discipline. They would apply my observation about most lawyers'
legal history to legal scholarship and education as a whole: the more it changes,
the more it stays the same. The "law student who fell asleep in 1963 and awoke
in 1993 would not be astonished by his new surrounds," Stanford Law School
Dean Paul Brest maintains. "If he had fallen asleep holding a law review—the
soporific power was no weaker in those days—the nature and language of some
of the articles would bewilder him, but he would find much that was familiar."
John Schlegel grieves: "Until one takes the 'and' out of 'law and...' there is no
point in talking." Pierre Schlag grumbles that "when traditional legal thought
goes traveling (in the footnotes) through the university, it never seems to encounter much of anything except itself. The interdisciplinary travels of traditional legal thought are like a bad European vacation: the substance is Europe,
but the form is McDonald's, Holiday Inns, American Express." Perhaps that is
universal. "Despite the recent millenarian calls to interdisciplinarity, disciplines
will prove remarkably resilient and difficult to kill," Stanley Fish predicts.

Nevertheless, the interdisciplinary gropings of law professors worry some of
the humanists that the legal scholars most admire. To put it colloquially, the humanists have responded: "Don't fool around with the rule of law and justice."
Richard Rorty cautioned one adoring law professor: "I must confess that I trem-
ble at the thought of Barthian readings in law schools. I suspect that civilization
reposes on a lot of people who take the normal practices of the discipline with
full 'realistic' seriousness." We also encounter postmodernism's prophet Jean-
François Lyotard "arguing that 'consensus has become an outmoded and suspect
value' but then adding, rather surprisingly, that since 'justice as a value is neither
outmoded nor suspect' (how it could remain such a universal, untouched by the
diversity of language games, he does not tell us), we 'must arrive at an idea and
practice of justice that is not linked to that consensus.'"

And we find English professor Jennifer Wicke, the keynote speaker at a conference on postmodernism and the law, cautioning that "these bedfellows could
make strange politics." The "more than thirty-one flavors of postmodernism,"
she warns, all promise indigestion for law. According to Wicke, in postmodernism "the legal text ceases to emanate from an origin, point of timeless authority or as a singular transmission." Postmodernism insists that "[l]anguage games
are all that are left," and it highlights the schizophrenic existence of the individual who lives in multiple worlds. Those characteristics endanger law's integrity
and potential for social change. Postmodern analysis may clash "with the need to
deploy a language of the legal subject, in other words, a language of rights and a
language of cultural identity, in securing cultural justice."

Wicke's warning may only increase the appeal of postmodernism for many
law professors. What is law if not "Word-Magic"? Who is the law professor if
not a schizophrenic, even pathologically so? As the gap between the law school
and the university narrows, that between the law school and the profession may
widen. Yet for all the disjunction between the legal academy and the profession,
that between law professor and student is greater. University legal education has

never prepared students for law practice. Even nearly thirty years ago, as Thomas Bergin saw, the law teacher was "a man divided against himself," a victim of the belief "that he can be, at one and the same time, an authentic academic and a trainer of Hessians" who practice law.

Today that schizophrenia is still more intense. Bergin spoke at a time when most law professors agreed that an "authentic academic" did doctrinal analysis. Now, however, as doctrinalists battle with those who would make the law school "a colonial outpost of the graduate school," doctrinal work may be dismissed as unprestigious and anti-intellectual. Law professors contest the very definition of authenticity. Further, though its connection with the Supreme Court has always made the work of academic lawyers more overtly political than that of scholars in other disciplines, the legal academy became polarized in the 1980s. Nor is today's law professor "divided against himself"—more likely, he or she feels fragmented.

Most law professors have learned postmodernism from other disciplines and have been speaking it for a long time. In fact, one scholar who surveyed postmodernism's influence concluded: "Legal theory is an arena where post-modern views of epistemology and method have created one of the most severe crises." Law professors have been speaking other languages as well. Some believe "there is much to be gained by introducing Barthian readings into the law schools." Perhaps we cannot expect academic lawyers to remain at the barricades valiantly holding culture together, while those outside the law schools pick it apart. But it would be unfortunate if law professors desert the barricades just as academics in other fields, such as historians, begin to show signs of appreciating what legal scholars are doing, and wanting to help.

Daniel R. Coquillette, "Introduction: The 'Countenance of Authoritie,'" *Law in Colonial Massachusetts* (eds. Coquillette, Brink, Menand) Boston, 1984, vii–ix.

Introduction:
The "Countenance of Authoritie"

*　　*　　*　　*　　*

"Legal" history has always been the special subject of controversy. Indeed, renaissance lawyers can make claim to the dubious distinction of inventing the "historicist fallacy," the idea that scientific study of the past can discover first principles "which will not only explain the present but reveal the future."[4] This notion stands in direct opposition to the idea that the study of history must be just an end unto itself, an idea tagged as "pure antiquarianism" by its detractors.

---

4. See Frank E. Manuel, *Shapes of Philosophical History* (Stanford, 1965), 137; Arthur Marwick, *The Nature of History* (New York, 1970), 227–279; Edward H. Carr, *What Is History?* (New York, 1961), 3–35; W. H. Walsh, *An Introduction to Philosophy of History* (Atlantic Highlands, N.J., 1951), 169–187. Grant Gilmore, "The Age of Antiquarius: On Legal History in the Time of Troubles," *University of Chicago Law Review*, XXXIX (1972), 484. As to the "invention" of legal history and "historical" schools of jurisprudence, see Donald R. Kelley, "Guillaume Budé and the First Historical School of Law," *The American Historical Review*, LXXII (1967), 833–834; Donald R. Kelley, *Foundations of Modern Historical Scholarship: Language, Law, and History in the French Renaissance* (New York, 1970), 53–148; T.G.A. Pocock, *The Ancient Constitution and the Feudal Law* (Cambridge, 1957), 8–17.

Lawyers have traditionally had a "pervasive fear of antiquarianism," probably because it appears to be—practically speaking—a waste of time.[5] On the other hand, it has been said that lawyers are especially susceptible to the "historicist fallacy" because they are in the business of predicting outcomes and legitimizing them. A rejection of *both* the "historicist fallacy" and pure "antiquarianism" leaves legal historians with an interesting problem of how to justify their existence, particularly to the legal community. As Felix Gilbert put it: "But what is our situation, for we believe neither in history as a means of teaching ethical values nor in the possibility of discovering laws to determine the process of world history?"[6]

I would like to suggest two answers to this dilemma, both well illustrated by this book. First, to the extent that the study of history is regarded as an end unto itself, there has been too little attention paid to the impact of legal ideas and legal institutions on the course of political, social, and economic events. The colonial history of Massachusetts is a prime example, and the essays in this book demonstrate the kind of benefits to be realized. Of course, as Michael S. Hindus has emphasized, not all power is "legal," nor can an isolated study of legal doctrine give a complete picture of anything, much less an operational legal system.[7] But, as this book illustrates, the old shibboleths dividing legal history from social history, political history, intellectual history, and economic history are crumbling, and cross-disciplinary cooperation is beginning to yield new insights into the past as it was.

But I am unwilling to stop with this relatively safe, limited answer. The reason is that I believe, and believe deeply, that the relationship between legal history and modern legal scholarship is a "special relationship" and, like most "special relationships," it is full of passion and danger. First, there is the relationship of historicism to modern legal scholarship and professional education. In particular, as Robert Gordon has brilliantly explained, any profession that attempts to legitimize existing procedures or rules will be tempted to demonstrate that such systems are inevitable, or are justified by "universal rationalizing principles."[8] Christopher Columbus Langdell, who established the model of "scientific" legal education that has dominated generations of American law students, was probably sitting in the front row of the audience when Oliver Wendell Holmes, Jr., warned that "[t]he life of the law has not been logic, it has been experience."[9]

Holmes was not just warning Langdell. He was warning all of us that our attempts to rationalize legal rules are "contingent" on the particular social and historical conditions of the times.[1] Gordon has suggested that lawyers and legal

---

5. Stephen M. Fuller, "Some Contemporary Approaches to the Study of Legal History and Jurisprudence," *Tulsa Law Journal*, X (1975), 576.

6. Felix Gilbert, History: *Choice and Commitment* (Cambridge, Mass., 1977), 452.

7. See Michael S. Hundus, *Prison and Plantation: Crime, Justice, and Authority in Massachusetts and South Carolina, 1767–1878* (Chapel Hill, 1980), 34–37. See also Hiller B. Zobel, "Law Under Pressure," 203–205.

8. See Robert W. Gordon, "Historicism in Legal Scholarship," *Yale Law Journal*, XC (1981), 1018–1024; Morton J. Horwitz, "The Historical Contingency of the Role of History," ibid., 1057.

9. O.W. Holmes, Jr., *The Common Law*, M. Howe ed. (Boston, 1963), 5. See Grant Gilmore, "The Age of Antiquarius," 480–481.

1. Morton J. Horwitz, "The Historical Contingency," 1057. Erich Auerbach defines this insight as "[W]hen people realize that epochs and societies are not to be judged in terms of a pattern concept of what is desirable absolutely but rather in every case in terms of their own premises; when people reckon among such premises not only natural factors like climate and

scholars avoid a frank recognition of this fact, as it threatens to expose the ideological and political assumptions of the law, and to weaken what John Winthrop would call the "Countenance of Authoritie."[2] But authority in a free society should be able to tolerate such scrutiny, and defend its legitimacy.

This second point gets me to my "bottom line." The major task of history is to make us aware of the character of our own times by seeing it in comparison and by contrast with others. This is especially true of the character of our law and legal system, *our* "Countenance of Authoritie." As Gilmore puts it:

> [T]he historian who shows us that what in fact happened need not have happened the way it did or need not have happened at all enriches our understanding of the past and, consequently, puts us in a position where we can deal more rationally with the infinitely complex problems which confront us. The argument that historical study which has no direct and immediate relevance to our present condition is "mere antiquarianism" is simply another aspect of the historicist fallacy.[3]

This has been demonstrated again and again by the insights of the contributors to this book. Whether the context be early professional history, lay judges, the use of the law to control the poor and provide welfare, early criminal law, the rights of defendants, the ideological background of lawyers approaching a revolution, or how an "illogical" doctrine developed to resolve conflict of laws, the benefits are better perspectives on our own hidden agendas and assumptions.

Clifford Shipton has observed that "Massachusetts in her first century and a half was an ideal proving ground for the principles on which our democratic way of life rests."[4] This is not to say the picture was always pretty, or progressive. There are the ghosts of the Antinomians, of Anne Hutchinson, of Mary Dyer, of the "strolling poor," of the victims of "spectral testimony," of the enslaved, of the dead on the streets of Boston and on the Green at Lexington—these do not represent triumphs of scientific jurisprudence or of human understanding. Yet, throughout all, a dominant theme of the colony's development was a pursuit of,

---

soil but also the intellectual and historical factors; when, in other words, they came to develop a sense of historical dynamics...when, finally, they accept the conviction that the meaning of events cannot be grasped in abstract and general forms of cognition..."Erich Auerbach, *Mimesis, the Representation of Reality in Western Literature* (W. Trask, Trans, Princeton, 1953), 391. See also Donald R. Kelley, *Foundations of Modern Historical Scholarship*, 301–309.

2. Robert W. Gordon, "Historicism," 1017. See Darret B. Rutman, "The Mirror of Puritan Authority," *Law and Authority in Colonial America*, George A. Billias ed., 149–152.

3. Grant Gilmore, "The Age of Antiquarius," 487. "If legal history does not tell us how things ought to be, it can at least tell us that they need not be the way they are." Adam J. Hirsch, "Pillory to Penitentiary," 1269. Arthur Marwick and Felix Gilbert have expressed the same idea in a broader context. "We cannot escape from history, our lives are governed by what happened in the past, our decisions by what we believe to have happened." Arthur Marwick, *The Nature of History* (New York, 1970), 319. "But, after all reservations have been made, we ought to remain aware that the man who acted and was acted upon in the past is the same man who acts in the present, and that the past is one way—and not the worst way—of acquiring the right and the criteria to judge the present. Our willingness to see the past as a whole, our willingness to take a stand, constitutes our card of identity." Felix Gilbert, *History: Choice and Commitment* (Cambridge, Mass., 1977), 453.

4. Clifford K. Shipton, "The Locus of Authority in Colonial Massachusetts," in *Law and Authority in Colonial America*, 147.

and adherence to, ideals of lawful authority. The traditions of local government, of lay justice, of legal representation, of social innovation through legal forms, of faith in the law—these things are more than part of our past—they are what Holmes would call our "experience," the experience which remains at the very heart of what our law has become.[5] To understand these failures and triumphs, to see them clearly and understand, remains important.

---

5. "Our recent preoccupation with the relation of law to the interests (primarily the material interests) of individuals and groups has led us to overlook the significance of legal institutions for the nature of man and his quest for a moral order." Danel J. Boorstin, "The Humane Study of Law," *Yale Law Journal*, LVII (1948), 960, 975.

INDEX OF NAMES

INDEX OF PLACES

INDEX OF TECHNICAL TERMS